THE COMPARATIVE STUDY OF CONSCRIPTION IN THE ARMED FORCES

COMPARATIVE SOCIAL RESEARCH

Series Editor: Fredrik Engelstad

Recent Volumes:

Volume 17: Regional Cultures, 1998

Volume 18: Family Change: Practices, Policies, and Values, 1999

Volume 19: Comparative Perspectives on Universities, 2000

COMPARATIVE SOCIAL RESEARCH VOLUME 20

THE COMPARATIVE STUDY OF CONSCRIPTION IN THE ARMED FORCES

EDITED BY

LARS MJØSET

Department of Sociology and Human Geography, University of Oslo, Norway

STEPHEN VAN HOLDE

Department of Political Science, Kenyon College, Ohio, USA

2002

JAI

An Imprint of Elsevier Science

Amsterdam – London – New York – Oxford – Paris – Shannon – Tokyo

ELSEVIER SCIENCE Ltd
The Boulevard, Langford Lane
Kidlington, Oxford OX5 1GB, UK

First edition 2002

Library of Congress Cataloging in Publication Data

The comparative study of conscription in the armed forces/edited by Lars Mjøset, Stephen van Holde.
p. cm. – (Comparative social research; v. 20)
ISBN 0-7623-0836-2
1. Draft. I. Mjøset, Lars. II. Van Holde, Stephen. III. Series.

UB340.C57 2002
355.2'2363–dc21 2001050639

British Library Cataloguing in Publication Data
A catalogue record from the British Library has been applied for.

ISBN: 0-7623-0836-2
ISSN: 1095-6310 (Series)

∞The paper used in this publication meets the requirements of ANSI/NISO Z39.48-1992 (Permanence of Paper).
Printed in The Netherlands.

CONTENTS

PART II: CONTEMPORARY PERSPECTIVES

PART III: REVIEW SYMPOSIUM SECTION

EDITORIAL BOARD

LIST OF CONTRIBUTORS

Rafael Ajangiz	Department of Political Science and Administration, University of the Basque Country, Bilbao, Spain
Tarak Barkawi	School of Politics and Sociology, Birkbeck College, University of London, UK
David Carey, Jr.	Department of History, University of Southern Maine, USA
Alan Forrest	University of York, UK
Paul R. Higate	School for Policy Studies, University of Bristol, UK
John M. Hobson	Faculty of Economics and Political Science, University of Sydney, Australia
Meyer Kestnbaum	Department of Sociology, University of Maryland, USA
Margaret Levi	Department of Political Science, University of Washington, USA
Lars Mjøset	Department of Sociology and Human Geography, University of Oslo, Norway
Bjørn Møller	Copenhagen Peace Research Institute, Copenhagen, Denmark
Paul Richards	Wageningen University and Research Centre, The Netherlands

Gretchen Ritter — Government Dept., U. T. Austin, USA

David M. Rowe — Department of Political Science, Kenyon College, USA

Stephen Van Holde — Department of Political Science, Kenyon College, USA

Michael Wessells — Department of Psychology, Randolph-Macon College, USA

INTRODUCTION

Throughout recorded history, the need for military manpower has challenged states and transformed societies. And, as states and wars have grown larger and more ambitious, the forces needed to advance state interests have also grown. While William the Conqueror defeated the Saxon army at Hastings with only 8000 soldiers, Napoleon was prepared to raise, and if necessary spend, a million men to conquer Europe. By this century, states had found the means to raise even larger armies in the service of national defense or conquest. More than two million men died on the Western Front in 1916, and even more were killed on the Eastern Front a quarter of a century later. Such wars would not have been possible without the development of rational and routinized means of military recruitment and military service. Conscript armies helped European states to win and hold colonies around the world, and colonial conscripts helped to fight and win the World Wars. Thus in some respects, the current international state system is an outcome of military conscription. And, because conscription both required and reinforced ties between states and their citizens, it transformed societies inside state borders as well. Conscription played a crucial role in creating the world we know today.

Yet, surprisingly, military conscription has not been a central topic of social science. This omission is especially odd considering that conscription and other forms of military recruitment directly relate to many of the central issues in social science, including state formation, state capacity, the legitimation of state claims to citizen sacrifices, social stratification, nationalist or separatist socialization, the spread of military skills, and the constitution of male identities. Moreover, military service has been, and remains, one of the central problems of the contemporary world, since this organized use of violence has always raised the question of how mankind could achieve a peaceful world. That military recruitment has been a central concern of states is obvious; that it should also be a central concern of social scientists seems to us equally obvious too. This volume attempts to help direct our disciplines' attention more fully to this important issue.

If social scientists have largely neglected military recruitment, so too have most military historians. With few exceptions, such historians have generally focused on military technologies, organization, leadership, morale, strategy and tactics, battles and campaigns, and accounts of how all these phenomena influence the fate of states, while paying little attention to military recruitment itself. Yet recruitment clearly is an equally if not more important topic, since it is only through successful recruitment that war-making and state-making can ultimately succeed. While its specific forms have evolved over time, from mercenaries and militias to modern conscripted armies and – perhaps – beyond, the importance of military recruitment to states and their armies has not declined. Consequently, it is only appropriate that this process of entry into the military should serve as the main focus of this issue of *Comparative Social Research.*

Any analysis of modern military recruitment must necessarily begin with the European state system, since this system lay at the war-ridden heart of international politics until its bloody breakdown in the First and Second World Wars. Consequently, this volume begins with a broad introductory article by the editors (Mjøset and Van Holde), which traces the historical development of conscription in, and eventually beyond, the European state system. It is argued that while conscription has proved to be a powerful and increasingly emulated means of military recruitment in the modern era, it may now be growing obsolete, at least in the developed world. We also develop a general typology of military recruitment which helps to "frame" many of our contributors' more detailed essays, as well as to indicate key questions for further investigation.

The other articles included in this issue of *CSR* address the development, impact, and implications of military recruitment from the eighteenth century to the present day. Several of our authors (Alan Forrest, Meyer Kestenbaum, David Rowe, and David Carey) focus on states' efforts to develop, implement, and impose conscription on often resistant populations, both within Europe and in peripheral regions and colonies. Others (Gretchen Ritter, Paul Higate) focus on the impact of military service in shaping gender roles, or in socializing children to accept casual killing and its corresponding dehumanization as normal (Paul Richards, Mike Wessells). Two of our contributors (Rafael Ajangiz, Bjørn Møller) trace recent trends in European states which suggest that conscription may, at least in that region, be increasingly obsolete. And in the final section of this issue, we feature a debate on Margaret Levi's recent work on conscription.

One major issue in the comparative study of conscription has focused on how, when and why states moved from earlier forms of military recruitment to modern conscription, which at once asserts and depends on an intimate connection between individual "citizen-soldiers" and the nation-states to which they belong. In discussing this important development, several of our authors demonstrate that the transition from old regime recruitment to modern conscription was complex, prolonged, and frequently contentious. According to Meyer Kestenbaum, the standard account which sees conscription as emerging solely or even primarily out of the French Revolution greatly oversimplifies a longer and more complex process which took place before, during, and after that seminal event. Tracing the emergence of citizen conscription in the eighteenth century American colonies, Revolutionary France, and in early nineteenth century Prussia, Kestenbaum shows that war forced *all* those states to develop innovative conceptions of a national citizenry, a mass army, and widespread popular mobilizations, innovations which then combined to create conscription as we know it.

Alan Forrest, in a detailed analysis of the French and British cases from the Revolution to World War I, largely agrees, but also shows that even in France, the principles and practices of universal conscription long were vigorously contested. It was only by constructing a highly stylized myth of a "nation in arms" that conscription was finally accepted for once and all. Acceptance of conscription was even slower in Britain where, according to Forrest, long-standing military tradition and a deep-seated suspicion of central state power made the imposition of a draft essentially impossible before 1916. David Rowe offers a different explanation, arguing that support for, or resistance to, recruitment in early twentieth century Europe depended on "the effects of globalization on civilian wages and whether militaries used conscription or voluntary" means to recruit their soldiers. Such factors also shaped the *forms* of resistance, which ranged from relatively apolitical British antimilitarism to the much more politicized outcomes typical of continental Europe.

Popular responses to conscription in peripheral regions and colonies were equally, if not more problematic, as David Carey shows. In a comparison of military conscription in two "peripheral" countries (Guatemala and Senegal) during and after World War I, Carey demonstrates that Mayan and Senegalese soldiers were able to use their military experience as a means of personal and sometimes political empowerment. In the periphery, therefore, conscription sometimes eventually undermined hegemonic powers, as the troops they drafted later organized insurgencies against them.

In short, the historical case studies in this volume clearly show that there were significant problems in legitimizing and implementing conscription from its inception, in European and peripheral states alike. Such difficulties are unsurprising, perhaps, since the bargain between citizen and state on which conscription depended had always been a conditional one. And, as our contemporary case studies demonstrate, that bargain has proven increasingly difficult to sustain, as citizens grew more politically sophisticated and powerful, and as states became increasingly burdened by obligations at home and abroad. Once a powerful means of popular mobilization and military recruitment, conscription may now be significantly or even fatally flawed.

One of the most problematic aspects of conscription lies in its complex and increasingly controversial relations to citizenship, civil society, military service, and gender – issues addressed in the articles by Gretchen Ritter and Paul Higate. For Ritter, the problems inherent in the "conscription bargain" are evident in the very different treatment of male and female soldiers and veterans in the United States during and after World War II. Although women served in unprecedented numbers during the war, persistent gender stereotypes meant that their contributions to the war effort were minimized and their citizenship rights significantly curtailed. And gender discrimination only increased after the War, as the state retroactively gendered service in the war – and the honors it conferred – as essentially male. Thus although Ritter, like Carey, demonstrates that military service *can* serve as a means of empowerment, she also shows that such empowerment all too often is limited and transitory.

Paul Higate's account of more recent developments in the British reinforces Ritter's conclusions, but also suggests that even the abolition of conscription would not resolve all of the difficulties Ritter identifies. While Britain's abandonment of a conscript army in 1962 decisively broke the link between citizenship and military service, older and possibly deeper links between such service and (hyper)masculinity have, if anything, been reinforced in the new army. Nor has the gradual incorporation of women into the Volunteer Force significantly reduced such hypermasculinity. To date, their presence has not led to any significant regendering of roles, and the AVF remains deeply committed to preserving a male "warrior ethic" among its recruits. In short, Britain's All Voluntary Force (AVF), despite its apparently modern character, has played a traditional or even reactionary role with regard to civil society.

Nevertheless, the gradual abandonment of conscription in favor of professionalized "volunteer" armies appears likely in the near future, at least in Western Europe. That trend began during the Cold War, when Western and Eastern powers alike grew convinced that peace was only possible if conscript armies were reinforced with highly sophisticated weapons systems. Thus while elaborate systems of peacetime conscription were developed in most NATO and Warsaw Pact countries, a turn away from "pure" conscription based simply on fielding huge civilian armies was already underway. That trend was further accelerated in Western Europe, where states became increasingly committed to ensuring the civilian security (via welfare state subsidies) rather than the military security of their populations. And, once the Cold War ended and the nation-state came under pressure from neoliberal and globalizing forces, the role of the military had to be rethought too. In sum, as Europe has come to play a less important role in the international balance of power in the last decade, the historic role of peacetime conscription is now also waning in the wealthy states of Western Europe.

There are, as Rafael Ajangiz and Bjørn Møller show, a variety of reasons for this development, both among state leaders and across European societies. Causes of this trend include the progressive extension of rights and social services to citizens, growing popular dissatisfaction with military interventions and "imperialism" in the developing world, and a sense that with the end of the Cold War, large conscript armies are no longer necessary or justifiable. All of these developments have worked to undermine the bargain between states and societies on which conscription ultimately depended. However, state leaders have also increasingly come to see universal conscription as an outdated practice. After all, as it has grown less popular, its political costs have become correspondingly higher. And, as Møller points out, conscript armies are not well suited to the multilateral peacekeeping operations which European states are increasingly required to perform. In such settings, readily deployed "volunteer" forces are greatly superior.

In the developing world, conscription appears to be equally if not more endangered, although for very different reasons. In many if not most developing states, military service has never served to incorporate previously marginalized groups or to extend citizenship rights to those previously denied them. In fact, in many states it has even failed to serve the narrower function of providing a means of social mobility via promotion through the ranks, as key opportunities and positions have often been reserved for dominant ethnic groups. Thus the conscription bargain has never really worked in these settings. Nonetheless, "third world" armies have continued to draw many of the poorest and most powerless into their ranks, using the mere promise of security as a means of recruitment. Such promises are often quite attractive in states plagued by serious economic and social problems, threatened by regional conflicts, or torn by civil wars.

Although this volume cannot begin to do full justice to the varied character of military recruitment in the developing world, it does address one particularly disturbing trend in war-torn developing states – the growing number of child soldiers. As Mike Wessells and Paul Richards show, state collapse and rebel insurgencies have led increasingly to the forced military service of children, especially in sub-Saharan Africa. Kidnapping is the most common means of procuring child soldiers, but insurgent armies are ready and willing to use other methods, including the murder of any and all adults who might otherwise prevent such tragic outcomes. Perhaps even more disturbing, children sometimes "choose" to join up, as poverty and civil war have destroyed their families, their villages, and have left them with no other means of survival. In paramilitary groups like Sierra Leone's RUF and Uganda's Lord's Army, such children can "apprentice" themselves to older killers, and may find a sort of family to replace the one they have lost to war. Not surprisingly, such experiences make successful reintegration into civil society difficult or impossible. Thus the military service of children entails a double tragedy, in that it not only devastates the lives of those recruited, but also jeopardizes lasting peace in the societies to which demobilized soldiers return. If child soldiering comes to play a significant role in the developing world, then the future of military recruitment there would seem to be very bleak indeed.

The last section of this volume addresses important questions of theory and method by focusing on one of the major recent studies in the field – Margaret Levi's *Consent, Dissent, and Patriotism*. Levi's analysis of conscription centers on three key questions: the reasons why democratic states choose to adopt and enforce universal conscription; the means by which democracies secure the "contingent consent" on which successful conscription depends; and the conditions under which citizens suspend or withdraw that consent. For Levi, conscription thus is the result of an extended bargaining process between states and citizens, where states extend certain rights to citizens in exchange for their willing acceptance of, and compliance with, personally costly policies. Conscription, as a vitally important yet supremely costly policy, serves as an ideal test of the extent to which such bargains are feasible and durable. And, as a carefully grounded and theoretically rigorous explanation of that important policy, *Consent, Dissent, and Patriotism* is a work which clearly warrants thoughtful analysis, assessment and critique.

John Hobson, Tarak Barkawi, and Margaret Levi clearly all have taken that charge seriously, and the resulting exchange is incisive and lively. Both Hobson and Barkawi find Levi's analysis quite problematic, and raise a number of fundamental questions regarding her model and method. In turn, Levi offers a thoughtful and tightly reasoned rejoinder to their critiques. We will not attempt to fully summarize that complex and often contentious debate here, but instead only indicate a few points on which there is fundamental disagreement. They include: criteria of case selection; the role of endogenous and exogenous factors in shaping state policies; the relative importance of consent and domination as means of legimitation; and finally, the role and relative impact of interest and power in explaining social action and institutions. Obviously, the resolution of such deep disagreements on theory and method is not possible in this volume. Yet the debate between Levi and her critics, as well as the analyses by our other contributors, will, we hope, allow our readers to more fully understand the complex dynamics of conscription as well as the many challenges this powerful yet contentious model of recruitment faces.

And indeed, the diverse patterns of military recruitment discussed in this volume clearly raise a number of intriguing and important questions. Are we now entering a situation where universal conscription – a very powerful model of mobilization and recruitment in Europe and North America during the 19th and 20th century – is in decline? Should conscription be regarded as a historically limited means of recruitment now destined to be replaced by other forms of service that demand less of states and their citizens? What will be the consequences of the increasing professionalization of first world forces – have democratization and strengthened civil societies proceeded far enough to ensure that such forces do not develop into tools of international or domestic aggression? What trends will affect young people – mostly young males – in the rest of the world now that Cold War polarization has been replaced by regional and civil strife? In particular, what role will conscription play in Asia's densely populated states? Is there any sense in which we can see conscription in the post-Cold War developing world as an instrument of peace? And finally, do these complex developments relative to conscription suggest that we are moving towards a less violent future or a more violent one?

Here we can only mention these challenging questions. We trust, however, that this volume of *CSR* will inspire further research into and analysis of these urgent and important issues.

Lars Mjøset
Stephen Van Holde
Editors

PART I:
HISTORICAL PERSPECTIVES

KILLING FOR THE STATE, DYING FOR THE NATION: AN INTRODUCTORY ESSAY ON THE LIFE CYCLE OF CONSCRIPTION INTO EUROPE'S ARMED FORCES

Lars Mjøset and Stephen Van Holde

INTRODUCTION

This essay provides a broad overview of the European experience with recruitment of military manpower. We combine a sequence – in the form of a periodization stretching from the early modern period until today – with a rough typology distinguishing the seawards, non-continental cases (with England as the archetype) from two continental types: one "seawards" (France as the archetype), the other "landwards" (Prussia as the archetype). We also include some remarks on the Nordic countries, which mostly approximate the French type of military recruitment. While this essay does not provide a fully articulated model of military recruitment – that would be the task of a much longer study! – it does develop a provisional typology of such recruitment. And that typology in turn provides a context by which regional trends and patterns in the recruitment of military manpower can be better understood, and can also serve as the basis for further comparative analyses of this important topic.

The Comparative Study of Conscription in the Armed Forces, Volume 20, pages 3–94.

ISBN: 0-7623-0836-2

HISTORICAL AND METHODOLOGICAL BACKGROUND

Although modern conscription dates from the eighteenth century, similar forms of military recruitment existed in the ancient world. There are allusions to conscription in the Old Testament and Homer's *Odyssey* and hints of rudimentary draft systems in Egypt and Assyria (Møller, 2000). Conscription also was employed by some of the Greek city-states and in Rome, particularly during the decline of the Empire. The Romans' increasing need for troops eventually led them to abandon the voluntary recruitment of propertied citizens in favor of the conscription of non-propertied plebeians. With the demise of the classical world in the fifth century AD, however, such systems of military recruitment collapsed as well, to be replaced by the more localized and personalized recruitment systems of the Middle Ages. Such systems obligated subordinates (vassals) to perform military (and other) services for their lords, in exchange for land and protection (Anderson, 1978, pp. 139–142, 147–153, 183ff.).

In the late Middle Ages, the basis of military forces in Europe began to change. In this era, military forces were composed primarily of militias linked to specific communities, frequently reinforced by heavy cavalry and a skilled fighting force of armored knights (Finer, 1975, pp. 102–103). In other settings, however, the forces of knights and those of communities – especially medieval communes – came into direct and violent conflict (Anderson, 1978, pp. 147–153; Anderson, 1979, pp. 29–33). In any case, the bases of military service for militias and knights alike were socially contractual ones; the first owed specific obligations to their communities, while the latter were obligated by ties of vassalage that bound them to feudal lords. As we will see, knight service was eventually replaced by service for pay; however, militia service persisted much longer, existing in some locales until the age of absolutism and beyond. For now, however, we will focus primarily on the transformations in the services of military elites, since it was this service which would have the greatest consequences for war-making and state-building during the next several hundred years.

This medieval style of warfare required a substantial investment in horses, armor and squires, and so generally proved prohibitively expensive to all but the wealthiest individuals (i.e. if a soldier today were to spend an equivalent amount on his arms, he could buy a tank). These rich self-equipped fighters often were relatively autonomous, which in turn created great problems of authority and loyalty vis-à-vis their liege lords. Consequently, the system eventually proved unstable, as knights became the core of a nobility supporting the military status quo, while kings and other state leaders increasingly sought to develop or acquire more easily controlled forces (Finer, 1975, pp. 102–103).

Let us clarify certain analytical issues. In order to elucidate the evolution of conscription and other forms of military recruitment during the last several hundred years, our analysis will build primarily on the work of Stein Rokkan (1999), and on Charles Tilly's (1990) extension of his studies of how states are formed and consolidated. As for the means of state-making, Rokkan emphasized the granting of citizenship rights and nationalism, while Tilly has added an emphasis on war-making. In our historical narrative, we shall employ significant aspects of both analytic approaches.

Beginning in the fourteenth century, a number of roughly simultaneous military, political and economic transformations helped to ensure that the medieval style of recruitment and warfare gradually lost importance. New weapons, such as the longbow in Britain, and the pike on the Continent, made knights increasingly vulnerable and feudal cavalry increasingly obsolete. Even more important were the state- and war-making innovations of the fourteenth century. Italian city-states began to find innovative solutions to longstanding political, economic and military problems, (re)introducing republican government, private banking systems, and a new form of warfare. The Italian city-states exemplify Tilly's *capital-intensive* path to state-building. The rulers of these city-states taxed traders and craftsmen – and increasingly borrowed money from the new banking houses – to finance the defense of their territories and the conquest of neighboring city-states. And since the forces they fielded were increasingly made up of mercenaries, the leaders of the city-states were able to construct states at once more independent and more sovereign than had their feudal predecessors.

In Europe's eastern landwards areas, state formation and the evolution of military institutions followed distinctively different lines. Russia and Brandenburg-Prussia show how state leaders employed coercion-intensive strategies of state-building and power consolidation, seizing resources and forcing military service on the peasantry, and using aristocrats and other landowners as middlemen (Tilly, 1990). In exchange for being granted certain rights and privileges, these middlemen were expected to keep peasants tied to their plots. The elites were also controlled through co-optation and forced service in state offices. In this way, huge agrarian bureaucracies developed. The basis of these states was feudal agriculture, which in turn engendered a "second serfdom" in reaction to the crisis of feudal government and warfare during the later middle ages (late 14th century). However, because this – what Tilly dubs *coercion-intensive* – path to state formation was not conducive to the development of trade and of civil societies, the Eastern states would eventually find themselves at a disadvantage in the era of popular conscription and modern warfare.

Between the fourteenth and seventeenth centuries, states and armies slowly developed into the forms familiar to us today. Tilly (1990, p. 30) views the later states that crystallized during that period as an intermediary form between the capital- and the coercion-intensive types of state formation, and labels this the capitalized coercion type. Here we find a main difference between Tilly and Rokkan: Rokkan is content to end up with a map of the factors that explain the political systems of the various nation states, while Tilly ends with an aggregation. Explicitly objecting to the common view of seeing Britain, France, Prussia and Spain as contrasting trajectories of state formation, Tilly holds that the similarities are important enough to subsume them all under his capitalized coercion type. As he notes, "in all four cases the coincidence of coercive centers with centers of capital facilitated – at least for a while – the creation of massive military force in a time when large, expensive, well-armed armies and navies gave those national states that were able to create them the overwhelming advantage in the search for hegemony and empire" (Tilly, 1990, p. 159). These states relied more on direct coercion of their citizens for resources and military service than had the Italian city-states, yet also depended on an evolving market and rudimentary civil societies to supply their militaries and ensure their states' security.

In our analysis of the evolution of military recruitment systems, we cannot accept Tilly's aggregations without modification. Rather, our typological sketch will follow Rokkan in treating each of the Great Powers as separate and distinct, while employing Tilly's terminology. Thus, we suggest – for the specific purpose of our analysis – that Britain, and even more the USA, should be viewed as cases where the capital/coercion combination is tilted towards the domination of capital (albeit in a large state setting rather than in a city-state variety). In France, capital and coercion were more evenly balanced, while in Prussia, and even more in Russia, the balance was sharply tilted towards coercion. Such a comparative sketch can also be viewed in accordance with the geographical west/east-axis employed by Rokkan. And finally, it can be seen in terms of relationships between state and civil society. Only by viewing military recruitment systems in this multidimensional manner can their complex evolution be properly understood.

If the movement of states towards modern centralized and rationalized "power containers" (Giddens, 1985) was relatively slow and uneven, the evolution of armies towards the mass armies of the modern era was slower still. The knight faded from history, but the aristocratic officers were his heirs. In much of Europe, such aristocrats remained in charge of the armies until the early nineteenth century, and in some states, like Germany and Russia, aristocrats continued to enjoy disproportionate influence until the First World War. The armies they commanded, by contrast, were generally recruited from the lower strata of society, and were in most states made up overwhelmingly of peasants. Such armies remained fundamentally dependent on aristocrats, however, who not only served as their commanders, but often directly recruited and outfitted them as well.

Not surprisingly, such armies often proved to be more loyal to that aristocracy than to the state leaders who they formally served, making them potentially dangerous to employ. Moreover, because generally only the aristocracy had the skills and knowledge to command them, state leaders often had a tenuous control over their own armies. Such problems would eventually force those leaders to abandon aristocratic armies in favor of larger and more meritocratic armies, where soldiers owed loyalty directly to the states they served, and where the most able of them were in principle able to rise to positions of command. Popular conscription would play a central role in sparking and accelerating that important trend, as we will see.

While the changing social relations between military elites and the state would eventually force a radical popularization of the armed forces, sheer demographics transformed the armies much earlier. As states grew increasingly large, powerful and ambitious, they required larger and larger armies. Although it is difficult to estimate the exact size of armies before the nineteenth century, there is no question that they increased markedly, particularly during the age of absolutism. According to Finer, for example, the number of (French) troops called up for campaigns (a useful, if somewhat rough indicator of army size) exploded between the beginning of the sixteenth and nineteenth centuries: 65,000 (1498), 155,000 (1635), 440,000 (1691), 700,000 (1812). In other, less populous, countries such as England and particularly Prussia, the numbers lagged somewhat, but the increases remain impressive all the same. At the height of the Napoleonic Wars in 1812 and 1813, England was fielding an army of 250,000 and tiny Prussia (with only about 3 million citizens) one of 300,000 (Finer, 1975, p. 101)! Other authors' figures are roughly similar. For example, Parker (1996, p. 45ff.) notes that the first really big leap in army size can be dated to 1670–1710, "a major manpower revolution", with the French army growing from 200,000 men in the 1670s to 395,000 by the end of that century. The rising trend peaked in the twentieth century's world wars, where literally millions of soldiers faced off in the fields of Flanders, Russia, Germany and France.

In order to better assess this trend, we shall supplement Tilly and Rokkan's typologies of state- and war-making with Finer's more specific typology of recruitment. Finer's typology of recruitment has three key dimensions: where soldiers are recruited from (native/foreign), whether they are paid or not (voluntary/conscripted), and whether they are mobilized on an *ad hoc* or permanent

Table 1. Typology of Army Formats.

	Ad hoc	Permanent
Foreign paid "volunteers"	(3) "Mercenaries"	(4) "Subsidy troops"
Native paid "volunteers"	(2) "Bandes", indentured companies	(5) "Regulars"
Native obligatory service	(1) Feudal Host Popular militia	(6) Universal military service

Source: adopted from Finer 1975, Figs 2–4.

basis (part-time/full-time) (Finer, 1975, pp. 95, 99–102; using only the two latter dimensions, we arrive at the typology used in Cohen, 1985, and by Kestnbaum in this issue).

By examining this table, we are able to trace a number of important trends in the evolution of military recruitment from the late Middle Ages to the current day. To begin with, we note that over time, armies increasingly shifted from *ad hoc* to permanent standing forces. This trend peaked in the early and mid-twentieth century, when entire male populations were employed to fight for the state. In many countries, they were also trained as a permanent reserve during peacetime. This is conscription in the strong sense, but we shall see that there are also a number of border cases – or conscription in a weaker sense – particularly varieties of what Finer dubs the "popular militia", and Kestnbaum (this issue, following Cohen, 1985) dubs the "militia draft."

The trend from *ad hoc* to permanent forces is from left to right in the typology, but we can also use the typology to sketch an "ideal-type" historical sequence, as indicated by the numbers listed in parentheses. This sequence moves from a pre-modern "community" at the regional level to a modern "community" in the form of the nation-state employing universal conscription in the twentieth century. It progresses via a commercialized phase in which rulers first pay *ad hoc* groups to defend and extend their territories. Later, these forces are made permanent, to the point where Europe's 17th century absolutist rulers could bring several hundred thousand men to the battlefield. These troops were partly foreign or native "volunteers"; a term that should be used cautiously, as most were paid, and many of them were forcibly impressed into service. Conscription in the modern sense of the word does not appear to have been implemented in Europe before the 17th century, and remained quite uncommon for at least another 150 years.

Conscription originally meant "the common writing down of eligible names for the purpose of a ballot, [with] only the unlucky numbers having to serve" (Finer, 1975, p. 94). It is important to note that neither mercenaries nor volunteers were conscripts in the strict sense, since they *chose* warfare as profession or employment and served in exchange for pay. In contrast, conscripts are *required* by a political authority to serve. In a sense, various methods of impressment, especially when sufficiently organized and on a large enough scale, can be said to constitute a rudimentary kind of conscription. And again, militia forces cannot usually be seen as conscripted, as they mainly serve local defense needs, and often involve a degree of voluntary choice as well. To the extent that various communities exert pressure on young males to participate, however, militias can be seen as a limiting case of conscription.

That being said, it is important not to conflate militia service with conscription into a regular standing army, as the features of the two systems are quite different. In militias, men serve part time with only a few weeks of drill and training, and generally are fully mobilized only in response to specific emergencies. Standards of discipline and expertise are relatively low, and militias are rarely if ever deployed far from home (cf. concepts of national guard, reserve forces, "irregulars"). A standing army, by contrast, implies regular military service (as opposed to service only during emergencies), the discipline and law of a standing force, isolation from civilian life and civil society, extensive training, and expertise in battlefield technology and tactics (cf. concepts of "regulars", "army of the line"). (See Kestnbaum in this issue.)

The first genuine cases of conscription in the modern era can be dated to the early seventeenth century, with the practice becoming more common in the eighteenth and (especially) nineteenth centuries. There was, as we shall see below, conscription of Swedish peasants by about 1620 and a parallel development in Norway some twenty years later. Such practices, however, were the exception rather than the rule. A wider and more socially transformative form of conscription arose in the late eighteenth century in the United States and France, with military service being directly and explicitly linked to the acquisition and protection of citizenship rights. However, such developments remained atypical for almost another century, as nineteenth century European states abandoned citizenship-based conscription in favor of more inegalitarian models. During the early and mid-nineteenth century, conscription generally took the form of lotteries, substitutions and replacements, and was clearly skewed to target the lower classes, especially the peasantry. In fact, substitutes and replacements often served as a kind of quasi-professional soldiers. It was not until the last quarter of that century that the Prussian model became widely emulated, if modified, so as to respect legitimate claims to democratic rights then largely ignored in Germany.

In the early twentieth century, conscription finally acquired its most general, egalitarian and deadly form. Universal military service became a condition for the enormous and fatal resource extraction and waste of the two world wars. Yet the human costs of wartime conscription did not significantly delegitimize the new model, as we will see. Instead, universal peacetime conscription was adopted by a number of countries during the Cold War, and would continue to be widely practiced in almost all of them until very recently.

MILITARY REVOLUTIONS IN EARLY MODERN EUROPE 1450–1660

Starting in the mid-fifteenth century, European states and armies began to be radically transformed. Such transformations centered on fundamental changes relative to the recruitment and structure of armies, the weapons they carried, and ultimately in the character of the states fielding those armies. By the end of the "long sixteenth" century, the groundwork had been laid for the even larger technical, political and social revolutions that army, state and society would see in the seventeenth and eighteenth centuries.

One of the most important changes in this era lay in the gradual "nationalization" of the armed forces, beginning in the mid-fifteenth century. In 1445, the French began to convert *ad hoc* military forces (what Finer refers to as "bandes") into centrally controlled "national" forces. Within fifty years, such forces were being used so frequently and generally as to constitute a kind of primitive standing army. Although such nationalization was quickly emulated in a number of European states, it was not universal; England reverted to popular militias in 1485 (Finer, 1975, p. 117). We should be careful not to overstress the national character of these armies, however, as they were and would long remain semiprivate. In such armies, an agent of the king typically received a commission to raise, equip and lead a force of mercenaries. Moreover, such armies' limited size and skill forced rulers to frequently resort to additional means of bolstering their forces, and consequently, to employ foreign troops and mercenaries on a contract basis. Such troops posed few dangers for domestic stability since they were not attached to any particular regional interests or powers. Consequently, they were widely used. Swiss mercenaries, in particular, served many of the European royal families, and would continue to do so until the end of the *ancien regime*. And in several states, such as France and Spain, armies acquired a complex heterogeneous character, as standing armies made up of native and foreign volunteers were combined with such mercenaries and local militias to make up a *de facto* national army.

At the same time, a number of significant technological developments began to transform the character of war. The most important of these revolutions was the development and spread of gunpowder, firearms and artillery. Gunpowder was first applied to field artillery. The first cannons were enormously heavy and difficult to transport, but even so, they soon transformed warfare. Beginning about 1420 (and especially in the French invasion of Italy in the 1490s), the new technology shifted military advantage decisively to the offense, as cannons proved able to destroy castle and city walls in a few days. Similar developments were taking place in the navies, where cannons were gradually integrated into naval design, tactics, and strategy. Heavy artillery was placed on ships by the 1440s, and cannons were placed in gunports by the 1470s. Design refinements enabled ships to fire broadsides beginning around 1510, and such "capital ships" became common in the next half-century (Parker, 1996, p. 160).

From artillery the new gunpower revolution spread more slowly to firearms, but as it did so, it further transformed the character of war. Hand-held firearms were first used in battle in the 1470s, but there were many technical problems, and it was not until the late sixteenth century that it was possible for an army to shoot a continuous barrage of fire (Parker, 1996, p. 161). Earlier, however, primitive firetubes were used together with other weapons such as pikes and halberds. Even such relatively primitive weapons transformed tactics and strategy, however. Commanders experimented with formations like the "Swiss phalanx", a square of 6000 men which made best use of the new weapons by insisting on a strict division of labour among the fighting forces.

As the weapons revolution of the fifteenth and sixteenth centuries progressed, the advantage shifted back to the defense, which again transformed tactics, strategy, and war itself. By the 1520s, Italian city-states threatened by aggressive monarchies in Northern and Western Europe (France, the Habsburgs) had developed new techniques of artillery-resistant fortification – fortresses with thick walls and angled bastions. Cannonballs against such thick walls might – after prolonged firing – create an opening, but the bastions allowed the defenders to prevent an attack (Parker, 1996, p. 165).

An additional and perhaps even more important consequence of this military revolution lay in the ways in which it shifted the balance of power in the European state system. That shift actually entailed two stages. The first change was characterized by a marked and general increase in the size of European states, with a corresponding eclipse of the small states which had previously predominated. States with populations sufficiently large to recruit and provision massive standing armies gained a considerable advantage, and used that advantage to secure substantial gains in territory and wealth at the expense of their smaller neighbours. Even the richest city-states increasingly found themselves unable to afford the large armies now required for territorial defense or aggrandizement (Tilly, 1990). While in the "dorsal spine" regions of Europe (Rokkan, 1999, p. 179), smaller states and city-states survived into the 19th century, their influence was quite limited.

A second major transformation in the European state system occurred during the "long sixteenth century", as power gradually shifted from inland to seawards states. Private interests financed expeditions of great strategic and military importance, but required that those expeditions be economically efficient enough to turn a profit. Expansion of the seawards states therefore often proved self-financing, reducing taxation pressures significantly. The maritime great powers thus were in a "virtuous circle" during this mercantilist period, easily conquering overseas areas flourishing with precious metals and other easily transportable tradeables such as spices. The first hegemons of the developing state system were the Iberian countries in the mid-sixteenth century, followed by the Netherlands approximately 100 years later. They would in turn be followed by Britain, which ascended to its eventual dominant position as a result of the chronic great power conflicts of the eighteenth century.

To the other side of the "dorsal spine" of city-states lay the inland states, virtually none of which could be counted as great powers in this period. The one true inland great power was the Austrian Hapsburg Empire (which by the mid-sixteenth century could field an army of almost 148,000 men in several different war theaters!), but this empire had a seawards orientation through its union with Spain as the United Habsburgs between 1519 and 1556. The reason for the failure of inland states to realize great power status lay in the difficulties they faced in fielding and financing the necessary armies. The more important the continental borders were to the inland state, the larger was the pressure to finance large armies. Yet such states experienced few economic benefits from their military organisation. Military leaders mostly became integrated in agrarian bureaucracies, and were driven by codes of honor rather than by business-minded attitudes. In addition, tax pressure was much stronger than in the seawards empires (McNeill, 1982, p. 101–105). In the seawards states, conquest and commerce went hand in hand. The inland states, by contrast, could only expand by provoking strong rivals.

The most populous European state in this period, France, combined all three of these elements. She was seawards, and thus competed with other seawards powers in building a navy (and would soon also compete for overseas possessions). But France was also oriented inwards, as the first country to establish a standing army in her quest for military hegemony on the continent. Finally, France also went through a long and complicated process of centralization, and so originally was in some respects fragmented, like the small states of the city belt. In fact, while England was already a unified kingdom in 975, France remained a motley collection of autonomous fiefs, counties and duchies until well into the sixteenth century.

The French case demonstrates eloquently that in the early modern period the extent to which most states controlled their territories remained quite limited. There were strong regional power-bases, some of which retained significant autonomy until the mid-seventeenth century. The central state was vulnerable to revolts, such as food and bread riots, peasant uprisings, and to resistance to military service in times of war. The economy was agrarian and feudalistic, and the social structure was marked by hereditary nobility. Numerous local assemblies and Estates had to agree to taxation, and whole regions and sectors of the population were exempted from state taxes. The absence of one central constitutional organ (like the British parliament) made the extraction of resources for war easier in France than in England, but at the threshold of the Thirty Years War (in the first decade of the seventeenth century), "neither the standing army nor the grossly overswollen bureaucracy was an effective instrument of unification" (Finer, 1975, p. 129). Only in the latter part of the seventeenth century was full absolutism established under Louis XIV.

The period from roughly 1550 to 1660 also saw further important advances in weapons technologies, the art of fortification and, most notably, in manpower organization. The turning point towards warfare dominated by firepower has been dated to 1580–1630 (Parker, 1996, p. 169). The lands of the Spanish Habsburgs were at the center of this military revolution. While smaller states built superfortresses, larger states erected networked systems of artillery fortresses. Warfare now took the form of frequent sieges, assaults, and skirmishes, but few real battles. Only by taking key fortresses could an invader hope to gain genuine control over the territories he occupied.

Traditional knightly cavalry could do little in a context of long sieges, so military leaders needed large numbers of disciplined infantry to wage and win wars. Consequently, armies grew markedly in size. In the mid-sixteenth century, 50–60,000 men were needed to successfully carry out a major siege; by the late seventeenth or early eighteenth centuries, the required forces had increased to 90–110,000 (Parker, 1996, p. 171). Sieges involved large concentrations of troops, as one part had to attack the fortress, while an observation army was needed to cover the routes by which the enemy could send relief troops to the besieged fortress. And within those fortresses, more troops were needed, so the size of the garrisons inside the fortresses to be defended increased as well.

Under the new conditions, wars became larger, more costly, and more long-lasting. For example, in the Thirty Years War (1618-1648), which eventually involved almost all of the major European powers, armies swept over – and devastated – much of the European continent. In the final, particularly bloody, period of the War (1635–1648), battle deaths rose to 12,933 per million. This unprecedented rate would not be equalled until the Napoleonic wars almost 200 years later (Levy, 1983, Tables 3.1. and 4.1).

The geography of fortifications was important to the outcome of these new longer wars. Thanks to its particularly strong system of fortresses, the Netherlands was never fully conquered during the Thirty Years War. In the late seventeenth century, the French started to erect a long line of mutally supporting positions between the North Sea and the Meuse. With the arrival of such fixed positions, it was no longer possible to win wars by knock-out blows.

The new technologies and tactics also posed new challenges in provisioning armies, financing the new warfare, and ultimately to the state itself. The costs of warfare were rising due to the increasing number of soldiers needed, the increasing price of arms, and the growing length of military campaigns. To the extent that troops had to remain stationary around a fortress, it was less easy to supply their needs by plundering local populations. Thus, a number of logistical challenges on how to feed and equip an army had to be addressed. There also were significant fiscal challenges in financing the escalating costs of large armies and expensive "ships of the line" equipped with the latest artillery. Confronted by these challenges, the new monarchies were forced to improve their bureaucratic capacities for raising and maintaining large armies, which in turn provided additional impetus to the emergence of absolutist states at the end of the sixteenth century.

European monarchies soon proved able to organize the use of force more efficiently and with more support from the participants than could any competing organizations. Tactical and technological innovations in warfighting – and particularly, the use of standing armies – spread rapidly between the units of the European state system, via rumors or intelligence by spies. By the end of the Thirty Years' War, an army was not just a collection of individually skilled mercenaries, it was a disciplined and tightly organized force of up to 30,000 men.

At the tactical level, perhaps the most important innovation occurred in the early seventeeth century, as Dutch commanders carefully studied the Roman art of war in order to develop a refined and accurate system of military drill. This innovation allowed a large number of soldiers to shoot with precision simultaneously, which meant that a disciplined army could thus expose its enemy to continuous volley fire. Together with other advances, such as smaller tactical units, this new military choreography turned the Dutch army into "an organism with a central nervous system." Not only were such innovations quickly emulated by other armies, similar tactical advances were being developed in the navies of the era. Both armies and marine forces were now becoming "works of art", where men, using ships and weapons, were assigned specific tasks according to an advance plan (McNeill, 1982, pp. 123, 129–130, 158; McNeill, 1995; Parker, 1996, p. 19).

The recruitment and socialization of military forces also witnessed a number of important innovations during this period. From the early seventeenth century, military service began to entail a process of socialization which created a military life style. The above-mentioned organizational innovations not only increased military efficiency, they also served to discipline young men. This had important consequences. Daily drill in a standing army created a deeply based primary community amongst the soldiers, who were often recruited from the lowest social strata (McNeill, 1982, pp. 131, 137–139; McNeill, 1995). This *esprit de corps* not only meant that soldiers were increasingly isolated from the rest of society, it also meant that they would not usually join popular uprisings. Instead, they generally acted to defend the privileges of absolutist rulers, a stance which once again helped to ensure the success of state-building and the consolidation of state power.

States were increasingly organized for war. Tax collection and military administration grew more and more centralized and bureaucratized, and the internal and external affairs of states became increasingly structured. In this era above all, the connection between warmaking and statemaking was a deeply intimate one, as the bellicose states of the seventeenth century found a way not only to successfully wage wars of an unprecedented scale, but also to consolidate their power over resistant societies and potential competitors at home.

As the power, ambition, and coordinating capacities of states grew, they also grew ever hungrier for military manpower. Yet in this era they were still unable to organize military recruitment on a national scale. Instead, they continued to rely on middlemen. During the Thirty Years War, for instance, roughly 1500 individuals raised armies from all over Europe, for one or more warlords (Parker, 1996, p. 64). Such armies were largely made up of volunteers, supplemented by foreign units and occasionally, by limited conscripted forces. Table 2 provides a summary outline of the character of such volunteer forces.

As Table 2 indicates, these armies were characterized by considerable diversity in methods of recruitment and in the personnel recruited. Such forces have been described as, "Noah's ark armies: volunteers and felons, international brigades, local militiamen, vassals, lieges and conscripts from many lands were all jumbled up together" (Parker, 1996, p. 60). Veterans were particularly valuable, given their rich experience and generally higher levels of skill. Veterans' motives for reenlisting undoubtedly varied, but probably usually included many of those listed in Table 2.

Table 2. Recruitment to Old Regime Armies.

Frequent motives of volunteers
- deteriorating living conditions (poor people striving to escape starvation, unemployment, tax-pressure, and/or harassment by soldiers).
- adventurism, religious motives.
- choice of the army as a professional career (clans, bands, families, military dynasties)

Border cases between volunteering and conscription: the use of foreign units
- membership in foreign units (e.g. Irish, German and Swiss regiments fighting for France). Some of these were criminals, beggars, vagabonds accepting military expatriation instead of execution or punishment
- Membership in defeated troops being enlisted by their enemy.

To the extent that the state needed exclusively national formations: conscription
- have local magistrates select "undesirables": criminals, unemployed, etc.
- select members of local militia (an unpopular move, last resort)
- compulsory military service

Source: Extracted from Parker 1996, pp. 46–52.

Despite increased degrees of discipline and organization, armies composed of the sorts of soldiers described above were less than perfect instruments of war. They were subject to high attrition rates and extensive internal mobility, and given their mixed and unevenly professional forces, often suffered from serious problems of discipline. Although "professional" soldiers were generally paid about the same as agrarian laborers in this period, they always tried to supplement those wages by "living off the land" and by collecting "protection money" reminiscent of mafia kickbacks in exchange for limiting the damage done to whatever unfortunate country they invested (Parker, 1996, p. 65ff.). Conscripted soldiers did the same. Armies were also plagued by chronic shortages of arms and artillery, generally of inferior quality. Such difficulties, especially when combined with the minimal training, undermined such armies' efficacy and reliability.

Although voluntary enlistment clearly seems to have been the most prevalent form of recruitment, other varieties were not unimportant, as Table 2 indicates. In all cases manpower usually was tapped from the lowest strata of the social hierarchy: the poor masses, as well as outcasts, criminals, or prisoners of war. The two purest cases of conscription (bottom of Table 2) seem to have been exceptions to the general pattern of volunteerism; in general, conscripting militia members was an unpopular move. Only in one European region – the Nordic states – during this period do we find a fully fledged system of compulsory military service.

We shall examine the Nordic trajectory more closely. Tilly (1990, p. 136) argues that in the Nordic area, we find varieties of the "coercion-intensive road to statehood." Sweden was the strongest unit in the Nordic area, and sought not only to dominate the region, but also to become a Great Power – a status it would briefly enjoy in the wake of the Thirty Years War. There was competition for regional dominance between Denmark-Norway and Sweden, but also tensions between Denmark and Norway.

Chronically short of money, the Swedish kings employed a variety of tactics to increase state power, including forced requisitions of resources and men, fiscal reform, and land-for-service bargains with the numerous (and previously autonomous) peasantry. Accordingly, the kings strengthened the state fiscal apparatus, made land grants that multiplied the number of small-holders (Tilly, 1990, p. 135), and, especially during the reign of Gustav Vasa (1521–1560), subjected large parts of the Swedish economy (iron, copper, and related proto-industries) to the military demands of the state. The Swedish kings also worked closely with the state's protestant clergy. The Protestant Reformation gave this small state a distinct homogeneity vis-à-vis the catholic great powers. The pastors of the (national) Lutheran church not only preached support for state policies, but also kept meticulous parish registers beginning in the 17th century. Such measures in turn allowed the state to keep track of taxpayers and potential military manpower.

Sweden also developed a proto-conscription system of military recruitment. Swedish conscription was developed by Charles IX (ruled 1599–1611) and Gustavus Adolphus (r. 1611–1632), and was organized as an allocation system (*indelningsverk*) covering Finland and metropolitan Sweden. By the late 1620s, the system was generating a very respectable number of soldiers for such a small (pop. of 1.5 million) state – roughly 10,000 soldiers a year (Parker, 1996, p. 53). The system required that each parish supply one soldier (equipped and fed) for every ten eligible male parishioners. Noblemen, clerics, miners, armaments workers and the only sons of widows were exempt, which meant that soldiers were largely drawn from the peasantry. Even though the state relied more on mercenaries than on conscripts to supply its armies during this period, the impact of the *indelningsverk* system on peasant communities could still be severe. Overall demographic estimates indicate that in early modern Europe, for each year of active service, one of every four or five enlisted soldiers died – a painful rate of attrition. Historical case studies also show how dramatically many parishes suffered: Parker refers to monographs on one parish (Bygdeå) in Northern Sweden which had 230 young men conscripted into Sweden's war with Poland and Germany between 1621 and 1639: of that number, 215 died and 5 returned crippled. By 1639 all but two conscripts were under 18, and half of them were no more than 15. The male population of the parish declined dramatically and the number of households headed by a woman increased sevenfold (Parker, 1996, pp. 52–53). While the *indelningsverk* system helped to facilitate Sweden's bid for power, and also set the stage for the far more extensive Swedish conscription of the 17th and 18th centuries (Tilly, 1990, pp. 135–136) its costs to the peasantry cannot be denied.

As for Denmark-Norway, Denmark clearly dominated. However, Norway was separated from Denmark by the North Sea and by Sweden, which made it difficult for the Danish king to manage wars and tensions with Sweden without allowing for some kind of autonomous administration in Norway. In 1643–1644 the Danish governor in Norway won a concession from the king that Norwegian farmers would finance their own military, and would in turn be exempted from Danish taxes. The result was a national Norwegian system of taxation, seen by historians as one of the main roots of Norwegian independence, since this required a Norwegian central administration (Jacobsen & Skauge, 2000). Innovative solutions were also found to the problem of actually staffing the Norwegian armed forces. While the first law on conscription in Norway would not be passed until 1705 (next section), it appears that some form of conscription had been institutionalized earlier, in connection with the 1644 settlement with the Danes. And, since Sweden had periodically occupied large sections of Norway in the 16th and 17th century, and had conscripted soldiers from Norway to fight its wars in the Baltic, it seems probable that the Norwegians emulated the Swedish system in designing their own.

Denmark also substantially reformed its means of military recruitment in the mid-17th century. Although the Danes had raised some of their troops through a militia system since the middle ages, by the 16th century mercenaries made up the bulk of their army. As the Danish king challenged the aristocracy and won absolutist powers (1660), a form of conscription was introduced – quite different than the one that had evolved in Norway. The Danish system was similar to Prussia's, with landlords being put in charge of conscripting their serfs. In order to escape this system, many young men fled the Danish countryside to Amsterdam or other freeholds (Hansen, 2001). In contrast, in Sweden it remained possible for the landlords to gain control over the conscription of peasants in the manner of their counterparts in Russia, Denmark, or Prussia.

In the late 17th century, parallel to the emergence of absolutism elsewhere, the Swedish king gained even more power against the nobles, repossessing crown lands that had earlier been sold off to pay for warfare. This land – or sometimes the income from crown lands – was allocated to part time soldiers (or militiamen) in exchange for military service. Thus, parts of the military personnel were paid in kind. Swedish farmers remained free, and by contributing soldiers, they were able to consolidate certain power positions in the system: there was a separate peasant Estate in the Estates system, and it actually exerted some influence on state action (with the three other estates: clergy, nobility and bourgeoisie). This class structure helped to shape the character of recruitment to the armed forces, and thus made its mark on the organization of the state (Tilly, 1990, pp. 27, 136). Tilly observes, that the Swedish "created a system of local surveillance and control that rivaled the Chinese and Japanese systems of their time." It was run by state bureaucrats and the clergy. While guaranteeing peasant rights, Sweden became "one of Europe's most militarized states", with about 5.5% of its entire population under arms in 1708 (Tilly, 1992, p. 18).

Tilly points out that in 1984, only 0.6% of the world population as a whole was serving in the military. That comparison not only conveys the ambitiousness of Swedish militarization during the 17th century, it also helps to explain why and how Sweden, despite its peripheral location and tiny population, was able to briefly become a Great Power.

Prussia was one of Sweden's main enemies, and would ultimately play a much more important role in the history of conscription. Brandenburg-Prussia was a small state (with between 2.5 and 3 million inhabitants in 1740), which gradually became a significant power in the century following the Thirty Years War. It was a prime example of Tilly's coercion-intensive model of state formation, and of the power of that path to state-building when systematically and energetically applied. At the beginning of the postwar era, Brandenburg-Prussia was an agrarian bureaucracy which had long been dependent on noble landowners to extract taxes and services from their peasants. On meeting resistance from the nobles in paying taxes for war efforts, however, the Great Elector Frederick William (1640–1688) forced peasants to pay their taxes directly, setting in motion a number of institutional innovations by which the state bureaucracy eventually gained direct control over the revenue extraction process. The Elector's reform was highly successful, and began the long process of transforming Prussia into a state of increasing capacity and strength. Between 1640 and 1688, Prussia's army grew by more than 2000%, from a measly 1300 mercenaries to a standing army of 30,000. Such growth was only possible through intensive and prolonged coercion, which in particular took the form of taxing the poor peoples of Prussia at more than twice the rate of states like France (Finer, 1975, pp. 134–142).

By the late seventeenth century, the Prussian state was becoming highly centralized and bureaucratized. Such developments meant that Prussia was able to efficiently finance, provision, and organize the military forces necessary for its bid to become a great power. State-appointed tax-councils (*Steuerräte*) recorded minute details on the regional economies, thereby fulfilling many modern functions of local administrations. But as Finer notes, this "extensive tax-gathering machinery had been devised and expanded solely in order to expand and maintain a permanent force of troops" (Finer, 1975, p. 139). And there was an equal, if not greater, centralization – and singlemindedness – in the military-administrative command structure, which was tightly and bureaucratically organized from the General War Commissariat in Berlin all the way down to local "war directors" (*kreisdirektors*) at the municipal level. The War Commissariat soon became the state's most general administrative organ, assuming responsibility not only for the army, "but also for revenue (apart from the Elector's own domains) and for administration *generally*" (Finer, 1975, p. 140). Such successes would eventually create strong incentives for Prussia's military competitors to adopt at least some features of its coercion-intensive model.

The bloody Thirty Years War (1618–1648) shook the whole European state system, and strengthened the general trend towards permanent standing armies. Such a trend is evident in the narratives sketched above. But within the post-1648 Westphalian system we can also see the contours of an increasingly complex evolution of military recruitment systems. That evolution contains at least four different approaches to military recruitment: France's old regime "Noah's ark" army, Britain's more austere standing forces, Prussia's state-directed and highly interventionist system, and the Swedish/Norwegian system of conscripting relatively independent peasants. In the following section, we will continue to describe the development of each of those approaches to military recruitment in greater detail.

THE ABSOLUTIST ANCIEN REGIMES OF THE 18th CENTURY

We have seen that the military "manpower revolution" in Europe came at the threshold of the 18th century, and we have seen examples of how local communities and villages were tapped for men in the prime of life. Such recruitment was possible because the military was the biggest, and often the only, branch of public administration in this era. All the same, states and elites alike were concerned that they not recruit too broadly among peasants and craftsmen. The elites knew that they needed both a tax base and sources of supply in order to maintain their power, and accordingly sought to limit recruitment by state agencies. Still, states now increasingly had to draw on peasants and craftsmen too – a requirement which could generate conflict between the needs of the state and of the dominant class elites (Skocpol, 1979, Ch. 2, esp. pp. 56–64; however, see Anderson, 1979, Ch. 2 for a slightly different view). The Swedish case, as discussed above, is an extreme but significant example of this trend.

Such large-scale recruitment of the common people would soon come to be the norm. The absolutist states of the 18th century maintained armies of a size and discipline not seen in Europe since the fall of the Roman Empire. Although tactical (from battalion to line and maneuver formations, such as the oblong formation) and technological innovations (flintlocks and bayonets) certainly played an important role in this change, the increasing importance of (primitive) conscription systems is the most important military innovation of this period. The share of domestic lower classes in the standing army increased in all the great powers, first in the Netherlands, then in Austria and France, followed by the other European states. Britain lagged behind. Mercenaries declined, as they were increasingly expensive – and unreliable, especially if and when states were unable to pay their wages on time. However, the advent of large-scale recruitment systems did not yet really amount to national conscription, as many of the recruits still came from other lands. Indeed, even in the late 18th century, as much as one-half of the men in European armies were foreigners. Only in the 19th century would armies become fully native and national.

In this period, the success of recruitment still depended on tapping two key groups: either the reservoir of non-working lower class people – the socially undesirable "dangerous classes" (criminals, vagabonds and the destitute) or, in the regions of the "second serfdom", a population of expendable serfs (Best, 1982, p. 30). As noted above, this kind of volunteerism can be seen as a primitive form of conscription. States also relied on the older and more costly method of using foreign troops, not just officers or mercenaries, but foreigners directly recruited into national regiments and to navies. While such soldiers were less desirable, the lack of a truly systematic system of conscription forced states to make use of them all the same.

However, when possible, the states of Europe increasingly preferred to avoid such tactics of recruitment. More genuine volunteers made up the better elements of the armed forces, and were most likely to rise to positions as non-commissioned officers (NCOs). To get volunteers, the state had to depend on local authorities: "The normal thing was for government to specify the proportion of liable men it needed – e.g. 'one in twenty-four' – and to leave the method of selection to the local authority" (Best, 1982, p. 31). Especially in periods of high interstate conflict, this method implied bargains between the state and local authorities. The latter in a sense related to the state in a "voluntary" way, often gaining concessions in exchange. The relationship between the local community and its citizens could then be more or less marked by force, informal pressure, etc. Only towards the end of the century did conscription become a more direct relationship between the state and its citizens. Let us consider more closely this question of the state encountering a rudimentary civil society:

For Foucault (1975) and other researchers inspired by his study of the history of the modern prison, the 18th century "enlightenment" saw the establishment of several nationwide institutions of social control and surveillance. A main task of these institutions was to prevent revolts against the state and its clients, but they also served to make larger parts of the population useful to the state. To that end, the treatment of criminals and deviants changed, with such groups now being locked into prisons and mental hospitals, unless they could be used in the army or in the navy. Foucault frequently employs military metaphors in his analyses of these 18th century trends. And indeed, it is well documented that the military organizations used strong discipline and punishments to keep men in line. For example, it was said of Prussia's Frederick the Great that "the secret of his troops' discipline in battle was that they feared death and the enemy less than they feared their NCOs and officers" (Best, 1982, p. 32). Another example of such "discipline" is the use of press-gangs in securing personnel for the British navy.

In comparative historical sociology, this transition generally has been seen as a move from indirect to direct rule (Tilly, 1985, p. 181, 1992). The thrust towards direct rule took very different forms depending on the prevailing pattern of state formation. In cases belonging to Tilly's capitalized coercion path of state formation – one that allowed autonomous roles for traders, craftsmen and protoindustrialists – attempts to establish direct rule clashed with trends towards the consolidation of distinct civil societies. This was typical of the northwestern seawards states. In contrast, in the eastern, inland areas, these elements of civil society development were much weaker.

Civil society is a complex entity, in that it incorporates two quite different and possibly opposed attributes. In one respect, it entails the articulation of straightforward economic interests (of producers, traders and financiers) vis-à-vis the absolutist state. In that context, representative institutions and courts were originally highly important for market actors in the early modernization of Europe (Habermas, 1961). But another, equally important, component of civil society is social mobilization by groups that make use of institutions consolidated by earlier processes of mobilization. The interests and worldviews promoted by the groups that mobilize need not always fit with the economic interests voiced. Social movements – most relevant here is the mobilization of peasants, craftsmen, etc. – in turn lead to institutions which put their mark on society even after the movements themselves have become less active, or at least integrated into the social and political structure.

Here Tilly's model (1990) of the capitalized coercion type of state formation is highly relevant, and implies at least two links to the development of civil society. The first link is between economic actors and the state: financiers and traders limit the ruler's capacity to mobilize military resources by command. The other link relates social mobilization to taxation and conscription, connecting money and men to military purposes. As Tilly (1990, p. 83) remarks with reference to the latter part of the seventeenth century, "reliance on mass conscription, confiscatory taxation, and conversion of production to the ends of war made any state vulnerable to popular resistance, and answerable to popular demands, as never before." Conscription now became visible as a form of taxation in kind. The need to secure military resources in the context of Europe's fragmented and ever-fighting sovereign states forced the rulers to make recurrent concessions as they faced their peoples' claim of "no taxation without representation."

In states that followed Tilly's coercion-intensive path of state-formation, however, state-building was organized via feudal ties, so the only resistance the king had to tackle was that of the agrarian aristocracy. In the western areas, by contrast, kings had to depend on regions in which feudalism had withered away, and where urban economies were quite influential. In these areas, regional leaders, or other groups with a strong position, would insist on institutions that could check whether the ruler actually was true to his promises to taxpayers and to the communities supplying soldiers.

This gave rise to the transformation of older institutions into legal and representative institutions. The early estates in which the church or certain privileged strata (e.g. the nobility and urban citizens) would appoint members, were thereby transformed into parliaments throughout the eighteenth century (Habermas, 1961, §8). We have seen above that in Sweden, the peasants maintained representation as an Estate. In other western states this trend was more gradual but remained steady all the same. A public sphere for political discourse emerged in the late seventeenth century in the western German principalities, in England by the early eighteenth century, and in France from the mid-eighteenth century. Courts and assemblies would give ever-larger groups the chance to ensure that the claims they had won against the ruler were actually met. In many cases these internal disputes interacted with high tension in the interstate system, and in such situations, it was particularly hard for the ruler to reject such claims for guaranteed rights. This trend would climax during World War I, and would play a significant role in the collapse of that era's remaining old regimes.

With reference to the historical documentation of such trends a debate has recently emerged. That debate turns on the question as to whether the increased state capacities mainly took the form of an ever-widening "microphysics" of discipline and detailed control (the post-structuralist perspective) or was instead a series of bargains between the state and groups in civil society (the collective action perspective). We see no need here to side completely with either view. The challenge is rather to analyze – with as much comparative detail as possible – how discipline and bargains were intertwined. Moreover, in providing such a comparative assessment of the mix between discipline and bargains, we must also pay attention to the institutionalization of normative concerns – however slow and fragile.

In addition to those broader pressures, coming from above and below, there also were important forces of integration functioning within the military institutions of the *ancien regime*. Although *ancien regime* armies certainly were highly authoritarian organizations that provoked desertion as often as allegiance, they did nonetheless produce a certain *esprit de corps*, as already noted in connection with the innovation of drill in the early 17th century. In such armies camaraderie and pride often worked effectively to produce a genuine solidarity between soldiers more effective than any indoctrination in this pre-nationalist era could be.

To see how such trends and patterns actually emerged and developed, it may at this point be helpful to again return to the typological sketch of recruitment patterns outlined in the preceding section. We will start by discussing two eastern inland and coercion-oriented states, Prussia and Russia.

In the early eighteenth century, the Prussian king gained control over the recruitment and appointment of officers. The aristocracy was forced to send their sons off for military education, a development which not only served to provide the armies with a large and relatively skilled officer corps, but also to effectively subordinate a potentially rebellious elite to central state control. Within roughly twenty years (by 1740) 90% of all officers were aristocrats. This thoroughly tamed aristocracy then enthusiastically turned its organizational talents and coercive powers to supplying the king's growing military machine, organizing troop logistics and services, extracting stiff tax contributions from the peasantry, and employing their own serfs as foot soldiers in the king's army (Finer, 1975, pp. 141–142).

Systematic conscription of peasants was introduced beginning in 1733. A recruiting officer would visit families to inspect young boys at the age of 10: those who the officers considered fit for the army would wear a red tie. There were many exemptions, so the main burden fell on the enserfed peasants (Finer, 1975, p. 142). Full-time basic training lasted two years (Best, 1982, p. 38). Since the concern for farm output could not be neglected, the serf was thereafter returned (in uniform) to the farm to work 10 months of the year, spending two months doing spring maneuvers (led by the same landlord). Only in times of war did the serfs spend more time with the army (Finer, 1975, p. 142). The stratification of the army reflected that of the countryside. Military uniforms were seen everywhere. Policemen and other local administrators were often ex-soldiers (Best, 1982, p. 38).

At the administrative level, civilian and military tasks, as well as local and central levels were united, with the result that the former War Commissariat "absorbed *all* the administrative jurisdictions in the state" (Finer, 1975, p. 143). There was one official per 450 inhabitants, and by the mid-18th century the king ruled there much more absolutely than in France. There were few traces of a civil society: local parliaments had insignificant powers, there was no free press. Prussia was at that time a virtual dictatorship, anticipating Napoleon's regime and later military bureaucracies.

The Russians resorted to cruder methods. Trying to catch up with the West, the Russians employed large numbers of foreign officers and technical experts, especially from Prussia. The regular army incorporated nearly half a million men, and various irregular forces probably accounted for about half a million more. Geoffrey Best paints a dark picture of that army, arguing that it brutally conscripted misfits and troublemakers the Russian landowners could not use for anything else. Earlier, peasants had been conscripted for life, but even when service was reduced to 25 years, the young men were "brainwashed with the standard mixture of militaristic manliness and religious patriotism", which made "wholly militarized creatures." Many soldiers even died – in action or from disease – well before their term was up, or they deserted. According to Best, the "gross average wastage *from all causes* must have been at least 50% every year" (Best, 1982, p. 44f).

In the *ancien regime*, troops became substantially more disciplined and in some respects more "national" then they had been in earlier periods. But the convergence between military, state, and society also ran the other way. Prussia built a state and society in the army's image and, in Russia as well, civil and military hierarchies increasingly coincided. Military uniforms became more homogenous, and militaries were less likely to victimize the rest of the population than previously. Soldiers were fairly closely integrated with the larger population, and in peacetime often worked in the communities where they were billeted. Thus in Prussia and Russia agrarian bureaucracies developed a specific, and quite effective, variety of direct rule in the virtual absence of civil societies. Other paths to direct rule – and to the increasing integration of military, state and society – were of course possible, as the sharply contrasting evolution in Western Europe clearly shows.

In the northwestern parts of Europe (cf. Rokkan, 1999), eighteenth century rulers also strove to establish more direct rule inside their territories. Here, the capitalized coercion type of state formation was the rule. Their more accommodating relationship to traders and entrepreneurs had given them advanced technological capacities. These areas became the sites of the "scientific revolution" of the 17th and 18th centuries and, as such, quickly became leaders in weapons production and ship construction. In fact, the link between the early development of manufacturing capabilities and increasingly military power was very close indeed (McNeill, 1982). Army units could only fight efficiently if their soldiers had highly standardized weapons. Beginning in the eighteenth century, state armories and early industrialists strove to standardize and routinize weapons production, a development which not only made weapons more reliable, but significantly cheaper as well. The 1770s and 1780s also saw important developments in logistics, as French military leaders found solutions to many longstanding organizational problems. Such innovations included improved supply systems, increasingly accurate maps, more educated officers, written orders, and a reorganization of the army itself along more rational divisional lines.

Such reforms played an important part both in rationalizing the military and in strengthening direct rule. However, rulers in the northwestern, seawards areas could not fully strengthen that rule without taking seriously the rudimentary civil societies developing within their territories. Yet while social pressures did significantly affect state- and army-building efforts in all of these states, their different geopolitical situations meant that such efforts would assume very different forms. In order to understand the dynamics of those processes, we will examine the cases of Great Britain, France and Norway.

Britain's insular location and detachment from some of the worst continental struggles are the main reasons why its standing army passed 100,000 only in the late 18th century (Best, 1982, p. 42). Army recruitment was very difficult in Britain, and frequently required that the military acquire its soldiers through press gangs and the seduction of potential soldiers with liquor and promises of a glorious career. The army's forces also were bolstered with paid troops, drawn both from the British population and hired out en masse from other states' populations (Best, 1982, p. 42; Colley, 1992, p. 300). Recruitment problems also forced riskier tactics, such as recruiting in colonial Ireland. Recruitment for the militia, which took care of inland defense, was based on conscription via local authorities. British peers and gentry freely bought officers' positions, and familiarity with this market mechanism helped prevent anti-bourgeois sentiments among the British military elite. In that respect, they were the total opposite of their Prussian counterparts.

Not surprisingly, given its geographic location, Britain cared most about its navy. And indeed, that navy was the world's best at the time, although its quality depended as much on "force and fear" as on patriotic enthusiasm (Best, 1982, p. 41). Recruitment mainly relied on impressment, which could be and was used to fill out a ship's crew at any time, and particularly when a ship was getting ready to sail. The men who were lured into a contract were committed for several years, and each ship had special marines who controlled the men and protected the officers from mutiny. Such control depended on the regular and ferocious use of coercion. Not surprisingly, perhaps, in an environment where "sadism . . . severity and . . . brutality . . . could make the atmosphere . . . rather like that of an early Nazi concentration camp", desertion was common. For example, during the years 1774 to 1780 there were about 42,000 desertions out of men 176,000 raised – a rate of almost one in four. Some ships eventually were stabilized by the "intoxicating mixture of patriotism, camaraderie, *esprit de corps*, self-preservation and combat frenzy" (Best, 1982, p. 41). Yet it would be both inaccurate and naïve to claim that in eighteenth century Britain patriotism rather than coercion served as the primary means through which the navy realized its outstanding victories. Indeed, in spite of a growing patriotic sentiment (Colley, 1992, pp. 4–5), such patriotism did not yet at this point translate into a general willingness to serve.

In France the situation was quite different. The French army was, at least when compared to the other armies of *ancien regime* Europe, something of a real volunteer force. The army contained many volunteer regulars, supplemented by men drawn from obligatory local militias (who were in a certain sense also volunteers, as previously discussed). In contrast to highly militarized states like Prussia and Russia, France was run by civilians, who constructed an extensive and sophisticated bureaucracy. As that civilian bureaucracy continued to expand during the second half of the eighteenth century, it assumed control of many military affairs, and of recruitment in particular (Best, 1982, p. 43). The French navy, by contrast, assembled crews via a fairly efficient naval administration, using a comprehensive seaman's register.

Yet the greatest impact of the French military of the later eighteenth century was an indirect one. The army and navy played a major role in the recurrent financial crises that plagued the French state during the eighteenth century, and so helped to drive France towards social revolution. With France's engagements in the wars of the American Revolution, this crisis became so grave that the lower layers of the armed forces were drawn into the sphere of national politics. The soldiers were obviously not sufficiently indoctrinated or disciplined, since they turned against their king. In the French Revolution, soldiers and lower officers would support the popular revolt, while the higher officers mostly emigrated. The impact of that military and political upheaval was enormous, and would draw all of the larger members of the European state system into long and dramatic wars at the century's end.

Finally, we turn to the Nordic subsystem. Sweden had been weakened by excessive continental war-fighting in the seventeenth century. The Great Nordic War (1709–1720) is generally seen as the end of its imperial phase. In this war, the Danish king sought to exploit the weakness of Sweden's Charles XII. In the context of these Nordic geopolitical tensions, innovative solutions to the problem of military recruitment were found. It can be argued that conscription in the modern era probably first developed in Scandinavia rather than Prussia, France, or the United States, as is usually claimed. The case of Sweden has already been presented. Furthermore, Jacobsen and Skauge (2000) argue that Norway was an example of the "nation in arms" already in the early 18th century. Norway's first general law on conscription stems from 1705, well before the Prussian system discussed above. By 1718, the system had been further refined. In this system, each farm would contribute one soldier. The army would decide which son to pick. Military service was for 10 years. The system was based on a direct relationship between the local Norwegian administration and the farmers. In Denmark, by contrast, a 1701 law consolidated the system in which the nobility conscripted young males from the rural population. In order to ensure a reliable reservoir of military manpower, for much of the century (1733–1788) farmers and their sons between 14 and 36 years of age were tied to their farms by law (adscription, *stavnsbånd*). This regulation covered both Denmark and Norway.

In spite of these draconian policies, however, draft evasion remained possible and common. Since the organization of military recruitment varied between the two countries, young men seeking to avoid military service in Denmark could flee to Norway, where the Danish feudal system of control could not reach them. Self-inflicted injuries, such as cutting off a thumb or index finger (essential for shooting) constituted another method of avoiding service. After 1788, Denmark turned to a system that established a more direct relationship between the state and the peasants; the system became personalized, conscripting all male persons in rural areas. This reform was linked to a wider process of liberation, as Danish peasants became free of all remaining feudal ties, thus approaching the wider Nordic model of free owner-occupier farmers.

Norway's relative administrative and military autonomy vis-à-vis Denmark increased through the eighteenth century. Regional administrative divisions were established, and military officers became civil servants. The military established the first autonomous Norwegian institutions: a military retirement fund, a military academy (the first national institution of education) and a military surveillance department. The number of officers increased sharply, especially in years of war, and the share of Norwegian-born officers reached nearly 70% in 1730–1814. The remaining foreign (mostly German) officers were really only needed for technical expertise in the construction of large fortresses. Norway became more independent of Denmark and was relatively uninvolved in that country's continental battles.

Autonomy increased in the social sphere as well, particularly among the lower classes. According to Jacobsen and Skauge (2000), the "wars and the military apparatus strengthened the farmers against the growing middle class and the steadily increasing number of public officials." Soldiers were badly needed and accordingly were able to win moderate taxation rates in return. Thus, in contrast to Prussia, the lower classes recruited into the army were not serfs, but independent farmers. This was a major cause of the "egalitarian" trajectory of modernization typical of Norway and other Nordic countries. Timing varied substantially: as we have seen, the trend was already underway in Sweden, with its tradition of independent peasants (partly an effect of the king's need for soldiers); by contrast, Denmark would adopt this egalitarianism only in the late 18th century. The military forces also served as domestic police forces, and were particularly instrumental in quelling tax rebellions. Usually the mere threat of force was enough, however. The period 1670–1770 was a relatively quiet period in Norway. It appears that taxation procedures were not blatantly unfair and that the public offices were generally attentive to the needs and interests of the farmers.

In conclusion, it seems clear that the viability of the huge forces mobilized depended as much on the limits of even the strongest *ancien regime* states as on the particular virtues of such armies themselves. In fact, *ancien regime* armies typically incorporated a motley assortment of soldiers, whose disparate levels of training and professionalization led to substantial irregularities in recruitment and staffing, as well as to strained and sometimes antagonistic relations between those troops and the societies from which they emerged. While the militias tended to be made up of largely untrained and often unwilling recruits who sought only to escape their service as soon as possible, the professional "line armies" tended to view civil society as a hostile and alien territory to which they owed little if any allegiance, and from which they could and should expropriate any booty that came their way. Not surprisingly, armies formed of such a strange amalgam of forces were difficult to discipline, and suffered from serious internal tensions, tensions that would surface as fatal contradictions as the *ancien regime* drew to a close.

THE FRENCH REVOLUTIONARY AND NAPOLEONIC WARS, 1789–1814 – THE FIRST EMERGENCE OF THE CITIZEN-SOLDIER

In the last quarter of the eighteenth century, *ancien regime* armies began to suffer surprising and sometimes catastrophic losses when faced with a new sort of army: a popular army of patriotic volunteers and, later, of citizen-soldiers. These losses convincingly demonstrated the weaknesses of the *ancien regime* armies. Although the wars of the French Revolution are usually, and perhaps rightly, seen as the watershed point when the *ancien regime* armies were shown to be distinctly inferior fighting forces, the definitive transition from one form of army to another actually was considerably more prolonged.

In fact, that transition had already been underway for quite some time, possibly for a century or more. Kestnbaum (this issue) points to the popular armies of the American revolutionary war (1770s), but there were even earlier cases of significant popularization of recruitment. In Norway and Sweden, for example, important steps in that direction had already been taken in the seventeenth and early eighteenth centuries (see previous section). While it would be mistaken to view such innovations as fully popular conscription, they did in many respects prefigure the more radical reforms of the late eighteenth century, reforms that would culminate in the French "nation in arms."

It was during the French Revolution, of course, that the really decisive transformation of the old regime armies took place. It was sparked by a combination of institutional collapse and ideological realignment (Forrest, 1990, esp. Ch. 2 and 4; Bertaud, 1979; Scott, 1978). Although the need for military reform had been evident even before 1789, with the coming of the Revolution the internal and external pressures on state and army increased sharply, making such reform absolutely imperative. As the old "line army" became increasingly unreliable in the years following 1789 (both because of officers' emigration and a lack of discipline in the ranks – see Forrest, in this issue), it became necessary to construct the French nation's military forces on a new basis. And, as France increasingly found itself threatened by invasion from without and counterrevolution from within during the turmoil of the early 1790s, such reform became increasingly urgent. The French revolutionaries responded rapidly to these challenges, completely reorganizing the army and eventually mobilizing the entire French nation for war. While some of those innovations, such as the *levée en masse* of 1793, would prove transitory, the larger changes that underlay them would revolutionize recruitment to the military, and, even the conduct of war itself. At the heart of that military revolution lay the idea of the citizen-soldier.

Kestnbaum (this issue) highlights the key features of this new paradigm of a citizen-soldier. First of all, with the rise of citizen-soldiers, a political definition of citizenship replaces a corporatist one. During the *ancien regime*, soldiers constituted a corporate group, *and as such* owed military service to the state. Under the political definition of citizenship, however, the citizen has a formally egalitarian, political relation to the state: only the individual owes a military service, solely due to his membership in a territorial political community. The national citizenship of individuals becomes the sole and sufficient basis for extracting obligatory service. Second, military service is *decommodified*, that is, political ties are substituted for earlier market ties. Recruitment on the basis of (formally) voluntary decisions in the labor market is increasingly replaced by a compulsory call to arms, backed by the laws and force of the state irrespective of the conscripts' preferences. Finally, the citizen-soldiers of the late 18th century served in standing armies, not merely militias (cf. Table 1).

This emergence of a citizen soldiery depended on "the mobilization of the previously excluded popular classes into national politics during an ongoing war in which the future of the state, and the independence of its people, were both at stake" (Kestnbaum, this issue). Thus, the revolutions in the United States and France, along with the French threat to Prussia, served to motivate and mobilize the reforms that led to the new paradigm of a citizen-soldier. But it is important to point out that the relations between state and civil society were very different in these three cases. Thus, to fully explain the further development of conscription we need to continue our typological investigation.

In France, the Revolution brought a number of radical changes to the French army, as well as to the relations between that army and the French state and society. And, because France was in a state of revolutionary turmoil and civil war for much of the 1790s, it was both possible and necessary to repeatedly transform the military during those years. The first of those reforms took place in the years between 1789 and 1792, when revolutionary France grew increasingly threatened by its reactionary neighbors, but was not yet in open conflict with them. During those years, the old line army was retooled, with a view to tying its allegiances to state and society rather than the (increasingly suspect) monarch, and conversely, to increasingly treating soldiers as full and equal members of French society by giving them increasing civil rights and duties. There also were cautious experiments in arming certain "safe" portions of the citizenry, experiments that resulted in the construction of a bourgeois national guard (Forrest, 1990, pp. 43–49).

The need for systematic reform grew even more urgent in 1792, as the French declaration of war quickly provoked an invasion by Austrian and Prussian forces. While the immediate threat of invasion was neutralized fairly quickly, the larger risks of counterrevolution and continental war continued to challenge the revolutionary state and its armies, and to force the pace of military reform. Although the revolutionaries had at first been uneasy about combining the troops of the line with the new revolutionary forces, such as national guards, pragmatism eventually prevailed over rigid principle. By joining two battalions of the national guards with one from the line army, they were able to construct a fighting force that combined the revolutionary enthusiasm of the former with the fighting skills and experience of the latter. The army also was increasingly organized along meritocratic and even democratic lines (Forrest, 1990, pp. 49–54).

Not even these reforms proved sufficient to satisfy the enormous manpower needs of France, however, especially once the Austrian-Prussian alliance was strengthened by the addition of Britain and Holland in early 1793. Drawing on widespread, although by no means universal, popular support (cf. Tilly, 1964), the French leaders soon turned to increasingly ambitious means of mobilizing and organizing their people. In February 1793, they organized a great levy of troops designed to raise the army's numbers by 300,000 men – and to put down the rebellion spreading in the western Vendée departments. When that measure proved inadequate, they ordered an even more sweeping levy, the famous *levée en masse* of August 1793. The levy in principle recruited the entire population for the war effort, although only young unmarried males between the ages of 18 and 25 were actually expected to defend the borders. It turned out to be a highly successful experiment in a situation marked by wide-ranging social destabilization and unemployment, and would help to point the way to the more institutionalized conscription of 1799.

Perhaps the most important element in the success of the levies of '93, and of the revolutionary reform of the army more generally, was its articulation and implementation of the idea of a citizen-soldier. While in retrospect it is tempting to see that development as logical or even inevitable, the notion of a soldier-citizenry was at first deeply controversial. Forrest (in this issue) shows that only when it became clear that patriotism alone could not provide the necessary numbers of men, did the leaders of the new Republic wholly accepted the necessity of conscription and consequently of a citizen-soldiery. Similar calculations, as well as renewed war against most of the European great powers in 1798, led the French to institute conscription in 1799. With the implementation of this new policy, which combined mass mobilization and administrative routine – the French "Directors" of 1799 found a potent yet attractively apolitical solution to the problem of raising mass armies. That solution was further refined by Napoleon. Rather than relying on a *levée en masse*-style universal mobilization, Napoleon convinced, and when necessary, compelled, the people of France and other occupied French territories to accept his new "blood tax" (as it was called by the French peasantry) as a burden not fundamentally different than the other taxes they already endured. And in exchange, he offered them unprecedented opportunities for personal advancement, honor and status. *Social mobilization* thus was replaced by *social mobility*, as Napoleon institutionalized the Revolutionary policies of "careers open to talent" while at the same time eviscerating the populist practices and democratic institutions which had been characteristic of civil society and the revolutionary armies alike.

This powerful new means of recruitment allowed Napoleon to quickly recruit armies of unprecedented size and ardor. An enormous number of citizens, by no means all of them French, jumped at the chance to join Napoleon's armies. They saw in a military career an opportunity to escape the "idiocy of rural life", the chance to make some real money as a replacement for a more reluctant countryman, or simply a hope of glory.

The new Napoleonic armies required radical innovations in strategy and tactics. Such armies' successes depended on their ability to "live off the land", as their enormous size made earlier traditions of extended supply lines simply infeasible. Consequently, Napoleon's armies resorted to the older routine of seizing resources wherever they happened to be encamped. This policy in turn allowed them to advance quickly and to change position or direction rapidly, and played an important role in Napoleon's brilliant use of "wars of maneuver." Tactical innovations also helped to ensure the army's success, with its mixed (infantry, cavalry and artillery) divisions and corps being particularly significant in this respect. Such heterogeneity meant that these forces were self-contained fighting units that could be rapidly deployed and operate either autonomously or in combination – a flexibility which Napoleon used to great advantage (Parker, 1995, pp. 196–203; Cowley & Parker, 1996, pp. 321–323).

But Napoleon's successes depended above all on his systematic development and refinement of conscription, which guaranteed him the enormous numbers of men he needed to carry out his ambitious program of conquest. Previously, military leaders had been painfully aware as to how difficult it was to recruit and train infantrymen. Now Napoleon could tell Metternich (1805): "I can afford to expend thirty thousand men a month" (quoted in Finer, 1975, p. 150). By 1813, Napoleon had called up 1.3 million Frenchmen. And even in 1813–1814, with his popularity plummeting after the disastrous Russian campaign, Napoleon still was able to use the conscription apparatus he had constructed to quickly find and field another million men.

Given the scale and severity of the challenge from France during the revolutionary and Napoleonic eras, the international wars that broke out in that period reached unprecedented proportions. In 24 out of the 26 years between 1789 and 1815, France was at war. This is not surprising when we consider how radical the ideological, political and military threat from France actually was. The French revolutionaries believed passionately in spreading reason and republican institutions to their reactionary neighbors; this was even Napoleon's belief, even as he grew increasingly conservative at home. Moreover, France was not shy about expanding its political sway, either via forced alliances or outright annexation, especially along its less secure eastern and northern frontiers. And finally, the military threat from France grew more alarming during the Napoleonic years. The result was war. From 1793 until 1814, France and its new armies appeared to be virtually unstoppable. Six great powers were involved at one time or another, and total battle deaths for the period eventually exceeded two million. The death rate per million Europeans rose to 16,112 during the Napoleonic Wars (1803–1815), an unprecedented rate which would only be surpassed in World Wars I and II (Levy, 1983, Table 4.1).

The French triumphs shook the other great powers. But none of them could implement equally radical changes, and so they were forced to implement only a few elements from Napoleon's model. The impact was probably most limited in England, which for fifteen years continued to rely mainly on its navy and on other troops (whether Prussian mercenaries or Spanish guerrillas) to defend the threatened balance of power. Finally in 1804, in response to the threat of invasion by France, Britain sharply increased its volunteer forces, and on occasion, allowed that "Home Guard" to serve overseas in the fight against "Boney" (Finer, 1975, p. 152). Even the redoubtable Royal Navy was substantially increased. Such reforms proved enormously expensive (entailing a 400% increase in the military budget 1780s–1810s), but were possible because of the enormous economic power of an industrializing Britain, creditors' willingness to underwrite increased debt (+350% 1780s–1810s), and because of the social and economic dislocations caused by industrialization and war.

Such dislocations allowed the state to recruit soldiers from the poverty-stricken agricultural south (and the periodically underemployed industrial north) by offering them advantageous employment at relatively high rates of pay. Britain's unequalled industrial power, economic resources, and overabundant labor force enabled the state to successfully tackle these challenges. Thus, if Britain is a case of Tilly's capitalized coercion model of state formation, its enormous capital allowed it to maintain a purer capital-intensive profile than France could. More fundamental reforms were neither necessary nor desirable. Nowhere was this truer than in the military. Even when confronted by the enormous challenge from Napoleon, the British army did not fundamentally change – it remained anarchic, non-cooperative, and run by officers with little formal education. It could remain an 18th century remnant, "obsolete" compared to the armies of the major continental states (Finer, 1975, p. 153).

The Prussian response to the French challenge was very different. Prussia's loss to Napoleon at Jena (1806) was a traumatic experience that forced a radical reform of its state, civil society and the military alike. Not only did the Prussians lose half their provinces, they had to pay a huge indemnity to the French and, perhaps most galling of all, enter into an alliance with the conquering enemy (Finer, 1975, p. 153; Best, 1982, pp. 154ff), and ally with France. The Prussians decided to adopt a limited form of popular conscription. According to the Prussians the close cooperation between rulers and the lower classes had been the key to France's success in the Revolutionary wars. The military leaders understood that there was a danger of popular revolt if some degree of citizen participation was not allowed. They thus pushed for a "revolution from above", although aristocratic and royal doubts and hesitations concerning such "revolution" prevented really radical reform until the winter of 1812–1813 (Best, 1982, pp. 156–161). All the same, there were substantial changes in the years following Jena. Serfdom was formally abolished, and municipalities and provinces acquired more representation and autonomy (Finer, 1975, p. 153). The army was extended by a force of conscripts (the first and second *Landwehrs* and, eventually, by a reserve of all males, the *Landsturm*). However, as we shall see in the next section, these changes were transitory, and ultimately proved to be more formal than fully genuine.

In the Nordic states, the major transformations during this period were political rather than military. Sweden and Norway already were close to some kind of citizen-soldier arrangement, and saw no major changes with regard to conscription in the period of the French revolution. But the unfolding of the Napoleonic Wars did lead to great changes in the Nordic subsystem. In the Vienna peace settlement, Denmark, which had sided with Napoleon, lost Norway to Sweden, a union that lasted to 1905. Denmark-Norway had the misfortune to be drawn into the war on the French side after a preemptive British strike against the Danish fleet (the attack on Copenhagen harbor in 1807). This alliance with France meant that during the Vienna peace settlement, Sweden, which had supported the British and earlier had lost Finland to Russia, was given control over Norway. The result was that Norway would remain a Swedish dependency until 1905.

At this point, it may be useful to review some of the broader trends in war-making and military recruitment from the end of the Middle Ages to the end of the Napoleonic era. We have previously discussed three major factors identified by Finer that are particularly important in tracking trends in military recruitment over time. They are the size of the armed forces; the permanence of such forces; and the contractual terms under which soldiers serve (Finer, 1975, pp. 99–101; above, pp. 7–8). For the first two factors, the trend lines appear to have been relatively straightforward, rising steadily – if not always smoothly – upward over the years. Thus armed forces grew continually larger from the late 15th century until the two 20th century World Wars. Similarly, the permanence of such forces – *ad hoc* or standing armies – increased until the end of the Second World War. Of course, there were and would continue to be significant short-term variations in such trends, as well as national and regional ones. For example, the "military revolution period" of 1550–1660 saw a steep rise in manpower needs, and the size of the Prussian armies increased sharply after the disasters of the Thirty Years War. Overall, however, the size and permanence of the armed forces increased consistently and would continue to do so.

With respect to the third trend, the contractual terms of military service, the progression was more complex. Here the terms of military service changed from obligatory service in the late Middle Ages (to a community or a local lord) to paid volunteer service during the early modern period and the era of absolutism, and then finally back to an obligatory form in the age of conscription (Finer, 1975, pp. 99–100; above, p. 8). Such periodization is necessarily approximate, of course, as here again there were significant national and regional variations, as discussed in the sections above. By the end of the 18th century, however, the trend was generally towards obligatory service, and in some places, conscription properly speaking. England was the only significant case where paid voluntary service remained.

In all other major states, the clear trend was towards conscript armies. It would take some states a while to get there, but by the end of the 19th century almost all of them had adopted conscription. Such service was not voluntary, but forced, and while sometimes paid, was a "job" very different from employment in the "outside" world of civilians. Moreover, the wages for military service generally were inferior to alternative employment in the civil sector. Only England, with its labor surplus and powerfully capitalized economy, could afford not to conscript its population but instead rely on the incentives of the marketplace to meet its military manpower needs. In other contexts, the limits imposed by pre-industrial societies on the one hand, and the need for ever-larger armies on the other, forced states of all ideological stripes into conscription. While such an outcome might be politically unpalatable, it was militarily necessary, and even the most reactionary states, like Prussia, adopted conscription in order to field the armies they now required.

In addition, Finer (1975, pp. 100–102, 145ff) points to two other important trends: the shift from multinational to national armies, and the shift from semiprivate to public control of the armed forces. These trends are best discussed in connection with the changes that occurred *after* the French Revolution and Empire. With respect to these trends, the revolutionary period must be seen as a period of transition, but one that in some respects anticipated the militarism that would develop in the late 19th century. Finer (1975, p. 146ff).

As for the public control of armies, European states in 1815 mostly only controlled the recruitment and appointment of officers. Only in Prussia did the state have more extensive control. By the 20th century the state would run it all – at least in the Western world. And, as for national armies, we have seen that the importance of mercenaries and other non-natives decreased as the need for more military manpower grew. But only later in the 19th century, following nationalist and democratic mobilization, would armies become fully national. Kestnbaum (in this issue) notes this trend, arguing that in "conjunction with citizen conscription, the exclusion of foreign soldiers and later even foreign suppliers and producers meant the almost unrivaled dominance of the national idiom in interstate war."

On the face of it, therefore, it would appear that the military reforms wrought by the revolutionaries of '93 were visionary but impermanent. After all, with regard to the trend from multinational towards national armies, the Napoleonic Wars were more similar to 18th century *ancien regime* wars than to the fully nationalized conflicts of twentieth century Europe. During this period, the armies were still multinational, even in France – half of Napoleon's soldiers in 1809 were foreigners. Furthermore, 18th century wars had been limited dynastic wars for colonies and provinces rather than the total mobilization of national resources. Here the revolutionary wars prefigured the total wars of the early 20th century, being at once ideological, popular and predatory. And, while Napoleon tried to establish full French hegemony over the rest of the European continent, he failed, not only because of the difficulties of the Russian campaign, but even more because the fiscal pressure of such wars on the French state simply became too large. Following that debacle, the scale and purpose of European wars again assumed a more limited character for most of the rest of the 19th century. Finally, 18th century wars were fought by regimes with no intention of improving the social conditions of their subject populations. The revolutionaries of '93 were indeed driven by such intentions, but within a few years regimes that had no social purpose soon once again dominated. Indeed, one of the most striking – and ironic – contrasts between the revolutionary warfare of the Jacobins and the campaigns of Bonaparte lies in precisely this difference.

Yet the apparently transitory innovations of the revolutionaries would ultimately prove more durable than Napoleon's brilliant old-new synthesis. The notion of military service as a sacrifice would prove surprisingly robust, as would its corollary, the general extension of civil and political rights to those willing to risk their lives for the nation. As Samuel Finer remarks, "sacrifice, hence equality of sacrifice since the fatherland was a common patrimony – this notion was destined to drive on. In the end it brought its obvious counterpart. Equality of sacrifice, equality of benefits. In the Swedish expression, 'one soldier, one rifle, one vote' " (Finer, 1975, p. 155). This notion of equal rights for equal sacrifice *was* a long term effect of the Revolution, although it would be temporarily eclipsed by the setbacks of the 19th century restoration all over Europe.

Similarly, conscription of citizen-soldiers was an important institutional and organizational innovation. Because conscription explicitly linked military service and citizenship, it could serve to tightly bind otherwise alienated social groups to state and the status quo. This was true not only for soldiers of the line who, in striking contrast to their *ancien regime* predecessors, now often saw themselves as serving a sovereign people rather than a ruler or a *corps*, but also for commoners, who saw in the equation of military service with citizenship a new means of access to status and rights previously denied to them. As Kestnbaum (in this issue) observes, the masses got "political recognition if not democracy, a way to participate in at least one of the state's chief endeavors, and a way – perhaps only symbolically – to appropriate the state as their own."

In some circumstances, therefore, conscription pointed towards a new relation between states and societies. It may have served as a sort of bargain, where in exchange for military service subjects would be granted full citizenship. Such a bargain could also serve state interests, as by incorporating previously marginalized populations into mainstream society, states could not only secure their borders against external enemies, but also protect themselves against the threat of further popular revolution from below. Yet we should be wary of reading too much into such developments, which were fragile and insecure, as social and political forces from "above" and "below" were in precarious balance. If and when wars proved long lasting, democratic rights were likely to disappear and elements of "discipline" prevail. As we shall see in the next section, such would be the case in France and Prussia alike for much of the 19th century. It would not be until the 20th century that the conscription bargain between state and society would prove entirely solid and durable.

Yet if the revolutionary and Napoleonic regimes did not complete the construction of a conscription bargain between state and society, deeper socioeconomic changes were now underway that would make later attempts to cement that bargain more successful. Through the 19th century conservative restoration on the European continent, there was a rapid spread of the British industrial revolution – and the socioeconomic changes it carried with it – to the continent. Accordingly, when the ideals of citizen-soldiers and a nation in arms reappeared towards the end of the century, they would be supported by the industrial development and national institutions necessary for their successful realization.

Armies of enormous size forced states to extract growing numbers of men from civil society. Before the modern era, soldiers had been either professional warriors, representing a separate "caste", or people who were fighting on behalf of their local community. With the rise of the enormous armies of modern Europe, however, soldiers increasingly were people who were taken out of their normal activities as producers (agrarian and industrial producers). Such developments had important consequences for the character of armies, since, with the rise of the industrial revolution, they were fighting wars in a state system with developed economies. As industrially based warfare developed, soldiers were not living off regions they invaded, but had to be supplied by thoroughly organized "national economies."

Moreover, such soldiers were *not* primarily defending their local community or region; they were fighting for a broader organization, the state. While helping to solve the problems of irredentism that regionally based forces had posed, this new nationally based organization posed a number of difficult challenges of its own. Foremost among such challenges was the threat of an armed people that might rise to insurrection or even revolution – a threat that of course eventually was realized in 1776 and 1789. Thus the European states faced an increasingly difficult dilemma as their size, power, and aspirations grew. As those states required ever-larger armies, they increasingly faced the challenge of controlling a population that increasingly knew how to fight.

MILITARY RECRUITMENT DURING THE 19th CENTURY RESTORATION

The century between 1815 and 1914 is sometimes called the *Pax Britannica*, in reference to Britain's role as architect and de facto hegemon of the European state system. British hegemony was based on its leading role in early industrialization (cotton-textiles, later railways), its powerful navy, and above all, on its crucial role in constructing and maintaining a "managed balance of power" in continental Europe. In the first half of this period there were still interstate conflicts, but no large wars, as we will see. Such international stability, especially when conjoined with growing domestic unrest, also meant that many of the military reforms of the revolutionary and Napoleonic eras were no longer necessary or desirable. Specifically, the conscripted armies of the earlier period were generally abandoned in form of more limited and professional armed forces. From 1860 onwards, however, the rise of the German Empire began to threaten the stable European status quo. And, as the states of Europe began to move towards another in another round of geopolitical conflict, those powers would once again be forced to adopt policies of military reform, particularly universal conscription.

In the 19th century context of managed peace and increasing social unrest, armies across Europe played important but increasingly varied roles at home and abroad, serving both to secure peace and to potentially threaten it. The evolution of industrial capitalism in a context of highly inegalitarian political frameworks created endemic rebellions across the continent. In response to these events – which were followed by significant extensions of the vote – domestic ruling elites gradually turned away from a policy of total resistance to change to a more subtle and varied policy of accommodation, repression, and cooptation. By contrast, in the "Anglo-democracies" of Britain, its settler colonies, and the United States, relations between armies and the societies from which they emerged were relatively stable. This may have been because in general those states staffed their armed forces voluntarily (with the significant exception of armed forces during the U.S. civil war). But such social peace between armies and their populations was more the exception than the rule.

In fact, continental European states during this period were subject to growing domestic tensions, which provoked increasing social unrest at home and eventually, eventually, increased state militarization and international conflict. Only Russia – industrially backward – was unaffected by the revolutionary republican movements of 1848–1851.

European states needed large standing armies in case of war or revolution, but such armies might also serve as sources of protest and unrest themselves. For example, in industrialized areas, the demobilization of troops after the Napoleonic wars led to unemployment and consequent social instability, especially as peace often was conjoined with economic recession or depression. In more rural settings, demobilized soldiers also frequently disrupted social peace as they sought to reintegrate themselves into civil society. Nor did finding "civil" uses for soldiers necessarily lead to peaceful outcomes. Armies were often used to perform domestic, police-like functions (Best, 1982, p. 205). In the coercion-intensive states of the Holy Alliance (Russia, Austria, Prussia), this was in line with earlier practice. Prussia did not have separate police forces until the mid-century. In France, especially considering the recent history of the French armed forces, this policing function posed more of a dilemma, as we shall see. And finally, the 19th century also saw the rise of national liberation armies, first in Spain, and then in a host of other European states (e.g. Poland, Italy, Belgium, Serbia, Greece). In all cases, therefore, armies played crucial, if highly varied, roles in the internal affairs of states.

Such variety was also characteristic of the means by which continental armies were recruited from their populations. In general, France and the westwards countries on the continent practiced a watered down system of peacetime conscription which accommodated social inequities through liberal "buying out" practices. In the eastern "inland" areas, by contrast, there was militaristic-authoritarian conscription – with few, if any, exemptions allowed.

Let us first consider the most dynamic developer in the second half of the 19th century: coercion-intensive Prussia. Not only was Prussia dominated by an agrarian bureaucracy centered in the army, it was largely run by a Junker (estate owner) aristocracy. The striking feature of its 19th century development is the coexistence of elements from the coercion-oriented state formation with modern, "liberal" features. We saw that the post 1806-reform of conscription was tied to modifications of the coercion-intensive pattern: the abolition of serfdom, the extension of regional representation, and the increasing use of conscripts in the armed forces. While such reforms appear impressive, in reality 19th century Prussia shared many features with the 18th century regime: peasants generally remained tied to the land, and had won few real concessions or liberties. The nobility's privileges remained correspondingly huge; it retained jurisdiction over the peasantry (to 1848), was still exempted from taxation (to 1861), and retained control of local police functions (to 1872).

Military reform in Prussia was also quite limited, and generally only proved possible when the aristocracy and the state leaders both saw it as necessary and desirable. When the conservative Junkers, the king, or both, sought reforms that would advance their own agendas, they almost invariably succeeded. By contrast, when liberals wanted to institute more egalitarian military reforms, they found them difficult to implement and even more difficult to preserve.

For example, repeated liberal pleas for reform of the officer corps went largely ignored. While the Prussian officer corps did remain more open to recruitment from the lower levels of society than did analogous corps in other European armies, the rigorous meritocracy of the post-Jena decade gradually gave way to a more traditional system of "reserved" places and special privileges for noble candidates. Meritocracy increasingly came to mean only that certain bourgeois groups were absorbed into the ranks of middle officers, since the aristocracy did not have sufficient numbers to fill the needed positions. Mainly NCOs, these officers helped to relieve the gentleman officers of exhausting drill and supervision of rank and file soldiers (Kiernan, 1982, p. 15). Thus reform was neither as systematic nor as successful as it first appeared to be.

The fate of liberal military reform in nineteenth century Prussia is perhaps best shown by the decline and eventual collapse of the citizen militia, the *Landwehr*. This people's militia incorporated "liberal" ideas of forging strong ties between the military and civil society, quite in contrast to the Prussian aristocracy's elite militarism. The liberal reformers in 1808–1809 had seen the *Landwehr* as a tool for the development of a civil society with some autonomy from the traditional ruling classes, and had designed the *Landwehr* accordingly. It was separated from the army (they were only under common command during war), and elected its own middle/upper class officers, based on nominations by local government authorities. Yet the *Landwehr* eventually disintegrated in the face of constant Junker pressure. After 1848, the principles of constitutionalism and parliamentarianism were to some extent strengthened in Prussia, but the Junker elites successfully prevented democratic control of "their army" (Best, 1982, pp. 212, 283). The *Landwehr* was judged by many royalist and aristocratic groups to be politically suspect, and eventually was absorbed by the regular army in the 1860s (Best, 1982, pp. 206–208).

By contrast, both universal conscription and the use of the army as a police force proved relatively easy to implement and maintain, once the social and political need for them was clear to the Junkers and the king. After 1815, the standing army no longer consisted mainly of paid volunteers, " but on the obligatory services of all the male population." In contrast, the granting of exemptions turned the French army into something more like an army of paid volunteers. Prussia would elaborate the organization of this conscript force and win three major victories in the 1860s, thereby serving as "the model format for all the states in Europe and indeed the world, with the exception of the Anglo-Saxon powers" (Finer, 1975, p. 154).

By 1848, the army was again the policing tool of the Junkers, which used it to repress social mobilization: first of artisans and peasants, then, after general male suffrage, the working class mobilization. Similarly, public administration in Prussia was completely dominated by the Junkers' military apparatus. Everywhere there were enormous numbers of soldiers (as many as one out of six inhabitants in the fortress towns, and more than one out of twenty in the garrison towns), who actively controlled the daily lives of more than 50% of Prussia's urban population. Until the establishment of an effective police force in the 1850s, military personnel did all "but the pettiest of police duties." And even later, "troops continued to be used whenever riots or strikes got serious" (Best, 1982, p. 211). The military was a state within the state, but at the same time was directly influential in the civil sphere.

Prussian leaders thus transformed the traditional coercion-intensive system so as to secure direct rule in a modernizing, defeudalized situation. They allowed bourgeois forces a limited role as economic entrepreneurs, a role that was strengthened with unification of the German Empire in 1871, with the addition of states that had more elements of capital-intensive state formation. However, Prussia's ruling agrarian-aristocratic elites created a system where the authoritarian state penetrated and controlled civil society, largely by military means. Prussia pioneered a number of "disciplinary tactics" that would later become generalized all over Europe. Austria and Russia followed Prussia during the 19th century, generally combining limited meritocracy with even more limited social reform from above.

Let us now turn to the northwestern seawards states, beginning with France. When the Napoleonic Empire fell, French conscription laws were abolished in favor of a purely volunteer force (see Forrest, in this issue; also Levi, 1997, p. 49). That arrangement did not last long, however, as declining patriotism and consequent manpower shortages quickly forced the French regime to reestablish its national army. In 1818, therefore, a new recruitment law was passed (Levi, 1997, p. 49; Best, 1982, pp. 217–218). This new law, which would serve as the basis of recruitment for the next fifty years, was deliberately eclectic, combining some of the aspects of Napoleonic conscription with other attributes of the old line armies of the pre-Revolutionary period. This eclecticism was necessary because the French needed to reconcile the state's need for a reliable supply of soldiers with the military's demand for a professional and apolitical army. Moreover, pressure from the conservative royalists made fully popular conscription along the lines of the *levée en masse*, the Napoleonic army, or even contemporary Prussia, politically impossible (Best, 1982, p. 217). Consequently a compromise was found: the army would "rely entirely on volunteers", but when volunteerism proved insufficient, conscription would be employed to make up the difference. The potentially conflicting interests of patriotism, professionalism, and privilege were accommodated and reconciled in other ways as well. Leftist and Bonapartist patriots could point with pride to the new army's principles of meritocracy, while the military got a six year term of service designed to socialize men into military careers and create a hardened professional army (Best, 1982, pp. 217–218). Finally, privileged groups saw *their* interests accommodated by liberal terms of "replacement" for reluctant conscripts who preferred not to serve – a point we will discuss at greater length below.

A particularly important set of developments in the French (and other Western) armies of the 19th century centered on the increasing use of inequitable conscription practices such as replacement, commutation and substitution. Even in the French system of 1799, conscripts had been chosen by lot (*tirage au sort*). But there were various ways of buying out of this, a feature which gave the lottery an element of "market logic" that was of course to the advantage of the rich. More specifically, the (officially sanctioned) policy of *replacement* meant that a person who had drawn a "bad number" could pay somebody to take his place as a soldier. Although this policy provoked considerable resentment and unrest and also probably encouraged the sale of illegal draft exemptions (Van Holde, 1993, Ch. 3–5), it remained in place in France in one form or another until the Crimean War (Schnapper, 1968, Sales de Bohigas, 1968). And although replacements were often very expensive (running to 10,000 francs or more), the demand for them was sufficiently high as to support a booming business in "replacement insurance " for those who received a bad number (Levi, 1997, p. 89).

Nor was replacement the only legal means of escaping unwanted military service during the 19th century. *Commutation* allowed a person with a "bad number" to buy themselves an exemption from military services by paying a fee or fine to the state. In France (Levi, 1997, p. 91), the state introduced this system in 1855 in a situation of extensive recruitment for the Crimean war (Best, 1982, p. 221). The French state used these fees to establish a fund from which they could pay a premium to re-enlistees and support veterans' pensions. In contrast to replacement, commutation thus made it possible to opt out of military service without having to find a substitute soldier. Like replacement, commutation soon became so widespread that there were insurance companies selling policies to cover the costs of a commutation in the event that a conscript drew a bad number (Levi, 1997, p. 91). Commutation was increasingly popular in Europe after 1848, and also was employed in the United States during the Civil War (Levi, 1997, pp. 99–100, 102–103). Finally, *substitution* was another means by which it was possible to legally avoid the draft. Although arrangements for substitution varied, they usually hinged either on a personal exchange between two individuals, as in France (Woloch, 1994, p. 399; Levi, 1997, pp. 85–86), or were arranged by local communities, as in the United States during the Civil War (Levi, 1997, pp. 98–99). In the U.S., at least, substitution often served as a way for communities to protect their own men and economy against government demands for troops.

Through replacement, commutation and substitution, the state was able to recruit men from the lower classes (including many who did not have the right to vote), while employing a seemingly fair system of recruitment. We have seen that in many cases conscription had been seen by the lower classes as a promise of citizenship. But as inequitable conscription practices expanded, the populace gradually grew more experienced and cynical about such promises. In the United States, for example, disillusionment about commutation probably was a significant cause of the 1863 conscription riots in New York (Levi, 1997, p. 99). The Thrane movement, the Norwegian equivalent of the 1848 revolutions elsewhere in Europe, saw the abolition of buying out arrangements as one of its main objectives. Why, then, did such inequitable systems of recruitment persist for as long as they did? While this is a hotly contested question (see Levi, 1997, esp. pp. 102–106, and the articles by Levi, Hobson and Barkawi in this issue), the apparent fairness – and de facto inequality – of replacement, commutation and substitution is surely significant. Because they effectively reconciled the principle of universal conscription with the practices of social privilege, such policies proved convenient and even popular in a wide variety of European states (e.g. Sweden, Holland, Spain, and Belgium) as well as the ones already discussed above.

Although military reform and replacement policies solved many of the 19th century army's most pressing problems, some significant difficulties remained, as the French case again clearly shows. In particular, the French army continued to be overly political and politicized, taking what state leaders, ruling elites and military commanders alike considered an inappropriate interest in social issues and civil society. During the Revolution of 1830, for instance, many soldiers were open republicans and many NCOs were in sympathy with their views – a situation that did little to promote military discipline or professionalism. In fact, the mass mobilization of 1830 was preceded by a number of protests in the army, which combined revolutionary rhetoric with more concrete dissatisfactions about terms of employment and living conditions in the new French army. Here again, we see the typical 19th century conjunction of trade unionist concerns and old-style appeals to republican ideology – a conjunction that lay behind much of the impetus to reaction in the conservative backlash of the 19th century monarchies. And here again, the state's response to pressure for reform was one of "divide and rule", albeit in a less repressive and more sophisticated manner than in the eastern monarchies.

Following the 1830 protests, the French military was reconfigured to prevent its political mobilization in the future: military service was lengthened to seven years, and new, more isolated (and comfortable) barracks were built so as to increase the isolation of the army from society. Such reforms served not only to increase army morale and professionalism, but even more to distance the army from those who sought to radicalize it via demands for shorter service and universal conscription. The strategy worked, as the army remained obedient and largely apolitical during the revolutions of 1848–1850 and the coup d'etat by Napoleon III in 1851 (Best, 1982, pp. 219–220).

By the middle of the century, therefore, any real possibility of a radical army in France had been largely eliminated. The appeal of republicanism had faded, while the romance of military service increasingly was focused on imperialist adventures in Algeria and elsewhere. And, while most soldiers still lacked the vote, they saw themselves as duty bound to serve France, the French people, and whatever political authority was ruling it at a given moment. In short, by the 1860s, the French army had drifted far from its revolutionary and Napoleonic roots, and the French soldier, once radical and even potentially revolutionary, had been transformed into a thoroughly socialized and conformist military professional. Only after that army's disastrous encounter in 1870 with the more politicized soldiers of Germany would French leaders seriously consider returning to the older model of a citizen-soldier.

At this point, it may be useful to temporarily set aside our typological analysis of specific state trajectories, and return to a more general narrative. That will allow us to see why the 19th century restoration ended, and how it produced the astonishing militarization and polarization of the late 19th and early 20th centuries. Accordingly, it is to that more general account that we now return.

The Crimean War of 1853–1856 and Bismarck's impressive geopolitical maneuvers in the 1860s undermined the early 19th century balance of power. The final humiliation of France in 1871 demonstrated that in international politics, as in military doctrine, it was Prussia that had found the principles on which successful states and military victories would be henceforth be organized. As one authority remarks, "France fought for the principle of territorial compensation, a legacy of eighteenth-century dynasticism, Prussia for the ideal of the nation state, a legacy of the French revolution" (Bridge & Bullen, 1980, p. 109).

Within a few months of 1871, France found herself attempting to defend her 1815 borders rather than to expand beyond them. She even had to cede Alsace and Lorraine to the Prussians and accept a huge indemnity. The outcome of Bismarck's byzantine maneuvers and campaigns was a radically changed balance of power in continental Europe, one that led to its destabilization and subsequent militarization. First Austria and then France had tried to benefit from the end of the Anglo-Russian equilibrium after 1855, but by 1871, the end result was a dramatically strengthened German state under Prussian leadership. This was a structural change in the European states system which England's balance of power strategy could not bar, based as it was on an "obsolete" army and remarkably low military spending of only 2–3% of GDP (Kennedy, 1984, p. 153).

Both the 1848 events and the Crimean war "proved" to the states and peoples of Europe that wars could be localized and limited – a dangerous "lesson" when we consider its consequences in the early 20th century. The experience of the revolutionary and Napoleonic wars had given Europeans the impression that any war would be long and costly. Now, however, war had "ceased to be regarded as a great danger to the social order and became instead the means by which political changes within states were consolidated and given the seal of popular and patriotic approval" (Bridge & Bullen, 1980, p. 82). This was confirmed by the European wars that followed in the 1860s.

THE LATE 19th CENTURY – THE RETURN OF THE CITIZEN-SOLDIER AND THE INDUSTRIALIZATION OF WAR

While states did gradually turn to popular conscription as the most efficient means of fielding large armies, they were slower to wholly embrace the related concept of a citizen-soldier, since that concept entailed unacceptable political costs. The gradual diffusion of the idea of a citizen-soldiery took the form of a back and forth movement of emulation (Prussia emulates France), institutional development (Prussia develops conscription within its social structure), and "return" emulation (France emulates Prussia). The unexpected Prussian victory in 1870 was a forceful reminder to the French of the virtues of popular conscription. As a result, France reintroduced general conscription in 1872: the new system was more universal, and the question of exemptions and shorter voluntary service became increasingly politicized. Forrest (in this volume) notes the irony "that the French were overwhelmed by a Prussian army which had itself adopted conscription in 1806 as a conservative, counter-revolutionary response to French victories in the Revolutionary and Napoleonic Wars."

Really huge conscript armies developed only after 1870, when most European states, as well as the United States, applied the format developed in Prussia. In 1874, Germany had 1.3 million men in the field or in reserve, while France had 1.75 million. By 1897, Germany had 3.4 million and France 3.5 million men (Finer, 1975, p. 159). Increases in most of the other Great Powers, especially Russia and the United States, were similarly impressive (Kennedy, 1987, p. 203, Table 19).

Although Prussia/Germany was widely emulated, the specific form of that emulation depended on the way in which various Continental states' specific social structures evolved under the impact of industrialization and nation-state formation. These were the two basic transformations indicated by Rokkan's (1999) analysis of the development of mass politics in 19th and 20th century Europe. These transformations meant that when the vision of the citizen-soldier was reintroduced in the latter part of the 19th century, both nationalism and industrialism had transformed the European states dramatically. In turn, those latter developments meant that the question of military manpower now had to be tackled in a far more complex sociopolitical context. That context was one of mass politics, in which the large masses were actually represented by political parties, and of emerging industrial relations systems, where unions played an increasingly important role. Keeping those points in mind, let us therefore specify the impact of the industrial and national revolutions, as well as the ensuing structures of mass politics, for our topic.

Between the middle and end of the 19th century, the industrial revolution swept across continental Europe and the United States, transforming the economies, military capabilities, and relative power of the states it touched. The mid-19th century saw the diffusion of a whole new transport infrastructure, based on railways and the steam engine. In the late 19th century, new technologies based on innovation in electricity and chemicals emerged. In the railroad phase, Britain was the dominant economy, but by the turn of the century, unequal development had turned Germany and the U.S. into significant challengers to British economic dominance. The British economy was hit by decline, and the French economy also lagged, both in terms of industrial innovation and population growth. In both states, the relative (and absolute) increase in German power caused great concern.

The impact of the industrial revolution on the means of warfare was equally dramatic. The industrialization of war was well on its way by around 1850, and was essentially completed by the end of the century. Weapons were now mass-produced, and, as the years passed, increasingly powerful and accurate. In the mid-19th century, the standard military weapons were rifled percussion muskets, rifled breech-loading artillery, and steam-powered armored warships. By the turn of the century a number of further innovations, including the magazine rifle, smokeless gunpowder, the rapid-firing field gun (1891), and the machine gun (1880–1914) had revolutionized weapons technology, and with it, the conduct of war itself.

Given the increased firing power of the new weaponry, Napoleonic offensive tactics were now suicidal. Rather than line attacks, tactics of maneuver, including flank attacks, skirmishing, and column formation, now were crucial. Shelters, breastworks and trenches played major roles, especially once the new heavy caliber field artillery began to be generally employed. With the introduction of these new weapons technologies, defensive tactics and strategy gained a decisive advantage over offensive ones – a point that would be brutally driven home during the bloody trench warfare of the First World War. Yet strangely, the evident advantage of the defense over the offense – a clear lesson of the American Civil War, the Franco-Prussian War and the Russo-Japanese wars alike – went largely unnoticed by military and aristocratic elites (Finer, 1975, pp. 159–160). Instead, as we noted in the previous section, those elites concluded that short wars could easily be waged and won, and that such wars would even bolster lower class support of and commitment to the "national cause." Thus in the face of overwhelming evidence to the contrary, an anachronistic belief in the feasibility of "short, sharp" wars survived (Mayer, 1981; Miller, 1985) to serve as a major cause of the "mutual massacres" of the First World War (Finer, 1975). It also helped to accelerate and exacerbate nationalism, a second major cause of the transformation of states, armies, and war in this period. It is to that topic that we now turn.

The impact of nationalism in this era was at once enormous and highly complex. The military-history literature tends to focus on "nationalism from above," on nationalism as a way to discipline the masses. While such "official" nationalism clearly was important, particularly with respect to state-directed education and military training, the impact of "nationalism from below" on nation building also was significant, especially with regard to national associations and nationally oriented political parties. In fact, because political mobilization and nation building so often were conjoined, many states judged it necessary to seize control of those processes (Anderson, 1991) for their own purposes. In the following, we will examine how these competing forms of nationalism helped to shape the character of the national state as well as to influence the means by which men were recruited and socialized in the armed forces.

For a number of reasons, the opportunities for popular nationalism increased markedly during this period. With the extension and concentration of industrial infrastructure and communities across Europe, particularly after mid-century, the conditions for political mobilization and organization sharply improved. While such organization often took the form of Marxism or other forms of class-based protest, nationalist mobilization also benefited from these changes. Such mobilization was further facilitated by the emergence of a national press, national associations, and political parties. Conscription systems had also originally been part of this popular nationalism. As we saw in the section on the revolutionary era, the original conscription of citizen soldiers in the late 18th and early 19th century expressed an early form of such "nationalism from below." All of these emerging institutions helped to create flourishing civil societies in European states – societies, which in contrast to "internationalist" working-class movements, were increasingly contained within, and defined, by state boundaries.

Such popular nationalism had an important impact on 19th century states, which devised a variety of strategies to cope with the challenges it posed. To the extent that citizens conceived themselves as members of a civil society within a national framework, they increasingly insisted on their rights, both procedural (freedom of speech, fair trials, etc.) and distributive (social welfare, etc.), and states responded accordingly. As European states grew richer through the 19th century, the scale of their social expenditures also had to grow if they were to continue to rule effectively. The civil share of state spending for the first time thus increased significantly, as states began to exert a more direct influence on the living conditions of various social groups. Income from taxation was no longer solely spent to run the state as a military machine, it also was spent to provide institutions and infrastructure (communication systems such as railways, post/telegraph, roads, modern mass media, nationally organized monetary systems, etc.) necessary to expanding industrial capitalism. Equally important, that income was increasingly spent to provide the social services and social infrastructure necessary for the growth of the states' "social capital" as well.

Education was especially important in this respect. States increasingly supported education, above all at the primary level, but partly also at the secondary and tertiary ones, in order to educate, socialize, and nationalize their populations. By committing substantial resources to education, states were increasingly able to buttress their economies, standardize national languages, and to consolidate national symbols (flag, national anthem) and national identities (Weber, 1976). State support for universities not only enabled more concentrated research in the natural sciences, which had important consequences for the continuing industrial revolution, but also facilitated modern historical research ("constructions of the nation's historical past") and linguistic research into the roots of national languages. Finally, and perhaps most importantly, states committed increasing resources to primary education. During this period, European states markedly raised the rate of enrollment in primary schools (schools containing students aged 5–14 years old): England lagged vis-à-vis France and Prussia in that respect, but caught up by the turn of the century (Flora, 1983, Ch. 10). While such education certainly helped to produce a skilled workforce and a politically literate population, its greatest impact probably lay in its ability to construct, stimulate, and reinforce nationalist identities and nationalist sentiments (Weber, 1976, esp. Ch. 18).

States also devised a variety of responses to the special challenges that conscription posed for their efforts to control nationalist agendas and idioms. As noted above, conscription was in some respects contested terrain between popular and state-directed visions of nationalism. Precisely because they *were* conscripted, citizens confidently insisted on certain rights from their states, rights that were more easily articulated and defended because of increased (state-provided) education and growing self-identification as members of a national community. Yet in the face of such pressures, states found a variety of ways to simultaneously accommodate popular demands for rights and services and to legitimate state control. Even in the most apparently republican regimes such as the French Third Republic, where conscription was framed and justified in explicitly revolutionary terms, there were significant elements of manipulation and legitimization from above. Aiming to create an army at once professional and patriotic, ardent and yet apolitical, Gambetta and his colleagues mythologized the draft as a heroic l*evée en masse*, while relying on routinized conscription to impose *de facto* military discipline and social control. Such artful combinations of heroic myth and routinized process served to mask the extent to which states actually had seized control of apparently popular conscription, and would be widely emulated by the "totalitarian" states of the 20th century.

But there were also cases of collision between nationalism from above and nationalism from below, where groups that were not in control of their own state successfully mobilized in order to gain independence. In Austria's multiethnic empire, for instance, the ruling elites feared nationalism from below so much that they were even constrained in their nationalism from above. Two other examples are Norway before 1905 and Ireland before 1921. Despite important differences, both cases illustrate how state attempts to secure popular loyalties from above led unassimilated minorities to construct separatist identities from below, and eventually to raise their own claims for sovereignty. This mechanism would become even more important during the decolonization processes of the 20th century (Tilly, 1990, p. 117).

In the face of such challenges to "official nationalism" (cf. Anderson, 1991), military service became an important institution for the nationalist socialization of young men. The loyalty of these men had traditionally rested with their local village or region. Now, the leading elites wanted people to identify with the state as their "community", and to serve as the loyal defenders of "their" nation. Accordingly, military service was now envisioned in far more ambitious terms as a form of national socialization, rather than simply as drill and training to ensure military efficiency. States used military service to instill discipline and loyalty to orders given by military leaders. And they increasingly also relied on the military, and the sometimes fierce nationalism it encouraged, to displace social unrest outwards against other nations in order to secure social peace at home. There is a school of historians and social scientists (cf. Mayer, 1981; Anderson, 1991) which – rightly, in our view – emphasizes how in the latter part of the 19th century, the aristocratic embrace of nationalism came to be an important cause of the First World War.

Finally, the emergence of mass politics also played an important part in these developments. We previously noted that during the absolutist era, representative assemblies had served as a base for mobilization and making claims against the state. Now these assemblies were transformed into bases for claims to democracy and universal voting rights, or new such bases were formed. Torn from the king's control, such institutions became arenas for political parties crystallizing in line with the major cleavages that divided the various civil societies (Rokkan, 1999). The timing of these reforms varied between countries, but for the core European areas, 1848 was a starting point (with the major extension of male voting rights in Germany and France) and 1917 an end point (when the same reforms were finally passed in Britain). The achievement of female voting rights lagged behind, as is well known. As a result of such changes, ever-larger numbers of the masses were integrated in a "national" community. At the core of this development stands the interplay between extended state capacities and the consolidation of political rights for ever broader parts of the population (Mann, 1993).

The notion of the citizen-soldier was generalized all over the European continent, but the form that notion now took was a historically new one. In this era there was a much greater emphasis on training of officers and ordinary recruits alike. More complex technologies, and the increasing importance of logistics in an industrialized army, meant that officers now needed to be far more professional than their 17th or 18th century counterparts. Recruits were no longer mostly illiterates, and were rigorously trained and retrained throughout their service. As one authority remarks, "though the German and French armies could now be described as conscript ones, based on universal obligation to serve the state, this conscription signally differed from the early experiments in the late seventeenth, in the eighteenth centuries, and during the Revolution and Empire. Napoleon never gave his new conscripts more than eight days drilling. After that they were expected to pick up their soldiering on the way to the battlefield. These new conscript armies insisted on a long and rigorous training of the conscript and constant retraining all the time they were on reserve" (Finer, 1975, p. 159).

The larger social climate surrounding conscription had also changed markedly. In the preceding section, we saw how conscription systems were fitted to social stratification by means of exemptions and "buy out" options such as replacement. But when the citizen-soldier returned in the context of mass politics, the options available to reluctant conscripts contracted strikingly. Analyzing the cases of France and the U.S., Levi (1997, p. 103ff.) denies that this change can be explained by considerations of military efficiency, pressure by military elites (who, she argues, saw replacement as counteracting their goal of acquiring fully professional forces), or problems in finding suitable replacements. Can it then be explained by increasing democratization? An early study by Sales de Bohigas (1968) suggested that commutation and other forms of elite "buy outs" declined as the voting franchise was gradually extended. With the coming of mass politics, and the increasing representation of workers and peasants in the political system, pressure therefore increased "to change a military system that was the product of unrestricted bourgeois and landed power. When the bourgeoisie constituted the bulk of the electorate, their consent was bought by the state; when the franchise was extended, policies changed" (Levi, 1997, p. 103).

The fit between the introduction of universal male suffrage and the termination of replacement, substitution, and commutation is not that good, however, as the abolition of these policies *preceded* the full extension of the suffrage (Levi, 1997, p. 103). Still, Levi's own preferred explanation also refers to democratization and mass politics. She notes that the political clout and political views of those who were expected to serve were changing, and that the consent of rank and file was increasingly necessary, both to the success of military recruitment and to social peace more generally. Already during the period of property-based voting systems, norms of fairness had been invoked to legitimate government policies as fair "to those not in the electorate but whose cooperation [was] essential to effective military organization" (Levi, 1997, p. 105). It was often claimed that the bourgeoisie provided more valuable services to the nation when *not* serving in the military. But such a strategy of legitimation gradually grew incompatible with the "increasingly universalistic norms of a broader electorate" (Levi, 1997, p. 104f).

Levi diagnoses an irreversible shift in states' conceptions of fairness, as they gradually moved towards an "ideology of universalism." These conceptions were increasingly protected by bargains and institutions formalizing the relation between state and civil society. By the last quarter of the century, even people who benefited from replacements and other forms of inequitable conscription were growing skeptical of such claims. As the ideology of democracy changed, civil rights and duties were increasingly linked to all adult males. The standards of fairness had now become "equality of service and sacrifice." As Levi remarks, "a democratic and universalistic ideology took hold that made unthinkable the direct exchange of money as a means to escape military obligations" (Levi, 1997, p. 106).

We must not forget that the consolidation of democracy took place in the context of further industrialization and urbanization. With the rapid growth of the working class and an industrial middle class in the mid-to-late 19th century, young men from these groups came to play an increasingly important role in the armed forces. And their arrival in force led to a number of tensions within those armies, as their ideological bias towards socialism and liberalism diverged sharply from the patrimonial-dynastic-autocratic ideology of the traditional military elites. Those elites, which were distinctly "aristocratic" on the continent, and at least "upper class" in Britain, had a world-view that ranged from strongly conservative (France and Britain) to unreservedly reactionary (Germany and Russia). The new officers, for their part, were increasingly professional, having attended military academies with updated curricula. And even the common soldiers were increasingly educated and articulate, particularly relative to the illiterate peasantry that had traditionally made up the armies' rank and file. This change in the armies' composition led to a number of further problems, as we will see.

To begin with, the officer corps still largely held highly aristocratic or even reactionary world-views, in spite – or perhaps because – of the recent incorporation of more professional elements. In France, the officer corps had been "rearistocratized", as can be seen by its support of Napoleon III's *coup d'etat* in 1851 and its even more reactionary attitudes during the Boulanger and Dreyfus Affairs of 1887–1888 and 1894–1896. Things were better in Britain, but there were tensions there as well. In the German Empire – as we shall see

– there were tensions between the emperor and his military cabinet on one side and the parliament on the other, over a host of issues, most notably that of war credits. And in Prussia itself there was extreme tension between the Junker nobility and the lower classes, especially the working class, which the Junkers feared would not only undermine army discipline but overthrow the state itself.

We have so far surveyed a number of aggregate trends relative to military recruitment, socialization, and the conduct of war in the late 19th century. A more regionally focused and disaggregated analysis may at this point be helpful, in that it can show how regional variation, as well as specific responses by particular regime types, can lead to quite different outcomes. The divergent trajectories we shall discuss are outlined in Table 3. The new normative standards relative to preferential conscription policies were applied in at least three quite different settings, marked by sharp differences in social structure and correspondingly divergent relations between state and civil society.

In the Anglo-American group, the elimination of inequitable conscription policies such as "buying out" did not pose much of a problem, as the universal conscription systems in which such policies arose were only used in times of war. In continental western Europe, by contrast, "buying out" was common, given the prevalence of universal peacetime conscription. Conscription was thus seen as a more or less permanent duty of citizens, and the reconciliation of universal conscription with preferential policies was correspondingly more difficult. And in the "eastwards" inland cases, finally, the more authoritarian conscription systems allowed little "buying out", as varieties of authoritarian rule continued even despite some degree of democratization. In such settings, therefore, the tensions between privilege, democracy, and military service took a different form.

We have seen that Britain's capital-intensive model of state formation implied a small regular army based on volunteers, while giving priority to the navy. Peacetime conscription was avoided for ideological reasons and also because it would undermine the continuity of industrial production. A geographical factor of some importance was of course the physical isolation of Britain (and the U.S.) from the European continent. Conscription was adopted only very reluctantly, once it became clear that Britain could not field the needed troops through volunteer forces alone. Accordingly, Britain would first try to mobilize the men it needed within the framework of voluntary service. If and when military manpower needs grew too great, however, the state resorted to a number of public opinion campaigns (such as the white feather campaigns, cf. Levi, 1987, pp. 111, 116) to raise political consciousness and thereby generate the needed numbers of soldiers. Only when these efforts proved unsatisfactory, *and* there was also state intervention against pacifists and other "shirkers", did the British state decide to resort to universal conscription.

Table 3. Dimensions of the Late 19th Century Situation.

	US	Britain	France	Norway	Germany
Industrialization	Catching up, new leader in some sectors	Lagging	Lagging	Relatively peripheral	Catching up, new leader in some sectors
Nationalism	Mainly from below	Relatively moderate, focus on the Empire	Early, balance from above and from below	Early, balance from above and from below	Early, but in a highly authoritarian framework
Civil society	Strong "state of courts and parties"	Early impact of business elites, but Late development of mass education	Early, relatively strong, but increasing direct rule by the state	Early, relatively strong	Weak. High tensions state/civil society at the end of the period.
Mass politics	Early	Late, slow, but stable emergence	Early, but more discontinuous than in Britain	Convergence with national independence from Sweden	Late, significant authoritarian restrictions
Conscription	Voluntary enlistment	Voluntary enlistment	Citizen-soldier revived	Citizen-soldier revived	Pioneer of citizen-soldier
Buying out options mid 19th century	Extensive during Civil War regime, then irrelevant	Irrelevant	Extensive	Extensive	Less extensive due to authoritarian system
Impact of aristocracy	None	"Gentlemanly capitalism"	Quite strong	None	Strong, military state in state
Geopolitical location	Island	Island	Continent	Continent	Continent

There are conflicting views as to whether resistance to military service was less or more likely in Britain than in other European countries. As long as the British government strenuously tried to motivate volunteers, workers who did not want to go were safe, and there was no coercion other than social pressure. To that extent, the data appear to agree with Rowe's (this issue) argument that resistance was weak in Britain. But once British authorities decided on the draft (1916), we have a case for Forrest's argument (this issue), that the absence of a tradition of conscription led young British men to more resistance. By then World War I had already started, and political opposition was difficult. In such a situation, even liberal states like Britain became strongly interventionist. That is hardly surprising, as the imperatives of all-out war force states to authoritarian actions where opportunistic choices, and the cost/benefit analyses that explain them, become largely irrelevant (see Levi, 1997, esp. Ch. 7, for various bans on anti-war opposition).

Let us now turn to the western parts of continental Europe, including some of the Nordic countries. We have already mentioned the different dynamic in continental Europe: here universal conscription was reintroduced or maintained in the context of increasing Franco-German tension. In France, we previously noted the very rapid extension of mass democracy after 1848. For several years after that date, preferential conscription policies flourished, but their costs became increasingly evident in the following years. As people with higher (bad) numbers "bought out" of military service, poorer people (who had initially drawn a low number) would end up having to serve. Republicans and liberals pushed hard for fewer exemptions and shorter service and, following their return to power in the years after 1879, were increasingly able to secure such gains. The law of 1872 was necessarily a compromise, since the Republicans were still politically marginalized, but in 1889, egalitarian political forces won decisively. Universal military service (first for two years, and then later for three), plus one year in the reserve, was generalized immediately. And in France, as opposed to Britain, longstanding traditions of conscription as well as the ability of Third Republic leaders to "sell" their people a romanticized vision of the draft largely ensured that even the enormous conscription of World War I would meet with little resistance.

In the Nordic countries, the trajectories were different again. In Sweden-Norway, the army had large powers and responsibilities for maintaining political and social order. There was extensive use of preferential conscription policies and "buying out" options. These were abolished when Norway introduced general conscription in 1876, although general male suffrage came about only in 1898. The extent to which this shift reflected Levi's notion of a change in normative conceptions of fairness, or simply the changing arguments of state elites (Jacobsen & Skauge, 2000), cannot be discussed further here. In Sweden, commutation lasted longer, and was not finally abolished until 1904. Yet even there "the writing was on the wall" – such policies would no longer be tolerated. By the interwar period even holdout states like Spain (1920) had abolished preferential conscription policies. It had, in Margaret Levi's words, become simply "unthinkable for a young man to contract with someone else to take his place in the military or to pay the state directly for an exemption" (Levi, 1997, p. 103).

In imperial Germany, the coercion-intensive Prussian state was the hegemonic power, but integrated with the smaller German political units which had earlier belonged to the "city belt", the smaller units of the European state system. Imperial Germany thus combined the Prussian military and agrarian bureaucratic state with the explosive industrialization of Westphalia and other regions bordering the Rhine. This created dynamic political-economic instability, including a tension between political forces pushing towards a liberal-democratic constitutionalist state and an autonomous-aristocratic military elite which sought to maintain the old regime that had brought them power. The number of workers multiplied and, once they were given practical universal male suffrage in 1871, began to play an increasingly important role in politics. Their political party, the SPD, gained ever more votes, from approximately 10% in the 1880s, to 30% by the turn of the century, and 35% in 1912 (Flora, 1983, p. 171).

Given the weakness of German traditions of civil society – particularly in Prussia – the mobilization of this labor movement emerged as a particularly radical threat to the ruling elite. The whole state apparatus was therefore used to repress this massive social change by containing, disciplining and assimilating the workers and their collective organizations. The history of this conflict stretches from Bismarck's laws against SPD activities outside of parliament to later efforts to use schools and the army to "nationalize" the workers. The army would be the "school of the nation", but at the same time, there was extensive discrimination against social democrats in the army (Groh, 1973, p. 55ff). Army leaders feared the increasing number of social democrat soldiers, while the SPD saw this as an indicator of the growing power of the labor movement and, accordingly, sought to exploit worker-soldier solidarity for political gain. There were extensive strikes in 1905, 1907, and 1909 and eager agitation by social democrats both against a "reform" of the electoral system that would harm the SPD and against state militarization and preparations for war. Imperial Germany thus serves as a particularly dramatic example of the tensions between a militarist state and social mobilization from below.

And, as we might expect in a state run by military elites yet beset by dynamic socioeconomic change, the heart of those conflicts lay in the army itself. At the turn of the century, the extension of the army had been postponed for fear of "democratization of the officer corps and social-democratization of the soldiers" (E. Kehr, quoted in Groh, 1973, p. 386). The risks that this conjuncture entailed led in turn to a unification of the political right. Military elites discussed the deliberate use of military forces in domestic politics, including systematic planning for the case of civil war (Geyer, 1984, p. 85). Considerations of military security implied continued reliance on universal conscription, but this created a serious dilemma for both army leaders and government. The huge Prussian estate owners saw the army and the bureaucracy as the main tools for protection of their political and economic interests. They thus protected these institutions both from liberal reform proposals (parliamentary democratic state, democratization of the army) and from social democratic mobilization. By contrast, the SPD had its own "military program of the left", which focused on issues such as the end of special privileges for Prussian officers, shorter terms of service, and religious and political liberalization. The Junkers' resistance to such reforms led to institutional inertia so severe that it reduced the state's capacity to pursue flexible policies in domestic and international affairs alike (Groh, 1973, p. 391).

In the face of the mounting crises in the army, an increasingly polarized society, and increasing conflict with other European states, even the Army General Staff began to call for sweeping military reform. Suggested reforms included democratizing the officer corps and even the possibility of arming the whole people in the event of war. And, while the Junkers accused military proponents of reform of opening the door to social revolution, the social democrats and the left generally supported such proposals. They hoped, not unreasonably, that the trend towards a more democratic army would make it impossible to pit soldiers against workers in the case of domestic instability (Groh, 1973, pp. 387–388). While such calculations were to prove disastrously wrong in 1919, in 1913 they probably seemed both reasonable and prudent.

In retrospect, the fatal decision of German social democrats to accommodate German militarism in the years before World War I has been much discussed. Our brief account above indicates the difficult balance: there was fear that the army could be used against the political left in a civil war, and there were tensions in the army with some chance that parts of the left's program would receive broader support. This analysis, however, moves only at the elite level. As emphasized by Moore (1978, p. 221ff), one must also investigate the extent to which the working class rank and file identified with the German empire. Moore finds a specific working class conception of German patriotism. The class antagonism was strong regarding daily life and material interests, but foreign affairs were more remote from this. Referring to studies within social history (1978, pp. 224–225) he argues that German working class patriotism flourished in the 1880s and 1890s. But of course these are regional studies, and it may be that national trends were quite different. Nor is it clear that this analysis can be accurately extended to the more polarized situation of the early 20th century.

We have seen how our typology, which identifies distinct Anglo-American, Western-Continental and Eastern-Continental models of conscription – points us to interesting variations in military recruitment, socialization, and relations between military and civil institutions. We now turn to the early 20th century drama that ensued when these different military machines clashed.

WORLD WAR I

In the period 1914–1945, the tensions that had accumulated within the European state system since the mid-19th century burst into two world wars. Their all-embracing scope and terrifying waste of human resources was due above all to the industrialization of war that had emerged as a possibility in the late 19th century. World War I was also driven by the influence of militarized aristocracies who had adjusted to industrialism and adopted nationalism (Mayer, 1981). Casualties totaled over eight million dead soldiers, with something like 20 million wounded and another 20 million civilian deaths (Bond, 1982; cf. Gilbert, 1984, p. 163 for slightly different estimates). World War II – "Act II of the Great War that ended Europe's hegemony" – would prove even more costly. Total deaths in that war were estimated as being between 35 and 50 million, and may well have ranged even higher (Nye, 1993, p. 82; Craig, 1966, p. 729). This section, however, will focus largely on the first of those wars.

The major combatants in World War I are well known. The Central Powers were made up of Germany, Austria-Hungary, the Ottoman Empire and Bulgaria, while the major Allied Powers comprised France, Russia, Britain and later, Italy and the United States of America. In the Central Powers, coercive styles of rule were predominant. While the German Empire was by now attaining several traits of the "capitalized coercion" type, it also retained many coercion-oriented features, particularly in the networks between the Emperor, the Berlin bureaucracy and the military elites. Germany's main ally, Austria-Hungary, also had a coercion-intensive background, but was at this point weakened and verging on dissolution, due to its multi-ethnic character. By contrast, the German state – and army – had linguistic and cultural unity, which served as an asset in the subsequent struggle. The two other units belonging to the alliance, the Ottoman Empire and Bulgaria, will not be dealt with here.

As noted above, the other major powers of the European state system allied against these central powers. This entente was led by Britain, facing its greatest challenge to its role as the "balancer" of continental powers. Britain allied with

France and Russia, and eventually, with many of the remaining smaller states of Europe as well. While the war did not directly oppose capital-intensive groups of states and coercion-intensive ones, it *is* clear that the Central Alliance was dominated by states with coercive-intensive roots, while, with the significant exception of Russia, the Entente was dominated by states with more elements of the capital-intensive pattern.

At the end of World War I, it also was obvious that the three great powers with strongly coercion-oriented traditions had been most dramatically affected by the war. Internal destabilization in Russia gave rise to the world's first socialist revolution, while the Austro-Hungarian Empire dissolved into several smaller central European states. As for Germany, not only did it lose a significant proportion of its prewar territory and population (13.1 and 10%, respectively) at Versailles, it also was forced to accept humiliating terms of peace and devastating reparation payments (Gilbert, 1984, pp. 185–187).

World War I brought two of Finer's stated trends – the nationalization of armies and total mobilization for war – very close to completion. Except in the Austro-Hungarian Empire, state armies were now national, and included few if any foreign volunteers. Furthermore, world wars in principle implied the mobilization of a country's entire resources for the purpose of warfare. A new notion, "the home front", which referred to the civilian population mobilized in support of the war effort, clearly indicated the total nature of these wars. This was something very different from the earlier rather limited dynastic wars for colonies and provinces, and even far exceeded the most ambitious mass levies of the Revolutionary and Napoleonic Wars. In the First World War and Second World War, states made everyone support the war effort, intervening strongly in the daily life of the masses.

Such developments helped to further strengthen the "conscription bargain" between states, armies, and the general population. Universal service or support for the war effort was demanded of all citizens, and in exchange, the state implicitly promised not only to defend those citizens, but also to provide for their welfare in times of peace. Such provision of social welfare would become especially important in the years following World War II, when it became in many respects the central function of the modern state. Yet even by 1918, that process was well underway, as states assumed an unprecedented interest and importance in the daily lives of their citizens. Unlike their largely oligarchic and paternalist 19th century predecessors, these states had to concern themselves with the welfare of all their citizens if their highly ambitious strategies of social mobilization – including but not limited to universal conscription – were to succeed.

Germany lost both world wars, but its unequalled ability to organize its society and economy on a wartime basis gave it a real chance of victory in both cases. That ability not only allowed it to massively increase its military resources in the early 20th century prelude to World War I (Kennedy, 1987, pp. 199–215, esp. Tables 19 and 20), but even more impressive, to counter the effects of devastating hyperinflation and depression during the 1920s and 1930s and fight yet another war between 1940–1945 (Kennedy, 1987, pp. 303–310). Thus among all of the states with a coercion-intensive legacy, Germany best managed to incorporate significant aspects of capital-intensive strategies of growth, particularly in establishing a controlled war economy. Indeed, the industrialist Walter Rathenau claimed that the war was "an education in state socialism." Germany soon introduced rationing cards and price controls, and went the furthest in militarizing all corners of society in order to more effectively mobilize it for war.

We have previously noted the "cult of the offensive", the belief in short wars, the enormous expansion of conscript armies, and the impact of nationalism both from above and below. By the summer of 1914 the myth and the mechanism of heroic yet routinized conscription were firmly in place in most European states. And, with the significant exception of Russia, most continental states encountered relatively few difficulties in implementing the draft. Thus France, where previously draft evasion rates had at times approached 50% (Forrest, 1989; Van Holde, 1993), had few such problems during World War I. Not before 1916 was there significant anti-war mobilization (see below). Popular antipathy to the draft was more pronounced in Britain, where, as we have already noted, there was a long tradition of aversion to forced military recruitment. Consequently, the British state relied instead on heroic appeals to volunteerism, which at first worked so well that they threatened to deplete vital sectors, such as the chemical and explosives industries of much-needed skilled labor (Bond, 1986, p. 106). Only in 1916, as casualties mounted and volunteerism flagged, was conscription finally introduced.

At first, World War I was almost universally judged to be necessary and even desirable, and popular enthusiasm and morale were accordingly high. Consequently, conditions, state leaders and social forces inside the contending states took a number of bold or even naïve actions to support the war effort, many of which they would later regret. Military authorities everywhere were lionized and given enormous authority and discretion over political as well as military affairs – a step which civilian state leaders would later come to regret. Continental Europe also witnessed the establishment of wartime truces (Burgfrieden – fortress truces – in Germany) between states and the left. The latter abjured their old internationalist principles, suspended all protests and strikes, supported their states' war efforts by voting war credits, and then enthusiastically marched off to fight (Bond, 1986, pp. 104-105). Russia, the site of an abortive revolution in 1905, also saw strikes sharply decline and popular patriotism surge (Bond, 1986, p. 100). Anti-militarist sentiments were stronger in Britain (cf. Forrest's argument noted above), but even there, old and bitter conflicts between liberals and conservatives were suspended in favor of patriotism and the war effort.

Because the war was widely expected to be "short and sharp", it was at first fought as a 19th century "war of movement" and maneuver (Finer, 1975, p. 161; Bond, 1986, pp. 100–101). But the troops soon became bogged down in trench warfare, with two million men at each side "staring at each other" from the Jura to the Channel (Finer, 1975, p. 161). In the subsequent war of attrition, all sides used any and all methods to gain an advantage over the enemy, all too often by winning a few miles of ground at enormous cost. Seemingly endless offensives and counteroffensives were maintained through massive artillery bombardments and the use of poison gas. In this industrially based war, the killing capacity of weapons increased more than ever, as Germany's ability to shell Paris from 70 miles away with "Big Bertha" clearly shows (Bond, 1984, pp. 102, 115–117).

Yet decisive victory eluded all of the combatants and the war dragged on. Because of this stalemate, there was a race to increase the manpower for war. 1916 probably saw the bloodiest fighting, with staggering death tolls; above 400,000 at Verdun, and more than 1,000,000 at the Somme (Craig, 1966, pp. 513–514). Such casualties drove the European states to previously unprecedented actions: in May 1916 Britain introduced the draft, while later that same year Germany created a "patriotic auxiliary service" that conscripted all remaining German men between 17 and 60 years of age (Bond, 1984, p. 118).

The increasing costs of war were also making themselves felt on the home front, as states were forced to radically reorganize their societies and economies for the war effort. States drained their populations and already stressed industrial sectors for badly needed skilled labor and war materiel, and on the whole succeeded brilliantly in overcoming the periodic crises created by the ever-increasing demands of total war. In Britain, shell production, loss of merchant ships and problems of raw materials supply due to blockade were main challenges. Things were far worse in Germany, which faced huge industrial bottlenecks and a severe economic crisis, having to finance this war alone (while Britain could rely on U.S. aid). Although the Germans used female labor as far as possible, and even forcibly conscripted Belgians to work in German plants, it became increasingly apparent that to meet their production targets, skilled laborers would have to be withdrawn from the army and returned to the factories. Such tactics further weakened the already decimated German armies, increasing war-weariness and damaging public morale. World War I had become "a conflict between economic systems as much as of armed forces" (Bond, 1984, p. 116).

Finally, the war turned into blockage warfare, a "ghastly exaggerated travesty" of 18th century siege warfare, where the sieges now were directed not against fortresses or cities, but entire nation-states (Finer, 1975, p. 161). Blockage warfare was entirely logical, since only through such means could states effectively prevent their enemies from using the natural resources on which the successful prosecution of total war depended. But it was also terrible, since it implied such activities as submarine attacks on merchant ships or passenger liners, and the even more unpalatable strategic bombing of cities. Both sides employed strategic bombing from 1915 on, and any claims that the primary targets were military ones became highly implausible once night bombing campaigns began (Bond, 1984, pp. 114–115). In such circumstances, the distinction between combatants and civilians was completely eroded. There was a certain justification to such a view; after all, if civilians were working on the home front busily making bombs, they were partners in war, if not quite combatants in the usual sense. And anyway, if the enemy's morale was to be broken, civilians could easily be seen as necessary targets – and thus as legitimate ones (Bond, 1984, p. 115). While such measures might seem morally repugnant to those schooled in older chivalrous traditions of war, in the era of total war they were logical and thus inevitable: total war meant the total mobilization of societies in the struggle.

By 1917, the struggle had become a terrible war of attrition that exhausted all combatants but seemed unable to promise victory to any of them. There was rising opposition to the war by civilians and soldiers alike, particularly in Russia, Austria and Germany. Draft resistance, insubordination and desertion were increasingly common in the Austrian army, and were even worse in Russia, where they played a major role in sparking and accelerating the slide to revolution later that year. Nor were the Western states immune: in France, as we previously noted, outrage at enormous losses (more than 3 million by 1917), increasingly suicidal offensives, and general mistreatment by their commanders drove several thousands of soldiers to open mutiny in April 1917 (Bond, 1984, p. 123). The state responded harshly, executing 49, sentencing thousands, and creating a national crisis. In Britain, things were somewhat better, but still, war-weariness was pronounced and suicidal battles like Passchendaele (where 300,000 British died) did little to improve declining morale.

The rising opposition to the war led to one event of truly world-historical significance. The Russian state's inept conduct of the war had by 1917 created a revolutionary situation in which the armed forces played a central role. The Russian army was enormous (with over nine million men by the middle of 1915), but it consisted mostly of ill-equipped, untrained, and illiterate peasants, who had little interest in the war, and even less in common with their commanders. The social distance and polarization between officers and men was enormous, and there was a serious shortage of NCO's, which made the already tenuous command and control of the peasant armies virtually impossible except through the most brutal methods (Bond, 1984, p. 111). As early as mid-1915, Russian forces were seriously demoralized and close to anarchy. The causes of this demoralization were numerous, ranging from chaotic management and endemic distrust at the top (between the general staff and the war ministry, as well as between business and government) to internal rivalries between military sectors, to prosaic but deadly problems like severe shortages of weapons, ammunition, and food. Above all, the soldiers were simply tired of fighting hugely costly battles hundreds or thousands of miles from home. By the end of 1916, the Russians had lost more than three million men and, with no end in sight to the carnage, many soldiers simply decided to desert and head back home (Kennedy, 1987, pp. 264–265).

The Russian regime's economic problems also helped to provoke its eventual collapse. The government financed the war by contracting international loans, and by liberally printing paper money, a measure that led to uncontrolled inflation (Bond, 1984, p. 108). And, as the state geared up for war, the polarization between the civil and military sectors of the Russian economy increased. Enormous growth in wartime industries contrasted with food and raw materials shortages, especially in urban areas. And, since the cities were the main location of industrial expansion, such shortages posed a serious risk of riots (Bond, 1984, pp. 117–118).

The first sign of the discontents that would lead to the October Revolution was the massive unrest that developed in the army during the fall of 1916 and the early spring of 1917. Soldiers openly accused their superiors of various abuses of power, including graft, cowardice and treason, clamored for unconditional surrender, and deserted *en masse* in the meantime (Bond, 1984, p. 119). Deserters were everywhere and, as their numbers grew, they posed a serious problem not only for the military, but for the civil government as well, since they frequently engaged in criminal activity and also radicalized the peasants on their return. Rather than acting as a force for order, therefore, the now disintegrating army actually helped to provoke disorder and accelerate the slide to revolution.

And that revolution was not long in coming. The revolution entered its first phase in March 1917 when, during a munitions strike, 200,000 men and women in the streets of Petrograd were joined by Cossacks and reservists. Other cities quickly followed Petrograd's example. Within a few days the tsar abdicated and a provisional government was set up, while the Russian people decided what form their new republic should take. This provisional government passed liberal reforms, such as a people's militia instead of police, and granted civil rights to soldiers. But mass opinion was more radical, particularly on the issues of peace, land and bread. And here again, the armed forces played a crucial role in escalating and radicalizing the revolution. In the armies themselves, the old hierarchical command structure was increasingly breaking down, to be replaced by democratic self-government and sometimes outright class war (Fitzpatrick, 1994, pp. 47–48, 53). And, as the long hoped-for redistribution of land began to look more likely, the peasant troops increasingly returned home. Desertion reached epidemic proportions in July, when the Provisional Government's disastrous attempt to push the Germans back in Galicia led to another 200,000 deaths (Fitzpatrick, 1994, p. 57). Encouraged by the deserters' evident war-weariness, the Bolsheviks adopted a policy of "revolutionary defeatism" which set them apart from all other parties, and helped to legitimate their seizure of power in October. True to their word – in this respect at least – within a few months, the Bolsheviks had taken Russia out of the war.

1917 also saw the United States enter the war. This development established a major 20th century trend, as the U.S. began to assist its allies, and especially Britain, in their war efforts by drawing on its huge productive capabilities. And, as the major industrial power in such alliances, the United States began to assume an unprecedented influence. In the postwar Cold War period, this Anglo-American dominance under U.S. leadership would become the main axis of Western international relations.

All great powers learned that defeat could bring social and political revolt. By the end of the Great War, Austrian soldiers were fighting in rags (Bond, 1984, p. 131). Under such conditions, the danger of state collapse as well as military disintegration was genuine in several countries. The stresses of war, combined with socialist antiwar mobilization, provoked revolution in Germany – the other main country with many coercion-oriented elements remaining – in the final months of 1918. Here again, however, war-weary soldiers served more to disrupt civil order than to ensure it – a striking contrast to the effective policing by their predecessors in Prussia and Wilhelmine Germany. In 1918, when German sailors in Kiel and Wilhelmshaven revolted, soldiers were once again ordered to restore order, but instead joined the revolt. Workers' and soldiers' councils modeled on Russian soviets subsequently emerged. The Kaiser abdicated, the social democrats were brought in, and armistice on the Western front was negotiated, marking the end of the First World War. The revolution was brought under control when the regime extended the franchise and accepted the idea of peace without annexation.

Finally, it should be noted that the Great Powers were also imperialist countries which freely used their colonial subjects as soldiers. Troops from the

British Empire and "Dominions" (e.g. Canada, Australia, and New Zealand) played an important part in the First World War (Levi, 1997, Ch. 5) and paid a proportionate cost; between 1914 and 1918 perhaps 250,000 of them died (Parker, 1995, pp. 275, 295). France went further, *conscripting* colonial soldiers in the Great War, using them both to secure and capture colonies, and as regular forces or even "shock troops" in the European theater (Craig, 1966, pp. 521–522; Carey, this issue). As colonial subjects, such troops were expected to serve the metropole loyally, although they generally received few social or political benefits in return.

In conclusion, by 1918 the character of war had changed forever. While not all future wars would be total wars like World War I, the possibility of escalation to such a war would henceforth be with us. And in that evolution, the role of the state as war-maker also changed irrevocably. As Samuel Finer remarks, "Now not only were the standard logistical requirements of armies catered for by the army or the state; the state went further: it nationalized the economy, it took technology into its own service, and it even took in *ideology* – in great lie-factories that turned out war-propaganda (Finer, 1975, p. 162). Once an affair of only a few armed men, war – and the struggle for "hearts and minds" it now entailed – had become total. And that change in turn suggests that the relationship between states and wars had now grown more complex. While states had long used war as *a* means to secure their ends, total war demanded that states commit themselves utterly to *its* means if they were to realize those goals. And yet, as the cases of Russia and Austria-Hungary show, those means could well entail the destruction of the states that employed them. In the following sections, we will examine the implications of the shift to total war in greater detail.

THE INTERWAR PERIOD

The fall of the tsar and the emperors of Austria and Prussia signaled a broader weakening of Europe's aristocracies after World War I. Aristocratic militarism had dissolved in the war, and even France and Britain had experienced radical mobilization in connection with its end. In the core western parts of the state system full democracy (political citizenship, voting rights) was instituted for males and in many cases also for women (female suffrage adopted by Germany in 1919, by Britain in 1918 and 1928, and by France in 1945). Moreover, in striking contrast to their war-making predecessors, all of the major states emerging from World War I were committed to providing for the social welfare of their subjects (Finer, 1975, p. 146). Such provision would henceforth be a central feature of state and nation building strategies. In the interwar period, this process took a variety of different forms: at one pole, we find the democracies emerging with a capital-intensive background, and at the other, we find several states in Eastern Europe, Central and even Southern Europe. In many of these cases the coercion-intensive background was still influential, now reinforced by the use of mass mobilizing techniques first employed during the Great War.

If states focused increasingly on transforming society in this period, so social forces bent on political mobilization now focused almost exclusively on the state. Before World War I, there had been a number of movements, particularly among liberals and anarchists, which envisioned a political future where the state would play a minor role. After the war, however, both extreme and moderate political movements increasingly regarded the state as the obvious vehicle for their moral projects (Mann, 1995, p. 111). The 19th century had brought both nationalism and industrialized class-divided societies, but only after the Great War did class and nation became the crucial points of reference for political mobilization. On the right, fascists sought to exterminate the enemies of the "nation", while on the left, communists took an equally extreme position in the name of the working class. Under their influence, Russia, Germany, and to a lesser extent Italy, were rapidly militarized, a transformation which played a crucial role in precipitating the final crash of the European state system into the Second World War.

In the states that did not develop along these extreme paths, the relations between class interests and nationalism were more ambiguous and complex. Their situation was characterized by considerable polarization between the bourgeoisie on the one hand, and the increasingly militant workers (and to a lesser extent, farmers) on the other. The Soviet example had a strong impact on the labor movements all over Europe. After all, the communists had ended the war and repudiated Russia's debts to the western countries – impressive victories in the eyes of those suffering from the traumatic social, economic and personal effects of World War I. In their own struggles, therefore, militants sought to emulate the organization of Russian workers and peasants. Yet at the same time, such militants often found themselves without broad support, as most members of their societies preferred social peace to class warfare, and political appeasement to policies of confrontation. Such isolationist quietism probably reached its apogee in postwar America, but was true to a certain extent of France and Britain as well.

While most societies were relatively peaceful during the 1920s, there were deep and unresolved economic problems in many of them, particularly in Britain which, because of the relatively minor damage it suffered during the War, was not forced to retool its industry and economy as were its continental neighbors.

Consequently, British industry began to lag further and further behind that of other countries. The effects of that lag were worsened by the decline of trade after the war, as key markets were lost to the Americans or "simply disappeared because of the rise of new manufacturing in the British dependencies" (Craig, 1966, pp. 668–671). And Britain was also still paying for the war. France, too, suffered from severe economic dislocations, particularly in the years before 1926, when a vigorous Conservative government under Poincaré began the systematic reconstruction of industry and the economy which the British were unwilling to undertake (Craig, 1966, pp. 684–685). While such reforms would for a few years shelter the French from the effects of the Great Depression, that economic crisis eventually affected all of the European states, and in so doing served as an impetus to wider social and economic transformations during the 1930s.

As the unstable growth pattern of the 1920s turned into a deep economic crisis from 1929 on, states were forced to reconfigure the means by which they organized their societies and economies. Ironically, while the relative social peace of the late 1920s had not allowed significant social or political reforms to be enacted in the Western states, the Great Depression did open up innovative alternatives to rule by the bourgeoisie. In France, the 1930s saw the rapid growth of communism as well as of quasi-fascist organizations like the *Action Française*, the *Croix de Feu*, and a host of others (Craig, 1966, pp. 687–688). In Scandinavia, by contrast, reform-oriented labor parties rose to power. The historically most important developments, however, were taking place in Britain and the United States, where the bourgeois rule of the 20ths increasingly gave way to the dirigiste liberalism of the National Government (Britain) and Roosevelt's New Deal.

The 1930s saw a new round to the early 20th century trend towards a more organized civil society. There was protectionism and import substitution as well as state intervention to reorganize the financial systems after the turmoil of the economic crisis. Additionally, the territorial borders of the state were drawn much more tightly, with state borders now serving also as the borders of economic networks. In Russia, Germany, and Italy, civil societies were fully dismantled and coercion-intensive control from above introduced. And in most of the remaining European states, a number of organizations in civil society were more tightly connected to the activities of the state.

In the interwar years, Britain and the U.S. demobilized rapidly, and retreated from wartime conscription to the less politically volatile approach of volunteer recruitment of professional forces. This essentially laissez-faire liberal approach accorded with longstanding traditions in both countries and accordingly was maintained as long as possible. Only when tension again arose in the European state system in the mid-1930s, would they begin to abandon their commitment to such "normal" recruitment systems. It was not until May 1938, with Hitler occupying Austria and eyeing the Sudetenland, that Britain finally introduced the draft in peacetime. And in the even more reluctant United States, Roosevelt would not succeed in establishing peacetime conscription until more than two years later.

On the continent, by contrast, a return to the *status quo ante bellum* was far more difficult. The interwar period was marked by polarization. The massive destruction wrought by World War I shattered state, societies and economies alike, producing social and political unrest within states. While the focus of conflict would shift outwards again with the rise of virulent Nazi nationalism in the 1930s, during the early part of the interwar period even global conflicts, such as the struggle between capitalism and communism, took place largely within states rather than between them.

That shift from conflict between states to conflict within them had important consequences for the internal politics of "external" institutions like the armed forces. Because the threat from the USSR was seen less as an external military one than as an internal political one, it became essential to police key institutions like the army. Domestic communist parties were generally seen as internal enemies, dedicated to the subversion of state institutions and military organizations (Bond, 1984, p. 136). And such a perception was in many respects accurate, for while the USSR had abandoned internationalism for "building socialism in one country", it was not above sponsoring social disruptions inside of other states. European leaders often concluded that communists should be excluded from the armed forces. The French strategy, for example, was "surveillance of all communist suspects, disciplinary maneuvers, transfer to special units, uncovering of regimental cells and an attempt to root out the distributors of political pamphlets" (Bond, 1984, p. 136).

The radical right also exploited its relations with the armed forces for the purposes of mass mobilization and political destabilization. Fascism and other hard right movements offered a natural haven for hundreds of thousands of ex-combatants in Germany, Italy and even France, who felt betrayed and disoriented in the postwar situation. Such men idealized the military hierarchies and, with their "nostalgic memory of the frontline comradeship" (Bond, 1984, p. 137) soon raised prewar "militarist nationalism . . . to a yet higher pitch of intensity" (Howard, 1976, p. 118f). Groups such as the German free corps and Italian fascists readily used violence against a variety of enemies, Jews and communists in particular. In Germany, they helped the social democrats crush the communist uprising in 1919. That even social democratic leaders were willing to sell out to an army connected with such paramilitary auxiliaries testified not only to the profound social dislocations wrought by the War but also to the fragility of nominally democratic politics and civilian institutions in the interwar era. These disturbing trends were only strengthened in the ensuing Great Depression, as groups such as Germany's *Shalhelm* and France's *Croix de Feu* dressed up in ersatz uniforms and engaged in generalized thuggery, while meeting with little government opposition (Best, 1984, pp. 138–139). Indeed, such groups played a crucial role in the anti-parliamentary right wings in several postwar states, where they often acted with the tacic or even explicit support of mainstream politicians and serving officers.

In Germany, Article 173 of the Versailles Treaty had banned general conscription and limited the army to 100,000 long-term (12-year) volunteers. While the French would have preferred a conscript army based on one-year service, Britain's Lloyd George insisted that, to destroy the militarization of German society, it was necessary to get rid of the "evil of general conscription." Pointing to the British experience, he claimed that a professional army could be democratically controlled, while a conscript army might prove more difficult to manage. In the event, however, things turned out quite differently. The army leadership was able to keep the German military organization functioning as a largely autonomous state within the state. Moreover, long-term volunteerism actually worked to promote militarism, since it provided an effective means by which potential officers could be screened, selected and trained (Best, 1984, p. 137). And, since the military saw the social democrats as responsible for the humiliating Versailles Treaty, they felt little obligation to support the Weimar Republic, seeking instead to subvert Versailles and Weimar, and to promote the continuing militarization of German society (Wette, 1994, pp. 95, 100). Finally, in keeping with longstanding Prussian traditions, the German army was used against popular mobilization, playing a role in the destruction of the Weimar Republic.

France was traumatized by the Great War, making military reform and the quest for national security imperative there as well. Yet reconciling those goals would prove to be very difficult. In a country where almost 1,500,000 soldiers had died and three million more had been wounded, there was no doubt that military service would be sharply reduced; the question was only by how much. In 1926, the terms of service were set at one year's conscription, in itself a compromise with the socialists, who had pushed for eight months service in a Swiss-style militia. There were no standing reserves whatsoever, which meant that in the event of conflict, mobilization would be slow and inefficient. Political controversies undermined reforms aimed to put "the nation on a war footing." Diplomatic attempts to guarantee national security also failed; in May 1930, French premier Aristide Briand issued a memorandum suggesting European political and economic integration, including measures for collective security. The plan was torpedoed by the British, who viewed it as posing a threat to their role as European "balancer" and to their "special relationship" with the United States (Heater, 1992, p. 143).

Although France had abandoned its tradition of revolutionary mobilization in favor of a timid "defencism", the notion of revolutionary armies was by no means obsolete. Drawing their inspiration from the French Revolution, revolutionaries such as Lenin and Mao emphasized the power of the potentially explosive linkage between military mobilization and political mobilization. Only bourgeois regimes saw that linkage as a liability. By alerting the people to the threats their nation faced, revolutionary leaders hoped not only to secure their states from external attacks and internal counterrevolution, but to recreate the heroic reign of virtue which had so energized the people of France in 1793. Such models would prove particularly important in the national liberation movements of the mid-20th century, as we will see.

There was a real difference between revolutionary rhetoric and the realities of organizing and disciplining a large army, however, as the history of the Russian Red Army clearly shows. After a brief flirtation with populist militias (the Red Guards) and volunteer forces, in 1918 the Bolsheviks adopted conscription in order to counter the growing security threats posed by counterrevolution and civil war. By the end of the Civil War in 1921, the Red Army was huge, numbering over five million enlisted men (mostly poorly trained peasants) although probably only about a tenth of that number actually served as fighting troops (the rest did supply, transport or administrative work). Although the Bolsheviks had supported "military democracy", including the election of officers, in the Imperial Army (probably in order to further destabilize it) and the Red Guards, in organizing their own army they were less principled and more pragmatic. Officers were appointed, not elected, and for several years included a large number (c. 50,000) of former officers from the Imperial Army, paired with Party commissars, so as to ensure that the new Soviet army would be both red *and* expert (Fitzpatrick, 1994, pp. 75–76). Military discipline was harsh, with desertion and even military failure punishable by death (Craig, 1966, p. 577). A reform in 1924 established a two-year conscription period together with a force of five-year regulars.

Systematic organization, brutal discipline and terror were typical of Stalin's industrializing efforts, and also extended to the Red Army itself. By the early 1930s, the Red Army had been thoroughly bureaucratized and appeared to be a stable and increasingly powerful fighting force. Its peacetime strength stood at approximately 1 million, but it could be increased to more than 10 times that size by general mobilization in the case of war. The red/expert dilemma in the officer corps had been resolved by requiring that all new officers should have a working class background; a step which helped to ensure their political reliability, if at the cost of some efficiency. More importantly, the armed forces were finally becoming modernized and industrialized, with a 1000% increase in tanks and the construction of three airborne divisions in 1933–1934 alone (Bond, 1984, pp. 160–161). But just when it looked as if the Soviets were on the verge of creating a "large, modern and, above all, *national* army", Stalin purged the military leadership. The Great Purge of 1937–1938 cost the army 35,000 officers, which completely disorganized and demoralized the forces that remained (Bond, 1984, pp. 161–162). Because the Red Army was still recovering from this blow when Hitler attacked the USSR in June 1941, it was quickly overwhelmed. Not until the end of 1942 would the tide really turn in favor of Russia.

The claim to protect the masses via revolutionary mobilization also got its right-wing version in the 1930s. While communism was emerging in Russia, the other huge state with a coercion-intensive background was experimenting with a quite different form of political mobilization, state *dirigisme*, and social control. In Germany, the fragile democracy of the Weimar Republic broke down, and the older authoritarian aspects of the German-Prussian state returned in a far more vicious form than ever before. For Nazism, as for communism, the experience of war planning shaped the broader mobilization and militarization of society. But here the goal was to organize capitalism in such a way that it would maintain and even promote the principles of private property – at least for supporters of the regime. Similar goals and methods prevailed in the south European periphery where, in the 1920s and 1930s, Italy and then Spain fell under the control of fascist movements (Craig, 1966, pp. 594–612 passim, 709–714; also cf. Rokkan, 1999, p. 235f). Such developments can be seen as a return of coercion-intensive states, although state power and social control in Germany at least were no longer primarily dependent on a feudal-agrarian system. Germany, after all, was one of the era's most developed industrial states. The fascist economy in Germany was a full-fledged planned command economy and, like its communist counterpart in the USSR, employed wartime principles of popular and industrial mobilization even during times of peace. Italy and Spain, while also seeking to develop command economies, were considerably less successful in doing so.

On the political and military fronts, fascism and related authoritarian movements also developed effective new strategies of coercion-intensive state building and social control. Except in Japan and perhaps Spain, traditional militarism was everywhere on the decline, being increasingly replaced by a sort of mobilizational populism where state leaders, rather than military elites, determined the course and content of state militarization. In the new coercion-intensive European states of the 1920s and 1930s, traditional militarists like Ludendorff were replaced by "civilian militarists" such as Mussolini and Hitler. They first bypassed and then subverted the general staff and army headquarters, and then subsequently mobilized and militarized their societies. By appealing to expansionist hopes, memories of victimization, dreams of revenge, and simple racism the new fascist leaders found an unparalleled means by which virtually the entire population could be consolidated, mobilized and disciplined (Bond, 1984, p. 158). Fascism and even more Nazism homogenized populations (and eliminated those who would not or could not go along) through highly coercive rule conjoined – at least in Germany – with unprecedented bureaucratization. In the 1936 Nazi Four Year Plan, civilian workers were subjected to military discipline and regulation, while highly militarized education guaranteed a constant supply of the desired "soldier products" (Bond, 1984, p. 149). More generally, beginning with the Enabling Laws of 1933, all major civil institutions were brought under state control or eliminated altogether (Craig, 1966, pp. 652–653).

Such systematic coercion and militarization was clearly designed to put the state on a war footing, as the other European powers slowly and unwillingly concluded. Although the Nazi regime did not directly violate the Versailles Treaty until March 1936, preparations for "defending the country by all means" had begun a year earlier, when Hitler denounced that Treaty's disarmament clauses and reintroduced general conscription (Gilbert, 1984, pp. 296–299). During the next 10 years, Nazi Germany called up 20 million men in this manner. As soldiers of the Reich, these men were subjected to rigid discipline and socialization in order to break their ties to civil society as well as to deprive them of the fear of killing. In this case, as in other coercion-intensive states such as Imperial Japan and Soviet Russia, therefore, conscription and democracy were decisively at odds (Wette, 1994, pp. 101–105). While most regimes in the modern era have found it necessary to make mass conscription contingent on the promise of social benefits or the franchise, the mass-mobilizing coercion-intensive states appear to have found a very different, and equally powerful, means of implementing the draft.

As German expansionism became increasingly evident towards the end of the 1930s, European war-weariness gave way to reluctant preparation for war. Recalling the disastrous offensive campaigns of World War I, strategists of the day placed their hopes in new weapons and doctrines which would allow them to fight a less costly "technical" war when and if it became necessary to move against Germany and her allies. On the ground, strategists hoped that new forms of mechanized warfare, and tanks in particular, would help to keep casualties down; others, as we have noted, had an even more naive belief in static defenses, such as the Maginot Line (Bond, 1984, pp. 153–154). The hope, then, was that the industrialization of war could reduce casualties rather than increase them, as it so clearly had in World War I. Yet such optimism was increasingly outweighed by an increasingly pessimistic vision of what the latest military revolution might in fact mean. Strategic bombing in particular worried military strategists, state leaders and the general public alike, who extrapolated liberally (but not, as it turned out inaccurately) from the limited devastation caused by strategic bombing in World War I to the prospect of the unlimited destruction of cities and civilians. Increasingly, as one author notes, "the message was that war had become so terrible that there would be no winners" (Bond, 1984, p. 151). Unfortunately, as Pearl Harbor, Dresden, Tokyo and Hiroshima were to show, that apocalyptic vision turned out to be true.

WORLD WAR II

Although World War I had been a war of unprecedented size and destructiveness, World War II soon eclipsed it. Even more than World War I, World War II was a truly global and total war, eventually reaching around the world. The costs of the war – both monetary and human – were proportionately immense: enormous property losses and military expenditures totaling more than a trillion dollars (Craig, 1966, p. 730). The human cost was equally great: between 1939 and 1947, over 16 million Europeans were permanently displaced, and in some areas, the destruction brought by the war was almost unimaginable. In the western USSR, for example, the war destroyed 50% of all urban living space, millions of rural houses and thousands of villages (Kennedy, 1987, p. 362).

At least 17 million soldiers died in the war, while civilian deaths cost at least another 18 million lives. Of the combatants, the USSR perhaps suffered the worst, with between 15 and 20 million dead, and another 15 million seriously injured. Germany suffered between four and six million combat deaths, another 1.5 million missing, and over one million civilian deaths. Germany also was responsible for the deaths of six million Jews, and another 4 million Slavs and gypsies (Craig, 1966, p. 728; Bond, 1984, pp. 196–197). Losses in Britain and the United States were considerably lighter, totaling about 450,000 and 400,000, respectively. All told, World War II's death toll may well have exceeded 50 million, but the damage was so great that the true numbers will probably never be known.

World War II also was an ideological war in a way that no wars since the French Revolution had been. In their twisted quest for racial purity and *lebensraum*, the Nazis developed a grand strategy of reorganizing Europe along racial lines. Although Hitler's use of the "big lie" allowed him to avoid fully explaining his "final solution" to all but a few initiates (see Arendt, 1973, Ch. 11), young men in Nazi uniform were regularly expected to exterminate Jews, gypsies, homosexuals and others stigmatized by Nazi ideology. The Nazis' horrendous doctrine naturally provoked ferociously ideological responses – and extensive propaganda campaigns – from all of Hitler's enemies. None of those responses, however, with the possible exception of Stalin's efforts during the "Great Patriotic War", approached the extremity of the Nazi doctrine.

While the battle for "hearts and minds" was fierce on all sides, the war ultimately was won by the forces who controlled the greatest resources and industrial capacity. During World War II all combatants developed and imposed highly centralized planned economies, continuing and greatly extending a process begun in World War I and the 1930s. Ultimately, both organized western capitalism and the communist command economy alike fared better than the fascist economies in mobilizing the enormous resources necessary to win the war.

Although the industrialization of war had really begun in World War I, World War II witnessed the culmination of that trend. And here the power of the Soviet and American industrial complexes really made itself felt. Once the Russians and the Americans both were fully engaged in the war (from 1942 on) war production became industrialized on an unprecedented scale, a development which led not only to the unprecedented destruction described above, but also to the virtually certain defeat of Germany and Japan. Allied production of such vital materiel as armaments, tanks and aircraft consistently outpaced Axis totals by between 200 and 400% (Kennedy, 1987, pp. 352–357).

Science and technology also played a much greater role in this war than in any preceding one. Science and scientists were enlisted by all combatants to develop cutting-edge weapons and weapons detection systems, many of which forever changed the character of war. In the last years of the war, scientists developed jet aircraft, missiles, and eventually, an atomic bomb, all of which anticipated the even more powerful integration of science and warfare in the contemporary age (Craig, 1966, pp. 728–729).

States willing and able to mobilize such enormous economic, industrial and scientific resources naturally had no qualms whatsoever about requisitioning whatever manpower was necessary to win the war. And indeed, during World War II, all states mobilized unprecedented numbers of their citizens to take part in the war effort. Such mobilization not only meant the military conscription of any and all able-bodied men, but also the recruitment of increasing numbers of women, to serve as non-combatant military personnel, as nurses, and to staff the factories on which weapons production depended. In Britain, the National

Service Act of 1941 conscripted men from 18 to 50 and made women between 20 and 30 liable for military or civilian war services. These age limits were later pushed upwards, dramatically increasing the number of gainfully employed persons as many women took up work outside the home (Bond, 1984, pp. 175–176).

Similar processes were at work in most of the other combatant countries, including the United States (Faragher et al., 2001, p. 467; Ritter, this issue) and Soviet Russia (Bond, 1984, pp. 177–178; Enloe, 2000, p. 217). In Germany, by contrast, the massive conscription of men was *not* met by an equivalent mobilization of women until the very end of the war. In accordance with policies of strict "maternalism" (where a woman's primary duty was to "maintain the race"), the Nazis "made every possible effort to eliminate women from the labor force" (Gilbert, 1984, p. 353). They would not relax those policies until late 1944, when the (labor) conscription of women up to the age of 50 was finally allowed (Bond, 1984, p. 189).

In this war, even more than in World War I, the distinction between combatants and civilians was erased. Strategic bombing became common as the war ground on, and led to enormous civilian casualties. Although the military value of such bombing has been questioned repeatedly, there seems to be little doubt that it did weaken civilian morale and disrupt war production (Bond, 1984, pp. 192–193). The Nazis were the first to perfect the "science" of war against civilians, resorting to random hostage-taking, slave labor, terror, and massive destruction, and above all, to the nightmarish bureaucratization of killing that reached its apogee at Auschwitz (Bond, 1984, pp. 181ff; Arendt, 1973, Ch. 12). However, they certainly were not the only ones to employ such tactics, as the raids on Hamburg, Dresden, and Tokyo, as well as the later atomic bombings of Hiroshima and Nagasaki clearly show.

The final, and in many way most revolutionary consequence of the war was the development of nuclear weapons. The "nuclear revolution" – especially the hydrogen bomb in 1952 – created an enormous disjuncture between the ends of war and the means now available to realize them, a disjuncture that actually worked to revive the concept of limited war. If total war would lead to total destruction, then it became an unusable means of realizing political goals. Accordingly, states were forced to look to other means by which to project power in the nuclear age. Even the superpowers might find themselves forced to concede defeat, if their enemy was sufficiently determined and the only means of victory would be through nuclear war. Such were the lessons of Vietnam and Afghanistan (Nye, 1993, p. 121).

Because nuclear bombs were cheaper to deploy than the massive armies on which success in conventional war now depended, even superpowers like the

United States increasingly sought to project power through such means. Rather than relying on mass mobilization and the rapid deployment of huge armies, nuclear weapons and the troops necessary to guard them could be "forward based" to accomplish superpower foreign policy goals (Kennedy, 1987, p. 370). Such forward basing would serve as a centerpiece of NATO doctrine in the postwar era. Thus nuclear weapons once again shifted the balance of power from large armies to technically advanced forces, and may have helped to prepare the ground for the progressive abandonment of general conscription at the present time.

THE COLD WAR PERIOD

Total war raged in Europe for about ten years between 1914 and 1945. Together with the social, economic and personal crises of the 1930s, such conflicts helped to delegitimize the European regimes that survived the World Wars. Yet while few citizens in 1945 remained enthusiastic about the idea of killing for the state, they clearly saw the importance of defending their countries.

Yet such decisions would no longer be entirely their own. In contrast to earlier peace settlements, the postwar framework for Europe was not decided primarily by the members of the European state system, but by the superpowers outside it. In the emerging Cold War system, Europe was split in two by its division into Eastern and Western blocs. The two parts of the European state system thus now became subsystems in the Cold War system of international relations.

While the U.S. had helped decide the outcome of the two world wars, in both cases she had entered late and her main contribution had been in terms of the productive power of her economy. Ironically, only with the advent of the Cold War – a period of "peace" – did the United States really begin to be concerned about foreign threats to the "American way of life." Developments in transport, communications and weapons technologies had all made the world smaller, and the threat from abroad correspondingly more real. According to Friedberg (2000), in this period, the USA became a garrison state, and its economy a permanent war economy (Melman, 1985). In preparation for an apparently inevitable war against the USSR, the U.S. allied with the European seawards and Western continental countries to form the North Atlantic Treaty Organization (NATO) in 1949.

American elites increasingly accepted that U.S. security was threatened by the powers of the Eastern bloc, and took action to counter that threat. Accordingly, in the 1950s and 1960s the U.S. became the military muscle of the West. U.S. military expenditures increased by 300% from 1950 to 1960, and surged still higher in the 1960s, as a result of the Cuban Missile Crisis and the Vietnam War (Kennedy, 1987, pp. 383–385, esp. Table 37). The main condition of U.S. leadership, however, was its dominant position in the development of nuclear arms, which not only allowed it to counter growing Soviet power, but also to dictate military policy to the rest of the Western world.

Nuclear arms also spelled real savings on soldiers. Particularly in Europe, where the Soviet Union had a vast superiority of men and materiel over the United States, it became necessary to find a way to counter that imbalance. Nuclear weapons provided the ideal solution. As Walter Lippman remarked, "nukes" allowed war with "no national effort, no draft, no training, no discipline, but only money and engineering know-how, of which we have plenty." The U.S. could remain the "greatest military power on earth" without incurring the "the cost of a great Army, Navy, and Air Force" (quoted in Beckman et al., 1992, p. 65). This was capital-intensive war-preparedness. In the new era ground troops meant less than they previously had, as wars now could be run by Dr. Strangelove-type scientists, engineers, and the Air Force.

That is not to say that conventional forces played no important role in U.S.-NATO strategy. After all, the doctrines of massive retaliation and flexible response both envisioned armies using smaller nuclear arms in "theater" and even "battlefield" settings. Particularly important for NATO was the doctrine of extended deterrence. Extended deterrence insisted on the importance of stationing American troops and nuclear weapons on European soil, not primarily to repulse a conventional Soviet attack but rather to serve "as a tripwire to force the United States to employ America's nuclear arsenal threat if Western Europe were invaded" (Beckman et al., 1992, p. 101). As especially pointed examples of the general "balance of terror" discourse then prevalent, extended deterrence and the associated doctrine of mutual assured destruction represented perhaps the most extreme outcome of the modern tendency to use populations as hostages in war.

As for the European members of NATO, they continued to conscript their populations because of the constant threat posed by the Red Army, and because of American pressure to meet their end of the security bargain. Although NATO never managed to realize its targets for conventional forces (In 1954, for example, they had wishful plans of reaching 96 divisions but could actually only field 15!), all scenarios for the defense of Europe relied heavily on a substantial conscript force. Indeed, the question of how much to spend on conventional defense was at the core of the perpetual controversies on burden sharing between the U.S. and its Western European NATO allies. In addition, there were a few neutral states, such as Switzerland or Sweden, which relied on peacetime conscription to guard their neutrality.

On the whole, however, during the Cold War the European continent, as well as outlying countries like Britain and Turkey, remained sharply divided between the NATO forces and Warsaw Pact states in the East. The Eastern bloc consisted of the USSR and the buffer states it had secured in the late 1940s. The situation here may briefly be contrasted with the Western model that we shall survey below. In the East there was first of all the Soviet Union itself, a self-declared socialist state characterized by very weak traditions of self-organization in civil society. That state had replaced, but also partially reproduced, agrarian-bureaucratic structures developed in the pre-communist coercion-intensive process of state formation. Some analysts (see Tucker, 1977) have even argued that the Stalinist state took its inspiration as much from the Russian monarchy in the era of Ivan the Terrible and Peter the Great as from Marxism-Leninism.

The trajectory was somewhat different in the other Warsaw Pact countries, which had, after all, gained some experience with democratization in the interwar period. But here Soviet-Russian client regimes were imposed, regimes that could not have survived without stringent social control and vigorous state repression of any attempts to spur independent mobilization of a civil society. In the whole area, therefore, the party sought to monopolize all civil society activities, and the secret police – a military kind of institution – was a crucial instrument in achieving this goal. There were also party spies. Finally, the discipline provided by long spells of peacetime conscription into the armed forces was one element in controlling civil society.

The Warsaw Pact armies themselves were quite formidable. The USSR's Red Army, which eventually stabilized at a peacetime strength of about four million, was based on universal eligibility for military service for all between 16 and 50, with a two-year term of service. Troops were subjected to strenuous and realistic training, to extensive political indoctrination (referring extensively to the "Great Patriotic War" of 1940–1945), and to regular police surveillance. They worked long hours and received little in return; pay was low, barracks accommodations were spartan, and leaves were limited and strictly regulated. Particularly in the USSR, the officer corps became a privileged stratum of society, receiving advantages such as free apartments and access to special stores with hard-to-find goods at reduced prices. In some respects, this was a remnant of the privileges that had accrued to military elites in the earlier coercion-intensive model. The other Eastern bloc armies were minor variations on the Russian model, with uniforms, drill, training and military textbooks all being derived or directly copied from the Red Army (Bond, 1984, p. 216).

Although the Eastern bloc forces were superior in conventional terms, the Western bloc countries tried to counter that superiority by mustering more highly qualified troops. Most of the continental Western European countries chose to do this through peacetime conscription. The trend in Western forces during this era thus generally was "away from semi-trained, primitively equipped, mass conscript armies towards more streamlined, highly professional forces relying increasingly on sophisticated technology and weapon power rather than sheer numbers for their effectiveness" (Bond, 1984, p. 214). Such strategies entailed certain liabilities, however, as defense costs skyrocketed, and the armies faced competition for skilled manpower with other economic sectors.

Especially during the 1950s (Bond, 1984, p. 207), all of Western Europe faced a clear contradiction between civilian objectives and military spending to satisfy NATO commitments. After all, while a strong military defense was considered essential to combat the communist threat, economic growth and development was itself crucial in the Cold War. The Americans held that if 1930s-style economic instability were to reappear, national communist and socialist parties might conquer important parliamentary positions, provoke popular unrest, and tilt Western countries into the Eastern bloc. But with steady economic growth, living standards would rise and radical mobilization would be undermined through what has been described as the "politics of productivity."

And indeed, the postwar period did produce an economic miracle, at least until the mid-1970s. We shall not deal with the main reasons for this here, but it should be noted that both in the U.S. and Western Europe, the interplay between state and civil society was crucial. In both contexts, but especially in Europe, development relied on the specific balance between them that had evolved through the European process of state formation: democratic control over military power, bureaucratic control over state finances and interest representation via courts and parliaments (Tilly, 1985, p. 186). Crucially, European states were never able to establish full control over two of these aspects (economic organization, law) of civil society, with law in particular remaining somewhat autonomous of the interests of ruling state elites. But those states (with the possible exception of France for a couple of years) did establish definitive control over the military. These outcomes meant that legal institutions and rules reflected not only state interests but also civil rights gained through processes of social mobilization. Western Europe's postwar regimes thus combined state interventionism, market economic principles and parliamentary democracy.

While the U.S. was becoming more "armed", the old Western members of the European state system were becoming less so. The military conflicts so long persistent in the European systems now were largely eliminated and replaced by broader East-West Cold War tensions. In Western Europe, therefore, Cold

War militarization was balanced by the development of relatively peaceful welfare states. With the U.S. as the guarantor of overall security, it was possible for the states of Western Europe to act as "free riders", and to focus their priorities on welfare state reforms rather than NATO burden sharing – butter rather than guns (Calleo, 1987). Western European postwar welfare states thus devoted themselves to taking care of societies' lower classes, providing them with pensions, health care and schooling. Such welfare policies, quite the opposite of squandering monies or masses of young men on war, testified to the increasing demilitarization of European states and societies, a process that would culminate in the sharp restriction or outright abandonment of conscription in the last few years.

A brief consideration of some national profiles confirms our earlier typology. Britain maintained general conscription in the 1950s, but began to phase out its National Service conscripts in favor of a professional "all volunteer force" (AVF) which would be stabilized at approximately 375,000 in the years following 1963. The United States also eventually decided to abandon conscription in favor of volunteer forces, although the demands of the Vietnam War delayed that decision for some years. In 1973, largely as a response to enormous popular protest against that war, the U.S. converted its army into a "voluntary" one made up of long-term professional forces. And, like Britain, the U.S. increasingly promoted capital-intensive, nuclear arms-based strategic concepts that emphasized military hardware over the huge conscript armies of the previous two wars. While in a few cases, as in the forward basing of NATO forces in Europe, soldiers were deliberately placed in "harm's way" for political reasons, U.S. military doctrine increasingly sought to eschew the large armies of an earlier era.

France's trajectory was quite different, as its army and society went through a difficult process of mutual readjustment during the postwar period. In the 1950s, France was plunged into the difficult process of decolonization, first in Indochina and then in Algeria. By that time France's army had expanded to approximately one million men, most of whom were fighting in Algeria. That conflict forced the French state to impose military service of 28 months on its people, to withdraw almost all of its armed forces from NATO, and finally, to leave NATO's strategic command in 1966. It also almost led to the collapse of civilian control over the army, as army leaders were again tempted to pursue strategies of right-wing *dirigisme*. Once the army was again brought under civilian control, it was extensively modernized and mechanized (and now included a nuclear strike force), in keeping with De Gaulle's vision of again making France a great power (Gilbert, 1984, pp. 449–451). Not surprisingly, given France's political and military aspirations, it long continued peacetime conscription (until the mid-1990s), and did not really allow conscientious objection on any scale until after 1968 (Ajangiz, this issue).

In the Nordic countries, social democratic parties (or political alliances with a similar orientation) became increasingly influential in the postwar period. These regimes viewed general conscription as a genuinely democratic approach to mobilization and defense, and therefore embraced it enthusiastically. In some settings, as in Sweden, Nordic conscription approached Swiss-style citizen militias, employing features such as extensive reserve training, personal storage of military weapons at home, and home guards which focused on social welfare and civil defense as well as on national defense. Such systems often proved highly effective; according to some authorities, the Swedish forces were the most impressive militia outside of Israel (Bond, 1984, p. 221).

In Germany, major changes took place. As the loser of the war, Germany was more strongly influenced by the Allied occupants than the Nordic countries or even France. As with Japan in East Asia, Germany was eventually fully integrated into the Western bloc of American-sponsored alliances. The program of a fully "pastoralized" Germany was never implemented. German reindustrialization was considered crucial to Western European recovery, and in the mid-1950s, Germany was even remilitarized within NATO (Bond, 1984, pp. 208ff). Even though the German people were reeducated in liberal-democratic values, the organization of the new *Bundeswehr* – however rigorously functional and bureaucratic – was a traumatic matter for the German public, as well as for certain other European states, France in particular. Arguments in favor of the new law on conscription emphasized an alleged connection between conscription and democracy. But this was highly controversial, especially considering that conscription had coexisted neatly with Nazism in Germany, while Britain and the United States had evolved democratic institutions and practices without resorting to the draft. Germany – like Japan in the east – remained antimilitarist, pacific, and anti-nuclear, and the status of military officers was understandably rather low.

The German army reflected that wider social ambivalence about military service, and sought to "package" itself as a skilled service dependent on its soldiers' quality and technical skills rather than on their numbers (there were only 12 divisions) and fighting spirit. Only one in four young males was conscripted in 1960, although the rate increased in the following years. At the same time, appeals for conscientious objector status also rose, from 3400 in 1960 to ten times that amount by 1970. In many respects, therefore, the German army was a "new army", closer in spirit to the "volunteer forces" of Britain and the United States than to the more popular conscript forces characteristic of France or its own history in the 19th and early 20th centuries.

In addition to constructing welfare measures such as pensions and health care, European elites in the postwar period followed the U.S. in emphasizing mass education. While basic education may serve to socialize people and strengthen their respect for authority, higher education teaches them to think for themselves. This educational revolution certainly had strong links to the Cold War, both in the USSR and in the West (where Sputnik in 1957 was seen as evidence of USSR strength in science and technology and caused a rush towards such investments). But the spread of higher education began to erode citizens' confidence in state strategies, as the events of the late 1960s demonstrated. And in the USSR the impact of higher education was especially powerful and ironic. Its last leaders were the first generation to complete a university education, which suggests that such education played a crucial role in sparking reform and revolution in the 1980s and 1990s.

Thus, the Cold War not only spurred the arms and space races, but also had a powerful unintended effect by educating an increasingly articulate and critical generation in the West and East alike. A main indicator here is the emergence of conscientious objection to military service in the years following 1968 (Ajangiz, this issue). The Cold War therefore created the modern postwar peace movement in a double sense: its obsession with ideologically driven wars, arms races and doctrines (containment, counter-insurgency, mutual assured destruction) provided the grist for antiestablishment movements, while its emphasis on higher education created the critical elites who would form the center of those movements. By the late 1960s, there was a conjunction between trends such as sexual liberation, the student movement, the peace movement, and feminist claims for equality for women.

While conscription is a remarkably effective means of recruiting and fielding armies, it may become increasingly infeasible if and when societies grow more peaceful, affluent, and content. Because general conscription means that soldiers are taken out of civil society – the society of civilians – the draft is most appealing when much of the population is poor, unemployed, or underemployed (e.g. late 19th century Germany – cf. Rowe), or when a war is on. Once those conditions no longer obtain, however, it may again be necessary to find and field troops on a different basis. And that is just what happened in postwar Western Europe. With the "takeoff" of the postwar economic miracle, living standards rose, which in turn produced an increasing divergence between the military and the larger society in which it was situated. Unlike their parents, who had lived through one or even two great wars, the generations born after 1945, "became accustomed to regular pay rises, high living standards, a great variety of leisure activities and, above all, minimal restriction on personal freedom as regards dress, behavior and travel" (Bond, 1984, pp. 221–222).

To that generation, the armed forces, which continued to stress discipline, regulations and routine, had little appeal. The rise of this "youth culture" as well as increasingly unpopular superpower military adventures in the developing world (the Vietnam war was the first one to be continuously covered on national television – cf. Cumings, 1992), may also explain the increasing prevalence and toleration of conscientious objectors in the postwar years.

The major shift in the global balance of power after 1945 also – especially in the 1950s and 1960s – had important results in the so-called Third World, as one European state after another abandoned their huge colonial holdings. Independence for third world states did not necessarily guarantee social, political or economic stability, however. Frequently the post-colonial states lacked anything like the balance that we traced between civil society and the state in Western Europe or the United States. Before colonization, their main institutions of civil society generally had been local ethnic or clan groups, many of which included just a few hundred or thousand members. On colonization, however, they were progressively amalgamated and reified as larger mutually exclusive "tribes" by colonial administrators. Those administrators, pursuing classic divide-and-rule strategies, subsequently gave one "tribe" preferential access to power and (subordinate) positions in the state. This approach allowed European states to control vast territories in the colonies, since they could rely on indigenous elites to help them to prevent or put down any resistance to their rule (Martin & O'Meara (Eds), 1984, pp. 153, 209; Ottaway, 1999).

But if divide-and-rule proved useful in the colonial era, it would prove disastrous in the states and societies of the post-colonial era. Decolonization created deeply fractured societies, as ethnic groups struggled to capture state institutions and use them to further consolidate their own power and wealth. One disastrous outcome was civil war and thus militarization, as in Sri Lanka, Nigeria, and most tragically in the Rwandan genocide of 1994. Another was the rise of predatory states, which at worst became "kleptocracies" like Mobutu's Zaire. While such examples are perhaps extreme, they indicate the depth and breadth of the problems associated with decolonization in the developing world. Significantly, the most striking successes in the developing world have turned out to be countries *not* colonized by Western powers (e.g. South Korea, Taiwan). In such countries, the state has enjoyed a kind of "embedded autonomy" vis-à-vis a relatively traditional civil society, which has led to relative stability and economic development (Evans, 1995).

In most post-colonial states, however, social divisions and political instability were the rule. The capture of state institutions proved too tempting and too easy, especially if and when certain ethnic groups already enjoyed unequal advantages and access to social benefits and state positions. And, among the captured institutions, the military frequently took pride of place, since by controlling it, dominant ethnic groups could marginalize and if necessary repress any and all competitors. Decolonization thus frequently created military organizations without strong links to the civil societies in which they were nominally situated. Being captured by an ethnic elite, such armies did not generally allow the mobilization and institutionalization of civilian interests, at least not beyond the ethnic elite. Not surprisingly, the military was naturally seen as political and politicized, and that (accurate) perception tended to provoke further political instabilities and social unrest. And finally, ethnic capture policies sometimes undermined the military itself. They made truly meritocratic recruitment and promotion effectively impossible, and also gave the lie to state claims that the army served the interest of all citizens rather than just that of a few. Under such conditions, the relationship between conscription and citizenship became precarious at best.

Seldom, it seems, have the effects of conscription in the developing world been similar to the effect it had in 19th century Europe where, in conjunction with "nationalism from below" it helped to serve as a force for the transformation of social relations. In that setting, universal conscription bolstered nationalist, lower class support for states, while in exchange helping to enfranchise the marginalized and institute irreversible ethical standards for the "conscription bargain" itself. By contrast, in developing countries, the isolation of the army from civil society has frequently blocked such social transformation, and in some cases the army has acted actively to repress social change rather than to promote it. Nor has military service in the developing world very often served as a means for the political co-optation of previously marginalized groups or for the extension of citizenship rights to those previously denied them. Indeed, in many states it has failed even to serve the narrower function of providing a means of social mobility via promotion through the ranks, as key opportunities and positions have often been reserved for a few members of the dominant ethnic group. (Still, it seems that even quite exploitative military service can empower those forced to serve. Cf. Our remarks on Carey, Introduction to this issue).

SOME TRENDS IN THE CONTEMPORARY WORLD

We can offer no full overview of the various ways in which military manpower is recruited today. But we shall look briefly at two extremes: the recruitment of children in some of the world's poorest countries today, and the demise of military conscription in some of the richest parts of the world. We also add some brief remarks on the former "second" world.

Many third world countries ran into serious trouble during the 1980s debt crisis. The problems in developing countries were exacerbated by the end of the Cold War, which led to greatly reduced aid, and at the same time, to increased – and increasingly expensive – arms purchases. Moreover, in much of the developing world already serious social, economic and political dislocations have been made even worse by a growing public health crisis. Such developments, each of which was destructive in its own right, have combined to send many developing countries, especially those in sub-Saharan Africa, into free fall.

The conjunction of these problems often stressed already weak states so far that they became difficult or impossible to govern or defend, leading to further unrest, which not infrequently exploded into war. War, both within and between states, has in fact plagued much of the developing world in the post-war era, especially in Sub-Saharan Africa. Not surprisingly, the threat of war in turn has led state leaders to invest growing proportions of increasingly scarce state revenues on arms. Here again the end of the Cold War has had the perverse effect of destabilizing states and societies, as poor states now are forced to pay full price for weapons systems they once acquired cheaply or even free of charge from the superpowers (U.S. DoD, 1994; Hughes, 1997, pp. 374–375). Not only has that shift meant a steady source of business for weapons manufacturing states (especially the U.S., Britain, and Russia) it has also meant the delegation of declining fiscal resources for weapons systems in impoverished and unstable states.

In the face of such developments, Third World armies have drawn many of the poorest and most powerless members of developing societies into their ranks, as the articles by Wessells and Richards (in this issue) clearly show. This is not surprising when we consider the desperate poverty of many people in the developing world as well as the relatively privileged position that the military enjoys in such states. With few if any social services or "safety nets" on which they can rely, the poor and powerless may view military service as one of the only options available to them. For some, service in the army means literacy and basic job training, highly valuable skills that promise a better life once the term of service is completed. For others, in poorer or more fractured states, the benefits of military service are more immediate: clothes, shelter, and an assured meal. And, for the most powerless of all – the perhaps 300,000 child soldiers in countries from Afghanistan to Uganda – service in an army may provide them with a "family" to replace those they have lost to war (see articles by Richards and Wessells; see also Wessells, 1997; *The Economist*, 1999, pp. 19–21; and Enloe, 2000, pp. 242–244). Ironically, while organized conscription may become impractical in the weakest states, the anarchy that results as those states collapse may serve as a powerful incentive for growing numbers to "voluntarily" enlist. Unable to provide their peoples with any of the traditional rights of citizenship, the most fractured states of the developing world may be able to use the mere promise of physical security as a means of recruitment. And, considering the other choices they have, many of those peoples may come to see that offer as one they cannot refuse.

Such stark choices are discussed in considerable and often painful detail by several of our contributors. If military service has benefited Mayan conscripts in Guatemala (cf. Carey in this issue), it has proved far more destructive to the young soldiers of Angola, Uganda and Sierra Leone (Wessells, Richards, this issue). In those countries, state collapse has led to civil war, rebel insurgency, and increasingly, to the forced military service of children. While the practice of inducting children into the military is largely confined to rebel groups or paramilitary allies of state forces, states are not always above using underage forces themselves, if and when adult conscripts cannot be found. More importantly, since those states lack control over large portions of their own territory, they are unable to prevent the much broader forced recruitment of children by rebel groups. And, because their countries are torn by violence, such states may also inadvertently encourage the "voluntary" recruitment of child soldiers seeking security in military service. As in Guatemala (and 18th century Europe) those who do "choose" military service tend to do so for opportunistic reasons, in an attempt to improve their futures or even just their chances of surviving a murderous civil war. In Sierra Leone, for example, children sometimes join the rebel RUF because they "need parent-surrogates and training in life-skills." Cynically, some RUF "recruiters" have encouraged such decisions by killing the recruits' families and destroying their villages! In other cases, however, children are simply kidnapped and forced into military service, recalling the 18th century practice of impressment. Although Richards is careful to stress that the "volunteers" do choose to "apprentice" themselves to skilled killers, to describe choices made under such conditions as fully free may be both inaccurate and cruel. Yet, tragically, in states where factional strife has created a de facto war of all against all, it may be only in the warring armies that any significant order or security can be found. These armies cynically exploit the tragic fact that, given the present technologies of light handguns and explosives, young kids can serve as efficient soldiers, and – compared to adults – are easier to grab, control and indoctrinate.

To speak of such military service either as voluntary or as conscription in any normal sense of the word risks emptying those terms of any real significance. But there are significant, if perverse, similarities, to voluntary service and conscription (Richards, Wessels, in this issue). In the forced recruitment and abductions characteristic of the RUF and Uganda's "Lord's Army", we see a sort of nightmarish extension of the principle of state compulsion as the basis of conscription, with local forces serving as the *de facto* state in conditions of civil war. As for the cases of "voluntary recruitment", such choices testify to the often intimate relationship between poverty, anarchy, and military service. When conditions are sufficiently hard and society sufficiently dangerous, the best remaining option may be for the most vulnerable to find security amongst those who would otherwise prey on them. In striking contrast to 19th century European society, where increasing wealth, security and political clout led the poor to turn away from military service as employment (thus forcing states to find other means to supply their armies), in Uganda, Angola and Sierra Leone, the collapse of state and economy have driven people *into* the armies, greatly worsening not only the war itself but the more general tendency of the society to drift towards war. And, as the consequences of that militarization for state and society in Sierra Leone and other sub-Saharan states have grown ever more devastating, the incentives to flee to the armies and paramilitary groups have grown increasingly powerful.

Let us now turn to the "first" world. In Western Europe, as we have seen, conscription has developed into a tacit bargain between citizens and states, whereby the former make themselves eligible for military service in exchange for rights, liberties, and social services. This bargain has grown increasingly tenuous as citizens have gradually grown more powerful and gained higher living standards, thereby decreasing the leverage that states could exert on them. And it has grown particularly difficult in the post-Cold War years. Neoliberal reforms and structural changes, such as the aging crisis, have put pressure on the state's ability to provide social services, while at the same time the collapse of the Soviet Union has made the need for large conscript armies increasingly implausible. In a certain sense, then, the increasing impact of neoliberalism and declining threat perceptions have combined to make Western Europe look more like the Anglo-American states where, except for a few years in the mid-20th century, conscription has always been viewed with considerable skepticism.

In continental Western Europe, therefore, the ties between military service, citizenship and popular consent have grown progressively weaker. The success of the first conscription bargain was prolonged by the Cold War, which made it an essentially non-negotiable arrangement. Several conditions were essential if that were to change: first, it was necessary that the bargain once again become something that *could* be discussed and questioned. Secondly, states had to be convinced to abandon the status quo in favor of (recently) untried recruitment systems, whether because of pressure from dissatisfied social forces, political and economic concerns of their own, or both. Abandoning conscription thus entailed a difficult and prolonged process, and the final conjunction of conditions developed in the years after 1989. The end of the Cold War, together with increasing fiscal and economic policy problems in all of the continental states, finally made such a change possible. In some countries the change was mainly an effect of budget cuts, while in other cases the peace movement played a significant role. By the year 2000, the Netherlands and Belgium had already abolished the draft, and France, Italy, Spain and Portugal "were in the process of phasing it out" (Møller, this issue).

Such developments appear to be part of a larger trend. Since the Cold War ended, Western European citizens have increasingly sought to retain and even extend their citizenship rights without incurring the obligation of traditional military service. They have frequently sought to replace military service with other, "substitutory" forms of service, as in Italy and Germany (Ajangiz, this issue, especially Table 4 and Figures 2 and 3). In Germany, in fact, such service has increasingly served to reinforce social welfare programs, as conscientious objectors now help to implement many of the social welfare functions of the state. It has been less successful in relegitimizing the conscription bargain, however, as the acceptance of substitute service does not translate into acceptance of conscription more generally. Such strategies have proved even less successful in Spain, where conscription has become so unpopular that citizens accept substitute service in order to escape the draft, but see it as having little or no educational or social welfare value. Instead, they view such service only as a ruse, an indefensible strategy of a state seeking to valorize a morally bankrupt policy (Ajangiz, in this issue). In some settings, therefore, citizens appear to be claiming that their citizenship rights entail *no* commensurate duties of national service, military or otherwise.

There could be a variety of reasons for this "distancing" between civil society and states. Some of those reasons are suggested by Ajangiz: the extension of voting and other political rights to women (who generally acquired citizenship rights without the obligation of military service), the rise of human rights concerns among European populations, and the impact of unpopular interventions by the superpowers and their less enthusiastic allies. Certainly, all of these developments served, even before the end of the Cold War, to divide conscription and citizenship and thereby weaken states' claims to the willing compliance of their peoples. In addition, it may be that secular trends inside the continental European states have led to a gradual rejection by citizens of the conscription bargain. Such trends might include the consolidation of postwar welfare states and "safety nets" with few attached obligations, an increasingly broad conception of citizen rights, the deaths of those who recalled the last world war, and the experience of relative peace in the richest and most democratic parts of the world.

Although such outcomes clearly provide sufficient reasons to call conscription into question, military strategists have also increasingly questioned the citizen-soldier model of conscription. With the rise of technology-intensive forces since World War II, some strategists have argued that conscripted armies are no longer efficient. Rather, they argue, smaller and more intensively trained "volunteer" (e.g. professional) forces can do the job better at a lower cost.

Finally, there is another important trend to consider which may be helping to promote the abolition of conscription in and beyond Western Europe. The increase of regional conflicts in the post-Cold War era has given rise to a number of "humanitarian" interventions and peacekeeping operations sponsored and implemented by multilateral institutions such as the United Nations, NATO, WEU and, recently, the EU itself. In contrast to the superpowers' Cold War interventions, which mostly centered on projecting power and prestige, such interventions have had broader and perhaps more ambitious goals, seeking to establish and guarantee peace in war-torn states and societies. Because such missions are not generally focused primarily on issues of "national interest" or national security (at least in the sense of a "war of national defense") it may be more difficult to mobilize and sustain popular support for them. And since professional forces generally can be deployed much more rapidly than conscript armies, they are better suited to carry out the new military missions of the post-Cold War era (Møller, this issue). Therefore, as Western European states increasingly begin to take part in such missions, they have also sought to restructure the armed forces so as to be best able to respond to the special military and political challenges that humanitarian intervention poses. On the whole, European states have preferred to avoid using conscript soldiers on such missions, seeing professional soldiers as at once more adaptable and more politically acceptable, especially in the event that the missions should prove unexpectedly lengthy or costly.

To some extent, the move towards voluntary forces in Western Europe can be seen as an adoption of the Anglo-American model of relatively small, professional armed forces. Yet the recent developments and missions in Bosnia and Kosovo also suggest that the Anglo-American model is itself being modified in the face of increasingly multilateral missions and foreign policy goals. In short, the growing integration of two important recent trends in the military – professionalization and "multilateralization" – suggests that armies in locations throughout the developed world are now assuming a form that they have never had before. At once professional and internationalized, such armies bear a superficial resemblance to the mercenary forces of the early modern era, but are sharply distinguished from those forces by their broadly conceived missions and purposes. To a certain extent, some developing countries, such as

Bangladesh, Ghana, and Jordan, have also adopted the new model of multilateralization, contributing disproportionately large forces to UN peacekeeping operations, possibly in order to secure much-needed resources and revenue (Møller, this issue). Yet if some developing states have gone into the "business of war", others have taken the opposite approach, hiring "contract soldiers" (mercenaries) to help them defeat insurgencies (Møller; cf. also Misser & Versi, 1997; Shearer, 1998). Such changes all suggest that the once intimate connection between military service, citizenship, and state interests now have been thoroughly eroded, a development which raises some disturbing questions concerning the relationship of military forces to the states and societies they supposedly serve.

In Eastern Europe and Russia, recent developments have taken a somewhat different course. With the end of the Cold War and the collapse of communism, the region's newly democratic regimes have become increasingly unwilling to accept the costs – both monetary and political – of maintaining large armies. Accordingly, military budgets have been slashed. Although several states in this region, including Russia, Bulgaria, Hungary, Ukraine, and the Czech Republic, would eventually like to eliminate conscription (Møller, in this issue), state leaders generally have refrained from pushing too hard for fully professional forces. After all, the full modernization of forces and equipment that such a transformation requires is not at this point financially feasible. And, especially in Eastern Europe, there is a real desire to see the armies "civilianized" before any other reform is undertaken (Joo, 1996). In those countries, where the military long remained essentially autonomous and often posed a threat to civil society (and personal safety!), there are good reasons to secure civilian control of the armed forces before proceeding with any other reforms. While the integration of Eastern and Central European forces with their NATO counterparts may eventually make professionalization necessary, at present these states are reluctant to commit significant proportions of scarce fiscal resources to such a project (Michta, 1999, Conclusion).

In Russia, military reform has been far slower and more difficult. That systematic reform in the Russian armies is urgently necessary is undeniable, but how such reform can be accomplished is unclear. In attempting to field an army equal in size to the United States forces on a military budget one-tenth the size of the latter's, Russia has seen its army slowly fall apart. Not only did military allocations fall continually during the 1990s, chronic budgetary shortfalls meant that even those meager sums were rarely made available to the increasingly strapped military (Herspring, 1997; Kokoshin, 1997). Unpaid soldiers, skyrocketing draft evasion, outdated equipment, the pressure of "rights" from a oversized officer corps, as well as a host of other problems, have combined to undermine morale and to render the army increasingly ineffective as a means of defense. Such developments have also exacerbated unrest and posed a real and growing threat of anarchy inside the armed forces (Herspring, 1997). The solution would appear to be a sharp reduction in the army's size and a professionalization of its forces, but such reforms are unpopular (especially in the Ministry of Defense) and politically risky, making any real reform in the near future unlikely. All the same, given the crisis in the Russian army, it seems probable that in the long run, such measures may well be adopted (Arbatov, 1997). As to when exactly that will be, it is virtually impossible to say.

CONCLUSION

In this essay, we have followed the "life cycle" of general conscription from the 15th century to the present day. We have traced its development in the European state system from early mercenary forces through a long and complex history of state-, nation-, and war-making, ending in two terrifying and bloody world wars, the militarized peace of the Cold War, and the rapidly changing political-military dynamics of the contemporary era. We have also emphasized the fundamental differences between conscription and other types of military service, whether voluntary or forced. And finally, we have concluded that, in the rapidly changing social, political and military environments of the contemporary era, the citizen-soldier born during the American and French revolutions may be about to be buried.

Throughout the introduction we have played with a rough typology distinguishing various forms of state-building and war-making: an Anglo-American type, a western continental type and a (mostly) eastern type in which the legacy of coercion-intensive state formation has always been present in some form (Germany, Russia). The 1945 war settlement and the Cold War period decisively transformed Germany, making it a trustworthy member of the Western bloc. The end of the Cold War put an end to the Soviet project of legitimating a coercion-intensive regime with reference to socialist ideals. East Asian areas and African states were fully integrated in this system of international relations only in the postwar period, and many of the generalizations that hold true for continental Europe and the Anglo-American states have only limited relevance there. In Africa, the continued social, political, and economic legacies of decolonization and neocolonialism have meant that bitter conflict and forced military service show little sign of decline. In that region, "killing for the state and dying for the nation" are all too likely to continue in the foreseeable future.

The outcomes in Asia are more complex. While the Cold War ended in Western Europe in the early 1990s, there was no equally clear end to the Cold War in Asia. Except for our very brief comments above on revolutionary armies, we have not discussed that part of the world. We shall not try to cover that region now, except to remark that China, as the world's most populous country and the home of the world's largest conscript army, should be a major focus of further research on conscription. However, to equate China (or Japan before 1945) with the coercion-intensive model is too simplistic. These countries are marked by their ability to resist the impact of the European state system, having successfully maintained a social collectivism (e.g. Confucianism) that bears little resemblance either to Anglo-American liberalism or to the more corporatist features of continental European states. They will thus require a quite different contextualization than the one we have used above with regard to the European state system.

War and armed forces constitute killing as an organized activity. The specific aspect of that activity we have traced in this introduction is the state's arrogation and concentration of the means of killing in its own hands. In the earliest phases of the modern European state system, the inability and unwillingness of state leaders to mobilize the common people for war forced them to *hire* soldiers to kill. Beginning with the conscription of citizen-soldiers in the late 18th century, however, regimes faced a new challenge: inspiring ordinary people to kill for the state. After some initial setbacks during the early 19th century restoration, popular acceptance and even enthusiasm for that task increased during the later 19th century, peaking in World War I. It was not until World War II, however, that the blood ties between states and their citizens reached their height. In that war, the complete disappearance of the distinction between soldiers and civilians was signaled by the "officially sanctioned killing of citizens" in strategic bombing and Nazi concentration camps (Gaddis, 2001).

Since the end of World War II, that trend has apparently been reversed, at least in the first world. Reviewing wars since 1945, Gaddis finds a downward trend in the number of casualties, and that trend is even more pronounced after the end of the Cold War. NATO's war against Serbia (2000) – which demonstrated the notion of surgical, "high tech" bombing, or even "remote control war" – was the first war ever in the history of any great power where combat forces suffered no casualties. Yet that should not lead us to readily conclude that we are emerging into an era which eventually promises a "democratic peace" or even an "end to war" (cf. Zakaria (Ed.), 1997, pp. 26–59). After all, since the end of the Cold War, the United States and Russia have continued to actively intervene in what they consider to be their proper spheres of influence

(Gulf War, Somalia, Chechnya, Kosovo, etc.), while at the same time becoming noticeably less peaceful at home.

And while it is interesting to speculate how a casualty-free operation in Serbia was possible, the more interesting question is *why* states today would feel the need to wage a casualty-free war. On the basis of his historical analysis of the postwar period, Gaddis concludes that the capacity of Great Power states to inspire people to kill is declining, a trend he links to their decreasing ability to wage traditional warfare, and to an even more general decline in the overall authority of states. The West won World War II, but according to Gaddis, this victory concealed a "less visible defeat of authority in all its forms." This defeat suggests that states are once again being forced to renegotiate key social contracts with their citizens as moral standards change.

It also suggests, especially in connection with the recent turn toward professional "volunteer" armies, that the days of the conscripted citizen-soldier may now be coming to an end.

CONSCRIPTION AS IDEOLOGY: REVOLUTIONARY FRANCE AND THE NATION IN ARMS

Alan Forrest

INTRODUCTION

Among the nations of Europe, France showed an early commitment to the principle of universal conscription – a commitment which dates from the institution of the *levée en masse* in 1793 under the Jacobin Republic and which entered republican memory during the long years of the Restoration and the July Monarchy. Conscription was for many an emotive cause – the mechanism by which the French people had risen against tyrants and turned early defeats into an unstoppable military advance across much of the continent. A conscript army, it was argued, had saved both the nation and the revolution, and the idea would be regularly revived in moments of national emergency during the nineteenth and twentieth centuries, most demonstrably in 1870 at the time of the Franco-Prussian War, and again in 1914. The idea, it is true, had clear ideological overtones and appealed especially to republicans. This can partly be explained by the fact that the Revolution had established a close identification between 'citizens' and 'soldiers' in the new secular state, and had questioned the wisdom of depending for national defence on professional troops or on hired mercenaries, the mainstays of the royal armies of the Ancien Regime. Only the citizen-soldier could be relied upon to defend his rights as no mercenary could be expected to do; in this way citizenship legitimised the army just

The Comparative Study of Conscription in the Armed Forces, Volume 20, pages 95–115.

ISBN: 0-7623-0836-2

as conscription provided the state with an added degree of legitimation (Le Cour Grandmaison, 1992). He could also be expected to defend the cause of the French people rather than that of a monarch or emperor, unlike, to take only the most notorious instance, the Swiss Guards of 1792, long reviled for firing on the crowd at the Tuileries in the service of Louis XVI. If the people were again to be sovereign, it required an army in its image whose loyalty to the national cause could never be in doubt, and that, too, argued for the personal service of all.

The long years of the Napoleonic Wars, fuelled by the annual *classes* of young conscript soldiers, helped acclimatise the country to conscription and to legitimise it as a necessary tool at moments of national emergency. Conscription was widely seen as the key to French military successes, as the necessary means to Napoleonic glory and to the creation of a mass army. But once the Empire fell, Napoleon's conscription laws were abolished. And there would be no continuous tradition of systematic conscription through the nineteenth century, or at least none that actually required personal service from the population at large. In part this was a matter of circumstance: in peacetime France had no call for the mass armies of the Napoleonic Wars. But, more significantly, it marked a change in military thinking in the army high command, with greater emphasis now placed on technical skills and the virtues of an *armée de métier*. Yet the use of conscription as a source of recruitment did not die completely, even in the years immediately after 1815 when royalists and ultras campaigned vociferously against it, and it would be reintroduced in a limited form under Gouvion-Saint-Cyr's important military law of 1818. Two major concepts dominated his thinking – the conviction that voluntary inscriptions alone could not provide France with the numbers of troops required and that some form of compulsion would therefore be needed; and the belief that a professional army had qualities which no conscript army could match. This had two important consequences. First, it led to a very watered-down form of annual conscription, one that required very few men to serve in person, though those who did had to serve for a long fixed term. Conscripts who drew a low number at the ballot and who had the money to buy themselves out could quite easily find a replacement. And secondly, it led to the run-down of the reserve, for which Gouvion-Saint-Cyr had little patience. The 1818 law marks something of a sea-change in French military recruitment policy, one which, complemented by Soult's Law of 1832, would remain influential for more than half a century. Though the detail might change, the fundamental principles underpinning Gouvion-Saint-Cyr's reforms remained in force under such contrasting regimes as the Restoration, the July Monarchy, the Second Republic and the Second Empire. It would take the shock-waves produced by defeat in 1870 and by the violence of the Paris Commune to raise the status of a conscript army once again (Schnapper, 1968).

The Third Republic's enthusiasm for a conscript army was partly a practical matter, as politicians drew lessons from France's crushing defeat at the hands of the Prussians in 1870. They concluded that professionalism had failed militarily as well as being politically suspect. In Richard Challener's words, 'the fact that army leaders had no faith in the conscript soldier and that the French people were unwilling to accept the rigours of compulsory military service is a significant aspect of the defeat' (Challener, 1955, p. 5). There was a certain irony in this, given that the French were overwhelmed by a Prussian army which had itself adopted conscription in 1806 as a conservative, counter-revolutionary response to French victories in the Revolutionary and Napoleonic Wars (Gates, 1997). The Franco-Prussian War proved to be a key moment in re-establishing France's faith in conscription, since it exposed the fallacies on which France's nineteenth-century military policies had been built and opened up once more the vexed question of how best to organise an effective national defence. History had persuaded the French, or at least French republicans, that their instincts were right, that conscription enabled them to rise to the challenge of war and to organise their defences when their territory was threatened.

For the issue of a conscript army was first and foremost a republican issue, one deeply embedded in political ideology. By 1870 it had become assimilated into republican memory, its imagery quite explicitly evoking the duty and obligation which the nation was entitled to demand, and linked to the mythology of the French Revolution and the army of the Year II. Thus when Léon Gambetta called for a new *levée en masse* to repel the Prussians in September 1870, his rhetoric was explicitly republican, his historical allusion unambiguous. He openly likened the present predicament of France with the *patrie en danger* of the Revolutionary wars. He appealed to the tradition of self-sacrifice which had saved France in 1792, calling for the spontaneous rising of the people against the German invader, and creating an auxiliary army of *corps francs*, resonant of the *élan* of the II, to fight alongside the regular troops in defence of their homes and villages (Cambon, 1976). The new language of patriotism and citizenship achieved instantaneous results, at least in Paris and the larger provincial towns. Patriotic enthusiasm reached unparalleled levels. The single month of September saw some 30,500 voluntary engagements in the military; young men of the *classe* of 1870 rushed to volunteer before they were called up, some even concealing injuries and infirmities from the medical officer in their eagerness to enlist (Audoin-Rouzeau, 1989). Of course this eagerness did not of itself create an effective army: the scale of the subsequent defeat and the chaos created by the Commune would lead to much republican rethinking in the years that followed. But they did not alter the Republic's deep commitment to conscription, nor yet to the principle of a citizen army. That commitment did not fade with time. As John Horne has recently reminded us, the political speeches of 1913 and 1914 serve to show how much the *levée en masse* of 1793 provided 'a potent and much cited precedent' for the total war of the twentieth century (Horne, 1997, p. 4).

For the political dimension of the debate was never eradicated. The victory of those who advocated conscription was also the victory of the Third Republic and of men seeped in the memory of the French Revolution – republicans who had instituted the fourteenth of July as France's national day in 1880 in commemoration of the assault on the Bastille, who had organised the celebration of the Centenary of the French Revolution in 1889 and of the Republic in 1892 – men who saw the legitimacy of their own republican institutions as being integrally bound up in the traditions of the Great Revolution (Garcia, 1989). For them the concept of the Nation-in-arms, and with it the idea that defence was the duty of all, was central to the idea of the Republic itself. Soldiers were once again seen as citizens, and citizens as potential soldiers. Léon Gambetta said as much in a notable speech in Bordeaux in June 1871, when he described quite starkly what he saw as the educative role of military service in the life of the nation. Gymnasts and soldiers should, said Gambetta, take their place at the side of schoolteachers in the task of training the next generation of Frenchmen, so that today's schoolboys could become tomorrow's soldiers in the war of revenge which he saw as inevitable. They must be prepared to hold a sword, manipulate a rifle, survive long marches and sleep under the stars. For, he insisted, no confusion could be permitted about the centrality of the army to the lives of all. In language that owed much to the Jacobins of 1794 he insisted that 'it should be clearly understood that when a citizen is born in France, he is born a soldier, and that anyone seeking to avoid this double duty of civil and military instruction would be mercilessly deprived of his rights both as a citizen and as an elector' (Crépin, 1998, p. 206).

Without a citizen army, republicans feared, the military could never be politically neutral: the army would be a natural hiding-place for discontented royalists and Bonapartists, for those men of the Right who dreamed of overthrowing the nation's cherished republican institutions. Hence the new National Assembly immediately turned its attention to military reform, and – as Douglas Porch has expressed it – the history of the French army between 1871 and 1914 became a battle between the professional army and the 'nation in arms'. That battle would finally be won by the professionals, but Porch is right to emphasise that the battle lines were not exclusively drawn on the basis of national politics; there were conservatives and reformers within the military, and they had their counterparts in the political sphere (Porch, 1981). Indeed, it would be simplistic to imply that the image of conscription in the later nineteenth century was just that of the Great Revolution. It had evolved with the passage of time, most particularly with the conflation of revolutionary memory and that of the Napoleonic era, to produce a mixture of voluntarism and universalism, citizenship and obligation. A conscript army was seen to provide the most effective form of mass defence, while accentuating those most revolutionary of military qualities, enthusiasm, bravura, and *élan*. In this respect it united Frenchmen of diverse political colours in its support, and not merely those belonging to the republican or radical camp.

CONSCRIPTION DURING THE FRENCH REVOLUTION

Given its clear relevance to the core issue of equality, conscription might seem to hold obvious appeal for the policy-makers of revolutionary France, especially after the summer of 1792, when war had been declared on Austria and Prussia and when in France itself the *patrie* was formally recognised to be *en danger*. Yet it is striking that conscription was not imposed by the revolutionaries either in 1789, when the whole issue of citizenship was being debated, or in response to the first threats of invasion in 1791, or even after the institution of the republic in September 1792. Indeed, early discussion of citizenship was conducted largely in the context of property rights, with the military rights of citizens discussed in terms of the property-owner's right to bear arms, on the grounds that arms alone allowed him to gain and maintain his liberty (Rétat, 1993). The first debates in the National Assembly on military recruitment revealed that there was strong opposition among the deputies to any system which smacked of compulsion. Such a system, it was argued, would recall the worst abuses of the Ancien Regime, when men were routinely rounded up and pressed into service (the system known in French as *racolage*). This would, the deputies believed, create immense resentment amongst the civilian population and result in unwilling soldiers being despatched to the front to fight in the name of the Revolution. Indeed, Dubois-Crancé, who would later serve as War Minister under the Jacobin republic, was in 1789 a lone voice when he proposed that France needed a truly national system of recruitment which would fall upon everyone alike, from 'the second person in the state' – the King himself, as supreme commander of the army, was to be excluded – to 'the last active citizen' (Crépin, 1998). At that time, of course, France was not at war, and the Assembly was talking of the measures that would be required at some future date if her frontiers were to be attacked. But already the deputies saw the need to define just how a revolutionary army should be recruited, whether they should depend on the generosity of patriotic volunteers or whether some form of compulsion should be sought. And if so, what sort? If there was general agreement that the Ancien Regime army did not provide an appropriate instrument to fight a war in the name of the French people – an army where the officer class was drawn from the nobility, and where few bar the very poor and vulnerable were attracted to the ranks – there was no clear vision of what should replace it. When Dubois-Crancé talked of 'conscription' and argued that the rich should not be allowed to buy themselves out of service, few were willing to commit themselves to his cause. The ideological attraction of equality was easily set aside in favour of arguments about military effectiveness and personal commitment.

Yet there was a certain logic to the case that a revolutionary war, declared in the name of the people, should be fought by an army which was drawn from the people and was devoted to its cause. No other solution seemed entirely apt. Hence the wide range of expedients that were turned to in the course of the Revolution in an effort to fulfil the manpower needs of the military while producing an army that would be worthy of the ideals to which France was committed. The deputies realised that they could not afford to leave things as they were. They were spurred, of course, by the resignation of many of the more conservative army officers, who held that their oath of loyalty had been to the King and was not to be transferred to the new political order; by 1791, in the months following Louis XVI's flight to Varennes, the initial trickle had become a flood, with many senior officers threatening to defect or joining the ranks of the emigration. In all, between mid-September 1791 and the beginning of December 1792 Samuel Scott has calculated that in the line regiments one-third of all units lost a third or more of their officer strength through resignations, illegal absences and emigration, and the politicians could not but be suspicious of the future intentions of many who remained (Scott, 1978). But the problems of the line army were not restricted to the officers. Just as alarming was the indiscipline in the ranks, the sympathy expressed by many soldiers for the cause of the populace and most especially of the Paris sans-culottes, and the incidence of open mutiny in 1790 – most famously, though by no means uniquely, at Nancy – frequently supported by revolutionary slogans and political pleading (Bourdeau, 1898; Scott, 1978). The creation of National Guard units among the sons of local *citoyens actifs* to defend property and maintain the Revolution in towns and villages across France, also created an anomaly, encouraging the more patriotic citizens to join the Guard, and bestowing on the Guard units higher prestige and greater respect than was accorded to the soldiers of the line (Dupuy, 1972). The politicians accepted that this anomaly could be harmful to the future defence of the Revolution, and they became increasingly convinced that existing systems of recruitment had to be quite radically reformed.

In particular, they were determined to rid themselves of the negative and highly damaging image of the military that had been so widespread in the eighteenth century, an image that was only compounded by the familiar spectacle of old soldiers, tired and broken by service and often abandoned to fend for themselves without medical treatment or a decent level of pension, reduced to begging or to seeking shelter in the local poorhouse. During the Ancien Regime the army had too often been a career of last resort – a life of drudgery and harsh discipline, uprooted from the community and often alienated from it, a life where there was little prospect of independence, marriage, or a family of one's own (Léonard, 1958). Soldiers, as they were portrayed in popular prints and images, were often seen as thieves and marauders, able-bodied strangers who posed a threat to honest citizens and who had a permanent eye on opportunities for booty and plunder. In seventeenth- and eighteenth-century woodcuts, for instance, in Germany and Switzerland as well as in France, mercenary bands were depicted almost as 'alternative societies, exciting, threatening and repulsive by turns', presenting as much danger to local people as the enemy they opposed (Hopkin, 1997). In these circumstances it is hardly surprising that those who offered themselves for service included many who, whether through poverty or inadequacy, could find no other source of livelihood – the younger son of a poor peasant family whom the land could no longer support; the apprentice driven by a natural rootlessness or by the consequences of a family quarrel to flee his father's home; the drunkard, the debtor, the young man who had dabbled in crime or who had served a prison sentence for some youthful felony. Nor is it to be wondered at if respectable society regarded the soldier with a mixture of fear and distaste, as a drifter who was naturally corrupt and devious, a trickster who had little morality and whom it would be unwise to trust. Some went further, Voltaire, for instance, denouncing European armies as 'a million assassins organised into regiments, rushing from one end of Europe to the other inflicting murder and pillage because they have to earn their living and they do not know an honest trade' (Léonard, 1958, p. 225).

Distaste with the image and lifestyle of the soldier constituted an important argument for change. A revolutionary army, it was agreed, had to enjoy the esteem and confidence of the population. Nor could it rely heavily, as Ancien Regime armies had done, on the systematic recruitment of foreign mercenaries. But that did not mean that the revolutionary authorities, sons of the humanist spirit of the age, would necessarily be attracted to ideas of compulsion or seek to impose a conscript army. There was a sense in which they even felt a degree of revulsion at the idea that serving the nation could be a requirement, a legal obligation on an unwilling individual, and they sought solutions which would, they believed, both meet the requirements of the armies and raise the status of the men fighting in the name of the French people. Hence in the pamphlet literature of the later 1780s there are numerous references to the need to appeal to the patriotic devotion of individuals and to the dedication of young Frenchmen to the revolutionary cause. Increasingly they looked for inspiration to writers like Joseph Servan, a noted pamphleteer during the reign of Louis XVI and the future Girondin Minister of War, whose long and influential work of 1780, *Le Soldat Citoyen*, had emphasised that the soldier's role must be first and foremost that of a citizen, whose identity as a fighting man was a secondary consideration, the outcome of circumstance. In a nation that was composed of citizens it was the fact of his citizenship that gave him status and respect, just as it was his citizenship which had inspired him to offer his services to the people and to defend their frontiers against foreign aggression. The soldier, in Servan's view, had to be decently remunerated and humanely treated; military and civil society had to become integrated parts of a single, holistic unity (Servan, 1780).

The route to conscription turned out to be a rather tortuous one for revolutionary politicians whose first commitment was to rid France of institutions that depended upon an outdated idea of privilege, where liberty had to be defended by the abolition of what the eighteenth century termed 'liberties', generally exemptions or monopolies which had been granted by the monarch or had been bought from privileged bodies like gilds or chambers of commerce. At the same time, if liberty was to be defended at all, politicians felt they had to take advice from their generals about the size of army and the kinds of qualities which they should be seeking out. For it was recognised that conscripting everyone of a particular age could not offer a practical solution: the army had no use for recruitment on that scale, and would not know what to do with the hordes of young, untrained and largely unskilled boys which any system of annual *classes* would produce. The revolutionaries therefore chose to retain the old line units which they had inherited, supplementing them with new battalions raised on what they saw as principles compatible with their political ideals. Reforms came in stages. First the Assembly endorsed the principle of a volunteer army, and in 1791 and 1792 it called upon the young and patriotic, especially those without family commitments, to step forward and offer themselves in the cause of the Nation. In 1791 there was still no war to fight; and by the following spring, when there was, it was clear that appealing for volunteers would not provide the manpower the armies required. For this reason the government was increasingly under pressure to find alternative means of persuasion, and from 1793 it was accepted that a degree of compulsion was inevitable.

A degree of compulsion did not necessarily, however, translate into conscription as the modern world has come to recognise it – a system that is systematic and bureaucratised, with each *classe* of young men, on reaching the prescribed age for military service, passing obligatorily before the recruiting-sergeant. That would come only in 1799 with the Loi Jourdan, following a decade of experimentation with various forms of levy and quota. Of the intervening years, 1793 was the one which saw the heaviest demands on the population, with first the *levée des 300.000* in the spring and then, more famously, the *levée en masse*, introduced in August in a bid to raise the numbers in uniform to three-quarters of a million. The *levée des 300.000* cannot be described as conscription. Departments (and subsequently districts and communes) were allocated quotas in proportion to their population which they were obliged to fill. But no one sought to prescribe how the soldiers should be found: the law states simply that 'in the event that the voluntary enrolment does not yield the number of men requested from each commune, the citizens shall be required to complete it at once; and for such purpose they shall adopt, by plurality of votes, the method which they find most suitable' (Stewart, 1951, p. 403). It was almost an open invitation to deceit and ingenuity, and there were many instances where the process aroused bitter resentment, with claims that villagers were volunteering the sons of their rivals, or were callously nominating outsiders – seasonal harvesters passing through in search of work, men drawn from marginal communities or living on isolated hillsides, and those who had been consigned by society to hospitals, poorhouses, and even prisons (Forrest, 1981).

The *levée en masse* in August 1793, by way of contrast, did constitute a form of conscription, though an exceptional, one-off variety born out of a military emergency rather than a systematic annual exercise. The decree began with these famous words: 'Henceforth, until the enemies have been driven from the territory of the Republic, the French people are in permanent requisition for army service'. In theory the decree placed the entire population, young and old, male and female, on a war footing. 'The young men shall go to battle; the married men shall forge arms and transport provisions; the women shall make tents and clothes, and shall serve in the hospitals; the children shall turn old linen into lint; the old men shall repair to the public places to stimulate the courage of the warriors and preach the unity of the republic and hatred of kings'. And in each district the battalion that was raised was to be united under a banner bearing the patriotic inscription: 'The French people risen against tyrants' (Stewart, 1951, pp. 472–474). The levy, it was explained, was general, though in practice it was the young, 'unmarried citizens or childless widowers from eighteen to twenty-five years', who were expected to defend the frontiers. It assumed spontaneity and enthusiasm, an upsurge of patriotic anger, and revolutionary commitment. The law was designed to avoid the worst of the abuses of the previous March, the government insisting both that communes hold ballots to choose those who should march first and that those nominated could not avoid their duty by the provision of a substitute. In this way, they believed, recriminations could be avoided and enthusiasm for the war maintained. This enthusiasm would be essential to success, since the law carefully failed to lay down the period of each conscript's service: he was to stay in the army until the end of the war, until victory was attained. It would be a long assignment. On the men sent to the battalions in 1793 the full weight of a decade's fighting would fall, as there would be no further major exercise in recruitment before 1799. Only then, with the Loi Jourdan, did France see the introduction of systematic conscription, with the annual levy, *classe* by *classe*, a necessary *rite de passage* to be borne by each succeeding generation as they reached their twentieth or twenty-first birthday (Castel, 1970; Vallée, 1936).

The image of conscription conjured up in the minds of young Frenchmen from the eighteenth century to the twentieth – of appearing before the recruiting sergeant, presenting themselves for measurement and medical examination, and drawing that fateful number from the barrel on the village green – was created under the Directory and imposed by the Consulate. It was not the revolutionary *demi-brigades* that were raised by annual *classes* in defence of France's frontiers, but the Napoleonic armies, pursuing their dream of imperial expansion across a continent at a time when the war had become institutionalised and when the army itself had lost much of its ideological gloss. For by 1799 few of France's soldiers were fighting for ideals of liberty and equality – they were more likely to be fighting for themselves, for their friends, their fellow soldiers, even the community of the army itself (Bertaud, 1985; Forrest, 1990). And the time was long past when officers won promotion on the basis of their ideological credentials. Napoleon's armies won so convincingly precisely because they had become professionalised and were superbly trained, many of them looking to make their career in the military. Napoleonic conscription was less a measure of revolutionary radicalism than part of the process of ending the Revolution in the armies, of moving from an army of militants to an army which won respect by its competence and tactical brilliance and sought rewards in glory and honour (Lynn, 1989). The transition would not always prove an easy one. In some regions of France where there had never been a strong tradition of military service, avoidance remained widespread, often with the connivance of parents and neighbours, priests and mayors (Bergès, 1980). It would take years of dogged enforcement by the army and the gendarmerie – and certainly until 1810 or 1811 – before the habit of conscription finally became engrained in the psychology of the young and of the communities to which they belonged. If young men obeyed, they obeyed out of fear rather than passion or belief. Napoleonic conscription was achieved by firm policing; but it evoked little enthusiasm amongst the population at large. In this respect it must be seen as quite distinct from its revolutionary predecessor, the republican project that was the *levée en masse*, with its overtones of revolutionary idealism and popular spontaneity.

CONSCRIPTION DURING THE THIRD REPUBLIC

Even in the twentieth century, with so much more coercive power at their command, states have not always shown an immediate enthusiasm for the idea of a conscript army, even in the quite exceptional circumstances of the First World War. In part this reflects a reluctance on the part of the military themselves to contemplate a reform which many saw as undermining the skills and patriotic enthusiasm on which a successful force might depend, and to which their existing ideas on training and discipline, tactics and manoeuvres were geared. In part, too, it exposes doubts among the high command about the wisdom of deploying conscripts alongside volunteers in the same units, with all the rivalry and mutual contempt which that might involve. Here we can see many parallels with the arguments propounded in 1789. The opposition to conscription within the military demonstrated a certain conservatism within the officer corps, combined with widely-held assumptions about morale and man management. But there was also a very significant political dimension, particularly, perhaps, in the more advanced democratic societies where governments faced re-election and felt answerable to (and vulnerable in the face of) public opinion. Only if conscription reflected the popular pulse would they be willing to embrace it, and the reluctance of governments to institute it from the outbreak of war demonstrates the unease which many still felt at compelling families to part with their sons and brothers. Whereas in some countries it seemed to be the necessary consequence of citizenship, in others it seemed like an unacceptable step along the path to centralised state power over the individual.

Hence the image of conscription remained curiously inconsistent, a blend of the equitable and mechanistic on the one hand – the qualities which had led Jourdan to reject any idea of *remplacement* in 1799, any thought that the unwilling or well-endowed could buy themselves out of service – and of the spirited and enthusiastic on the other, the antithesis of the normal image of a conscript army. This owes much to the power of the revolutionary tradition and of the mythology built around the soldiers who had defended the Revolution at Valmy and Jemmapes; or to the lionisation of revolutionary heroes like Bara and Viala who, though mere boys, had sought to fight and die for the republican cause (Musée Calvet, 1989). More recently the myth had been revived in 1870 by the *francs-tireurs*, who combined the qualities of resistant and martyr in the face of the Prussian onslaught. Again the image was ambiguous, since some of them were organised into effective military units, while others were little more than peasant guerrillas, acting on their own and shooting at Prussian soldiers from behind hedges (Cambon, 1976). In Paris, indeed, the majority of the *francs-tireurs* were avowed revolutionaries, remaining in the capital after the armistice to take part in the insurrection. Sacrifice and nobility, courage and spontaneity, all were rolled into a single image of the revolutionary armies which continued to inform the French concept of a conscript army and would be revived, quite unashamedly, in the recruitment propaganda of the Great War (Paret et al., 1992).

Valmy, in particular – the famous battle on 20 September 1792 in which the French revolutionary armies had first defeated the enemy and 'saved the revolution' – was the object of a recurrent republican myth. The men who had fought there were not, of course, conscripts. They were a somewhat haphazard mixture of volunteers, some of whom had first demonstrated their enthusiasm for the Revolution in the National Guard, and soldiers of the line, men inherited from the regiments of the Ancien Regime; the majority of them were seasoned professionals. In the same way the young men recruited by the *levée en masse* would be a rather uneasy mixture of idealists stirred to defend the frontiers from royalists and tyrants and those who had simply had the misfortune to draw a *mauvais numéro* in the ballot on the village green. These awkward realities were not, of course, allowed to get in the way of republican myth-making. The cult of Valmy, and to a lesser degree that of the *levée en masse*, had their roots in revolutionary ideals of self-sacrifice and heroism. They did not directly refer to conscription and should perhaps have had little direct relevance to the conscription debate; yet the representation of the French soldier became blurred, a confusion of two very different images. Taken together they symbolised an ideal *soldat-type*, personifying at one and the same time the routine duty of the conscript and the commitment and enthusiasm of the young citizen thirsting to defend his country. It was, in short, the military form of a more general image of legitimation, that of the democratic nation-state which could draw upon the strength and the participation of its citizens. It was reinforced by a strong sense of national identity, which was regularly threatened by aggression from across the Rhine.

The cult of Valmy might seem far removed from the reality of the conscription process, carefully burnished by selective memory and republican myth-making. But it cannot be ignored. It was Valmy, after all, which was given pride of place in the centennial celebrations of 1889, Valmy which came to epitomise the martial spirit of the French people. Here myth is everything: what Valmy came to represent rather than what it had actually been. Some historians even question whether Valmy should be regarded as a great military victory at all, whether it really constituted a true battle in the military sense. But its symbolic power is not in doubt. Morale had been saved and the victorious Prussian armies turned back, and it would prove to be a key turning-point in the fortunes of the revolutionary battalions (Bertaud, 1970). More crucial still is the fact that the outcome came as a complete surprise, since few, even among France's leaders, had expected the French to emerge triumphant. They had, it was generally believed, poorer weapons and inadequate training, and they were up against the most professional soldiers in eighteenth-century Europe. It was their spirit, their fervour, and their revolutionary self-belief which won the day and which captured the popular imagination. This was the explanation offered by those romantic writers of the nineteenth century who sought to keep the revolutionary tradition alive. For Michelet 'it was really the people who were fighting at Valmy far more than the army . . . On that young army shone something resembling a heroic glow, of which the King had no understanding. That glow was Faith'. Victor Hugo, writing in the same tradition and reflecting on the spirit of the soldiers that for him explained the victory, talked of 'a mystique of the people that is formidable when it is aroused' (Crépin, 1994, pp. 470–472).

This version of events would take a long time to die. During a conversation with Foch in 1908, Georges Clemenceau would express the awe he felt faced with the memory of these young men and of the manner of their victory. Valmy, he said, defied rational explanation. 'It is a dawn, a dawn of our hopes . . . a moral phenomenon; at present the buoyancy is missing, we have to recreate it' (Hublot, 1987, p. 373). The spirit of Valmy and the enthusiasm of the revolutionary soldiers had become a source of inspiration to future generations of republicans. In the process two competing images of military service – voluntarism and conscription – tended to become confused. The idea of a citizen army, the myth of the nation in arms, became permanently linked to the notion of spontaneity, and *élan* found its way into military manuals of the Third Republic. For this reason myths of military service in nineteenth- and early twentieth-century France were multi-dimensional. Frenchmen had a duty as citizens to serve the state, and conscription was the most obvious of the administrative mechanisms at the state's disposal. But, like their forebears in the 1790s, they were also revolutionaries, committed to the ideal of the republic. When both the *patrie* and the revolution were in danger, the citizen became once again a soldier and sprang spontaneously to the defence of both.

After 1871, it is true, the romance of this part of the revolutionary tradition was tarnished by the sheer scale of France's defeat when faced with a huge Prussian army that was itself the product of conscription. But what was really at issue was the failure of the nineteenth-century French *armée de métier*, in many ways the antithesis of the revolutionary dream; and with the electoral victory of the republicans, military reform was again high on the agenda. The conscription law introduced by the Third Republic – a compromise measure between conservative and radical factions passed by the Chamber in 1872 – was scarcely the product of lyrical idealism. Instead, it was rooted in political pragmatism and designed to serve the needs of the military, who were deemed to have lacked the manpower resources they needed during the Franco-Prussian war. It prescribed two different degrees of military service, one far more arduous and time-consuming than the other, with the individual's fate resting on the outcome of a ballot. At the same time it took a step in the direction of demanding personal service from all, including those sons of the bourgeoisie who were widely supposed to have left soldiering to others. In the event it was to prove unsatisfactory both to the more radical republicans, who objected to the maintenance of the ballot and the two distinct classes of service which it created, and to the army, who found themselves desperately short of officers and NCOs to assume military responsibilities (Jauffret, 1987). Others were to claim that it lacked the overtly educative role which the Republic required, and once the radical republicans replaced the opportunists in power they did not hesitate to mould conscription more tightly to their tastes. This was, after all, the high period of the *lois scolaires*, and conscription law was seen by this generation of republicans as a legitimate area of education. The result, after thirteen years of debate and reflection, was the law of 1889, which instituted a three-year period of service and raised the total manpower available to the army by one-third (Porch, 1981). A hundred years after the Revolution, the myth of Valmy had given way in the republican Pantheon to an egalitarian approach to conscription, through systematic annual *classes*.

Yet parts of the myth endured, in particular the attachment to the idea of a national army that would be representative of the French people, the idea of the *nation armée* which would not be read the last rites. In the opinion of many Frenchmen, an army of mercenaries, of hired professional soldiers, had proved inadequate on many occasions before, and there was no reason to suppose that it could suffice in another major crisis in the future. Nor did they necessarily trust such an army to carry out the wishes of elected governments, in particular of republican governments. Republicans were always prone to suspect generals of caesarism, and with the upsurge of popular support for General Boulanger and the threat which that posed, these fears were as rife in the 1880s as at any time since the Revolution itself. They therefore believed, as had Robespierre and Saint-Just before them, that it was prudent to entrust their defence not to professional soldiers (whose focus of loyalty would be to their own commanders), but to conscripts who would return to the people from whom they had sprung. And if, in the course of the nineteenth century, memories were dimmed, if revolutionary soldiers became confused with those of Napoleon in his pomp, if volunteers tended to merge with conscripts to form the single canvas of achievement that was the Revolutionary and Napoleonic Wars, the persistence of the myth helps us to textualise the willingness of successive republican regimes to turn to conscripts almost as a matter of faith. It would be as true of General de Gaulle in 1958 as of the Popular Front in 1936.

It also helps explain the apparent enthusiasm of the French population when war once again threatened in 1914. The people had, of course, been well prepared by a barrage of patriotic propaganda and anti-German invective during the previous months; and neither the radical republicans nor the nationalist right were minded to forget France's ravished provinces of Alsace and Lorraine. The young, in particular, had been thoroughly inducted in nationalism and republican dogma in the schools of Jules Ferry – an education many transferred to the battlefield by way of the *clubs de gymnastique* and *sociétés de tir* which so characterised the provincial towns of fin-de-siècle France and where so many were encouraged to hone their skills in marksmanship and to develop their sporting prowess. In popular memory as in the novels of the immediate pre-war era – especially those relating to the life of Parisians – an inordinate part of the hot, glorious summers of 1912, 1913 and, however fragilely, 1914 was spent in running, fencing, cycling and swimming, whether in the Seine as it flowed lazily through the outer suburbs or in the refreshing waters of the Piscine Hébert, recently opened to serve the working-class *quartiers* to the north and east (Cobb, 1988). The preparation for war may have shattered the calm of the summer holidays in the last days of July, but in truth many young Frenchmen were already well prepared, both physically and psychologically, to perform the service which they knew would be demanded of them.

But what is more striking even than this general acceptance by the population that another war was unavoidable is their seeming agreement that France should resort to some form of conscription to find the manpower required. There was curiously little opposition to the idea, and that in a country where Jean Jaurès and many other socialist leaders were committed pacifists, opposed to the very idea of a war of revenge against Germany which would condemn a generation of young Frenchmen to misery and destruction. For Jaurès believed, with an equal passion, that for however long France had to have an army – and he accepted that there was a case for an army for defence – it should be based on conscription, on the grounds that 'it would be a crime against France and against the Army itself to separate the Army from the Nation' (Jaurès, 1910, p. 44). That argument was by 1914 as good as won. The principle of conscription had been accepted; if there had been a debate about citizenship and about equality of sacrifice, it had taken place back in the 1880s and was now past history. Egalitarian republicans had been outraged by the law of 1872 which had allowed 30% of each contingent to escape active service, and they had concentrated on making legislation that was visibly fair. By 1905 they had achieved this, with a conscription law which laid down a two-year period of service for all. In the years preceding the declaration of war that principle was never seriously questioned. Public debate centred rather on manpower needs and the inerasable fears that France's population was dwindling and would prove incapable of sustaining the war effort. In 1913 Louis Barthou responded to this by pushing a three-year service law through the French parliament, increasing France's standing army to three quarters of a million men in arms. Interestingly, the debate did not spread to matters of principle, but limited itself to logistical questions – the belief that the existing two-year obligation could not supply the country with sufficient defences against the Germans (Challener, 1955). As Charles de Gaulle noted with evident approval in *La France et son Armée*, 1914 was a triumph of national unity. 'Not a single group to protest against the mobilisation. Not a single strike to interfere with it. Not a single vote in parliament to refuse the war credits' (Werth, 1965, p. 71).

There is nothing to suggest, either, that the youth of France refused the call to arms or tried to dodge the draft of 1914, quite unlike their response to the *levée en masse* during the First Republic or to the early conscriptions of Napoleon. There were some pacifist meetings in the final days of July 1914, mainly in working-class areas of Paris and its suburbs, and in a few provincial towns, most particularly in the industrial Nord, but they remained largely orderly, expressions of peaceful protest rather than of militant defiance. Only during one meeting, in the railway workers' suburb of Sotteville, near Rouen, did protest get out of control and rioting ensue. More generally, people accepted their lot and adjusted to the new circumstances which threatened them. By 31 July the youth of the working classes, whose loyalty had seemed least certain, appeared, in the main, to be resigned to the war, some even relieved that the waiting and uncertainty were finally over. Richard Cobb sums up their response with typical warmth and humanity. With the announcement of mobilisation the boys who were conscripted knew where they stood, where they would have to go, 'above all with whom they would have to go'. He goes on: 'What was written in each individual *livret militaire* would put an end to the speculations of the previous days; it would also provide the comfortable feeling of being *encadré*. This was a crisis one didn't have to face alone, but with one's mates' (Cobb, 1988, pp. 138–139). The camaraderie that would be so vital to maintain any vestige of morale in the trenches of the Somme and the Marne, the sense that they were fighting to help one another, was already important in buoying up their spirits even as they prepared to leave. And leave they did. Between August 1914 and the end of the year the number of cases of desertion and draft-dodging that came before *conseils de guerre* would be a mere 841 (Cobb, 1988).

Once the war began this image would be sustained and regularly refreshed by the rhetoric and the imagery in which French republicans enshrined their military mission. The culture of an entire society was involved, the interests of the people being defended by the bravery and sacrifice of its young. As in the 1790s, the Republic was presented as being virtuous, and the republican armies as fighting for an ideal. As the philosopher Henri Bergson wrote in the *Bulletin des Armées de la République*, it was that quality which guaranteed victory. 'The conflict before us', he told the military in September 1914, is between two opposing forces – the force which wears itself out because it is not supported by a higher ideal, and the force which can never be spent because it rests upon an ideal of justice and liberty' (Ferro, 1999, p. 295). The fact that the French based their defence on the collective strength of the people, on those who had inherited the traditions of the *nation en armes* and the spontaneity of the *levée en masse* of the revolutionary years, was perceived to be a central part of that 'higher ideal' and one which – in France as in other European countries with an established tradition of conscription in hours of danger – was assumed, not agonised over, either by the political leadership or by the population at large.

THE CONTRAST WITH BRITAIN

The contrast with the situation in Britain at the start of the war could hardly be more succinct. Here nineteenth-century political traditions were, of course, very different, and the government, which took overt pride in the professionalism of its soldiers, was not attracted by the prospect of conscription. They did not see it as a political principle to be admired and applied in the interests of equality, even if that case was increasingly being voiced. Rather it was seen as a desperate pragmatic response to the huge scale of the losses which were incurred during the first months of the Great War. Even then the decision was slow in coming and was taken with every show of reluctance – not in 1914 when war was declared, but considerably later, in 1916, at a time when the draining campaigns on the Western Front had exposed the wafer-thin reserves available to the army, and when more conventional calls to patriotism and self-sacrifice were becoming inadequate to the army's needs. The long and often acrimonious arguments which preceded the introduction of conscription provide a good instance of the reluctance of politicians to grasp what was seen as an unpalatable political nettle, an issue which, in the British context, risked dividing public opinion and putting support for the war effort at jeopardy. The debates in parliament lack the idealistic fervour which the issue might seem to command. Indeed, such principles as might underlie the case for a conscript army remained largely subsumed as soldiers and politicians argued about matters of public acceptance and political cost, questions which were seen as more central to the success of recruitment and to winning the war. Here we can sense not just a reluctance to institute root-and-branch change in a situation of grave national crisis but also something of the initial French dilemma back in 1789. Britain in 1916, like France at the beginning of the Revolution, was conscious that there was no tradition of conscription to build on. The principal difference, of course, is that Britain in 1916 was proud of her established military and imperial traditions and defensive of her institutions, whereas revolutionary France had been eager to replace any structure which smacked of hierarchy and privilege. Indeed, many saw the arguments advanced for conscription as an unwarranted attack on British traditions and military culture.

The debate raged for over a decade before conscription was finally imposed by parliament in the Military Service Act of May 1916, and the intemperate language used by both sides shows the extent of the fissures that existed in both political and military circles over the issue. The Boer War had left a profound mark on public consciousness, and there was a flurry of military preparations and a growth in paramilitary youth organisations in expectation of a war with Germany, which had momentarily replaced France as the subject of that popular genre of British writing, invasion literature. In the eyes of a part of the population the principal lesson to be learned from the Boer War was that Britain needed to show greater preparedness in advance of the next conflict, and that fighting should not be left solely to those brave enough to volunteer. This belief led to the creation in 1902 of the National Service League, set up by a group of nationalist political and military figures at Apsley House, the London home of the Duke of Wellington. Its members were fiercely patriotic and strongly committed to the principle of conscription, and they pressed for legislation to institute compulsory drill in school for all boys and compulsory military service for all young men, as part of a necessary militarisation of British society.

At first the League seemed somewhat patrician, since its more prominent members included high-ranking army and naval officers, peers, bishops and protagonists for Empire; they appealed especially to the county elite, its membership including thirteen of the Lords-Lieutenant (Spiers, 1980). This impression was only heightened by the lack of interest shown in the movement by the main political parties. Both Conservatives and Liberals were wary of any measure that seemed to have its roots in continental practice, with the Liberal Party, in particular, finding it difficult to contemplate the idea of compulsion or to extract itself from its Gladstonian legacy. Nor did the Labour movement show any enthusiasm for conscripting factory workers. The fact that the Liberals held office after 1905 did little to help the cause of the National Service League. The new War Minister, Haldane, was more concerned to enact other reforms in the interests of military efficiency: a drive for cost savings in the regular army, an expansion and major restructuring of the reserve, the resuscitation of the Officers' Training Corps in schools and universities, and above all the creation of a general staff. He believed that the young should be encouraged to acquire the elements of military training voluntarily and to avoid unnecessary compulsion. 'I do not see', he told Parliament, 'why the rifle club, cadet corps, the Volunteers, all the different forms of military organisation which we have at present, should not be encouraged, so that the people should be able to organise themselves' (Haldane, 1907, p. 29). Haldane did insist that young men aged between 18 and 24 should serve for four years in the Territorial Army, but that required a commitment of no more than a fortnight's attendance at camp each year. He had no plans to introduce conscription; indeed, he saw his plans not as a first step towards a conscript army but rather as a means of beating off any threat of compulsion (Adams & Poirier, 1987).

The egalitarian arguments for conscription, which were so powerful in France, seemed to evoke little sympathy in England. It is true that after 1905 the National Service League did build up a degree of popular support, when it recruited Lord Roberts, the veteran field marshal from the Boer War, as its new president and began to play on his undoubted popularity in the community at large. In his person he symbolised both military prowess and devotion to the British army, qualities which endeared him to large sections of the public, with the consequence that his well-publicised views could not be so easily swept aside. Fear of a German invasion was also growing during these years, and this, too, played into the NSL's hands. And yet its levels of membership remained modest (10,000 in 1907, 62,000 by 1910) until just before the outbreak of war in 1914, when anti-German paranoia was at its peak. Only then did the League swell into a movement with a sizable popular base, claiming a membership of some 270,000 (Adams & Poirier, 1987). And increasingly its cause was winning broader support from within the armed forces themselves.

If by 1914 the case for conscription was being aired, loudly and persistently, in the press, that does not mean that the public, or parliament, was yet convinced. Support was stronger, it is true, on the Conservative side than among the

Liberals, many of whom still abhorred any idea of compulsion, though the years of exposure to conscriptionist propaganda were beginning to have some effect even amongst traditional Liberal-voluntarists. Even in 1915, in the face of mounting mortality figures, there was still no Commons majority for compulsion: public opinion was simply not ready for it. In March 1915, for instance, Lloyd George could answer a parliamentary question with the clear message that 'the Government are not of opinion that there is any ground for thinking that the war would have been more successfully prosecuted by means of conscription', since the call for volunteers had met with an adequate response (Hayes, 1949, p. 153). This approach was somewhat disingenuous since the number of men refusing to come forward was causing real concern and the possibility of introducing conscription had already been discussed in cabinet. But the principled case for conscription seemed to have made little impact. Instead, when the case was made, it was put in a deeply pragmatic form. The needs of the military could not be met by existing mechanisms. Too many young men in the categories who were being called upon to volunteer – in essence, those without wives and dependents – were failing to come forward. There was also the issue of civilian needs, the fact that too many of those who did volunteer were needed elsewhere. The case was well summarised in these terms: 'The voluntary system enlists unsuitable men. It takes skilled mechanics who ought to be making munitions; and it takes married men whose maintenance is costly, whilst there are many single men who do not enlist' (Hayes, 1949, p. 139). Britain, it was clear, was faced with a war on a scale that was previously unknown, and it was this new element which called for regulation and manpower planning to a degree which, even a few years previously, would have seemed unthinkable. Only for a small minority was conscription a question of equality or of the implications of citizenship.

The arguments against came from both the traditionalist Right and the pacifist Left. There were fears that conscription would enlist reluctant recruits who would make resentful and incompetent soldiers; but there were also fears that the introduction of conscription would unleash an intolerable succession of measures extending the power of the state into other aspects of the individual's daily existence. Even those who accepted that compulsion might one day be required – like Tennant, the Under-Secretary of State for War in 1915 – showed no liking for a system that was identified with continental practice and which seemed 'foreign to the British nation, to the British character, and to the genius of our people' (Hayes, 1949, p. 155). And from the Left came fears that the measures would override questions of conscience and pacifist belief, as well as more ideological claims that the powers that the government would acquire might be used to force workers to die in wars for capitalist profit that were rightly none of their concern. In the words of the No-Conscription Fellowship, a left-wing pacifist organisation led by socialist politicians like Clifford Allen and Fenner Brockway, conscription undermined the most fundamental rights of the individual and should therefore be vigorously opposed by socialists as it should by libertarians of every political hue. 'Conscription is now law in this country of free tradition', they declared; 'Our hard-won liberties have been violated. Conscription means the desecration of principles that we have long held dear; it involves the subordination of civil liberties to military dictation; it imperils the freedom of individual conscience and establishes in our midst that militarism which menaces all social progress and divides the peoples of all nations' (Hayes, 1949, p. 177).

Perhaps so, but, as we know, these arguments cut little ice with the public, and the enormity of the task which Britain faced meant that here, as in other European states faced with the slaughter of the trenches in 1915 and 1916, the resort to conscription could no longer be denied. The reasons for adopting it remained pragmatic rather than ideological – the need for a large pool of manpower, the failure to produce the necessary numbers by voluntary appeal, the desire of the state to prioritise among potential recruits, the need to reserve certain occupations to protect the home front. There was also, of course, an awareness that more discriminatory forms of recruitment would create animosities and jealousies and would give rise to charges of favouritism and cronyism which could be damaging to the war effort. But it would be difficult to claim that conscription, even in 1916, had become part of a political ethic. In France, by way of contrast, it had been integrated into republican ideology as providing a fair and equitable way of raising armies for national defence, one which reflected on the duties and obligations that accompanied the benefits of citizenship. As such, it had achieved a rather different status, both amongst politicians and with the public at large. It was, in Annie Crépin's felicitous phrase, part of the 'triple apprenticeship' which young Frenchmen had to undergo, at once for the Nation, for full citizenship, and for the Republic. That does not mean that there was no debate in France about conscription; but the debate focussed on what type of conscription was most appropriate to a republican regime, on what definition of conscription would most accurately reflect the aspirations of the Nation. On that conservatives and radicals could and did disagree. But on the general principle of conscription to ensure the defence of the nation in an emergency there was quasi-unanimity. That battle had been fought and won in the parliamentary debates which followed the Franco-Prussian War and the re-establishment of republican institutions after the Paris Commune (Crépin, 1998).

CITIZEN-SOLDIERS, NATIONAL SERVICE AND THE MASS ARMY: THE BIRTH OF CONSCRIPTION IN REVOLUTIONARY EUROPE AND NORTH AMERICA

Meyer Kestnbaum

INTRODUCTION

By the late-1870s, after more than a decade of expanding conflicts in both North America and Europe, the institution of conscription emerged as one of the chief solutions to manpower shortages available to warring states (see Howard, 1961; Forster & Nagler, 1997; Murdock, 1971; Geary, 1991). Only a century before, however, the compulsory service of citizens in the line army was not only militarily suspect but also politically threatening (Kestnbaum, 1997; Chorley, 1943; Rothenberg, 1978; Sheehan, 1989). In less than a hundred years, conscription had undergone a dramatic transformation, becoming both an accepted military expedient and a way to raise national and massed armed forces.

Through the work of historians as well as historically oriented social scientists, the broad strokes of conscription's ascendance from an untried and untested policy to a source of military power demanding emulation has become more or less familiar by now. Typically, the story goes something like this. The military conscription of national citizens emerged suddenly and

The Comparative Study of Conscription in the Armed Forces, Volume 20, pages 117–144.

ISBN: 0-7623-0762-5

spectacularly in the French *levée en masse* of 1793, a draft nominally of all citizens undertaken by the newly declared Republic during the wars of the Revolution. In the face of protracted conflict, and with the product of this first extraordinary draft depleted, the French state then adopted a routine and regularized system of annual conscription after 1798, drawing altogether more than two million young men into their forces to wage a coalition war against much of Europe. Near the conclusion of those wars, and more than twenty years after the famous *levée*, Prussia instituted the Boyen Law of 1814, establishing that all citizens owed military service that could be exacted by their state, and putting in place a socially comprehensive system of conscription that nonetheless offered favorable treatment to the middle and upper classes.

A retrenchment of sorts then followed after the conclusion of the Revolutionary and Napoleonic Wars, in which no new moves toward citizen conscription were made and only Prussia retained a nearly universal system of compulsory military service. This retrenchment was broken only with the eruption of the American Civil War, where first Confederate and then Union forces turned to conscription in an effort to form field armies sufficient to cope with the demands of war as it began to change in the era of the steam engine and rifled weaponry. But it was the Franco-Prussian War, and especially the Prussian reliance upon the extensive and nearly universal conscription of citizens that made the military power of the institution patently clear. Not only was France driven to imitate Prussia, collapsing its universal national guard into its standing army and demanding the service of all young men in the forces of Third Republic, but much of Europe proceeded to emulate the victorious Prussian reforms, putting in place systems of extensive compulsory service in the line army based on national citizenship (see Kiernan, 1973; Maude, 1910–1911).

The story of conscription's ascendance can perhaps best be understood in two parts, focusing on two periods of substantial reform. In the first, between 1790 and 1820, it is a tale of institutional origins and emergence, observed initially in France and then Prussia. In the second period, between 1860 and 1880, it is a story of institutional elaboration, consolidation and ultimately dominance, in which the American experience reasserted the military power of conscription as an emergency measure, and Prussia was distinguished as the standard bearer for the military potential of routine and extensive citizen conscription. The conventional story to this point, however, misses a crucial historical precursor from North America, also embroiled in the revolutionary tumult of the age that spawned the *levée en masse*. For in the newly United States, the Continental Congress mandated the several states to draft American citizens into the Continental line army, directing the implementation of federal conscription between 1778 and 1781 (Kestnbaum, 2000). Often ignored, the

United States was in fact an early innovator, instituting citizen conscription fifteen years before its more celebrated fellows in Revolutionary France.

The precocious innovation of the United States throws much of the conventional tale of conscription's emergence into question. No longer is it sufficient to suggest that the origins of conscription lay primarily in the desire of reformers to expand the military power of the state by increasing numbers alone. This is the case precisely because conscription was not used to enlarge forces dramatically in the U.S., and in Prussia it was instituted amidst the demobilization following the apparent end of the Napoleonic wars. Nor is it clear, or plausible to maintain, that the emergence of citizen conscription was tightly linked to the establishment of political democracy, as is sometimes proposed in the case of Revolutionary France. That both the *levée en masse* and the Boyen Law were put in place by authoritarian regimes – the Montagnard Jacobin dictatorship in France and a Prussian monarchy just beginning to throw off the mantle of autocracy – makes the democratic character of the reforms quite problematic. How, then, are we to explain the birth of citizen conscription at the end of the eighteenth century? This becomes our central question, on whose answer hinges any effort to make sense of the modern institution of conscription across its first hundred years.

The argument that follows begins from the proposition that the birth of citizen conscription lies at the intersection of three distinct historical processes, each unfolding around the turn of the nineteenth century. The first historical process was the emergence of the national citizen as an organizing principle in politics. The second process was the formation of state policies of compulsory service in the line army based on national citizenship, or conscription proper. And the third was the initial mobilization of the wide swath of 'the people' for war by the state. The invention of the national citizen produced both a popular politics and a new idiom with which to talk about those politics, around which the modern institution of conscription itself was built. The conscription of national citizens, in turn, offered the policy instrument used by the state to mobilize the masses into war. The birth of conscription lay at the center of these three tightly interwoven processes, binding them together. Tracing out the links among these three historical processes allows the analyst to situate the emergence of citizen conscription within its wider historical and institutional context, while at the same time avoiding the partial treatment or distortion that may come from examining any one of these historical processes in isolation from the others.

Identifying how the emergence of the national citizen, the formation of conscription policies and the mobilization of the masses into war fed one into the next around the turn of the nineteenth century is quite suggestive, but the analysis may be taken substantially further by looking at the *roots* of these three historical processes as they unfolded over time. There we see something startling, which forms my central argument. The key to all three processes lies in a single historical conjuncture – a conjuncture that may be observed emerging between the 1770s and 1810s in a small number of polities, one after another, on both sides of the Atlantic. In this conjuncture, the previously excluded popular classes were mobilized into national politics while the state was drawn into a war in which its future, and the independence of its people, were both at risk. The significance of this historical moment becomes clear when we recognize its remarkable generative effect. It sparked the invention of the national citizen; it spurred reforming elites to institute policies of conscription based on national citizenship; and it opened the way to raise 'the people' by means of citizen conscription to serve the state in war.

To specify precisely how the peculiar historical conjuncture around the turn of the nineteenth century shaped the three historical processes in which conscription's birth was intertwined, this account proceeds in a distinctive manner. The account focuses on concrete sets of institutional arrangements in three spheres – citizenship, military service and war-making – corresponding, respectively, to the three historical processes – the invention of national citizenries, the formation of conscription policies, and the mobilization of the masses into war. The account then examines the transformation of institutions in each sphere as part of a distinct historical process driven by the confluence of popular political mobilization and ongoing war.

Building such an account in institutional terms, however, requires great precision concerning the institutions themselves. In particular, to be able to specify the relationship between clusters of institutions and the critical conjuncture that led to their transformation, it is necessary to be able to distinguish clearly among types of institutions within each sphere. Thus, we can see that in order to make an argument about the emergence of the national citizen, it is necessary to distinguish carefully between corporative and national understandings of citizenship. To make an argument about the formulation of conscription policies, it is necessary to distinguish compulsory from voluntary military service, and service in the militia from a standing force. Only in this way may the particular salience of the obligatory service of national citizens be captured, and the full implications of realizing that obligation by means of conscription properly understood. Lastly, to make an argument about mass military mobilization, it is necessary to distinguish between the kind of service performed by citizens and the actual military organizations constructed from such materials by the state. In this way, we are forced to confront the difference between reliance upon the conscription of national citizens and its use in the formation and maintenance of mass armed forces.

The account to follow is organized into three main parts. The first examines the invention of the national citizen, approaching it through the lens of one of its principle expressions – the citizen-soldier. The citizen-soldier opens the door to the second part, examining the formation of conscription policies based on national citizenship. That these novel policies constituted a form of explicitly national service forms the link to the third part, examining the use of conscription based on national citizenship to mobilize the masses into war. There, it becomes clear that citizen conscription gave rise to a revolution in warfare among states, the organizational centerpiece of which was the mass army, although the historical link between conscription and massed armed force was not always to remain as strong in the two centuries following conscription's birth.

NATIONAL CITIZENSHIP AND THE CITIZEN-SOLDIER

Upon first inspection, the notion of the citizen-soldier appears fairly straightforward. With only a little probing, however, it becomes substantially more complex. In order to see this most clearly, it is necessary to move from the abstract principles governing military service to the particular institutions which breathe life into those principles and realize them practically on the ground.

What is clear from the outset is that to be a soldier, one must be a member of the community of citizens.[1] Immediately, this formulation draws our attention to two elements of the institution. First, the citizen-soldier is predicated on the recognition of the fundamentally trinitarian character of military service, identifying the particular ways in which prospective soldiers are raised from some wider, 'non-military' society to be formed into an armed force, over the constitution and employment of which the state claims a legitimate monopoly.[2] At its root, therefore, the citizen-soldier is built on the distinction – acknowledged if only tacitly – between the armed forces and the society or societies from which they are drawn. Brought into bold relief historically only with the invention of standing armies by state-building princes and monarchs in Europe after 1500 AD, this distinction was renegotiated and reaffirmed in the course of subsequent military reform, forming one of the building blocks of every concrete military institution in Europe and North America to follow. Second, making the distinction between the armed forces and society permits the analyst to examine precisely how the relationship between military service and membership in some wider, non-military society was historically established and regulated. Put another way, it draws our attention to what may be called the social basis of military service: the particular way in which the pool of persons who are permitted to serve, or may be compelled to serve, is defined and given force by state policy.

Since the distinction between the armed forces and society became an organizational reality, specifying the social bases of military service has been primarily a question of the categorical status or statuses occupied by persons in the wider, non-military society. Foremost among the statuses available was citizenship, understood to define a membership group both legally constituted and formally recognized by the state.[3] By the middle of the sixteenth century in Western and Central Europe, citizenship as membership came to comprise the primary criterion for defining the social basis of military service (Delbrück, 1990[1920]; Corvisier, 1979, 1985a). By the close of the nineteenth century, it formed the preeminent basis for socially and institutionally meaningful circumscriptions of the militarily mobilizable population not only in Europe and North America, but in almost every nation-state the world over (Brubaker, 1992; Anderson, 1991).[4]

While citizenship proved increasingly central to the specification of who could and would be mobilized into the armed forces, the institution of citizenship itself underwent a dramatic transformation. Characteristic of the *ancien régime* in Europe, citizenship in the earlier period was understood in corporative and capacitarian terms. Such citizenship was based upon membership in one or another of the formally or conventionally recognized estates into which society was organized and to which distinct privileges accrued. It was by definition unequal, defined with respect to one's greater or lesser capacity to exercise the prerogatives of citizenship. However, around the turn of the nineteenth century, we see the emergence of a new understanding of citizenship in national and formally egalitarian terms that was to challenge and ultimately replace the corporative citizenship of the old regime. This new form of expressly national citizenship was defined with respect to the individual's unmediated and explicitly political relationship to the state as the sole legitimate ruler of the territory in which he lived; the state, in turn, derived its authority from the people themselves as sovereign. National citizenship was formally egalitarian, admitting to no distinction in principle among the individuals who made up the political community of citizens. Membership in the community, however, varied with the degree of its social inclusiveness, for example in terms of the extent to which the mercantile or laboring classes were understood to constitute part of the sovereign collective (See Brubaker, 1992, pp. 14–15, 27–29, 35–49 and note 24).

Let us set this into motion. What is crucial here is that politically defined, formally egalitarian national citizenship began to replace socially defined, formally differential corporative citizenship as part of a secular trend, beginning in the last decades of the eighteenth century and continuing through the nineteenth and even into the twentieth century.[5] Wherever popular political movements undermined institutional supports for privilege and threw off the shackles of imperial or absolutist domination by force of arms, often replacing both with sovereign republics, the groundwork for a new, national citizenship was laid. We can see this with striking clarity in the United States during the American Revolution. Whatever corporatist and socially capacitarian foundations citizenship maintained from its British, colonial origin, were practically abolished with the political and military reality of independence, when the former colonies asserted their power as a sovereign nation to establish their own form of republican rule. In so doing, the former colonies reconstituted American citizenship along explicitly political and formally egalitarian lines as membership in the community of all nationals who would now rule themselves (Wood, 1991; see also Anderson, 1991). We see this same process in the foundation of the Batavian Republic in the Netherlands, the Helvetian Republic in Switzerland, as well as in the Cisalpine, Roman and Neapolitan Republics in Italy. In each of these instances, the example of the United States was known; but it was the French efforts to export their own revolution that were decisive, as was the model offered by Revolutionary France. There, in the French Revolution, we see perhaps most spectacularly how the mobilization of the previously excluded popular classes into national politics transformed citizenship. Not only was the absolute monarchy sundered and the institutions of governance remade, but also state support for the corporative arrangements of the *ancien régime* was abolished and a new social order formally enshrining equality erected in its place (Brubaker, 1992; Hobsbawm, 1996; Van Kley, 1994; and Markoff, 1996). France's exportation of revolution, moreover, was not limited to the creation of its sister republics. Partly as a product of military defeats at the hands of Napoleon's *Grande Armée*, reform in Prussia advanced through the abolition of serfdom to the formal recognition of the so-called bourgeois rights of association. Further, French military domination provided the impetus for Prussia's own war of liberation, in which an autocratic ruler mobilized the people as one nation to reassert their claim to independence (Hintze, 1975a; Craig, 1955; Meinecke, 1977; Sheehan, 1989, 1992, pp. 42–53).

When popular involvement in politics was wed to a call to arms to defend the power of the people to rule themselves as one nation, the citizen-soldier was born. At that moment, in the ferment of the democratic revolutions at the turn of the nineteenth century, the citizen who became a soldier to defend the sovereignty of the nation emerged not only as an historical actor, but as an ideal.

VOLUNTARISM, CONSCRIPTION AND NATIONAL SERVICE

In its first incarnation, the citizen-soldier was firmly rooted in individual volition. Indeed, what greater testimony could be given to the power and promise of national citizenship than the willing commitment of citizens to their common defense. However, as part of the revolutionary process of popular mobilization and national self-definition, where the citizen-soldier emerged, compulsory service replaced putatively pure expressions of voluntarism as the way in which the citizen could distinguish himself as a member of the national community. As this transition unfolded, citizen service took on a meaning quite apart from merely the service of citizens. Increasingly it became identified with service as an obligation of citizenship. At the heart of this historical transition lay the birth of conscription based on national citizenship, an unprecedented institution that emerged from the tumult of popular uprisings and protracted war. When citizen conscription was embodied in authoritative policy and implemented by the state, not only was national citizenship made socially consequential in the most visceral of ways, but the military obligations of citizenship were transformed into national service.

From Volition to Compulsion

To begin to make sense of the transformation from volition to compulsion, it is necessary to move back into the realm of the careful analytic specification of institutional arrangements at the end of the eighteenth century. For the differences between voluntary and compulsory military service were not merely differences in principle. They were first and foremost an issue of the particular, concrete mechanisms employed by the state to induct persons from the wider, non-military society into the armed forces. The state confronted a choice between two fundamentally distinct ways to recruit prospective soldiers: either it could issue a voluntary appeal, drawing on a formally free labor market in soldiers; or it could issue a compulsory call to arms, relying on public authorities or their representatives to induct men into the military according to formally defined criteria, backed implicitly by the legitimate threat of force against those who do not comply.[6]

In voluntary induction, what is pivotal is that at one or both points in the recruitment process – either when the pool of those eligible for service is identified, or when some from that pool are designated to serve – the individual is able to exercise his volition.[7] For military service to be compulsory, public authorities must make persons members of the duty-eligible ranks irrespective of their wishes, AND those authorities must select such persons from the lists for active duty irrespective of their preferences to serve, all according to some formally designated criteria.[8]

The mechanism of induction, however, cannot be said to determine either how military service is offered or experienced. Unwilling and more especially reluctant service may of course be given when the state is seeking volunteers. Conversely, even when the state has the power to compel military service, that service may be offered not only willingly but zealously. As a rule, military service during the latter eighteenth and nineteenth century was extraordinarily harsh, placing the individual under often brutal discipline and subjecting him to privation and suffering – devastatingly threatening while in combat and unrelentingly tedious when waiting to engage the enemy. For many, military service was simply the more appealing of several unattractive options, and certainly for some, there was no reasonable alternative. The absence of a reasonable alternative or the low esteem in which service might be held, however, does not amount to an order from the state to serve in the armed forces. Such service even when compelled, on the other hand, may appear as something to be undertaken as a point of honor, or even something to be entered into with great excitement as a sign of one's patriotic commitment (Keegan, 1976, pp. 117–206; Redlich, 1964–1965, Vol. 2, pp. 191–230; Bertaud, 1985; Elting, 1988).

Two additional qualifications help to clarify the distinction between voluntary and compulsory induction. Neither categorical nor arbitrary exclusions from the service-eligible ranks undermine the voluntary character of recruitment in which choice is offered either to join the lists or to enter active service from the lists. Take for example the elite *Jäger* detachments formed during the Prussian war of liberation, open only to the educated and better off, or the citizen militias of France open only to those with sufficient property. Exclusions by social status or wealth may be formally prescribed, or they may simply operate *de facto*, as in those cases where the uniform and weapon needed to serve in the militia had to be provided by the prospective soldier. In all of these examples and their like, those excluded may be deprived of the opportunity to serve, but in no respect are they compelled to serve. Furthermore, actually performing the military service demanded by the state is not necessary for recruitment to be compulsory. If this were the case, draft resisters, evaders, and deserters would have to be seen as 'volunteers,' in the sense that they have elected not to serve. Here the decisive factor is provided by the state's command that an individual must serve, irrespective of his wishes, and that this command is backed by the threat of force in the absence of compliance. Even if they are not caught, evaders, resisters and deserters are all subject to punishment for their refusal to comply with the state's demand.[9]

When states began to define the pool of people who might be compelled to perform military service in terms of a socially expansive national citizenship around the turn of the eighteenth century, a notable transformation ensued. In a series of official acts, sweeping and novel service obligations of citizenship erupted to the surface and were rapidly formalized in state policy. Whether in the Revolutionary United States, when the militia, symbolic of citizenship and the protection of liberties, was itself liberated from British control in 1774; or in Revolutionary France, when the *gardes nationales* that had formed spontaneously in opposition to absolutism and privilege at the local level during the municipal revolutions of 1789 were formally recognized by the National Assembly as an institution 'of the nation'; or in Prussia, when Frederick William III formed the *Landwehr* as a force of citizens with whom to fight a war of liberation from France in 1813 – in every instance, extraordinary and unprecedented service obligations of national citizenship were first articulated in the citizen militia (Shy, 1990; Bertaud, 1988; Paret, 1992b; and Showalter, 1971. See also Delbrück, 1990[1920]; Corvisier, 1979; Corvisier et al., 1975).

From this initial institutional assertion of the obligations of national citizens, two matters of interest emerged. First, we see the crystalization of a striking new formula. Military service was a responsibility incurred solely because of one's membership in the national community of citizens. And precisely because of this duty owed, the state may legitimately compel military service from its citizens.[10] In this manner, state power to compel and citizen obligation to serve were forged into the two complementary halves of a single principle of citizen service, animating the very institutions in which the principle was embodied on the ground. Citizen service involved the military service of citizens, surely – but it was something more: it was service entered into and performed *as a citizen* (Paret, 1992b, c, 1993; Royster, 1979; Cress, 1982; Bertaud, 1982). Second, by distinguishing service as a citizen from the service of citizens, compulsory induction had the effect of elevating acts of obligation relative to acts of volition. Because state compulsion defined obligatory service as the exclusive preserve of national citizens, obligatory service was rendered simultaneously one of the clearest expressions of political commitment and participation as well as the surest defense of a free people. Moreover, state compulsion asked citizens to make the ultimate sacrifice willingly for their nation in the service of their state.[11] Stripped of any mercenary quality, service was made a duty to be embraced, and sacrifice was transformed not merely into a virtue but also a privilege (see Mosse, 1990; Bartov, 1996). As an expression of duty and sacrifice born solely because one was a national citizen, obligatory service supplanted the enthusiasm of nationals as the exemplary expression of the citizen who took up arms as a soldier.

The Revolutionary Birth of Citizen Conscription

While the citizen militia offered the institutional context in which the service obligations of nationals were initially articulated, the shift towards valorizing obligation itself depended upon the birth of an entirely new military institution: conscription based upon national citizenship. To understand the impact of citizen conscription, and to begin to explain its origins, me must first examine what about the organizational conditions of military service made this kind of compulsory service distinctive.

Around the turn of the nineteenth century, soldiers served the state in two basic types of military organizations. Military service might be in a part-time force, such as a militia, or in a full-time force, such as a standing army.[12] In part-time service, men are mobilized only to meet particular emergencies. Commanding officers may remain mobilized when there is no pressing need, but part-time soldiers return to their homes, families and livelihoods, awaiting the call to arms. Typically a few weeks a year, those performing part-time service are mustered to train and drill, in order to maintain a minimum of readiness in case of emergency. While demobilized, part-time soldiers are not subject to the command and discipline of military authorities; even when mobilized, their standard of discipline and expertise is generally lower than that of full-time soldiers, owing to the irregular and infrequent periods of training. While there is a tremendous range of variation in actual deployment of these forces, only in the most extraordinary circumstances are part-time soldiers asked to serve more than a few months continuously, and then, generally not very far from home, and almost never abroad.

Alternately, in full-time service, men are on active duty even in the absence of a particular emergency. Since they are mobilized for the period of their service, full-time soldiers are held in abeyance from civilian life and instead are governed by military command and law. Full-time soldiers are prevented in this sense from participating in the routines of civil society, most especially from earning a livelihood outside of the military itself. During the period of their sequester, full-time soldiers are put through repetitive drill and training in an effort to instill discipline and expertise in battlefield weapons and tactics. It is they who are expected to shoulder the burden of interstate war, and may as a consequence expect to serve in long campaigns and far away from home.[13]

Taken together, the distinctions between mechanisms of induction and conditions of service permit the specification of four ideal-typical modes of recruitment. Each combination of induction mechanism and conditions of service constitutes a distinct organizational structure of recruiting, expressed in Fig. 1.[14]

		Mechanism of Induction	
		Voluntary	Compulsory
Conditions of Military Service	Full-time	Regular (1)	Conscription (4)
	Part-time	Militia (2)	Militia Draft (3)

Fig. 1. Modes of Recruitment.

Moving counter-clockwise from the upper-left, the four modes of recruitment are:

(1) full-time, voluntary or 'regular' recruitment;
(2) part-time, voluntary or 'militia' recruitment;
(3) part-time, compulsory or recruiting through a 'militia draft'; and
(4) full-time, compulsory recruitment or 'conscription.'

These names are not random, but instead correspond to more generic labels sometimes given particular military forces raised in each of these ways.

The critical point of this figure and the set of distinctions it represents, of course, is that it is possible to specify with some degree of firmness the differences among modes of recruitment, and especially among different types of compulsory service. It would seem quite easy to distinguish between conscription and recruitment as a militiaman. After all, where conscription is full-time and compulsory, militia recruitment is part-time and voluntary. Yet even here there is potentially room for confusion, and I must be explicit. As I have underscored, even among those recruited as volunteers, compulsory elements may persist – whether in the form of obligatory enrollment or engagement from the rolls. Because these are not *combined* in the militia, however, recruitment is not compulsory. A similar point may be made about regular recruitment. Conscription may be distinguished from regular recruitment because it relies on state compulsion, but that does not mean coercion is never applied in raising forces through an appeal to volunteers. To suggest so would be ludicrous. What distinguishes conscription from regular recruitment is that while soldiers raised by both means serve on a full-time basis, only in the case of conscription is there a state-mandated system of compulsion in place, rendering all other forms of forced service just that, coercive. In turn, the quality conscription shares with regular recruitment – full-time service – is precisely what distinguishes it from militia recruitment. Militia drafts share with conscription their formally compulsory quality, but they must be seen as distinct since they raise soldiers only for part-time service. Conscription is properly reserved for that particular case of compulsory recruitment into full-time service.

With this set of distinctions in place, both the institutional logic and historical process through which the transformation of the citizen-soldier unfolded may finally be seen. The sea change in compulsory induction emerged as national citizenship became the sole and sufficient basis for exacting obligatory service around the turn of the nineteenth century. Militia forces played a central role in this transformation, not only as specific sites at which citizen obligations of military service were articulated in distinctly national terms, but also as the primary institutional vehicles by which the social composition of the national citizenry initially broadened. As entry into the citizen militia was opened to persons both up and down the class scale, including those of the higher orders who under the regime of corporative citizenship were subject only to demands against the privileged as well as those of the lower orders who had formerly been subject only to the demands registered against the dependent classes, national citizenship became more socially inclusive. What is striking, however, is that only the *voluntary citizen militias* – built around the obligation of all citizens to enroll on lists of those who may be called, but whose operational companies were almost uniformly formed of volunteers from the lists – played this critical, dual role. We see this clearly in the revolutionary United States, with its decayed colonial compulsory militia and the revivified voluntary militia which formed the backbone of early armed resistance. We see it again in France during the first four years of the Revolution, with the suppression of the *milices bourgeoises*, a voluntary civic militia, as well as the *troupes provinciales*, a compulsory militia of the lower agrarian and artisanal classes, both of the old regime, and the spontaneous eruption and efflorescence of the *gardes nationales*. And we see it in Prussia during the war of liberation, with the emergence of the *Landwehr*, where in the prior century the compulsory militia had been suppressed in favor of the canton-system of corporative conscription. In each case, we observe an extraordinary outpouring of voluntary militiamen in cities, towns and villages, mobilized as members of a single political community sharing one fate. And we see how the opening of the voluntary citizen militias helped bring about a progressive redefinition of that community in socially expansive terms (Kestnbaum, 2000; Shy, 1990; Bertaud, 1988, 1991; Hunt, 1976; Clifford, 1990; Hunt, 1976; Paret, 1992b, c; Showalter, 1971).

State compulsion based on national citizenship emerged most urgently and entered social life most forcefully around the turn of the nineteenth century not in the form of the militia draft, but rather in the birth of citizen conscription.

First to formulate a policy of conscription based on national citizenship was the newly United States, when in 1778 the Continental Congress directed the states to draft American citizens into the Continental Army in the midst of a crisis of enthusiasm not for self-rule, but for continued armed struggle to achieve that self-rule. Fifteen years later in August of 1793, the Montagnard Jacobin dictatorship introduced the *levée en masse*, in principle drafting all French citizens to play whatever role they might in a war to defend the Revolution against enemies both from within and without. At the conclusion of its own war of liberation more than twenty years later, Prussia then instituted the Boyen Law of 1814, exacting the military service owed by national citizens to their state in the form of a conscript army. Not again for nearly fifty years did another European or North American state impose conscription on its citizenry defined in national terms.

This pattern of institutional innovation leads to one essential question. How can we explain the origins of citizen conscription in France, Prussia and the United States? How was it that compulsory military service in the standing army ever became attached to national citizenship in the first place? The answer to these questions lies in a particular and unprecedented historical conjuncture, a conjuncture defined by the mobilization of the previously excluded popular classes into national politics during an ongoing war in which the future of the state, and the independence of its people, were both at stake.

First in the newly United States, when rebellion turned into a war to secure independence; then in Revolutionary France, facing invasion and counter-revolutionary uprisings at home; and then in Prussia, as part of the struggle to be freed from the grip of Napoleon's Empire, popular political mobilization within national states became intimately intertwined with inter-state war. Mobilization of the previously excluded popular classes into national politics became an integral part of armed struggle to seize or hold state power. Facing extensive political mobilization and inter-state war together, political and military elites were confronted by a new set of urgent imperatives: build a viable regime around the previously excluded popular classes, while also organizing and deploying the force of arms in an effort to insure the future of that regime. Under these conditions, and facing this imperative, coalitions of reformers regardless of their constitutional orientation determined that the conscription of national citizens was a *politically desirable* response to the conjoint military and political challenges they faced. By incorporating the wide swath of 'the people' as citizens, conscription offered a way to build popular support for the regime in power and to gain a measure of central direction over those newly mobilized into politics. Bringing the people into the regime as citizens by force of state policy, binding them into a political community and to the state through obligation – *that* was the key to consolidating a regime suddenly dependent on popular mobilization, strengthening the hold of elites over state power, and building the military means necessary to contend with the crises they faced.

We can see how both reformers and the representatives of those newly mobilized into politics understood citizen conscription to help consolidate a politically mass-mobilizing regime in three distinct ways, each corresponding to a different sense in which the policy incorporated the people as citizens: in the first, by rendering all citizens formally equal; in the second, by integrating them and their state into a single polity; and in the third, by politicizing them, their relations to one another and to the state. The key to all three was the manner in which citizen conscription, as a way of redefining the relationship between the military and society, in turn would reshape relations between the state and society on the one hand and between the state and its armed forces on the other.

By making military service contingent on national citizenship, national conscription would level social differences in the political as well as military spheres. For the masses mobilized into politics, this was a powerful formulation. Even the lowliest of those previously excluded from politics now had an unimpeachable claim to be included as an equal citizen solely by virtue of the military service he performed.[15] Conversely, the burden of that service would no longer be borne solely by those who had been excluded from regular participation in politics, but instead in principle would be borne by all (Levi, 1997, pp. 80–106; Janowitz, 1975, pp. 70–88). And what is more, the policy itself institutionalized national citizenship in formally egalitarian and socially inclusive terms and made that very status more politically salient. It made formally equal national citizenship a social fact, and gave the principle of formal political inclusion on an egalitarian basis a tangible expression, embodied in law and enforced by public authorities.[16]

That the popular classes mobilized into politics desired formal equality was crucial to reform coalitions in national assemblies and councils of state. It meant that national conscription could comprise a means to secure the support of the people behind the regime in power and help form them into a broader ruling coalition under the stewardship of reformers (Paret, 1992b, p. 64ff; Mosse, 1990, pp. 3, 6–11, 15–21, 32–33; Bartov, 1996, p. 35ff). It also provided the means to undercut attempts of some elite groups to delegate martial participation to others, thereby broadening the web of service to include more than the lower strata who had formerly made up the vast bulk of the rank and file of the standing army. Moreover, since all were formally equal in the eyes of the state, national conscription would help to undercut intermediate institutions, remnants of privilege and corporate law, between the state and its citizens – institutions that might constrain the action of the regime in power or alternately form the basis around which opposition or resistance might organize (see de Tocqueville, 1955; Weber, 1978, Vol. 2, pp. 983–987).

Second, national conscription would break down the insulation of the line army from society and instead bring the army closer to the people. Building an army of citizens, the line army would increasingly appear to soldiers and civilians alike as an integral part of the nation, not as an institution outside of or alien to the nation. There would be less reason to fear that it might be used as a repressive tool against the people. At the same time, the previously excluded popular classes would acquire a very real presence within the state. Whichever came first – whether army or people were to be made by the other – the army would be the people's army.

This proprietary and constitutive sense of a citizen's army held out a definite appeal to reforming elites as well. By encouraging the people to identify with the state, citizen service would make it easier for the state to mobilize and retain the support of the people. Moreover, this identification with the state would help undercut insurrectionary threats from the rank and file of the armed forces. Soldiers would identify their new-found place in politics with the mass mobilizing regime that had made it possible. Precisely because their stake in the new regime *as citizens* was the result of the actions of the regime in power, they would share an interest *as soldiers* in sustaining that regime.[17]

Third, by drafting men as citizens to defend the nation, conscription would politicize service and the struggle underway. From the perspective of the people, that military service was undertaken as a formal obligation of citizenship invested such service with an essentially political significance.[18] It helped forge in each soldier as well as each potential soldier a definite stake as a citizen in the regime demanding his participation, as well as in the struggle in which he was a participant. Unlike a mere oath, the administrative and military reality of service amounted to a moment of political conversion, in which the individual publicly declared and visibly acted upon his political identification with the state as a citizen. The experience and even the example of compulsory citizen-service, in turn, constituted a sort of political education, in which the demands of citizenship were made clear, participation in public terms was made possible and rendered meaningful, and the unity of the people as a nation of citizens was dramatized publicly. As a consequence, answering the call to give one's life if necessary was transformed into *the* constitutive political act. It offered to all citizens the foremost opportunity to participate as equals in a national endeavor of the utmost importance and urgency, both morally and politically.

The state, in turn, could draw upon the express politicization of its citizen-soldiers, and their investment in the regime occasioned by the state's military demands. Citizen conscription not only made it possible to channel political mobilization into military affairs, it transformed military mobilization itself into a massive political mobilization on behalf of the regime in power. Moreover, by extending the net of military service to draw in all forms of armed citizen involvement in public life, conscription would politically encapsulate 'independent' armed forces and help reassert the state's monopoly over the use of force.[19]

What conscription based on national citizenship offered reformers was political stability – a way to attach the people and their representatives to the regime in power, and then to foster and channel the mobilization of the popular classes. What it offered the masses was a newly authorized place in the regime as citizens: political recognition if not democracy, a way to participate in at least one of the state's chief endeavors, and a way – perhaps only symbolically – to appropriate the state as their own. In any particular historical crystallization, elements of popular participation or state control might receive priority in the plans and aspirations of reformers and popular groups, just as these groups might place one or another sense of incorporation above the remainder. In all cases, however, it was the way in which conscription incorporated the people as national citizens that held out its promise as a tool of war.

Conscription and National Service

As conscription based on national citizenship emerged around the end of the eighteenth century in the newly United States, revolutionary France and reforming Prussia, the principle of citizen service which it realized in socially and institutionally consequential terms acquired a newfound salience. Not simply the exemplary manner in which citizen-soldiers served, the particular relationship created by conscription was expressed in a new idiom conscription itself helped to foster: the idiom of national service.

That conscription based on national citizenship from its very birth may be identified with national service is perhaps not surprising. In many respects, national service inheres in the very formulation of the distinctive claim of the state against its citizenry, and the conditions under which citizens responded to that claim. Under corporative systems of compulsion, discrete corporate groups not any one of their members owed a military obligation to the state. Compulsory service based on national citizenship, on the other hand, is rooted in the premise that the individual owed military service, for no reason other than the fact that he was a member of the political community of nationals from whom the ultimate authority of the state itself derived (see de Cardenal, 1912; Godechot, 1985, pp. 499–503, 601–603). What makes such conscription constitutive of national service, then, is that it comprises not only service owed *by* the entire social extent of the national citizenry but also service performed *as* a member of the nation *on behalf of* the community of fellow citizens.

Just because every citizen owed an obligation to serve in the armed forces, however, did not mean that all national citizens were equally subject to conscription in fact, and even less, that the burden of military service itself was to fall equally across the new-born nation. National citizenship was egalitarian not in terms of the particular allocation of political rights or duties to the many members of the political community, but rather in terms of the juridical entity of individual membership itself (Walzer, 1970, pp. 77–98, 105–111, 211–217, 226–228; Rosanvallon, 1992, pp. 45–101). That is to say, formal equality before the law existed in perfect harmony with differential powers and responsibilities under that law. This, in turn, was entirely consistent with the understanding, dominant amongst all but the most radical revolutionaries, that the burden of military service was not to fall upon all. Rather, it was to be borne by some on behalf of the rest, based largely on the differential powers and responsibilities accruing to groups of national citizens.

To understand how citizen conscription provided the framework within which compulsory service was simultaneously national in extent and content, but nonetheless unequal, it is necessary to probe further two aspects of its development: the creation of openings in the mechanism of compulsory induction, and the definition of portions of the national citizenry as exempt altogether from military service obligations. The prerequisite for both lay in the view, conventionally held and embedded in law at the end of the eighteenth century in polities from the most reactionary and monarchical to the most revolutionary and republican, that individual obligation to serve did not simply translate into the power of the state to compel service from particular individuals. That is, the obligation of national citizens did not amount to personal service to the state.

From its birth, citizen conscription was accompanied by a variety of ways for the prospective soldier to avoid the ranks with impunity by paying a fee in lieu of military service. This practice took several discrete forms, including commutation, substitution or replacement, and the paying of non-service fines. Each was a legally regulated form of intervention in the compulsory selection process. Commutation was the practice of paying a fee to have one's name removed from the list of the duty-eligible, avoiding the risk of selection altogether. Since payment was generally made before the state had selected men to serve, the fee was often a small fraction of that paid by a man seeking a replacement to serve in his stead. Substitution typically involved paying an exorbitant fee to another man to replace the selected individual in the armed forces, and was sometimes accompanied by a fine paid to the state for the privilege of hiring a replacement. Having secured a substitute on the private market, however, generally entitled the selected man to be free of the obligation of service for the duration of the substitute's stay, or for a specified period as long as the substitute served at least a predefined minimum number of months or years. In some cases, all that was required to avoid induction into the armed forces was that men selected who did not wish to serve simply paid a fine directly to the local authorities. In this instance, the fines constituted a type of non-service impost, or what may be considered a 'patriotic tax.'

Substitution, commutation and fines for avoiding service are all ways of introducing the market in a qualified way back into the de-commodified process of compulsory selection. This can be seen clearly since each proposes to establish a price for non-service, and then offers the opportunity of a reprieve to all who can afford to buy one. Furthermore, exacting fines for non-service and permitting substitution frequently gave rise to secondary insurance arrangements. Individuals paid a fee to private associations or publicly regulated corporations which in whole or in part was returned to them if no member was selected; but in the case that a member was selected, the sum of the individual fees went toward paying the fines or acquiring the replacement for the selected member of the association. Replacement has the additional distinction of giving rise to markets in soldiers willing to fight as substitutes at a substantial premium over the bounty they may be offered to serve as a volunteer. Unlike refractory conduct, which may lead to the avoidance of service but does not absolve the individual of the obligation to serve, fines, substitution and commutation constitute an alloying of a pure compulsory mechanism of recruitment, just because they create a voluntary way for those who can afford it to avoid personal service.[20]

Modifying the mechanism of compulsory induction through commutation or substitution, however, stands in marked contrast to the other primary way in which the risk of conscription was increased for some, and diminished for others: the systematic and legally regulated circumscribing of the pool of national citizens themselves. We can see this in several senses. Designation by estate of that portion of the male population subject to compulsion, typical of corporative and capacitarian citizenship, was replaced almost uniformly under regimes of national citizenship with designation by age, and secondarily by marital status. As a consequence, rather than those drafted coming from particular corporate groups, they were at first cut limited to the young and often unmarried men from a variety of social strata.[21]

Systems of national service also generally provided for exemption from or deferment of service for whole categories of citizens of appropriate age who were otherwise fit to serve. These exemptions in the latter eighteenth century were typically linked to property ownership, or what became its proxy, the paying of taxes; and although based no longer on birth, they nonetheless replicated the privileges of the 'higher orders' under corporative regimes. Increasingly through the late eighteenth and nineteenth century, however, exemptions were formally extended on the basis of education and occupation, enlarging that proportion acquired by the urban and bourgeois population, and especially shielding those who might elect to enter a career as a state official (see Craig, 1955; Bertaud, 1982, 1988; Sales de Bohigas, 1968a).

Commutation, substitution, categorical exemptions and deferments undercut the egalitarian nature of citizen conscription – but they did not make it any less national. Only when national citizenship was defined in the broadest possible social terms; the pool of prospective soldiers was reduced by exemptions for prior military or current alternative state service alone; and the compulsory selection mechanism allowed for neither commutation nor substitution, did national service become universal in extent and formally democratic in character. Once fraud and corruption were also rooted out of the process, only then were national citizens equally subject to compulsory service, irrespective of distinctions in birth, wealth, ethnicity, language and so on.[22] Seen from the perspective of the state, the democratization of citizen conscription had a further implication. By offering national citizens no legitimate way of avoiding military or alternative service, the state acquired the power to compel personal service from designated individuals that it had been denied at the birth of citizen conscription. Democratic citizen conscription, however, is still quite a ways from universal service proper. Only when it is the case that not merely all are subject to serve, but all must serve in some capacity, may service national both in extent and content be said to constitute universal service.[23]

CONSCRIPTION AND THE NATION IN ARMS

More than half a century before policies of universal military service in the standing army were first implemented, the introduction of the wide swath of 'the people' as citizens into war between states precipitated a major upheavel in the nature of war-making itself. In the words of Peter Paret, what we see most especially in Europe is nothing less than a "revolution in war at the end of the eighteenth century," defined by the way in which "the assumptions and practices of the ancien régime [were replaced] with new methods of raising and organizing armed forces and of employing them in ways that could add tremendous power to the policies of state."[24] Not only historians such as Michael

Howard (1976a), Jeremy Black (1991, 1994, 1995), and Omer Bartov (1994, 1996), but political scientists such as Barry Posen (1992) and Deborah Avant (2000), as well as contemporary observers such as Clausewitz (1976, pp. 587–594, 1992) echo the sentiment: what we observe is a dramatic break from the past, one that ultimately unleashed awesome and even terrible military power, born of the new role given to national citizenries in war. And at the very heart of this military revolution lay the institution of conscription itself.

The revolution in war at the end of the eighteenth century can be understood most clearly if we examine it in four discrete senses. In the first, the extensive and repeated use of conscription by states at war made possible the formation of a new type of military organization: the citizen or mass army.[25] These armies were perhaps somewhat larger than the forces assembled by corporative conscription or appeals to volunteers at the end of the century. More importantly, however, they were comprised of national citizens, who generally acknowledged that as soon as their period of service ended, they would resume the more peaceful pursuits of citizens. Coerced surely at times, reluctant if not resistant to serve certainly, this was the nation in arms, animated by that very sense of membership in a common political community that conscript service itself helped to foster.[26]

Second, the mass army became the center piece of a new mode of warfare. By tying the state powerfully to the armed forces and to society in general, conscription laid the groundwork for a new form of state-led military mass-mobilization. Expressed of course in extensive conscription used to build the mass army, mass mobilization extended from manpower to material resources to moral as well as political support for ongoing conflicts. Military mass mobilization as well as the endurance of widespread privation, suffering and sacrifice were accomplished not by means of state compulsion alone, of course – although these were indeed crucial, as can be seen in the legitimizing of requisitions, forced loans and ultimately compulsory labor during war. Rather, state compulsion was used in conjunction with appeals to the people as members of a national community, appeals whose resonance only increased in an environment of military emergency in which the state was explicitly and extensively making the service obligations of citizens and the duties to nation clear through its own policies.

Third, military mass mobilization had the further effect of producing an almost complete nationalization of war between states. Not only did the state direct its compulsory efforts and popular appeals explicitly at members of the national community; but increasingly as it did so, it began systematically to exclude non-nationals. Initially, the institution of the foreign regiment collapsed, as fears over their political reliability mounted in the context of coalition warfare against Napoleon (Scott, 1984, 1986). Accompanying this transition was a somewhat more protracted one, in which the trade in foreign mercenaries that had sustained the most powerful armies of the eighteenth century also collapsed, and employing such mercenaries became increasingly intolerable (Thomson, 1994; Avant, 2000). Ultimately, this was expressed in the desire to limit dependence upon foreign trade and production, including not only foodstuffs but also materièl deemed essential. In conjunction with citizen conscription, the exclusion of foreign soldiers and later even foreign suppliers and producers meant the almost unrivaled dominance of the national idiom in interstate war.

Fourth, the effect of the foregoing was to expand the scale and intensity of war-making. War of this type was quite literally more encompassing in social and political terms, mobilizing more people in more ways as part of the war effort than previous forms of war had been on either side of the Atlantic. But more than that, suddenly political goals of unprecedented magnitude were within its reach, and powerful sentiments including nationalism animated their pursuit. This form of war, ultimately, broke free of many shackles that had bound conflicts under the old regime, unleashing the power of the people into conflicts between states.

As was the case with the birth of citizen conscription that comprised its core, we may explain the revolution in war at the end of the eighteenth century primarily in political terms. Clausewitz was perhaps the first to articulate the close connection between the socio-political circumstances of revolutionary Europe and the dramatic change in war-making he observed (Clausewitz, 1976, pp. 587–594; see also Paret, 1992e, pp. 4, 78 and *passim*). Ultimately, it was the dynamic of popular political uprisings and foreign responses to those uprisings that led to the revolution in war. When the popular classes were mobilized as citizens into national politics, suddenly a whole host of new resources – from political support to material assistance to the very lives of the people themselves – were within reach of the regime in power. Spurred by a credible threat to the future of the state and the independence of its people, conscription provided the instrument to raise the nation in arms and to martial the vast, previously unavailable energies of that new-born nation into war that would now be waged in a novel and extraordinary way.[27]

Once the revolutionary period had drawn to an end, however, the close connection between citizen conscription on the one hand, and the mass army as well as military mass-mobilization on the other, was substantially loosened. We need only look at the armed forces of the period of restoration after the French Revolution, even those of France and Prussia, to see how this was so. In both these cases citizen conscription was employed, but the service of extraordinarily large numbers of citizens who would return to civilian life after a brief period in arms was replaced by a much smaller contingent of men whose protracted service transformed them into career soldiers. This pattern continues more or less to the present, in which conscription is used to form something other than massed forces and as part of mobilizations whose scale and social extent are comparatively limited (Haltiner, 1998; Burk, 1992; Boëne & Martin, 1991). Furthermore, the converse has held true since at least the beginning of the twentieth century. In that instance, states form mass armies by means other than conscription. One need only examine the great outpouring of volunteers in Britain during the first months of World War I to see how this was achieved. The loosening of the link between conscription and mass mobilization underscores both the unusual nature of the period around the turn of the nineteenth century, as well as the contingent quality of the ties among institutions it helped forge (cf. Avant, 2000).

Although the complex of relationships that gave rise to the citizen-soldier, national service and the mass army may have been peculiar to single historical moment, citizen conscription's legacy has been durable and far-reaching. Clearest, of course, is that as the institutional foundation of mass war, conscription lives on even where it is no longer practiced – precisely because the experience and memory of this kind of war persist long after the guns have gone quiet, and families have received what consolation they may (Mosse, 1990; Winter, 1995; and Horne, 1997). Nearly as clear is the way in which conscription expressed and helped spur the reorientation of politics around citizenries defined in national and socially expansive terms (E. Weber, 1976; Mosse, 1990; Brubaker, 1992; Paret, 1992e; Bartov, 1994, 1996). Thus, just as conscription created the nation in arms, so too it fostered the political community of citizens understanding themselves to be one nation. Conscription's powerful duality, at once military and political, forms its third legacy. As popular politics were brought squarely into military affairs, military considerations loomed large in the public life of regular people. Suddenly, in Clausewitz's memorable phrase, "war became the business of the people" (1976, p. 592) – their support essential, its impact inescapable. As conscription fused the political and the military in the lives of national citizens, so too did it intertwine the lives of those same citizens more tightly with their state, forming the institution's fourth legacy. In unprecedented terms, the conscription of national citizens brought the state into the daily lives of its people, and drew the people at-large directly into the operation of the state (see Mann, 1986, 1993). Together, these four legacies live on into the twenty-first century, marking nearly every state in the states system today, more than two hundred years after the birth of citizen conscription.

NOTES

1. This should not be confused with the substantially different claim that all citizens must be soldiers, something that will be addressed explicitly with respect to national and universal service.

2. This formulation of course is derived from and inspired by Max Weber (1978, Vol. 1, pp. 50–56). However, I have gone out of my way to distinguish one of the organizational structures of which the state is typically said to consist – the armed forces – and to hold it in particular tension with the remainder of the state apparatus and the state elites whose political power that military force guarantees. On the specification of the trinity of state-army-society and its role in analysis of the military as a political institution, see Clausewitz (1976[1830]); Delbrück (1990[1920]); and Mann (1993).

3. For an exemplary specification of membership issues, see Walzer (1970, 1988, pp. 29–34, 40–51). On citizenship as an historically created categorical status, linked to military service, see Marshall (1963); Brubaker (1992, pp. 21–29); Rosanvallon (1992, pp. 41–180); and Tilly (1995).

4. It is important to note, however, that the major exceptions to this are religious and ethno-cultural groupings distinct from and not congruent with citizenship per se.

5. Tocqueville (1966, 1969) offers the seminal formulation and analysis of this general transition toward what he calls democratic society, understood not in terms of suffrage and representative assemblies but in terms of formal and conventionally embraced equality of conditions. On the prolonged character of this transformation – and the persistence of corporative social arrangements well after the invention of the national citizen – see Mayer (1981).

6. While there is a rich and extensive literature on compulsory as opposed to voluntary recruitment that includes both examinations of military manpower policies and historical studies of military institutions, it is among the latter that the most careful specification of the various mechanisms of induction may be found. This and the next several paragraphs draw heavily on a few exemplary works of the latter variety, the bulk of which are extensive studies of French Revolutionary recruitment and reforms of the line army, and the last an extremely valuable examination of the highly contested reform of the English militia through the same period: de Cardenal (1911, 1912); Vallée (1937); Bergès (1987); Forrest (1989); and Western (1965). On the general distinction between compulsory and voluntary recruitment, see Delbrück (1990[1920], pp. 223–319, 387–449), Corvisier (1979, pp. 21–60, 131–136, 142), Corvisier et al. (1975), Godechot (1985, pp. 499–503, 601–603) and Rothenberg (1978, pp. 98–102, 169–197). On compulsory as opposed to voluntary recruitment to the line army, see Redlich (1964–1965, Vol. 2, pp. 170–190) and Paret (1992a, b). On compulsory as opposed to voluntary recruitment to the militia, see especially Morton (1958) and Hennett (1884).

7. That is to say, a soldier is a volunteer under any of three different conditions: first, if he chooses to put himself on a list of those to serve, even though he may be compelled to enter active duty thereafter; second, if he is placed on a roster of prospective soldiers irrespective of his choice, but still retains the power to choose whether and when to go into active duty; or third, if he chooses both to put himself on the lists and actually to enter active service.

8. Impressment occupies a peculiar position in this dichotomy. As a practice, it resembles compulsory induction insofar as it relies on compulsion to induce men to

serve. It is different, however, in two fundamental ways. First, some non-trivial number of those conscripted by the state in fact serve willingly; or, they volunteer when faced with the prospect of being compelled to serve, often in order to take advantage of available bounties or to receive preferential conditions of service. All those impressed, however, were by definition inducted against their will. More importantly, however, impressment lacks the formal designation of membership in a class and contingent by a public authority that marks compulsory induction. Instead, coercion is the particularistic response of recruiting officers to a situation in which monetary inducements as well as deception or fraud have failed to produce voluntary enlistment. If the inducements or deception had worked, recruiting officers would not have resorted to force, and there would be no grounds on which to suggest a resemblance between impressment and compulsory induction. Historically, impressment grew up alongside voluntary recruitment, and may best be understood as a by-product of the conditions and demands placed upon recruiting officers by voluntary induction, forming what Redlich has called 'strong-arm methods of recruiting' as distinct from conscription (Redlich, 1964–1965, Vol. 2, pp. 173–181). On the distinction between compulsory selection and impressment in the English experience, see especially Western (1965, pp. 443–444).

9. On the various forms of refractory conduct and its prosecution by the state under the regime of conscription, see especially Forrest (1989); Bergès (1987); Arnold (1966); Woloch (1986, 1994, pp. 380–426); Van Holde (1993); and Grab (1995). Of the extensive monographic and regional literature on refractory conduct and insubmission, see especially Cardenal (1911); Sangier (1965); Legrand (1957); Manry (1958); Vidalenc (1959, 1975); Waquet (1968, 1974); Castel (1970); Chatelain (1972); Suratteau (1974); Boudard, (1985); and Hudemann-Simon (1987).

10. Put another way, the principle of citizen service involves a radical de-commodification of military service itself. Rather than organizing a market in military labor through which the state then hires soldiers as volunteers, citizen service supplants that market with a mechanism of compulsion. In this environment, military service may be freely offered and surely receives compensation. But it is not remuneration per se that elicits service; rather, it is the state's compulsory call to arms, deriving from the obligation of citizens to serve.

11. In this, the principle of citizen service mirrors the particular construction of the enlightenment philosophy of right, running from Rousseau through Kant, built on the notion that the individual wills to do precisely what it is that he ought to do (Cassirer, 1945, 1954).

12. This distinction between the 'kinds of service performed' cuts across a more commonly made distinction based on the duration of service commitment, and they should not be confused. Part-time service may entail a commitment to muster in emergencies across a span of forty years or more, but for any given muster it does not require more than a few months of service, nor in repeat calls would it necessarily involve the same men serving back to back periods of a month or two. On the other hand, men serving on a full-time basis could run the gamut, from a ten month recruit who declines to re-enlist, to a career soldier having put in many years under the colors. On the utility of distinguishing between long-service and short-service troops in political analysis, see for example Chorley (1943, Ch. 10–12).

13. In addition to Delbrück (1990[1920]) and Corvisier (1979), see Redlich (1964–1965, Vol. 2) for an extended examination of the transition from part-time to

full-time forces, and the role often relegated to part-time forces after this transition in Continental Europe. On part-time forces in differing socio-political and military contexts, see especially: Western (1965); Hennet (1884); Corvisier (1985b); Chagniot (1985); Showalter (1971); Morton (1958); Gross (1976); and Shy (1990). In contrast to the Continental, especially Central European view of the military potential of part-time forces, see also Higginbotham (1971), Kohn (1975) and especially Millet (1991) on the United States.

14. Compare to Cohen (1985, pp. 22–24, 42–59), whose bases for distinction, like so many in the field of comparative recruitment institutions, follow along only grossly similar lines.

15. On the power of the military service of citizens to establish a claim to equality or equal membership, see: Weber (1981, pp. 324–337); Hintze (1975b, pp. 184, 187–188; 206–208, 211); Paret (1992b, pp. 64–65, 73); Foner (1988, p. 9ff); Berlin et al. (1992: 193–196); Janowitz (1975); and Segal (1989, pp. 9–12). See also Peled (1994), on the analogous logic of appealing to ethnic youths on the basis of the 'benefits' that could be acquired by performing compulsory service in contract relationships within multi-ethnic states which lack strictly unitary national citizenship. A further line of support for this account comes from arguments that citizenship itself was consolidated or expanded as a way to encourage more to serve. On this perspective, see: Chorley (1943, pp. 168–169); Howard (1976b, pp. 217–218); and Tilly (1995).

16. See especially Mosse (1990, pp. 17–19, 22–25). De Tocqueville (1966, 1969) provides the seminal and eloquent argument that equality, regardless of whether it is equality in liberty or in subjection, offered its own distinct and irrepressible appeal, spurring attempts to acquire and consolidate the conditions of equality – especially among those who had tasted it in some measure. On the ways in which the categories or statuses of citizen and state are institutionalized by state policies such as citizen conscription, see Brubaker (1996, Ch. 1).

17. On the gap between the armed forces and society and bringing the army closer to the people, see: von der Goltz (1887, Ch. 1); Chorley (1943, pp. 153–187); Challener (1955, pp. 3–9); Janowitz (1960, 1971); and Huntington (1957, pp. 37–39 and *passim*). This particular line of reasoning concerning the reciprocal nature of identification when armies are made of citizens through conscription animates Bartov (1991, 1994, 1996). On the converse of this account, stressing the gap between army and society when the army is recruited by other means and becomes therefore institutionally insulated, in addition to the sources cited above, see: Tocqueville (1966, 1969, pp. 651–653); Segal (1989); and Moskos and Wood (1988).

18. See Weber (1978, Vol. 1, pp. 50–56), on compulsory association as constitutive of the state and territorially defined political organization generally. On commodification of service and its rejection, see Redlich (1964–1965, Vol. 2, pp. 77–112); Kiernan (1967); and Scott (1984).

19. The politicization produced by incorporation as a citizen is treated at length primarily in two discrete contexts, each of which forms its own distinct thread of scholarship and argument. With respect to the ways in which service as a citizen makes soldiers see themselves as expressly political actors, and conversely the ways in which states are able to draw upon that self-identification for military purposes, see: Shy (1973, pp. 146–153); Royster (1979, pp. 25–53, 1986); Hunt (1976); Bartov (1994); Mosse (1990); Enloe (1980, pp. 51–54); and Posen (1992). This perspective also finds its adherents in a much older line of argumentation, in which citizen service provides the

institutional means by which individual zeal and commitment to the state in war is cemented and thus can be drawn upon by the state.(see: Clausewitz, 1976, pp. 591–594; Hintze, 1975b, pp. 202–213; Millis, 1956, pp. 23–28; Janowitz, 1960, 1971; Segal, 1989, pp. 1–12, 17–27; Paret, 1992c, d; Lynn, 1996; Bartov, 1996).

These politicizing effects of national conscription as a mode of recruitment must be distinguished, however, from attempts by the state to 'politically educate' the rank and file through propaganda, oration, sermonizing, and so on. Nearly all revolutionary military forces have been subject to more or less explicit attempts to indoctrinate the line army in order to insure its political reliability. While quite different in form and execution, these political education efforts are entirely compatible with – but not necessarily dependent upon – reforms in the manner of recruitment undertaken with an eye toward the political character of the line army. What political education studies underscore, however, is the pressing nature of elite concerns over the political stand of the army once formed, and the willingness of political and military elites to undertake extensive efforts to shape the political views of soldiers with the express intent of making the army an institution more serviceable to the regime in power. (Bertaud, 1988, pp. 133–156, 191–230; Lynn, 1996, pp. 119–162; Charnay, 1964; and Chorley, 1943).

20. On the operation of substitution, commutation and fines for service avoidance, (see: Western, 1965; Schnapper, 1968; Sales de Bohigas, 1968a,b; Bertaud, 1982; Forrest, 1989; Levi, 1997; Murdock, 1967, 1971; and Geary, 1991). On the disappearance of these "alloying mechanisms," (see: Choisel, 1981; Levi, 1997). The regional, more historically circumscribed and particularistic literature on these questions is quite extensive, and several elements repay investigation, including: Vallée (1937, 1926); Cardenal (1911); Desert (1965); Maureau (1957); Alexander (1945a, b, 1947); Murdock (1967, 1971); Geary (1991); and Kestnbaum (2000).

21. Moreover, levying an army even for protracted and large scale war rarely could be said to require, and never to have set out to achieve, the mobilization of all men even of any one broadly defined age group in the eighteenth and early nineteenth centuries. The economic and administrative dislocations and disruptions engendered by such a mobilization – were it possible or desirable otherwise – were prohibitive. As a result, selection from amongst the young is always implied in even the most ambitious and inclusive systems of compulsory service.

22. This complex process of the democratization of citizen conscription has been eloquently and powerfully examined in Levi (1997).

23. On the creation of universal systems of compulsory service, in addition to Levi (1997), see: Maude (1910–1911); de Cardenal (1912); and Choisel (1981).

24. See Paret (1986, 1992e, pp. 3–4, 16–17, 26–27, 32–38, 77–80, 136 and 151); quotation to Paret (1992e, p. 3).

25. We must be careful, however, when we sketch out the relationship between citizen conscription and the mass army. There is a strong affinity between the two, but not a one to one identity.

26. On the ways in which conscription helped foster a distinct understanding of nationhood as well as membership in a particular national community, see especially: E. Weber (1976); Mosse (1990); Brubaker (1992); Paret (1992b, c, 1993); and Bartov (1994, 1996).

27. Skocpol (1994) offers perhaps the clearest and most powerful formulation of the political dynamics of mass military mobilization in the midst of revolutionary war, although she pays little attention to citizen conscription per se; cf. Posen (1992).

ACKNOWLEDGMENTS

I would like to thank Cynthia R. Cook, Steve Van Holde and the two anonymous reviewers for Comparative Social Research for their insightful and constructive comments on this article during its preparation. For their sharp questions and unceasing willingness to challenge not only their own preconceptions but also my arguments, I would like to thank my students as well as the participants in the monthly Research Seminar in Military Sociology at the University of Maryland. This article could not have been written without the generous support of the Center for European Studies of Harvard University, the Krupp Foundation, the Center for Research on Military Organization at the University of Maryland, and the U.S. Army Research Institute for the Behavioral and Social Sciences under contracts DASW0195K0005 and DASW0100K0016. The views expressed in this article are the author's own, and not necessarily those of the Army Research Institute, the Department of the Army, or the Department of Defense.

GLOBALIZATION, CONSCRIPTION, AND ANTI-MILITARISM IN PRE-WORLD WAR I EUROPE

David M. Rowe

ABSTRACT

This chapter explains the emergence and complex pattern of popular resistance to military recruitment in pre-World War I Europe by pointing to two factors: the effects of globalization on civilian wages and whether militaries used conscription or voluntary recruitment. By increasing civilian wages, globalization also increased the potential opportunity costs of military service in Europe. How these economic pressures became manifested in the state's military politics was determined by the institutions that states used to mobilize labor into the military. In conscripted systems (continental Europe), recruits were compelled to serve despite the growing cost of military service, thus politicizing popular opposition to military service. In voluntary systems (Britain), labor could respond to the rising opportunity costs of military service by simply not enlisting, meaning that the growing burden of military service did not become strongly politicized. Consequently, anti-militarism was strongest on the continent and weakest in Britain.

The Comparative Study of Conscription in the Armed Forces, Volume 20, pages 145–170.

ISBN: 0-7623-0836-2

INTRODUCTION

Popular resistance to the military loomed large in the security politics of the European great powers before World War I. Strident anti-militarism was a constant feature of continental socialist politics, as socialist parties sought both to minimize the burdens of military service within in their own countries as well as to coordinate working class opposition to militarism across Europe. In Germany, the Social Democratic Party won its biggest electoral victory in 1912 by campaigning against "dear bread and militarism," capturing 4.25 million votes or 34.8% of all votes cast (Ferguson, 1999, p. 26).[1] The most contentious issue in French politics before the war was the reintroduction of a three-year term of compulsory military service in 1913, a move strongly opposed by the French left. Rampant rank and file discontent in Russia's armed services raised considerable doubts about the military effectiveness and political loyalty of its forces. Even in Britain, where socialist politics made the fewest inroads, widespread domestic political opposition prevented the substantial army reforms necessary to solve chronic manpower problems, despite the growing awareness among state and military elites that British security rested ever more heavily on its ability to intervene meaningfully in a European land war (Rowe et al., 1999; Skelly, 1977; Spiers, 1980). "The evidence," writes Niall Ferguson (1999, p. 30), "is unequivocal. Europeans were not marching to war, but turning their backs on militarism."

The emergence of popular resistance to military service in the decades before the war defies easy explanation. Usually scholars point to the rapid industrialization and urbanization of European society to explain the social tensions of this era (Van Evera, 1986, p. 98). Yet these factors fail to explain why popular resistance to military service emerged in all of the great powers despite dramatically different levels of industrial development and urbanization, nor the important puzzle of why rural recruits were perceived to be the most desirable and politically loyal soldiers in industrial countries, but were disloyal in Russia, Europe's most backward and overwhelmingly agrarian great power. Moreover, even among the industrialized countries of west and central Europe, the strength of anti-militarism and the political demands of similarly situated political parties towards military service varied considerably. In Britain, anti-militarism played almost no role in the electoral politics of the Liberal and Labour parties (Newton, 1985). Yet anti-militarism was a centerpiece of the electoral strategies of the left in both France and Germany. And whereas the British Labour party adamantly opposed any form of compulsory military service, the socialist parties of France and Germany demanded the creation of "nations in arms" in which all citizens were required to perform military service.

This complex pattern of prewar anti-militarism means that most explanations for popular resistance to the military tend to be idiosyncratic and country-specific, grounded in each country's unique political traditions and cultures. In France, popular resistance to military service is argued to reflect a longstanding struggle between right and left over the role of the military in French society (Kier, 1997, Ch. 4; Challener, 1955). Likewise, the conflict between militarism and anti-militarism Germany is often interpreted as a struggle between modernity and feudalism, in which industrial society threatened the social integrity of a feudalistic monarchy and the army that was sworn to protect it (Fischer, 1969/1975; Berghahn, 1973; Förster, 1985). As one scholar recently argues, the fact that the political left in Britain and France could hold such diametrically opposed positions regarding conscription and a professional standing army strongly suggests that country-specific political and military cultures play the key role in determining a country's security politics (Kier, 1997, p. 142).

Yet country-specific explanations of the popular resistance to the military before World War I are unsatisfactory because they cannot explain the simultaneous emergence of anti-militarism in all of the European great powers. Just as differences between political left in France and Britain on military issues suggest an important causal role for domestic factors in determining a country's security politics, so too does the common emergence of anti-militarism across Europe strongly suggest a causal role for systemic factors. In this paper, I will explain the common emergence and complex pattern of European anti-militarism using two factors: one systemic and one domestic institutional. I will argue that the systemic "shock" responsible for the common emergence of popular resistance to the military in pre-World War I Europe was the rapid globalization of the international economy in the late-nineteenth and early twentieth centuries. This economic development fueled popular anti-militarism by raising substantially the opportunity costs to the rank and file soldier of performing military service. How these rising opportunity costs manifested themselves as popular resistance to the military in different countries depended, in turn, on whether the state used conscription or voluntary enlistment to mobilize labor from the economy.

I. LATE NINETEENTH CENTURY GLOBALIZATION

The late nineteenth and early twentieth centuries were a period of rapid economic globalization. Technological innovations such as railroads, steamships, and the telegraph dramatically reduced the costs of transacting over substantial distances, linking previously isolated regional and national markets into a larger world economy. Trade blossomed as commodities previously too heavy, perishable, or bulky to enter international commerce could now be shipped across oceans and continents. Between 1870 and 1900, world trade almost doubled and in the remaining years before World War I grew by nearly half again (Rogowski, 1989, p. 21). These technological innovations also spurred dramatic factor migrations as it now became less costly for capital and labor to relocate to take advantage of relative factor price differentials between markets. Massive outflows of capital materialized from the rich industrial core in western Europe, flowing mostly toward capital scarce but resource rich lands of recent settlement in the Americas and Australasia. At their peak, these outflows were nearly 9% of GDP in Britain and almost as high in France, Germany and the Netherlands (Bordo et al., 1998, p. 4). Falling costs of passage likewise spurred large labor flows, as labor emigrated from the populous and low wage Old World to reap the much higher wages in the thinly settled New.[2]

Globalization had several important consequences. Falling transport costs promoted the deepening integration of commodity markets, causing commodity prices to converge. In 1870, for example, the price of wheat in Liverpool (the major port handling British grain) was 57.6% greater than in Chicago (the U.S. port closest to American wheat producers); in 1913, the price spread had fallen to only 17.9% (O'Rourke & Williamson, 1994, pp. 899–900). Nor was this development linked solely to the North Atlantic trade. Wheat price spreads between Britain and Odessa fell from 37.9% in 1870 to only 6.5% in 1913 (O'Rourke, 1997, Table 1). These changes were mirrored by most other traded commodities which also saw price differentials fall (O'Rourke & Williamson, 1994, pp. 901–902). To grasp the magnitude of the fall in transport costs, one need only consider that the often more than 40 percentage point fall in transport costs between 1870 and 1913 was a vastly greater change in trade barriers than that embedded in the Smoot-Hawley tariff (an increase of eight percentage points over the levels implied by the 1922 Tariff Act), or even the much celebrated postwar decline of tariffs under the GATT in the three decades after the 1940s (Williamson, 1996, pp. 8–9).

Globalization also meant that factor markets became more integrated. On the one hand, falling transport and communication costs made factor mobility between national markets less costly. Because there were few legal restrictions on the movement of money and people across national boundaries in this era, capital and labor could now respond to relative price differentials by relocating from countries where they were relatively abundant and cheap to countries where they were relatively scarce and expensive. On the other hand, the boom in commodity trade also affected factor markets, raising the demand and prices of factors that were locally abundant, while depressing demand and prices of those factors that were locally scarce.[3] As a result, relative factor prices across national economies also converged in the years before World War I. Between 1870 and 1910, the ratio of wages to land rents in labor abundant but land scarce Europe rose by a factor of 2.7 in Britain, 1.8 in France and 1.4 in Germany. Conversely, the wage-rental ratio fell in the land abundant and labor scarce economies of the New World. Between 1870 and 1913, the Australian ratio had fallen more than 25%, while the United States' ratio fell by more than half. The Argentine ratio in 1913 was only one-fifth its level in the mid 1880s (Williamson, 1996, p. 13). (See Table 1.)

These global economic trends had profound social implications for the European continent. As labor abundant but land scarce economies, the countries of west and central Europe experienced falling social inequality as incomes derived from the ownership of land, which in Europe was usually concentrated in relatively few hands, fell while real wages rose. Social inequality fell fastest in the poorer countries of the European periphery and more moderately in the richer industrial core (Williamson, 1996, pp. 13–15). The growth of real wages was especially striking in Ireland, which was an important source of Britain's military labor. Irish unskilled real wages grew by 84% over this period; rising from 71% of British wages in 1870 to 82% by 1913. British unskilled real wages rose 59% between 1870 and 1913; French real wages 32%; and German real wages 59% (Williamson, 1995, Table A2.1). (See Table 2.)

In land and labor abundant Russia, on the other hand, economic theory suggests both land values and wages should raise as this country was abundant in both resources (Rogowski, 1989). A paucity of good data, however, makes these economic trends harder to discern. Whether the Russian peasantry (which possessed the vast bulk of Russia's land) experienced rising living standards in

Table 1. Ratios of Wages to Land Values 1870–1910 (1901 = 100).

Country	1870	1890	1910
Old World			
Britain	42.28	84.99	115.42
Ireland	12.61	66.86	70.31
France	59.97	112.97	122.36
Germany	67.51	86.47	95.57
New World			
Argentina	167.58	106.45	31.95
Australia	289.74	118.54	75.64
United States	127.99	103.23	64.07

Source: O'Rourke et al. (1996), Table 2. Index numbers are not comparable across countries.

Table 2. International Real Wages, 1870–1913.

Country	1870	1880	1890	1900	1910	1913
Britain	69	84	97	101	105	110
France	50	57	64	69	71	66
Germany	58	62	76	84	87	92
Ireland	49	56	75	89	91	90

Source: Williamson (1995), Table A2.1. 100 = British real wage in 1905. Index numbers are comparable across countries.

the late nineteenth and early twentieth centuries, which would lessen inequality, or declining standards, which would exacerbate it, has been a highly contentious issue in Russian historiography (Vasudevan, 1988). Yet recent scholarship makes the argument that living standards declined for the Russian peasantry increasingly difficult to sustain. Peasant housing standards rose during this period, mortality rates fell, nutrition improved (Bushnell, 1987, pp. 80–81; Hoch, 1994). The mean height of Russian army recruits, a good indicator of living standards, appears to have risen between 1890 and 1899 (Hoch, 1994, pp. 68–69). One scholar has estimated that the "rye equivalent" peasant wage rose from 10 to 15 kilograms per day in 1882 to 15 to 20 kilograms per day in 1914, an increase of 40% (Stephen G. Wheatcroft cited by Hoch, 1994, p. 49, n. 24). All these indicators suggest narrowing social inequality because even though peasants were still poor in 1914, they were less poor than in times past.

Moreover, one can plausibly link the rising living standards directly to the globalization trends that affected the rest of Europe. The penetration of railways into Russia's interior lowered transport costs and raised the demand for Russia's agricultural produce. Wheat price spreads between Odessa and Britain fell while Russian grain prices rose, causing farm rents and land values to rise (Stone, 1984, p. 208; Williamson, 1998, p. 57). Rising prices spurred production as per capita grain output rose during the last thirty years of the empire, as did per acre yields and the amount of land devoted to cereal cultivation, which expanded 62% between 1872 and 1911 (Hoch, 1994, p. 52; Bushnell, 1987, pp. 78–79; O'Rourke, 1997, Table 4). These developments benefitted directly Russia's peasantry, who were not only the intensive users but also part owners of Russia's abundant agricultural land. "The picture," according to Paul Gregory (1983, p. 26), "is one of an agricultural population that was experiencing rising per capita income and living standards." And, because the peasantry comprised the vast bulk of Russia's population, rising peasant standards of living implied narrowing social inequality as well.

Table 3. The Military Strengths and Potentials of the European States in 1914.

Country	Peacetime Strength	Wartime Strength	Population	Men of Military Age
Russia	1,445,000	3,400,000	164,000,000	17,000,000
Serbia	52,000	247,000	4,000,000	440,000
Montenegro	2,000	—	400,000	60,000
France	827,000	1,800,000	36,600,000	5,940,000
Britain	248,000	162,000	46,000,000	6,430,000
Belgium	48,000	117,000	7,500,000	—
Germany	761,000	2,147,000	67,000,000	9,750,000
Austria-Hungary	478,000	1,338,000	51,000,000	6,120,000
TOTALS	3,861,000	9,211,000	376,500,000	45,740,000

Source: Ferguson (1999), Tables 9 and 10. Missing information denoted by "—".

By raising wages and narrowing social inequality, globalization thus unleashed powerful economic forces in Europe that would have affected any enterprise that required the intensive use of large quantities of labor. This would have been especially true of the European militaries which drew more than a million men from their national economies each year for military service and which, by 1914, maintained peacetime forces of 3,861,000 men (Ferguson, 1999, Table 9, p. 92). (see Table 3.) Most directly, the growing ease of emigration to seek fortunes elsewhere deprived the militaries of young men who would otherwise have been available for military service. In the early 1890s, German Chancellor Leo von Caprivi worried that growing emigration would leave Germany unable to field an army (Calleo, 1978, p. 17). Likewise, British army recruiters often blamed emigration as one significant cause of the army's severe recruiting difficulties (Rowe et al., 1999). Europe's most infamous draft dodger was Adolf Hitler, who fled his obligations to the Austrian army by emigrating to Bavaria.[4] But globalization affected the European militaries not only by depriving them of young men who emigrated, but even more important by reducing the willingness to serve by those who stayed behind.

II. GLOBALIZATION, MILITARY RECRUITMENT AND ANTI-MILITARISM IN PRE-WORLD WAR I EUROPE

Globalization was a substantial common shock to the European economies that narrowed social inequality by raising incomes in the lowest strata of society and depressing them in the highest. Yet globalization alone cannot explain the emergence and complex pattern of popular anti-militarism before World War I. There is no intrinsic reason why narrowing social inequality *must* increase popular resistance to military service. And, as we have seen, manifestations of anti-militarism varied greatly among the great powers. It was strongest on the continent and weakest in Britain. In the labor abundant and land poor great powers of west and central Europe, military elites perceived anti-militarism to be greatest among the urban working classes, and rural recruits to be the most desirable and reliable soldiers. In populous, land abundant Russia, however, peasants ultimately proved unreliable, mutinying against the military in the wake of the abortive 1905 revolution. Finally, the socialist parties of France and Germany favored short-service universal military conscription, a stance that was diametrically opposed to that of the Liberal and Labour parties in Britain, which rejected conscription in favor of a standing professional army. This complex pattern strongly suggests the necessity of domestic factors in determining how the common shock of globalization manifested itself as popular resistance to military service in the individual great powers.

To determine how globalization fueled popular anti-militarism one must show how globalization affected the attitudes of individual soldiers and potential soldiers toward military service. This, in turn, requires an examination of the domestic institutions by which individual states mobilized labor into the military. For it was these institutions that determined who would serve in the military, how they were compensated by the state for their service, and ultimately how they would be affected by the narrowing social inequality wrought by globalization.

The European great powers used two different institutions to mobilize labor into the military. The continental states conscripted military labor. All young men were eligible for military service and required to perform it if chosen, although the percentage of men actually inducted into the ranks varied greatly. France conscripted approximately 84% of all men eligible for military service; Germany 53% and Austria-Hungary only 29% (Ferguson, 1992, p. 734, 1994, p. 155). Britain, on the other hand, used voluntary enlistment to fill the ranks of its world-wide navy and small, professional standing army. Its intake of men was considerably less than the continental states. Its standing army in 1914 comprised less than 4% of males of military age, compared to the standing armies of the continental powers which comprised 8% of military aged males in Germany and Austria-Hungary, 9% in Russia, and 14% in France (Ferguson, 1999, Tables 9 and 10, pp. 92–93).

Continental Conscription

Figure 1 presents a stylized model of European military conscription *prior* to the onset of globalization. The state's demand for military labor is given by the curve **D**. I assume this demand to be relatively inelastic with respect to military wages for two reasons. First, each state's demand for recruits was roughly set by its strategic circumstances, regardless of its ability to pay. This point was forcefully made by the British Lord Wolsely in 1896, who wrote to the Permanent Under Secretary of State for War, Sir Arthur Haliburton (War Office, 1896), that:

> It is no answer to say that the inducements we offer do not get us sufficient men; if they do not, they must be readjusted until they do . . .. My point is that the strength of our Army must be fixed by the work it has to do and not by the rates of the recruiting market. The latter we can command, the former is imposed upon us. The imperious pressure of Imperial needs will not yield to consideration of home thrift, and an enemy will not weaken his attack. . . . because rather than increase the soldier's pay, we give it too weak a garrison.

Second, technological limitations, especially in the critical area of battlefield mobility, severely limited the extent to which pre-World War I European armies could substitute weapons for men in military competition. As a consequence, the sheer number of men that a state could field in battle was the most important component of landward military power (Stevenson, 1996, p. 62; McNeil, 1982, p. 283; Herrmann, 1996, p. 228; Storz, 1992, pp. 295–297; Rowe, 1999, pp. 201–202).

The supply of potential conscripts is given by the curve **S**. This curve traces out the number of men willing to voluntarily serve at different levels of military wages. It also represents the opportunity cost to individuals of performing military service, or, in other words, the costs that an individual bears in terms of not being able to pursue other opportunities while in the military. These costs will be determined by the basket of skills, opportunities, and assets that an individual possesses, allowing us to array individuals along the curve roughly according to income and class. For example, in a labor abundant, land-scarce economy typical of prewar western Europe, an individual at **a** could be an unskilled landless peasant; **b** an unskilled urban worker; **c** a skilled worker; **d** the son of a middle class professional; and **e** the son of a wealthy land-holding aristocrat. In short, the greater one's potential income, earnings, and opportunities in civilian life, the more the state must offer to induce voluntary military service.

Because this is a system of compulsory military service, the state, not the market, sets the level of compensation offered for military service, given here by the military wage **W**. This wage should be broadly interpreted to include a soldier's money wages, the value of payments in kind such as room and board while under the colours, the value of acquired skills and training, and finally the satisfaction derived from performing one's civic duty. It is critical to recognize that the value of the military "wage" offered by the state *must* be less than

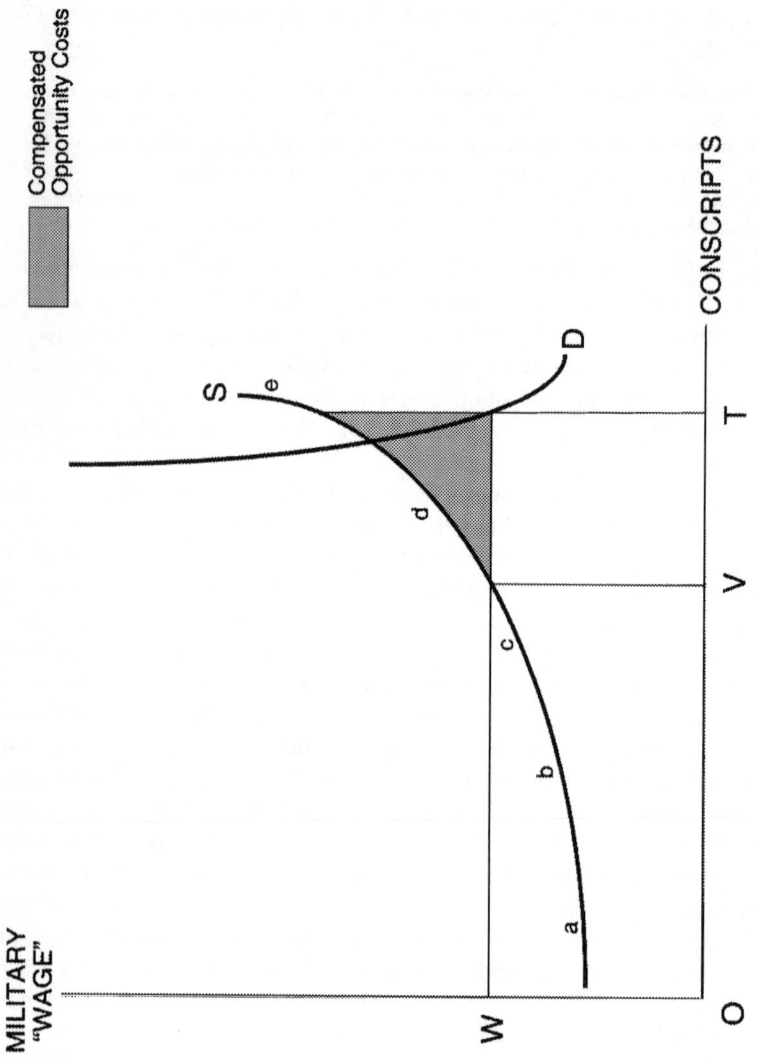

Fig. 1. A Stylized Model of European Military Conscription.

the equilibrium military wage implied by the intersection of the state's demand for military labor **D** and the supply of military labor **S**. The reason is simple. Wages at or above the equilibrium level would render compulsory military service superfluous because sufficient quantities of labor would voluntarily present themselves to the state for military service. At the prevailing military wage **W**, the state will draft OT conscripts for military service.

Several important implications follow from this stylized model of conscription. Because the equilibrium military wage always exceeds the actual level of compensation offered by the state, conscription divides each recruiting class into two components which roughly reflect the class divisions in society. Lower class conscripts over the distance OV (where **V** represents the threshold beyond which conscripts will no longer serve without the threat of compulsion) will voluntarily comply with conscription because the compensation offered by the state equals or exceeds the opportunity costs of military service. This is not the case for middle and upper class conscripts over the distance VT. To elicit compliance from these conscripts, the state must either coerce them, or offer additional compensation to offset the greater opportunity costs they bear, represented in the model by the lightly shaded region. In fact, the state's need to offer middle and upper class conscripts additional compensation corresponds closely to the actual practice of the European states in the prewar era, which offered various forms of compensation to the sons of middle and upper class families. Conscripts from these social backgrounds typically needed serve only one year of active duty compared to the two to four years that were required of ordinary conscripts. Even in France, which abolished one-year volunteers in 1889 to make conscription correspond to egalitarian ideals, the state exempted from military service those studying for many middle and upper class professions, such as medicine, the bar, education, and the priesthood (Krumeich, 1994, p. 142). In addition, the European militaries also compensated these conscripts by offering them greater levels of privilege and command authority. In the Russian army, for example, one year volunteers were not obliged to live in the barracks, exempted from work details, and addressed by officers and non-commissioned officers (NCOs) with the title "volunteer so and so" or the formal form of "you" ("vy") rather than the familiar (and in the social context degrading) form of "you" ("ty") (Wildman, 1980, p. 28). The European militaries also typically named their reserve officers from the "one year volunteers" of the middle and upper classes, even though these recruits possessed less military training and experience than ordinary conscripts, and considerably less than professional non-commissioned officers.

Although European prewar conscription reflected the overall class structure of society, it would be mistaken to conclude that this institution possessed an inherent bias *against* the lower classes. Even though the European armies often treated conscripts harshly (especially in Russia), life in the military could well be no more trying than civilian life for lower class conscripts who faced few real opportunities. As Allan Wildman (1980, pp. 33, 36) observes in regard to Russian conscription, peasant soldiers often ate better in the army than the villages and the indignities they suffered "were simply a part of the tribute that a peasant was expected to pay to outside society, along with taxes, passports and bribes to rural police officers." Likewise, Douglas Porch (1981, pp. 54–55) notes that as late as the 1880s French peasant conscripts often found military service superior to the "backbreaking tedium" of farm life, and that army living standards exceeded those in much of France. In the 1860s, for example, the soldier's daily ration amounted to 1.4 kilograms of food, above the national average of 1.2 kilograms.

In reality, if there was any bias inherent in conscription, it would have been a bias against the middle and upper classes. The fact that military service was compulsory for all young men opened the door to state-practiced extortion. The height of the curve **S** represents not only the opportunity costs to an individual of performing military service, but, critically, what one would pay the state to be freed from that obligation. For example, a middle class son at **d** who pays the state the military wage **W** to free himself from military duty is better off than if he performs his military service. In the first instance, the potential conscript captures for himself the difference between payments to the state to be freed from military obligations (the military wage **W**) and the greater rewards he reaps from using his time in other ways (the height of the curve **S** at **d**). In the second instance, the costs of military service to this middle class conscript are the value of his lost opportunities (the height of the curve **S** at **d**), a value that far exceeds the compensation offered by the state (the military wage **W**). The European states often exploited this structure of incentives to extort payments from the families of middle and upper class conscripts. Until 1872, for example, France practiced "replacement" in which wealthy sons would be freed from their military obligations so long as they found a replacement willing to perform their military service, thus creating a market for soldiers in which wealthy families paid other people to perform their sons' military duties (Levi, 1997, pp. 85–96). Because this system created a cohort of privately financed, long-service professional soldiers in the French army, it essentially generated a subsidy for the army that was paid by the middle and upper classes. More generally, the continental European states did not provide exemptions from military service to the middle or upper classes for free, but usually extracted some form of cash payment. One year "volunteers" were typically required to reimburse the state for the costs of training, food, and lodging while under the colours, a payment that was often quite steep.[5] Moreover, during their tour of duty, one-year volunteers could also be subjected to petty extortion by their poorly paid non-commissioned officers (NCOs) in a rough form of "barracks socialism." For example, one joke that surfaced in Germany in 1905 has one NCO ask another "How is your recruiting class this year?" "Excellent," replies the second, "I have wonderful one-year volunteers in my company. One has an uncle who owns a sausage factory, another owns a cheese factory, the third is himself a producer of cognac and the fourth is the son of a major wine distributor. I have never had a better crew" (Klingenschmidt, 1997, pp. 45–46).[6]

Figure 2 represents the effects of globalization on the continental practice of conscription. As we saw in the first section, globalization narrowed social inequality in Europe. In the land poor but labor rich countries of west and central Europe, globalization depressed the incomes of the wealthiest land-holding strata of society, while raising real wages among the lowest. In terms of the model, narrowing social inequality compresses the shape of the supply curve of military labor **S** by pushing downward the height of the curve to the right of C′, representing the highest strata of society, while raising the curve to left of C′, representing the lowest. This yields a new, post-globalization, supply curve which is given by **S**′.

The changing shape of the supply curve indicates that narrowing social inequality does not affect all social classes equally with respect to universal military conscription. Among the highest and lowest strata of society, narrowing inequality appears unlikely to substantially alter attitudes toward military service. Falling incomes among the wealthiest middle and upper class conscripts over the distance C′T lessens the value of the exemptions they receive from the state for military service as well as the amount the state can extort for them. This group's basic attitudes toward military service, however, are likely to remain unchanged so long as the state continues to compensate them for their opportunity costs **S**′, and ensures that any payments extracted for exemptions from service remain less than the costs they bear. For the poorest class of conscripts over the range OV′, globalization reduces the surplus they reap from military service, but does not reduce their willingness to voluntarily comply with conscription because the compensation offered by the state continues to equal or exceed what they could earn elsewhere.

Potential middle class conscripts over the range VC′ experience rising incomes as a consequence of globalization and narrowing social inequality. How these changes affect attitudes toward military conscription depends critically upon the practices by which the state compensates this class of conscripts for the excess opportunity costs of military service. For example, if the conscript's compensation is simply a cash subsidy equal to the difference between the military wage **W** and his position on the old supply curve **S**, that subsidy would

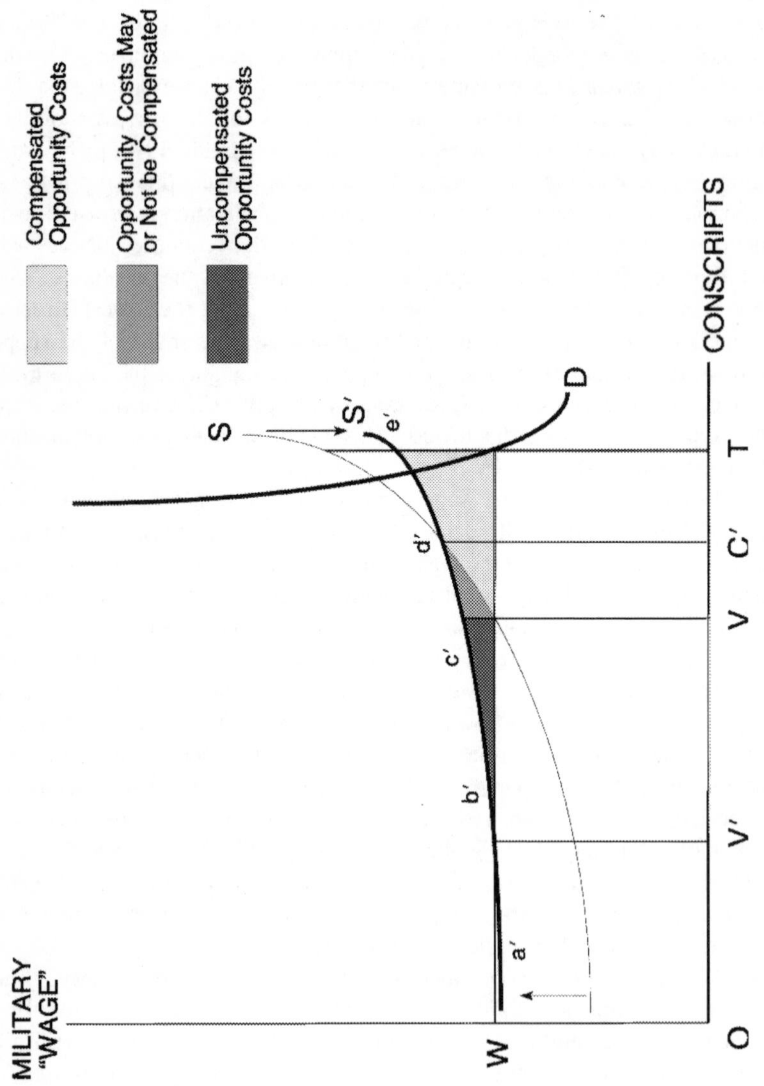

Fig. 2. Narrowing Social Inequality and Military Conscription.

no longer compensate adequately for the opportunity costs of compulsory military service. To the extent that these costs remained uncompensated by state policies, they will generate either potential resistance to military service or political demands on the state to increase the compensation offered to this class. If, on the other hand, special exemptions such as reduced lengths of service could be purchased with cash payments to the state, as was true of the "one-year volunteers" in most continental militaries, the potential burdens of military service would become less onerous the more incomes rose. Consequently, a middle class son along the range VC′ would find that the value of his exemption from military service had risen, as he could now reap a greater net benefit from being freed from military service.

The most interesting consequences of globalization and narrowing social inequality for military conscription occur among lower and working class conscripts over the range V′V. This is a class of conscripts who previously complied voluntarily with military conscription, and did so without the offsetting exemptions and privileges offered to the middle and upper classes. Yet rising civilian wages mean that military wages no longer fully compensate these conscripts, as this portion of the supply curve of military labor now lies above the level of military wages **W**. How this development affects this group's attitudes toward military service again depends critically on how the state compensates these individuals for their opportunity costs that now exceed the military wage. Where the state grants access to extra-compensation, such as that available to the middle and upper classes, narrowing social inequality will not affect attitudes toward service. Although the costs of military service have risen, so too have the rewards. In the absence of offsetting compensation, however, members of this class will cease to comply willingly with conscription. The more civilian wages exceed the military wage, the more their behavior becomes determined by the naked threat of punishment for non-compliance. They continue to serve only because they are compelled to do so. In other words, rising wages change military service into an increasingly onerous and resented activity that one preforms not voluntarily, but only under the shadow of state coercion. This model captures several critical aspects of popular resistance to military service in prewar Europe. First, it explains how globalization generated the simultaneous emergence of prewar anti-militarism throughout continental Europe. The lower classes of Europe were generally excluded from the exemptions that compensated the middle and upper classes for the excess opportunity costs of military service. What determined eligibility for these exemptions was not one's potential income, but class markers such as father's profession, family wealth, or university education. The common practice of extorting expensive "reimbursements" from one-year volunteers also excluded the lower classes from this form of "compensation." Few working class families possessed sufficient savings to cover these costly payments. As a result, globalization transformed universal military conscription from an institution that was either class neutral or even biased against the middle and upper classes, to one that now favored the middle and upper classes and possessed a distinct class bias *against* all but the lowest of the lower and working classes. And rather than merely reflect the underlying class divisions of society, conscription now exacerbated and politicized them. Unlike the middle and upper classes, who could at least purchase exemptions to offset the excess opportunity costs of military service, the lower and working classes were simply compelled to serve without offsetting compensation, thus generating considerable popular resentment against the state and military.

Moreover, there is considerable evidence to suggest that rising wages and living standards among Europe's laboring classes fueled popular anti-militarism. In France, poor quarters, bad food, and lack of leave became the pretext for numerous soldier revolts after 1905 (Porch, 1981, p. 130). Anti-militarism was also closely linked to socialist agitation for better pay and working conditions for the working classes. The *Confédération Générale du Travail*, which was founded in 1895, made anti-militarism a centerpiece of its politics. Likewise, *Sou du Soldat*, trade union societies established to aid needy members in uniform, became centers of anti-militarism within the military. Soldier revolts and insubordination were often accompanied by socialist symbols, such as the singing of the *Internationale*. As one French police report noted, "anti-militarism [has conquered] a great portion of the working masses, who are in the habit of confusing syndicalism with anti-militarism" (Krumeich, 1984, p. 34; Porch, 1981, pp. 110–111). More broadly, French socialists consistently demanded reductions in the terms of service. In 1905, leftist pressure forced the government to cut the length of military service by a third, from three years to two. These trends culminated in Jean Jaures' call for a "nation in arms" manned by one-year conscripts (Jaures, 1972). Immediately prior to the war, the most controversial issue in French politics was the Three Year Law of 1913, which required all eligible males to perform three years of active military service. The government was able to pass the law only after it amended the law to lower the age of induction from 21 to 20 so as not to delay the entry of young men into the working population (Krumeich, 1984, p. 112). Even so, the law was extremely unpopular, sparking soldier riots among the rank and file and unable to command a stable political majority in parliament. Bolstered by electoral victories in May and June 1914, the socialists would have challenged the law in the fall of 1914 had the war not intervened (Stevenson, 1996, pp. 358–359). The German military, for its part, judged that the Three

Year Law would so disrupt the professional education and vocational training of French youth, that France would soon be forced to return to a shorter term of service (Generalstab, 1914a, p. 32). And as Tony Judt finds in a study of French socialism in Provence, widespread opposition to conscription in this region sprang less from ideology than from the economic and social costs of military service, especially the fact that the small peasantry of the region could not afford to hire labor, which was in short supply and very expensive, to replace the loss of their sons to the army (Judt, 1979, p. 85).

In Germany, anti-militarism was likewise strongly linked to the Social Democratic Party and the trade unions movement. Fears that conscripts from working class backgrounds would infect the ranks with socialist anti-militarism led the army to induct an increasing number or conscripts from rural backgrounds, so that two-thirds of conscripts as late as 1911 had rural origins even though only 42% of the population lived in the countryside. A mere 6% of conscripts were from large cities and only 7% from mid-sized cities (Kitchen, 1968, pp. 147–148; Förster, 1994, pp. 59–60). Likewise, the army also excluded active social democrats from one-year voluntary military service and forbid their promotion to the ranks of non-commissioned officers (Kriegsministerium n.d.). Significantly, the efforts of the Social Democrats were directed less toward revolutionary subversion and more toward reducing the burdens of military service and improving the working conditions for the rank and file. In 1892, socialist pressure in the Reichstag was critical in forcing the state to reduce the term of active military service from three years to two. Although Kaiser Wilhelm II protested that he would "never ever" allow a two year term of duty, he relented once it became clear that opposition to a three-year term was so deep and widespread that it threatened the very existence of the German Reich (Kaiser Wilhelm II, 1891; Reichskanzler, 1891). The Social Democrats subsequently advocated reducing the terms of compulsory military service to one-year for all conscripts, as well as making working class conscripts eligible for "one-year volunteer" status should a general reduction in military service not be forthcoming.[7] In 1907, a majority of the Reichstag approved a Social Democratic resolution that demanded rank and file pay be increased to a paltry 10 pfennig per day, a demand that went unfulfilled because the war ministry considered it too expensive (Kriegsministerium, 1908).[8] Yet by 1912, the pressing need to expand the peacetime size of the German army, a development that would force it to induct greater numbers of working class recruits, convinced the war ministry that it could no longer avoid raising pay for rank and file conscripts and non-commissioned officers. Grievances about poor military pay had become fertile ground for socialist anti-militarist agitation, and according to War Minister Heeringen, now stood in the way of any army expansion. Electoral competition caused other parties in the Reichstag to echo socialist demands to raise pay for the rank and file. (Kriegsministerium, 1912; Königliche Bayrische Bevollmächtiger, 1912a, b). The failure to pass a pay increase, Heeringen warned Reichskanzler Bethmann-Hollweg, would give the Social Democratic Party a "powerful, material issue" which would achieve its goal of bringing political agitation directly into the barracks (Kriegsministerium n.d. (1912?)). In 1912 and 1913, the Reichstag, again under significant socialist pressure, passed majority resolutions to lower the term of military service to one year for all foot soldiers.

Likewise in Russia, rising wages and standards of living among the lower classes appear directly related to the emergence of popular anti-militarism. Inadequate pay and conditions of service made naval conscripts receptive targets of socialist agitation, and played a central role in the naval mutinies of the 1905 revolution (Lieven, 1983, p. 108; Mawdsley, 1978, pp. 7–9). They also played a considerable role in the army revolts that that engulfed the countryside between 1905 and 1907 when more than one-third of European infantry units mutinied. Soldier demands for higher pay, shorter active duty, and an end to the onerous practice of hiring out conscripts to local landowners featured prominently in almost every mutiny (Bushnell, 1980, pp. 563–569, 1985, pp. 100–101). Soldier revolts were also fueled by an oppressive system of property rights and government policies that sought to extract the maximum available agricultural surplus from the peasantry and thus deprive peasants of the gains that would otherwise flow to them from an expanding world economy. Peasant grievances thus fed soldier grievances, causing the pattern of army mutinies to mirror peasant revolts in the countryside (Bushnell, 1985). As one regiment wrote to a Trudvik deputy in the newly established Duma, "We soldiers are poor, we have no money to buy land when we return home from service, and every peasant needs land desperately . . .. This land is God's . . . and on this, God's free land, should toil God's free workers, not hired laborers for the gentry and Kulaks" (Bushnell, 1985, p. 180). In the end, brutal repression and the fact that the government capitulated to the soldiers' economic demands for better conditions of service ended the rebellions. The government raised the soldier's meat ration from one-fourth to three-fourths pounds; increased enlisted pay two and one-half to three fold (varying by rank); and reduced the term of compulsory military duty by one year. It also provided free handkerchiefs to the soldiers, to show the soldiers that, according to War Minister Rediger, "they were given not only what they demanded, but even a luxury that had not occurred to them" (Bushnell, 1985, pp. 112 and 140–141). The government did not, however, accede to the political demands to restructure property rights over land, with the result that fundamental soldier grievances continued to fester.

This model also explains the varying social location of anti-militarism among the continental states. Anti-militarism was strongest in the urban working classes in the land scarce and labor abundant states of west and central Europe and closely associated with the rise of socialism. In fact, in both Germany and France, the history of the left is inextricably linked to struggles over the terms of military service and the role of the military in society (for example, Porch, 1981, p. 109; Berghahn, 1973; Fischer, 1969/1975). Anti-militarism was weakest in the rural countryside. For labor and land abundant Russia, however, both industrial workers and the peasantry resisted military service and possessed questionable loyalty to the state. This pattern follows directly from the ways in which globalization affected military conscription in these countries. For the labor abundant, land poor states, wages would initially rise fastest in the country's rapidly expanding labor-intensive industrial sectors and lag or even decline in its contracting land-intensive agricultural sectors. Although labor mobility would equalize wages over the long run as labor flowed out of low-wage agriculture and into high-wage industry, over the short run considerable gaps in wages could emerge. These lags meant that agricultural workers faced fewer opportunity costs for military service than urban workers, causing anti-militarism to be weakest in the countryside and strongest in the cities. On the other hand, in land abundant Russia, the peasantry either worked or owned this country's most abundant resource. Unlike agricultural laborers in the rest of Europe, peasants therefore benefitted directly from globalization and grew increasingly resentful of the structure of property rights, government policies, and social obligations (including military service) that denied them the full extent of their gains. Consequently, the "peasant problem" and the questionable loyalty of peasant soldiers were the most serious problems facing the Russian army command on the eve of the war (Wildman, 1980, p. 38; Fuller, 1985, p. 207; Kennedy, 1987, p. 236).

Finally, the model explains the pronounced preference for rural recruits by the militaries of the labor abundant, land poor states of west and central Europe. It is interesting to note that most justifications of the superiority of rural recruits were grounded in part on differential opportunity costs of military life for rural and urban recruits. Not only were rural recruits perceived to be more loyal than urban recruits, they were also believed to tolerate better the harsh rigor and many indignities of military life (Stone, 1984, p. 333). City people, according to the French General Francois-Osker Nègier, were not used to the "walking, hauling, and starving" that comprised a soldier's lot. Likewise, Johann Bloch wrote that rural soldiers were vital to the army because they were accustomed to a hard and simple life, much more so than urban workers and especially men from the well-to-do classes (Storz, 1992, p. 310). Again, we can trace the origins of this preference to the differential effects of globalization on conscription in these societies. Because agricultural wages lagged behind urban wages, rural recruits faced fewer opportunity costs for military service and were thus less likely to resent the military burdens imposed on them by the state.

Voluntary Enlistment

How would globalization and narrowing social inequality have affected Britain, which unlike the continental states used voluntary enlistment to fill the ranks of its military? Figure 3 represents a model of voluntary military recruitment. Demand for military recruits is given by the curve **D**, which, as before, is highly inelastic with respect to wages. The initial, pre-globalization supply of labor is given by **S**. It is important to realize that this curve does *not* represent the total supply of labor willing to serve at a given level of military wages, but only those recruits who meet the military's minimum selective physical and mental quality standards. Because enlistment is voluntary, the military wage is set not by the state, but by market forces, and is determined by the intersection of the state's demand for military labor **D** and the supply curve of military labor **S**. Thus, prior to globalization the state inducts OR recruits at the military wage **W**.

Because Britain was a labor-abundant, land poor economy, globalization raised real wages among the lowest strata of society from which Britain recruited its military labor. In terms of the model, rising wages shift the supply curve of military labor upward to **S′**. Given the higher wages and greater opportunities elsewhere in civilian society, fewer men will now present themselves for military service, causing the number of recruits inducted at the pre-globalization wage to fall to OR*. The state can respond to these changing economic circumstances in one of two ways. On the one hand, it can raise wages to the new equilibrium level **W′** indicated by the intersection of its demand for labor **D** and the new, post-globalization supply curve **S′**. This solution therefore implies that rising civilian wages will lead to substantial increases in the military's wage bill. On the other hand, the military can hold wages constant, but expand the size of the pool of military labor by choosing a new, lower quality standard for recruits that yields the desired number of recruits OR at the pre-globalization wage **W** (see Rowe et al., 1999). This solution is represented in the model by the new, lower quality supply curve **S*** and implies an erosion in the quality of recruits.

Britain consistently chose the second path for responding to the pressures of globalization. Parliamentary opposition to higher taxes and military spending meant that it was impossible for the state to raise military pay. This resulted in recurrent recruiting crises as traditional sources of military labor, such as

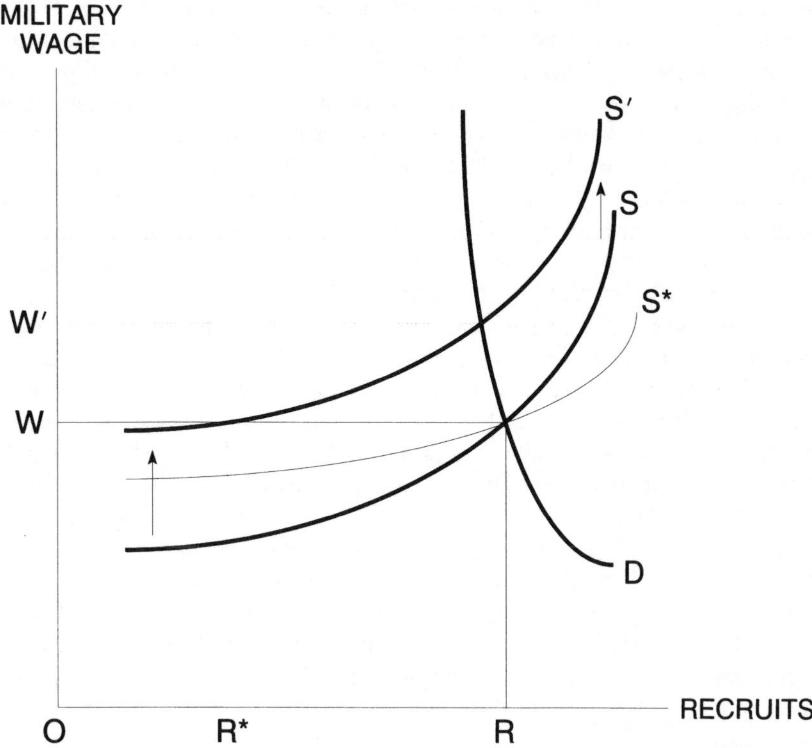

Fig. 3. Globalization and British Military Recruiting.

Irish peasants, pursued better opportunities in the civilian economy, as well as a dramatic decline in the physical qualities of the British recruit as the army was continually forced to lower standards to maintain numbers. Between 1861 and 1914, for example, the *minimum* required height for an infantry recruit fell from 5'8" tall to 5'3" and at times was even relaxed to 5'0" (see Rowe et al., 1999). In addition, the army also inducted a high number of "special enlistments" that failed to meet one of the army's minimum physical standards (Spiers, 1980, p. 40: Skelley, 1977, p. 238). Between 1892 and 1901, more than one-quarter of the army recruits fell into this category. Nor were the standards demanding. The army's minimum physical requirements in this period were for a soldier to weigh 115 lbs., be 5'4" to 5'3" tall, and have a chest size of 33" (Skelley, 1977, p. 238). In 1903, the army abolished the fixed minimum weight of 115 lbs, giving considerable discretion to the military's medical officers to induct recruits who would have previously fallen below the existing standards (Inspector General of Recruiting, 1903, p. 4; Skelley, 1977, p. 238).

In short, the history of the British army in the late nineteenth and early twentieth centuries is one of lagging military wages, chronic recruiting shortages, and falling physical standards (Skelley, 1977; Spiers, 1980). As is the case with continental Europe, there is considerable evidence to suggest that these problems were directly linked to Britain's deepening integration into the world economy. British military recruiters, for example, consistently blamed the growth of British trade for bad recruiting years. The growth of trade also appears responsible for a significant degree of the decline in physical standards and the erosion of the physical qualities of the British recruit (Rowe et al., 1999). Notably absent from the military's problems, however, were the working class antagonisms and rank and file resistance to military service that were so evident in the continental militaries. British military elites worried considerably about their ability to mobilize sufficient, high quality men into the armed forces, which they attributed to very poor rates of military pay; but in comparison to the continental states, they worried very little about the political loyalty of the troops or their willingness to serve. Popular anti-militarism did not find deep roots in British soil for the simple reason that military service in Britain was voluntary. Unlike continental Europe, men for whom the opportunity costs of military service exceeded the benefits simply did not have to serve, meaning that rising civilian wages did not politicize military service as was the case on the continent.

In fact, the most politically significant example of popular resistance to military service was the conflict over conscription. By the early 1900s, the abysmal performance of the British army in the Boer War and the growing threat of a continental conflict had convinced many among Britain's state and military elites that only a policy of universal military conscription would raise sufficient manpower to safeguard British security. The National Service League was founded in 1902 as an advocacy group for compulsory universal military training, and grew to some 250,000 members before the war (Adams & Poirier, 1987, pp. 10–11). Lord Roberts, a hero of the Boer War and Britain's most distinguished soldier, became the leader of the National Service League in 1905 and conscription's most vocal advocate. In public, Lord Roberts argued that some system of universal military training was needed for home defense and privately that conscription was essential to waging a successful war on the continent (Adams & Poirier, 1987, pp. 12–15; French, 1982, p. 24). Yet despite the growing strategic need for conscription, tremendous latent opposition made compulsory military service impossible. The National Service League did not gain widespread popular support and attracted members almost exclusively from the middle and upper classes (Adams & Poirier, 1987, pp. 16–32). Moreover, all of Britain's political parties distanced themselves from the idea. There were few gains to the Conservative party from proposing a policy that would only rally the supporters of the opposition; likewise a policy of conscription by the Labour and Liberal parties would have meant political suicide as its cost fell primarily on the constituencies of these two parties. Interestingly, it was militarism in the form of conscription, not anti-militarism, that for Britain appeared to pose the greatest threat to social stability before the war. As Herbert Henry Asquith later observed, the imposition of conscription "would have split the Cabinet, split the House of Commons, split both political parties, and split the nation . . ." (Adams & Poirier, 1987, p. 16).

But why did the British left oppose universal military service while the German and French left supported it? We can now explain this apparent conundrum by considering the different opportunity costs to labor of conscription in Britain and Europe. The Liberal and Labour parties opposed conscription because Britain's working classes had already demonstrated that existing rates of pay did not compensate sufficiently for the opportunity costs of military service. Conscription would have solved Britain's recruitment problems not by raising the level of compensation and therefore attracting more recruits, but by simply forcing people to serve who had already demonstrated their unwillingness to do so at present rates of pay. In essence, conscription amounted to little more than a highly coercive and regressive form of blood tax that would fall disproportionately on the populous working classes. These costs far outweighed any potential benefits in terms of democratization and social leveling that conscription was argued to bring. It is therefore not surprising that the Liberal and Labour parties opposed this proposition. For the socialist parties in France and Germany, on the other hand, conscription was a long-established practice that predated the rise in wages and which, because of globalization, now possessed a considerable bias against the working classes. Thus, the desire to create "nations in arms" was aimed directly at reducing the opportunity costs of conscription for the working classes. Truly universal military service would end the unfair and discriminatory exemptions available to the upper and middle classes but not to labor. Likewise, by reducing compulsory military service from two years to one, the socialists would cut the time spent under the colours, and hence the opportunity costs of service, by half. In short, there was no contradiction between the policies of British labor and the continental left. Both sought to minimize the costs that military service imposed on labor. The British Labour and Liberal parties opposed conscription because they wanted to prevent the imposition compulsory military service on the working classes; the French and German socialists favored short-service universal military conscription and a the creation of "nations in arms" because these steps would rectify the most unfair and egregious flaws in the long-standing systems of compulsory military service that already existed in their countries.

CONCLUSION

Widespread anti-militarism in pre-World War I Europe was a direct consequence of the effects of the late-nineteenth and early twentieth century globalization of the world economy. By raising wages and narrowing social inequality, globalization thus raised the opportunity costs of military service, and in so doing, altered the fundamental terms under which the state could use its citizens' lives for public purposes. Anti-militarism was weakest in Britain because its voluntary system of military recruitment left potential soldiers free to pursue the new opportunities created by the expansion of the world economy. It was strongest on the continent because long-standing systems of conscription denied continental conscripts this opportunity, thus politicizing military service.

At least three broader implications follow from this study. First, the effects of globalization on security are far from straightforward. The idea that trade and deepening international integration promote international peace is a staple of liberal thinking and dominates much of the current popular debate about late-twentieth century globalization. Yet it is far from clear that globalization's effects on prewar European security were entirely beneficial. The growing anti-militarism of prewar Europe progressively constrained the abilities of these states to use their citizens to maintain peace and engendered deep domestic conflicts as the lower classes sought to renegotiate the terms of duty. These were forces that destabilized European relations. They contributed to the growing belief among state and military elites that they now faced intractable but linked crises in both their domestic politics and external security.

Second, to understand the impact of globalization on domestic society requires an understanding of the institutions that comprise domestic society. The strength of anti-militarism depended critically on how the state mobilized manpower to fill the ranks of its military, for it was these institutions that determined who bore the rising opportunity costs of military service. Anti-militarism was weakest in Britain because military service was voluntary; it was strongest on the continent because conscripts were compelled to serve regardless of the personal costs of doing so. In determining how changes in the world economy reverberate within the struggles that characterize domestic society, institutions are key.

Finally, this study demonstrates that globalization affects domestic politics in ways that go far beyond influencing the positions of domestic groups on economic issues such as free trade and protection. By altering the opportunity costs of military service, late-nineteenth century globalization raised one of the most fundamental questions of social order in any society: the terms under which states may lay claim to the lives of their citizens. This suggests to me that we have barely scratched the surface in our understanding of this important phenomenon.

NOTES

1. "Dear bread" refers to the SPD's opposition to the Reich's practice of using tariffs (especially on grain) to raise revenues for military expenditures, thus linking the two themes of this paper, the international economy and anti-militarism.

2. Although globalization is often defined as the increasing penetration of international trade in the world's domestic economies, an exclusive focus on trade is too narrow. Trade flows are only one force that can drive the deepening integration of national economies. Migrations of capital, workers and productive technology can also respond to relative price differences between countries, flowing from countries where these resources are relatively abundant and cheap toward those countries where they are scarce and expensive (Williamson, 1996, p. 10; Richardson, 1995, p. 44).

3. This, of course, is the Stolper-Samuelson result derived from the Heckscher-Ohlin trade model. O'Rourke and Williamson (1994) generally confirm the accuracy of the model for the period of late nineteenth century globalization.

4. After the outbreak of hostilities in 1914 Hitler volunteered for service in the Bavarian army.

5. In France, this sum in 1889 amounted to 1,500ff (Porch, 1981, p. 25). By comparison, the annual salary of a French army sergeant in 1913 was only 1,368ff (Generalstab, 1914b). France abolished payments in 1889. This practice persisted in other continental European states until the war.

6. See also various issues of *Der Einjährige Freiwillige*, a private publication for one-year volunteers in the German army which often complained bitterly about the petty extortions exacted from these privileged soldiers. The publication was banned from the army in 1910. Some issues can be found in the archives of the Bavarian War Ministry in Munich, file MKr 4951.

7. See, for example, the parliamentary debate over an SPD bill to shorten conscription to one year in Reichstag 1912.

8. 10 pf a day would earn a conscript RM36.50 per year not including payments in kind such as room and board that were provided by the army. In comparison, a textile worker earned RM786 per year in 1913 and a steelworker RM1513. Although workers, unlike conscripts, paid room, board and other costs directly from their earnings there is no doubt that conscripts (and non commissioned officers) were extremely poorly paid (Klingenschmidt, 1997, p. 36).

ACKNOWLEDGMENTS

I thank the anonymous referees, Pamela Camerra-Rowe, Stephen van Holde, and Jytte Klausen for their many helpful comments. Errors are the responsibility of the author. This research was supported by the National Science Foundation, grant SBR-9709556.

WHO'S USING WHOM?: A COMPARISON OF MILITARY CONSCRIPTION IN GUATEMALA AND SENEGAL IN THE FIRST HALF OF THE TWENTIETH CENTURY

David Carey, Jr.

INTRODUCTION

Military conscription has long been used by elites and colonial powers to fulfill their need for soldiers and laborers. While this relationship is inherently exploitative, in some cases recruits have been able to use military recruitment to their advantage. While Maya of Guatemala and Africans of rural Senegal suffered distinct methods and outcomes of military conscription, they also realized fundamental changes in their worldviews and relations with their hegemons. A comparison of the oral histories of Maya-Kaqchikel and rural Senegalese soldiers (*tirailleurs*) shows how knowledge and experience gained from their military service resulted in an improved quality of life and sense of efficacy for many.[1] Paradoxically, despite its hierarchical nature, the military was more egalitarian than civilian life in Guatemala and Senegal. The majority of conscripts would have preferred not to have fallen victim to the voracious desire of the State to utilize their manpower, but many gleaned some benefits from their trials.

The Comparative Study of Conscription in the Armed Forces, Volume 20, pages 171–199.

ISBN: 0-7623-0836-2

A case study of Senegal and Guatemala is compelling because both are developing nations with diverse historical backgrounds and ethnic tensions. Unlike Senegal, Guatemala has long been a sovereign nation (since 1823) where a minority of primarily mixed-blood elites known as Ladinos[2] has controlled the government. These leaders subsequently forced indigenous peoples of Guatemala to serve in the military and engage in domestic conflict. In the case of Senegal, a European imperialist country forced natives of Senegal to fight in a distant war that held little relevance to their lives in Africa. Interestingly, the results of military conscription on these ethnically distinct soldiers bears some resemblance to the situation in the United States, an ethnically segmented, yet developed society. Scholars who have studied the integration of African Americans in the U.S. military have argued that the military is one of the most egalitarian institutions in the U.S. They assert race relations are better in the army than in civil society (Moskos & Butler, 1996). Generally, the military provides more equitable ethnic relations than civilian life in developed and developing nations.

Scholars have long recognized the role of the military in social and political change in developing nations. Claude Welch, Jr. (1985, p. 194) emphasizes the importance of examining the ways that the military imposes "its perspectives on society". However, much of the literature has focused on officers and those who voluntarily make a career of the military and utilize it as a means of social mobility. Furthermore, studies recognize the role of active military recruiting, but not necessarily conscription.[3] Morris Janowitz emphasizes the egalitarian qualities of the military and that it is more representative of less advantaged social classes than other professions. He notes, "In the ethos of the profession . . . social background is de-emphasized once a man has been accepted into military service. The military has a combat ideology and is preparing for war – real or imaginary. As a result, it tends to stress the personal worth of the individual man and to ignore his social background" (Janowitz, 1977, pp. 129–130). He argues that as a result of the greater probability of equal treatment, a sense of social cohesion and solidarity develops (Janowitz, 1977, p. 157). Likewise, in his study of Mexico's officer corps, Rod Camp adeptly shows, "that discipline facilitated the formation of a homogeneous, obedient officer corp" with "an extreme sense of loyalty to superior authority" (Camp, 1992, p. 11). In the case of Africa in the First World War, Melvin Page (1987b, p. xi) asserts that Africans' participation in war as opposed to hegemonic policy decisions is the key to understanding the impact of military service on Africans. The military experience for conscripts is remarkably distinct from that of those who enter the army of their own free will. For many conscripts a sense of a common identity with each other develops and to a lesser extent with those who have forced their participation, however, I argue that the military provides conscripts with the self-confidence to challenge and resist hegemons. It exposes subalterns to various means to confront injustices inherent in power structures maintained by the ruling social classes (oftentimes also representing ethnic divisions) at the local and national level. While Maya and Senegalese had distinct experiences through military conscription, both groups emerged from their experience with greater capacity and confidence to resist domination by Ladinos and French colonials (*colons*).

BACKGROUND

Guatemala, a multi-ethnic Central American nation of ten million people, has just ended the longest continuous armed conflict in twentieth century Central American history. The military played a central role in politics and society during Guatemala's thirty six year civil war that began in 1960. Guatemala's most recent elections in January 2000 endorsed the political party of former military dictator José Efraín Ríos Montt, evidence that Guatemala's military continues to play a dominant role in the political and social life of the nation. In fact, since the failure of Guatemala's democratic experiment in 1954, the majority of presidents have been military officers. Despite the signing of the Peace Accords in 1996, researchers know little about the inner workings of the military as an institution, the process and effects of conscription, the training of its conscripts or the evolution of its relationship with society and politics. Military conscription began well before the civil war. An essential component of this conscription has been the majority population of the Mayan people. The goal of military conscription was not simply to take advantage of this vast labor source, but also to indoctrinate (or in some cases simply eliminate) indigenous people into Ladino society. Dictators, such as General Jorge Ubico who ruled from 1931 to 1944, perceived military conscription as a means to keep Maya at peace. Ladinos argued that military conscription would force the indigenous population to integrate into national society and thereby result in a more peaceful, united, and developed nation. Many scholars argue that military conscription has attacked the traditional communal structure of the Mayan people and thereby led to increased acculturation. Mayan leaders have fought military conscription and today it is outlawed, but what has been the impact of forced participation in the military on Maya from their point of view?

In their oral traditions, Kaqchikel, the third largest of Guatemala's twenty one Mayan language groups, reveal their perceptions of military conscription. Most Kaqchikel men served as conscripts in the Guatemalan military. Their accounts of their experiences in the military and the effects of military service differ considerably from what the Guatemalan State hoped to achieve with military conscription. Prior to the onset of Guatemala's civil war, Kaqchikel did not simply succumb to this pressure to change, but rather, many worked military conscription to their benefit. While men suffered due to poor living conditions and separation from their families, they also used the institution to empower themselves. For many men, the military provided their only access to education. They learned how to speak, read, and write Spanish. The skills and experience they gained in the military gave them confidence to confront Ladinos in their communities. Today, however, most Kaqchikel avoid the military, because it attempts to change their character. This government institution, designed to force the incorporation of Maya into national society, resulted in the Kaqchikel's renewed confidence to stand up to Ladino persecution.

Senegal is a multi-ethnic, pluri-cultural nation in West Africa. It makes an excellent comparative case study with Guatemala because France was the only European colonial power in Africa in the twentieth century to institute universal male conscription during peace as well as war times (Echenberg, 1991, pp. 4, 25, 28–30). While the experience of rural Senegalese men in the military was distinct in many ways, they too were able to increase their efficacy in their communities and homeland as a result of their experience. In comparison, hardship imposed on Senegalese was greater than their Guatemalan counterparts. They too suffered from poor sanitary and hygienic conditions, but more acutely they were faced with intense combat in World War One and many of their brethren died in battle. Death and violence had a profound effect on these veterans. Furthermore, unlike Kaqchikel conscripts, they received little in the way of education or training beyond military matters. Nonetheless, their self-perceptions changed as did their images of Europeans. They no longer would stand French exploitation, abuse, or corruption. In fact, these transformations served as an important, albeit yet distant, catalyst to their nation's independence movement.

Military conscription has a long history in both Guatemala and Senegal. The Guatemalan government has conscripted young Mayan men into the military since Rafael Carrera led his revolt in 1837 to remove the national government and establish his Conservative regime (1844–1848, 1851–1865). However, a significant change occurred in the Guatemalan army when Justo Rufino Barrios became the first president (1873–1885) to professionalize the military. Originally, Barrios' liberal government did not deem Maya worthy of military service, either because they believed Maya incapable of arms training or unable to be trusted with that ability. However, only the poorest Ladinos, who were few in number, joined the military to become soldiers. Wealthy and educated Ladinos either avoided the military or became officers. As a result, beginning in the twentieth-century, the military came to depend on Maya to comprise the majority of their troops and achieved this support through conscription (Recopilación, 1881, pp. 115–118, 143–145, 151; Woodward, 1985, pp. 114, 154, 166; Adams, 1995, pp. 14–17, 30; Handy, 1984, p. 6; McCreery, 1994, pp. 180, 236–264; Carmack, 1990, p. 121, 1979, p. 277, 1995, p. 344). Kaqchikel oral histories recount each male between the ages of 18 and 60 had to perform at least one year of military service (Jun Kawoq, 1998; Ka'i' Kawoq, 1998; Wo'o' Kawoq & Waqi' Kawoq, 1998; Oxi' Kawoq, 1997; Ixkawoq, 1998). At the same time, Ladino images of the utility of Maya in the military began to change. Ladinos wanted to take advantage of Maya because the "tribes that anciently populated Guatemala were valiant and accustomed to war" (Anónimo, 1904, p. 66). Likewise, French advocates of conscription stressed the "warlike" character of the African "races" to justify their policy. Concurrently, they emphasized that Africans lacked intellectual prowess and became easily confused and unreliable. Nonetheless, their "bestial" impulses and "[highly] developed warrior instincts" made them exceptional candidates for the front lines (Lunn, 1999, pp. 45, 123–127, 139, 158; Echenberg, 1991, pp. 2, 32–33, 37–38, 63).

In Senegal, the French had utilized African troops since the early nineteenth century although they did not officially mandate military conscription until 1912. France resisted any international attempts at agreements over the nonmilitarization of Africans during the colonial period. In fact, they regarded Africans as "reservoirs of manpower" for the defense of their nation. Senegalese troops fought in Madagascar in 1828, French Guinea in 1838, the German war in 1871, and in the Moroccan War of 1912. They also fought in the Mexican war. French military conscription in Senegal lasted from 1912 to 1960. The most intense period of military conscription (and consequently Senegalese participation in the military), however, was from 1914 to 1918 in an effort to provide Senegalese soldiers for the French in World War One (Crowder, 1978, p. 108; Coleman & Brice, 1962, pp. 361–363, 376; Echenberg, 1991, pp. 4, 27; Davis, 1934, p. 50). In fact, historian Joe Lunn (1999, pp. 33, 46, 49) argues the French demand for African soldiers was more intense than the expropriation of Senegambian men in the eighteenth century trans-Atlantic slave trade. The realization that their services were needed for combat made military conscription more daunting for Senegalese than for Kaqchikel, who did not face armed conflict in the military until 1944.

THE PLIGHT OF MILITARY CONSCRIPTION

Oral histories assert that few men joined the military by choice. In the case of Guatemala, Kaqchikel attest local military commissioners organized a day (typically a market day when town squares were teeming with people) when officials would go to communities and grab men as young as fifteen years old off the street. They note officials then shipped the young men out in trucks destined for military quarters and oftentimes, families were unaware that their sons had been kidnapped. Sometimes, military officials would wait anxiously outside school doors and force boys into trucks and buses just as they were dismissed from classes for the day (Waqxaki' Kawoq, 1997; Junlajuj Kawoq, 1997; Lajuj Kawoq, 1998; Wuqu' Kawoq, 1998; B'eleje' Kawoq, 1998; Kab'lajuj K'ej, 1998). Kaqchikel were also susceptible to this disregard for their rights when they visited other regions of the country. For example, one Kaqchikel man was grabbed in Totonicapán, a K'ichee' speaking area (Kab'lajuj Kawoq, 1998). Few Kaqchikel resisted this inevitable service.

French officials proved more ruthless than their Guatemalan counterparts. Recruiting agents (both African and French) would also raid villages to acquire young men. However, when met with resistance, they would destroy crops and livestock, burn homes, and even kill family members and villagers. While measures this harsh were the exception, other agents bound Senegalese after capturing them. In another strategy, French utilized local chiefs and Muslim clerics to recruit young men. Most Senegalese assumed they would not return alive from the war so they employed numerous methods to avoid recruitment including self-mutilation, flight, and armed resistance. At the same time, some men viewed flight as dishonorable or perceived their fate to be inevitable and simply accepted conscription. Finally, in 1918 when French Premier Georges Clemenceau appointed Blaise Diagne to head the recruitment drive as Commissioner for the Republic in West Africa, military conscription became persuasive, not coercive. Diagne tied military service to French citizenship and emphasized promotions (Crowder, 1978, pp. 107, 109–110, 113–114, 116; Johnson, 1966, pp. 247–248; Echenberg, 1991, pp. 42–46, 71–75, 85; Lunn, 1999, pp. 38–44, 49, 73–84).[4]

Oral histories attest harsh treatment ensued after such physical coercion. Kaqchikel assert officials hit Mayan men during their training at times. According to some Kaqchikel men, discrimination against Maya was prevalent in the military. Some Kaqchikel viewed their military service as a punishment (Wuqu' Ajpu', 1998; Oxlajuj Kawoq, 1998; Wo'o' Ajpu', 1997; Oxi' Ajpu' et al., 1997; Waqi' Ajpu', 1998). Likewise, Senegalese soldiers were victims of beatings, insults, and racial slurs. Furthermore, they attest fighting increased when Europeans became inebriated (Lunn, 1999, pp. 96, 107).

Few men looked forward to military service. In the case of Guatemala, historian David McCreery asserts, "The indigenous population with few exceptions abhorred service in the regular army and did all they could to avoid it. To be drafted into the army means brutal treatment under Ladino officers, poor food, harsh and humiliating living conditions, and, often, years away from one's home community and interests" (McCreery, 1994, p. 181). For Senegalese soldiers, communications with their families were also minimal, but the physical distance was even greater than that of Kaqchikel from their families (Lunn, 1999, pp. 108–109). Abusive conditions, coupled with the loss of time with one's family and work, dispirited many. In Guatemala, despite improved racial relations in the barracks, anthropologist Richard Adams (1995, pp. 22, 57) asserts many Ladino officers discriminated against Mayan soldiers because they found them to be ignorant, lazy, and miserable. He also notes that only on rare occasions did Maya become officers, the majority of Mayan men were soldiers. Furthermore, Mayan conscripts received less food and salary than their Ladino cohorts. Even Mayan men who advanced through the military ranks were paid less than their Ladino counterparts (Carmack, 1979, p. 278). Likewise, Senegalese received less compensation and after the war their pensions were about one third of those who had French citizenship (Crowder, 1978, p. 108; Lunn, 1999, p. 230). While ethnic relations in the military were better than in their communities, racism continued to surface.

Oral histories also recount that living conditions in the military were less than desirable and food provisions were poor. One Kaqchikel elder explains, "We only got beans and half-cooked rice with no onions, oil or tomato in it" (Waqxaqi' Kawoq, 1997). In addition to less than palatable food, Kaqchikel assert many men suffered from bugs in their clothes and mattresses. Others complained that the soldiers consumed excessive amounts of alcohol, which made the situation uncomfortable. Kaqchikel recount that in some cases, men either were not paid, or the salaries were too small to contribute to their families. Kaqchikel opine many men suffered during their military service because the military did not take good care of its conscripts (Junlajuj Ajpu', 1998; Oxlajuj Ajpu', 1998; Kab'lajuj Ajpu', 1997; Waqxaqi' Ajpu', 1998; B'eleje' Ajpu', 1998; Lajuj Ajpu', 1998). Western scholars concur that the allocation of resources to the enlisted troops remained negligible. They received minimal, if any, pay, no uniforms or boots, and little education. The military provided limited social mobility and generally this movement was restricted to Ladinos (Woodward, 1985, pp. 78, 169–170; Adams, 1995, p. 11).

Living conditions in French and Senegalese camps proved to be worse than in Guatemala. Many of the camps were not completed and soldiers had to sleep in tents, some without beds. In fact, most provisions and military equipment were in short supply. Hygiene and sanitation were poor, consequently disease was not uncommon and some men died in the camps. The lack of medical personnel and supplies compounded the problem. In addition, Africans were unaccustomed to and unprepared for the winters. As a result of these harsh conditions, some men attempted desertion, although few succeeded. Most Senegalese opined, however, that they had been better treated in French camps than in African ones. Even after the war, conscripts continued to suffer from the military's inadequate provisions. In some cases, men had to march hundreds or thousands of miles to reach their induction sites (Crowder, 1978, p. 108; Lunn, 1999, pp. 93, 106, 108; Echenberg, 1991, pp. 35, 76–77, 164).

BENEFITS

Despite the sacrifices, some men appreciated the opportunities provided them through military service. In Guatemala, ethnohistorian Robert Carmack (1979, p. 278) points out the military provided an education that included the Spanish language, the opportunity to travel, the opportunity to develop leadership skills, and a familiarization and increased level of confidence with Ladino culture. Kaqchikel oral histories express that most men appreciated the experience because without their military service they would have been unable to communicate in Spanish. According to oral histories, the military offered Spanish classes for one and a half hours each day. In general, oral accounts assert most men welcomed the opportunity to learn to read and write Spanish (Waqi' Imox, 1998; Jun Imox, 1997; Wo'o' Imox, 1998; Ixtijax, 1998; Ix'imox, 1998; Jun Ajpu', 1997; Wuqu' Imox, 1997; Oxi' Imox, 1998; Wuqu' Kan, 1998; Ka'i' Imox, 1998; Kaji' Imox, 1998). An 82 year old Kaqchikel man who stands at about four feet and nine inches explains, "I never went to school. I do not know the numbers, but I do know how to write because I did school in the military under [President Jorge] Ubico" (Ka'i' Imox, 1998). While reading and writing skills gained in the military were only rudimentary, most conscripts learned to communicate in Spanish and that proved to be an invaluable asset. Prior to Juan José Arévalo's administration (1944–1950), the only schooling most Kaqchikel received was through the military. As a result of the educational opportunities, some men volunteered their services. In some cases Mayan men not yet of the eligible age volunteered to join the military (Adams, 1995, p. 24; Carmack, 1979, p. 288). One former Kaqchikel soldier states, "I was in the army in 1944. I went to the *Matamoros* [military quarters]. I was not grabbed. I wanted to go. We presented ourselves and I had to sell my machete to get a ticket to get there" (Waqxaqi' Imox, 1997). That this man was willing to sell an essential agricultural tool to pay for his transportation to the military showed he was determined to gain some experience outside of his community and expand his knowledge.

A similar phenomenon occurred in rural Senegal once Diagne instituted his recruitment drive based on citizenship, equal rights, and assuaging the fears of combat. In 1918, nearly a quarter of all recruits volunteered for their service. A stark contrast to the early years of French recruitment based on terror. For the first time, West Africans witnessed the possibility of African power over Europeans when Diagne dismissed French officials for abusive or corrupt actions. One Senegalese recruit notes, "When Diagne came more respect was given to 'black' people [by the French]" (Lunn, 1999, p. 80). Senegalese realized the potential for escaping their second class status and developing equitable relations with Europeans in their nation (Crowder, 1978, p. 117; Lunn, 1999, pp. 77, 80, 110; Johnson, 1966; Echenberg, 1999, pp. 44–46).[5] As Diagne heralded and demonstrated the benefits of military service it became more attractive for some Senegalese.

The military also appealed to some men's sense of adventure. Kaqchikel oral histories attest that through the military, enlisted men traveled to areas they never had seen before and in some cases, the military sent them to foreign countries. Informants point out for this reason, some men served the military through three administrations. Some Kaqchikel assert that their experience in the military gave them more confidence to explore areas outside their communities for both pleasure and employment (B'eleje' Imox, 1997; Lajuj Imox, 1997; Kaji' Imox, 1998). Likewise, before World War One, most Senegalese recruits had never traveled more than a few miles from their home. In fact, for most *tirailleurs* their military service was the first time they had any significant contact with Europeans. After the war nearly one third of rural Senegalese soldiers decided not to return to their homes (Lunn, 1999, pp. 91, 209). For some soldiers, the military offered an escape from the quotidian reality of their communities.

For some men, the military offered a livelihood and a chance to set their lives in a new direction. One Kaqchikel woman explains her father's experience, "When [my father] was fourteen, he went to the military. He was looking for work and did not know what to do. He was working in a small restaurant and only earned his food. He had to sweep and clean out trash, so then he decided to go to the military where he could sleep and eat well. He did that for six to eight years" (Ixiq', 1998). Some men joined the military because they had few other options. This Kaqchikel man used the military to bring stability to his life and later he began a successful career as a painter.

Kaqchikel men learned skills beyond Spanish. According to some men, the military educated them in the use of firearms that required an understanding of mathematics so they learned how to multiply and add. Some men were content that the military taught them how to swim. In other instances, men learned a skill that allowed them to earn a living in their communities. For example, one local barber learned how to cut hair in the military and today he continues to use the same implements for his trade that the army gave him in 1944. In addition, oral accounts note the military gave some men musical instruments that they continued to use in their communities (Oxi' Imox, 1997; Junlajuj Imox, 1998; Lajuj Imox, 1998; Ixk'at, 1998; Oxlajuj Imox, 1998; Kab'lajuj Imox, 1997; Junlajuj Ajpu', 1998; Wuqu' Imox, 1997).[6] Furthermore, Kaqchikel men who already had some education taught classes. One Kaqchikel musician explains, "I went to school and earned a third grade education. I knew how to read and write. The army liked that, so I gave classes to others" (Junlajuj Ajpu', 1998). In addition, oral accounts attest that during the Arévalo administration the military offered scholarships to talented soldiers to study in the military academy (Ka'i' Kawoq, 1998). The majority of Kaqchikel men appreciated the opportunity to expand their talents, intellect, and employment opportunities. Nonetheless, the overwhelming majority of men returned to their communities to live.

In contrast to Kaqchikel reactions, most Senegalese men who parlayed a skill they learned in the military into new employment entered the French sector of the economy outside their communities. New jobs included: medical assistants, policemen or guards, carpenters, lorry drivers, and mechanics. In fact, some men chose to pursue new locations because they feared members of their communities would no longer understand or identify with them. Conversely, in some cases ethnic pressure kept men in the community (Echenberg, 1991, pp. 63, 82, 84). One soldier explains:

> [Although the *commandant* offered me the option of a job in the police force] I didn't want to become a policeman because I didn't want the people of my village to be angry with me. Because they might [have] said that [I did] it because I had been in France and in the war that I had kept French habits. So that's why I wanted to come back to my village and to remain a farmer like before (Lunn, 1999, p. 210).

Like Kaqchikel, the majority of Senegalese (two thirds) returned to their communities and pre-war livelihood. One soldier recalls, "When [we first] returned to Senegal, I was eager to see my family and to [be with] them. But, then I started [doing my] daily work as I had done before the war. [I was] farming, fishing, and learning the Koran; these were my [only] occupations" (Lunn, 1999, p. 209).

In addition to intangible qualities, such as education and leadership skills that the military provided, financial compensation satisfied many soldiers. Kaqchikel oral histories note in some cases, conscripts earned money for their service. Kaqchikel recall during the Ubico regime, the military paid its conscripts three *quetzals*[7] per month, a daily wage of ten cents which was on a par with their earning potential in their communities. They also note that during the Arévalo administration, wages were higher in the military than in the highlands. They assert this compensation provided them with a valuable contribution to their livelihood. They point out men could buy land or cows with their income (Kab'lajuj Tijax, 1997; Ixkawoq, 1998; Jun K'at, 1998; Wuqu' Ajpu', 1998). Senegalese also returned with surplus income. Oftentimes they would contribute it to their families or in some cases attempt to begin new endeavors (Lunn, 1999, p. 192). The military provided the means for some men to establish a source of income independent of what they derived through their families.

Most Kaqchikel soldiers appreciated the military's emphasis on discipline. They argued that their own self-discipline made their transition into the military easier. Informants assert that they displayed orderliness in marching drills and other assignments. Some opine that the reason young people today fail to display good discipline is because they never served in the army when it was respectable (before the civil war) (Oxi' Kat, 1998; Ka'i' K'at, 1998; Ka'i' Imox, 1998). Kaqchikel appreciated that the military operated with a clear set of rules. As long as they adhered to the physical and mental demands they were free from abuse and in most cases they were respected as soldiers.

EMPOWERMENT AND VALUATION OF SUBALTERNS

In addition to the emphasis on discipline, the military also provided Kaqchikel with an escape from an oppressive situation in their villages. One elder explains, "I went to the military in 1925. I liked it because here [in my town] was a big problem. We were exploited and abused by the Ladinos. They did not like us, so they fought us" (Junlajuj Imox, 1998). When Kaqchikel returned from the military, Ladinos knew they had received training so they left them alone. A former Kaqchikel mayor shares his father's opinion:

> In those days the Ladinos did not like 'our people' and they did not treat us well. You always had to walk on the side of the road. If you got in the Ladinos' way, or even if not, they would push you or hit you. You let them have the middle. Thirty years ago that settled down a bit, but the Ladinos are still bad people. My dad got people together and told them it was wrong what the Ladinos do to us. They kill us. We are dumb. Back in those days, there was no school. He told them not to be afraid. He said they should go to the military because it makes you tough. That is how we can rise up. Go to the military, because it is tough. When you leave the military you have changed from a boy to a man (Wo'o' K'at, 1998).

The military provided a means for Kaqchikel to defend themselves against Ladino abuse. A forty five year-old van driver notes, "When studies and military service came, they gave value to our people. We fought Ladinos and then we could read. There was no more *ixto*" (Waqi' K'at, 1998).[8] Likewise, some scholars recognize the military was the only institution that offered an outlet from the racist system that inhibited Maya from a better quality of life. Carmack (1979, p. 277) asserts, "The military organization showed the least indigenous-Ladino caste stratification in comparison with any other formal institution of the community, and provided the Indian with the best opportunity to reach a high public position." Oral histories note Kaqchikel appreciated the military for its ability to level race relations. Another Kaqchikel elder asserts, "That is what I liked about the military. Everyone was equal. We worked and stood side by side with the Ladinos. Justice and rights were equal with the Ladinos" (Junlajuj Ajpu', 1998).

Senegalese soldiers also experienced a transformation in their relations with and perceptions of the powerbrokers in their homeland: the French. Lunn (1999, p. 92) observes, "The soldiers' view of themselves, other Africans, and the French first began to change," as a result of their experience in the training camps in Senegal and France and their involvement in the war. Unlike Kaqchikel, for many Senegalese it was the first time they had personal contact with Europeans and consequently they were exposed to new worldviews, institutions, realities, and personalities. A few even had French girlfriends and were invited to their homes. For most tirailleurs, however, contact with French civilians was limited because they spoke little French. Nonetheless, it was considerably more interaction than they had experienced previously and through these relations they realized that Europeans were as human and diverse as themselves. For example, many Senegalese were amazed to learn that some Frenchmen could not read. Certainly, they no longer feared Europeans and the more Senegalese interacted with French people, the better their images of them became. Senegalese also appreciated the system of justice in the army. Unlike in their native country, European wrongdoings were met with punishment. Furthermore, racist overtures were met with Senegalese reprisals such as beatings. In general, most soldiers felt they were treated fairly by the French and respected more than they ever had been in the colony. They were excited to discover that for some French people the color of one's skin was irrelevant and they all might be accepted as brothers (Echenberg, 1991, pp. 63, 77–78; Lunn, 1999, pp. 91–92, 111, 165, 172–123, 176–179). One rural Senegalese soldier stressed, "We were in the same army . . . so we were all equal; we were all the same" (Lunn, 1999, p. 111). In contrast to civilian realities at the time, social leveling was common in many European armies during World War One (Leed, 1981, pp. 24–27, 198–200, 210).[9]

In some cases French-Senegalese relations went beyond equality. One Senegalese soldier who participated in the famous retaking of Fort Douaumont explains:

> We felt very proud after the attack because the French had tried many times to retake the fort, but finally we [were the ones] that took it . . .. And in every town we crossed, the French were clapping their hands and shouting: "*Vive les tirailleurs sénégalais!*" . . . And afterwards, whenever we were walking in the country – everywhere we used to go – if we told people that we made the attack on Fort Douaumont, the French were looking at us with much admiration (Lunn, 1999, p. 137).

Many Senegalese would carry this sense of pride, equality, and justice with them when they returned to their native land and their sense of efficacy increased dramatically.

Another outcome of military service for Senegalese was the amelioration of historical ethnic animosities. While Kaqchikel do not emphasize relations with other Maya during their military stints, many Senegalese soldiers noted a certain amount of social leveling among and between ethnicities. Lunn (1999) points out that age and precolonial social standing were irrelevant in the French army. One *griot* noted, "We all joined the same army – the French army . . .. So we did not think about our [previous] way of living, our behavior, our kingdoms . . .. [Although] little arguments sometimes [occurred] between soldiers of the same country . . .. There wasn't any [social] differentiation because we were following another system – another [way of] life – which was the French one" (Lunn, 1999, pp. 97–98). Despite occasional tensions, as ethnic interactions increased a general sense of unity developed among African soldiers (Lunn, 1999, pp. 97–98, 109).

Kaqchikel oral traditions most fondly recall their military service during the Ubico regime (1931–1944). Kaqchikel note his government constructed military quarters in Chimaltenango. They assert Ubico cleaned up the military, because he took pride in it. They recount that prior to Ubico, lice and other vermin inhabited the uniforms, so Ubico burned all the clothes and ordered new ones (Jun Kawoq, 1998; Ka'i' Kawoq, 1998; Wo'o' Kawoq & Waqi' Kawoq, 1998; Oxi' Kawoq, 1997; Ixkawoq, 1998). Informants argue that his government valued conscripts and compensated them for their service. Furthermore, they opine that Ubico respected them as Maya. They point out that in some cases, he allowed them to wear their *xerkas*[10] over their uniforms (Wuqu' K'at, 1998; Waqxaqi' K'at, 1997). A forty year-old artist argues that the military helped to give Maya self-esteem:

> Now military service is bad and repressive, but during the time of Ubico, it helped our people. For example, when a young man went to the army, he gained self-esteem. He had never been to school, but they taught him things, like how to write and speak Spanish. So

> he no longer was afraid of the Ladinos. During Ubico's time, Ladinos had to perform military service also. Now men are not required to enter the military and only Mayas go, so many people do not understand that it was a good thing under Ubico (B'eleje' K'at, 1997).

The military gave Kaqchikel the self-confidence to confront Ladinos and therefore helped to reduce the racial separation of Guatemalans. Oral histories note that prior to Ubico, only Ladinos achieved the status of officers in the military, but Ubico changed that and some Kaqchikel became officers (Jun Kan, 1998). Like Senegalese soldiers, the self-esteem Kaqchikel gained from their military experience allowed them to return to their communities and change their reality.

Some Senegalese soldiers returned to their communities and had the confidence to confront oppression and corruption. As the son of one former rural soldier explains:

> When [my father] came back, he had learned many things from the war and [about] the 'white man' . . .. He had gained more understanding about the kind of ways officials should [behave]. So he contributed a lot to the change of many things. Because he said 'no' when he was [within his rights] to say 'no' and 'yes' [only] when he [decided] to say 'yes'. And he didn't accept any longer this official cheating [of] people or telling [them] something that was not [true] (Lunn, 1999, p. 192).

Many became involved in veterans groups and were active in local and national organizations and politics, demanding representation and organizing labor unions. Some returning soldiers demanded their rights as full citizens. Those who had been serfs refused to resume their obligations to overlords. Manumission was a direct result of the war. Veterans had a profound impact on Senegalese society; in ways that the French did not welcome (Lunn, 1999, pp. 194, 204, 207, 226; Crowder, 1967, pp. 18–20; Page, 1987a, p. 20).[11]

Some French leaders quickly became aware of the impact that participation in the military would have on Africans. A 1922 report from Senegal of the Inter-Ministerial Commission on Recruitment in French West Africa noted:

> The former slave population has also accepted the principle of conscription with less difficulty than have the aristocratic element. The former slaves correctly regard military service as an excellent means of levelling social classes. They have everything to gain in the future in seeing their masters served cheek by jowl in the same ranks with them. It can be said without exaggeration that certain population groups did not really achieve their complete autonomy until the day when their children, definitely liberated by military service, returned from duty to their homes, thereby instructing all as to the equality of every one before the white man's law (Echenberg, 1991, p. 70).

The combination of transformed Senegalese self-images and the assertion of African pride, forced French colonists to respect them. These psychological reconstructions and an increased sense of potency on the part of Senegalese meant French abuses diminished. One Senegalese corporal explains:

> I received many lasting things from the war. I demonstrated my dignity and courage, and [I] won the respect of the people and the [colonial] government. And whenever the people of the village had something to contest [with the French] – and they didn't dare do it [themselves] because they were afraid of them – I used to do it for them. And many times when people had problems with the government, I used to go with my decorations and arrange the situation for [them]. Because whenever the *Tubabs* [Europeans] saw your decorations, they knew that they [were dealing with] a very important person. . . . And I gained this ability – of obtaining justice over a *Tubab* – from the war.
>
> [For example], one day a *Tubab* came here [to the village] . . . to make an examination of the people . . . and there was a small boy who was blind and . . . walking, [but] he couldn't see, and he bumped into the *Tubab*. And the *Tubab* turned and pushed the boy [down]. And when I saw that, I came and said to the *Tubab*; "Why have you pushed this boy? [Can't] you see that he is blind?" And the *Tubab* said: "Oh, pardon, pardon. I did not know. I will never do it again, excuse me!" [But] before the war, [no matter what they did], it would not have been possible to do that with a *Tubab* (Lunn, 1999, p. 232).

Some veterans believed that the alterations initiated after the war played an important role in the eventual independence of the country in January 1959 (Lunn, 1999, pp. 232–233; O'Brien, 1972, p. 107).[12]

Prior to the 1940s, the military served as a vehicle for Mayan males to acquire an education that otherwise the government denied them. In many ways, their experience in the military capacitated them to better achieve their goals in national society. They learned how to read, write, and speak Spanish, do basic mathematics, interact more efficaciously with the State and Ladinos, and perform a variety of technical and vocational skills. In addition, they explored their own country and learned more about its geography, topography, and diverse population. Some Mayan men were able to use these new talents and skills to improve their economic situation (Adams, 1995, p. 11). Despite advantages, however, the military appealed to only a few Maya. Most Mayan men preferred to end their obligation quickly and return to their communities.

DISTINCT ASSIMILATIONIST GOALS AND RESULTS

Both Senegalese and Kaqchikel were able to empower themselves through their military experience, but unlike Senegalese, for many Kaqchikel their military obligations ensued even after they returned to their communities. Oral histories attest Ubico designed volunteer companies to ensure military participation of all men in the community. Kaqchikel assert when a man completed his military obligation in one of the regional military quarters, he had to "volunteer" each Sunday morning for local military drills in the unit called "the voluntary company". They point out, however, that the voluntary company was a misnomer because Ubico required everyone to contribute their time and effort. He wanted to have prepared soldiers (Jun Kawoq, 1998; Ka'i' Kawoq, 1998; Wo'o' Kawoq & Waqi' Kawoq, 1998; Oxi' Kawoq, 1998; Ixkawoq, 1998). Kaqchikel recall even men who had not served at a military quarters had to volunteer. One man elucidates, "I participated in the volunteer company for four years beginning in 1936 during Ubico's time. It was pure instruction and mobilization of arms. We did not get paid, but I was good at it. I never went to school, but I learned how to read in the army . . .. Then I bought a dictionary to improve" (Oxlajuj Ajpu', 1998). The volunteer company provided this man with Spanish skills and the confidence to continue to teach himself.

Other men assert they resented this obligation, however, because it eliminated their only day of rest, and their only compensation was a signature on their control card. Oral histories show most Kaqchikel believed they gained something from the one or two year stints in the military quarters, but they viewed the voluntary company as a waste of time. Kaqchikel assert they had to report at six o'clock and march until eleven o'clock each Sunday morning, and they could not miss sessions because of an illness. They recall each Sunday officers stamped the men's books to prove they had participated. They also recount if the men did not have their stamps, the police would incarcerate them, and a jail term meant five days without pay. They point out these voluntary companies essentially eliminated any respite they would have had from their week's work (Wuqu' Imox, 1997; Ka'i' Kawoq, 1998). One man expresses the mixed reaction to obligatory military service, "I served in the army for one year. The lieutenant instructed us. We had to carry arms and we also learned Spanish. I liked the military, but it was also a loss of my time" (Kab'lajuj Imox, 1997).

Ubico's volunteer companies and conscription were part of his attempt to incorporate Maya into the army and national life. He said, "They come [to the military] rude, brutish, and with primitive origin, but they return learned, *desnados* [transformed from donkey-like condition] with good manners and in a condition to face life with improved personal faculties" (Hernández de León, 1940, p. 17). Ubico viewed military training as an educational device. He wanted to militarize the society and make all men, especially Maya, soldiers. Consequently, Maya comprised the majority of the troops in the military.

In addition to the state's demand to fill its military ranks, many Ladinos believed that military service would be a good influence on Maya. One Ladino author opines, "Although the physical conditions promise great success, the Indian is extremely self-denied, malnourished, and under-clothed," but the author concludes that many Maya become good soldiers and, "although the Ladino is much more intelligent, the Indian possesses some military qualities of a higher level than that of the Ladino" (Kuhsiek, 1915–1916, pp. 4–6). Military education combated illiteracy and included reading, writing, basic math, grammar, geography and other subjects (Gaitán et al., 1940, p. 34; Anónimo, 1911, pp. 9–11; Adams, 1995, p. 26). Another author emphasizes the importance of the role of acculturation in the military, "Here is the principal and most useful part. The Indian in the army will have to abandon his primitive outfit to dress in uniform . . . sleep in a bed, in a room that is much better than the home he left, eat at a table and bathe in a bathroom, in the daily ablution, acquire the habits of an exterior that better conforms to civilization" (Anónimo, 1911, pp. 9–11).

Interestingly, French public perceptions of Senegalese were similar to Ladino perceptions of Maya. French representations of Africans identified them as a mix between animals and humans mainly because their intellectual and moral capacity lacked development. Some asserted that they were lascivious and lazy beings who practiced human sacrifice and other uncivilized customs. In fact, many French asserted that Africans lacked any praiseworthy civilization or indigenous culture (Crowder, 1967, pp. 2–4; Lunn, 1999, p. 158).[13] One Senegalese soldier attests, "The French thought we were cannibals, [even though] we never ate anybody" (Lunn, 1999, p. 158). Slowly, French perceptions began to change as a result of increased interaction between Senegalese and French, and a public campaign to correct popular misconceptions (although seldom were Africans viewed as equals). For the most part, military officials respected the Senegalese soldiers (Cohen, 1980, pp. 283–284; Lunn, 1999, pp. 159, 174–176). One general lauded them for, "their marvelous courage, their indomitable tenacity, their impetuosity of spirit . . . [and] their loyalty and absolute devotion" to the French cause (Lunn, 1999, p. 159).

Despite their negative perceptions of these subalterns, the ruling powers advocated the utility of military conscription. The Guatemalan press praised obligatory military service for Maya. *El Imparcial* (July 10, 1940), a daily newspaper, applauded the government's efforts that resulted in "dignifying the life of the soldier." Reporters noted "the obvious transformation" of Mayan participants. They also asserted, "Many indigenous troops have been educated by the military . . . a beneficial change is reflected in their customs, clothing and self identity" (El Imparcial, January 2, July 10, 1940). Another newspaper, *El Liberal Progresista* (February 14, 1941), also recognized a transformation that occurred in Maya which would help them "to conduct themselves better in society." This source reported that demand to join the military exceeded the number of spaces available. During her travels through Guatemala, Erna Ferguson (1938, p. 317) opined that through military conscription Maya gained a sense of nationalism that subsumed their ancient tribal allegiance. According to these authors, the military facilitated the government's goal of the incorporation of Maya into national society and most Ladinos were not striving for a multi-ethnic and pluri-cultural country.

The Guatemalan military's attempt at acculturation was only mildly successful, however. One female Kaqchikel activist from Poaquil explains, "The ideology of the military is very different from our own" (Ixkan, 1998). Many Kaqchikel observe that today when men return from military service, they have lost much of their respect for their culture and community; their character has changed. For example, in the 1980s one Kaqchikel man rose up through the military ranks and eventually became Guatemala's Vice-Minister of Defense. However, Kaqchikel emphasize that as a general in the K'ichee' military zone he killed many Maya. Informants point out that this man assumed Ladino values and structures and in the process violated the Mayan respect for life. Consequently, his actions disenfranchised him from Kaqchikel and he is no longer considered one of "our people" by most of them (Jun Kan, 1998; Lajuj K'at, 1998). His drastic acculturation and subsequent rejection sharply contrasts the reality of the majority of Kaqchikel conscripts who performed their military service in the first half of the twentieth century.

For the most part, prior to the civil war, indoctrination was not as intense and few men remained in the military long enough to lose their attachment to their homes and people. Kaqchikel oral histories point out that as a result of their talents, discipline, and diligence, the military promoted a few Kaqchikel men to sergeant. In fact, some Ladino officers preferred to work with Maya rather than Ladinos because they were better soldiers.[14] Most Mayan men succeeded in this environment because they knew what was expected of them and as long as they accomplished their tasks for the most part they were not victims of capricious acts. Kaqchikel oral histories assert most Kaqchikel men gained confidence from their military service, but few accepted promotions that required a continuation beyond their stipulated time. Kaqchikel note most men missed their families and community life. Furthermore, they point out some men viewed the military as a waste of time that took away from their responsibilities at home (Lajuj Kan, 1997; B'eleje' Kan, 1997; Jun Iq', 1998; Oxi' Imox, 1998; Kab'lajuj Imox, 1997; Waqxaqi' Kan, 1998). One elder states, "I learned Spanish in the military. I did it for two and a half years. I was a first sergeant. They wanted to promote me, but I did not want to stay. I wanted to come back to Comalapa. It is better that I work in the fields" (Junlajuj Imox, 1998).

Ironically, Senegalese soldiers acculturated more than Kaqchikel soldiers despite (or perhaps due to) the fact the Guatemalan State's assimilationist policies were more overt. The French policy of assimilation was never significantly extended beyond the Four Communes to the interior of Senegal. In fact, by 1910 the French had shifted to a policy of association because they believed Africans were too distinct to assimilate into their culture. Nonetheless, residents of Senegalese rural communities noted that their men had acquired European traits. For example, many wore European not their traditional clothes and began smoking tobacco among other changes. At the same time, their increased knowledge and experience challenged the traditional hierarchical system that reserved expertise for elders. In addition, those who retained their money could enter into marriage contracts without the traditional outside assistance. Concurrently, some transformations were gladly welcomed as in the case of one woman who recalls that her cousin helped her in the kitchen; a gender role seldom mixed prior to the war. Generally, most veterans eventually acculturated themselves again to their communities to the extent necessary for conformance (Crowder, 1967, pp. 3, 17; Lunn, 1999, pp. 191–192; Echenberg, 1991, p. 3). Naturally, the effects of acculturation were more intense on Senegalese than Kaqchikel because for the most part they had longer stints in the military and their stations were not only further from their homes, but in another culture and country.

In further contrast to Kaqchikel conscripts, many Senegalese soldiers sought promotion and desired to become noncommissioned officers (NCOs). This promotion included additional language and weapons training as well as increased prestige and salary. It also allowed them the opportunity to assert authority over European soldiers and lower ranking NCOs (Lunn, 1999, p. 108). The majority of Kaqchikel refused promotions to quickly escape military life, whereas Senegalese soldiers knew their service would not end until the war did (or they were killed or mamed) so they sought advancements through the ranks.

TERROR OF COMBAT

Kaqchikel benefited from military education, but they understood the real motivations behind this schooling. They assert the military trained men for combat (Oxlajuj Kawoq, 1998; Ixkame, 1998). One man explains, "I just learned a little how to read in the military. There was a quarter hour of school, then a quarter hour of instruction. They do not teach you to read, they teach you more how to use arms" (Junlajuj K'at, 1998). A local painter takes it one step further, "I never wanted to be in the military because they teach you how to kill people" (Kab'lajuj K'at, 1998). A store owner who served in the military for two years said, "I hated it. They taught you how to kill. Some of my friends were even killed. I was [only] seventeen years old" (Oxlajuj K'at, 1998). A rural farmer succinctly states, "Ubico sent men to the military to exploit them" (Ka'i' Kan,

1997). Kaqchikel knew the government did not send them to the military quarters for their own benefit. More importantly, military training starkly contradicted Kaqchikel upbringing and respect for life.

Senegalese soldiers reacted similarly to their experience in the military. In their case they were trained for combat and war was ensuing; there was never any illusion of instruction beyond military concerns. As one rural Senegalese soldier recalls:

> We went to France, we fought for France, and the French took us by force to fight for them. [But] we learned nothing [there] – [not] even the French language. They only taught us some rudimentary [commands], [in order] to use us in the war. But they didn't care about teaching us the structure and sound of their language. So [although we] went to war, [we] came back here without any real knowledge of the French language (Lunn, 1999, p. 230).

Many felt the French had exploited them. Senegalese soldiers' combat experience was also considerably more intense than that of Kaqchikel soldiers. Senegalese suffered high casualty rates because the French used them as shock troops. Many had to engage in hand to hand combat. Men describe, "soldiers falling all around you" and literally "walking over the bodies of the dead" as they advanced on the Germans (Lunn, 1999, pp. 6, 95, 120–147, 167, 230).[15] One soldier recalls

> The first thing we saw when we [disembarked from the ships] were boots just coming out of the ground – they were dead soldiers that had been buried by the shells . . .. The soldiers had been bombed by the shells . . .. Both the French and Germans were bombing everywhere when we arrived. I was in the crowd and was advancing. [And a shell] dropped near my legs, and I was blown up about 20 meters [in the air] from where the cannon ball fell. I was not wounded, but I had a stomach full of air . . . because of the impact of the [explosion]. And I was lying there for . . . hours [because] I could not move (Lunn, 1999, p. 147).

Some Senegalese wept, drank, sang, prayed, fled, wore protective charms or found other means to deal with omnipresent death, but those who survived had to live with physical, pyschological, and emotional scars. Sadly, while some Senegalese expressed anti-German sentiment or claimed to be fighting for their own rights to citizenship, most Senegalese were uncertain as to the reasons for the war (Echenberg, 1991, pp. 34–37; Lunn, 1999, pp. 132–137).

While many Senegalese valued the knowledge they gained from their military experience, most would have preferred never to have left. One rural soldier opines, "Nothing I saw [overseas] was worth our [sacrifices], and the [loss] of all the people who died during the war" (Lunn, 1999, p. 229). Others felt they had changed little as a result of their military experience. Soldiers from the rural areas bore the brunt of Senegalese casualties and consequently, most of those who survived viewed any benefits (personal or national) as immensely disproportionate to the horrors of the war (Lunn, 1999, p. 229). Another Senegalese soldier adds, "I don't know whether there was anything lasting [that resulted] from the war, but [I do know] that no one can replace a human life" (Lunn, 1999, p. 229). The intense combat to which Senegalese were exposed resulted in more embittered recollections and evaluations of their military service than that of Kaqchikel.

Many Kaqchikel men experienced some combat during their military service, although not to the extent of Senegalese soldiers. The 1944 revolution is a vivid memory in Kaqchikel oral histories. One Kaqchikel participant explains:

> I joined the military because I was obligated to. At first I was in it for one and a half years. Then they grabbed me again and I did another term during the October Revolution in 1944. I was in the palace, but my barracks were San José Fort. In the palace nothing happened, shots just passed overhead, but hundreds died in [the military barracks of] Matamorros, Honor Guard and San José Fort (Oxi' Kan, 1998).

Oral histories recall many soldiers died in the 1944 revolution. A painter recounts what her father told her, "My father was in the military in 1944, when they revolted and took out Ubico. It was a war between military quarters, so he [my father] had to kill others. Many people died" (Ixiq', 1998). For some Kaqchikel, the military was not just training; they engaged in mortal combat. Kaqchikel were not opposed to weapons training, but few wanted to utilize these skills. Others add that in October, two military quarters burned to the ground and all the soldiers present died (Ka'i' Kawoq, 1998; Ixkej, 1997). Although most Kaqchikel thrived in the military because they could abide by its clearly defined rules of conduct and expectations, they did not agree with the military's agenda. Kaqchikel lament that they had to participate in the death and violence associated with the military.

By 1944 the country was ripe for revolution. Labor unrest, middle class pressures for democratization and reform, and a loss of U.S. support all weakened Ubico's position. On July 1, 1944, faced with an extensive petition from some of Guatemala's most respected professionals and business people in solidarity with striking workers, Ubico resigned and turned power over to a military junta composed of three generals. General Federico Ponce Vaides quickly dominated the junta and ordered congress to appoint him provisional president. He threatened to forestall the elections. Finally, in October, cadets from the *Escuela Politécnica*, the Guatemalan military academy, and progressive members of the military Honor Guard in Guatemala City joined students in a bloody battle that forced Ponce's capitulation and established a more democratic political system with Arévalo at the helm.

The subsequent democratic administrations of Arévalo and Jacobo Arbenz Guzmán (1950–1954) curtailed the role of the military in society. Arévalo and

Arbenz reduced both its size and resource allocation. During the Ubico regime, the military received seventeen percent of the national budget, but by the end of Arbenz' administration, military spending comprised only ten percent of the national budget (Woodward, 1985, p. 237). The democratic government was a reprieve from a militaristic society, but this opening did not last long.

Ten years after the October revolution, Kaqchikel were involved in another internal military struggle. Arbenz' government came to an abrupt end when Colonel Castillo Armas led a group of Guatemalan exiles supported by the CIA, to overthrow the president. The army refused to resist the invasion and Arbenz resigned on June 27, 1954 (Woodward, 1985, pp. 238–240). One Kaqchikel soldier who was in the military when Castillo Armas invaded Guatemala says:

> Jacobo Arbenz was the president when I was in the military. Then one month later [Castillo] Armas came from Honduras to oust Arbenz. Some people died. [Castillo] Armas had a lot of arms, but I do not know what nation they [the arms] came from. Arbenz did not have an airplane, but Castillo [Armas] had an airplane and flew it over the capital. Soldiers shot at his airplane, but could not shoot it down. It was Arbenz's fault because he did not prepare to have an airplane and defend himself. I was in Matamorros and we had a gun there that shot across at the Honor Guard. We had weapons to kill each other (Junlajuj K'at, 1998).

This man faults Arbenz for his failure to protect the nation from Castillo Armas' invasion. The Castillo Armas administration, and especially the subsequent military governments, began a period when military service lost its appeal to Maya.

NO WINNERS

Some Kaqchikel leaders opposed military conscription because it infringed upon their freedom and rights. Oral traditions share that in the early twentieth century President Manuel Estrada Cabrera (1898–1920) conscripted Mayan men into his military. Kaqchikel assert that a local leader wrote the president a letter to tell him that Comalapa (a Kaqchikel town) did not approve of a military that accosted its men and boys and forced them into the military. They proudly recount that the president responded to this admonition and while men did not escape forced labor, they no longer had to endure military indoctrination (Junlajuj Ajpu', 1998). Kaqchikel lament that subsequent governments reinstituted military conscription in Comalapa and the practice remained through the civil war. Informants point out finally, in the early 1990s a Kaqchikel congresswoman from Comalapa named Rosalina Tuyuc successfully pressured the government to end this intrusive process (Kaji' Kan, 1998; Wo'o' Kan, 1998).

Likewise, Senegalese were subject to military conscription for an extended period. In fact, France maintained military conscription until Senegal's independence. Although in the 1940s France attempted to make the military more attractive. In 1946, they extended the right to vote to all African veterans and soldiers, as well as to widows of veterans killed in service. The following year they established pay scales commensurate to duties and rank to eradicate pay differentials based on race or citizenship. Finally, they provided increased opportunities for Africans to become officers. Prior to World War Two, only one African achieved the rank of major and held a regular commission. Nonetheless, Senegalese were content when military conscription ended in their homeland (Coleman & Brice, 1962, pp. 377–379; Echenberg, 1991, pp. 2, 38–42).[16] Only one quarter of the veterans said they would have reenlisted in the army. One man concludes, "I [would have] run away to the furthermost place possible" (Lunn, 1999, p. 214).

The violent and aggressive actions inherent in the military led many Kaqchikel and Senegalese to oppose the military and especially war. A thirty one year-old Kaqchikel evangelical teacher, concludes, "The military is an institution that has nothing to do in Guatemala . . .. In a democracy it should not exist. Look at Costa Rica. They should invest the money into the country" (Waqi' Kan, 1998).[17] Similarly, one Senegalese veteran asserts, "War is a very terrible thing. Even if you are the victor you lose [much]. And if you are defeated, you lose everything. So [regardless] of whether you win, or you are beaten, you lose, because war [itself] is evil" (Lunn, 1999, p. 215).

CONCLUSION

Kaqchikel and Senegalese oral histories present complex assessments of military conscription and participation in the military. Few men freely chose to enroll in the military. Nonetheless, they realized and took advantage of the benefits that this unavoidable military service offered. However, they did not seek to prolong their experience in these Ladino and French institutions. Most accepted their conscription into the armed forces as an inevitable obligation and willingly performed this service. Many appreciated the educational, employment, and social empowerment opportunities the military provided them. They gained respect and confidence and they utilized these attributes to interact assertively and efficaciously with Ladinos and French *colons*. In fact, in the case of Senegal, the changed perceptions and mindsets of men who served in the military contributed to the independence movement forty years later. Kaqchikel and Senegalese made good use of the military's "benevolence".

These oral histories reveal two seemingly contradictory conclusions. First, military conscription is a crime against the natives involved. They were torn from their communities and placed in foreign environments without language or other skills to assist them in preparing for this drastic transition. They were trained for combat, sent into battle and in the case of Guatemala pressured to assimilate into the hegemonic culture. The process constituted a complete disregard for the rights of the individuals involved. One the other hand, conscripts realized some benefits from their participation in the military. The military allowed these subalterns to gain a degree of acceptance in their respective nations, legitimacy for their demands, and capacities (through literacy skills and/or increased confidence to confront powerbrokers) to voice their opinions. Kaqchikel and Senegalese conscripts were agents in turning this crime committed against them to their advantage.

Experience in the military improved the quality of life for many Kaqchikel and Senegalese. The military provided exposure to life outside their communities as they traveled to other areas and learned more about their own and other countries. They also gained leadership skills in these hegemonic institutions. Furthermore, Kaqchikel conscripts learned Spanish and other basic subjects in addition to skills they could parlay into livelihoods. In contrast, for the most part Senegalese did not benefit from language or other skills that they could then use in their homeland. Unless they were promoted to NCOs, their training focused on military concerns. Nonetheless, both groups earned income to contribute to their families or begin their own endeavors. More importantly, they earned the respect of their leaders and learned how to operate in these respective Ladino or French-dominated environments. While ethnic relations remained skewed in favor of the powerbrokers, these interactions were more benign in the military than in their communities. In these two nations wrought with racism, the military was the one institution that mitigated this discrimination. Many Kaqchikel and Senegalese felt they were treated on an equal basis with Ladino and French conscripts in the military. Kaqchikel gained confidence and language skills to confront Ladinos. Likewise, Senegalese no longer feared Frenchmen and henceforth commonly challenged them. Exposure to outside influences, newfound respect and self-esteem, and Spanish language skills (in the case of Kaqchikel) resulted in more efficacious interactions within and outside their communities. These subalterns could escape the racism of their communities and return with an empowered outlook about their reality and improved quality of life.

In Guatemala, both Ladinos and Maya perceived the military and indigenous men to be a good match, but for distinct reasons. Ladinos believed Maya would incorporate into national society as a result of this influence. One of the government's goals was to change the dress, language, and mentality of Mayan men through the military. Many officers appreciated Mayan conscripts for their ability to withstand harsh conditions and apply the skills they learned. Kaqchikel assimilated well to the demands of discipline and diligence. Consequently, the military promoted a few Maya to officer level positions and gave them the opportunity to continue their studies and military careers. Ladinos respected these Mayan leaders. However, few Maya chose to remain in the military and pursue a career, because, while it mitigated racism, it remained a Ladino institution that attempted to acculturate them. Consequently, Kaqchikel men never felt comfortable in the military and they refused to surrender their lifestyles and worldviews to its indoctrination. In fact, community members ostracized those who failed to maintain Kaqchikel values. Most Kaqchikel proved they could succeed in a Ladino setting and not become dominated by it.

French motivations for conscription were more focused: to fill their military ranks. They seldom intended incorporation and in fact were dismayed when Senegalese became more involved in politics and society in West Africa. In contrast to Kaqchikel, Senegalese sought promotions because it meant more training (including language), money, prestige, and most importantly power over Europeans. In general, Senegalese experienced a more powerful acculturation process than Kaqchikel conscripts did. Consequently, their economic, social, political, and cultural integration was more significant than Kaqchikel transformations. In fact, some Senegalese decided not to return to their home communities. Senegalese appreciated the more egalitarian treatment in the military as compared to their country and they sought to enforce these relations when they returned. Consequently, soldiers formerly entrapped in domestic servitude enacted manumission. Senegalese were content to have survived their trials and most had little interest in returning to the military, much less another war.

The Guatemalan and French militaries had to conscript young men because the conditions were horrendous, dangerous, and exploitative. In most instances, Senegalese conscription was more violent and demeaning than Kaqchikel experiences. In both experiences the food and living quarters were not hygienic. Health hazards were abundant and medical care minimal. Abusive relations were prevalent. For example, some Ladinos and Frenchmen hit their charges, and in many cases conscripts were paid less than their lighter skinned counterparts, and received lower quality and quantity provisions. Alcoholism was also a problem that exacerbated the already uncomfortable conditions. Kaqchikel and Senegalese who advanced beyond these abusive conditions tended to be the exception, not the norm. Moreover, conscripts lost time they could have dedicated to their farms, and they missed their families and communities. Most Kaqchikel simply fulfilled their obligation and returned to their communities to incorporate into their lives whatever knowledge and skills they had gained from their military experience. Similarly, although some rural Senegalese applied newfound skills to employment away from their communities, most, like Kaqchikel, also returned to their homes and incorporated their burgeoning self-esteem in ways to improve their quality of life.

The case of Senegalese soldiers is distinct from Kaqchikel because, among other reasons, they suffered severe combat situations. Many lost brothers and friends; some returned mamed. Even those who displayed no physical scars, suffered pyschological damage that in some cases prevented them from returning to their families and communities. Their physical displacement was also much greater than it was for Kaqchikel who served in their own country. Many Senegalese expressed that the cost of human lives lost and forever damaged was not nearly commensurate with any benefits gained from their experience.

Kaqchikel were also especially disturbed by the demand to put their military training into practice by engaging in battle. They did not appreciate the combat experience in the 1944 and 1954 political coups. They recall violent and bloody outcomes from these military campaigns. Kaqchikel had hoped their weapons training never would be called upon, because they did not want to kill other people, let alone their own countrymen. Shortly after the Castillo Armas invasion of 1954, as the military assumed control of the government, the Kaqchikel willingness to participate in military training declined. Today, some Kaqchikel fail to see the need for Guatemala to maintain a military force.

Many Kaqchikel and Senegalese empowered themselves through military service. They took advantage of the training to improve their communication skills and increase their efficacy with Ladinos and French *colons*. The military served as a leveling institution during their service and when they reintegrated into their communities. Ethnic relations did not become egalitarian, but they did improve. Kaqchikel and Senegalese came to know these powerholders better, so their ethnic relations were no longer based on fear, intimidation, or inferiority, but rather, on equality and justice. These subalterns enhanced their bargaining power vis-à-vis their hegemons, refused to accept flagrant abuses, and created spaces where their self-valuation and self-esteem could grow. A strong connection can be drawn between military service and the eventual outcomes of Kaqchikel regaining control of their communities, and Senegalese gaining their independence. Certainly, the French and Guatemalan governments used, abused, and imperiled conscripts, but they also unwittingly empowered them. Kaqchikel and Senegalese soldiers endured hardships and returned to improve their lives and those of their comrades and family back home with their expanded knowledge, worldviews, and self-confidence.

NOTES

1. The Senegalese oral histories are from *tirailleurs* (riflemen or infantrymen). Their situation contrasted sharply with *originaires* (originally a person from the Four Communes) who (potentially) enjoyed French citizenship. *Tirailleurs* tended to be from the rural areas of the interior and the French treated them as subjects. They had to perform forced labor and generally had to comply with French governance with no recourse or political rights. Their reality most closely resembled that of Maya-Kaqchikel in Guatemala, who in many ways were treated (and continue to be) as subjects by Ladinos. Consequently, I selected *tirailleurs*' testimonies as the basis for comparison. For a discussion of *tirailleurs* and *originaires* see Lunn (1999, pp. 10–21). On *sujets* and *originaires* see Crowder (1967, pp. 17–18).

2. Ladinos are non-indigenous, Spanish, or ethnically mixed Guatemalans. In fact, in many ways ethnicity in Guatemala is self-defined. Most Ladinos have some Mayan blood, but choose not to recognize or represent these cultural, social, or historical aspects of their identity. They are the minority in Guatemala yet they are also the political and economic powerholders.

3. For theory on the military in developing nations see Janowitz (1977); Welch (1987, 1985); Camp (1992); and Fitch (1978).

4. In fact, Diagne had been spearheading military recruitment drives that focused on patriotism, the need to aid the French, and citizenship rights in the four communes (urban areas predominantly inhabited by Europeans) since 1915, but the Protectorate did not experience this campaign until a few years later. Needless to say, the reactions of conscripts in the communes differed significantly from those in the Protectorate. Interestingly, in the late nineteenth century France (along with other European nations) had come to the realization that, among its own population, constitutional rights must accompany compulsory military service; see Keegan (1990, p. 22).

5. Sadly, Diagne was unable to secure the reforms he had promised his people.

6. Scholars also note the military provided instruction for Mayan men, and as a result, few deserted (Adams 1995, p. 24 and Carmack 1979, p. 288).

7. *Quetzal* is the Guatemalan currency and during the 1930s, 1940s and into the 1950s it was roughly equal to one U.S. dollar.

8. *Ixto* is a pejorative term used in Guatemala for indigenous people.

9. At the same time, Leed (1981, pp. 25–26, 81–91) does not idealize or oversimplify this assertion. He emphasizes that tension over class differences and racism remained, for example, between volunteers and common soldiers, and among soldiers from India.

10. Knee-length cloth traditionally worn by Kaqchikel males.

11. Interestingly, Page (2000, pp. 104, 184, 188–189, 206–210) found that Malawians had a similar transformative experience as a result of their military experience in World War I. They no longer were fearful or intimidated by the British because they came to view them as human beings subject to the same physical and emotional pressures as themselves. They directly and indirectly expressed their dismay with colonial rule as they gained a sense of equality with Europeans. In fact, many comparisons can be drawn between the Kaqchikel, Senegalese, and Malawian cases.

12. For an examination of the role of African veterans in French West African politics leading up to independence see Echenberg (1991, pp. 146–170).

13. For an analysis of the development of French impressions of Africans since the sixteenth century see Cohen (1980).

14. Carmack (1979, pp. 277–278, 288) asserts superiors also recognized K'ichee' men's inherent ability as good soldiers and promoted a few to officer ranks. He concludes, "The indigenous people who remember that period [early twentieth-century] sustain almost unanimously that, yes they were exploited by the military, but they were respected nevertheless as soldiers."

15. Lunn (1999, p. 147) estimates that at least 6,000–7,000 Senegalese soldiers died in battle.

16. For an analysis of the Conscription Law of 1919 and its effects see Echenberg (1991, pp. 47–64, 84). Also for an examination of African officers see Echenberg (1991, pp. 64–69).

17. Waqi' Kan refers to Costa Rica because it is the only Latin American nation without a professional army (although it does maintain an extensive Civil Guard force). For an analysis of how Costa Rica achieved this status see Bird (1984).

*Oral Interviews of Kaqchikel Informants**

Towns/Names**	Dates
San Antonio Aguas Calientes (SAAC)	
B'eleje' Kan	11/9/97
Ka'i' Kawoq	2/7/98
Oxi' Ey	11/28/97
Waqi' Ajpu'	2/28/98
Waqi' Kan	Ix'ey interview, 1998
Waqxaqi' K'at	11/8/97, Jun Tojil interview 1998
Waqxaqi' Kawoq	11/8/97, 11/28/97
Wuqu' Imox	11/12/97
Santa Catarina Barahona (SCB)	
B'eleje' Ajpu'	Jun Tojil interview, 1998
Waqxaqi' Ajpu'	Jun Tojil interview, 1998
Wuqu' Ajpu'	Jun Tojil interview, 1998
San José Poaquil	
Ixkan	3/29/98
Junlajuj Kawoq	11/17/97
Kab'lajuj Kawoq	3/23/98, 8/30/98
Ka'i' Raxche'	3/16/98, 4/1/98
Lajuj Ajpu'	3/29/98, 4/19/98, 6/6/98, 8/30/98
Oxlajuj Kawoq	3/18/98, 4/19/98, 8/30/98
San Juan Comalapa	
B'eleje' Imox	9/20/97, 1/11/98, 4/17/98, 4/26/98, 5/19/98, 5/25/98, 8/1/98, 8/9/98
Ix'imox	8/23/98, 9/6/98
Ixiq'	1/12/98, 7/9/98

Ixkame	8/17/98, 8/22/98
Ixkawoq	4/17/98
Ixk'at	1/7/98, 2/9/98, 4/7/98, 4/20/98, 4/26/98, 8/15/98
Ixtijax	2/9/98, 2/14/98, 4/22/98, 8/17/98
Jun Ajpu'	9/26/97, 10/21/97, 10/24/97, 10/27/97, 12/20/97, 1/14/98, 4/7/98, 4/10/98, 4/13/98, 4/26/98, 5/1/98, 5/25/98, 6/11/98, 9/7/98
Jun Imox	12/9/97
Jun Imox, Ka'i' Ajpu' and Oxi' Ajpu'	12/2/97
Jun Iq'	4/6/98
Jun Kan	8/15/98, 8/19/98, 9/3/98, 9/14/98
Jun K'at	2/11/98
Junlajuj Ajpu'	8/2/98
Junlajuj Imox	5/23/98, 6/23/98, 7/11/98, 8/29/98, 9/14/98, 9/15/98
Junlajuj K'at	3/20/98, 7/9/98
Kab'lajuj K'at	6/27/98, 7/11/98, 7/18/98, 8/1/98, 9/9/98
Kab'lajuj Ajpu'	11/14/97, 5/5/98
Kab'lajuj Imox	9/28/97, 10/23/97, 11/5/97, 1/5/98
Kab'lajuj Kej	4/26/98, 8/2/98
Kab'lajuj Tijax	9/13/97, 9/28/97, 4/7/98, 7/12/98, 7/19/98, 7/25/98
Ka'i' Imox	1/21/98, 4/14/98, 8/5/98, 9/12/98
Ka'i' K'at	2/12/98, 4/5/98, 5/16/98
Kaji' Imox	12/13/97, 4/12/98, 8/2/98
Kaji' Kan	8/16/98, 9/6/98
Lajuj Imox	12/20/97, 1/18/98, 3/3/98
Lajuj Kan	10/12/97, 10/15/97, 10/29/97, 12/20/97, 1/30/98,
Oxi' Ajpu', Ka'i' Ajpu', and Jun Imox	12/2/97
Oxi' Imox	11/13/97, 2/10-1/98, 5/1/98, 8/11/98, 9/14/98
Oxi' Kan	8/19
Oxi' Tz'ikin	8/1/98, 8/5/98, 8/8/98, 8/11/98, 8/17-8/98, 9/11/98
Oxlajuj Ajpu'	1/19/98, 4/14/98, 4/17/98
Oxlajuj Imox	1/13/98, 8/17/98, 9/1/98
Waqi' K'at	5/3/98, 8/21-2/98, 9/6/98, 9/19/98
Wo'o' Ajpu'	11/6/97, 11/11/97, 1/20/98, 1/31/98, 4/21/98
Wo'o' Imox	5/23/98
Wo'o' Kan	4/26/98
Wo'o' Kawoq and Waqi' Kawoq	3/3/98
Wuqu' K'at	4/5/98, 4/6/98, 7/25/98
Wuqu' Kawoq	1/6/98, 1/10/98, 1/29/98, 2/7/98, 4/7/98, 4/14-5/98, 5/15/98
Tecpán	
B'eleje' Kawoq	6/9/98
Oxi' K'at	6/5/98
Waqi' Imox	5/3/98

* Unless otherwise indicated, the author conducted the interview.

** Unless otherwise indicated the interview was conducted in the informants hometown or aldea.

OF WAR AND VIRTUE: GENDER, AMERICAN CITIZENSHIP AND VETERANS' BENEFITS AFTER WORLD WAR II

Gretchen Ritter

INTRODUCTION

What is the relationship between war and citizenship? Most scholars and pundits agree that World War II changed American society and the political system for the better. America's victory in the war was itself testimony to the strength of our democracy and the power of our economic enterprise. Further, the war experience helped to create an ethos of civic engagement for those who contributed to the military effort at home and abroad (Putnam, 2000). The gradual disappearance of this "Great Generation" (Brokaw, 1998) of Americans may be part of the reason behind the decline in social capital today. Nor, as some would theorize, was civic engagement contrary to social provisioning (Skocpol, 1996). Veterans' programs constituted a major expansion in national social programs. It was precisely these programs – especially the educational and employment benefits attached to the G.I. Bill – which provided social mobility and security to the members of the Great Generation. In this case, social provisioning positively effected the civic engagement and political participation of a generation of Americans.

The Comparative Study of Conscription in the Armed Forces, Volume 20, pages 201–226.

ISBN: 0-7623-0836-2

The experience of World War II seems, to provide an easy answer to the question about what is the relationship between war and citizenship. War helped to create a civic ethos that enriched citizenship. War also expanded social provisioning and thereby gave substance to American social citizenship. Finally, war gave weight to the claims of African Americans and Latino Americans seeking to secure full civil and political rights. A democratically fought war expanded the democratic nature of the American political system.

This is an appealing account and one with a great deal of merit. Yet our view of the effects of war on citizenship are complicated when we consider gender. Many women participated in the Second World War, as members of the nurses' corps and military auxiliaries, laborers in the war industries, and as the makers of domestic life. Did the war effort accord new rights claims to women as well as men? Did the establishment of veterans' benefits create a social citizenship in which all citizens, men and women, were equal? In the long fought effort by American women to achieve equal citizenship, was the war a moment of progress or one of regress? It is the argument of this essay that while the war expanded the terms of citizenship for many American men, it also created a new gendered hierarchy of citizenship in which male citizens (particularly veterans) were more entitled and rewarded than female citizens.

This essay analyzes two different aspects of the relationship between gender, citizenship and the Second World War. The first concerns the experience of military service and its relationship to claims for political rights. There was a revival of interest in the Equal Rights Amendment during the war and the justification for the amendment was framed in terms of women's war participation. Despite these claims, the effort to pass the ERA in the mid-1940s failed. Further, it may be that there was an elevation in men's civic standing as a consequence of their military service which ultimately disadvantaged women. The second issue this essay explores is the relationship between the development of veterans' benefits and American social citizenship. T. H. Marshall argued that programs that contributed to the social rights of citizenship – that is, rights to social provisions such as education, housing, and full employment – helped to expand the terms of citizenship in the direction of equality and universalism (Marshall, 1964). Yet, while veterans benefits appear to have expanded social citizenship for many men they did so in ways that elevated the civic virtue of male veterans while offering fewer rewards to the female dependents of veterans and less status to female veterans.

Before analyzing the development of citizenship in the mid-1940s, let me specify my approach and define some terms. Citizenship is understood here as a status that is defined both legally and culturally (Shklar, 1991). Citizenship as a legal status connotes membership within a particular political community.

Attached to the legal status of citizenship may be a set of rights (such as voting and social provision) and responsibilities (such as taxpaying and military service) that bind citizens to their states (Kerber, 1998). The meaning of citizenship status may also be found within political culture where distinctive notions about the roles and virtues of different groups of citizens may be present. As a term of political identity, citizenship is associated with nationalism (Brubaker, 1992). To be a citizen of the United States is to be an American. There is overlap between these conceptions of citizenship, as when nativism results in the legislative exclusion of certain immigrant groups, or when popular gender ideals are reflected in court rulings that limit women's citizenship rights. Since both popular conceptions and legal doctrines help to define the place of different citizen groups, each is consulted here, though the stress is on the legal (or constitutional) construction of citizenship. I trace the legal debates about citizenship primarily through court rulings and explore cultural notions of citizenship through contemporary popular periodicals and political debates.

The concept of equal citizenship may be addressed at three levels. At the broadest level, equal citizenship pertains to civic status. All of those considered as "full" or "first class" citizens may be thought of as holding the same high civic status. The second conception of equal citizenship is more specifically rights focused, and holds that any differences in the rights afforded to citizens constitute unequal citizenship. It was this view which informed the effort to pass an Equal Rights Amendment for women. Finally, a third conception of equal citizenship examines not only rights and status, but also the duties and obligations of citizens. Many women political activists who believed in equal citizenship for men and women at the level of civic status and rights differed over what the duties and obligations of male and female citizens ought to be. Thus, it was possible to believe in equal citizenship while thinking that men and women would remain distinct in their political interests, outlooks, and roles (Ritter, 2000a).

Finally, to say that citizenship is gendered means that the rights and responsibilities of citizenship differ by sex. Such differences may be fairly minor and inconsequential, or they may be substantial and coherent. In the latter case, I argue that these differences may reflect the existence of distinct gendered ideals of citizenship for men and women that may be found in both the law and in popular understandings of what it means to be a citizen. Thus, the argument here is not concerned merely with whether there are any differences between the positions of male and female citizens. Rather, my interest is in determining whether gender operates as an organizing premise in the distribution of rights and responsibilities among citizens. My research suggests that it does to different degrees at various times in American political history (Ritter, 2000a).

The essay proceeds as follows. The first section offers a discussion of three theoretical and historical frameworks that guide my analysis of gender, war and citizenship. The first framework reviews the debate on war and democratic rights, the second involves a discussion of T. H. Marshall's theory of the development of citizenship, and the third is a historical and theoretical account of the development of women's citizenship between the passage of the Nineteenth Amendment and the advent of World War II. Each of these frameworks contributes something to the analysis, but is also found to be insufficient on their own. The second section addresses the relationship between military service and the political rights of citizenship. There I argue that the claims of civic virtue associated with military service have a powerful effect on claims for political rights, but that in World War II the impact of those claims were clearly gendered. The third section reviews the development of veteran's benefits in mid-1940s and their impact on American social citizenship. Contrary to Marshall's theory, I find that American social citizenship as it emerges in the late 1940s is compartmentalized and hierarchical, particularly along gender lines. In the conclusion, I consider the larger implications of this work for understanding gender and citizenship in American political development.

I. FRAMEWORKS

In looking at the relationship between gender, war and citizenship, we begin with a discussion of three theoretical and historical frameworks. Each of these frameworks focuses on a different aspect of the issue at hand – the first on war, the second on citizenship, and the third on gender. The first framework considers the relationship between democracy and war in both the international relations literature and the American political development literature. The second framework discusses T. H. Marshall's theory of the development of the social rights of citizenship. The third, more historical, framework examines the relative positions of men and women in American politics between the passage of the Nineteenth Amendment and the Second World War. From each of these frameworks we develop a set of expectations and questions about the relationship between gender, war and citizenship that can be used to guide our analysis of the development of gender and citizenship in the United States in the 1940s.

(A) War and Democracy

Democracy and war, it appears, are intimately related. Democratic countries are less likely to enter into wars, particularly with other democracies. But once a democracy does enter into a war, it is more likely to win (Reiter, 1998). The ability of a democratic country to fight effectively has to do not only with its capacity to mobilize resources and to strategically plan military campaigns, but also, and perhaps most importantly, it reflects the commitment, morale, and resourcefulness of the citizen soldiers who fight in the national interest.

It appears that democracy helps to maintain peace and win wars. But is war also good for democracy? (Downing, 1992). Does the effort made by the citizenry to support their country in time of war result in extensions of rights and privileges by the government to the citizens? In particular, what of the role of politically less privileged groups? Are claims for political rights made more effective by a record of war service? This is a point of debate both for scholars of international relations and students of American politics. Some stress that democratic governments are made more beholden to their citizenry by the service that citizens offer in support of wars. Others contend that wars make even democratic governments less tolerant of political dissent and more willing to exercise authoritarian control measures against their own populations (Kryder, 2000). The American historical record appear mixed on this point, marked, as it is, both by instances of wartime political repressions and war related extensions of political rights (Rousseau & Newsome, 1999).

The Second World War and its aftermath are also marked by instances of government repression (for instance, with the internment of Japanese Americans in relocation camps [Smith, 1995]) and calls for extending the political rights of socially marginalized groups on the basis of their war service. Given the appearance of both of these tendencies, this theoretical debate on war and democracy might help us to focus the present analysis as follows. First, if women were not seen as a potential disturbance to the American war effort, then there ought not to have been any repressive measures directed toward them. Second, we need to explore more carefully the nature of the connection between war service and claims for political rights. Do social differences, such as gender or race, and differences in the contributions made to a military effort (e.g. the distinction between combat and noncombat roles) matter for claims of civic virtue and political rights? Finally, do the claims of different social groups involved in a military effort compete against each other or help to frame one another? Given women's cooperative and supportive role in support of the American military in World War II, it might be expected to have strengthened their claims for political rights and equal citizenship. As discussed below, the historical record suggests that such an effect was present, but this effect was limited and complicated by the particular terms under which women's military service was understood and the competing claims to civic virtue by male veterans.

(B) T. H. Marshall and the Social Rights of Citizenship

T. H. Marshall's famous 1949 article, "Citizenship and Social Class," (1964) laid out a theory for the development of citizenship in liberal democratic countries such as Great Britain. The article remains a standard point of departure for contemporary studies of citizenship through much of the western world (Barbalet, 1988, van Steenbergen, 1994). In his essay, Marshall lays out a developmental view of citizenship as beginning with the appearance of civil rights such as free speech, freedom of assembly, and trial by jury; then expanding to include political rights such as the right to vote and the right to hold elective office; and finally extending to the development of social rights such as entitlements to education, housing, and medical care. With each new stage, citizenship was expanded both in terms of the proportion of the population it included and the content of citizenship as a status. Citizenship became more equal and universal as well as more robust.

According to Marshall, there were significant differences in the character and impact of civil, political and social rights in their effects on an individual citizen's relationship to the state. Yet, by the end of the eighteenth century, when the courts had established civil rights throughout the nation, the overall character of modern citizenship was established. "When freedom became universal, citizenship grew from a local into a national institution" (p. 84). As political rights became more universal in the nineteenth and early twentieth century, and social rights were added, then citizenship became a status under which all were entitled to "share to the full in the social heritage and to live the life of a civilized being according to the standards prevailing in the society" (p. 78). In Marshall's account, it is civil rights that initially secures a notion of individual freedom for all, (in which there is "one law for all men") thereby providing the foundation for a more expansive civic status.

What would it mean, then, to have a social group that did not acquire civil rights, or legal personhood, before they acquired other rights, such as the right to vote? Would they also acquire full citizenship? Marshall notes in passing that "the status of women, or at least married women, was in some important respects, peculiar" (p. 84). Indeed, it was, since under the common law rules of coverture a woman upon marriage lost her status as a legal person as she became one with her husband. A married woman could not contract, write a will, own property, establish her own domicile, or testify in court. In short, she lacked the basic civil rights of a free individual. Was such a woman a citizen? It was a question with which the nineteenth century American courts wrestled (Kettner, 1978). Nor did the issue end with the passage of the Nineteenth Amendment in 1920, which secured the right to vote for women. Though women had political rights after the Nineteenth Amendment, married women still did not have full civil rights since in many respects the rules of coverture still applied to them. Did the development of social rights in the twentieth century complete women's incorporation into a universal civic status in which they shared fully in the social heritage of the nation, or did it continue the peculiar trajectory of the women's separate citizenship? This is a question we shall explore more fully below.

Political theorist Nancy Fraser and historian Linda Gordon have taken up Marshall's theory of citizenship and the development of women's citizenship in "Civil Citizenship Against Social Citizenship?" (1994). They argue that in the United States the relationship of male citizens to the state is premised on a notion of contract, while that of female citizens is premised on a notion of charity or dependency. While white men developed the civil and political rights of citizenship in the nineteenth century, women, especially when married, were excluded from these rights. So while men became possessive, rights bearing individuals in the eyes of the state, women were cast as family dependents under the authority of men and beyond the public sphere. The legacy of this distinction between contract and dependency in the twentieth century appears clearly in the arena of social policy where men are covered by social insurance (e.g. old age retirement benefits) and women are given public assistance (e.g. Aid to Families with Dependent Children). As Barbara Nelson also notes, men are able to make political claims in their status as workers, while women's political claims (often made for them) revolve around their status as mothers or wives (Nelson, 1990). Instead of trumping other social status distinctions such as gender, it appears that civic status has become imbricated with these social status distinctions.

What, then, can Marshall's theory tell us about gender and the development of citizenship after World War II? The theory is particularly useful for thinking about the role of veteran's benefits in developing social citizenship in the United States. In Marshall's original theory, the social rights of citizenship enrich a universal civic status that is founded on common civil and political rights. Yet implicit in the theory as well is a question about whether women (or, at least, married women) were ever truly incorporated under the universalistic citizenship that began with civil rights. Absent a foundation of universal civil rights, the addition of political and social rights for women might either help to equalize women's civic status or might continue a pattern of differential citizenship for women and men. In their critique of Marshall, Fraser and Gordon suggest that the latter is the case – that since women were never fully awarded the civil rights of citizenship they continued to be seen as dependent citizens rather than independent, contract based citizens. An analysis of the impact of veterans benefits on concepts of social citizenship suggest that Fraser and Gordon are largely correct.

(C) Women's Citizenship from the Nineteenth Amendment to World War II

While the first theoretical framework focused our account on the effects of war, and the second examined the development of citizenship, this last framework considers the historical trajectory of women's place in the constitutional order. Such an examination may illuminate the role of gender in the political order of citizenship, and suggest whether there is a historical pattern of movement toward civic equality.

When the Nineteenth Amendment was adopted in 1920 it held out the promise of making women equal citizens and full persons before the law. Yet in the two decades after suffrage was implemented, the promise remained unrealized for several reasons. The suffragists had argued that the vote would help to make them equal citizens for normative, instrumental, and constitutional reasons. Normatively, the right to vote would elevate women's status as citizens, helping to make them full persons before the law. Instrumentally, the right to vote provided women with the means to defend their interests and secure their rights through political representation. Constitutionally, the right to vote would fully incorporate women as equal citizens under the Fourteenth Amendment. Instead, in the 1920s and 1930s, the courts construed the Nineteenth Amendment narrowly, as having little impact on women's constitutional status. Where impact was granted it was within the domain of negative rights granted men under the principle of freedom of contract. Further, within the arena of electoral politics, it became quickly apparent that there was no distinctive women's vote and that fewer women than men voted at all. Finally, normatively, women activists of the 1920s divided over what equal citizenship meant, how it should be pursued, and even whether they wanted it.

While the story of the Nineteenth Amendment's impact on women's political position has been able told elsewhere (Cott, 1995, Andersen, 1997), my concern here is with the its impact on women's citizenship, particularly on their place within the constitutional order of American politics. After the passage of the Nineteenth Amendment, gender distinctions remained part of the substratum of women's citizenship. Consequently, for instance, when the courts considered whether women's status as electors made them eligible for jury service, most state courts found that it did not and that statutory provision was required before women could serve on juries.[1] In these cases, common law restrictions were frequently cited as creating legal disabilities for women. The claim to equal citizenship after the Nineteenth Amendment was also obstructed by the continued vitality of the rules of coverture. Married women found that even with the right to vote, the fight for civil equality – with regard to property, domicile, contracts, and parental rights, etc. – was ongoing. In the early 1920s, this led the National Women's Party to propose an Equal Rights Amendment to the Constitution. Social feminists and other labor feminists quickly came out against the ERA proposal as a blunt instrument that would sacrifice protective labor laws for women in the name of an abstract equality. By the mid-1920s, it was clear to all the former suffragists that women still did not have equal citizenship. What was less clear was precisely what equal citizenship would mean and how desirable it was (Zimmerman, 1991).

Ironically, the one place where the Nineteenth Amendment was taken as having a broader constitutional impact was in the realm of protective labor laws. In *Adkins v. Children's Hospital*, 261 US 525 (1923), the Supreme Court ruled that a federal law providing for minimum wages for women workers in Washington, D.C. was unconstitutional. Before *Adkins*, women could be covered by protective labor laws because it was assumed that they were socially and legally unequal and could not fully defend their own interests in bargaining over employment contracts (Baer, 1978). That changed with the Nineteenth Amendment. The court wrote,

> But the ancient inequality of the sexes, otherwise than physical, as suggested in the *Muller* Case has continued 'with diminishing intensity.' In view of the great – not to say revolutionary – changes which have taken place since that utterance, in the contractual, political, and civil status of women, culminating in the Nineteenth Amendment, it is not unreasonable to say that these differences have now come almost, if not quite, to the vanishing point (261 US 525, 552).

Now women were part of the same freedom of contract regime that covered men. Under this regime, in the *Lochner* era (named for the famous case of *Lochner v. New York*, 195 US 45 [1905]), the freedoms enjoyed by American citizens were defined negatively as freedom from state interference in their labor contracts.

The incorporation of women into the negative freedom of the *Lochner* regime only deepened the divide among feminists between those who desired to pursue broad constitutional equality for women versus those who were willing to accept women's special or peculiar civic status in some areas. In the 1930s, there were further assaults on the effort to establish constitutional equality for women. It became more difficult for married women to legally obtain public employment. Further, the 1939 amendments to the Social Security Act incorporated the wives and widows of male workers were under Old Age and Survivors Insurance, while women workers were often left out of coverage for falling into excluded job categories (Ritter, 2000b). Finally, the *Lochner* regime was overturned in the 1930s, beginning with *West Coast Hotel v. Parrish*, 300 US 379 (1937), a women's labor case that resurrected the *Muller v. Oregon*, 208 US 412 (1908), decision that originally established women's special civic status in this area. In changing the terms by which civic freedom was understood (and thereby opening the way to government regulation in the general interest), the court found it easiest to do this first for women, who were never more than tentative members of the *Lochner* regime.

The change made by the court in the *Parrish* case was twofold. On the one hand, the court made claims for equality for women more attractive when equality no longer meant access to negative freedoms, such as freedom of contract. But on the other hand, the court made claims for treating women as different more constitutionally acceptable as well. In the decade following this ruling, both tendencies were visible though ultimately a more gender distinctive order of citizenship emerged. Meanwhile, in the process of considering the relationship between labor status and gender status in *Parrish*, the court began remaking the political order of citizenship by bringing the *Lochner* era to an end. At this crucial turning point in American political development, gender played a key role.

The war gave renewed energy to the advocates of equal citizenship for women. More women than ever before, including married women and mothers of young children, were gainfully employed. Further, women took jobs from which they were previously excluded, including jobs in heavy industry. Their performance in these positions exceeded the expectations of their employers and the general public. Finally, women entered the armed forces in record numbers and were accorded regular military status for the first time. In all of these respects, women's position in the public realm was more visible and universal than ever before. Consequently (as elaborated below) the Equal Rights Amendment came closer to passing in 1945 and 1946 than at any other time until the 1970s.

How does this historical account of the constitutional development of women's citizenship in the 1920s, 1930s and early 1940s bear on our analysis of gender and citizenship in the aftermath of the Second World War? Even after the Nineteenth Amendment, women had, at best, a tentative hold on equal citizenship. Having been awarded suffrage, the highest political right of citizenship, their civic status was elevated to a point closer to the status of native born white men. However, women's pursuit of further equality proved contentious during the *Lochner* era when equality meant the loss of government labor protection for women. Yet the terms of citizenship were changing. The Supreme Court finally moved beyond the negative rights model of citizenship in *Parrish*. This was followed shortly thereafter by *NLRB v. Jones & Laughlin*, 301 US 1 (1937) a case which displaced the freedom of contract principle for all citizens regardless of sex. As of the early 1940s, it appeared that gender retained it's a appeal as a principle for ordering the rights of citizenship, but that it was a distinction that could be overcome in the expansion of the social rights of citizenship. Consistent with this trajectory, women's war related experiences and the development of social citizenship in connection with veteran's benefits, could either lead to the continuation of a gender hierarchical and divided social citizenship, or to the realization of a more universal and equal citizenship.

In sum, these three frameworks leave us with the following expectations and questions. The first framework on the relationship between war and democracy might lead us to expect an increase in support for women's claims for political rights in light of their contributions to the war effort. Yet, I have also argued that we need to further analyze the relationship between war service and civic virtue, to consider whether it is a qualified relationship, a gendered relationship, and an interdependent relationship amongst war supportive social groups. The second framework on T. H. Marshall's theory of citizenship might lead us to expect the development of an American social citizenship that is inclusive and egalitarian. Still, as Marshall's own essay implies and his critics assert, such a view neglects earlier differences between those who did and did not obtain full civil rights, differences that could continue with the further development of political and social rights. Likewise, the third framework on the development of women's citizenship after the Nineteenth Amendment reveals the competing trends toward more equal and more gender differentiated citizenship. Either trajectory seems capable of further development at the end of the Second World War.

II. MILITARY SERVICE AND THE POLITICAL RIGHTS OF CITIZENSHIP

> May only those Americans enjoy freedom who are ready to die for its defense.
>
> Toast on the First Anniversary of the Declaration of Independence (Kerber, 1998, p. 240).

The Second Amendment to the Constitution asserts "the right of the people to keep and bear arms." It was a right that was also reflective of a duty – the duty to serve in the militia and contribute to the common defense (Levinson, 1989). As a right, the right to bear arms is both personal and social. Personally, it is what Blackstone called an "auxiliary right" intended to secure an individual's fundamental rights of life, liberty and property. Socially, and this was especially relevant at the time of the American Revolution, the right to bear arms reflected republican concern with the oppressive potential of a standing army. Thus, a well-regulated militia was important for the "preservation of the entire constitutional structure." During colonial times, many colonies mandated that all men, white men, freemen, citizens, masters of families, or householders should be armed and should bear their arms in public places (Malcolm, 1994, p. 139). Often these mandates carried with them racial restrictions to exclude blacks and Indians. From at least the founding, then, arms bearing has been intimately connected to civic status and the political order of citizenship in America.

There are different ways of understanding the civic virtues involved in military service. Virtue may lie in one's willingness to surrender their personal autonomy in service to the nation in a time of national need. Or it may lie in one's willingness to risk personal safety and perhaps even to die for one's country. Further, war service may involve not just the risk of death but the willingness to kill for the good of the country. Morris Janowitz (1983) argues that a democratically based military (that is, one based upon universal conscription or voluntary militias) contributes to a democratic culture through "the obligation of the citizen to the nation state" (16) and through the role of military experience in providing civic education. Depending upon how military service is conceived, its civic virtues have been more or less accessible to different social groups.

During the nineteenth century, military service was strongly associated with claims for the political rights of citizenship, while during the twentieth century it is also associated with the development of social citizenship. In the republican ideology of early America, citizens demonstrated their civic virtue through their martial service (Kann, 1991). The civically virtuous, in turn, expected to be granted political rights. In the Jacksonian period, the ideal of the citizen soldier was used to challenge the property qualification for voting. Comparing service to rights, one speaker at the Virginia Convention of 1829–1830 said,

> If landless citizens have been ignominiously driven from the polls, in time of peace, they have at least been generously summoned, in war, to the battlefield. Nor have they disobeyed the summons, or less profusely than others, poured out their blood in defense of their country (Shklar 1991, p. 48).

Democracy in military service provided a claim for a democracy of political rights. The result of this particular effort was an expansion of democracy to include all white men within the category of first class citizens. The extension of the vote effectively gendered citizenship, thereby creating a citizenship that was divided into separate male and female spheres (Baker, 1984). The connection between voting, military service and citizenship was sustained after the Civil War when partisanship and the social rewards of citizenship were deeply connected to veterans' status (Skocpol, 1991).

The citizenship status of African American men was also defined in relation to military service. In *Dred Scott v. Sandford*, 60 US 393 (1857), Chief Justice

Roger Taney contemplated the issue of whether African-Americans, slave or free, were citizens of the United States. In answering that they were not, Taney cited the "first militia law, which was passed in 1792." The law directed every "free able-bodied white male citizen" to serve in the militia. Thus, Taney concluded "The African race . . . is repudiated and rejected from the duties and obligations of citizenship in marked language" (Brest & Levinson, 1992, p. 199). Later, the freedmen would articulate their claims for citizenship rights in terms of their military service in the Civil War. As Frederick Douglass said, "It is dangerous to deny any class of people the right to vote. But the black man deserves the right to vote for what he has done, to aid in suppressing the rebellion . . . He deserves the right to vote because his services may be needed again" (Shklar, 1991, p. 52). Hence Douglass clearly demonstrates his understanding of the logic of war and democracy. Voluntary military service required citizenship rights and rewards. Formally, African American men were granted full citizenship, including the right to vote under the Fifteenth Amendment. Yet in the South and elsewhere, their rights continued to be denied in practice for decades to come. After World Wars I and II, the call for civil and political rights for African Americans was once again justified by their martial service records (Kryder, 2000).

(A) Women and the Military

For women, there was also an association between war service and the political rights of citizenship. The effort of women as part of the Sanitary Commission in the Civil War bolstered the claim of the Woman's Rights Movement to extend the right to vote to women. When women finally did get the right to vote in 1920, President Wilson cited their contribution to the war effort in World War I as justification for his own belated enthusiasm for woman suffrage (Flexner, 1973). Women's war service during the Second World War is credited with prompting renewed support by both parties for an Equal Rights Amendment. Summarizing the Congressional debate in 1943, historian Susan Hartmann writes, "Women's tremendous contributions to the war effort earned them equal opportunities: to refuse them their rights was 'a stain on our flag.'" (1982, p. 130) Whether in uniform or outside of it, women's contributions to the national defense validated their civic virtue.

During the Second World War, women participated in the military effort to a greater extent than they ever had before or would afterwards. Some 350,000 women served in the military in World War II, in the women's units that were attached to each branch of the military. For the first time ever, and as a result of pressure from women's organizations and members of Congress, these women were awarded full military rank. The only exception was the Women's Airforce Service Pilots (WASPs), the women's unit attached to the airforce (Merryman, 1998). These women, some of whom died in war service, were not awarded military status until the 1970s. But for the women in the WACs (army), WAVES (navy), SPARS (coast guard), and MCWR (marines) full rank and equal pay were provided. There were still, of course, differences in the treatment of male and female service members. Most women were never sent out of the country. There were restrictions against the enlistment of married women, and a prohibition against women with minor children. Women were barred from higher ranks and were not generally allowed to supervise male servicemen. Finally, the military's concern for the moral reputation of service women was expressed in policies that restricted their off duty behavior and prevented the distribution of contraception or information about venereal disease to women (Hartmann, 1982, Ch. 3; May, 1988, Ch. 3).

Shortly after Pearl Harbor, a bill introduced by Rep. Edith Nourse Rodgers was given approval by the War Department and brought before the House. The bill called for the creation of a Women's Army Auxiliary Corps (or WAAC, later changed to WAC). In signaling his support for the bill, General George Marshall wrote "there are innumerable duties now being performed by soldiers that can actually be done better by women." (Weatherford, 1990, p. 30) Women would free men for combat, and they would bring their own particular "womanly" skills to the tasks at hand. After WAAC was successfully established, the other armed services followed suit with their own women's auxiliaries.

Military service did not necessarily reduce perceptions of gender difference. Commenting on women's service within the military during World War II, Christine Williams writes,

> Women and men were often engaged in identical tasks, but official military policy and the dominant ideology of gender perpetuated the division of labor by sex. Thus, women's nontraditional activities were interpreted in ways that supported a traditional sex role arrangement. This meant that women could maintain their femininity in spite of the military's traditional identification as a masculine occupation (1989, p. 20).

The women's auxiliaries were originally envisioned as temporary, war emergency measures.[2] Even their proponents, including General Eisenhower, did not foresee women having military careers: "after an enlistment or two enlistments women will ordinarily – and thank God – they will get married." Further, the work of women in the military corps was strongly gendered. Even when women were given jobs previously held by men, these jobs were regendered to highlight women's special abilities to perform the work. "They are superior to men in all functions involving manual dexterity . . ." While in some respects, women's military experience contributed to calls for gender equality, in others it helped to affirm the importance of gender difference (Williams, 1989, Ch. 2).

As it had been for previous generations, military service was an important affirmation of masculinity for American men in the 1940s (Hoganson, 1998). Consequently, many of the rank and file soldiers and sailors resented the presence of women in uniform. In 1943, there was a widely publicized smear campaign in which rumors were spread regarding the sexual promiscuity of the members of the women's auxiliaries. This grassroots campaign had such a negative effect on morale and recruitment, that the top commanders began a counter-propaganda campaign to bolster recruitment efforts among women. The women in the service understood the motives behind the slander campaign.

> As Brigadier General Jeanne Holm recalled, "In the machismo world of barracks humor, where women and sex are a primary topic, military women had become fair game. Having joined what was a masculine domain, the women were 'asking for it.'" As one WAC commander explained the underlying motive, "Men have for centuries used slander against morals as a weapon to keep women out of public life" (Campbell, 1990, p. 115).

Both the smear campaign and the counterpropaganda campaign took as their premise the differences between the sexes. For some, the presence of women in the services affected not only their civic status, but the masculinity and political status of men as well (Honey, 1984, pp. 113–119).

During the midst of the war, when it appeared that the effort would continue for quite some time, Congress considered a bill to establish a National War Service under which men and women could be required to give civilian service in war industries. Such an effort had public support. As historian William O'Neill writes in *A Democracy at War*, "In January 1942 Gallop reported that 68% of the public favored a labor draft for women aged 21 to 35; among women, the majority rose to 73%." (1993, p. 132) The national service bill exempted women who cared for children under 18 years of age or for elderly parents. In introducing the bill in the Senate, Senator Austin of Vermont explained,

> We have founded our political life and our social life upon the doctrine of relative equality . . .. Therefore it is necessary to declare an equal liability of all mobile men within the range of 18 years and 65 years of age, and all mobile women within the ages of 18 and 50 (*Cong. Rec.*, February 8, 1943, p. 668).

Provided that women were not obliged to care for their children, then, they, too, could be asked to serve their country during wartime, albeit in noncombat positions. Yet this was a distinction that mattered. Austin was interrupted during his presentation of the bill by Senator Walsh of Massachusetts, who was concerned about the fate of young men ordered to work in a civilian rather than a military capacity.

> The impression among many seems to be that unless one has a military service record, after the war his opportunity for civic advancement, and for political preferment in the future, will be handicapped (*Cong. Rec.*, February 8, 1943, p. 669).

For men, the virtues of martial service exceeded the virtues of civilian service. So, too, did the expected rewards.

But the senator need not have worried. The prospect of women being drafted prompted the formation of the Women's Committee to Oppose Conscription. During a radio interview, the organization's leader Mildred Scott Olmsted explained her opposition to the national service idea.

> Woman are naturally and rightly the homemakers . . .. They play their part during the war by 'keeping the home fires burning' . . . and by carrying on the services that hold the community together (Kerber, 1998, 249).

Or, as a member of the Mothers of Sons (another conservative women's group) put it: "this bill would nationalize our women and complete the sovietization of our country" (Kerber, 1998, p. 249). Although the opinions of these organizations may have been extreme, it seems that there were many in Congress who shared their concerns about the consequences of drafting women. The bill was not made into law.

There were also nurses corps attached to the various branches in the military. Nurses often operated closer to combat areas. They were therefore more likely to risk being injured or taken as prisoners of war. Indeed, both fates befell many of the army nurses who served in the Philippines. Some were killed in the intense fighting between the Japanese and American forces in Bataan and Corregidor in 1942. Under horrible siege conditions, these nurses provided the wounded soldiers with both medical attention and feminine nurture. One nurse recalled "It meant a great deal to the wounded and sick men to have American women to give them the expert care their mothers or wives would have wanted for them" (Weatherford, 1990, p. 4). When the American forces finally fled Bataan and Corregidor, some nurses became prisoners of war and remained in a Japanese prison camp in Manila until 1945.

The need for nurses motivated President Roosevelt to call for a draft of nurses early in 1945 when it appeared that the war would drag on for some time longer. Congress responded positively to this initiative – a bill to initiate such a draft passed in the House and was pending in the Senate when victory was declared in Europe. The Congressional response to this effort stood in contrast the negative reaction that accompanied the initiative to draft women in the women's military auxiliaries in 1942 and 1943. The reason for the distinction was not a matter of the greater danger to members of the women's auxiliaries as opposed to the nursing corps – indeed, just the opposite was true, nurses were in greater danger than auxiliary members. Rather, it appears that there was perceived to be a greater need for women nurses, and that their role in the military was more accepted both by men in the military and by the general public. Women nurses did not challenge gender roles in the way that women army or navy officers did.

Popular journals of the early 1940s are full of images of men in uniform. There are fewer, but still frequent, images of women in uniform as well. Yet what is striking about these images is their tendency to portray women nurses rather than women from the military auxiliaries. Thus, for instance, an ad for stockings in *Good Housekeeping* shows a woman in uniform and is entitled "She's the BUSIEST woman on the block." The text reads in part "Red cross classes ... Nurses' aid ... Bauer & Black Elastic stockings ... makes it *possible* for her to *do* those important tasks that women *can* do to help win the war" (*Good Housekeeping*, August 1944, p. 226). Another truly extraordinary ad that appeared in *Good Housekeeping* is of a woman in uniform in front of an airplane. It is entitled "I Looked Into My Brother's Face" and tells the story of a nurse treating combat wounded and coming across her wounded brother. The narrative represents a wonderful mixture of female valor and feminine identity.

> And suddenly we were children again, playing nurse and wounded soldier on the battlefield of our yard back home, and I was crying because it seemed so real and I was scared . . .. Out here, I've seen my share of war . . .. And I've stood it, because I'm an Army nurse and that's my job. But a nurse is a woman first. And when someone you love is wounded, something breaks inside, and the war hits home (*Good Housekeeping*, September 1943, p. 145).

The ad celebrates this woman's contribution to the war and calls upon the nation to support her and her brother. Yet it is also careful to assure readers of her femininity (and her brother's masculinity) through the recollection of childhood gender role playing, through an emphasis on her emotional state, and through the assertion that gender identity ("a woman first") trumps any public role. Finally the contribution being celebrated is that of a nurse (a role already deeply feminized), rather than that of a women's auxiliary member.

When the war closed, women came closer than ever to seeing the Equal Rights Amendment passed. Both parties endorsed the amendment in their 1944 platforms. Congress held hearings in 1945 and the amendment was favorably reported to the floor of the House and the Senate. President Truman was on record in favor of the amendment, as were thirty of the nation's governors, and dozens of national women's organizations (*Equal Rights Amendment*, 1946). In the Congressional hearings on the amendment that year, a great deal of stress was put on women's war service as a justification for the amendment. The 1945 New York State legislature's resolution in favor of the ERA began, "Whereas they have shared equally in the pain and distress which have been involved in the maintenance of the American Republic . . . and are today participating in the battles precipitated by the enemies of freedom" (*Equal Rights Amendment: Hearing before a Subcommittee*, September 28, 1945, p. 20). Not only was war service cited as evidence of civic virtue, it was also taken as an indicator of women's abilities. As one member of the National Woman's Party testified, "During the two wars that have just come to a close no burden has been too great for women to bear; no responsibility too great for them to undertake; no hazard they have not been called upon to meet. . . . They answered every call" (*Equal Rights Amendment: Hearing before a Subcommittee*, September 28, 1945, p. 46).

Finally, at the close of World War II, the parallel was drawn to the close of World War I and that war's contribution to the passage of the suffrage amendment. "Wars are terrible things, but they bring reformations. At the end of World War I, the women's suffrage amendment was passed and made a part if the Constitution of the United States, but women found that they had but one thing and that was the right to vote . . .. Is it too much to expect that at the end of World War II the Congress of the United States would pass onto the states the opportunity to ratify the equal rights amendment?" (*Equal Rights Amendment: Hearing before a Subcommittee*, September 28, 1945, p. 34). Eventually the amendment was altered on the floor of Congress and it lost support. But the experience of women in the war contributed strongly to arguments in favor of the ERA at the close of World War II.

The association between military service and civic virtue was configured differently for men and women. For men, willingness to both fight and risk one's life for the nation were clear acts of civic virtue. Indeed, for men who were physically able to fight, a lack of willingness to serve in combat was a signal that they were lacking in civic virtue. Women were also expected to support the war effort, but in different ways – by supporting their men, contributing to the economy, aiding the war wounded, or even participating in the women's military auxiliaries. Yet, women's war contributions were sometimes greeted with ambivalence. Ironically, the actions of women in the military auxiliaries were sometimes regarded as less virtuous, because the presence of women in uniform (other than nurses) threatened gender standards. As the next section's discussion of veteran's rights reveals, the nation was more comfortable with rewarding the widows of servicemen than with rewarding women veterans.

III. VETERANS' BENEFITS AND SOCIAL CITIZENSHIP

Military service is related to citizenship both as a civic obligation and as the source of citizenship rights. The rights which military service helps to generate are not just political rights, but social rights as well. Since at least the Civil War, veteran's status has served as the most compelling justification for the development of social citizenship in the United States (Skocpol, 1992, Ch. 2). Yet the history of veterans' benefits in the United States calls several aspects of Marshall's model into question. In particular, the history of veterans' benefits suggests that the expansion of certain social rights may produce a more narrow and hierarchical rather than a more universally based citizenship. And, of course, a social citizenship that is based on veterans' benefits is a social citizenship that is strongly gendered.

(A) Male Veterans

The Roosevelt administration began giving serious consideration to veterans' benefits in 1943. Several concerns shaped their approach to this issue. Administration officials wanted to avoid the experience of the World War I veterans who suffered high rates of unemployment. Further, disgruntled veterans were a politically dangerous group, as the recent example of WWI veterans who marched on Washington demonstrated. Moreover the enormous size of the demobilization expected at the end of the war meant that the administration would have to think carefully about how to manage the economic and social dislocation that would accompany this task. Finally, the administration wanted to pursue the expansion of veterans' rights within a broader context of the establishment of social rights for all citizens – a project that began with the passage of the Social Security Act in 1935.

As the administration slowly formulated its plans in 1943, the American Legion took the initiative in putting together a comprehensive veterans' benefits bill. The Servicemen's Readjustment Act (popularly known as the G. I. Bill of Rights) was introduced in Congress in February, 1944. The Legion proposal would centralize benefits under one agency, the Veterans Administration; it would authorize benefits equal or better than those given to World War I veterans; and it would allow for the resumption of civilian status at the point where the veterans were before they entered the military. After debate in Congress over the extent of the unemployment and educational benefits that should be included in the bill, it passed and was signed into law in June, 1944. At the signing ceremony, President Roosevelt commented "apart from these special benefits which fulfill the special needs of veterans, there is much to be done [for reconversion and readjustment]" (Olson, 1974, p. 19). The administration did not see the GI Bill as a substitute for broader social welfare measures.

The sixteen million veterans of World War II were provided a broad and generous package of preferences and benefits at the end of their service. These included educational benefits, medical benefits, unemployment benefits, low interest housing and business loans, job training and placement services, and civil service job preferences. Generous as these benefits were, they received further expansion after the war. By 1948, 20.1% of the federal budget went to pay for veterans' benefits. The benefits made a substantial impact on the opportunities and social position of veterans. Ten years after the war a government study found that veterans had higher pay and more education than nonveterans at all age levels. They also owned more homes (Ross, 1969, p. 289).

Though initially the extension of veterans benefits proceeded within a vision of the broader establishment of social citizenship, eventually the political justification for these benefits changed. As Congress turned increasingly conservative in the mid-1940s and as veterans organizations articulated a logic of political obligation as the justification for veterans benefits, there developed a separate ideal of martial citizenship. Emblematic of this shift is an editorial that appeared in *Stars and Stripes*:

> Unlike our economy minded enemies, who hate to pay for the expense of a war once it is won, unlike those socialistically-minded do-gooders who would make veterans line up at a clinic along with local unfortunates, unlike the American Medical Association that has formed its trust in order to combat socialized medicine and has caught disabled veterans right in the middle, men who have worn the uniform have by that very act been placed by their Government in a class by themselves to be considered above all other classes, and as such the country has so considered them since its inception (Mosch, 1975, p. 6).

Veterans were cast as a political class apart – a class "above all other classes." They were not to be confused with "local unfortunates" who received benefits from the government as a result of socialism or paternalism. The source of this separate civic status was not disability per se, but the simple act of wearing a uniform. Here we see the ideal of martial citizenship being constructed as contrary to the development of social citizenship for the broader population.

The attachment of veterans' rights to citizenship status received further elaboration by the Supreme Court in *Fishgold v. Sullivan*, 328 US 275 (1946),

> The Act was designed to protect the veteran in several ways. He who was called to the colors was not to be penalized on his return by reason of his absence from his civilian job. He was, moreover, to gain by his service for his country an advantage which the law withheld from those who stayed behind . . .. This legislation is to be liberally construed for the benefit of those who left private life to serve their country in its hour of great need (328 US 275, pp. 284–245).

Thus, the benefits and preferences afforded to veterans for their service were intended not merely to compensate them for time lost from their civilian endeavors, but to positively advantage them over nonveterans. Interestingly, many of the Supreme Court cases which addressed veterans' preferences after World War II were ones in which the court was called upon to adjudicate between claims of labor rights and veterans' rights.[3] In the hierarchy of civic standing of the late 1940s, the citizen soldier stood above the citizen worker.

(B) Female Veterans and Veteran's Dependents

Women might have benefited from veterans' rights in two ways – as veterans or as veterans' dependents. Even with the large number of women who joined the armed forces, as a proportion of those who served, women constituted only 2% of World War II veterans (Hartmann, 1982, p. 26). Thus far more women were likely to be affected by the veterans' dependents category. Further, it seems that the military and the public were more willing to be generous with the wives and widows of veterans than they were with women veterans. Fewer women veterans made claims for benefits for which they were eligible (Willenz, 1994). Those that did sometimes experienced discrimination in the application of benefits. Women veterans were evidently refused reemployment by many private employers, despite their legal obligation to do so. In their efforts to assist female veterans to new job placements, the federal government generally directed them to lower skilled "women's" jobs. When women veterans sought to claim dependent benefits for their own families, they were obligated to demonstrate their status as the primary economic provider in the family – an obligation not imposed on male veterans. One of the two major veterans organizations of the period, the VFW, refused to admit women as regular members and lobbied against benefits for military women (Hartmann, Ch. 3). Finally, since the WASPs were not accorded military status, they remained ineligible for veterans' benefits.

What accounted for the elevation of *male* veterans and their rights over those of female veterans? Was it that there were far more male veterans so they constituted a more effective voting block? There are two problems with this argument. First, why should male veterans regard themselves as having a separate political interest from female veterans? The presumption of a gender distinction itself needs explaining. Secondly, no American politician was opposed to veterans' benefits for men in the 1940s. There was a very general sense of national obligation to the male veterans. The claims of male veterans rose above distributive political calculations. For instance, in an article written for the *Ladies Home Journal* in 1944, Dorothy Thompson (who usually wrote in favor of women's rights) expressed the view that "If there are not jobs for women and soldiers [after the war], the soldiers will get them, and no one will want or dare to protest." (Thompson, 1944, p. 6) The question was merely who would be able to attach themselves positively to this support for male veterans and use it as a means of gaining support for other social groups or social programs. Male veterans were seen as having a clear claim to civic virtue and social reward. The claims of women – as veterans or as war workers – was not as clear or absolute.

Even in the original legislation, there were differences in the ways that male and female veterans were regarded. This was most apparent in the civil service preferences which were expanded in 1944 to include able-bodied, as well as disabled, veterans. During hearings on the Act, Representative Charles LaFollette (R-Ind) noted that while the wives of disabled servicemen were awarded their husband's preference, the husbands of disabled servicewomen were not afforded a similar advantage. LaFollette sought to rectify this inequity, but he faced opposition from those who feared that men might marry disabled servicewomen just to receive their preference. LaFollette commented,

> Can we presuppose that every girl that a soldier marries necessarily on the home front makes any real contribution to the war effort? We know, as a matter of fact, that unfortunately some women who have married soldiers are little strumpets (Ross, 1969, p. 194).

LaFollette's argument's proved unpersuasive. The amendment failed and the bill was passed with discriminatory benefits for the dependents of male veterans.

A 1946 article published in the *Reader's Digest* found that women veterans were reluctant to claim veterans' benefits and that many felt discriminated against in their search for civilian employment.

> In one voice the girls of the Wac, Waves, Spars and Marines complain that prospective employers completely disregard their two or three years experience in the services. Some employers even count it against them, the women veterans believe .... Two thirds of a group of 150 women veterans who met recently at the New York Veterans Center felt they had been discriminated against by employers (Quoted in Weatherford, 1990, p. 106).

Employers were not inclined to believe that women learned anything useful in the services, and may have had questions about the moral standing of women veterans given the slander campaigns of previous years. The Army's official history of the WACs confirms these findings (Treadwell, 1954). Discrimination was that much worse for the African American women veterans. Given the public's ambivalence about women's service in the military, women veterans were more reluctant to discuss their war experiences than were their male counterparts in the years that followed World War II (Treadwell, 1954).

There was a more sympathetic attitude shown toward the wives and widows of veterans then to many female veterans. Women dependents received a lower level of financial assistance than male veterans' under the G.I. Bill, but many more women received assistance as dependents than as veterans. In a 1948 case, *Mitchell v. Cohen*, 333 US 411, the Supreme Court ruled on whether members of the Coast Guard Reserve were covered under the Veterans' Preference Act of 1944. In doing so, the Court offered their interpretation of who the "ex-servicemen" were that the Act intended to cover.

> Such ex-servicemen are those who completely disassociated themselves from their civilian status and their civilian employment during the period of their military service, suffering in many cases financial hardship and separation from home and family. They formed the great bulk of the regular armed forces during World War II. In the popular mind, they were typified by the full-fledged soldier, sailor, marine or coast guardsman (333 US 411, p. 418).

Thus, the veterans that the government desired to reward and privilege were the full-fledged soldiers, sailors, and marines; the servicemen who left behind their families and jobs to serve the nation. The popular image cited here is a strongly, if implicitly, masculine one. Making the gender of these servicemen more explicit, the court goes on to discuss their dependents.

> It is true that . . . the Act establishes preference eligibility for the unmarried widows of deceased ex-servicemen . . . But the preference rights thereby granted are derivative in nature. They are conferred on the widows because of the dislocation and severance from civil life which their deceased husbands suffered while performing full-time military duties and in partial substitution for the loss in family earning power occasioned by their husbands' deaths . . . The widows of ex-servicemen are in a special category which cannot be compared, in terms of sacrifice or need for reëmployment and rehabilitation, with any group of individuals who performed part-time military duties (333 US 411, pp. 420–421).

Several things should be noted here. First, in this passage there are male servicemen and their widows. So the categories of veteran and dependent are clearly gendered. Second, the rights of dependents are derivative rights, not the rights of citizens for themselves, but rights they receive on the basis of their relationship to another citizen. Third, these widows are welcomed into the job market because they have no husbands in that market ("loss in family earning power"). Upon remarriage, widows lose their job market privileges, since there is now a man in their lives to provide for them. Fourth and finally, war widows fall into a "special category" which justifies the state's protective attitude toward them (filling in the role of the lost husband), just as the state used to treat women workers in such protective, paternalistic terms.

When FDR first gave his support to the GI Bill in 1944 he saw it as a part of a larger program to expand and establish American social citizenship. But instead of leading to the creation of more comprehensive system of social security for all Americans, veterans' benefits lead to creation of a separate system of social provisioning for male veterans and their dependents. This consequence furthered the gendering of American social citizenship, such that male citizens – as workers and veterans – were the direct beneficiaries and their female dependents had derivative beneficiary rights through their men.

IV. CONCLUSION

In both political and social terms, it is hard to underestimate the significance of World War II for the development of American citizenship. The Second World War remains the model of the good war. American victory in this war is still taken as an expression of the virtues of American democratic culture, American economic might, and American patriotism. It was a war that produced a sense of national unity and confidence in our nation's ability to succeed in the face of international challenges. It was a war to which all groups contributed and a war that inspired new claims for political rights on the part of African Americans, Latinos and women. Yet, in the end, the virtues of women's military service were regarded differently the virtues of men's military sacrifice. Ironically, then, a democratic military victory provided the basis for a new civic hierarchy in which male veterans obtained exclusive title to the status of "first class citizens".

Social scientists often speculate about the failure of the United States to develop more robust social citizenship rights and social welfare policies during the 1930s and 1940s (Noble, 1997; Skocpol, 1992). Often this literature focuses particularly on the failures of the American labor movement to have a citizen's economic status translate into political rights. Yet it may well be that such an approach neglects a more important site for the development of citizenship rights in the 1940s. Veteran's status provided the most robust claim for social welfare and political entitlement after 1945. When American liberals dreamed in the 1940s of emulating the British effort to establish a cradle to grave system of social provisioning and social citizenship, their vision included all of the programs incorporated under the GI Bill (Ritter, 2000b). Veterans' rights did provide the basis for an expansion of social citizenship in the 1940s. But contrary to Marshall's theory it was an expansion of social citizenship that created a greater degree of political hierarchy than political equality.

This essay has considered the relationship between war, gender and citizenship in the United States in the 1940s. The argument has been that the war contributed to both the call to extend equal political rights for women and to the development of a social citizenship for male veterans in which women were seen as secondary. In terms of the three frameworks with which the article began, the following conclusions can be drawn. First, this essay offers a small correction or addition to the literature on war and democratic rights. Women were not disruptive so they faced no government repression. Further their war contributions gave strength to claims for equal citizenship for women. However, what the war and rights literature neglects is the relative standing of different social groups and the way that claims about the relationship between war service and civic virtue for one group (male veterans) can help to negate similar claims by another social group (female veterans and war workers). The gendering of civic virtue and male military service raised questions about the relative virtue of women's war service. Hence, Congress and the public appeared to be more comfortable with the service of nurses, who were clearly feminized, than with the contributions of women in the military auxiliaries.

Second, this essay sides with the critics of T. H. Marshall who argue that the historical development of citizenship is not universally in the direction of greater equality (Fraser & Gordon, 1994). For Marshall, social citizenship provided a capstone to the development of robust, egalitarian membership for all the nation's people in the polity. Yet even Marshall knew that there was something different in the experience of women. Marshall's own theory, with its emphasis on the importance of civil rights as the basis for the further development of equal individual rights, provides the basis for grasping the competing tendencies toward treating women's citizenship as equal or different in the 1940s. Setting aside Marshall's larger view of social citizenship, then, his theory still provides a potentially fruitful means for analyzing the intersection between the civil, political, and social rights of citizenship.

Third, the historical account of women's citizenship between the Nineteenth Amendment and World War II provided two expectations for our analysis of the late 1940s. First, this account suggested that there were two deeply entwined and competing tendencies, expressed by both the public and the courts, to treat women's citizenship as fundamentally equal to men's or to regard them as substantially different. These two tendencies were expressed in the near victory of the ERA in 1945–1946 and in the construction of a hierarchical social citizenship founded on veterans' benefits. Second, this earlier history suggested that the pattern of the political development of American citizenship was not clearly progressive. For women, for instance, the gains of the 1920s were followed by losses in rights and political standing in the 1930s. That pattern, too, was upheld in the late 1940s when women became more firmly positioned as secondary figures in the American system of social citizenship.

The place where the hierarchy of American social citizenship was most apparent was in the division between male and female citizens. Although veterans' rights were available to all veterans regardless of their sex, they were understood juridically and in popular culture as rights that applied primarily to the men who had seen battle and secondarily to the wives or widows they left behind. Since gender had historically worked as a reliable organizing principal for the development of citizenship, it continued to be an acceptable basis for the reformulation of citizenship ideals at the end of World War II.[4] The consequence for women was a reversal in the movement toward greater civic equality that had been gaining momentum in the early 1940s. This analysis suggests that citizenship development in the late 1940s proved more regressive than progressive, as the gendered terms of citizenship became more distinct rather than less. Yet it is not clear that this was all bad for feminist politics. After the Nineteenth Amendment, the highly mobilized and effective women's movement of the Progressive Era faded. It may be that the reemergence of gender distinctiveness in the late 1940s and 1950s helped to provide the foundation on which the next phase of the women's movement would be built.

NOTES

1. Some of the cases here include *State v. James*, 16 ALR 1141; *Palmer v. State*, 150 NE 917; *Commonwealth v. Maxwell*, 16 ALR 1134; *Harland v. Territory*, 13 PAC 453; *In re Grilli*, 179 NYS 795; *In re Opinion of the Justices*, 130 NE 685; *Parus v. District Court*, 174 PAC 706; *State v. Walker*, 185 NW 619; and *People v. Barke*, 180 NW 423.
2. After the war, in 1948, Congress passed the Women's Armed Services Integration Act, which made the presence of women in the military permanent.
3. In addition to *Fishgold v. Sullivan*, see *Trailmobile Co v. Whirls*, 331 US 40; *Hilton v. Sullivan*, 334 US 323, and *Aeronautical v. Campbell*, 337 US 521.
4. See, for instance, *Goesart v. Cleary*, 335 US 464 (1948) which upheld Michigan's law that barred women from seving as barmaids unless they were the wife or daughter of the male bar owner.

ACKNOWLEDGMENTS

The author wishes to thank Ira Katznelson, Eileen McDonagh, Suzanne Mettler, Anne Norton, David Rousseau, Stephen van Holde, and the anonymous reviewers for helpful comments and suggestions.

PART II: CONTEMPORARY PERSPECTIVES

TRADITIONAL GENDERED IDENTITIES: NATIONAL SERVICE AND THE ALL VOLUNTEER FORCE

Paul R. Higate

INTRODUCTION

Writing in 1987, David Morgan posed the question 'Does National Service (NS) make a man of you?' Drawing on the method of intellectual autobiography, he discusses elements of his gendered experiences of conscription in the Royal Air Force (RAF) between 1955 and 1957 in order to make sense of this particular masculinised *rite-de-passage*. His suggestive findings illuminate the nature and characteristics of a particular cluster of dominant gendered attributes National Servicemen learned to use in their everyday lives. Morgan (1987, p. 79) stated that NS:

> [P]rovided an arena in which young men might deploy various masculine attributes . . . making men was as much to do with what the recruits brought to the experience as with what the system might do for them once they were there.

The most striking aspect of Morgan's article was the extent to which it resonated with my own experience of the RAF between 1983 and 1991, over 26 years later within the context of what is popularly considered to be a modern (or even 'postmodern') volunteer military – an organisation one might assume to be considerably different to its citizen-soldier predecessor.

In this brief paper, a number of comments are made with regard to the high levels of 'gendered continuity' between institutions separated by three decades.

The Comparative Study of Conscription in the Armed Forces, Volume 20, pages 229–235.

ISBN: 0-7623-0836-2

The points raised in these discussions, whilst largely heuristic in intent, nonetheless, are derived from considerable biographical overlap; both myself and Morgan served as RAF clerks in parallel roles within 'orderly rooms', against the backdrop of historically discrete institutions. Given the overall paucity of analyses dealing with NS, these provisional comments are intended to throw light on the nexus that links voluntary/conscripted service with issues of structure and agency.

STRUCTURAL OVERVIEW – NATIONAL SERVICE AND THE ALL VOLUNTEER FORCE

National Service 1945–1963

Between 1945 and 1963, over two million men were conscripted into the three branches of the armed services. Whilst the army received the bulk of young enlistees, the RAF and Royal Navy (RN) also paid host to tens of thousands of conscripts during this period. The RAF was often considered to be the 'easy option' with discipline less stringent than that of the army, and with a 'better educated' and more technically able citizen enlisting for periods of between one and two years (Morgan, 1987; Royle, 1997). In conscripting citizen soldiers, NS necessarily placed in uniform young men originating from a broad social spectrum. These individuals tended to see their service as an interruption to the flow of the life-course, where employment or education might be delayed (Morgan, 1987).

The All Volunteer Force 1963 – Current

The current RAF differs in many respects to its conscript forerunner. It is a considerably smaller organisation (currently standing at around 50,000 personnel and during the 1980s and early 1990s at around 85,000 personnel), characterised by professionalism, reliance on 'state of the art' technology, a changed and changing role (towards policing/peacekeeping, rapid reaction and possible European integration), together with a career structure that is oriented at long service engagements when contrasted with NS. In addition – and of significance for the following discussions – around 8% of its members are women (Dandeker & Segal, 1996). The public and media perception of the armed forces more generally is vulnerable to fluctuation, and contingent (amongst other things) on the current global-economic climate. For example, whilst the following negative headlines (appearing on the BBC news website under the search phrase 'armed forces)' appeared: *Army rifles: what's gone wrong?*

(25 February, 2000), *Catalogue of MoD misery* (25 February, 2000), *£1bn jets "unfit" for combat* (23 February, 2000), *Damning report into Kosovo campaign* (3 January, 2000), *Defence cash shortfall fear* (10 February, 2000), *RAF faces "pilot morale crisis*" (14 September, 2000), nevertheless during particular moments (for example the Malvinos/Falklands and Gulf conflicts), the host society's attitude is noted to change. This appears to increase the attractiveness of the military career option (Shaw, 1991), and in a more positive sense, through the significant outcry from both the media and the public when it was suggested that ex-servicemen represented up to one in four of the single homeless population (Braid, *Independent on Sunday*, 29 May 1994; Kelly, *The Times*, 8 June, 1994).

Military service (and perhaps to a lesser extent, the RAF) continues to be understood by many – though as Morgan reminds us, he did not encounter the phrase at the time – to 'make men out of boys'. In the contemporary period, whilst we might be less inclined to label late teenage/adolescent men as 'boys', nevertheless, a broad perception remains that military service is characterised by a 'maturing' process understood along the lines of gender (Pleck & Sawyer, 1974).

Making Men – The RAF Clerk and National Service

Morgan's analysis of the gender-transformative effects of RAF NS are somewhat circumspect, and in pursuing the nexus that links violence with men (the original impetus for the work) he recalls a 'taboo on tenderness' (1987, p. 48; see also Segal, 1990) rather than the experience of being trained in the 'legitimate discharge of violence' (Huntington, 1957; Janowitz, 1971). Other substantive themes linked to the fostering of RAF NS masculinities concerned the ways in which women were categorised as either 'girl friends' or 'tarts'. To attain a consensually revered aggressively heterosexualist masculinity is undoubtedly to have 'had it' as Morgan (1987, p. 59) states, with a somewhat distanced female 'other'. Physical/mental hardship and deprivation are also discussed as formative masculinised experiences together with camaraderie, smoking, swearing, drinking and sport. In summary, Morgan argues:

> If it did make a man of you, National Service achieved these ends largely indirectly or in a round about manner – it did so through encouraging some distinctly unheroic and presumably unmasculine traits to do with skiving and avoiding responsibility (1987, p. 78).

These comments remind us of the part-unintended features of military life whereby resistance arises within the context of a strict institutional hierarchy, yet this cementing of camaraderie is undoubtedly functional in terms of organisational prerogatives (Hockey, 1986). Overall, Morgan's account was largely interchangeable with my own experiences, not just in terms of being a clerk, but also with regard to the broader context of the RAF.

Making Men – the RAF Clerk and the All Volunteer Force

I have already commented on the depth and breadth of experiential overlap in terms of my own service with that of Morgan. Like Morgan, I suffered little physical hardship during my military career (see Higate, 1998), conceived of women in terms of the binary opposition sketched above, despite the presence of members of the Women's Royal Air Force (WRAF's) in the workplace, and utilised dominant 'masculine scripts' in terms of camaraderie, swearing, drinking and sport. Similarly, the 'anti-masculine' traits of skiving and shirking responsibility – clear strategies of resistance – preoccupied large proportions of the routinised working day.

Whilst the academic neglect of NS limits the confidence with which we might generalise about the commonality of my experiences with those of Morgan, nevertheless, fictionalised and 'empirical descriptive' accounts of the armed forces (for NS see: Thomas, 1966; Thorne, 1998; Royle, 1997) and the contemporary AVF (Beevor, 1991; McCallion, 1996; McNab, 1995), when subject to gendered readings, also reveal striking cultural continuity between these historically discrete organisations. This is particularly surprising given the differences in both military structures (enforced *versus* voluntary service) and the civilian-social context in which these institutions were and are nested. The notion that the military is a 'society within a society' or a 'microcosm of society' would suggest that the AVF of the late 1980s and early 1990s – in the face of the alleged ascendancy of the so-called 'New Man' and other changes in gendered ideology in the host society (notably towards homosexuals and women) – should differ sharply from the citizen-soldier institution of the 1950s. The immediate post-war period, (the environment within which conscriptees-to-be were socialised) as Segal (1990) has argued, was distinguished by the relative fixedness of gendered roles – for example between the 'male breadwinner' and 'the housewife'. Why, given that citizen soldiers originated from *all* walks of life, and were not self-selecting, might it appear that little has changed in terms of the dominant military masculine ideologies within the RAF of the 1980s and early 1990s, and beyond into both the army and the RN?

THE TRADITIONAL MILITARY

One response to this question is to argue for the powerful influence of military socialisation, in other words, an understanding in which structure is prioritised over agency. As a traditional environment (Beevor, 1991; Downes, 1986; Dunivin, 1988), its key socialisers deal in unquestioned and durable 'formulaic truths' (Giddens, 1991). Here, RAF Station Warrant Officers (SWO's), RN Master's at Arms (MAA's) and army Regimental Sergeant Majors (RSM's) ensure continuity through their static attitudes and beliefs. McNab captures this traditional environment in the following extract:

> We seemed to have the culture of the seventies but the army of the fifties. It felt as if I was living in one of the black-and-white movies I sometimes used to watch on a Saturday afternoon. Each morning we had to drink a mugful of 'screech' the old army word for powdered lime juice. The colonel must have been reading a book about Captain Cook and thought it would stop us getting scurvy (1995, p. 19).

And, more recently:

> The armed forces tend to recruit people who are quite well-educated. One set of people are good at one thing, but no so good at another. Your Afro-Caribbean is a big chap, often very athletic and more interested in sport and music (RAF Squadron Leader Cowan, *The Guardian*, 23 March, 1996).

This military-cultural inertia is apparent in many other accounts, and in the late 1980s senior army officers were commenting that this was a positive feature of the armed forces, and that they should be 'at least half a generation behind' their host society (Beevor, 1991). No doubt their desires implicitly touched on the importance of retaining traditional (military) masculinities the likes of which were under increasing challenge in the civilian society.

Service Person Agency

The structural view tends to predominate in the literature with the notion that military training 'breaks people down to build them up' and, in a Goffmanian total institutional sense, 'mortifies the self' through the ritualistic humiliations characteristic of basic military training (though see: Hockey, 1986). Similarly, the notion that military personnel are homogeneous, implicit when the labels of 'tommy' 'squaddie', 'pongo', and 'GI Joe' are used, tends to downplay agency. However, the central hypothesis of this paper – and one way in which to account for continuity in military masculine culture sketched above, is to suggest that military culture is largely self-regulating and in a state of equilibrium because volunteer enlistees *tend* to be characterised by their traditional (pre-military) masculine identities. This 'raw identity material', in terms of gender, is then developed in a range of complex ways, and is 'steered' within largely consensual and familiar parameters. This formulation provides conceptual space for the frequently neglected concept of recruit agency, as it is very much alive, even within the intensive basic training endured in the most physical of regimes, the infantry (Hockey, 1986).

The Importance of Pre-Military Experience

The conscripted military, by its very nature, tended to reflect the host society in which it functioned. In turn, military gendered culture of the 1950s resonated more closely with that to be found in civilian life in ways outlined above with regard to traditional masculinities. In contrast, the military of the 1980s and early 1990s had 'fallen behind' and could be described as suffering from 'cultural lag' (Jolly, 1992), with the differences between military and civilian cultures becoming increasingly pronounced. In particular, the challenge of the feminist critique was largely ignored by the military and female service personnel were being treated as second class citizens, not least when it was established they were pregnant. Similar issues arose within the context of serving personnel found to be homosexual (Hall, 1995). Those attracted to the military life, and once again it is important to reiterate the provisional framing of these comments, brought with them beliefs and identities that might be described as 'outdated' or 'traditional'. For example, in the case of the army, many of the youngest recruits originated from poor socio-economic backgrounds (Beevor, 1991) where traditional masculine pursuits are everyday currency (notions around the 'place of women', homophobic and aggressively heterosexualist beliefs, use of physical capital as key element of masculine identity and so on) (Connell, 1995; Mac An Ghaill, 1994). A significant number of others (known as 'scaly brats') follow their father's military footsteps, and we could speculate, are familiar with these gendered attitudes and beliefs. Commentators have remarked on the importance of pre-military experience before (Beevor, 1991; Edmonds, 1988; Morgan, 1987), but tended not to have made the links between cultural continuity and the extent to these traditional identities (agency) are mobilised and developed. Ultimately, these dispositions contribute towards the relatively static constellation of military-gendered identities, dynamically produced and reproduced. Any cursory reading of Mac An Ghaill's (1994) '*The Making of Men*', an ethnography dealing with formations of masculinity within the school context, underlines the importance of immersion into the military as *secondary* socialisation, a point that is often sidelined by an overemphasis on the apparently *primary* influence of military training and subsequent experience. Other examples highlighting the tenacity of agency within the conscripted military context are touched on by Bourke (1998) who illuminates the fascinating examples of both men and women in times of war relishing (or loathing) combat and killing, together with other troops who, when out of earshot of their commander, would cease firing at the enemy.

CONCLUSION

In this brief paper I have argued that RAF NS and the AVF RAF of the late 1980s and 1990s were (and likely remain) characterised by high levels of gendered continuity. Though the empirical basis for this assertion is based on autobiographical experience, supporting literature tends to reinforce the relatively static nature of military-masculine culture, in particular the existence of traditional masculinities. Yet, whilst recent changes in the volunteer military have been far-reaching (the formal 'acceptance' of homosexual service personnel and an increasing gender consitution/opening up of roles for women), it is speculated that the *informal* gendered culture of today's armed services is unlikely to differ markedly from that described above. This can be partly explained by the 'traditional masculine dispositions' brought to the environment, particularly amongst the lower non-commissioned ranks. That said, there exists anecdotal evidence to suggest that enlistees from the non-state education boarding sector – destined for the officer corps – also bring 'traditional masculine' dispositions to bear on military socialisation. It is also worth considering that the media perpetuated 'New Man', and other such constructions may over emphasise the extent to which traditional masculinities have given way to more enlightened gender identities. The need for further research is clear, and a study of the recently established AVF in the Netherlands, draws our attention to the importance of understanding the nature and content of volunteer assumptions, as it is those who originate from disadvantaged backgrounds that are most likely to be repatriated from peacekeeping duties (Moelker, 2000). In sum, whilst these arguments are orientated at recentering agency in the military – particularly in terms of gender, the question remains: Is it possible to have a military devoid of some of the less desirable (traditional) military masculine traits that serve to oppress homosexuals and women, and fuel misogyny within military communities and perhaps beyond? (Kovitz, 2000). Are these gendered attributes a necessary pre-requisite for a fighting force in an increasingly 'detraditional' context or is it possible that military gendered culture can reflect changes in the civilian environment whilst still getting 'the job done'?

ACKNOWLEDGMENTS

Thanks to the two anonymous referees and, in particular to Antonia Parera for helpful comments in respect of the above.

RECRUITMENT OF CHILDREN AS SOLDIERS IN SUB-SAHARAN AFRICA: AN ECOLOGICAL ANALYSIS

Michael Wessells

INTRODUCTION

Contrary to images of children as passive victims of war, children are increasingly prominent actors in armed conflicts that are fought predominantly in and around communities (Wessells, 1998). Although hard figures are unobtainable, the Global Coalition to Stop the Use of Child Soldiers estimates that approximately 300,000 children, defined as people under 18 years of age, are engaged in military activity. Children serve a wide range of roles depending on the situation, the age, size, and gender of the child, the needs of the recruiters, and the level of secrecy that military commanders can maintain regarding their exploitation of children. Frequent roles include cooks, porters, spies, informants, bodyguards, and combatants. In many situations, girls perform roles such as these and may also serve as "concubines" or "soldier's wives," euphemisms for sex slavery. Both girls and boys are used as mine sweepers and suicide bombers.

Child soldiering is a global phenomenon, and at present includes Asian countries such as Afghanistan, Burma, Cambodia, Indonesia, Philippines, and Sri Lanka; Latin American countries such as Colombia, Mexico, and Peru; and African countries such as Angola, Burundi, Sierra Leone, and Uganda. But it is not only developing countries that recruit and use child soldiers. Northern countries such as the U.S., Norway, and the United Kingdom allow voluntary

The Comparative Study of Conscription in the Armed Forces, Volume 20, pages 237–254.

ISBN: 0-7623-0836-2

recruitment of children under 18 years of age, and the U.K. regularly sends children under the age of 18 into armed conflict. The recently adopted Optional Protocol to the U.N. Convention on the Rights of the Child bans compulsory recruitment by states of under-18s but allows voluntary recruitment by governments starting at age 16 provided that states specify the steps they will take to ensure protection of those under 18.

Children's association with armed conflict is hardly new. In Sparta, 7-year-old boys were reportedly taken from homes for military training (Stavrou, Stewart & Stavrou, 2000). In feudal Europe, boys assisted and trained to become knights, and in the 13th century, children participated in the Children's Crusade, although the children never reached Palestine or engaged in combat (Boothby & Knudsen, 2000). In rural Africa, boys have long fought beside their fathers to defend their villages in the same way that they have worked alongside their fathers in the fields. In the Revolutionary War that led to the formation of the U.S., child drummers led armies into combat.

Still, there are new, disturbing facets of child soldiering. In previous eras of hand-to-hand combat, children's small size limited severely their combat efficacy. Due to the widespread availability and low cost of lightweight, automatic weapons such as AK-47 assault rifles, even children of relatively small stature can now be useful fighting forces. As a result, children now comprise a significant percentage of combatants in some armies (Brett & McCallin, 1996), and children under 10 years of age are put into combat roles (Wessells, 1997). Commanders often prefer children because they are relatively manipulable, willing to take risks, and fearless. In addition, children are often highly accessible, leading to their recruitment in significant numbers. Facing troop shortfalls and eager to maintain strength, commanders may abduct or forcibly recruit children from local villages. Access to children is also linked to deprivation. Contemporary wars, which are fought in and around communities and target civilians, destroy schools, health posts, and other structures; displace large numbers of people; separate children from families; and amplify poverty. In such situations, the choice to join an army may be a child's best chance for survival, hope, money, or fulfillment of basic needs for security, belonging, and materials such as food and water.

Comparative studies of conscription stand to benefit from analysis of forced recruitment of children. Although studies of conscription typically focus on compulsory, legal conscription by states, in contemporary conflicts much of the non-voluntary recruitment is achieved illegally through abduction or coercion. Further, most armed conflicts are now fought within state boundaries (Wallensteen & Sollenberg, 2000), and non-state actors such as rebel groups, militias, paramilitary groups, and armed opposition groups forcibly recruit children and draw significant strength from the use of child soldiers (Brett & McCallin, 1996; Cohn & Goodwin-Gill, 1994). Exclusive focus on state policies and practices would limit the field prematurely and reduce the contribution that studies of conscription might make to the protection of children's rights.

Analyses of conscription practices and forced recruitment of youths face significant problems of time frame, data quality, and definition. Since forced recruitment often occurs opportunistically and practices coevolve together with rapidly changing conflicts, it is useful to examine practices over a period of several decades. Regardless of the time frame, however, accurate quantitative data are difficult to obtain as war scuttles data collection efforts and imposes enormous barriers to researchers' security and access. Groups that exploit children as soldiers are eager to hide this practice and seldom recruit according to written policies and procedures. Indeed, in many parts of Africa, written birth records are seldom kept, making it difficult to determine accurately the age of children. Troop hungry commanders often pay attention to children's size rather than their age. Few accurate data are available regarding girl soldiers (McKay & Mazurana, 2000).

Serious problems also arise in regard to definition of basic terms such as "child." Contrary to universalized views of childhood, many African societies regard 13-year-olds who have participated in cultural rites of passage as adults. Even the term "soldier" can be vexing to define in contexts in which one is dealing less with organized, governmental armies than with paramilitaries, rebel groups, warlord-led bands of youths, or groups of stone-throwing adolescents engaged in liberation struggles. Amidst the early stages of research, it is best to cast a relatively wide net, avoiding narrow definitions that limit inquiry or fail to capture the diversity that exists in the field. Consistent with international legal standards, this paper defines children as people under 18 years of age, and it defines child soldiers as people under 18 years of age who participate directly or indirectly in military activity, including peacetime training and preparation.

The purpose of this paper is to analyze practices of forced recruitment of children in sub-Saharan Africa, where child soldiering has occurred on a relatively large scale and children have played an important role in various armed conflicts. Across Africa, there are an estimated 120,000 child soldiers. The paper uses a case study methodology because a complete data set on sub-Saharan Africa is unavailable. Comparison of a small number of different cases illustrates the diversity of recruitment methods and conflict contexts in sub-Saharan Africa. Although it is not comprehensive, this case based approach provides a platform for the construction of wider comparative analyses.

The first part of the paper examines forced recruitment in Angola, Uganda, and Sierra Leone. These countries were selected because in each case, significant numbers of children have engaged in soldiering and relatively extensive documentation is available. Collectively, they exhibit wider themes evident in regions of Africa and yet also embody the diversity of patterns of armed conflict and recruitment practices. Currently active yet protracted, they are among the most pressing situations that warrant the attention of the international community. Of necessity, the focus is on qualitative descriptions, including testimony from former child soldiers that gives them a voice. The second part of the paper presents an ecological systems framework that analyzes the factors that place children at risk of child soldiering and heighten vulnerability to forced recruitment. This framework attempts to show that there are multiple pathways into soldiering and that difficult life conditions and victimization blur the lines between voluntary and forced recruitment.

THREE CASE STUDIES

Although conscription is prevalent in sub-Saharan Africa, nearly all governments have legal restrictions against the recruitment of people under 18 years of age. A noteworthy exception is South Africa, the Constitution of which allows recruitment in state emergencies of people over 15 years of age. Unfortunately, many governments have engaged in forced recruitment practices that violate their own national legislation. Nevertheless, the largest and worst violations of children's rights have occurred in connection with the actions of non-governmental actors. Accordingly, the case studies emphasize the importance of non-state actors.

Angola

In Angola, government legislation and practice regarding conscription has changed with the tides of the conflict that began in 1961 as a liberation struggle from Portugal and continued since 1975 as an internal war fought mainly between the Government of Angola and UNITA, the National Union for the Total Liberation of Angola. In 1993, the government introduced compulsory conscription for Angolan men between 20 and 45 years of age.

In practice, however, the Angolan government has used child soldiers. Child soldiering was a common practice on both sides of the conflict through the 1980s (Arlacchi, 1998). The Bicesse Accords of 1991 established a ceasefire and provided for demobilization, and the Minister of Defense reported in 1992 that Angolan armed forces contained 1,656 soldiers under 18 years or approximately 2% of armed forces. It is not known how many of these were forcibly recruited. When the Bicesse peace process fell apart as UNITA rejected the 1992 election results, war re-erupted with some of the worst fighting occurring between 1992 and 1994. Voluntary service by children occurred in many areas such as Kuito, which for 18 months was under seige and where it is commonly said that children won the war (i.e. prevented UNITA domination).

Even following the introduction of compulsory conscription, troop shortfalls led the Angolan government to engage in forced recruitment of youth, although the scale remains uncertain. With the signing of the Lusaka Protocol in 1994, it became possible to interview some of the approximately 9,000 youths who had been registered and were waiting in quartering areas. It also became possible to interview people in communities to learn about methods of forced recruitment.

Roundups of young people and kidnapping were the main methods of forced recruitment used by the government. According to a 17-year-old Private in the Angolan armed forces, soldiers had burst at night three years earlier into his home in Bie province and had taken him away. He said "I didn't want to join the Army, they made me join . . . All these years, all I have wanted to do is go home" (Fleming, 1997). Although roundups may not have targeted children specifically, they often snared youth who were large for their age. Such forced recruitment is made possible by the lack of proper birth records and identification, a problem that pervades much of sub-Saharan Africa.

It would be a mistake, however, to imply that there was no deliberate recruitment of children. As described by an Angolan boy now 24 years old, "I was walking with two girls. And they called me. I was too close to them, so I couldn't run. Even though my identification card said I was underage – and that was true – I was big, they insisted I was old enough, and they grabbed me and took me to a police station. It was full of kids . . ." (*New York Times*, January 20, 1999). The young man reported that typically, youths caught in roundups are taken for training to distant provinces where they do not know anyone. Fortunately, this young man's uncle secured his release by talking with the station commander. Today, reports of group roundups of youth continue, although the practice occurs mostly in rural areas rather than Luanda and is believed to be less frequent than in the pre-1994 fighting.

Turning next to UNITA, it is important to note that since 1975, Angola has been virtually a country inside a country, with the government controlling some areas and UNITA controlling others which have changed over time. UNITA controls communities through terror and has tightly limited the access of the international community (Human Rights Watch, 1994; Minter, 1994). Talk of peace or criticism of recruitment practices can get one killed. As a result, it has been difficult to estimate reliably the numbers of child soldiers among UNITA forces. It is widely believed that some of the youth presented for demobilization at quartering areas under the Lusaka peace process were not actually former soldiers but civilian stooges who had been ordered to present themselves as soldiers while the real troops remained in the field. Of the more than 9,000 underage soldiers were registered for demobilization under the Lusaka process, 520 came from the government forces while 8,613 came from UNITA forces (Verhey, 1999). Of the registered children, the median age was 13–14 years, the median length of time spent in combat areas was two years, and over 75% reported that they had shot someone (Christian Children's Fund, 1998).

UNITA uses ideology and propaganda to attract voluntary youth recruits. Children who grow up in UNITA-controlled areas are taught to revere UNITA's leader, Jonas Savimbi, and to call him "father." Forced recruitment, however, is widespread, and during the pre-Lusaka occurred often through a community tariff process (Verhey, 1999). In this system, UNITA forces entered rural communities and demanded that the traditional chief (*soba*) present a complement of young people (boys and girls) to serve as soliders lest the community suffer the consequences. Abduction also occurs in the current round of war, which reerupted in December, 1998. It is reported that people, including minors, who are abducted, are forced to serve, with deserters being executed. Reports of sexual abuse against girls are also widespread (U.S. Department of State, 1999).

It should also be noted that on both sides, children in desperate circumstances may join a military group because it provides security, health care, or food. Often it is children who have been separated from parents who tend to take up with a military group out of necessity and lack of better options. Unaccompanied children are more likely to be recruited as well since they lack adult protection. In such situations, it is difficult to know where to draw a line between forced and voluntary recruitment. Particularly in UNITA controlled areas, where the grip of terror is strong, what appears to be a choice to join may in fact be tacit submission to terror.

Uganda

Northern Uganda, home of the Acholi people, is the site of a prolonged power struggle involving Joseph Kony, leader of the so-called Lord's Resistance Army (LRA), whose rebel forces oppose those of the Ugandan army. Since Uganda has legislation against the use of child soldiers and has not in fact used children as soldiers, the emphasis here will be on the LRA. The shocking practices of the LRA provide what is perhaps the purest case of forced recruitment through abduction and terror (Amnesty International, 1997; Muhumuza, 1996).

Kony and the LRA have no political constituency in northern Uganda, but he professes spiritual leadership as a relative of Alice Lakwena, an Acholi woman who claimed to be possessed by the Holy Spirit and who had in 1987 led Acholi soldiers against government troops. Although Lakwena had promised her troops, armed mostly with rifles and stones, spiritual protection against bullets, the Ugandan army dealt them a crushing defeat, leading Lakwena to flee to Kenya and creating an opportunity for Kony. Under Kony, the LRA over the past decade has survived largely by terrorizing and raiding communities in northern Uganda, stealing animals, raiding and burning homes, and abducting children. Attacks on villages have displaced approximately 200,000 people, many of whom sleep in the bush at night to avoid LRA patrols. Following attacks and looting, the LRA often slips across the border into Sudan, where captured children receive brutal military training which involved frequent beatings which may be administered for no reason. The Sudanese government supports the LRA, which it uses as a proxy in its own fight against the Sudanese People's Liberation Army.

The LRA achieves its military strength in no small part by systematically stealing and brutalizing children. Since 1992, an estimated 14,000 children have been abducted as child soldiers and sex slaves (Stavrou et al., 2000). At present, the LRA is believed to include nearly 6,000 children as young as seven years. The typical pattern of abduction involves raids by small bands of five to twenty rebels who have radio contact and move swiftly. In the bush, they loot homes, steal food and tools, beat or kill adults as a means of achieving control through terror, and abduct children. The children receive death threats, which they know from experience are far from idle. Usually, the abducted children are forced to march rapidly into the bush, carrying heavy loads and having little water or food. Those who cannot keep up or whose feet become infected and swollen are killed. Part of the indoctrination for newly abducted children is to force them to kill or beat weaker children or escapees.

The pattern of abduction is indicated best by the testimonies of children (provided by Human Rights Watch, 1997) who escaped and found their way to reintegration centers or returned home.

> Thomas, age 14: "In our village, we realized the rebels were coming, and my whole family hid in the bush at night. At dawn, we thought they were gone, and I went back to the compound to fetch food. But they were still there, and they took me. It was very fast . . .. I had to carry a bag of groundnuts, maybe twenty kilos. It was heavy but there was no alternative to carrying it. Some young children were given very heavy loads, but with any load you must struggle to carry it, or otherwise the rebels say "You are becoming stubborn and rebellious!" And they kill you. If your feet swell they also kill you. I saw quite a number of children killed."

> James, age 14: "Me and my brothers and cousins were playing football. Five rebels came and took all six of us, my three brothers, two cousins and myself. They tied us with ropes

> around our waists and gave us heavy loads to carry. [They led us to a larger group.] There were about eighty rebels and fifty abductees in the group. At night, we stopped to rest, and they beat us – they used a bicycle chain to beat us. The next morning we came to the government soldiers when we were walking. They were firing at us. We ran with the luggage. My eldest brother escaped but the rebels caught him and they killed him. They beat him on the back of the head with a club. I watched him being killed . . ."

> Stella, age 15: "They came to our school in the middle of the night. We were hiding under the beds but they banged on the beds and told us to come out. They tied us and led us out, and they tried to set the school building on fire. We walked and walked and they made us carry their property that they had looted . . .. On the third day a little girl tried to escape, and they made us kill her. They went to collect some big pieces of firewood. Then they kicked her and jumped on her, and they made us each beat her at least once with the big pieces of wood. They said, "You must beat and beat and beat her." She was bleeding from the mouth. Then she died . . .."

By making children commit horrible acts, the children are made to believe that they have become unacceptable, have nowhere else to go, and have the best chances of survival by staying with the LRA. To strengthen this belief, the LRA generates a steady stream of propaganda, insuring the children (falsely) that if they are captured by the Ugandan army, they will be killed. These psychological tactics are an integral part of the forced recruitment process, which would be ineffective in the absence of deterrents against escape.

The deterrents against escape, however, are internal as well as external. The frequent beatings, progressive exposure to and normalization of violence, and the belief that one has a future only with the military help youth to build military identities that make it very difficult for them to return to or to stay at home. Over time, youth become accustomed to violence and may accept their part in it, seeing themselves as soldiers. To build soldiers' identities, the LRA uses positive incentives as well as tactics of victimization and threat. According to a former rebel commander, "I was abducted at the age of nine, I was a 'good' soldier and by the age of 14, I was 'given' my first wife (she was 17 years old at the time). When I turned 18, I was rewarded with a second wife (then 14 years old). I have had two children with the one and one with the other. We are a family" (Stavrou et al., p. 7). In effect, the LRA provides a "changed moral universe" that honors the reverse of what most societies revere and prepares youth to kill and to abduct and sexually violate other children (Rubin, 1998).

Even if they escape the LRA, young people may be highly vulnerable to reabduction. Affected by their war experiences, they may find it difficult to concentrate in school, and many display angry outbursts and difficulties forming relationships with other children or adults. Most former child soldiers lack marketable job skills, see few options for themselves in civilian society, and feel hopeless about the future. Many have no parents or have difficulty reintegrating with families, as it is hard for former rebel fighters and commanders to submit to parental authority again. In addition, fear, suspicion, and stigmatization may undermine the youths' attempts to reintegrate socially. In northern Uganda, previously abducted youth have told the author that they were called "rebel" when they returned to school and that they saw few options in civilian society. Spending large amounts of time idling, living away from home, and having no adult supervision and protection, these youth are at high risk of reabduction. In fact, forced recruitment of children in northern Uganda is often cyclical.

Sierra Leone

The literature on children and war has vacillated between extreme images. Whereas some portray children as innocents who need protection, others emphasize hardened adolescent killers. Similarly, some discussions of children's entry into military activity present grim images of children forced to join and to kill. Others show images of volunteers who actively seek the power achieved through the barrel of a gun and relish the excitement of military activity. Perhaps more than any country, Sierra Leone presents a complex mosaic that shatters such simplistic images and invites analysis of the diverse pathways through which children enter into soldiering.

Begun in 1991 as a spillover from the Liberian civil war, the war in Sierra Leone has pitted mainly the Armed Forces of Sierra Leone (SLA) against the Revolutionary United Front (RUF), the rebel group known to commit the worst abuses of children's rights. Allied with the SLA against the rebels are the Civil Defense Forces (CDF), including the Kamajors, a traditional hunters society and now a paramilitary group that in rural areas protects villages against the RUF. Driven in no small part by quest for power and control over diamonds (Smillie & Gberie, 2000), the war has created lawlessness and opportunistic fighting and has killed over 75,000 people. It has also displaced nearly half the population of 4.5 million people, destroyed many homes and large amounts of infrastructure, amplified already acute poverty and inflation, and confronted the world with horrifying atrocities such as mutilations and rapes. Many atrocities involve child soldiers, as girl soldiers report consistently that they have been raped and forced to serve as sex slaves. Further, youth have been perpetrators of atrocities, as adolescent soldiers in the RUF have committed mutilations such as cutting off people's arms or hands.

It is primarily the RUF and the CDF that recruit child soldiers deliberately and systematically. An estimated 5,400 children are associated with the RUF at present (UNICEF/Sierra Leone, 2000). Following the January, 1999 attack on Freetown, nearly 4,000 children were reported missing, and research has indicated that 60% of these had been abducted by the RUF, which has taken children as young as seven years (UNICEF/Sierra Leone, 2000; Wessells, 1997). Children have also fought on the government side through the CDF, as the Kamajors recruit young children and regard as adults youth who have completed the cultural rites of passage.

Methods for recruiting child soldiers in Sierra Leone exhibit complexity and vary according to the group as well as the local situation. The RUF recruits children extensively using a mixture of forced and voluntary recruitment. Forced recruitment typically entails abduction of either individuals or groups combined with threats and terror tactics designed to deter escape. In some cases, abductees have been forced to kill or to mutilate members of their own family or community. In addition to intimidating communities and shattering social trust, this practice is designed to break the bonds between child and community, to brand the child as a killer who cannot return home for fear of revenge, and to force the child to stay with the military for protection. In addition, RUF abductees and other troops have been fed drugs, including gunpowder, marijuana, alcohol, and cocaine, to numb pain, instill fearlessness, and encourage children to fight (Smillie & Gberie, 2000). According to one former child soldier in the RUF, "Our superiors put gunpowder in our food and gave us brown pills which they called cocaine to take with our drink. The drugs make your heart strong, make you feel that you are not afraid of anything" (*The Independent*, 1995; cited in Smillie & Gberie, 2000, p. 3).

Many of the RUF recruits, however, are volunteers, who express diverse motives for joining. Some express frustration over the lack of education and job opportunities and report that the military provides better life options than civilian life (cf. Peters & Richards, 1998). Youth volunteers have also reported that joining the army was their best means of meeting basic needs for survival, food, health care, and protection. Still others report that their friends have joined and they wanted comeraderie and excitement. Based on these reports, Richards and Peters have suggested a rational actor model in which youth assess their options and make rational choices about how to best meet their needs, with soldiering not infrequently emerging as the preferred option. At present, there are no reliable estimates of what percentage of RUF soldiers are volunteers.

With regard to the CDF, voluntary recruitment of children is prevalent. For the Kamajors, a strong ethos of protecting family and villages exists. Over the years of the war, the hunter traditions have evolved such that it is the role of men and older boys to join in paramilitary groups to fight the RUF and defend their villages. Young boys often join because their fathers, brothers and other family members belong.

Although it is tempting to accept at face value the distinction between voluntary and forced recruitment, war zones such as Sierra Leone often blur this distinction and demand alternative conceptual frameworks. In many cases, it is unwise to accept so-called voluntary recruitment as a matter of free, rational choice. Children in war zones may have so few options that it is not clear whether it is meaningful to speak of free choice. What appear to be rational choices may be matters of survival, necessity, and dealing with extreme adversity. If, for example, a hungry youth decided to join the military to obtain food on a regular basis, this choice would not constitute a free choice in any coherent sense of the term. Similarly, if a young boy were separated from his parents, lived in fear, and decided to join a military group for protection, this would be less a free choice than one dictated by harsh realities and survival needs. At best, the decisions of youth in war zones must be viewed as bounded and guided by the necessities of life and the fact that the conditions threaten the very right to survive.

Further, exposure to violence, displacement, and related stressors may have powerful cognitive effects, making it questionable to assume that decision-making follows a rational calculus. For youth who grow up in zones where violence and armed conflict are normalized and where family and friends are involved in armed conflict, peer and family pressures to "volunteer" may be so powerful as to overshadow or render meaningless other options. This is not to deny that youth make choices but to suggest that in war zones such as Sierra Leone, their choices may reflect difficult life conditions, a history of deprivation and victimization, pre-existing psychological problems, and a host of other variables that severely reduce the utility of the category of voluntary recruitment.

Ultimately, it would be futile to debate where to draw the line between voluntary and involuntary recruitment in zones of active conflict. What is needed is a rich conceptual framework that embodies the diversity and complexity associated with children's entry into military activity in cases such as Angola, Uganda, and Sierra Leone. The following section develops an ecological, interactive framework, which is intended to stimulate additional research into the factors that enable children's participation in the military.

AN ECOLOGICAL FRAMEWORK

Analyses of children's entry into soldiering may be enriched by drawing on the now extensive literatures on children's social ecologies and on risk accumulation. Ecological approaches to child development feature children's interactions with various actors in the nested social systems such as family, community, ethnic groups, and society (Bronfenbrenner, 1979; Dawes & Donald, 2000). The term "ecological" underlines the importance of the social context, though it does not imply a passive child who only reacts to the social environment. At every stage, children are actors whose temperaments, competencies, and decisions help to shape the course of development.

During development, children may encounter a variety of risk factors such as poverty, child abuse and neglect, deprivation of education, and exposure to violence that can delay development or lead to negative developmental outcomes such as heightened aggression, substance abuse, and involvement in crime. Children's response to risk exhibits enormous individual and cultural variation and depends on their developmental stage, temperament, interpretation of their situation, history of pre-existing problems, coping strategies, and the presence of protective factors such as the availability of a caring, competent adult (Garbarino & Kostelny, 1996; Garbarino, Kostelny & Barry,1998). In fact, children exhibit significant resilience, defined as the ability to withstand exposure to risks without experiencing negative developmental outcomes. A well-established principle, however, is that the likelihood of long-term developmental damage, including psychological and behavioral disorders, increases as a function of the number, frequency, and severity of the risk factors to which the child is exposed. As risk factors accumulate, the likelihood of developmental damage increases exponentially (Rutter, 1979).

In a discourse on risks and negative developmental outcomes, it would be simplistic to assume that soldiering is entirely negative. As discussed previously, a child's entry into a military group may have positive effects such as meeting basic needs for food, security, and health care. Moreover, soldiering may be attractive to some children because it helps to meet social needs for power, belonging, respect, and identity. These are evident to nearly everyone who has seen a child proudly wearing a uniform and carrying a weapon. Still, it should be recognized that soldiering has adverse outcomes for children and violates their rights as guaranteed under the CRC and the Optional Protocol. Through soldiering, children may be wounded, raped, maimed, emotionally scarred, stigmatized, deprived of education and basic life skills, and wrapped in warrior identities that make it difficult to reenter civilian life.

Functionality in civilian life is the main criterion against which developmental outcomes may be judged. After the fighting stops, the true cost of child soldiering becomes visible, as former soldiers encounter difficulties building civilian lives. Having little education or job preparation, they are often disadvantaged economically. Socially, they may be disadvantaged by stigmatization and, in some cases, by living in fear of retaliation. Former child soldiers may exhibit cognitive and emotional difficulties or substance abuse problems that make it difficult to participate meaningfully in school, jobs, or family life. In sub-Saharan countries such as Angola, many child soldiers are viewed as spiritually contaminated since they are believed to be haunted by the unavenged spirits of the people they have killed (Wessells, 1997; Wessells & Monteiro, 2001). Without spiritual cleansing, they may not re-enter communities since doing so would visit spiritual contamination on the community, risking disaster, misfortune, and even war. In countries such as Angola and South Africa, waves of political violence have been followed by waves of crime and banditry. Much crime is committed by former child soldiers who lack education and job training, know the power of wielding a gun, and choose to follow the familiar pattern of using violence to obtain their goals.

From this perspective, it is appropriate to focus on the risk factors that lead children to enter solidiering either through decisions or through forced recruitment. As depicted in Fig. 1, an ecological framework suggests that children who grow up in war zones may be exposed to a wide array of risk factors at multiple levels. Exposure to risk factors varies across conflicts and according to the local situation of children in particular communities and families. Broadly it is useful to distinguish between macrosocial and microsocial risk factors, recognizing that processes at these levels interact extensively. The framework is outlined below with reference to a variety of African countries to show its breadth of applicability.

Macrosocial Risk Factors

Children in war zones frequently grow up amidst societal conditions such as oppression, militarization, ideology, and armed conflict. Among macrosocial risk factors, poverty is perhaps foremost. In situations of abject poverty, children's basic needs often go unmet, and, as in the case of Sierra Leone, weakened educational systems and the paucity of job opportunities create a pervasive sense of frustration and hopelessness. In such contexts, joining a military group may provide a channel for meeting basic needs, and disadvantaged youth are particularly vulnerable to being drawn into soldiering. Indeed, in some countries, children join military groups in part to earn money to send home to help support their families (Brett & McCallin, 1996). Poverty and armed conflict are linked in circular causation, as poverty is both a root cause and a product of armed conflict.

Oppression, too, is a major risk factor since it fuels armed conflict (Gurr, 1993), plants seeds of hatred and fear, creates difficult life conditions for youth who then see military activity as a likely path toward social change or achieving revenge. In South Africa, for example, the oppressive system of

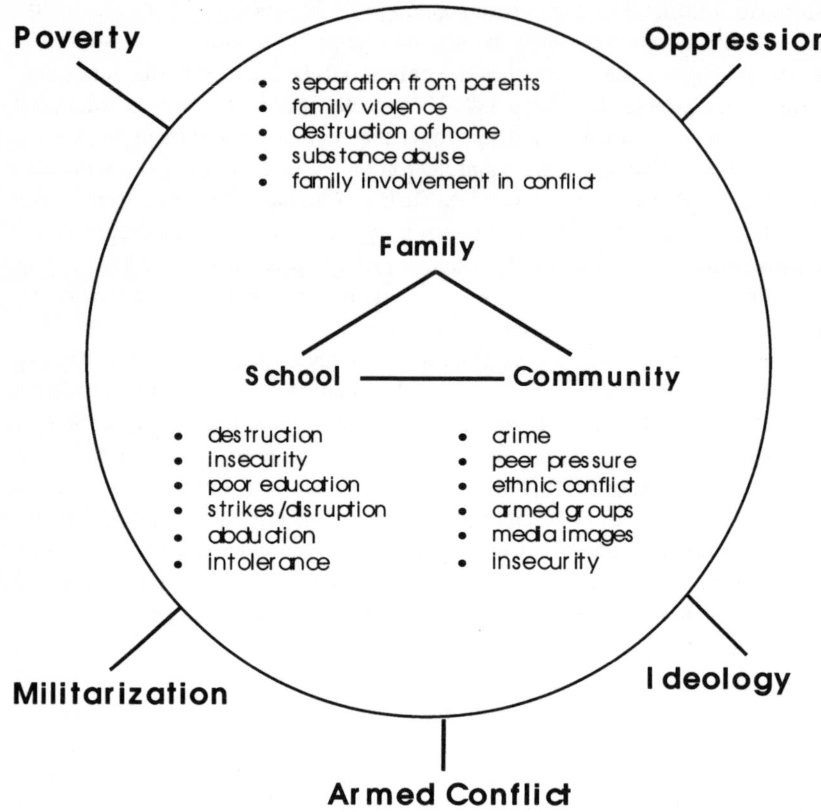

Fig. 1. Macro-level and Micro-level Risk Factors for Child Soldiering.

apartheid led to a liberation struggle that engaged large numbers of youth in fighting and militarized activity. Similarly, the current fighting in Northern Uganda is rooted in part in the historical oppression of the Acholi people (Rubin, 1998).

Groups in armed conflict use ideology not only to legitimate and strengthen their cause but also to awaken patriotic sentiments and attract youth into the struggle. In Angola, both UNITA and the government use propaganda to create mass support for their causes. In regard to the 1994 genocide in Rwanda, much of the killing was orchestrated by radio, which spread an ideology of hatred and encouraged people to kill all Tutsis (Prunier, 1996). Youth who participated in paramilitary groups such as the Interahamwe, which had received particularly heavy doses of propaganda, were among the most willing killers. Ideology influences youth not only because of their limited knowledge and life experience but also because it provides meaning and identity during adolescent years when young people typically seek to construct their identity. In liberation struggles such as that in South Africa, young people often find meaning by participating in violence (Straker, 1994). The perception of meaning in violence serves to buffer or protect young people from some of the most damaging emotional effects of experiencing violence through direct attack, witnessing, or perpetration of violence (Punamaki, 1996).

Armed conflict and militarization provide channels for child soldiering through participation in national armies, militias, opposition groups, paramilitaries, and related groups. Since both factors drain vast amounts of social and financial resources away from civilian pursuits and enterprises such as health and education, they effectively reduce the civilian supports and options of youth. In addition, significant numbers of youth are affected by attack, loss of parents and loved ones, displacement, destruction of homes, sexual violence, and landmines. Whether through fear or desire for revenge, the victimization of children often leads to their involvement in soldiering. Further, armed conflict and militarization serve to normalize violence. In countries such as Angola, several generations have grown up with war as a constant in their lives, making it difficult for young and old alike to imagine living in other conditions. Seeing soldiers in the streets and exposed to heroic images of violence on television, children learn to valorize war and can often be seen playing war games. In most war zones, children learn at a young age to accept war and the system of violence it creates. This system is evident also at microsocial levels.

Microsocial Risk Factors

A variety of family issues such as separation from parents heighten children's risk of involvement in military activity. Unaccompanied children, many of whom are displaced, orphaned, or both, are easy targets for abductors, and their insecurity and inability to meet basic needs leads them to join armed groups. In countries such as Sierra Leone, the involvement of older brothers, fathers, or members of one's extended family often creates social pressure or insecurity that leads to joining the armed group. In addition, children who have seen their families attacked, their homes burned, and their parents killed or harmed may join armed groups in hopes of gaining revenge on the attackers. Within the family, the economic and social stresses associated with war often lead to increased substance abuse and family violence such as spouse abuse and harsh corporal punishment. These and related difficulties within the family can propel young people out of the home, to seek belonging with youth gangs, and to idle with peers in public settings where they may be rounded up for recruitment. Throughout sub-Saharan Africa, the HIV/AIDS pandemic imposes on families heavy losses and powerful economic pressures which can lead youth to join military groups.

Although schools ought to protect and educate children, advance their cognitive and social competencies, and help prepare them to pursue positive developmental pathways, the reality in war zones falls far short of this ideal. In northern Uganda, schools have become likely sites of abduction. The wars in countries such as Angola, Sierra Leone, and Sudan have destroyed large numbers of schools, created climates of insecurity that block the conduct of classes, and imposed heavy economic burdens on governments and local communities. Many teachers receive no regular pay or get such low salary that teacher strikes and attrition become the norm. Affected emotionally and socially by having lived through horrible events, significant numbers of children may be unable to concentrate well or to benefit fully from participation in school. In situations of armed conflict, problems of intolerance and heightened aggression among students often occur, thereby creating a context in which children learn skills and values related to violence. Collectively these problems lead to poor education, attrition, absenteeism, and loss of educational opportunities for children. In Sierra Leone and other countries, this creates feelings of frustration and hopelessness that may lead youth to join armed groups.

Outside schools, various community pressures can heighten risks of child soldiering. High crime rates, prevalent in Angola, Sierra Leone, South Africa, and other sub-Saharan countries, can help to strengthen norms of violence that help to fuel armed conflict. Youth who become involved in crime and have learned relevant skills of using violence to obtain money may find a ready "market" for their services in armed groups that engage in raiding. In communities racked by ethnic violence and intercommunal fighting and raiding, youth may join armed groups in order to gain the protection and security their families are unable to provide. The activity of armed groups such as paramilitaries in a community can help to normalize and glamorize military activity, leading youths to pursue what they perceive to be the prestige and power associated with wearing a uniform and carrying a weapon. Further, peer norms may value fighting and toughness, leading boys in particular to pressure each other to join. On all sides, youth are often attracted into military activity by romanticized images of soldiers that typically exploit deep sentiments concerning masculine identity, patriotism, or struggle for liberation.

Toward the Future

Child soldiering is not a unitary phenomenon, and conceptualizations about the origins of soldiering need to take into account the influence of the social context and the multiplicity of factors that can lead children into military activity. The ecological framework presented here constitutes a first step that may help to move beyond single-factor views of entry into child soldiering and to caution against reified dichotomies such as forced versus voluntary recruitment. The framework emphasizes that many different factors operating at different social levels may lead children into soldiering. Although not a precise model, it offers an organized way of conceptualizing the diverse elements of the social context that heighten the risk of children becoming involved in soldiering.

Since the framework is intended to inform prevention and research efforts, it is useful here to identify two key themes that could profitably guide future inquiry. The first concerns children's pathways into military activity. Although the framework suggests that risks for soldiering accumulate at multiple levels, it is unlikely that the risks have equivalent influence. A reasonable hypothesis is that separation from parents is likely to place a child at greater risk of soldiering than substance abuse does. Few data exist, however, on the relative influence of different risk factors and combinations thereof. Further, very little is known about whether microsocial and macrosocial risks accumulate in similar manner and how they interact. Similarly, since forced recruitment by armed groups is not contractual, a significant question is what considerations lead them to stay. Although this may be a matter of terror in cases such as that of Uganda, situations such as that in Sierra Leone are more complex. Here, as is true in regard to the questions raised previously, it is vital to understand children's choices and subjectivities, which in turn requires understanding local beliefs, values, perceptions, and world views. Anthropological research will be particularly helpful in addressing these issues, as will analyses of how gender and class shape children's experiences. Research on subjectivity needs to address issues of identity and to clarify how young people forge identities as soldiers and what enables or impedes the change in these identities.

The second theme – prevention – presents a host of issues concerning the protection of children's rights. Powerful need exists for comparative studies that examine the efficacy of different prevention strategies, including local strategies such as educating commanders about human rights, meeting basic needs such as those for food or medical care, posting international monitors in zones where abduction frequently occurs, or having returning soldiers help educate youth and encourage them not to participate in military activity. Careful studies of international efforts are also warranted. For example, pressure from UNICEF and other international agencies resulted in 2001 in the release and flight to safety of 2,500 underage soldiers from Sudan. It is important to examine whether such efforts can have preventive effects, by for example, increasing international awareness of the problem and enabling more effective monitoring. Since re-recruitment often results from failures of reintegration, more systematic research is needed on the efficacy of various programs for the reintegration of former child soldiers. Relatively little is known about the role the former combatants themselves might best play in aiding the reintegration process.

The process of the research may be as important as the themes, however. Research can cause damage if it exploits local people, raises unrealistic expectations that food or other aid will soon be available, or does nothing to improve their lives. In most war zones, people report having strong feelings of resignation and hopelessness. Often the war that racks African areas is rooted in a colonial past that has implanted a sense of inferiority. Research that objectifies people can contribute to problems of disempowerment, resignation, and doubts about self-worth. What is needed is participatory action research that partners with local communities, gives them an active voice and role, and enables them to test the approaches that will most effectively limit child soldiering. The conscription of children as soldiers challenges all researchers to think carefully about their own place in the social ecologies of local children and to reflect on their role, ethics, and responsibilities.

MILITIA CONSCRIPTION IN SIERRA LEONE: RECRUITMENT OF YOUNG FIGHTERS IN AN AFRICAN WAR

Paul Richards

SOME COMPLEXITIES OF DEFINITION

By definition "conscription" is "compulsory enrolment for military service" (Penguin English Dictionary). It is distinguished from volunteering ("to offer oneself spontaneously for military service"). To oppose these terms is problematic in many respects, and it might be more helpful to envisage a continuum of military incorporation, with "conscription" positioned towards one extreme and "volunteering" towards the other. Here we deal mainly with "youth volunteers" and "abductees". Neither are "conscripts" in the dictionary sense, but the element of compulsion (whether of circumstances or capture) is never far away.

By "abduction" (perhaps a less loaded term than "kidnapping") we refer to compulsory enrolment without (state) authority. Historically, African armies were sometimes made up of abducted warrior slaves. Abduction has revived in post-Cold War conflicts. In some cases a majority of fighters has been made by abduction. Abduction seems shocking to modern citizens of well-founded states, especially when it involves children. But to populations with histories of enslavement and colonial forced labour, or enforced membership of adult sodalities with responsibilities for security in "stateless" societies, "abduction" may seem little different to, or no more (or less) morally objectionable, than other forms of conscription.

The Comparative Study of Conscription in the Armed Forces, Volume 20, pages 255–276.

ISBN: 0-7623-0836-2

Being a "young volunteer" is also a term that requires to be placed in its social and historical context. Peer and societal pressure, or a sense of fate, danger or desperation, have always been very important components of any decision to volunteer. Where children are concerned the issue of adult dependency also enters the equation. As we shall, see children often "volunteer" where parents or care-givers have been killed. They become fighters because they need parent-surrogates and training in life skills. If the militia band is the only source, then children become militia "volunteers". In these cases we might talk of "conscription through circumstances". But we ought also to note that ideas about when children become adults varies quite widely across cultures, and a practical (though not always *de jure*) "adulthood" (i.e. material self-reliance) often arrives early – especially for children from poor families, on a continent where half the population is below eighteen. We must be careful, therefore, not to deny the agency of young teenage "volunteers", who are consciously taking "adult"decisions. Moral opprobrium tends to attach to those who recruit them, but in our experience young teenage "volunteers" are often doing no more or less than "beg" for an apprenticeship from a skilled professional whose trade happens to be war. It might be as appropriate to "blame" poverty, or ideas about apprenticeship, for the phenomenon of young volunteer soldiers, as to place all responsibility on the "warlord".

THE SCOPE OF THE PRESENT ESSAY

The purpose of this essay is to review what is currently known about the realities of incorporation of young people into the fighting forces, in the ten-year civil war in Sierra Leone. The essay divides into three main sections – an overview of the conflict, a description of the main militias and their recruitment, and a brief assessment of demobilization and reintegration prospects. Knowledge of some of the issues is, as yet, rather limited, so the current account should be regarded as a report on work-in-progress.

There have been five main elements involved in fighting the war: the rebel guerrilla force (the Revolutionary United Front, henceforth RUF), Liberian irregulars c.1992–1994 allied with the RUF, the government army (and various splinters), army-linked irregulars (both local and Liberian), and "traditional" hunters forged into a national civil defence force by the newly elected democratic government in mid-1996.

There have been two formal demobilization programmes for ex-combatants. A 1996–1997 programme achieved little before the Abidjan peace agreement on which it was based (signed November 30th 1996) foundered. A second programme, consequent upon the signing of the Lome peace accord (July 7th

1999), dealt with up to 24,000 fighters, before it, too, was disrupted by renewed hostilities, in April–May 2000.

Where materials on combatant motivation and experiences are cited, these derive partly from a series of interviews with participants in a programme to demobilise child soldiers launched in 1994. Twenty such interviews were mainly carried out in 1996–1997 by Krijn Peters, prior to and just after the signing of the Abidjan accords. The bias of this data set is towards "volunteers" with militia factions loyal to the government army. The balance of the interview material relating to RUF "abductees" was mainly compiled in 1996 (cf. Richards et al., 1997), with some up-dating, October 2000–February 2001. Some of the interview material has been published, *in extenso*, in Richards (1996) and Peters and Richards (1998a, b). The reader is referred to these items for interview transcripts, description of methods, and more background on the war.

The present essay is ethnographic in orientation. Although the purpose is descriptive it may be useful to remark that the essay is backed by analytical perspectives deriving from neo-Durkheimian cultural theory (cf. Douglas, 1986, 1993; Douglas & Ney, 1998; Perri 6 1999). This is a functional, or operational, approach to the formation of social solidarities, in which norms, values and cultural orientations are seen as variables dependent upon the way social bonding and social control (so-called "grid" and "group" factors) intersect. The advantage of the neo-Durkheimian approach (in the current context) is that it allows us to view the values, orientations and motivations of militia fighters not as deeply-held political commitments but as "beliefs" produced by contingent social circumstances. In particular, our work suggests that abduction (a kind of initiation process), peer pressure and social isolation combined to induce in fighters social solidarities and patterns of behaviour more normally associated with life in a closed sect (Sivan, 1995; for further information and arguments, cf. Richards, 1996, 1998; Richards & Fithen, 2001).

AN OVERVIEW OF THE SIERRA LEONE CONFLICT

The civil war in Sierra Leone began on March 23rd 1991, with the incursion of two guerrilla groups, each of about 50 fighters, from war-torn Liberia. The aim was to encircle the diamond-rich and forested border region and establish an interim capital in the central Sierra Leonean town of Bo, before pressing on to Freetown with the objective of overthrowing the All People's Congress (APC) one-party regime. The guerrillas called themselves the Revolutionary United Front (RUF), and claimed inspiration from Pan-Africanist student revolutionaries and the Green Book of the Libyan leader, Col. Gadaffi (Richards, 1996; Abdullah, 1997). They also enjoyed the patronage of the insurgent Charles

Taylor, later elected president of Liberia. Several founding cadres in the RUF were young Sierra Leoneans from the border zone who had sought political refuge or economic opportunities in Liberia and Côte d'Ivoire. The collective leadership included Rashid Tarawallie, an unemployed revolutionary activist, Philip Palmer, a graduate engineer, and Foday Sankoh, a former army corporal who had earlier served time in jail for his part in the attempted coup of Col. John Bangura against the APC government of Siaka Stevens in 1969. Sankoh was the oldest member of the leadership group. To begin with he claimed to be no more than the group's spokesman. Later, he imposed himself as the undisputed leader of the RUF. The insurgents were accompanied by Liberian and Burkinabe fighters "on loan" from Charles Taylor's National Patriotic Front of Liberia (NPFL). These Liberian "special forces" introduced brutal tactics associated with the Liberian war.

The RUF's sweep through the south and east of the country quickly lost momentum. Opposed by government troops and irregular fighters recruited from among anti-Taylor Liberian refugees sheltering in Sierra Leone, the rebels became bogged down in a remote section of the forests on the Liberia-Sierra Leone border, and by the end of 1993 were contemplating defeat and retreat (RUF/SL, 1995). The movement subsequently adapted to forest survival conditions, and continued to pursue a long-term goal of undermining the wider society to the point of collapse.

The RUF angled its appeal at the disgruntled rural populations of the border region. In particular, it appealed to young people – school children from ramshackle rural schools in which teachers' salaries were paid only irregularly, and to sweated labour in remote alluvial diamond pits. Some young people rallied voluntarily, attracted by the populist rhetoric of the Green Book. Many were abducted. One tactic to enforce loyalty among abductees was to compel local children to assist in public executions of parents and elders, thus more or less making it impossible to return home. Recruits were also branded by the movement. Once scarified or tattooed, to run away was to risk summary execution at the hands of government forces (Amnesty International, 1992). In Sahun-Malen there is a mass grave, reportedly containing the remains of 17 village children, eliminated after government troops over-ran RUF positions in August 1991. Internally, the movement also ran an elaborate system of passes, and ringed forest camps with mines, to control unauthorised movements of conscripts (Richards, 2001). To try and quit the movement was to risk death (Richards, 2001). Some tried, but very few ever made it (Peters & Richards, 1998a).

Thus, a "Darwinian" process of selection operated upon the young abductees. Run-aways or prisoners-of-war were eliminated. Other abductees perished due to privations in the bush. Some were used as cannon fodder. Others with scruples were culled by the movement for weakness or cowardice, or were killed attempting to flee. Only the physically strongest, those with the least scruple, or the faintest memories of the social reality from which they had been snatched, survived. Over ten years of intense "selection pressure" these hardened survivors have become the backbone of the movement. Many have proven uncontrollable, even by the movement that created them (Richards, 2001), and stop at no atrocity to stay alive.

Initially, the RUF had hoped the Liberian border region (strongly opposed to the APC government in Freetown) would rally to its cause. This was never to be; the APC had conceded a return to multi-party politics in 1990, and the spokesman for the RUF – Foday Sankoh – although (historically) a supporter of the banned Sierra Leone People's Party (SLPP), a political group dominated by Mende-speakers from the south and east, was a Temne from the north. Thus the ethnic cues were wrong, and the local support enjoyed by Charles Taylor in launching his insurgency in Nimba County in North-eastern Liberia never materialised in Sierra Leone. The puzzled Liberian "special forces" increasingly fell back on crude terror tactics. Increasingly counter-productive for the RUF they were dismissed and returned to Liberia in early 1992.

The movement struggled on alone. Cut off from wider social contacts, after being backed into the border forests by government troops (of the Republic of Sierra Leone Military Force [RSLMF]), the RUF based its war economy (from 1993) on camping in forest reserves, with fighters emerging periodically to loot villages for food and medicine, ambush the army for supplies, or dig diamonds in remote border-zone pits. The diamonds were swapped for weapons and ammunition, some supplied by local traders, others by corrupt elements in the government armed forces.

Over time the leadership sought to attract international sympathy by representing itself as an environmental cult (Richards, 1996). The claim is made in the movement's main propaganda document, published with help from International Alert, a U.K.-based conflict resolution agency (RUF/SL, 1995). But the RUF's overall aim of destabilising, and eventually taking over, the Sierra Leone state had not altered. Internal expansion continued through raids to acquire weapons, resources and abductees.

Backed by International Alert, the RUF entered a tentative peace process in 1995, but this proved stillborn because the military regime of Capt. Valentine Strasser lost control of its war-bloated army. In opposing the Strasser regime it became common, in a capital remote from the war in the bush, to deny the existence of the RUF, and claim the only problem in Sierra Leone was the indiscipline of the government army. Video footage of RUF camp life made by International Alert was shown to the world's media in August1995, including impressive evidence of the extent to which abductees had "taken training" under the RUF, to comprise a formidable force of child guerrillas. But the focus of both local and international attention was already swinging from ending the war to the possibility of democratic transition as a means of ousting a corrupt and inefficient military regime.

With international backing, elections were held early in 1996. Attempts, both by the government army (afraid to lose its privileges) and the bush-mired RUF, were made to disrupt the voting process. The RUF interpreted elections-before-peace as an attempt to deny its existence as a political movement. Election irregularities were discounted by the international community as an artefact of the war-torn conditions under which the election took place. In the interests of reaching an end to the war opposition democrats conceded defeat, despite the irregularities.

The new regime was a coalition led by the Sierra Leone Peoples Party (SLPP), historically the party of the south and east (the region at the time worst damaged by the war). While announcing it intended to carry forward the peace negotiations begun under the previous military regime the new government was also taking advice from British and South African security experts (connected to mining companies pursuing diamond concessions) that the RUF could be overcome on the battle field. The key to this plan was air-support, weapons and training for a new pro-government militia to be created from the rapid expansion and modernization of localised "traditional" hunter civil defence militias. In part, the political appeal of this option was that it permitted the new government to sideline the northern-dominated army, disgruntled that it had lost power, and that northern civilian politicians were on the losing side in the election. In the event, the army was stood down as a token of government sincerity in the peace process, even while civil defence units were taking up positions against the RUF under cloak of a general cease fire. This caused the collapse of the Abidjan agreements almost before the ink was dry. The RUF had signed only under duress, after several of its key bases were destroyed in mercenary-backed civil defence attacks in the weeks before the signing ceremony, 30th November 1996 (cf. Shearer, 1997).

Then, in early 1997, the IMF pressured the new government to suspend subsistence (rice) subsidies to army personnel, as an unwarranted drain on public revenues. This was a last straw for many side-lined soldiers, already fearful that the peace dividend from any eventual victory over the RUF would pass straight to civil defence fighters. Army mutineers removed President Kabba in May 1997. A military junta (the Armed Forces Ruling Council, AFRC) took power.

The AFRC promptly tried to end the war by including the RUF in a power-sharing regime. In offering terms to such an unstable enemy straight from the bush, the calculation was that many ordinary Sierra Leoneans cared more that the war would stop than which political elite faction ruled in Freetown. But the result (since the junta was ostracised internationally, before being pushed aside by Nigerian-led peace-keepers) was to provide the paranoid and distrustful RUF leadership with access to new supplies. Restored by the Nigerian army in 1998, the legitimate government halted any further negotiations with the RUF. Instead, it placed rebel leader Foday Sankoh, detained in Nigeria in the aftermath of the Abidjan negotiations, on trial for treason. The courts found him guilty, condemning him to death in October 1998. The RUF resumed its forest campaign, but this time strengthened by resources and contacts acquired through its short and unstable partnership with the AFRC.

Meanwhile, overseas interests, seeking to wrest the rich kimberlite concessions (valued at one billion dollars) from the security and mining consortium backing the restored democratic regime, attempted to re-arm and re-train the RUF as it retreated into the bush. Assisted by Ukrainian and South African mercenaries the rebels were on the march again in a matter of months, fighting a swift, conventional campaign to take the Kono diamond fields in the east of the country in October-November 1998, and then linking up with dissident AFRC units from the now disbanded government army for a subsequent raid on Freetown in January 1999. Some within the AFRC hoped to return to power, but others were as concerned to destroy the records on which the cases against AFRC prisoners rested (police stations were destroyed and many police men lost their lives). RUF fighters were mainly interested in freeing their jailed leader from the condemned cell. Large parts of the east and centre of the capital were sacked, and many atrocities committed, in bitter street fighting, before peace-keeping troops regained control.

A traumatised government hung on by its finger nails (the president conducted business from the international airport, and slept at night in the Guinean capital, Conakry), and then, after a degree of calm had been restored, sued for peace. A controversial deal was signed in Lome, Togo, in July 1999, providing for the incorporation of the RUF within government. But full control of the main alluvial diamond fields remained with the RUF. Many RUF rank-and-file, having grown from childhood to adulthood in an atmosphere of violence and atrocity, with kith and kin only a distant memory, were in no hurry to re-enter mainstream society.

A new phase of the war began in May 2000. Externally-devised schemes to end the war by military means were dusted off, but this time using regular British military technical inputs (Operation Basilica), legally supplied weaponry,

UN ground forces to "fill in" behind advancing Sierra Leonean troops, and a clearer separation of military responsibility and private gain (in the form of diamond concessions). The RUF leadership, based in Freetown under the Lome accords, was rounded up and jailed, pending trials for war crimes.

The RUF forces returned to a war footing. The tactic of expanding numbers through abducting youngsters was resumed. A series of low-key cease-fires commenced in late 2000. UN troops resumed tentative confidence-building measures. By early 2001 the RUF was divided internally. Some of the bush command considered the movement might get a better deal by assisting a group of dissidents establish a new bush war in Guinea. Others were more interested in UN troop deployments and a return to discussions about demobilization options.

THE MAIN MILITIA AND THEIR MODES OF RECRUITMENT

(i) RUF Conscripts

At the time of the Abidjan peace accords in 1996 the RUF numbered about 3000 fighters (six battalions). A War Council – a tiny group of about 20–30 persons, half civilians and half leading fighters – led the movement. The rank-and-file were mainly abductees, but there were also some voluntary adherents. How many is a vexed question. One view is that quite large numbers of disgruntled and socially-excluded youngsters volunteered. This may have been the case in some border-zone communities alienated from Freetown rule, where families sometimes encouraged teenage sons to join the rebels, harbouring grievances to the days of British rule or earlier. Others grudges stemmed from APC suppression of political opposition, or from violence associated with attempts to control the lucrative smuggling trade into Liberia. An estimated 5–10% fighters were female. The RUF also had large numbers of women recruits enrolled in its "combat wives unit" and "combat support unit". These mainly abducted (and brutally abused) young women from war-zone regions became partners of combatants, and many have had children in the RUF.

As regards ethnicity, the majority of RUF rank-and-file, some now risen to leadership positions in the bush, were Mende-speakers, seized in a largely Mendephone border region. Others were, by background, Kissi, Gola, and Krim – groups at times disaffected from Mende-speaking chiefly families by a long and tangled history of mutual land grabbing and slave dealing. The largest single group of RUF adherents seems to have come from the south-eastern border region in Pujehun District, where families on the losing side in a bitter political conflict in the 1980s (the "bush devil war") were still living scattered in the forest. A number of young people from these families rallied to the RUF (or were volunteered) to revenge earlier oppression.

From 1994 the RUF established bush camps in the north of Sierra Leone, and began a process of raiding local communities for abductees from among the Temne, Limba and other northern groups (some early recruits from the diamond camps along the Liberian border were also northerners). Attempts were made to suppress ethnicity in camps (e.g. by enforcing the national *lingua franca*, Krio). Raiding parties sent out from camps, often covering long distances on bush paths, would include one or two local guides among a majority of non-local fighters (the guides were closely watched in case they attempted to abscond, especially recent abductees).

Upon reaching Freetown in May 1997, having been invited to join the army junta, the RUF also recruited among "ghetto" youth in the slums of East Freetown. Some estimates suggest thousands may have joined, but how many completed training and followed the RUF back into the bush in 1998 is unclear. A good number of those who drifted back into street life appear to have met a summary fate at the hands of peace-keeping troops.

Back in the bush, the RUF resumed recruitment through abduction in rural areas, in the north especially. They also quite rounded up quite large numbers from the main northern urban centres (Makeni and Magburaka). Numbers of RUF combatants seem to have peaked at about 10–15,000 when the RUF seized the Kono diamond fields, just prior to the January 1999 strike against Freetown.

At the signing of the Lome accords in July 1999 total numbers of combatants of all factions was estimated at 45,000 (15,000 RUF, 7,000 AFRC, 15,000 CDF, 6,000 loyalist armed forces of Sierra Leone, and 2,000 paramilitaries [Christian Aid, 1999]). Of 24,000 (53% of all combatants) entering demobilization post-Lome only 4,000 belonged to the RUF (27% of RUF forces). After the collapse of the Lome agreement, RUF numbers were estimated at about 10–15,000 (August 2000). It is not clear whether these numbers refer strictly to fighters, or include women "mobilised" in the "combat wives unit", and "combat support unit", dependent children, domestics and slaves. But the figures suggest that RUF losses in combat and through demobilization may have been quite rapidly made up through continued abduction. Eye-witnesses make it clear that the movement in the bush was highly "numbers conscious", even seeking to compile monthly reports of recruits in different classes, and keep track of losses through combat, sickness, etc. (Richards, 2001).

From 1991 to date opposing forces (reflecting the extreme civilian distaste for the RUF) have continued to "lock" the movement in place through summary executions. The first reports concerning summary executions of RUF prisoners were made in the earliest days of the war (Amnesty International, 1992). After fighting in May 2000 at the major road junction at Masiaka human rights agencies protested that bodies of RUF fighters had been found shot at close-range with bullets through the backs of their heads. It can be concluded that lacking safe surrender options the movement, however war weary and disillusioned with its leaders' struggle, will submit to demobilisation only as a final resort.

(ii) The RSLMF and Successors, and Army-Linked Irregulars

The British-established army in Sierra Leone was known as the Republic of Sierra Leone Military Force (RSLMF), and had a fighting strength of about 3,500 in 1991. Recruitment under APC rule was less on ability than according to political patronage. A majority of officers came from the North, where APC support was strong, and included a praetorian guard from among the Limba (an ethnic group within which presidents Siaka Stevens and Joseph Momoh cultivated connections). Only the less well-protected officers and other ranks were ordered to the war front in the south and east in 1991. These soldiers were badly supplied. The government preferred a strategy of arming Liberian dissidents opposed to Charles Taylor (the group that later emerged as the ULIMO – United Liberian Movement for Democracy – faction in the Liberian war). The bulk of ULIMO moved back into Liberia in 1992, but some still remained with the RSLMF. One reason was that this group "diverted" diamonds, loot and NPRC weaponry to the main ULIMO group in Liberia. They were generally referred to as RSLMF "special Liberian forces", to distinguish them from the Liberian Taylor-loyalist "special forces" serving with the RUF. In 1996 they had a main base at Mattru-on-the-Rails, near Bo.

At the outset of the war in 1991 a few junior RSLMF officers from the region worst affected by the early fighting quickly worked out the rather novel means by which the RUF was expanding (i.e. through abduction of rootless young people). Some of these officers were not unfamiliar with the mix of Green Book populism, Pan-African radicalism and drug-inspired Reggae-revolutionary talk through which young people throughout the country had been led to half-expect the RUF uprising. There was some fraternization with the enemy, feeding off Green Book themes and contacts (RSLMF officers were probably mainly protecting their backs, at the end of a very long and uncertain supply line, but the RUF clearly hoped to "turn" some of the more radicalised junior officers). Others in the RSLMF surrounded themselves with young fighters they could trust. Mainly they did this by inducting young kin as apprentice irregulars.

In Segbwema, Lt. (posthumously Capt.) Prince Ben(jamin)-Hirsch (grandson of a German trader) formed, trained and armed an irregular *hindo-hindo* squad, based on Poro (the major male sodality of the Upper Guinean forest region). In Kenema, a university lecturer, the late Dr. Alfred Lavalie, also experimented with forming a civil defence corps based on Poro solidarities. It was formerly a duty of young Poro initiates to defend their communities. In Joru and Mendekelema two RSLMF officers, Major Yaya Kanu and Lt. Tom Nyuma, trained an irregular "Border Guard". Even a sergeant-major commanding a forward position in Jimi-Bagbo in 1992 had a small platoon of hand-picked village fighters as his own security force. By day they helped out on the large rice farm through which the soldier fed more than forty orphan dependents. Thus every war-front officer, almost of necessity, had a retinue of local recruits trained to fight the RUF using RUF-style tactics (based on tracking and ambush). A number of officers supplied their young irregulars confidence boosting drugs. Regular soldiers were frank that they found it otherwise hard to cope with amphetamine-drugged under-age cadres of the RUF lacking any sense of their own self-preservation. "They did not know when they were out-gunned", one experienced but exasperated RSLMF sergeant explained, interviewed in Pujehun in 1992.

Most army irregular recruits were young (many were under-age) and linked to the local commander through extended family ties. They were, in effect, apprentice "war-boys" trained by a "master of war", in a reversion to a 19th century organizational model. Mainly they fought in short bursts and spent long periods working on other tasks, like growing rice, for their *bra* (Krio for "big brother", the name by which commanders were known). Some girls were also recruited under this system, and sometimes proved effective fighters, though they were very vulnerable to military rape, a routine "punishment" meted out for military failures, and to other forms of sexual abuse (Peters & Richards, 1998a).

At times the volunteers were simply looking for some training, or wanted to assist a military "big man" in their family. At other times they were children from villages attacked by the RUF who had lost their parents. They volunteered out of desperation, having no further sponsorship for education, food and clothing. Some had revenge in mind. Others were on a youthful adventure. Peters and Richards (1998a) recorded an interview with one girl from a secure middle-class Freetown background who had followed an army boyfriend to the war-front, where she volunteered to fight the RUF. Assigned the task of routinely killing RUF prisoners (a task she described as *wassing*, i.e. "wasting"), she became averse to the smell of blood, and quit.

A few irregulars belonged to a class of "special hunters". On the Liberian border in 1991–1992 these were mainly from the Koinadugu District in the north, and thus properly termed "*tamaboro*" (the equivalent in Koranko of the

Mende "*kamajoi*"). They were mainly professional bush-meat hunters very familiar with the border-zone forest reserves. They were used by the RSLMF to help set up ambush points and track RUF concentrations. Some were employed for their knowledge of hunter magic, and supplied army officers with "iron vests" (i.e. the magic gowns widely thought to protect against enemy bullets).

RSLMF irregulars ((including the Liberian "special forces") were often effective fighters, and could claim much of the credit for driving the RUF back towards the border in 1992–1993. But without an army induction number youth irregulars were highly vulnerable to the loss of their *bra*. Ben.-Hirsch was killed in an ambush (according to some accounts set by jealous rivals on his own side) in 1992, leaving his little band of irregulars to find new protectors (Peters & Richards, 1998a). Their fighting achievements unrecognised by civilians inclined to lump all young fighters as "rebels", many irregulars became deeply disgruntled as time went by. Some switched sides (especially when there was the option to join the AFRC/RUF alliance). Others compensated the loss of a *bra* by "freelancing" (as armed robbers).

After the 1992 coup the border-zone irregulars (a group perhaps totalling 1,000) was dwarfed by a new intake of unemployed youths from the city. The regular army quadrupled in size during this period to an estimated 15,000 (actual numbers may have been closer to 10,000, with corrupt officers claiming salaries for fictitious recruits). The National Provisional Ruling Council (NPRC), formed by junior officers from the war front, understood well enough that the RUF intended to appeal to the young unemployed. Drafting "idle youths" was a way of separating the RUF and its intended constituency. But an unforseen consequence was that this boosted APC-loyalist officers as patrons to new recruits from their home areas, and intense (ethnically-based) factionalism spread within the army, with long-lasting adverse consequences for the NPRC regime.

Some of the factionalism centred on opportunities for enrichment. Many recruits had hardly completed basic training when their officers ordered them to the war zone, but not necessarily to confront the RUF. The recruits served as little more than predatory gangs, either mining alluvial diamonds or looting prosperous mining communities. Officers might declare an area "closed", perhaps after an RUF pin-prick raid, only to take out truck-loads of items, from televisions to roofing sheets. The raw city recruits were often little more than the labour force to head-load the loot. Rival battalions struggled to control the asset-stripping opportunities, while in Freetown the regime badgered donors to overlook overruns on IMF spending limits "because of the war situation", and begged for extra assistance to help train and equip ever larger numbers of regular forces.

Officers and irregulars still trying to fight the war looked on in dismay, or gave up and joined the jamboree. One disillusioned commander ordered his men to open fire on a group of men from a rival battalion busy loading the spoils of the war, with the rather startling words "genuine soldiers do not exit a battle zone carrying television sets". Even army sources reckoned that by 1996 only "about 40%" of officers and men were serious about confronting the RUF.

The main beneficiary of this break-down was the ideologically-committed and weakened but fast recovering RUF. Its long-term strategy was based on undermining trust between civilians and the army, e.g. by embroiling dishonest officers in swapping rough diamonds for weapons, or by confusing civilians through carrying out raids kitted out in army standard-pattern fatigues. A new civilian president, recently arrived from several decades overseas, and anxious to rid himself of the problem at a stroke, stood down the entire army in mid-1996, except for some specialist units, preferring to pin his faith on mercenary-backed civil defence.

Post-Abidjan the pattern became even more complicated. Army elements unsympathetic to the democratic regime concocted the power-sharing AFRC/RUF alliance, while other army commanders (and their platoons of battle-front irregulars) remained loyal to the civilian president, and found themselves incorporated within the civil defence forces that never ceased field operations throughout the period of junta rule. When the AFRC was deposed by Nigerian-led West African peace-keeping forces in 1998 some RSLMF units surrendered, losing key patrons in a subsequent purge (when 24 northern officers were shot by firing squad on 17th October 1998 after being found guilty of treason before courts-martial). Others fled into the bush, where they took up the style and tactics of their erstwhile partners, the RUF, hoping to gain leverage in Freetown, and secure amnesty and reinstatement in the army.

Some of the die-hards were, indeed, reinstated, after Lome, to confront the continuing menace of the RUF. Deposed leader of the AFRC coup, Major Johnny-Paul Koroma, having become chair of the committee for the consolidation of the peace under Lome, rallied ex-AFRC fighters to stem a threatened advance on Freetown by the RUF in May 2000.

But others remained on the outside. One such group became known as the West Side Boys. It comprised mainly prisoners escaped from Pademba Road jail after the RUF attack in January 1999, and a handful of die-hard APC loyalists. From its earliest days the RUF had a policy of attacking jails (e.g. Pujehun, 1991), and encouraging prisoners either to join the movement, or foment local trouble the RUF could exploit. Movement strategists appreciated that long-term prisoners had less reason than most ever to surrender to the authorities. The government announced no amnesty conditions for such fighters. Unable to quit, the West Side Boys harassed travellers through the Okra Hills to the east of Freetown until August 2000, when they were flushed out of their bases by specialist British forces, having earlier trying to bargain their freedom in return for some hijacked British military observers.

(iii) Civil defence[1]

The third main fighting faction in the Sierra Leone war is the civil defence force. This is sometimes referred to as a "Kamajor" militia, because it draws on the lore and initiation practices of the specialist hunter, known in Mende (the main language of southern and eastern Sierra Leone) as *kamajoi* (pl. *kamajoisia*). Hunter "civil defence" can be traced back to the outset of the war. In one case in 1991 a professional hunter in Lalehun, Gola Forest succeeded in driving off a small and lightly-armed RUF raiding party single-handed, using only a shot gun and stalking tactics (Richards, 1996). It helped that he recognised the leader of the RUF band as a former schoolboy from the village in question. Specialist hunters in the Gola Forest tended to be northerners, and (as noted) some were used as auxiliaries by the RSLMF as early as 1992.

Civil defence organised by *kamajoi* hunters (i.e. hunters initiated according to Mende traditions) first arose in the Southern Province. According to Muana (1997) an innovative hunter worked with a small group of initiates out-manoeuvred RUF raiding parties in Jong Chiefdom in 1992. The initiates had the advantage of a more thorough knowledge of the local terrain. Lack of modern weapons proves no handicap in close quarters combat where the knife is as good as a gun. The idea quickly spread through the south and parts of the east, and chiefs began to call initiators, and sponsor local young men in the craft. As with the army irregulars, initiates were in some sense apprentices. They were known to local chiefs, and villagers were able quickly to reassure themselves about these Mende-speaking fighters, where uniformed soldiers were as likely to be disguised RUF as renegade RSLMF. Muana (1997) comments that the embryonic hunter militia developed what he terms a "rigidly hierarchised" command structure headed by a Grand Commander, founder of the movement and apparently residing in Bonthe District, but whose identity was a closely-guarded secret. "He is represented in different sectors by lieutenants who have been apprenticed to him and who have been granted licence to initiate other *kamajoisia* . . . [and heads] a 'super council' of Chiefdom and sector representatives . . . called Chief Kamajoi . . . most [of whom] are resident in hotels within the townships of Bo and Kenema" (Muana, 1997, p. 13).

When the government of President Ahmad Tejan-Kabba was elected in 1996 there were perhaps not more than a few hundred hunter militia fighters operating against the RUF. Looking for an alternative to the national army it so deeply distrusted the new government decided to build on this embryonic solution. Much of the organizational impetus was provided by Deputy Minister of Defence Samuel Hinga Norman (arms supply came through an Israeli agent working for an Antwerp-based company with diamond interests in the south-east of the country close to the Liberian border). Several thousand initiates (including many under-age volunteers) were undergoing military training by the end of 1996. Four years later total numbers (including equivalent hunter forces in the north) were probably somewhere in excess of twenty thousand (all males).

Concerns about the militia's ethnic character resulted in the launching of a national Civil Defence Force (CDF) in 1997, though northern units, based on broadly similar local hunter traditions, were never so well armed or supported as units from the south and east. Ethnic tensions at times hindered CDF cooperation, but in one remarkable case (Bonkolenken Chiefdom in Tonkolili District) the local Paramount Chief had several thousand young volunteers (all Temne speakers) initiated according to the Mende rite, and concluded a mutual defence pact with *kamajoi* fighters in Southern Province. This force of c. 9,000 fighters proved effective in ridding the area of the RUF.

That the CDF draws upon traditional hunter lore and technique should not be allowed to obscure an important point that it is a largely unprecedented mode of military mobilization in the Sierra Leone countryside. Hunter-based civil defence organised along militia lines is a specific military response to the challenge posed by the RUF. Specialist hunters in the Sierra Leone forests work alone, and hand on their skills via apprenticeship (i.e. through a master-pupil relationship). This individualism is clearly seen in the use of magic to render hunter activities invisible (and thus by implication unaccountable to a wider group). Even in thickly-forested areas such as the Gola Forest there are only one or two specialist hunters (mainly immigrant *tamaboro*, not native *kamajoisia*) per village. In cases where several such hunters operate from the same village they are rivals, not partners. Farmers trap animals around their farms, but hardly enter the forest to hunt. If they do so, it is mainly with dogs and nets on a cooperative expedition. Specialist hunters, by contrast, use guns, and roam alone over large tracts of forest in silence, drawing as little attention as possible to their craft.

It follows that hunters are not organised as a corporate group or caste, as in some other parts of Africa, still less is there anything approaching a traditional "militia" with the "rigidly hierarchised command structure" Muana (1997) attributes to the CDF. In pointing to the institutional basis of the specialist hunter tradition Muana (1997) speaks, helpfully, of the *guild* of *kamajoisia*. Hunters are craftsmen, and the craft is kept alive and handed on through initiation from master to apprentice.

Given the individualism of the specialist hunter tradition it is perhaps not surprising the Kabba government's attempt to create an effective militia force from volunteers mobilised around initiation procedures associated with the specialist hunting tradition ran into some difficulties of command and control. "Rigidly hierarchised command" well conveys what the innovators of the modern movement had to attempt if they were to attempt to bind local recruits into an effective regional or national force. Whether this was fully achieved is open to some doubt. Who exactly commanded the CDF, and whether units in the bush respected cease-fire agreements and the rules of war, was at times unclear. Complaints came from the communities civil defence set out to defend. Travellers in southern Sierra Leone in 1999 reported chaos on road blocks manned by civil defence, with no evident chain of command (the order for a vehicle to advance would be immediately countermanded from some other quarter within the group of hunters controlling the gate). Some initiates were said to retain such little respect for the masters who initiated them that they considered the payment of the necessary fees freed them to pursue war as a business at will. And concerns were not only voiced by villagers. In 1998, Maxwell Khobe, the Nigerian general invited to develop a new national army, rejected the idea of building it around CDF units on the grounds of "lack of officer potential".

CDF recruits are in effect all volunteers. We have some basic information on their background and formation. A passing out ceremony for the first cohort of around a thousand recruits to the new SLPP-backed civil defence force took place in Bo in June 1996. Most of the fighters were young men with rural backgrounds, recruited from refugee camps in and around Bo. Earlier civil defence action to defend Bo (April 1991 and December 1994) had been undertaken by ethnically mixed urban youngsters from Bo, mobilised through sports clubs and masquerade societies (Richards, 1996). But the war bore down hardest on the isolated and undefended farm villages. The greater part of the population of rural Pujehun District had been displaced to camps south of Bo, and there was considerable concern in these communities to develop militia capacity to the point where their villages could be resettled. The longer people remained displaced the greater the opportunity for both rebel and army units to harvest tree crops and dig alluvial diamonds on chiefdom land. It was in the hope of reconstituting communities and resurrecting the local economy that many young men from the displaced camps volunteered for the new force.

Trainers at Sugar Bowl camp in Bo (June 1996) claimed their ultimate aim was to secure at least one hundred civil defence volunteers for each of 80 or so chiefdoms in the Mende-speaking region, at that time the worst war-affected zone in Sierra Leone. Each recruit had to seek the approval of his paramount chief, have at least one parent from the chiefdom, and speak Mende. Initiation secrets and secret passwords served to ensure fighters could identify each other on operations and protect against enemy infiltration. Civil defence fighters were supposed to operate only in their local area, where they knew tracks and terrain, but where – equally importantly – they would be known and accountable to the civilian population. However it was clear, even in 1996, that many of the leaders in the movement were men with experience of urban employment and an expectation of government jobs after the war, that CDF units were operating well beyond their local domains, and that ethnic markers were not completely effective in keeping *kamajoisia* and enemy distinct. Popularly, the RUF was thought to be entirely alien (mainly made up of Liberians) but in fact large numbers of rank-and-file were Mende speakers, abducted from rural backgrounds close to those of the *kamajoisia*.

The CDF forces remained loyal to the Kabba government after the AFRC mutiny in 1997 and continued operations in the south and east, both against RUF groups and against the AFRC. This further changed the character of the expanding militia, which now absorbed Kabba-loyalists from the RSLMF, some war-front irregulars, and some educated, urbanised volunteers, as well as continuing to recruit and initiate young men from rural backgrounds (by 1998 it was thought that up to 10% of CDF fighters were graduates or college-trained). Despite the hunter costumes, strange to outsiders, it was clear that by 1999 the CDF had become a thoroughly modern militia force, and, apart from its ethnic and regional "lean" towards the south and east of the country, not much different in social composition from the RUF, or the rough-and-ready NPRC-expanded army in 1992. Like the RSLMF from 1992 the CDF became as much an employment agency as fighting machine, in a country in which war had destroyed most jobs in the formal sector. Like the RUF, the CDF recruited many under-age fighters (some as young as ten), but unlike the RUF had few female combatants. Some CDF fighters stand accused of war crimes, including summary execution of prisoners. Human rights agencies have lobbied hard for the internationally-supported war-crimes court for Sierra Leone to be even-handed in bringing perpetrators from all factions before it.

DEMOBILIZATION NEEDS AND OPPORTUNITIES

Mode of incorporation, gender, age, social and educational background are important factors determining demobilization needs and prospects, while perhaps varying quite markedly across the estimated 45,000+ combatants from the war in Sierra Leone.

(i) Incorporation

Although voluntary adhesion to the RUF tends to be underestimated it seems clear that most RUF fighters are abductees. The paradox is that many have developed considerable loyalty to the RUF leadership and cause. Whether this is because of indoctrination, the social dynamic of group operations, or a manifestation of so-called "Stockholm Syndrome" (in which traumatised hostages develop a sense of identification with and dependence on their captors), is not fully understood (Richards, 1996). Some adbuctees taken in the early 1990s have fought with the movement for up to a decade. They hardly know any other social reality than the battle groups and bush camps within which they have been raised. Having committed many appalling acts of violence it is clear they could only be re-integrated within their original communities with the greatest difficulty, and may have to be settled long-term on secure schemes.

Having been abducted and locked within the movement by fear of summary execution, many RUF fighters are themselves the victims of human rights abuse. Bearing this in mind, the Attorney General of Sierra Leone, Solomon Brewa, suggested, in June 2000, that no under-age RUF abductee will be charged with war crimes, but will instead be unburdened before a truth and reconciliation tribunal. Opinions in the international community have been divided over this issue. Human Rights and child advocacy groups favour Mr. Brewa's proposal, but others in the UN system want some older child soldiers to stand trial for war crimes. A compromise is that some fighters under 18 might be tried before a war crimes court, but will not be punished as adults. But whether this would apply only to those who remain under-age, or is a dispensation that can be claimed also by those who were under-age when abducted, or when the alleged crime was committed (and how ages will determined) is unclear.

Broadly speaking, nearly all other combatants in the Sierra War can be considered volunteers (but with the reservations that some were unemployed and desperate for work, and that some under-age army irregulars and CDF fighters were war orphans with perhaps no choice than to respond to offers of militia training).

(ii) Gender

A few females fought as army irregulars. The CDF was exclusively male. Female combatants were more prominent in the RUF (some estimates suggest up to 5–10% of fighters were female). An important difference is that the RUF was a social movement (with all its social functions contained within the mobilised group) whereas in the opposing militia social functions were maintained within the larger civil society. Within the RUF a large number of females was mobilised within "combatant wives" and "combat support" units. Many members of the former have had children with RUF fighters. These females were mainly inducted by capture, and are terribly abused and traumatised by their experience, but nevertheless evince considerable loyalty to their partners, offspring, and the RUF more generally. Very little attention has so far been focused on this especially vulnerable group, shunned by the wider society and suffering many burdens, including sexually transmitted diseases (many may be HIV positive) and the physical and mental scars of repeated rape. There is an urgent need to find out more about RUF mobilised females (including female fighters) and their needs for rehabilitation, counselling, medical care and employment.

(iii) Age

Most wars are fought by young people, but the age profile in African civil wars tends to be tipped towards the especially young (and Sierra Leone is no exception). This is partly due to the fact that children and young teenagers are good at low-intensity bush warfare (largely a matter of unobtrusive movements and ambush tactics), and that modern semi-automatic weapons are light enough to be handled by children. But it also reflects the general age profile in Africa. Due to high rates of population increase from a low historical base (the result, *inter alia*, of the slave trade and colonial epidemics of venereal disease) Africa is now the youngest continent. In most countries half or more of the population is under eighteen. Youth unemployment would be a major factor even without the economic decline of recent years. A recent study (Collier, 2000) suggests that having large numbers of young people in the population and economic decline are better predictors of rebel war than dictatorship or inequality. The RUF abducted from rural primary schools, and tends to be an exceptionally young movement, with its attitudes shaped not only by a crisis of national educational collapse (Joseph Momoh, the [APC] president, once told students education was a privilege not a right) but also by videos of violence, gangsta rap and other manifestations of global youth cultures (Richards, 1996). Army irregulars were mainly teenagers or pre-teenagers when recruited. The CDF has also extensively recruited under-age fighters.

Probably too much emphasis is placed on the phenomenon of *current* child soldiers. It is more important to know whether or not a combatant has been formed as an under-age fighter. The greater number of fighters in the war in Sierra Leone are either former child soldiers (who have grown to maturity in an atmosphere of exploitation and violence) or teenage combatants. Many now look fully adult, and society views them as if they had always been responsible for their actions. This causes difficulties, since a former child soldier is often a formidably hard fighter to have survived the experience of abduction, but views demobilization with suspicion if it means being treated as an adult war criminal. It may help that the authorities in Sierra Leone propose that no under-age abductee of the RUF will be so treated, but the provision may have to be extended to all combatants who have experienced abduction under the age of eighteen (or perhaps abductees in general, since they only became human rights abusers when their human rights were abused).

(iv) Social and Educational Background

The RUF abducted mainly children with basic literacy, though largely from rural backgrounds. Due to the RUF's long years in the border region perhaps three-quarters of the movement is Mende-speaking, though Sankoh (and the current interim leader of the RUF in the field, Issa Sesay, are both Temne-speakers from the north). The movement depended heavily on hand-written communications in the bush, and rejected illiterates for guerrilla training. RUF volunteers were often disgruntled products of educational collapse (sometimes the school ceased to function after teachers were unpaid for months on end, in other cases children were excluded for failure to pay fees). Many "sand sand boys" (labourers in alluvial diamond pits) drifted into the mines after being excluded from school or when their sponsorship ran out. Some RUF leaders (members of the War Council) were living in rural penury with a history of grievance against one or other educational establishment when the movement recruited them. Several key RUF figures came from the teacher's college at Bunumbu, close to the Liberian border (to this day an RUF stronghold). Fayia Musa – RUF "minister of agriculture" – was rusticated from Njala University College (in rural southern Sierra Leone). A known radical, Musa cited Momoh's remark on education as a privilege as his reason for joining the RUF. At one stage the War Council contained quite a sprinkling of abducted engineers, doctors and college lecturers aligned with, and helpful in developing, the movement's radical stance (Richards, 1996). Other members of the War Council were long-term exiles (for economic or political reasons) in Liberia and Cote d'Ivoire, where they fell under the influence of Burkinabe radical leader Thomas Sankara, and later Liberian warlord Charles Taylor. Some come from the border region, with dual Liberian and Sierra Leonean identity. One such is the 1998–1999

RUF field commander Samuel Bockarie, a Temne by birth adopted by a Kissi from Kailahun District. The Kissi have a complex history of opposition to Mende and Gbande warriors in the 19th century, and are currently split between three countries (Sierra Leone, Liberia and Guinea).

Army irregulars were mainly recruited at the war-front (and therefore come mainly from Mende-speaking communities). Some are war orphans, as a result of RUF atrocities. Several state clearly that they joined not only for revenge but also to secure replacement for lost educational sponsorship. The army was seen as a trade like any others (some informants were very proud of their technical accomplishments in handling weapons), and a source of food, clothing and the companionship that somewhat assuaged grief at the loss of beloved parents and elders (Peters & Richards, 1998a, b). NPRC army recruits tended to be from Freetown, some with a background of street life and unemployment. Many were recruited via officers still loyal to the deposed APC, and may still retain this "northern" political orientation (it seems likely that the West Side Boys enjoyed some clandestine encouragement from Freetown-based politicians opposed to the SLPP government). Certainly, demobilization remains deeply entangled with party politics based on regional loyalties. But many combatants are as much interested in employment prospects as remaining in the army (or militia group) for political reasons.

A problem in Sierra Leone is that the urban and formal-sector job markets are simply not capable of absorbing all these ex-fighters. Many will have to find self-employment in activities linked to agriculture and mining. Fostering functional links between the agricultural and mining sectors (so that most food for the mines is sourced within Sierra Leone, instead of being imported as at present) may do a great deal to absorb ex-combatants with low educational attainments (Richards, 1999). CDF fighters at first were mainly rural young men, many without formal education, hoping to return home to reclaim cash crop plantations and alluvial diamond pits. From 1997 the CDF absorbed other elements, and now contains significant numbers of unemployed university and college graduates with high expectations of any peace dividend. If the SLPP was to lose at the polls these expectations might be dashed. The CDF might then become something of a loose cannon. It follows that furtherance of democracy in Sierra Leone requires full and rapid demobilization of armed factions.

CONCLUSION: SIMILARITIES AND DIFFERENCES

Interviews with young combatants tend to confirm that this war has been about access to education and employment, rather than about political oppression and one-party rule (cf. Collier, 2000). As in any war, control of resources (in this case alluvial diamonds) has been key to funding the means to fight. A young CDF fighter told us (Peters & Richards, 1998a) that although he hated the rebels for killing his parents and wrecking his own chances of schooling he knew and understood the educational frustrations that drove RUF members to fight, not least from the letters they scattered during their campaigns. Even government-supporters among interviewees openly criticized politicians for sending their own children overseas while mis-using money that would otherwise have paid for schools in Sierra Leone. One or two were frank that had things been different (had the RUF not started to kill the rural poor) they too would have joined the rebellion. In some respects, war has come to represent a kind of self-help approach to training and employment for many young people. They are not necessarily ashamed of the skills they have acquired, as jungle fighters or defenders of their communities, however appalling the methods they deploy. But there is a major difference between army and CDF combatants on the one hand (mainly volunteers, with civil society support in varying degrees) and RUF combatants (mainly abductees, with no social support beyond the introverted world of the bush camps). The rather peculiar nature of RUF social experience – as much induction into a cult as conscription into an army – is still not yet fully understood (cf. Richards, 1998, 2001), and requires further anthropological research if die-hards are to be coaxed into eventual demobilization and social re-integration. There may be little option to some kind of semi-protected "marroon" existence for ex-RUF fighters for some years to come, as new social links are forged with the wider community, perhaps initially based on acquiring practical skills needed for physical reconstruction (Richards, 1999). The special problems of the many young women mobilised in and damaged by this war, but not necessarily taking part as combatants, are hardly known at all, and require major new research effort. This is where our notions of what happened are least well served by conventional ideas about "conscription", and new concepts and ways of envisaging the issues are urgently needed, sensitively framed by anthropological and feminist perspectives.

NOTE

1. This section draws on material from Richards and Fithen (2001)

ACKNOWLEDGMENTS

I wish to thank Krijn Peters for access to his field interview data, and for the considerable assistance he has provided in the preparation of this essay. He is not to be held responsible for any of the opinions expressed.

CONSCRIPTION AND ITS ALTERNATIVES

Bjørn Møller

INTRODUCTION

The Historical Background

> The LORD spoke to Moses (. . .) He said: "Take a census of the whole Israelite community by their clans and families, listing every man by name, one by one. You and Aaron are to number by their divisions all the men in Israel twenty years old or more who are able to serve in the army. (*Numbers*, 1.1-3)

The social organization of war has changed through the ages, the pendulum swinging back and forth between professionals and conscripts or citizen's militias (Hale, 1998; Best, 1998; Anderson, 1998; Bond, 1998; Foerster (Ed.), 1994; Opitz & Trennen (Ed.), 1994). The quote above from nothing less than the Old Testament thus shows that something like conscription is far from a recent phenomenon, but one that has been around for as long as war. Not only the Israelites of the Old Testament, but also the Egyptians and Assyrians periodically relied on modes of recruitment resembling conscription (Wallach, 1994; Ferill, 1985, pp. 51, 70–71, 82). The same was the case for the Ancient Greeks, where the hoplite armies represented an arming of the male citizenry. (Murray, 1980, pp. 120–131, 153–172; Andrews, 1971, pp. 161–183; Sealey, 1976, pp. 78–88; Bowra, 1969, pp. 20–41; Vassiliopulos, 1995; Stephan, 1998, pp. 51–84). Even though the Roman Republic had preferred volunteers, during the Empire Rome occasionally had to resort to

The Comparative Study of Conscription in the Armed Forces, Volume 20, pages 277–305.

ISBN: 0-7623-0836-2

forms of recruitment resembling conscription as well (Campbell, 1994, pp. 9–10 *& passim*). However, for most of the Middle Ages wars were predominantly fought by the nobility and their subjects. Even though in most countries the legal instruments for a levy of most of the male population were available, administrative capacities were quite inadequate for implementing anything deserving the label "conscription" (Ayton & Price, 1995; Prestwich, 1996, pp. 12–157; Howard, 1976, pp. 1–53; Stephan, 1998, pp. 102–108; Partner, 1997, pp. 110–132; Tallett, 1992, pp. 69–104; Ropp, 1962, pp. 19–40). This situation persisted through the renaissance and the Ancien Regime, where the State was able to enrol mainly riffraff and other undesirable social elements-something that did little to enhance the status of the soldierly profession. As late as in the 1780s, French War Minister Comte de Saint-Germain thus wrote:

> It would undoubtedly be desirable if we could create an army of dependable and specially selected men of the best type. But in order to make up an army we must not destroy the nation; it would be destruction to the nation if it were deprived of its best elements. As things are, the army must inevitably consist of the scum of the people and of all those for whom society has no use (Quoted in Anderson, 1998, p. 163).

Armies thus comprised a blend of local militias, locally recruited soldiers (usually of very poor quality) and mercenaries (Hale, 1998, pp. 75–99; Anderson, 1998, pp. 45–55, 111–130). The latter were a constant feature of all European wars, but were described in very unfavourable terms by Machiavelli (1469–1527), himself a staunch advocate of a citizens' militia:

> Mercenaries are disunited, thirsty for power, undisciplined and disloyal; they are brave among their friends and cowards before the enemy; they have no fear of God, they do not keep faith with their fellow men; they avoid defeat just so long as they avoid battle; in peacetime they are despoiled by them, and in wartime by the enemy (*The Prince*, 1999, pp. 39–40)
>
> . . . surely no one can be called a good man who, in order to support himself, takes up a profession that obliges him at all times to be rapacious, fraudulent, and cruel, as of course must be all of those – no matter what their rank – who make a trade of war (*The Art of War*, 1965, pp. 14–16, see also Hale, 1998, pp. 127–152; Anderson, pp. 45–63).

The origins of modern type conscription are usually traced back to the French revolution with its famous *levée en masse* (1793/1794) under the parole "*tous les Français sont soldats*" – or, in the words of the 1793 constitution, "*Le force générale de la République est composé du peuple entier*" (arts. 107 & 109, quoted from Godechot (Ed.), 1970, p. 90). By this means the French republic managed to mobilize more than a million men under arms (Léfebvre, 1951, pp. 380–386; Soboul, 1973, pp. 83–89, idem, 1975, pp.

332–335; Bouleoiseau, 1968, pp. 65–88; idem, 1972, pp. 133–170; Lynn, 1984; Howard, 1976, pp. 75–93; Best, 1998, pp. 82–98). This inaugurated the era of what Martin Van Creveld (1991, pp. 35–42) has called "trinitarian war", where wars were waged by the trinity of State, people and army, an innovation which went hand-in-hand with a Rousseau'ist conception of "sovereignty of the people" (Rousseau, 1966; Léroy, 1946, pp. 132–193, 221–229; Hoffmann, 1965).

These ideas (albeit without any infatuation with people's sovereignty) were partly taken over by military reformers in Prussia such as Scharnhorst, leading to the establishment of a *Landwehr* (Schnitter, 1994; Stübig, 1994; Förster, 1994; Bald, 1994; Best, 1998, pp. 150–167, 207–214; Anderson, 1998, pp. 167–180; Plantze 1990:I, pp. 167–172; 1990:III, pp. 17–18; Jones, 1988, pp. 392–398). Similar reforms were gradually introduced by most other European nations from the latter half of the 19th Century until the First World War (Ropp, 1962, pp. 195–206; McNeill, 1983, pp. 223–261; Paret, 1992; Krumeich, 1994; Marcinkowski & Rzepniewski, 1994; Lapin, 1994; Amersfoort, 1994; Bond, 1998, pp. 40–71. A good contemporary overview is Engels, 1855; 1870/1871).

Some have even argued that conscription was a direct reflection of the new basis for state-building, namely nationalism, as the conscripted armies served as "melting pots", bringing diverse strands of the population together and thus furthering a sense of community. Because of the "natural" link between rights and obligations, universal conscription was usually accompanied by political rights for the lower classes (Posen, 1993; Hettne, Sörlin & Østergård, 1998, pp. 172–183; Janowitz, 1976; Wakenhut, 1979; Grazia, 1981; Bald, 1997; Giller, 1992). In Denmark conscription was thus introduced in 1849 with the first democratic constitution. (Forsvarskommandoen, 1998). Moreover, conscription was accompanied by industrialization and may even have been preconditioned on this, as the equipment of mass armies required very capable arms industries. It thereby promoted the growth of capitalism (McNeill, 1983, pp. 223–306), as it did with the other pillars of "modernity".

While mass armies such as those made possible through conscription were extremely powerful military tools, they were also unwieldy and dangerous in at least three respects.

- First of all, the interaction between such mass armies had a tendency to escape control, beyond a certain point in the mobilization process, whence have ensued wars which neither side wanted, notably the First World War (Taylor, 1969, pp. 21–33; Afflerbach, 1994; Howard, 1984. For a critique see Levy, 1990/1991; Trachtenberg, 1990/91; 1991).

- Secondly, the mobilized forces (most of them belonging to the working classes) have proved dangerous to demobilize, especially for vanquished states. Both the 1917 Russian and the 1918 German revolutions bear witness to this risk (Kolko, 1994, pp. 139–179). In fact, this risk (albeit viewed as an opportunity) was exactly the reason why the founders of modern socialism such as Engels and Lenin had favoured conscription (Engels, 1972, pp. 66, 76; Lenin, 1970, p. 878).
- Thirdly, as the United States experienced during the Vietnam War, there are limits to what the public will accept in terms of casualties among conscripts, as well as limits to the treatment that conscripted soldiers from all walks of life will endure. Hence the opposition to the war at home, widespread draft dodging and desertions and other disciplinary problems at the front (Shills, 1977; Gibson, 1986, pp. 155–224; Record, 1998, pp. 41–42, 97–98, 146–147; Kimball, 1998, pp. 73–74; Glenn, 2000; Wolpin, 1994, pp. 37–68).

In addition to these risks to the country relying on conscription, one country's conscription may also constitute a threat to other countries, if only because of the military potential that it entails, for good or bad. Hence, for instance, the British-French disagreement in 1918/1919 about the regulation of the armed forces of the defeated Germany. The end result, satisfying mainly French security concerns, was a an compulsory abolition of German conscription and a general ceiling of 100,000 troops placed on the German army (Tanner, 1992; Wette, 1994a). Far from preventing a new war, however, these 100,000 (mostly officers, many of them trained in the Soviet Union, see Zeidler, 1993, pp. 33–38 & *passim*) simply became the cadres of the *Wehrmacht* when conscription was reintroduced by the Nazi regime, in preparation of its aggression (Wette, 1994b).

Despite these problems conscription became the predominant form of recruitment in the 20th century, at least as far as land powers were concerned. Insular states such as the United States and the U.K., however, only reluctantly introduced the draft during the world wars, only to abandon it again as soon as the opportunity arose (Roberts, 1977; Fabyanic, 1976).

Present Trends

By the turn of the millennium the picture of military personnel structures was a mixed one, even in Europe (Rödiger, 1994; Dertouzos & Nation, 1993). As Table 1 shows, countries in fairly comparable positions had opted for different modes of recruitment, ranging from militia systems to professional (all-volunteer) forces. Moreover, in the course of the nineties, several countries had second thoughts on conscription, albeit for different reasons:

- The Netherlands and Belgium have already abolished conscription (Meulen & Manigart, 1997; Huber, 1999; Manigart, 1999) and both France, Spain, Portugal and Italy are in the process of phasing it out in favour of all-volunteer, professional forces (*Jane's Defence Weekly*, *25*: 9; *25*: 20; *27*: 12; *30*: 10; *30*: 21; *31*: 6; *32*: 4; *32*: 11; *33*: 17; *33*: 22; cf. Boëne & Martin (Eds), 1991). The main rationale for this seems to have been a recognition that a war of national defence had become a highly unlikely eventuality, and that the armed forces were much more likely to be used for peace support operations or (at least since NATO's war against the Federal Republic of Yugoslavia, FRY) for "humanitarian interventions". For that purpose professionals are deemed more appropriate, if only because they can be more rapidly deployed.
- Russia is clearly interested in substituting smaller, professional armed forces for the present large conscript army, and is merely waiting for the economic situation to allow it to implement this (*Jane's Intelligence Review*, *3*: 7; 12: 1. The rationale seems to be a desire to rationalize and to capitalize on the improved security political situation facing the country after the end of the East-West confrontation.
- The situation is the same in other parts of the former USSR (e.g. Kazakhstan and Ukraine, see *Jane's Defence Weekly*, *29*: 5; *31*: 10) as well as in former Warsaw Pact countries such as Bulgaria and even Hungary or the Czech Republic, the latter two since 1999 members of NATO (*ibid.*, *28*: 2; *Jane's International Defense Review*, *33*: 4).

Table 1. Conscription in European Countries.

Conscription		**Abandoning Conscription**	**No Conscription**
Regular		**Political decision**	**Recent Abolition**
Albania	Poland	Russia	Belgium
Belarus	Romania	Bulgaria	Netherlands
Bosnia	FRY	Hungary	
Croatia	Slovakia	Ukraine	
Cyprus	Slovenia	Turkey	
Czech Republic			
Denmark	**With large**		
Estonia	**militia**		
Germany	**elements**		
Greece	Austria		
Latvia	Finland	**Under implementation**	
Lithuania	Sweden	France	**Tradition**
FYROM		Italy	Ireland
Moldova	**Pure militia**	Spain	Luxembourg
Norway	Switzerland	Portugal	United Kingdom

- Even Turkey, which in 1990 decided to phase out conscription but subsequently abandoned this plan, is seemingly now in the process of moving towards all-volunteer forces (*Jane's Defence Weekly*, *30*: 7; *32*: 23).

Even those countries which have taken no decisions on reform have seen serious debates on possible alternatives to whatever happens to be the prevailing form of recruitment, as was the case of the German debate on alternatives to conscription (*Jane's Defence Weekly, 33*: 20; cf. Kaldrack & Klein (Eds), 1992; Klein (Ed.), 1991; Klein & Zimmermann (Eds), 1997; Groß & Lutz (Eds), 1998) or the Swiss debate on a complete abolition of the militia army (Gross et al., 1989).

Table 2. Military Personnel.

	I. Population (1000)	**II. Armed Forces (Act.)**	**III. Conscripts**	**Cons. share (III/II)**	**IV. Reserves**	**AF Share (II/I)**	**Mob pool (II+IV/I)**
USA	275,636	1,365,800	0	n.a.	1,211,500	0.5%	0.9%
Canada	29,512	59,100	0	n.a.	43,300	0.2%	0.3%
Belgium	10,126	39,250	0	n.a.	152,050	0.4%	1.9%
Czech Repub.	10,290	57,700	25,000	43.3%	0	0.6%	0.6%
Denmark	5,267	21,810	5,025	23.0%	64,900	0.4%	1.6%
France	59,425	294,430	58,710	19.9%	419,000	0.5%	1.2%
Germany	82,112	321,000	128,400	40.0%	364,300	0.4%	0.8%
Greece	10,602	159,170	98,321	61.8%	291,000	1.5%	4.2%
Hungary	10,005	43,790	22,900	52.3%	90,300	0.4%	1.3%
Italy	57,930	250,600	111,800	44.6%	65,200	0.4%	0.5%
Netherlands	15,794	51,940	0	n.a.	32,200	0.3%	0.5%
Norway	4,443	26,700	15,200	56.9%	222,000	0.6%	5.6%
Poland	38,648	217,290	111,950	51.5%	406,000	0.6%	1.6%
Portugal	9,875	44,650	5,860	13.1%	210,930	0.5%	2.6%
Spain	39,237	166,500	51,700	31.3%	447,900	0.6%	1.6%
Turkey	66,130	609,700	528,000	86.6%	478,700	0.9%	1.5%
U.K.	58,882	212,450	0	n.a.	302,850	0.4%	0.9%
NATO Total	**784,004**	**3,941,880**	**1,162,866**	**29.5%**	**4,702,130**	**0.5%**	**1.1%**
Austria	8,138	35,500	17,500	49.3%	75,000	0.4%	1.4%
Finland	5,183	31,700	23,100	72.9%	485,000	0.6%	10.0%
Ireland	3,723	11,460	0	n.a.	14,800	0.3%	0.7%
Sweden	8,947	52,700	32,800	62.2%	570,000	0.6%	7.0%
Switzerland	7,090	3,470	n.a.	n.a.	351,200	0.0%	5.0%

Source: Figures from ISS: *The Military Balance 2000–2001*, pp. *25*, 53–108. Oxford: Oxford University Press, 2000.

Other countries have seen a "creeping professionalization" without any major debate, producing a growing share of professionals in the mixed personnel structure, tantamount to a piecemeal phasing out of conscription – as in the Nordic countries (Sørensen, 2000). The share of conscripts in the total armed forces is thus steadily declining so that most West European countries are now fielding either mixed or predominantly professional armies (Haltiner, 1998, 1999), as set out in Table 2.

This development has gone hand-in-hand with a substantial reduction in the size of most of these armies as well as of military expenditures since the end of the Cold War, with Denmark, Luxemburg and Turkey as the only exceptions within NATO.

Table 3. NATO Military Expenditures and Manpower.

	Mil. Exp. US$mil. (1997 prices)		**Increase**	**Armed forces Increase (Thousands)**		
	1985	1998	1985–1998	1985	1998	1985–1998
Canada	11,147	6,637	−40.5%	83.0	60.6	−27.0%
USA	367,711	265,890	−27.7%	2,151.6	1,401.6	−34.9%
Belgium	5,863	3,698	−36.9%	91.6	43.7	−52.3%
Denmark	2,978	2,799	−6.0%	29.6	32.1	8.4%
France	46,522	39,807	−14.4%	464.3	358.8	−22.7%
Germany	50,220	32,807	−34.7%	478.0	333.5	−30.2%
Greece	3,317	5,720	72.4%	201.5	168.5	−16.4%
Italy	24,471	22,633	−7.5%	385.1	298.4	−22.5%
Luxembourg	91	139	52.7%	0.7	0.8	14.3%
Netherlands	8,470	6,634	−21.7%	105.5	57.2	−45.8%
Norway	2,948	3,133	6.3%	37.0	28.9	−21.9%
Portugal	1,746	2,334	33.7%	73.0	53.	−26.6%
Spain	10,731	7,272	−32.3%	320.0	194.0	39.4%
Turkey	3,269	8,191	150.6%	630.0	639.0	1.4%
U.K.	45,4083	6,613	−19.4%	327.1	210.9	−35.5%
"Old NATO"	584,892	444,307	−24.0%	5,378	3.882	−27.8%
Czech Rep.	n.a.	1.132	n.a.	n.a.	59.1	n.a.
Hungary	n.a.	647	n.a.	n.a.	43.3	n.a.
Poland	n.a.	3.356	n.a.	n.a.	240.7	n.a.
"New NATO"	584,892	449,442	−23.2%	5,378.0	4,224.7	−21.4%
World	1,213,197	785,269	−35.3%	27,161.6	22,083.4	−18.7%

Source: Figures from ISS: *The Military Balance 1999–2000*, pp. 300–301. Oxford: Oxford University Press, 1999.

We have thus seen that there remains a significant diversity with regard to the personnel structures of the armed forces, even in a fairly homogenous "region" such as "the North". Different countries have made different choices, and it is difficult to discern a clear trend. The reasons for this diversity is the topic of the remainder of this paper. The focus is placed on Europe (with a few scattered references to other parts of the world). A comparative study of similar questions, however, is in preparation by the author, dealing with Southern Africa.

RELEVANT CRITERIA FOR COMPARISON

Before starting comparing conscription with its alternatives, it is important to determine what are the relevant criteria for such comparison. In the following these are subdivided into strategic, economic, social and political criteria.

There is no a priori reason to expect all of these to point in the same direction, i.e. one should not be surprised to find that the strategically most appropriate option might be economically unaffordable, or that it could have unacceptable social or political consequences. Politics is almost always about making choices, which often means weighing incommensurable considerations against each other.

Strategic Criteria

In a certain sense, strategic considerations have first priority. If a country has no need for armed forces, for instance, it could abolish them altogether, making all other considerations irrelevant. Conversely, if only one particular personnel structure could ensure national survival, a state would have to adopt if, regardless of the implications for other fields. In most cases, however, states do have a choice.

In such cases there is no obvious answer to how much, or which kind of defence, a state needs. In depends on an a political definition of what should be defended, as well as on an assessment of probabilities as well as on (likewise probabilistic) scenarios. Based on this, a state may define its national strategy or "grand strategy" (Hart, 1974, p. 321), which can then serve as a guideline for military planning, including the personnel aspects thereof (Sude, 1993; Deibel, 1993). Relevant elements of the political determination of national strategy include the following:

- What to defend, depending on definitions of "national interest" and "national security". These may range from a modest ambition to defend national sovereignty and territorial integrity, over further-reaching ambitions to defend "nationals abroad", or exercising control over a "near abroad", to very open-ended ones of defending economic interests or a specific world order (Chafetz et al., 1999).

- Against what to defend it? The answer hinges on assumptions about potential threats to this national interest. The more narrow the definition of what to defend, the fewer and the more concrete are the conceivable threats likely to be, and vice versa. In the absence of a stipulated threat military planning becomes complicated, as "uncertainty-based planning" is a rather fuzzy and almost metaphysical endeavour, open to all sorts of abuse (Davis, 1994; Kent & Simons, 1994; Blair, 1991; Kaufmann, 1992: O'Hanlon, 1995; cf. for a critique Klare, 1995).
- Under what general conditions to defend it? The answer to this question hinges on assumptions about the nature of a future war: How likely is it? It is likely to remain limited or to escalate? If the latter, will it escalate horizontally (from a local or regional to a world war) or vertically (e.g. from conventional to nuclear war), or both? (On Soviet and Chinese planning assumptions see MccGwire, 1987, 1991; Nan Li, 1996; Goodwin, 1996).
- Under what specific circumstances to defend it? Is a surprise attack conceivable, or can the country count on ample strategic and tactical warning? In what form will the attack occur? And where? Will it be a short and decisive, or a protracted war? In most cases several (but a finite number of) scenarios will have to be taken into account.
- With whom to defend it? Is the country alone and unlikely to receive any assistance? Is it a member of an alliance? How credible are the security guarantees? Can it count on the UN or other collective security arrangements as a partial substitute for self-help?
- How best to defend it? This hinges on assumptions about trends in military technology, e.g. on whether the alleged Revolution in Military Affairs (RMA) is a reality or not (Schneider & Grinter (Eds), 1995; Arquilla & Ronfeldt (Eds), 1997; Biddle, 1998); and on questions of strategy and tactics, as well as on questions of terrain and similar factors.
- With how much to defend it? Force comparisons are one element in this assessment, but the answer also depends on assumptions about the relative strength of offensive and defensive strategies (Møller, 1991, 1992, 1995; Lynn-Jones, 1995). Does a country need to be superior to its likely attacker, or of equal strength, or can it even make do with somewhat less – e.g. by specializing on the defensive?
- Within which limits to do so? In some cases, the size of a country's armed forces – occasionally also their composition – are determined by

international regulations, which sometimes deal directly with personnel issues. Even if they do not, they usually have personnel implications.

Depending on the answers to all these questions, planners will be able to specify personnel requirements, both with regard to the requisite size of the armed forces, the distribution of troops among the services, and the required skills. These will not merely be combat skills, but also organizational, technical, and social ones, in addition to which come skills for all those tasks that are, by their very nature, "civilian", but which are often performed by military personnel, e.g. those of cooks, cleaning personnel, chaplains, physicians, etc. (Brinkerhoff, 1993).

Ideally, defence planning should proceed as outline above, but in practice this is rarely the case. Because of the complexity of the issue, most countries tend to "satisfice" rather than optimizing, also with regard to their defence planning. Moreover, because of the uncertainties inherent in even the best assumptions on the above, states have an understandable preference for "flexibility" and for being "on the sure side". Rather too much defence than too little, and the more flexible and all-purpose the better.

This disposition allows all the other criteria to come to the fore, aided by the strong factor of "bureaucratic politics", where the selection of one option over its alternatives tends to depend less on "rational choice" on the part of the State as such than on the domestic strength of particular pressure groups (Halperin, 1974; Huntington, 1965; Trice, 1983). "Bureaucratic inertia" (e.g. in the form of "service culture") may also come to play an important role in the sense that once an option is selected, it will take very good arguments to opt for something else (Allison, 1971; Builder, 1997; Dunivin, 1994; cf. for historical perspectives Posen, 1984; Kier, 1997).

Economic Criteria

Economic considerations usually weigh heavily in military planning, also with regard to manpower. For rather obvious reasons, governments want to get a maximum (or at least a sufficient amount) of military power for the minimum costs. To determine how best to achieve this is, however, extremely complex (Sandler & Hartley, 1995, pp. 156–176; Warner & Asch, 1995; Jackwerth, 1998).

One sometimes encounters simplistic cost estimates which simply compare the wages (and/or other pecuniary compensation) of conscripts and professionals, multiplied with the required number of troops (presumably determined according the reasoning described in the previous section). Such estimates, however, disregard several factors such as the following:

First of all, we face the difficulty of assessing comparative "productivity". As armies (except for mercenaries, *vide infra*) do not sell their produce, it is very difficult to measure their "productivity" (Hofmann, 1993). It nevertheless stands to reason that some armies are more proficient than others, and that part of the explanation thereof is that some soldiers are more skilful, "productive" or cost-effective than others (Horne, 1987). For instance, there has been some talk about a Chinese realization that their huge but low cost PLA (People's Liberation Army) is also so low on quality that it is not cost-effective (Shambough, 1996). On the other hand, exactly the PLA is also known for its extensive non-military activities in agriculture, industry and housing, the output of which is quite measurable, and which would have to be subtracted from the aggregate costs (Kondapalli, 1996; Joffe, 1995; Karmel, 1997).

Secondly, there is the problem of measuring what might be called "human capital (or human resources) investment costs" (Nübler, 2000). While the costs of military training are quite measurable, the benefits thereof are not. Indeed, even the cost issue may be more complicated than what meets the eye. If the trainers are officers and/or NCOs (non-commissioned officers) who would in any case be required for defence purposes, the actual costs of having them train recruits in times of peace rather than doing nothing at all may be rather insignificant.

As far as the benefits of training are concerned, it stands to reason that there is a difference between the skills of conscripts and professionals. However, depending on the planning scenario, the fairly elementary skills which conscripts are able to acquire may suffice. Indeed, it may even be preferable to have access to a large pool of former conscripts possessing only elementary military skills, but comprehensive training in other fields that might be militarily useful. This may, for instance, apply to forces for traditional peacekeeping or other peace support operations, where organizational, language, psychological and conflict resolution skills weigh at least as heavily as combat skills. Under other circumstances, however, only "real" military skills may really matter, in which case the "investment" in military training is likely to yield higher returns for professionals, serving for several years, than for conscripts. What matters just as much as such combat training, however, is the "morale", i.e. combat motivation, which is rather a social than an economic question (*vide infra*).

Thirdly, there is the tricky problem of how to account for opportunity costs. On the one hand, both conscription or Swiss-type militias are clearly cheaper than the other personnel structures if one only compares the direct costs in the form of wages and/or other forms of pecuniary compensation.On the other hand, the actual costs to society depend on what the conscripts would have been doing if they had not been drafted, or what the militia members are prevented from doing by having to perform military duties. Important factors in this respect are:

- What is the level of unemployment in general, and that pertaining to young people in particular? The higher the unemployment rate, the greater the chance that conscripts would otherwise have been on the dole, and the lower the opportunity costs – and vice versa.
- What is the average productivity in those jobs that are not filled because of military service? For doctors, lawyers or bankers to perform military duties (as in Switzerland) is, in a certain sense, much more expensive than to employ labour with lesser (but more targeted) skills.

As far as professional armed forces are concerned, the market should be able to handle the above in the sense of transforming opportunity costs into actual costs.

Fourthly, both as far as direct and opportunity labour costs are concerned one must distinguish between gross and net costs to the national economy. For instance, if an otherwise unemployed youth is conscripted, his or her total income is usually increased, i.e. the labour costs grow. However, depending on the level and form of taxation, some of these costs return to the state in the form of income and consumer taxes. Moreover, what is left of the additional disposable income is spent on consumer goods. While the money spent on imported good "disappears" (from the point of view of the national economy) the purchase of those goods that are produced domestically produce additional income for other members of society, who also pay taxes, but spend some of the rest for domestic goods, etc.

All this can, in principle at least, be calculated by means of sophisticated input-output models which factor in the "multiplier effect" (Gleditsch et al., 1994; idem et al. (Eds), 1996). While the exact formulas for translating gross into net costs will vary from country to country, and from one period to another, the "bottom line" will always be that net costs are smaller than gross ones as far as conscripts are concerned. The same complexity is involved in comparing the net costs of replacing conscripts with professionals, or vice versa.

Finally, both logistics and infrastructure costs are influenced by the choice of personnel structure, as both conscripts, militias and professionals require arms, munitions, uniforms, food, barracks, and the like – albeit not necessarily in the same amounts. This also has to be considered.

All of the economic considerations listed so far point to the rather unsurprising conclusion that "it all depends . . .". In some cases, conscription may be cheaper than professionals, whereas in others the opposite might be true. In principle it should be possible to devise a computer programme, into which one could feed all of the above economic factors, on the basis of which the programme might come up with the (economically) best option for a particular country at a particular time. In practice, however, no such programme yet exists.

Social Criteria

As personnel questions have to do with people, social criteria are of obvious relevance for the comparison between different modes of recruitment.

First of all, demographic factors obviously play an important role, if only because fertility patterns determine the size of the age cohorts from which to draft the armed forces, or recruit the professionals (Kutscher, 1983). If strategic considerations were the only determinant, we should expect to see an extension of the length of military service to compensate for small age cohorts, and vice versa. However, this is a rare exception to the rule that the total size of the armed forces tends to fluctuate with the size of the age cohorts. At most, countries modify their rejection criteria to compensate for changes in the size of the total manpower pool from which to draw (Sørensen, 2000), regardless of their personnel structure.

A special problem arises when countries have to limit the total number of forces for non-demographic reasons, as was the case of post-unification Germany. There are inherent limits to how short the length of service can be without becoming pointless, but there are also limits to how small a percentage of an age cohort can be drafted (often in the form of a lottery system) without thereby creating the impression that the state is inflicting arbitrary "punishment" on the few draftees – a problem referred to in Germany as "*Wehr(un)gerechtigkeit*" (Kuhlmann & Lippert, 1992).

The economic factor probably plays an important role as an intervening variable. Times of "demographic shrinkage" tend to also be ones of high employment, implying both high direct and opportunity costs for conscripts, and rising wage levels for professionals. The opposite tends to also be the case, as demographic growth is often associated with unemployment (not least among the young) and falling wages.

As national and racial minorities almost everywhere have a below-average level of employment, it is reasonable to expect all-volunteer armed forces to be able to recruit a higher percentage of these. Hence, these minorities would tend to be over-represented in the armies, as is the case of blacks in the U.S. armed forces after the abolition of the draft. Such ethnic or racial biases may, in turn, create problems for those enlisted, e.g. because of clash of cultures; or it may cause problems for unit cohesion, hence also for combat effectiveness

(Janowitz & Moskos, 1974; Moskos, 1980; Segal & Verdugo, 1994; Elron & Ben-Ari, 1999; Ball, 1994; Peled, 1998). On the other hand, one could also see the phenomenon in a more positive light, as the armed forces could arguably play a "melting pot" role which could also serve as a ladder of social mobility for the members of disadvantaged minorities.

In addition to impacting on fertility and thereby determining the age cohorts available for recruitment, the family structure may also impactmore indirectly on personnel policies. Edward Luttwak (1996) has thus argued that the typical nuclear family size with between one and two children places severe limitations on a country's military options. With less than one son per family, parents are presumably less willing to place his life at risk than if they had several. If there is any truth to this theory (which the present author would doubt), the effect would probably be stronger under conscription than if military service is voluntary, which should speak in favour of the latter.

Besides such "hard" social factors as the above, social norms and culture undoubtedly also play a role as background conditions for decisions about personnel structures. For instance, the women's liberation movement has, on the one hand, opened up the military profession to women, in most Western countries at least (Stanley & Segal, 1993). This development has also been facilitated by the changing demands of soldiering which now requires less brute physical strength or other, presumably male, qualities than previously. Not only have modern weapons become increasingly automated, but modern combat has also become "depersonalized", rendering mental predispositions less important. When combat is less a matter of "eyeball-to-eyeball" duels than of pressing buttons, there is surely a lesser need for the (allegedly) innate masculine aggressiveness.

On the other hand, only one state (Israel) has introduced female conscription in peacetime. Herein lies the seeds of conflict, as women cannot well demand equal rights in all other respects without accepting the obligation to defend their country. To introduce female conscription would, however, merely exacerbate the aforementioned problem of "*Wehr(un)gerechtigkeit*", by doubling the total pool from which to conscript soldiers for whom there is little actual need.

Furthermore, certain social norms characterizing "postmodern society" may place constraints on the personnel choices. While there is much disagreement on what postmodernism entails, there is widespread agreement that individualism and anti-authoritarianism are among its distinguishing traits, partly as a reflection of the high level of education in late modern societies (Heller & Fehér, 1988). The average postmodern citizen may thus be much harder to discipline, as is called for in the military, than was his ancestors (Moskos & Burk, 1994: Rosenau, 1994; Shaw, 1991; Gray, 1997, pp. 195–211; Micewski, 1995). This may be especially true in times when the very legitimacy of the military is in doubt, as was the case in Germany during the 1980s (Vogt, 1989; Bald, 1994, pp. 123–132). However, it is not obvious that professional armed forces would always be more pliable in this respect, as they are members of the same societies, as a reflection of which they are, for instance, becoming unionized to an increasing extent.

Combat skills are not the only ones that matter, but in some cases they obviously do, as do intangible factors such as morale and combat motivation, both individually and for military units (Manning, 1993; Kellett, 1990, 1993). If the tasks which the armed forces are set to perform collide with prevailing social norms, it will usually require a lot of training to overcome them. One of these "skills" that soldiers have to acquire is, alas, that of killing their fellow human beings, in violation not only of social norms, but perhaps also of an instinctive aversion to the shedding of blood (Bourke, 1999; Ehrenreich, 1997). Professional armed forces would probably be easier to train in this respect, and the more so, the less integrated they are with the rest of society, thus shielded against the influence of its prevailing norms.

As far as some of the other required skills are concerned, however, they are in perfect harmony with the prevailing social norms of post-modern or late modern society. This is, for instance, the case of most of the skills relevant for peacekeeping operations: psychologial and social skills, the ability to take independent decisions, etc. (Däniker, 1995; Bellamy, 1996; Battistelli, 1997; Segal & Tiggle, 1997). Hence, the more integrated with the rest of society the are forces are, the more will they share its norms, and the better will they be at the "peace tasks" of the modern military.

Political Criteria

However much "Realists" refuse to distinguish between states, not all states are alike. Hence is should come as no surprise that their preferred personnel structures also differ according to political criteria.

A very relevant distinction is between strong and weak states, the latter referring to states lacking in either internal legitimacy and cohesion, or in administrative capacity, or both – a phenomenon which is not confined to, but particularly widespread in the Third World (Buzan, 1991, pp. 153–160; Ayoob, 1995; Holsti, 1996, pp. 82–120; Reno, 1998). When weighing the pros and cons of various personnel structures the governments of such weak states have to consider, among others, the following factors:

- Are the armed forces "only" required for "real" national defence duties, or also for policing and/or administrative functions?

- Does the regime in power need to defend itself against its own citizens, and will a general arming of the latter (as implied by a Swiss-style militia system) therefore represent a threat to their rule?
- Will a conscripted army be reliable against an external threat? or against an internal one, say from a secessionist or revolutionary movement?
- Are professional armed forces likely to "go praetorian" and stage military coups? (Huntington, 1991, pp. 231–251; Finer, 1976; Pearlmutter, 1977).

Weak states are the product of unsuccessful state-building, a failure which is often due to lack of congruity between state and nation. However, armies can sometimes play important roles in both state-building and nation-building, and in bringing about harmony between the two. An often-cited example is the role of the IDF (Israeli Defence Force) as a "melting pot" for the diverse (ethnic and other) strata of Israeli society, including immigrants from the scattered Jewish diaspora. David Ben-Gurion made this point in 1952:

> We do not have hundreds of years [to build a nation], and without the institution of the military, a compulsory, educating, unifying institution, we will not become a nation in time. We cannot rely on a historical process only . . . Through the Israeli Defence Force we can do in a short time things that would otherwise require dozens of years . . . (Porter, 1994, p. 18; cf. Barnett, 1992, pp. 153–209, 225–243; Creveld, 1994; 1998, pp. 103–126 and *passim*; Ben-Eliezer, 1998, pp. 1–15, 193–206 and *passim*; Goldstein, 1998).

That armies can play such role, however, does not mean that any mode of recruitment is equally suitable for it. It stands to reason that conscription and militia arrangements will be more efficient melting pots than professional forces, if only because they provide a more representative sample of the nation *in statu nascendi*.

A related problem affecting many weak states is their ethnic heterogeneity, which raises complicated questions with regard to the manning of their armed forces (Peled, 1998). It is possible to argue that their component parts (regiments, divisions. etc.) should be as ethnically homogenous as possible, which might make them more effective military tools (by virtue of better unit cohesion), but which might also represent problems of loyalty. An alternative position would be to make military units and formations as diverse as possible in line with the "melting pot philosophy", but at the possible expense of combat efficiency. It may even be possible to combine the two sets of considerations, as was attempted in the former Yugoslavia, with a complex structure featuring a combination of "ethnic quota" in the regular army (YPA: Yugoslav People's Army) and ethnically fairly homogenous units making up the territorial army –

or, as it turned out: armies (Roberts, 1976, pp. 124–217; Bebler, 1993; Gow, 1992; Remington, 1996).

In both weak and fairly strong states, the problem of civil-military relations is important, but considerations in this respect do not necessarily point in the same direction with regard to personnel policies (Desch, 1999; Lovell & Albright (Eds), 1997; Diamond & Plattner (Eds), 1996; Snider & Carlton-Carew (Eds), 1995; Luttwak, 1999):

- Governments usually want a maximum of control over the armed forces, if only because of fear of their developing praetorian tendencies. This is especially the case after the (re-)introduction of democracy, as in the former USSR (Nichols, 1993; Davenport, 1995; Arbatov, 1998), the Eastern block (Bebler (Ed.), 1997; Danapoulos & Zirker, 1996; Szemerkényi, 1996; Michta, 1997; Bald (Ed.), 1992; Gießmann, 1992; Klein & Zimmermann, 1993) South Africa (Griffiths, 1995; Nathan, 1996) or several Latin American countries (Millett & Gold-Bliss, 1995). This may, but must not automatically, point towards conscription, as the main problem is that of the officers corps, which in any case consists of professionals.
- Civilian supremacy may require controls which will often be seen by the military as unduly intrusive. But governments also want armed forces that are loyal to both state and nation, and form an integral part of society – something which may require granting the armed forces a considerable autonomy. Viable guidelines for how to strike a compromise may be the concepts of "professionalism" in the sense of Janowitz (1960) or Huntington (1957) and the French notion of "*citoyen-soldat*" and its German equivalent "*Staatsbürger in Uniform*" (Müller (Ed.), 1995; Borkenhagen (Ed.), 1986; Abenheim, 1990; Bald & Prüfert (Eds), 1997). Whether this ideal presupposes conscription or militias, however, or whether it may be compatible with professional armed forces, remains disputed.

In countries with well-established democratic forms of government, the above rarely presents serious problems, but it may well be so in less stable polities. In certain countries, the military as an institution thus sees itself as "the guardians of the State" (or Nation), even against the "wims" of the government in power. This may, for instance, have been the case of Poland or Chile, and it may still be the case of countries such as Turkey (Birand, 1991; Hale, 1994; Heper & Hünai, 2000), Taiwan (Bullard, 1997) and Pakistan (Shafqua, 1997). Whether this points towards conscription or professional armed forces is far from obvious, but the assessments thereof will surely influence the preferences of both the military and the politicians.

Summary

As will be apparent from the above elaboration of the various criteria there is a plethora of factors to take into account when comparing the alternative options for how to field the armed forces. Indeed, the list makes no claims to being exhaustive, but merely enumerates some of the relevant factors.

The following tentative comparison will therefore also be unable to provide clear answers, but will merely venture some *prima facie* pros and cons of the alternative options.

CONSCRIPTION AND ITS ALTERNATIVES

It is counter-intuitive that one personnel structure should be superior, by its very nature, to all others, as this cannot explain the actual diversity. That countries have actually opted for different personnel structure for their armed forces could safely be taken as strong *prima facie* evidence to the effect that this is very context-dependent, i.e. that some structures may be appropriate for some countries in certain periods, but not for others.

In real life we find few "pure cases", but personnel structures are almost always blends of different forms. It nevertheless seems useful to compare the pure cases for their advantages and disadvantages. These pure cases could be ordered along a continuum ranging from the "citizen in arms" model to complete professionalization (see Table 4). This continuum describes different degrees of division of labour between the armed forces and the rest of society, which also corresponds (albeit not completely) to degrees of statehood. This is not particularly surprising, in view of the several recent studies about the intimate relationship between war and the State (Mann, 1986, 1988, 1993; Giddens, 1995; Tilly, 1990; Krippendorff, 1984; Porter, 1994; Spruyt, 1994; Holsti, 1996).

At one pole we have the almost stateless society (or one where State and nation are almost synonymous) where the army *is* the population; at the other we have a situation where the State has subdelegated the use of armed force to private companies. However, neither of these are compatible with "strong states" enjoying a Weberian "monopoly on the legitimate use of force" (Weber,

Table 4. The Personal Structure Continuum.

Citizen-in-arms pole ◄------				------► Privatization pole
Ad-hoc Mobilization	Permanent Militias	Conscription	All-volunteer forces	Mercenaries

1958, p. 78). Statehood is more compatible with either of the three intermediate personnel structures, i.e. "swiss-type" militias, "European-style" conscription and "U.S.-style" professionals. As a preliminary to these more relevant options, however, it seems appropriate to give a short account of the extremes, i.e. "ad-hoc mobilization" and "privatization".

Ad-hoc Mobilization

States may abstain from fielding armed forces for different reasons: Because they do not perceive any threats to their sovereignty and territorial integrity; because they are so small that defence is obviously futile (which may be the case for, e.g. Liechtenstein); or because they rely on external protection (as is the case of Costa Rica and Iceland today); or because they rely on a non-military form of defence, as proposed by various peace researchers and others (Boserup & Mack, 1974; Mellon et al., 1985; Niezing, 1987; Sharp, 1985), but so far not implemented by any country. Such instances, however, fall beyond the scope of the present analysis which deals with countries acknowledging the need for some kind of national defence by military means.

It is, however, conceivable for such states to rely on "ad hoc mobilization", referring to a stance without any standing armed forces, yet still with a latent military potential. Surprising though it may seem today, the United States came close to such a situation until the Second World War. Indeed this was implicit in the Hamiltonian admonition that "Extensive military establishments cannot, in this position, be necessary to our security" (Hamilton, 1787). Before the First World War the United States thus had only very modest armed forces. As a result, its entry into the war necessitated a mobilization that was accomplished with impressive speed. Following the termination of hostilities, moreover, the U.S. undertook a far-reaching demobilization which was only reversed after the start of the Second World War – once again with impressive results. In continuity with this "strategy of unreadiness", the defeat first of Germany and subsequently Japan was soon followed by yet another demobilization. Only the onset of the Cold War reversed this trend, necessitating a high level of peacetime readiness (Betts, 1995, pp. 3–19; Koistinen, 1997; Cohen, 1994; Porter, 1994, pp. 243–296; Friedberg, 1992).

As will be apparent from Table 5, ad hoc mobilization seems to have few features that would be appealing to a "modern state". It presupposes that a significant proportion of the citizenry are armed, something which could well produce more widespread domestic violence, thereby constituting a security threat (to the population) rather than a means of national security. Moreover, it would tend to weaken the State considerably vis-à-vis society, hence would

Table 5. Ad Hoc Mobilization.

	Advantages	Disadvantages
Strategic	Some mobilization potential	No standing forces or command structures; low level of training
Economic	No costs for the state	n.a.
Social	No risk of militarization	Proliferation of arms
Political	No risk of praetorianism	Weak state
Other	No threat to other states	Only usable on national territory

probably appeal only to anarchists, both "classical" leftist ones and "modern" ones on the extreme right. Finally, while one cannot rule out that it may have a certain defensive potential, there is no way of knowing this in advance, as it would be based on improvisation. Hence it would neither provide reassurance (to the rest of the population) nor deterrence (of aggressors). I shall therefore disregard this option in the following.

Privatization

At first glance the privatization option appears appealing, also because is seems in line with fashionable trends in other fields. Its attractions may be illustrated by an example from ordinary life.

Most consumers have chosen to have neither resident dentist nor live-in plumbers, but simply hire their services if they should get a tooth-ache or a pipe should burst. This makes a lot of economic sense, because most teeth and pipes cause no trouble most of the time, so that resident plumbers or dentists would be idle most of the time, while other members of the same professions are quite willing to do the job for money, if and when the need arises. Countries are in an analogous position, as most of them are at peace most of the time, hence have no immediate need for any army to defend them. To have idle armies is not only expensive, but may also be hazardous, at least according to some analyses. This was, for instance, the reason why Immanuel Kant proposed an abolition of standing armies in his 1795 treatise *On Perpetual Peace* (Kant, 1963, pp. 17–18).

If states were to abolish their armed forces, they would have to rely on "guns for hire" in a "dial an army" mode. According to the principles of market economy, such a demand for hired armed forces would automatically (albeit perhaps with a certain time-lag) create its own supply, most likely in the form of private military companies (PMCs) offering mercenaries for hire. Most of these "hired guns" would surely be more or less permanent soldiers assigned to standing military units, but their services would be leased to the highest bidder. Not only states but also private firms might be among their customers. We would thus be the paradoxical situation of having "standing soldiers" and maybe even "standing armies", but ones that were "free agents" rather than instruments of states. It is even conceivable that certain states might make this their national business, so that we would have standing armies belonging to states, but tasked with defending other states, rather than with truly national duties.

Baroque though the above may appear, it is not without real-life examples:

- Large PMCs do exist, most (in)famously the South African-based Executive Outcomes (EO), which was dismantled in 1998 following the introduction of a set of government regulations deemed too rigid by the EO. Other companies such as Sandline and MPRI (Military Professional Resources Inc.), however, continue their activities. Both private firms, insurrectionist movements and governments have occasionally been among their customers. (Shearer, 1998; Cilliers & Mason (Eds), 1999; Mills & Stremlau (Eds), 1999; Musah & Fayemi (Eds), 2000; Reno, 1998, pp. 61–67, 130–139).
- Certain very small countries have made the surprisingly large contributions to UN peacekeeping operations. While part of the explanation thereof may certainly be genuine veneration for the United Nations, it is also conceivable that some of these countries are in the "peacekeeping business" mainly for the money and other resources to which it gives access. If so, the label "mercenary states" might be appropriate.

Table 6 merely enumerates the advantages and disadvantages of private armies from the point of view of the state that might rely on them.

While the list does not provide much support for using PMCs as an alternative to traditional armed forces, quite a strong case could be made for using PMCs as a supplement, say for particularly risky deployments (under UN or other auspices) for which there would be no domestic support in those countries usually providing peacekeepers. For such companies to enlist the services of PMCs might well seem attractive, and it might thus ensure that necessary, but risky or otherwise unattractive, missions are undertaken at all.

I shall disregard, in this connection, two phenomena which arguably belong in the same category as the above, namely that of terrorists functioning as "lone warriors" on their own behalf or in the service of sects and extremist political groups; and that of armed gangs (and child soldiers) roaming wild in "collapsed states". Not because they are umimportant, but because their inclusion would take us completely beyond the realm of national defence, however permissively defined.

Table 6. Privatization.

	Advantages	**Disadvantages**
Strategic	Skilled soldiers	No immediate defence capability
Economic	No peacetime costs	Higher wartime costs
Social	No risk of militarization	Risk of brutalization
Political	Small risk of praetorianism	Undermines the state monopoly on the legitimate use of force
Other	?	Danger of lawlessness

Swiss – Type Militias

Switzerland has for centuries relied on a radical form of "citizens in arms" model. The present militia system entails compulsory military service for all male citizens; all members of the militia are required to keep their weapons at home; and all are called up for periodic training (Cramer, 1984; Däniker, 1987; Bald (Ed.), 1987; Fuhrer, 1994). Other countries have included elements of the same model in their personnel structure, e.g. in the form of a home guard assigned to more or less important tasks in the defence of national territory (Roberts, 1976; Fuhrer, 1987; Ries, 1989; Agrell, 1979). This might be depicted by a continuous scale as in Table 7.

Table 7. The Role of Militias.

Switzerland	Finland, Austria	Denmark, Norway	U.K., United States
◄-------	-------	-------	-------►
Central military role	Partly independent military role	Auxillary military role	Non-military role

The advantages and disadvantages of militias are summed up in Table 8.

The most obvious strategic advantage of a militia system is that it allows for the mobilization of a very large part of the population, which may be relevant in cases of national defence against large-scale invasion. A country with a very substantial proportion of its adult male population under arms would be very hard for an invador to "digest", also because a militia might resort to guerilla strategy and tactics, and would be well-adapted to "swimming in the country-side like a fish in water" (Mao, 1975: 1, pp. 179–254, 2, pp. 79–19, 219–235; cf. Guevara, 1976; Giap, 1970; Chaliand (Ed.), 1982; Beaufre, 1972; cf. for the historical background Laqueur (Ed.), 1978, pp. 42–44; Gates, 1986; Clausewitz, 1976, pp. 479–483; Hahlweg, 1986).

The question is whether the kind of war against which a militia system provides a strong defence remains relevant today. It would probably be

Table 8. Militias and Home Guards.

	Advantages	**Disadvantages**
Strategic	High mobilization potential	Few standing forces Low level of training
Economic	Low direct manpower costs High equipment costs	High indirect manpower costs
Social	Civil-military integration	Risk of "militarism" Proliferation of arms
Political	No risk of praetorianism	Risk of militarization of politics
Other	No threat to other states	Only usable on national territory

premature to discount this eventuality for, for instance, small countries facing large, but not particularly technologically sophisticated, enemies harbouring territorial ambitions against them, which may be an adequate description of many Third World countries. However, most countries in Europe, are not in this situation – even though the experience from the dissolving Yugoslavia seems to show that guerillas are not entirely obsolete. For countries such as those in Western Europe, however, the risk of large-scale invasion has receded well into the background, providing a warning time of about a decade – which makes the militia model rather irrelevant. For such military tasks as are now given the highest priority, militias are clearly unsuitable: peacekeeping operations and (humanitarian and other) interventions, taking place outside national territory, often far from home.

While this would, in most cases, be an argument against militias, it could also be turned around. Should one favour a "Swiss-style" policy of neutrality, the inability to send forces abroad would not matter, because the country would not want to go abroad under any circumstances. Moreover, to have merely such forces could be seen as material evidence of defensive intentions, which could help mitigate the security dilemma (Collins, 1997; Møller, 1992). Several proponents of "non-offensive defence" (Møller, 1991, 1992, 1995) have therefore favoured militia structures. Unfortunately, others have come to see the two concepts as inseparable, hence have found the very notion of defensiveness to have been discredited by the experience in the former Yugoslavia (sometimes referred to as a model of defensive, territorial defence).

As far as the economic criteria are concerned, the picture is not totally clear. The low direct manpower costs are, of course, a function of the militias receiving no salaries (but sometimes compensations and per diems). However, there may be substantial "opportunity costs" involved in having people in other occupations performing military duties. The national costs and benefits, in both cases, depend on such factors as the level of unemployment.

Furthermore, to the extent that the equipment for the militia is of comparable sophistication as that of (more) professional armed forces, it would tend to be more costly, if only because of the larger quantities required. On the other hand, there does not seem to be any clear correlation between aggregate military expenditures and the role played by homeguards and militias. In terms of per capita military expenditures countries with substantial militia elements such as Finland or Austria ($328 and $205, respectively) rank below a country with a full-fledged militia system such as Switzerland ($439), but even further below states with quite insignificant militia elements such as the UK ($628) or the United States ($1,036) (IISS: *The Military Balance, 2000–2001,* pp. 297–298).

How to assess the social advantages and disadvantages depends very much on the context. It stands to reason that a militia eliminates the danger that the armed forces might come to constitute a virtual "state within the state", but in stable democracies this is probably no serious danger anyway. The constant influence of civil society on the military may be valuable, but is surely not essential – and it must be assessed against the danger that military values come to permeate civil society. A further problem is that the total number of small arms increases, which may tendentially both undermine the state's "monopoly on the legitimate use of force" and lead to a higher incidence of armed violence. On the other hand, there does not seem to be any strong correlation (if any) between militia systems and crime rates, Switzerland ranking rather low on a scale of violent crime, and certainly much lower than the United States.

Conscription

There is little doubt that the institution of conscription has played an important role in the past, both in narrow defence terms and with regard to beneficial effects for society as a whole. The advantages and disadvantages of conscription are summed up in Table 9.

As far as its defence functions are concerned, the following are especially noteworthy:

- It has provided states with substantial military power, combining a significant readiness with a large mobilization potential – and at rather modest costs.
- On the other hand, by thus paving the way for true mass armies, it has been a contributory cause of some of history's greatest catastrophes such as the

two world wars. The longer-term effect of this may, however, prove to be an "obsolescence of major war" (Mueller, 1989).
- Its compulsory nature has given the state access to average-quality military manpower at moderate costs, where volunteers (i.e. professionals) might be either prohibitively costly, or of low quality. In fact, as the military can always reject conscripts, they are usually able to enlist manpower somewhat above the national average.
- A conscripted army is fairly easy to partially demobilize, as this is simply a question of not drafting specified age groups.

Table 9. Conscription.

	Advantages	**Disadvantages**
Strategic	Large mobilization potential "Average quality" manpower	Moderate defence readiness Only elementary military skills Possible "casualty scaredness"
Economic	Modest direct manpower costs	Higher opportunity costs
Social	Socialization of the young	Gender inequality Possible "*Wehr(un)gerechtigkeit*"
Political	"Melting pot" effect Civil-military integration	?
Other	Easy demobilization	Politically difficult to send abroad

From among the several beneficial non-military (side-)effects of conscription, one could mention the following:

- Conscription has served as a "melting pot" for diverse ethnic groups, as mentioned above, thereby sometimes contributing to forging a sense of national identity and loyalty to the State.
- It has, likewise, served a "melting pot" function for social strata that might otherwise have had little mutual contact. This has probably contributed to the "egalitarian ethos" characterizing many modern European states.
- It has often contributed to the development of democracy, as military service obligations have usually been accompanied by voting rights.

What may, however, have rendered conscription obsolete, at least in some countries, are the following factors:

- While it may be debatable whether large-scale conventional war is obsolete as such, it is clearly believed to be so by a number of countries, facing only very insignificant and/or remote military threats. Their fatherlands are simply not believed to stand in need of any defence, and certainly not by means of mass armies (Haltiner, 1998, 1999).

- For the other functions currently performed by the armed forces of these countries (peace support operations, military interventions, etc.) conscripts are ill-suited. There is no need for mass armies for such missions, but only for contingents of some thousands of troops, at most. Moreover, it is not obviously fair to use compulsory military service for missions which have next to nothing to do with national security (Segal & Tiggle, 1997).
- Conscription entails considerable material and infrastructural requirements, as the draftees will have to be housed, fed, equipped and trained at society's expense, regardless of the actual need for the troops.
- Conscription may not only produce armies larger than required, but in some cases also larger than permitted (by international treaties, for instance), unless the rejection rate is increased substantially-which would be perceived as unfair by those few who are drafted.
- Exclusively male conscription seems hard to reconcile with the general principle of equal rights for the sexes.
- There have been some proposals to expand conscription to include both sexes, while including non-military functions, i.e. to create a general service obligation in analogy with the alternative services for conscientious objectors (Zimmermann, 1993; Bahr (Ed.), 1990). While this might seem reasonable in times of high unemployment for young people, the opportunity costs of such a scheme in times of full employment would be very high.

The above applies only to countries such as those in Western (and perhaps partly Eastern and East-Central) Europe. In other parts of the world, considerations such as these may be entirely irrelevant.

U.S./U.K.-Type Professionals

The United States has relied entirely on professional ("all volunteer") armed forces since conscription was abolished in 1973 (Janowitz & Moskos, 1979; Lockman & Quester, 1985; Gilroy et al., 1990; Sarkesian et al., 1995; Griffith, 1985; Burk, 1989; Sinaiko, 1990). The U.K., likewise, has since 1963 relied on professionals (Bond, 1984; cf. Booth, 1983), and several European countries have, since the end of the Cold War, moved in the same direction (*vide supra*). The advantages and disadvantages of professionals are summed up in Table 10.

Strategically, professionals possess some obvious advantages. First of all, training can be more targeted and cost-effective than that of conscripts, simply because it is intended for "the long haul". Secondly, all-volunteer forces are politically less problematic to deploy for whatever missions the government decides, e.g. for interventions far beyond national territory. Whether to regard this as an advantage or a drawback, however, depends entirely on one's general attitude to interventions as such.

On the other hand, depending on specific contractual arrangements, the number of mobilizable reserves will usually be lower than those "produced" by conscripted forces (Walker, 1992; Brown & Merrill, 1994; Kirby & Naftel, 2000). The mobilization potential is thus tendentially inferior to that of conscription, except for the obvious possibility that professional forces might serve as cadres for a larger (conscripted) army in the unlikely case of an emerging need for such a mass army – as was the case of the German *Reichswehr* in the inter-war years (*vide supra*).

Table 10. Professional Armed Forces.

	Advantages	**Disadvantages**
Strategic	Many standing forces High level of training	Low mobilization potential
Economic	Low indirect manpower costs	High direct manpower costs Expensive demobilization (McCormick, 1998; Jolly, 1996)
Social	Division of labour	Danger of low-quality personnel
Political	?	Danger of civil/military bifurcation
Other	No deployment constraints	No deployment constraints

It is a widespread assumption that professionals are always expensive. However, just how expensive they will be depends on the market, as the soldierly profession will merely be one line of occupation that will have to contend with others. In cases of (close to) full employment, the armed forces will either have to make do with less qualified soldiers, or pay them more in order to attract more qualified manpower – just as is the case for any other profession. The "correct" wage level will, of course, have to take into account the risks involved in soldiering, including the ultimate one of risking one's life in mortal combat. However, in most cases (and certainly in those of the West) the risks incurred are fairly modest and compare quite well with hazardous civilian trades such as working on an oil rig or as a fire fighter. Moreover, the risks depend entirely on political decisions, as countries can choose to only send their soldiers into battle in a low-risk environment – as has been the case for the United States (*vide supra*). Should the government change course and be prepared to send soldiers into "real" battle, it might cause problems in the short term. In the medium-to-long term, however, there would surely be levels of compensation that would suffice for attracting personnel, even for more risky deployments.

According to some analyses, professionalization will produce armed forces out of touch with the rest of society. Serious though these concerns about civil-military relations may certainly be, closer analysis reveals some of the argument as possessing questionable validity:

- First of all, officers are always professionals, but they are the ones referred to in the often-heard arguments about creating a "state within the state". Whether the rank-and-file are professionals or conscripts probably matters much less.
- Secondly, all professional groups develop ties among themselves, but this is rarely seen as a problem as such. Unless there are serious praetorian tendencies, and/or risks of a military *coup d'état* it is not obvious why such ties among the military should be particularly worrysome.
- Thirdly, if the armed forces should show tendencies to distance themselves from the rest of society, there would surely be ways of contravening this. To relocate military barracks from distant locations into the midst of civilian society, perhaps requiring a certain dispersal, might, for instance, go a long way to integrate the troops with the rest of society.

Indeed, the very fact that so many democratic and stable countries have chosen to rely on professional armed forces constitutes a very strong argument against the above concerns.

CONCLUSIONS AND LOOSE ENDS

As argued along the way, it is impossible to conclude anything in general terms. There are arguments in favour of both militia systems, conscription and professional armed forces which may well be valid for particular countries at specified times. Indeed, it is even conceivable that some form of privatization will gradually come to be seen as the least unattractive option for certain countries, and that others will come to rely exclusively on improvisation in the form of ad hoc mobilization. It all depends on the concrete circumstances and on political decisions. Needless to say, this does not imply that "anything goes", but merely that one should beware of generalizations.

Its length notwithstanding, the above analysis has left a number of relevant questions unasked and unanswered. As it would be foolhardy to attempt to answer any of these questions I shall confine myself to concluding by enumerating some of these "loose ends":

- To which extent, if at all, can the experience from Europa and North America be transposed to the Third World? Not only will the typical missions of the armed forces be different (constabulary as opposed to "defence" duties), but the social and political setting will also be radically different.
- What are the implications for personnel policies of the apparent transition from an era of international wars to one where intra-state war has become the predominant form of armed conflict–not least in the Third World? (Wallensteen & Sollenberg, 2000).
- It is one thing to create armed forces, but how does a state get rid of them, once it no longer experiences a need for them, i.e. how can forces be demobilized? This question, of course, has both strategic, economic, social and political aspects, and it is very likely that there will be significant variations between, e.g. First and Third world settings as well as between post-war situations (Kingma (Ed.), 2000; Berdal, 1996) and situations of a "normal" improvement of a country's security situation allowing it to build down the size of its armed forces.
- Is there a need to expand the concept of civil-military relations to account for variuous new phenomena. Not only is the concept of the "civilian" thus being expanded to include both national and international NGOs, but the category of relevant military agencies is also growing, e.g. with the aforementioned significant (and perhaps even growing) role of PMCs (private military companies). We may thus need a more all-embracing concept of civil-military relations.

Most of the above topics appear to stand in need of further research, but that will have to be the topics of other papers.

THE EUROPEAN FAREWELL TO CONSCRIPTION?

Rafael Ajangiz

ABSTRACT

The latest developments of conscription in Western Europe are framed in the long-term process of the decline of the mass army. Ten measures of that decline are reviewed to conclude that the social forces, namely democratic reason, have been much more influential in the decision-making process of this policy than is commonly admitted. Although on the short-term, with the exceptions of Spain and Italy, it is reason of state that better accounts for the end of conscription, on the long-term this is partly regarded as a direct or indirect outcome of social mobilisation. However, the completion of the process toward the all-volunteer force does not necessarily bring the end of conscription and a specific analysis of every country is presented to assess the rationale and prospects for change concerning this policy.

INTRODUCTION

The European map of conscription has changed radically in very few years: Belgium took the decision to abolish compulsory military service in 1992, Holland in 1993, France and Spain in 1996, Italy in 1999, Portugal is in the process of doing so, Germany and Austria are engaged in its discussion, Denmark and Sweden might be next. The countdown seems underway. Of the fifteen countries that make up the European Union, twelve made use of forced

The Comparative Study of Conscription in the Armed Forces, Volume 20, pages 307–333.

ISBN: 0-7623-0836-2

recruitment ten years ago; today that number is eight, and it might be no more than four within another ten years.[1] But, are the days of conscription really coming to an end? In any case, what are the reasons that govern both continuity and change in respect to this policy.

THE CRISIS OF CONSCRIPTION

Any answer to these or similar questions needs to concede that conscription suffers from a very serious crisis today. There are some political explanations to this crisis; globalisation or the end of the Cold War are usually the points on which they coincide. Concepts such as the development from the state-centric world into a multi-centric world (Rosenau, 1994) or the arrival of new times (Dandeker, 1994b) refer to two circumstances that directly affect the role played by mass armed forces at the turn of the century: (a) the crisis of the nation-state, which logically affects the national armed forces, and (b) a new geostrategic scenario, within which the traditional argument used until now to justify the existence of mass armed forces, territorial defence, no longer holds verisimilitude in most European countries. [2] The New Strategic Concept of the Atlantic Alliance is the realisation of the new circumstances; it refers to risk uncertainty as the new source of insecurity that replaces the traditional arguments of threats to the territorial integrity of the member states.[3] Its policy, which embodies the relocation of authority to regional agencies, consists of the formation of multinational forces and their involvement in out of area operations, e.g. the interventions in the Gulf and in the Balkans (Burk, 1994; Carr & Ifantis, 1996; Dorman & Treacher, 1995).

In addition to this, the crisis of conscription is social as well. This dimension, commonly unmentioned and neglected in spite of its visibility, needs to be stressed to fully understand the recent changes. The sharp increase in the figures for conscientious objection in Italy, Spain and Germany, for instance, is a sign that, when the alternative to military service becomes less disproportionate, conscripts choose not to join the armed forces. This is a reluctance that extends beyond Europe, one that is almost global in scope. Protests and resistance to recruitment are events common to all cultures and socio-political contexts. To give some examples, it was this context of mobilisation which led South Africa to abolish conscription in 1991, which led Argentina to do the same in 1994 and to Chile cutting the length of military service by half in 1994, the same as Vietnam, South Korea or Taiwan. In Brazil it has resulted in parliamentary motions calling for its abolition, while conscientious objection is growing rapidly in other countries of Latin America such as Paraguay, Guatemala or Colombia. In Russia the great majority of conscripts evade recruitment, while in Israel conscripts avoid the positions involving greater risk and prefer office work.[4]

Nevertheless, the crisis of conscription is not something new either; it arose long before the end of the Cold War. In the early 1970s, the works by Janowitz (1972; with Moskos, 1979) and Doorn (1975, 1976) already diagnosed the difficulties of conscription as a main feature of the *decline of the mass army*.[5] In their opinion, there were four structural changes, political and social, that indicated such decline: (a) the nuclearisation of defence, (b) military intervention in other countries, (c) the change of values and priorities in postmodern societies, and (d) the crisis in the social legitimacy of compulsory military service.

Nowadays this social dimension of the crisis is rarely mentioned, but at that time the protests were salient. Indeed, the North American mobilisations against the Vietnam War coincided with protests in Europe and Latin America, and were accompanied by an exceptional growth in conscientious objection, in Denmark, Norway, Holland or Germany for example (Mellors & McKean, 1982). Although there are different interpretations, we can easily agree with Janowitz (1971) that mobilisation was the major driving force for the abolition of conscription in the case of the United States. There is an extensive literature at this respect. However, it is interesting to note the little known fact that at that time, alarmed by the mobilisations, the authorities of some of those European countries, France, Belgium and the Netherlands among them, seriously considered that very same possibility, whereas Denmark installed a system of selective conscription, and all of them devised different measures to prevent future protests (Kelleher, 1978; Martin, 1977; Mellors & McKean, 1982; Meulen & Manigart, 1997).

In sum, there are two guiding ideas that underpin this article. First, that the crisis of conscription is not something recent, but instead it dates back some thirty years at least and has merely deepened since then; it should be regarded as a structural crisis on a *macro* level, affecting all countries. And second, that the social forces have been much more influential in the decision-making process of this policy than is commonly admitted. To assess the accuracy of these ideas we will now examine the values of ten measures that we have deemed appropriate to the case after a careful review of the existing literature. They are: (a) the evolution of military expenditure, (b) the volume of the armed forces in relation to population size, (c) the technological improvement and nuclearisation of armed forces, (d) the resistance to forced recruitment, namely conscientious objection, (e) the stance of public opinion concerning conscription, (f) the position of public opinion regarding the despatch of conscripts on interventions in other countries, (g) the development of *rapid action forces,* (h) the ratio between volunteer forces and conscripts, (i) the input of conscripts, and (j) the input of volunteers.

MILITARY EXPENDITURE, SIZE AND TECHNOLOGISATION OF THE EUROPEAN ARMED FORCES

Since conscripts are replaced by technology and volunteer soldiers, every transition to the all-volunteer armed forces entails an extra effort in budgetary terms; the case of the United States is a good example (Janowitz & Moskos, 1979). Accordingly, higher levels of **military expenditure** in the long term can be considered as a good asset to achieve such a transition. On top of that, the behaviour of this variable in the last decade will indicate which governments have allocated special resources to secure the final step.

In principle, France, Portugal, Norway, the Netherlands, Germany and Belgium, who followed the 3% criterion of NATO during the Cold War, were in a better position to accomplish the end of conscription than Italy, Denmark or Spain. Now, the generalised reduction in military expenditure in the 1990s in relation to the previous decade emerged as an opportunity to advance in that direction and lessen the differences between countries. Much of that peace dividend was used to confront the crisis of the 1980s and the requirements of European monetary convergence – value for money has been the motto in all armed forces since then (Dandeker, 1994a) – but every country has taken its own choices. The retention of conscription in its two forms, military and substitutory, has helped Germany to reduce its military expenditure by up to a 54% in ten years in order to meet the costs of reunification. The large savings of Belgium (53%) and the Netherlands (43%) result from the disbanding of some units and, paradoxically, the abolition of conscription itself; the reform has caused serious alarm among the Belgian military

Table 1. Average Level of Military Expenditure in Recent Decades.

	U.K.	Fra	Por	Nor	Neth	Ger	Bel	Ita	Den	Spa
Average military expenditure 1970–1998	4.2	3.8	3.6	2.9	2.9	2.9	2.7	2.2	2.2	1.9
Military expenditure in 1998 (% GNP)	2.6	2.8	2.4	2.1	1.8	1.5	1.5	1.7	1.6	1.3
Value given in the summary table	++	++	++	+	+	+	+			

Sources: *The Military Balance*, London: The International Institute for Strategic Studies and Oxford University Press; *World Development Indicators,* Washington: World Bank; *SIPRI Yearbook of World Armaments and Disarmament*, Stockholm, Stockholm Peace Research Institute, and Oxford: Oxford University Press; *Statistics from NATO*, NATO web page.

authorities. With smaller reductions in military expenditure, it would appear that military policies in Denmark (32%), Norway (31%), France (30%), Portugal (27%) and Italy (24%) have been more demanding on the national budget. Interestingly enough, France, Portugal and Italy are moving in the direction of the all-volunteer force.

Spain is a very unusual case. Already with a very modest military expenditure in the past, it is paradoxically one of the countries that has made higher savings in the last ten years (45%) and, on top of that, has also engaged in the abolition of conscription. Of course, this is not what the Spanish authorities had in mind. As a matter of fact, in 1991 the two majority parties agreed a substantial rise in military expenditure, as much as 2% of GNP, in order to ensure the modernisation of the armed forces and to improve their employment ratio. But the percentage kept shrinking instead. Then, in 1996, the newly elected conservative leaders were compelled to abolish conscription and again planned a substantial increase in military expenditure to make such a major reform possible. In practice, they have been unable to overcome zero growth and, off the record, they have acknowledged that, aware as they are that social expenditure and military expenditure have traditionally had a relationship of substitution, the voters would have reacted against any increase in military expenditure (Cosidó, 1994, 1996). This contingency could also apply to other national governments, specially the weaker or less authoritarian ones; conversely, the French government would be largely immune to it.

The **size of the European armed forces** follows a pattern that is very similar to that of military expenditure. In the last twenty years, but above all since 1989, there has been an important reduction in the number of military personnel

Table 2. Evolution of Military Expenditure and Total Number of Military Personnel Between the 1980s (average) and 1998.

	Bel	Ger	Neth	Spa	Por	U.K.	Fra	Den	Ita	Nor
Military Expenditure	−53%	−54%	−43%	−45%	−27%	−47%	−30%	−32%	−24%	−31%
Total Military Personnel	−53%	−50%	−45%	−42%	−38%	−35%	−27%	−20%	−23%	−22%

Sources for military personnel: *The Military Balance*, London: The International Institute for Strategic Studies and Oxford University Press; Patrice Buffotot (Ed.) *La défense en Europe*, Paris: La Documentation Française; White Papers of Belgium, Greece, and Great Britain; *Projet le Loi relatif à la programmation militaire pour les années 1997 à 2002*, Assemblée National, 7-6-1996 (France); *Nuevo Modelo de Fuerzas Armadas*, Ministerio de Defensa, 5-12-1996 (Spain); web pages of the Ministries of Defence of Denmark, France, Germany, Norway, Great Britain, Italy, the Netherlands, and Spain.

throughout Europe. In overall terms, the armed forces are now one third smaller than in 1980. This is not a new tendency, nor should it only be explained away to the end of the Cold War, since the scale of armed forces has constantly varied over the course of this century, basically as a result of the variations in recruitment that followed the cycles of war and peace. In fact, the present period is inserted in a longer cycle that started in the 1970s as a result of the policy changes than took place then.

Varied policy choices and structural strains have resulted in a substantial transformation of the military map of Europe. Until recently – if we do not consider Turkey – there were five big armed forces, Germany, France, the United Kingdom, Italy and Spain, and a long way behind in terms of size, a host of little armed forces; however, at the start of this 21st century we account for three first division armed forces – Germany, France and the United Kingdom; three second division armed forces – Italy, Spain and Greece; and a fair number of armed forces of slightly lesser size. In some cases, the latter will be better equipped in technical and human terms and will have a more clearly defined role in the new world scenario than those immediately above them in size, such as Spain or Italy, which, in addition, will have to compete with the new incorporations, such as Poland for example.

Table 3. Evolution of the European Armed Forces by Categories and Size.

	1980	1989	1998	2002
Major armed forces	Germany (654,000) Turkey (570,000) France (500,000)	Germany (659,000) Turkey (651,000) France (466,000)	Turkey (640,000)	Turkey
Large armed forces	Italy (370,000) Spain (340,000) UK (325,000)	Italy (390,000) U.K. (312,000)	Germany (330,000) France (360,000)	Germany (320,000)
Medium-size armed forces (1)		Spain (285,000) Greece (208,000)	Italy (290,000) UK (215,000)	France (250,000) UK (225,000)
Medium-size armed forces (2)	Greece (190,000)		Spain (185,000) Greece (150,000)	Italy (200,000) Greece (140,000) Spain (130,000)
Small Armed Forces	Netherlands (100,000) Belgium (90,000) Portugal (70,000) Norway (38,000) Denmark (32,000)	Netherlands (100,000) Belgium (92,000) Portugal (75,000) Norway (34,000) Denmark (32,000)	Netherlands (57,000) Belgium (45,000) Portugal (43,000) Norway (29,000) Denmark (24,000)	Netherlands (60,000) Belgium (40,000) Portugal (38,000) Norway (29,000) Denmark (23,000)

Table 4. Projection of the Probable Size of the European Armed Forces in the Year 2002 and Existing Relation to Population Size.

	Gre	Nor	Den	Fra	Por	Bel	Ger	U.K.	Neth	Ita	Spa
Military personnel	140,00	29,000	24,000	250,000	38,000	40,000	320,000	225,000	60,000	190,000	130,000
Ratio	13.21	6.55	4.55	4.22	3.89	3.88	3.87	3.85	3.82	3.35	3.26
Value		++	++	++	+	+	+	+	+		

Sources for poulation size: Wistat – CD, New York: United Nations Population Fund.

The evolution of the number of military personnel is determined by five factors: (a) the international disarmament decisions, (b) the national decisions of readjustment of strength, (c) the abolition or change in the length of compulsory military service, (d) the natural evolution of the recruitable population, and ultimately (e) the volume of the recruited population. The impact of each of these variables varies by country, but in general we have observed: (1) that the international decisions have not forced any country – if we except Germany – to reduce its number of military forces (Carr & Ifantis, 1996), so the decrease in the size of the armed forces is better explained as resulting from processes and causes that are internal to each country; and (2) that the reductions basically affect the compulsory component, that is to say, there are less young men carrying out compulsory military service and they do it for less time.

The authorities in most countries commonly argue that this change towards professionalisation results from the **nuclearisation and technological improvement** of the armed forces. On the one hand, armaments potential replaces human force. On the other, that type of armament requires military personnel who are more specialised, more motivated and more stable, more *professional* (Burk, 1994). The fact that the two European armed forces with nuclear arsenals have taken this step provides confirmation to this thesis; indeed, the nuclear tests in Mururoa were a prior condition to abolishing conscription in France. However, this decisive criterion which, in principle, appears to answer to a strictly defence and security logic, must be seen in relation to the social setting. The need for such more specialised personnel rests on the idea that the conscripts' military training period is too short: twelve months barely provide basic training, inadequate for more technical posts (Estrella, 1993, p. 30). But conscription lasted an average of 18 months in the Western European countries in the 1960s and 24 months some years before that. Therefore, the simplest and most economical solution for confronting the lack of preparation and, at the same time, the falling birth rate, would have been a return to tradition. This did not happen, though, because there existed a social mandate for its progressive abolition – the fact that it was never mentioned should not prevent us from recognising its decisive influence.

That mandate began to become effective with the mobilisations of the 1960s and 1970s; the reductions in the length of military service resulted in the armed forces starting to remunerate the longer periods of service associated with those technical functions. France is a good example: its military service lasted 24 months until 1965; the mobilisations in the 1960s resulted in its reduction to 12 months in only four years, and it was then that volunteer recruitment was promoted (Martin, 1977). Consequently, the reduction in the length of military service has never resulted from the progression towards an all-volunteer force, but the other way around. This is what happened in the 1920s and 1930s (Weber, 1964), in the 1960s and 1970s (Martin, 1977), and also in the 1990s (Ajangiz, 2000). The sequence is the same in all cases: first the duration of military service is reduced and immediately after or at that moment plans are decided upon and implemented to reorganise the armed forces and to strengthen the volunteer component. That is to say, the so-called professionalisation of the armed forces occurs as a result of the progressive distancing and lack of collaboration by society with respect to questions of defence. Belgium, Denmark, France and the Netherlands introduced that change mainly in the 1970s, while Italy, Portugal and Spain have initiated it in the late 1980s, already in a context of a massive flight from military service.

This reduction in the length of military service is one principal cause of the loss of manpower volume in the armed forces. The other basic reason is the smaller contribution of conscripts. There are three variables that determine this contribution: (a) the evolution of the recruitable population, that is to say, the demographic factor, (b) resistance to recruitment, normally conscientious objection, and (c) the recruitment pressure decided upon by the government in each period. The impact of demographic evolution is insignificant in the majority of European countries because military recruitment is normally situated at around 50% of the recruitable population and the armed forces enjoy sufficient margin of manoeuvre to regulate the rate of recruitment depending on the number of personnel that are considered to be necessary.

As a matter of fact, only three countries, Germany, Italy and Spain, have undergone a decrease in the contribution of forced recruitment in recent years. While it is true that there has been an important demographic decline, above all in the two former countries, the true cause of the reduction in the number of military personnel that can be observed today is, however, conscientious objection. If Germany, Italy and Spain had today the same levels of conscientious objection as in 1990, or those of the other countries, never higher than 10 or 15% of the conscript population, there would be no crisis of recruitment.

	1980	81	82	83	84	85	86	87	88	89	90	91	92	93	94	95	96	97	98
Belgium	10	—	—	—	—	—	—	12	—	—	—	11	10	8	—	0			
Denmark	9	—	—	—	—	—	—	—	—	—	—	—	—	—	—	—	—	—	—
France	12	—	—	—	—	—	—	—	—	—	—	—	10	—	—	—	—	—	—
Germany	15	—	—	—	—	—	—	—	—	—	—	12	—	—	—	10	—	—	—
Greece	24	22	—	—	—	—	21	—	—	20	—	19	—	—	—	—	—	—	—
Italy	12	—	—	—	—	—	—	—	—	—	—	—	—	—	—	—	—	10	—
Netherlands	14	—	—	—	—	—	—	—	—	—	—	12	—	—	9	—	6	0	
Norway	12	—	—	—	—	—	—	—	—	—	—	—	—	—	—	9	—	—	—
Portugal	16	—	—	—	—	—	—	—	—	—	15	—	12	—	4	—	—	—	—
Spain	15	—	—	—	—	—	12	—	—	—	—	9	—	—	—	—	—	—	—
Turkey	20	—	—	—	—	18	—	—	—	—	—	15	—	—	18	—	—	—	—

Fig. 1. Length of Compulsory Military Service (in months), 1980 to 1998.

Sources: Horeman et al. (1997); Kiljunen and Väänänen (1987); Quaker Council for European Affairs (1984); War Resisters International (1990); newspaper data.

This crisis is maturing in the case of Germany and has already broken out in those of Spain and Italy. As a result, the armed forces of these two countries have experienced a substantial devaluation on the European security stage that does not correspond with the public speeches and the diplomatic efforts of both states to join the group of countries that will decide the future of the new European fortress. In the case of Spain, the policy of socialists and conservatives during the 1990s aimed to establish a force of 180,000 military personnel, first with conscription and then without it. But, in the end, it has been the society which has had the final say: the high figures of conscientious objection and the reluctance to be recruited on a contract basis have downsized the armed forces to a manpower figure of 130,000; the revised new ceiling of 150,000 that the Spanish government established in January 1999 seems, once more, a formidable goal. Italy could find itself in a similar situation: the reform envisages 190,000 military personnel in the second decade of the 21st century, but the progressive deficit in recruits anticipates a future that will in fact be considerably less ambitious. A progressive demilitarisation of the foreign and security policies of both countries is foreseeable.

RESISTANCE TO RECRUITMENT AND THE STANCE OF PUBLIC OPINION CONCERNING CONSCRIPTION

Historically, on almost all occasions when governments have intensified forced recruitment, this has led to protest (Forrest, 1989; Levi, 1997; Lucassen & Zürcher,

1998; Sales, 1974; Young, 1984). If social compliance with this policy has always had its limits, then the change of values and priorities that has taken place in society in recent decades has further lowered them. Following Shaw (1991), we can argue that, in recent decades, there has been a sociological shift towards demilitarisation of: (a) everyday life, and (b) national and international policy. This finds expression in: (a) a growing dislike for, sometimes resistance to, military recruitment and the armed forces, and a basic discrepancy between the priorities of the military strategy designed by governments, the central axis of which is national strategic interests, and (b) the priorities of their societies, which centre around human rights or peace. Shaw judiciously speaks of a *post-military society*.

The position of Defence at the bottom of the scale of social priorities in all European societies in the early 1970s (Inglehart, 1977, p. 49) provides ground for thinking that disinterest in military questions, in short the growing distance between the armed forces and society – some authors openly speak of divorce – , is not a recent episode but rather a structural trend. Basing themselves on an antagonism between *warfare* and *welfare,* which in itself can be traced back for more than a century, Harries-Jenkins (1982) argued some years ago that the development of the welfare state had favoured a progressive change in the forms of social legitimisation of the military institution. That the traditional, fundamental legitimacy of the armed forces, on the basis of which they were assigned a central role in the building of national identity, had already been replaced by a functional legitimacy in which the armed forces were understood as forming no more than a further part of the state administration.

Conscription to the citizen army – a hallmark of national identity – specifically involving the younger cohorts, which were regarded as the bearers of post-materialism (Inglehart, 1976), became the most vulnerable part of the military institution. That is why in the late 1960s and the early 1970s, in a general context of mobilisation – May 1968, Mexico, Czechoslovakia, revolutions in the South, the Vietnam War, nuclear energy, etc. – it experienced a major crisis. First, conscientious objection ceased to be an option of minorities – always less than 2% of the call-up – and began to grow significantly, reaching 17% in Denmark, 15% in Germany, 9% in Norway, 8% in Holland and 6% in Belgium (Mellors & McKean, 1982; Moskos & Chambers, 1993). Second, in countries that banned conscientious objection, like France, Italy and Spain, this was also when mobilisation began demanding its formal recognition (Albesano, 1993; Ibarra, 1992; Martin, 1993). Third, soldiers and serving conscripts began to organise in unions (Cortright & Watts, 1991). And fourth, the government of the United States desisted from conscription in a context of general protest against the war in Vietnam (Chatfield, 1995; Useem, 1973).

***Table 5*. Conscientious Objection in Europe.**

	Ger	Spa	Ita	Fra	Nor	Bel	Neth	Den	Por
1965	3,437			67	*400*			490	
1966	4,431			59				540	
1967	5,963			65				672	
1968	11,952			101			*700*	1,107	
1969	14,420			151				1,766	
1970	19,363			261		89		2,456	
1971	27,657			606		112		4,200	
1972	33,792			789		272		4,489	
1973	35,192		143	586		792		3,987	
1974	34,150		219	596	2,675	607	*2,000*	4,161	
1975	32,565		238	770		766		3,136	
1976	40,618	597	628	766	2,090	913		2,255	*20*
1977	34,692	650	790	878	2,120	897		814	*20*
1978	39,698	*700*	1,103	1,200	2,020	1,190		763	*20*
1979	45,454	726	1,769	1,208	2,224	1,448		909	*20*
1980	54,193	*800*	2,375	1,148	2,543	1,339	3,845	816	
1981	58,051	*900*	2,559	1,312	2,690	1,171	3,341	606	
1982	59,776	*1,000*	6,917	1,147	2,812	2,011	2,936	466	
1983	68,334	1,106	7,557	*2,250*	2,372	2,023	2,705	366	
1984	43,875	*1,500*	9,903	*2,510*	2,070	1,886	3,037	319	
1985	53,907	*4,191*	7,430	*2,600*	2,094	1,720	2,953	218	
1986	58,693	6,407	4,282	2,737	2,497	1,356	3,017	232	
1987	62,817	8,897	4,986		2,360	1,078	2,936	355	
1988	77,048	11,049	5,697	2,950	2,281	949	2,768	484	704
1989	77,432	13,130	13,746	2,861	2,286		*2,900*	590	
1990	74,309	27,398	16,767	3,172	2,539	*1,600*	*3,000*	*500*	
1991	151,214	28,051	18,254		2,666	*6,000*		*400*	
1992	133,868	42,454	23,490		2,542				501
1993	131,057	68,209	28,910		2,358	737			624
1994	125,765	77,121	33,339	*8,000*	2,061				425
1995	160,569	72,832	44,342	*7,200*	2,110				382
1996	156,763	93,279	47,824		2,302				*1,000*
1997	154,972	127,304	54,867		2,300				
1998	171,657	150,581	71,043						

Sources: Agirre et al. (1998); Albesano (1993); Auvray (1983); Horeman et al. (1997); Ibarra (1992); Kiljunen and Väänänen (1987); Moskos and Chambers (1993); Quaker Council for European Affairs (1984); War Resisters International (1990); web pages of concerned governmental departments and peace groups; newspaper data; personal communications from activists. The figures in italics are approximate.

This specially resistance had important consequences, indeed a generalised reduction either in the scope or the length of forced recruitment, to half in many cases, e.g. from twenty-four to twelve months. As we have noted before, conscription lost much of its military value because of that, and it was then when the trend to increase the volunteer component in the majority of those armed forces began. But unlike the United States, it did not spell the end of conscription in Western Europe. Though it is true that the traditions on conscription were different in both regions and that Europe was not engaged in a war, two other major facts need to be mentioned in this respect. First, that in Europe there was no organised mobilisation to politicise that sum of individual options and expressly pose the suppression of compulsory military service; activists never pursued the end of conscription and the issue did not enter the political agenda. Some activists did share that goal – e.g. the FOGA network in Germany, which promoted total objection in the early 1980s – but presumably the bulk of them, indeed the main leaders, were partisans of the citizen army; they still are to some extent.[6] This circumstance prevented further developments. Shaw (1991, p. 8) has stated that, considering the great potential for anti-militarist protest that became visible in the early 1980s, contention might have had profound consequences had it been organised against conscription. The mobilisations of United States, South Africa or Spain, successful at this respect, provide support to this hypothesis.

The second reason for the durability of conscription rested on the painstaking application by governments of sufficient holding measures to normalise and integrate that dissidence: obstacles to the recognition of conscientious objection; restrictive laws; systematic rejection of a significant number of requests – Germany in the 1960s, France in the 1970s, Norway from that time until the present; a deterrent length to substitutory service – twice as long as military service in France, a progressive increase in Germany; prison and repression for the total objectors and, finally, a total closing of the political agenda to the question of compulsory military service. On the one hand, the authorities needed time to accomplish the changes that a prospective abolition of conscription implied. But, on the other hand, these measures were well-known to them; they had used them in the past to secure consent in regard to forced recruitment.

The decade of the 1990s brought a certain re-run of that cycle. Conscientious objection underwent a visible increase in gross numbers and the discussion about conscription re-entered the political agenda. A first sign of this circumstance was the general reduction in the length of compulsory military service that the authorities implemented around 1991, in some cases as a prelude to its abolition.

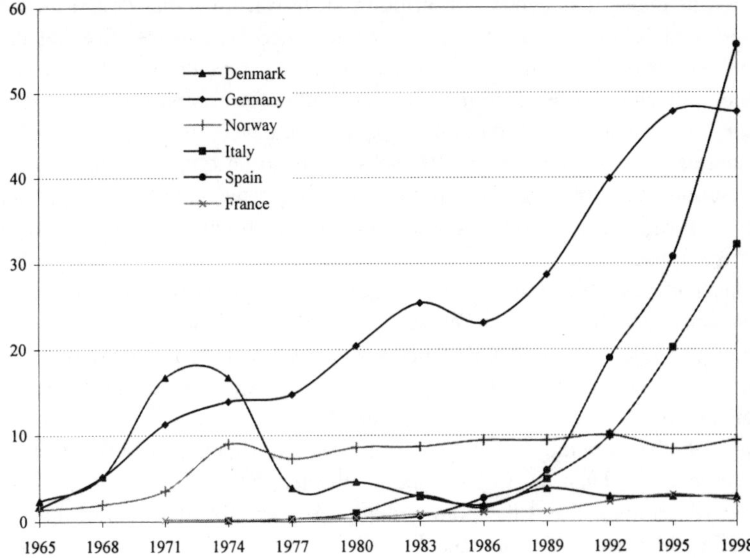

Fig. 2. Rate of Conscientious Objection.

The spread of conscientious objection has been described by some authors as the result of the modernisation process undergone by our societies in the last fifty years: with greater welfare there is less affinity for military questions (Moskos & Chambers, 1993). However, in some countries it would be more accurate to speak of a growing attraction of conscientious objection in comparison with military service. When examined in detail, we observe extensive dissimilarities in the magnitude of conscientious objection among the European societies. Countries like Spain, Italy or Germany, already have as many conscientious objectors as conscripts doing military service; figures were 48% in Germany and 56% in Spain in the year 1998, and 49% in Italy in the year 1999. In contrast, others like France, Belgium or Portugal, although having experienced a visible increase in the decade, have always benefited from very low figures, some 5% at the most. And, more interestingly, there are countries, Denmark or Norway for instance, that have today fewer objectors than thirty years ago. In our opinion, the thesis of cultural change is not fully comprehensive and needs to be complemented with political variables such as the policy-making process, where the interaction between the institutional actor and the movement actor is of great interest, in order to better understand the vicissitudes of forced recruitment.

It is our thesis that, when conscription suffers from social delegitimisation, it is not convictions but a rational calculation of costs and benefits that guides the behaviour of the majority of conscripts. In such a setting, it becomes vital for the authorities to penalise the possible routes for escaping military service, conscientious objection in particular, because the very moment this penalisation ceases to exist, the military barracks begin to empty. As a matter of fact, penalisation measures against conscientious objection have been implemented since its formal recognition, becoming harsher in the cyclical periods of crisis of conscription.

Conscientious objection is often described as an individual act rooted in convictions, whether religious or secular. However, it is its manifestation as collective political action that explains most policy changes related to it. To begin with, its legal recognition is frequently a by-product of civil disobedience. Instances are Norway, where mobilisation took place between 1890 and 1922 (Agøy, 1990b), Spain, between 1971 and 1996 (Agirre et al., 1998), and Turkey, now underway.[7] Then, at a certain point, the institutional actor takes over, the protest is terminated and the policy change is assimilated, opening up a calm period in which conscientious objection, now individualised, does not exceed the security threshold of military recruitment; this calm is the best proof that the penalisation measures have been effective. Yet, contention may appear again and occasionally succeed in bringing about the end of conscription, as happened in the United States or, more recently, in Spain and Italy. This would close the life cycle of forced recruitment. Obviously, the possibility must also be considered that this contention does not manage to pass the threshold and the result is a new normalisation that improves, for the time being, the anchoring of conscription.

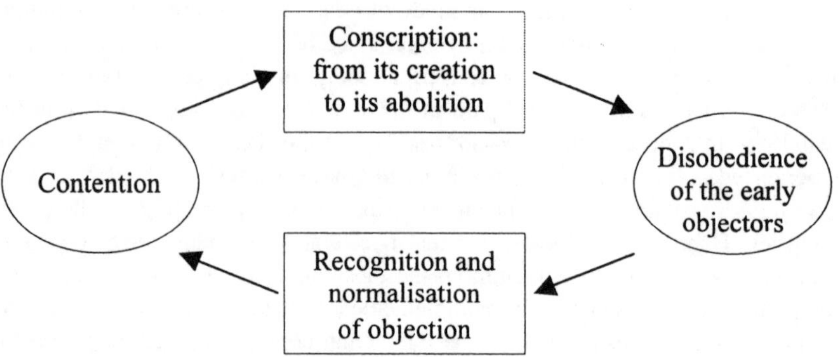

Fig. 3. Lyfe-Cycle of Conscription from a Mobilisation Point of View.

This thesis applies to the present situation. In the cases of Germany, Italy and Spain there has existed contention, lively enough to incapacitate, to various degrees, the usual measures of containment of conscientious objection. As a result, this behaviour has experienced an outstanding increase. In Germany, contrary sentiment and mobilisations against involvement in the military interventions of NATO were allied to the power vacuum concerning questions of conscription that existed in former East Germany between 1989 and 1991. The situation is stable now and the authorities have space to manoeuvre – not all military recruits are enlisted for the service – but conscientious objection is so high that any extra rise, allied with the prospective decline in the age-cohorts, can make military conscription unsustainable. In Italy, the movement actor struggled for years to obtain an equalisation of the length of substitutory service and military service; it did this through a strategy of reform that consisted of a systematic recourse to the law courts (Albesano, 1993). Eventually, when equalisation was granted, that made the option of conscientious objection much more desirable – substitutory service may be burdensome, but it is performed in an unthreatening and reasonable environment near home – and has unexpectedly resulted, for the time being, in the decision to end forced recruitment.

In Spain, the movement launched full-scale civil disobedience in 1988 – about 20,000 total objectors between 1988 and 1999–, which was highly successful in politicising the latent demand for the abolition of conscription existing in that country. The results are there to be seen: the impossibility of guaranteeing a sufficient number of recruits in the short term – the rise of conscientious objection is exponential – has led the authorities to get rid of conscription; the year 2001 will see the last recruits. The key to this expansion of customary conscientious objection was the deficit of posts for substitutory service: so many obtained either total exemption or an extreme reduction in the time of service that, as a matter of fact, conscientious objection became a likely way out of all duty (Agirre et al., 1998). A major reason for this deficit is the late implementation of this substitutory service, introduced when the leading conscientious objection organisations had already engaged in nonviolent civil disobedience with the aim of abolishing conscription. In this context of mobilisation, inasmuch as the service was understood to be an instrument for legitimising the punishment of those total objectors, and, in the final instance, for safeguarding the continuity of conscription, most of the welfare organisations and the other bodies that usually employ objectors in the other countries declined to do so in Spain. Posterior sanctions reversed that non-cooperation but the number of posts remained insufficient to contain the situation and substitutory service in itself never managed to become institutionalised.

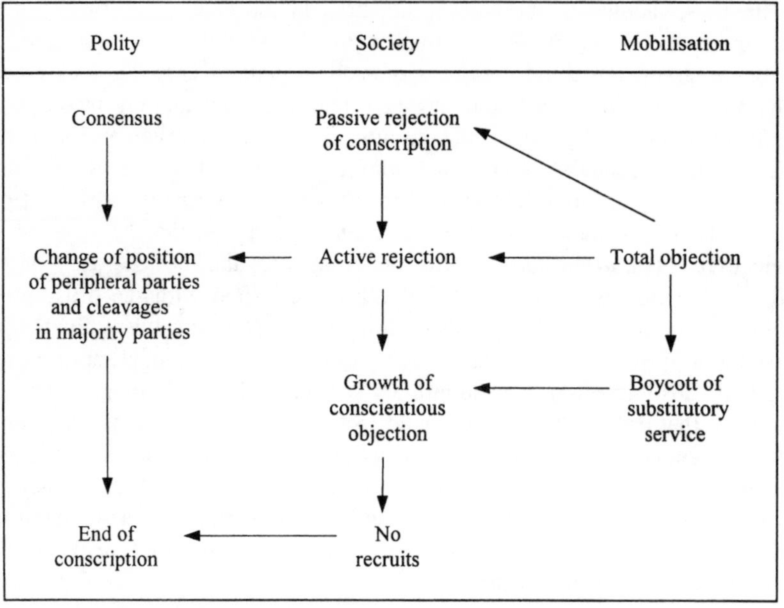

Fig. 4. The Process of the Abolition of Conscription in Spain.

We have stated above that social delegitimisation of conscription was a precondition for contention to develop successful in undermining the containment policies that ultimately safeguard forced recruitment. We have already mentioned that the European populations have become more and more distant from the armed forces in the last thirty years. However, until very recently **opinion polls** have shown regular support for conscription. This apparent inconsistency needs to be examined in detail. In this regard, it is highly revealing that in some European societies the favourable stance concerning conscription changed suddenly and radically in the 1990s following the decision by a neighbouring country to abolish conscription, or when an outstanding political leader distanced himself from the institutional defence of conscription that, without division, had predominated until then. France is a good example: opposition to conscription was 41% in 1994 (*Le Figaro*, 3 February 1995) and rose to 72% when a year and a half later Chirac announced his commitment to abolish it (*Le Monde*, 22 February 1996). Spain, where the peace movement was very active against conscription already in the 1980s, is the only country where disagreement with conscription became visible earlier.

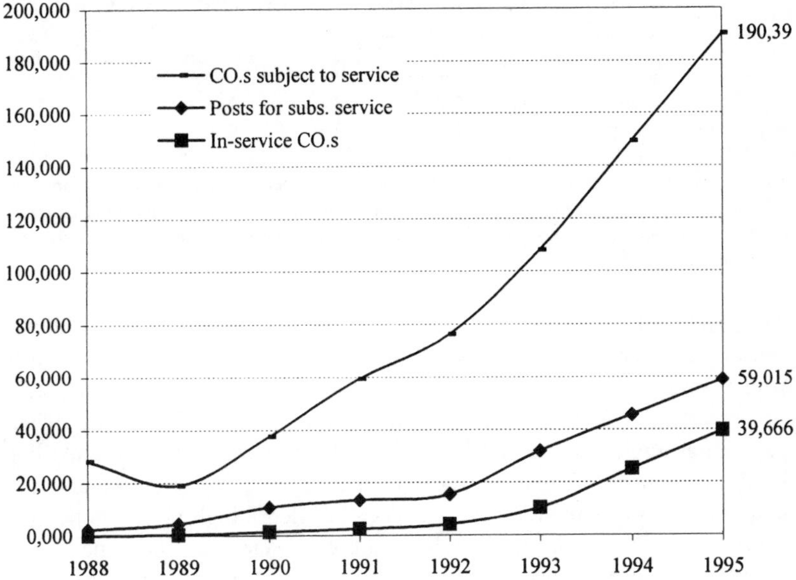

Fig. 5. Management of the System of Substitutory Service in Spain: Figures of those Awaiting Incorporation Before the Decision to Abolish Conscription.

Source: Oficina para la Prestación Social de los Objetores de Conciencia, Ministry of Justice. The difference between posts for substitutory service and serving conscientious objectors is partly explained by the 13-month duration of the service.

This change of positions, a sudden one indeed, leads us to believe that, for many years, public opinion was expressing what it thought to be possible rather than its own convictions. Its favourable position towards conscription derived from the certainty that military service was inevitable since, in fact, the issue was out of the question, no political actor disagreed and those who governed did not even consider – in public, obviously enough – the possibility of its abolition. We know today that they contemplated this and that studies were commissioned on the viability of such a measure. France serves as a good example (Chicken, 1996). Precisely because of that, the discourses legitimising compulsory military service can be regarded as another measure of social and political containment, consistent with the repression of those resisting recruitment and the penalisation of conscientious objection, with respect to any change that might affect military policy in general. The fact that those who transmitted these discourses were almost always representatives of parties in office lends strength to this assertion.

Table 6. Change of Public Opinion with Respect to Conscription.

	Spain	France	Netherlands	Italy	Belgium
Rejection of conscription in 1980s	63%	24%	No	34%	No
Rejection of conscription in 1990s	75%	72%	70%	53%	Yes

Sources: ECO, October 1985, and CIS n. 2,234, September 1997, concerning Spain; SOFRES, September 1986, and *Le Monde,* 22 February 1996, concerning France; Meulen and Manigart (1997, p. 322) concerning the Netherlands; Battistelli (1997) concerning Italy; and Thuysbaert (1994) concerning Belgium.

In spite of the official framing of the issue, we tend to think that conscription was primarily a means of the state for providing the armed forces with a certain quantity of troops. In these circumstances, the governments' main concern dealt with enforcing conscription, independently of what the population might think about it, its social legitimacy. Reason of state imposes itself on democratic reason. As a matter of fact, the security and defence policies typically integrate what has been labelled a high profile policy domain (Burstein, 1991). High profile policies are customarily decided upon by a very limited number of actors, in this case the civil and military authorities and the parties that usually hold government office (Hilsman et al., 1993; Pagnucco & Smith, 1993). Such a format of decision making, to a great extent immune to electoral consultation, results in a top-down style of government and makes it considerably difficult for other political actors to intervene or for there to be an effective control by civil society (Lindblom, 1980).[8] In this setting, only a very high profile disagreement in society or, more commonly, contention by non-governmental actors, can aspire to become influential and eventually affect the policy-making of conscription.

THE STANCE OF PUBLIC OPINION CONCERNING MILITARY INTERVENTION AND THE DEVELOPMENT OF RAPID ACTION FORCES

The recourse to all-volunteer forces for missions involving foreign intervention is partly, if not primarily, a result of the pressure exercised by public opinion, which has reiterated its opposition to the mobilisation of conscripts on such missions. There are experiences of resistance in this respect in the history of all countries, but it was following the World War II when, in the industrial advanced societies, it became decisive in terms of policy-making. Much of the society censured the dispatch of forced recruits on this type of mission during the Korean war and the Suez Canal campaign in the case of the United Kingdom

(Dietz & Stone, 1975), the Algerian war in the case of France (Martin, 1977), and the Korean and Vietnam wars in the case of the United States (Cohen, 1985; Janowitz, 1975), bringing about the decision to replace them with volunteer forces as a consequence. This same situation has arisen in the 1990s: in the cases of France, Spain, Italy or Germany at least, the social veto on the dispatch of conscript soldiers to the Gulf war led the authorities to strengthen the all-volunteer model. They found out that they could not rely on conscription for what was meant to be the central axis of future defence and foreign policies, military intervention, and they concurrently began to devise its abolition (Dandeker, 1994b; Huesca González, 1994; McKenna, 1997), just as happened in the 1960s and 1970s in the case of the United States (Downes, 1988). In summary, we can say that there is a sure, historical sequence, which relates foreign intervention missions and the process of decline of conscription in the following terms: intervention abroad → social criticism → abolition of conscription.

In this transition from territorial defence to intervention armed forces, where new structures should be secured before breaking with the old ones, the development of rapid action forces becomes one prerequisite for the abolition of conscription. Correspondingly, we can regard it as a proxy measure of change in this policy. As we observe in Table 7, in the mid-1990s the United Kingdom, France, Germany, Belgium, Holland, Italy and Germany: (a) had programmed the rapid reaction forces to form approximately a quarter of the total size of their armed forces; (b) they were assigning between 4 and 6% of their total military personnel to foreign intervention missions; and, except Germany, (c) they also had a prior tradition of those missions. Denmark and Norway, in spite of the resistance to participation in such missions by their soldiers, were very

Table 7. Projected Rapid Action Forces and their Maximum Deployment in Bosnia (SFOR) or Kosovo (KFOR).

	U.K.	Fra	Ger	Neth	Bel	Ita	Den	Nor	Spa	Por
Previous experience	Yes	Yes	No	Yes	Yes	Yes	No	No	No	No
Year of creation	–	1993	1993	1993	1993	1993	1994	1996	1995	1994
Projected no. of troops	60,000	60,000	54,000	15,000	10,000	30,000	–	–	–	–
% of total size	27%	24%	28%	25%	24%	16%	–	–	–	–
SFOR/KFOR	13,000	10,500	8,300	2,300	1,700	5,900	850	900	1,700	240
% of total volunteers	6.0%	4.6%	4.4%	4.0%	4.0%	4.2%	3.4%	3.1%	1.8%	0.8%
Summary Value	++	++	++	++	++	++	+	+		

Source for deployment: NATO web page.

close to the countries of the first group. Conversely, the armed forces of Spain and Portugal were still a long way behind: they had no programs in this respect and they were assigning fewer personnel to this type of force.

PROGRESSION TOWARDS THE ALL-VOLUNTEER ARMED FORCES

The central vector of the restructuring of the European armed forces, aside from the technological component and advances in the strategic field, is the replacement of conscripted soldiers by volunteer forces. This restructuring must be understood as a slow and progressive process that requires many years. In fact, the countries that today find themselves closest to the organisational model proposed by NATO are those that began restructuring thirty or forty years ago. The movements of resistance to recruitment were an important factor in this respect. At that time many armed forces started to resolutely strengthen the volunteer component and in the 1980s the armed forces of Denmark, Belgium, Germany, Holland, even France, responded to a greater or lesser extent to the mixed model, that is to say, conscription continued but they had a high percentage of volunteer soldiers, around 50–60%.

That progression once again accelerated in the 1990s. The generalised reduction of military service, on the one hand, and the social veto on the employment of conscripts in the new priority of foreign intervention missions, relaunched the drive to recruit volunteer forces. The evolution of the volunteer component in the 1990s has actually been a return journey: first the number of officers was reduced – Belgium, France and Italy are still in the process of doing this – and then new soldiers were recruited. At present, in any case, nearly all the countries have completed this journey or are very close to doing so, thanks

Table 8. Evolution of the Proportion of Volunteer Personnel Since 1970.

	1970	1980	1989	1999
United Kingdom	100%	100%	100%	100%
Denmark	32%	69%	70%	68%
Belgium		66%	64%	100%
Germany	40%	57%	58%	57%
Netherlands	30%	52%	57%	100%
France	35%	47%	48%	67%
Portugal		47%	44%	87%
Italy	15%	35%	32%	52%
Norway		29%	35%	47%
Spain	15%	24%	26%	45%

to the fact that they had, to a great extent, evolved towards the zero-draft model in the two previous decades. The changes that occurred in the 1990s could, in this context, be considered as a final adjustment associated with the overall reduction of personnel. On December 31st 1998 the United Kingdom, Holland, Belgium and France had carried out over 90% of their plans for entering the new millennium; only Italy and Spain were still a long way from this target.

Since these programs might still be readjusted in the future and there is in this respect a very evident tendency and commitment towards homogenisation within the European framework, we have set up an integrated zero-draft model in order to establish a comparative framework. The criterion for this zero-draft model is the figure of 3.9 military personnel for every 1,000 inhabitants, which is the arithmetical average of the targets in the United Kingdom, Belgium, Holland, France and Spain. In relation to this criterion, Belgium, France and Denmark were at the beginning of the 1990s in a fairly good situation to dispense with forced recruitment; the Netherlands, Germany, Portugal and Norway could also do so without too many complications; and Spain and Italy still continued to need compulsory military service in order to have sufficient military personnel in relation to their population size.

Amongst these countries, those that effectively decided to abolish conscription in the 1990s were Belgium, the Netherlands, France, Spain and Italy. At the time of decision-making, the Belgian armed forces were practically at 100% in volunteer troops and only had to cover the cases of expiry of contracts and retirement, the Netherlands were 15,000 soldiers short, France 50,000, Italy 78,000 and Spain 90,000. Thus, the change in the policy implied a minor effort for the first two countries, which have today almost accomplished the targets, and a greater effort for the others. If the rhythm of evolution between 1996 and 1999 were to be maintained, the French would reach their target in the year 2005, two years later than envisaged, the Italians

Table 9. Degree of Completion of the Recognisation Programs of the Volunteer Component.

	U.K.	**Neth**	**Bel**	**Fra**	**Ita**	**Spa**
Volunteer component in 1992	293,000	47,000	49,000	219,000	130,000	78,000
Volunteer component in 1998	217,000	57,000	43,000	229,000	140,000	96,000
Target no. of volunteers	225,000	60,000	40,000	251,000	200,000	150,000
(year)	(2002)	(2000)	(1996)	(2002)	(2008)	(2002)
Degree of completion	96%	95%	93%	91%	70%	64%

Table 10. Distance Relation to the Zero-draft Force Model (3.9 Servicemen for every 1,000 Inhabitants) at the Early 1990s and at Present.

	Bel	**Fra**	**Neth**	**U.K.**	**Den**	**Por**	**Nor**	**Spa**	**Ita**	**Ger**
Volunteer component in 1992	4.88	3.82	3.10	5.05	3.48	2.84	2.80	2.00	2.29	3.04
Zero-draft force	125%	98%	80%	130%	89%	73%	72%	51%	59%	78%
Volunteer component in 1998	4.21	3.89	3.65	3.62	3.19	3.12	2.71	2.44	2.43	2.31
Zero-draft force	108%	100%	94%	93%	82%	80%	70%	63%	62%	59%
Summary Value	++	++	++	++	+	+				

would reach it in the year 2016, six years later than planned, and the Spanish in the year 2014, twelve years later than programmed. At the beginning of 1999, the Spanish authorities decided to reduce the final target from 120,000 to 102,000; this advances its foreseeable completion to the year 2010.

These figures confirm that the abolition of compulsory military service in Italy and Spain was not a very convenient decision, at least from the point of view of the structure of their armed forces and the fulfilment of their defence programs. Another factor that lends weight to this evaluation is that the structure of recruitment of volunteer military personnel was already showing signs of exhaustion, that is to say, not enough volunteers were enlisting. The leaders of both countries were perfectly aware of this crisis – the statements made by the Italian president Romano Prodi (*Le Monde*, January 25, 1997) and the Spanish defence minister Julián García Vargas (*El País*, May 29, 1994) are good examples; indeed, they opted for a mixed force model and ruled out the abolition of conscription until the very end, when it became clear that the armed forces were being left without forced recruits.

The reform initiated in Spain and Italy is thus highly problematic, sufficient volunteer soldiers must be recruited in the most unfavourable conditions: decreasing levels of unemployment, poor levels of pay, armed forces that are institutional rather than occupational, a profound indifference of society with respect to the armed forces and, in the case of Spain, persistence of contention connected with military policies. In this country, in spite of a very intense recruitment campaign, the vacant posts already outnumber applicants. This reality has pushed the authorities to invest a greater effort in the recruitment of women and also to test the employment of natives from Latin America and the Magreb.

SUMMING UP

The ten variables analysed have enabled us to construct a model that explains governmental decisions concerning conscription at the turn of this century. The first conclusion offered by this study is that it is essential to understand this decision as the point of arrival of a process that started four decades ago. Although factors like the nuclearisation and technologisation of the armed forces played a certain role, in that process we have observed how democratic reason, understood as the alliance between a post-military society and the resistance mobilisations that have taken place in this period of time, has progressively set limits on the strategic usefulness of conscription to such a point that it has become, in some military and political contexts, an accessory, expendable institution (Buffotot, 1997). The progressive reduction of the length of military service or the veto on the employment of conscripts in military interventions abroad have been the two major axes of this limitation.

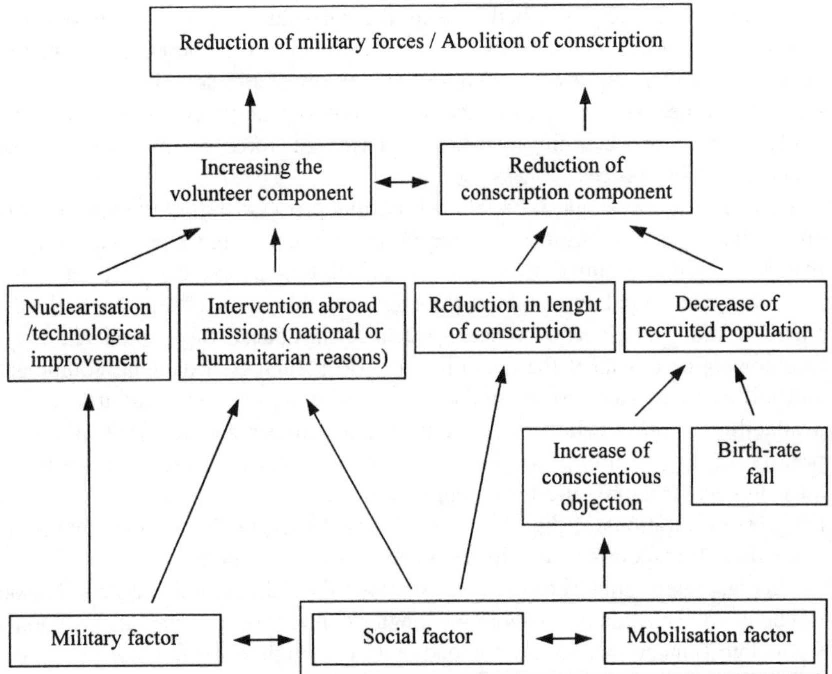

Fig. 6. Determinants in the Abolition of Conscription.

If the reason of state had prevailed or if conscription had really enjoyed the social legitimacy that the institutional actor publicly attributed it with, it would be conscripts and not volunteer soldiers who would participate in international missions today, enrolling in the armed forces for a minimum period of two years, just as they did in the 1950s and before; this would have been a choice far more convenient both in terms of costs and of liaison between the society and the armed forces. But the empowerment of democratic reason left no choice than to evolve towards the all-volunteer-force that is predominant today.

It was in the 1990s when the final reform for such a force took place. Along with it, the authorities in Belgium, the Netherlands, France, Spain and Italy have decided to do without forced recruitment, while Portugal is apparently moving in that direction as well. Conversely, Denmark, Norway and Germany are to retain conscription for the time being. This diversity does not dispute the evidence of a general trend towards the all-volunteer-force, it only verifies that the end of conscription is not a necessary consequence of that trend. All-volunteer force does not equate with zero-draft force: the core of the armed forces can be entirely all-volunteer and yet retain conscription; likewise, conscription can be abolished before the all-volunteer-force is developed. Besides, the end of conscription is not a technical or inconsequential matter either; instead, it implies a complete redefinition of the security and defence map of Europe. As a matter of fact, some countries are improving their assets while others are becoming weaker in terms of force as a result of that decision-making process.

There is not one single rationale behind this process: the intervening factors are manifold and, among them, domestic factors have a more profound impact than it is usually admitted. This is our conclusion after reviewing a pool of ten measures that suited this policy. At one end, the cases of the Netherlands, Belgium and, particularly, France – we have introduced the United Kingdom as a control case – meet the conditions of: (a) sufficient armament, equipment and military capacity, (b) a satisfactory level of military expenditure, (c) the availability of rapid action forces, adjusted in number and format to the new priority of intervention, (d) the existence of a consolidated and sufficient all-volunteer structure, and (e) an appropriate relation to population size and to the power aspirations of the *élite* which is usually expressed as "occupying the place that corresponds to us" in the scenario of power politics.

This fact lends support to the understanding that, although democratic reason lies behind the change in policy in the longterm, it is reason of state that accounts for its latest materialisation; in the end, with the single exceptions of Spain and Italy, the authorities, not the societies, have decided the pattern and timing of the conclusion of conscription. The French authorities have patronised a more convincing all-volunteer force in their determination to become the continental military power *par excellence* and ameliorate its foreign projection.[9] In Belgium and the Netherlands they have preferred to place themselves strategically at the centre of co-ordination of the new multinational forces, to a great extent dissolving their own national armed forces within the latter; formal statements like "it is what had to be done" concede, though vaguely, that some citizen influence has existed (Dumoulin, 1997; Meulen & Manigart, 1997).

The options taken by Denmark, Norway and Germany demonstrate that implementing of the zero-draft model is not a predestined pattern. The consideration that territorial defence continues to be its basic defence priority has led Norway to maintain conscription. Denmark has also preferred to maintain selective recruitment based on conscription – but very close to the all-volunteer force that it introduced in the 1970s. Germany is a case apart; it could have evolved towards the zero-draft force like neighbouring France, but in the 1990s it preferred to carry on with the system of conscription (Schmitz, 1994). Three basic reasons have been mentioned at this respect: (1) this is the most economical option, (2) substitutory service has become an essential element for maintaining the services of the welfare state (Kuhlmann & Lippert, 1993), and (3) the armed forces recruit 50% of their volunteer personnel from amongst the forced recruits.

Table 11. Variables that Determine the Abolition of Conscription in the Present Day.

	Fra	**U.K.**	**Neth**	**Bel**	**Por**	**Den**	**Nor**	**Ger**	**Ita**	**Spa**
Reason of state										
Technological improvement and nuclearisation	++	++	+	+			+	+		
Military expenditure	++	++	+	+	++		+	+		
Rapid action forces	++	++	++	++		+	+	++	++	
All-volunteer force	++	++	++	++	+	+				
Size of armed forces	++	+	+	+	+	++	++	+		
Democratic reason										
Public opinion	+		+	+					+	++
Resistance to despatch of armed forces	+		+	+				+	+	++
Mobilisation against recruitment									+	++
Deficit of forced recruitment								+	++	++
Difficulties in voluntary recruitment		+		+			+		++	++

The risk in this design is that the growth of conscientious objection or political pressure might finally force the abolition of compulsory military service and do with it its "defence plus welfare" device.

Finally, at the other end, Italy and, particularly, Spain have terminated with conscription, not because the authorities had long ago anticipated this and moved forward to the all-volunteer-force – both Spain and Italy began this adaptation in 1987 at a very slow pace – but because in the recent years: and (a) public opinion has expressed itself clearly against conscription; (b) it has opposed the despatch of conscripts on the military interventions that occurred in the 1990s; (c) there has been a weighty mobilisation in the form of civil disobedience; and (d) a very important increase in conscientious objection has produced a sustained deficit of forced recruits that has challenged the very existence of their conscription-based armed forces; it must be added that the current problems in voluntary recruitment concur with this state of affairs. In sum, democratic reason has prevailed over reason of state. In this respect, it is interesting to note that, although the timing of the decision and implementation of the end of conscription is exactly the same, the cases of Spain and France are at almost opposite extremes in the rationale behind that policy-process; the rest of the countries fall somewhere in between.

The answer to the question posed at the beginning of this article, whether the days of conscription are coming to an end, depends on each country rather than being an obvious yes. On the one hand, the trend toward the all-volunteer force, though certain and comprehensive, is being embraced to various degrees in the different countries. On the other hand, the completion of this process does not necessarily bring the end of conscription. As a result, it is difference that prevails behind this façade of a common trend. In sum, the answer to that question must be referred to a specific analysis of the vicissitudes of this policy of conscription in every country. The tension between democratic reason and reason of state is, in this setting, a very relevant one.

NOTES

1. The decision-making process for the Netherlands is outlined in Doel (1994), and Meulen and Manigart (1997); for Belgium in Thuysbaert (1994); for France in McKenna (1997), and Szarka (1996); for Germany in Manfrass-Sirjacques (1997), and Kuhlmann and Lippert (1993); for Portugal in Buffotot (1997); for Spain and Italy in Ajangiz (2000); and for the Scandinavian countries in Sørensen (2000).

2. Actually, public opinion today prefers that it should be the European Union rather than national governments that decides on foreign, security and defence policies (Manigart & Marlier, 1994).

3. The New Strategic Concept was first formulated at the NATO summit in Rome, November 1991. It has been agreed upon once more in the 1999 Washington summit.

4. For an up-to-date survey of conscription in the world, see Horeman et al. (1997), and Horeman and Stolwijk (1998).

5. Some years before, the seminal work of Janowitz (1960) had already argued that major changes were forthcoming. He also became a leading figure in the formation of the influential Seminar on *Armed Forces and Society*, which later gave birth to the periodical *Armed Forces and Society*. Its first issue was precisely dedicated to such decline.

6. Accounts of the peace movement of the 1980s and its position on conscription can be found in Agøy (1990a), Albesano (1993), Cattelain (1973), Della Porta and Rucht (1995), Duyvendak (1995), Gleditsch (1990), Ibarra (1992), Kiljunen and Väänänen (1987), Klandermans (1991), Koopmans (1995), Lyons (1999), Meulen and Manigart (1997), Moskos and Chambers (1993), Rochon (1988), Seegers (1993), Sørensen (1993), and Useem (1973).

7. The striking similarities among these three episodes of mobilisation in terms of political process, protest action, goals or discourse, which blur the alleged cross-time and cross-country social and cultural differences, suggest that the cultural change in our advanced societies is more a matter of quantity than quality.

8. To illustrate this, along with the issues of conscription or the military expense, we will mention the fact that the greater development of armaments during the Cold War was out of harmony with the social conviction that, contrary to the arguments of governments, there were no substantial threats to the territorial integrity of the Western European countries. Quite the opposite, the greatest threat perceived by public opinion in some European countries was represented by the aggressive military policy of their ally the United States (Ramos, 1987; Smet, 1990).

9. Declaration by Jacques Chirac (*Le Monde*, 24 February 1996).

PART III: REVIEW SYMPOSIUM SECTION

CONSENT, DISSENT, AND PATRIOTISM: A SUMMARY

Margaret Levi

With the *levee en masse* of 1793, France became the first country to introduce universal conscription and certainly the first country to justify such an imposition with democratic principles. Subsequently, many other democracies have also struggled to develop government capacity to compel conscription and to win citizen acceptance of some variant of compulsory military service. Through a series of comparative case studies drawn from six countries over 200 years, *Consent, Dissent and Patriotism* explores changes in the forms of military service in response to transformations in the state and to shifting citizen demands, concerns and power. As state building progresses, a wider range of military service policies become available to government. As the institutions and norms of democracy develop and change, so, too, do the conditions under which citizens will consent with or resist military service.

Democratic governments are able to elicit, legally and legitimately, both money and men from their populations. Conscription is just one of many ways democratic governments employ their immense power to tax. Often, there is tax evasion, draft evasion, and various other forms of disobedience and even outright resistance. Even so, it is remarkable the extent to which citizens acquiesce and even actively consent with the demands of governments, well beyond the point explicable by coercion. This is a puzzle for social scientists, particularly those who believe that individuals are self-interested, rational actors who calculate only the private, egoistic costs and benefits of possible choices. In this view the provision of collective goods would never justify quasi-voluntary tax payments; and the public benefits of a war could never exceed the cost of dying to an individual.

The Comparative Study of Conscription in the Armed Forces, Volume 20, pages 337–346.

ISBN: 0-7623-0836-2

The obvious response is that governments have solved the free rider problem by enhancing their capacity to monitor and enforce compliance. Yet, this leads to a second puzzle. However well elaborated and competent the state, however long its reach, successful implementation of democratic taxation requires legislative approval and a significant degree of quasi-voluntary compliance, compliance with a law when the actor chooses to comply but faces punishment if caught not complying (Levi, 1988, pp. 52–55). Few governments of any type can survive without a high degree of quasi-voluntary compliance if not active consent, and democratic governments cannot survive at all – at least not as democracies – if they totally ignore the preferences of the populace. Effective imposition of military, tax, and other political obligations depends on the willing compliance of large numbers of individuals who, albeit obligated to obey the laws and compelled to do so if necessary, comply because they choose to. Otherwise, both the political and economic costs of governance become too high.

Recognizing the need for a parsimonious but realistic account of the variation in compliance and consent with military service, I developed the model of contingent consent. Contingent consent is a citizen's decision to comply or volunteer in response to demands from a government only if she perceives government as trustworthy and she is satisfied other citizens are also engaging in ethical reciprocity by contributing or complying. The model of contingent consent (see Fig. 1) can account for when individuals will be compliant even when their individual material costs exceed their individual material benefits and even in the absence of strong ideological convictions that make costs totally irrelevant.

An assessment of costs and benefits also influences the decision to comply, but they are not the only consideration of contingent consenters. Even when short-term material self-interest would make free riding the individually best option, the contingently consenting citizen still prefers to cooperate.[1] However, if the costs of compliance become too high, then a cost-benefit calculation will probably trump other considerations.

Contingent consent encompasses quasi-voluntary compliance, but it is a broader category that also includes compliance and volunteering not required by law, e.g. voluntary military service or donations of blood. Contingent consent is reducible to neither material self-interest nor normative and moral considerations. Given a set of ethical standards about what makes a government just and what is involved in being fair, contingent consenters are those individuals who want to act ethically, who would like to contribute to the collective good, all things being equal, but who will do so only under certain contingencies: when convinced that government's commitments are credible

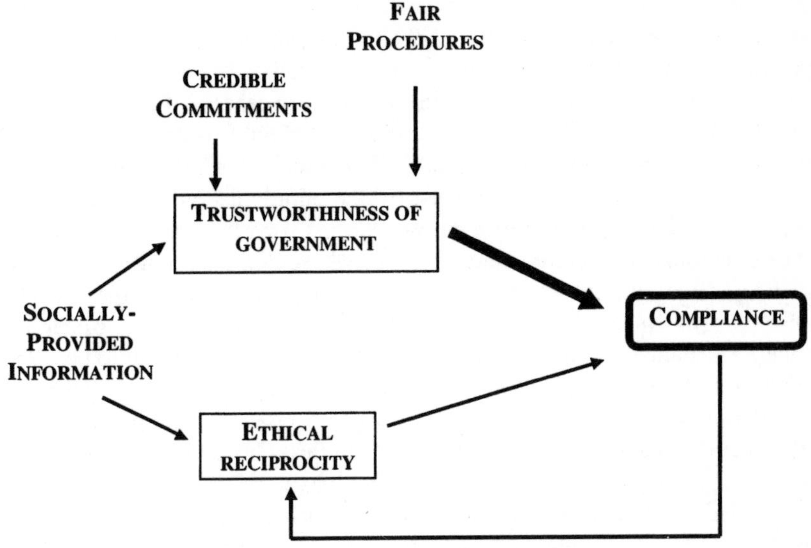

Fig. 1. The Model of Contingent Consent.

and its policies and implementation fair; and when convinced that other citizens are also doing their share.

The model of contingent consent implies a relationship that requires ongoing sustenance. It involves give and take, trust, and knowledge between those being asked to consent and those doing the asking. It is both fragile and resilient. Consent withers easily, but it sometimes withstands gale force winds. The strength of ethical reciprocity among citizens and their confidence and trust in government determine the durability of consent.

To understand the variation in contingent consent requires understanding the nature of the state, its history with various subgroups, and the norms that have developed among these subgroups. Part of the project of the book is elaborating the evolution of state capacity and democratic practices, the factors that make a government trustworthy. But equally important is documenting when and why groups within the polity feel excluded from representation in lawmaking, believe themselves discriminated against by the provisions or enforcement of the law, or encourage their members to resist certaingovernment imposed obligations. Trustworthy governments are those that have the capacity to enforce the laws but will do so fairly as well as competently. The more citizens believe their views were adequately represented in the policy making process and that the rules will be applied evenhandedly, the more they are likely to consent to and comply with the implementation of the law – in this case, the draft.

A generally trustworthy government is a necessary but insufficient condition for large-scale contingent consent. Although the perception of a trustworthy government might explain the choices of some individuals, its effects will be significantly enhanced by the additional presence of ethical reciprocity. Even when government appears trustworthy, the possibility of contingent consent is remote among groups whose dominant norm is "amoral familism" (Banfield, 1958), who defect from cooperative and reciprocal relationships. Among those who are ethically reciprocal but who are solidaristic in their resistance to government, contingent consent is also unlikely. The probability of an oppositional norm is greatest among those who believe that their demands and concerns are ignored in the decisionmaking process, even if they believe that government will treat them fairly once the law is imposed. The strength of the oppositional norm obviously grows with evidence of discrimination, which through the filter of socially-provided information, undermines their perception of government as trustworthy.

Thus, this book has two principal explananda: the institutionalization of policy in response to anticipated and actual citizen behavior; and conditions under which citizens give, refuse, or withdraw their consent. The central claims flow from the argument that citizen consent is contingent upon the perceived fairness of both government and other citizens. Most citizens of democracies, most of the time, are more likely to give their consent if they believe that government actors and other citizens are behaving fairly towards them. Fairness is a critical element in effective and democratic governance. Yet, the standards of fairness vary over time and place and among groups within the polity; so, too, do the democratic rules that will determine whose and which standards of fairness dominate. Consideration of how the standards of fairness emerge and change is an additional theme of the text.

Understanding the role of consent in governance advances democratic theory. Recognizing fairness as an important influence on behavior helps put to rest critiques of rational choice as a model that unrealistically assumes only narrowly self-interested actors. An equally important goal of the book, however, is the development of an empirical model that combines the microfoundations of methodological individualism with historically-grounded case studies of macro-events; it represents an analytic narrative (Bates, Greif, Levi, Rosenthal & Weingast, 1998).

Although governments often evoke political obligation as one basis for compliance, few issues permit observation of both the decisions that produce government policies and citizen choices in the face of government demands. Military service satisfies both criteria.[2] To join the army, to be a conscientious objector, to resist the draft are publicly recorded behaviors. The data may be messy, but the data on who pays or evades taxes is even more difficult to obtain and often even more suspect. Moreover, military service is an important obligation of democratic citizenship, at least male citizenship. Noncompliance with this obligation has implications for the efficacy of government. Although each act of noncompliance may have a singular motivation, an ensemble can constitute a political statement and, on occasion, an actual rebellion.

There are further justifications for the investigation of military service. In recent years, scholars attempting to develop a more adequate theory of the state have given considerable attention to the relationship between states and citizens in regards to social welfare and taxation. Variations in the form of the military obligation and the institutions that enforce this obligation have received some descriptive but far too little theoretical attention. Yet, military service is demonstrably as important an aspect of the state-citizen relationship as any that exists. There has not, of course, been total neglect. There is a growing literature that considers variation in military formats over time and among states as a means to appreciate their development and change (e.g Finer, 1975; Janowitz, 1980; Giddens, 1985, esp. Ch. 8 and 9; Mann, 1986 *passim* and, 1993 *passim*; Birnbaum, 1988; Gillis (Ed.), 1989; Tilly, 1990; Hooks & McLauclan, 1992; Downing, 1992; van Holde, 1993; Thomson, 1994; Rowe, 1999; and Katznelson forthcoming). But there has been little systematic investigation of how governments induce citizens to accept military service, even in important works like that of Huntington (1957) or Enloe (1980).

The study of military service contributes to the construction of a more satisfactory theory of the state than is currently available, but it also illuminates what it means to be a liberal and democratic state (see Cohen, 1985; Silver, 1994). Debates over the introduction of obligatory military service in democracies rehearse themes of ennobling self-sacrifice, nationalism, and the superiority of the needs of the state to the rights of the individual, on the one hand, and of the nature of full citizenship, fears of standing armies, and the superiority of the rights of the individual to the needs of the state, on the other. Military service is one of the central dilemmas for the liberal social contract as initially formulated by Thomas Hobbes (1985[1651]). It is to protect one's life that an individual agrees to submit to the regulations of states. The demand by government that a young man potentially give up his life for his country puts a tension at the heart of political life, a tension Hobbes recognizes but does not satisfactorily resolve.

The issues of consent, fairness, and obligation are clearly and unquestionably present in the institutions of military service in liberal democracies. Conscription is possible only with some form of permission by the citizenry. At the least, conscription, like taxation, demands representation. To what extent democratic conscription actually rests on the more exacting standard of consent is one of the empirical – and theoretical – questions at the heart of this book.

Using a simple rational choice model and comparative statics, I derive a series of hypotheses concerning the conditions for state introduction of universal conscription as opposed to another military format and for the variation in compliance. I then evaluate the plausibility of these hypotheses through a series of case studies. Cases drawn from six countries over the past two hundred years provide the illustrative material. The countries are the United States, Great Britain, Australia, Canada, New Zealand and France. Five are Anglo-Saxon democracies that share a political tradition affirming local rights, setting constraints on state incursions on those rights, and making conscription for a national military the exception rather than the rule. Even so, there are interesting differences among the countries that may account for differences in both government demands and citizen responses: in the granting and exercise of suffrage; the organization of both government and parties; the nature of the cleavages that are politically salient.

France makes an interesting contrast, permitting exploration of the effect of underlying legal and state traditions. The Napoleonic Code, *etatism*, and the numerous French experiments with forms of governance distinguish France from the common law, more decentralized, and relatively more stable regimes of Anglo-Saxon countries. To study military service in democracies and not include France would be indefensible. Modern conscription has been an aspect of French national life since the Revolution. France, like Britain, is an old country with centuries of experience with military service that was more impressment than civic obligation. To establish an army of citizens required first the destruction of the army of the king and the lord. France was the first of the democracies to transform the very meaning as well as institutions of conscription; by the twentieth century, military obligation was a rite of passage to citizenship for young French males. Its purpose was as much nation-building as nation-protecting. This makes Jacques Chirac's abolition of military service all the more interesting.

The choice of case studies among these countries reflects three criteria. The first criterion is the availability of comparable information over time or across countries to provide the basis for comparisons based on variations in the independent variable. All of the case studies consider either several countries or compare groups within a country, and all compare behavior at different points in time. The second is the extent to which it is possible to investigate competing explanations. Meeting these two criteria means that these are not necessarily the best of all cases in the best of all possible worlds. Unfortunately, the world with which a social scientist has to deal is far from perfect. There are few natural experiments and, in this instance, none.

The third criterion reflects the issues the case raises for the model. All of the case studies emphasize government design of military service institutions against a backdrop of variation in likely contingent consent. However, the first three focus on policy making and the precipitants to reform of military service policy and the last two on the three possible citizen choices in relation to the institutions that government develops: (1) to enlist in the military in the absence of conscription; (2) to protest or support the introduction of conscription; and (3) when conscripted, to comply or conscientiously object.

The cases vary government demand for troops due to the needs of defense and war and the extent of citizen compliance. The matrix of case studies (see Table 1) lays out where each of the cases fit.

There are several examples for most cells, and only one cell (high demand, medium compliance) is null. Moreover, in each cell, there is significant variation in the military service policies, defined as voluntary service, obligatory service with socially discriminatory exemptions, and obligatory service with relatively impartial exemptions.

The outline of the book is as follows. After a brief introduction, chapter 2 lays out the model of contingent consent. Chapter 3 documents the nineteenth century of history of military service in all six countries. Chapter 4 traces the transformation of socially selective exemptions to a policy of more impartial exemptions. The major empirical example is the elimination of various forms of "buying out" of the draft in France and the United States. Chapter 5 is a broad comparison of the introduction of conscription in the five Anglo-Saxon democracies of the U.K., U.S., Canada, Australia, and New Zealand during World War I. The focus is on the variation in the timing of and in the level of opposition to universal male conscription. This chapter considers the ways in which governments achieve the construction of contingent consent and the circumstances that lead citizens to vote against conscription, protest it, or otherwise refuse to give their consent.

The next two chapters analyze the behavior of citizens in response to wartime government requests for volunteers and demands for conscripts. Chapter 6 analyzes francophone opposition to and anglophone support of conscription in Canada during both world wars. Why did individuals from one group tend to refuse their behavioral consent and why did those from the other tend to give

Table 1. The Matrix of Case Studies.

	Citizen Compliance		
Government Demands	High	Medium	Low
high	WWI U.S. (P3) U.K. (P2) France (P3) New Zealand (P3) anglophone Canada (P3) WWII U.S. (P3) France (P3) anglophone Canada (P1–P3)	Napoleonic Wars (P2) U.S. Civil War (P2) WWI Australia (P1) WWII Australia (P1)	WWI francophone Canada (P3) Catholic Irish (P2) WWII francophone Canada (P1–P3)
medium		19th century wars, France (P2–P3)	New Zealand Wars (P1) 19th century wars, Britain (P1)
low	Vietnam France (P3)	Vietnam U.S. (P2) Australia (P3)	19th century U.S. (P2) 19th century Canada (P3) 19th century Australia (P1)

P1 = preference for voluntary enlisments.
P2 = preference for exemptions by socially discriminatory devices.
P3 = preference for selective service.

theirs? Chapter 7 considers the variation in reliance on conscientious objection over time as a form of refusing consent in the US, Australia, and France. Here the explicit contrast is between a model derived from contingent consent and one that privileges ideology. Chapter 8 presents the implications of my empirical findings for democratic theory and institutional design.

The case studies do not cover the whole range of possible choices by citizens or decisions by legislators. I was unable, for example, to study draft evasion because of the impossibility of sorting out exemptions granted for actual health versus manufactured health problems, for real versus paper marriages, etc. Nor do I deal with desertion, about which there is data; I confined my researches to choices around joining military service rather than the choices made once a man puts on a uniform. These cases are far from natural experiments, but the findings generally prove consistent with the model. The diversity in time, place, and variables adds further plausibility to my explanations of institutional change in military formats and variation in compliance and consent with military service.

This book suggests that there is unquestionably an historical and political context to preferences about conscription, and it also suggests that the plurality of preferences and interests democratic institutions permit is a palliative against allowing alternatives to remain unthinkable or particularistic for too long. First, not all citizens perceive government the same way. Not only are there individual variations in beliefs, information, economic incentives, ideologies, and other factors that influence compliance, there are also systematic variations by groups that have distinct experiences with the fairness of government or distinct differences in their standards of fairness. Second, not all citizens use the same strategies to achieve their ends. Some citizens will refuse their consent to the extent possible. Others will try to impose their will on the rest. There are also important instances where members of the group attempt to demonstrate even greater commitment to the state than the majority, perhaps as a way to signal loyalty and to win improved rights for their group within society.[3] Blacks and Nisei Japanese in the United States, the Druse in Israel, and the Sikhs in India are among the most notable instances. The effect of diverse strategies is, over time, a multitude of pressure points on democratic institutions to change and respond.

The existence of contingent consent provides stability for democracies. The process of establishing – or reestablishing – the conditions for contingent consent is a source of democratic change. The negotiation of concessions and commitments by government actors to citizens contributes to the transformation. Equally important is the periodic reevaluation of what constitutes a fair policy. The norms of fairness citizens and governments apply are a product of experience with previous practices, but they also may emerge from new ideologies that increase citizen pressure for reform. As standards of fairness change, so, too, do the institutions that demand consent.

The model of contingent consent should be able to explain (and predict) the general pattern of compliance within a society. It cannot, however, offer an account of individual motivation. It is an explanation of the aggregate, not the particular. Yet it is an explanation fundamentally grounded in a conception of citizens as ethically constituted rational actors. Democracies depend on citizens who have an ethical commitment to comply with the demands of their governments. Democracies equally depend on citizens who are rational in the pursuit of their self-interest "rightly understood". When ethics and rationality contradict each other, the result is the loss of self that makes possible either extreme nationalism and fascism or opportunistic disrespect of others. The model of contingent consent offers a perspective on how these two requirements of democratic citizens reinforce each other. Trustworthy and responsive government and citizens concerned with promotion of their individual ends within a context of ethical reciprocity are the foundational elements of democracy – rightly understood.

NOTES

1. I am purposely avoiding the debate about whether such actors are "quasi-rational" (Thaler, 1991).

2. Thus, once again I find myself studying armed young men in uniforms. My dissertation and first book (1977) was on police unions. My husband notes that *Of Rule and Revenue* was a study of old men in uniform.

3. Petersen (1989) offers the best available explanation of this phenomenon, but also see Enloe (1980).

STATE THEORY, HISTORICAL SOCIOLOGY AND THE CHALLENGE OF THE INTERNATIONAL

John M. Hobson

I was very pleased to receive a review copy of Margaret Levi's new book, *Consent, Dissent and Patriotism (CDP)*, not least because I was particularly impressed by her 1988 book, *Of Rule and Revenue (ORR)*. Her new book echoes the hallmarks of her previous work: it is very clearly expressed and leaves the reader with no doubt as to what her main argument comprises (something which is sadly all too-often not the case with many books); is well researched; covers a range of case studies; and develops an important argument – as far as it goes.

Being involved in a journal debate is no easy thing, especially for the author who is subject to critical review. I wrote a piece a few years ago which was subject to three critical reviews. Only one of the reviews critically engaged with my piece. The other two proceeded to lay out an entirely different agenda to the one that I had stipulated, leaving me with only a very limited target to respond to. I mention this initially because I will in fact at the end of my piece, call for a research agenda that is meant to *complement* the approach developed by Levi. And I think it important to note from the outset that while I have a few problems with some of what Levi has argued, I am however, generally sympathetic with the central arguments that she has developed in both *CDP* as well as *ORR*. Before I begin discussion of her new book, it would be useful to lay out the core propositions of her earlier book, as well as point to what I believe are its strengths. This is useful for contextualising the discussion of *CDP*.

The Comparative Study of Conscription in the Armed Forces, Volume 20, pages 347–359.

ISBN: 0-7623-0836-2

In *ORR,* Levi sets out to produce a theory of the state and a historical sociology of taxation. This came at a particularly apposite time, given that these areas were receiving renewed attention from a number of historical sociologists – mostly working from within the neo-Weberian inspired tradition. As is well-known, these included the writings of Theda Skocpol (1979), Michael Mann (1986, 1988), Randall Collins (1986), John Brewer (1989) and, not least, Charles Tilly (1990), all of whom developed the arguments made by earlier writers on taxation such as Rudolf Braun (1975), Gabriel Ardant (1975), Fritz-Karl Mann (1943) and Joseph Schumpeter (1954), in addition to building on the theory of the state laid out by earlier writers such as Max Weber (1978), Otto Hintze (1975) and Norbert Elias (1994). This research was interesting above all because it drew connections between the international realm (usually in the form of warfare and military costs), the state, and state-society relations, thereby implicitly laying the groundwork for a synthesis of Historical Sociology and International Relations (IR). This also enabled the development of what I call a 'neo-integrationist' theory,[1] which refuses to reify one particular spatial plane within an explanatory model, and seeks to produce a sociological analysis that combines all three spatial arenas: the international, national and sub-national. Such works were also important in that they enabled the development of a fresh theory of the state – 'fresh' within the discipline of Historical Sociology that is, though arguably less so within International Relations, given that such writers often relied on a traditional neorealist definition of the international.[2] In the process, such historical sociologists, though they were largely unaware of it at the time, were implicitly sketching a new agenda, which crosses Historical Sociology with International Relations. And unbeknown to them, moves were afoot within the discipline of IR to draw explicitly upon such historical sociological works in order to rethink IR. I shall return to this later in more detail.

The general argument made in *ORR* is captured in Levi's 'theory of predatory rule', which stipulates that rulers 'maximise revenue to the state, but not as they please. They maximise subject to the constraints of their relative bargaining power vis-à-vis agents and constituents, their transaction costs, and their discount rates' (Levi, 1988, p. 10). At first sight, given her claim that rulers are predatory 'in that they always try to set the terms of trade that maximise their personal objectives, which . . . [requires] them to maximise state revenues', it might seem that she is developing a theory of the pure autonomous state. Such an approach would appear congruent with a statist model (found typically in Skocpol's theory of state autonomy) or from within IR a realist, or more accurately, a neorealist model. But Levi provides a much more subtle analysis of the state by embedding it within the constraints of society (though she also stipulates various institutional constraints).

Her specific claim is that tax revenue extraction can be maximised only when a sufficient dose of what she calls 'quasi-voluntary compliance' exists. For the purpose of this present review, it is important to note that she adds the adjective 'quasi', because while revenue extraction can be maximised when there is voluntary compliance, it is nevertheless the case that it is always *quasi*-voluntary in nature because ultimately coercion can be deployed by the state against recalcitrant tax-payers. The key to the argument is that such compliance rests on reciprocity: 'It is a contingent strategy in which individual taxpayers are more likely to cooperate if they have reasonable expectations that both rulers and other taxpayers will also cooperate' (Levi, 1988, p. 69). In her historical work she convincingly argues that the existence of a liberal parliamentary regime in England was one of the most important factors in that state's highly effective system of fiscal extraction (Levi, 1988, Chs. 4–5). The presence of a parliament was crucial in that it forced rulers to negotiate with key social constituents, which ultimately decreased the costs of revenue extraction and enabled a high yield to the state. Logically, for this argument to have salience, we would predict that absolutist France, where such parliamentary institutions were relatively under-developed, would extract lower amounts of taxation. In Chapter 4, she argues convincingly that this was indeed the case, as others have attempted to demonstrate (e.g. Brewer, 1989; Mann, 1993; Weiss & Hobson, 1995, Ch. 4).

There are several points that I find interesting and important about this analysis; first is her suggestion that liberal parliamentary states are paradoxically more effective in ruling or enhancing their governing capacity than are their authoritarian or absolutist counterparts. This stands the usual argument on its head: authoritarian or autocratic states might be high in terms of 'despotic power', but paradoxically, they are much weaker in terms of governing capacity precisely because they are unable to rule *through* or *with* society (see especially Mann, 1993). Indeed, partly under the influence of *ORR*, I developed a similar argument comparing liberal Britain, autocratic Russia and authoritarian Germany for the years 1870–1918 in a recent book (Hobson, 1997). I argued that the British state's deep embeddedness throughout society meant that it was better able to extract taxation during times of war than its authoritarian and autocratic counterparts, which were either completely isolated from society (Tsarist Russia) or only partially embedded (Imperial Germany).[3] Britain's superior fiscal yield was secured by its ability to extract the income tax, which in turn was only possible when the state was widely or deeply embedded within society. By contrast, Germany and Russia relied on indirect taxes (which is why they chose tariff protectionism as opposed to Britain's policy of free trade), which in turn, had a far inferior fiscal yield. This gave Britain a relative advantage in the First World War.

Secondly, Levi's theory of the state is important above all because it goes beyond the antinomies of prevailing state theory. Broadly speaking, sociological liberals and Marxists tend to conceive a zero-sum contest between state elites and key social actors in domestic society. Both theories tend to treat the state residually, reducing it to its core constituents – the dominant class (Marxism) or individuals (liberalism); and of course, even those Marxists who have pushed the 'relative autonomy' argument as far as it will go, merely reduce the state to the 'long run' needs of the dominant class, or to the functional requrements of the mode of production 'in the last instance' (see Hobson, 2000, Chs. 3–4). At the other extreme are what I call 'first-wave' neo-Weberians – e.g. Skocpol – as well as neorealists, who tend to exaggerate the domestic autonomy of the state, and effectively refuse to accord non-state actors/structures any significant causal power (Hobson, 2000, Ch. 6). Levi's model goes beyond this 'binary' framework and in effect, treats states and social forces as partially autonomous, such that the state cannot be reduced to social actors' needs, nor can social actors be reduced to the state. This has much in common with what I have called the 'second-wave' of neo-Weberian sociological state theory (see Hobson, 2000, pp. 192–213). This approach lies at base of both *ORR* and *CDP*. The paradox here is that states can enhance their governing capacity (i.e. revenue-extraction) when they are embedded within social actors.

The third important aspect of her model lies with the fact that she integrates the three spatial planes – the international, national and sub-national – together into one seamless whole. Thus she hypothesises that changes in the format of war-making lead to an increased fiscal impact upon rulers' tax policies and their relationship with domestic social actors (cf. Finer, 1975; Poggi, 1978; Mann, 1986; Tilly, 1990; Elias, 1994). A fundamental argument in *ORR* is that external pressures leading to rising military costs enable rulers to convince constituents to yield more tax revenues (Levi, 1988, pp. 96, 105–108, 123, Ch. 7). While she tends to neglect the social dimensions of the international realm, preferring to equate it with a realm of military conflict, nevertheless the integration of the international into her theory certainly improves upon traditional 'endogenous' or 'internalist' accounts. This also enables an 'outside-in' approach (or what the IR theorist Kenneth Waltz (1959) calls a 'third-image' analysis),[4] which simultaneously complements her 'inside-out' approach (i.e. a 'second image' analysis), where she pays specific attention to domestic state-society relations in the shaping of the international realm. This makes for a rich historical sociological analysis both with respect to its 'integrationist' nature as well as its ability to unpack the 'black-box' of the state, and thereby open up the state-society relationship to a deep and sustained analysis. As I shall argue below, such ingredients of her model provide an important lynchpin for developing an historical sociology of IR as well as an IR of historical sociology.

Turning to her recent book (*CDP*), although Levi draws heavily from the earlier analysis she nevertheless seeks to build on that argument. Here she turns her attention away from taxation and focuses instead on the effectiveness of states' conscription policies. In particular, she develops a model of what she calls 'contingent consent'. It encompasses 'quasi-voluntary compliance' in that actors can face punishment by the state should they not comply. But it goes beyond this in that it also incorporates *volunteering which is not required by law*. This, therefore, makes conscription policy an excellent case study in determining the degree of 'voluntary compliance' that citizens offer their state. The main area of overlap between the two books lies with the central argument deployed: that social actors or individuals choose to comply and engage in conscription (or tax-payment) to the extent that they perceive that the government is trustworthy and fair. There are other factors that are important too. Taxpayers become increasingly 'recalcitrant' when others are perceived to be avoiding their fair share of taxation, no less than individuals become increasingly resistant to joining the draft should a significant number of others manage to successfully avoid it. Thus in both cases the condition of 'ethical reciprocity' must hold (Levi, 1997, Chs. 2, 8). So as with her analysis of taxation, she argues for a 'bargaining model': the more the state is embedded within society such that it meets prevailing standards of fairness, the more citizens are willing to be conscripted in times of war.

While I find her various hypotheses attractive, as I hope should be apparent by now, I do, however, find a number of problems. The most obvious problem lies with her choice of case studies, all of which were carefully chosen on the grounds that they are liberal-democratic states. Given her central claim that 'the more democratic the regime and the more universalistic its laws, the more likely it is that citizens will comply with a policy of universal conscription' (Levi, 1997, p. 35), it would surely be necessary to enquire into the ability of authoritarian states to manage such a universal conscription policy. Paradoxically, she notes correctly that the deepening or broadening of French conscription after 1870 was a function of the state's desire to emulate the Prussian conscription policy (Levi, 1997, pp. 91–92, 207). This is interesting for two reasons. First, because it brings in an 'international' factor into the analysis – military pressures emanating within the inter-state system. Such a conceptual variable is surprisingly absent from her analysis, given her exclusive focus on domestic state-society relations (of which more below); surprising, that is, because *ORR* sought to include the international as conditioning state policy, and also because

CDP engages with a state's military policy. Second, it is interesting because, of course, Prussia/Germany was an authoritarian state, and yet it was able to bring in a universal conscription policy. This potentially brings her whole 'democratic state' thesis into jeopardy. She rebuts this on p. 106, were she argues that,

> later in the nineteenth century [i.e. after 1870] Prussia . . . reverted . . . back toward privileging the aristocracy and wealthy . . . The commitment to universalism and the recognition of the importance of contingent consent that motivated the Prussian reformers could not be sustained without democratic institutions.

While this *might* answer this particular problem at least with respect to Prussia/Germany, it is nevertheless a surprisingly thin response to such an important challenge at a more general level – not simply on empirical grounds, but especially on conceptual grounds.

It would surely be important, if not imperative, to demonstrate that authoritarian states are unable to produce universal conscription policies (i.e, the null hypothesis). This would require a discussion of conscription policy in several authoritarian states. Ideally this would involve more than one chapter, though arguably, several cases could be dealt with in one chapter. But without even one chapter on non-democratic cases, she leaves herself open to the charge that she has skewed her choice of cases, and in the process skewed the argument. Authoritarian states have been able to achieve universal conscription outside times of war. *If* this has entailed a degree of contingent compliance/consent, then it is likely that the roots might lie in ideological or normative factors such as the strength of nationalism, and/or the degree to which militaristic norms are widely diffused throughout society. This would present a strong challenge to her 'democratic state' thesis, and would also pose a challenge to her rational choice methodology, which downplays the causal significance, or autonomy, of norms and ideas. Of course, it could be replied that to the extent that universal conscription policy has been effectively deployed in authoritarian states, it has only been so because it has been *coercively* managed by the state, thereby implying that such policies are not a function of 'contingent consent'. But we cannot know this unless authoritarian conscription policies are subjected to sufficiently detailed analysis. And whatever the reply, it is surely vital to consider in some detail such cases, even if it is only to secure her central hypothesis.

My other criticisms are less direct and are both concerned with what I see as a problem of 'narrow focus'. Not only has Levi narrowed the focus to a discussion of *liberal-democratic* states, but she has also narrowed the focus only to cases of *wartime* conscription policy. I have argued elsewhere that had

Britain been able to deploy conscription prior to the First World War, she might have been able to indefinitely deter Germany from going to war (Hobson, 1993). Of course, the ability of the British state to achieve this was highly circumscribed by the prevailing norms of society – such a policy would have been seen as too militaristic and in all likelihood would not have been successfully instigated. Levi herself notes from the outset that it is only in wartime that success viz universal conscription can be achieved – though arguably she would need to explain why liberal-democratic states have for the most part been unable to secure conscription outside of war-time, even if it is only to secure her central hypothesis. It could be hypothesised that in general, authoritarian states tend to rely on more militaristic societal norms compared to their liberal-democratic counterparts. Again, as with the point made above, such an analysis might operationalise a normative or constructivist approach, which would of course, offend Levi's materialism. Either way though, this omission necessarily leads to a narrowing focus, which tells us only about conscription during wartime in liberal-democratic states. We thus learn less about conscription policy than one might initially expect.

Moreover, as she herself notes, various liberal-democratic states had problems with conscription policy during the Vietnam War (most notably Australia and the U.S.). One of the reasons that Gough Whitlam was able to return the Australian Labor Party to power in 1972 was his decision to withdraw the troops from Vietnam, given the considerable domestic opposition to sending conscripts overseas. Although she notes the problem here, as discussed in Chapter 7, she never actually answers the question as to why resistance developed, and why there was from the outset of the war resistance to sending Australian conscripts abroad. Instead she comes at the problem in terms of the desire by individuals to rationally engage in conscientious objection. This diverts attention away from the problem that led to the increasing resistance to conscription as the war progressed. Undoubtedly the problem was concerned with the issue or legitimacy of the Vietnam War. And yet the issue of the *legitimacy* of a war itself is not addressed in her formal model, which is restricted to the issue of a state's relationship with its population. Arguably a full account would also look at the *international* factors that surround a particular war as well as the perceptions that a population have of it. It could be hypothesised that as the war progressed it became increasingly harder to recruit Australian conscripts to send to Vietnam because, with the exception of the notion of 'forward defence', the national interest was not directly threatened. Moreover, in the various polls conducted by Morgan Gallup, a clear majority of the Australian population were against sending conscripts to fight in Vietnam even at the outset of the war (Goot & Tiffen, 1983). Similarly, in the U.S., it could equally be hypothesised that there was less resistance to the draft during the Second World War than there was in Vietnam, again because the territorial integrity of the state in the latter case was not threatened. Moreover, from the specific angle that Levi comes at this problem, it could surely be hypothesised that the costs of conscientious objection would decrease in those wars where the national interest is not at stake – a point to which she alludes in the final chapter (Levi, 1997, p. 208). This suggests that the actual war itself will have an impact upon the success of the conscription policy, quite independently of the degree of trustworthiness that the populace may have for the government at the time; and yet to reiterate, no sustained analysis is forthcoming. So as to prevent any possible confusion over the point being made here – I am *not* saying that issues connected with contingent consent are not important. I am merely suggesting that international factors concerning the war itself might *also* be factored into the model. This could not only enrich her model but also broaden it into areas concerning International Relations expertise and theory.

The second area of 'narrowing' – which follows on from the previous point – is one that my own work is chiefly concerned with: namely to go beyond the limits of *pure* IR and *pure* Historical Sociology, both of which are, in my opinion, inadequate on their own. I was pleased to receive Levi's new book, not simply because I had been impressed by the arguments deployed in *ORR*, but also because her work potentially stands at the interface of Historical Sociology and IR. In *ORR* she was sensitive to changes at the international level (in this case military changes), and how these interfaced with state policies and changing state-society relations (as was noted earlier). This focus has been surprisingly absent in the recent book, as noted. With the receding of the international from view, her analysis narrows to one that is centrally concerned to tease out specific state-society relations that lie at base of universal conscription policy during war-time. I have no *direct* problem with this – this is of course her choice and it is one that is, I believe, important in its own right. And in any case, no author should be criticised for not writing what one particular reviewer would like to have read! But in another sense, a harsh criticism could be that she has not really added much to her original arguments laid out in *ORR,* and has done little to push the theoretical frontier of her earlier work, nor advance Historical Sociology more generally by engaging in some kind of dialogue with International Relations. This, I believe, is a shame, because Levi is one of the main historical sociologists, who, along with Michael Mann, Anthony Giddens and Randall Collins, could develop such a broader analysis. The final section elaborates on why historical sociologists should consider entering into a dialogue with IR theorists.

BEYOND A BOUNDARY? THE CHALLENGE TO SYNTHESISE HISTORICAL SOCIOLOGY AND INTERNATIONAL RELATIONS THEORY

At the time when Levi's *ORR* first appeared, there was an implicit movement developing within Historical Sociology that was working its way towards the discipline of International Relations. As already noted Mann, Tilly, Giddens, Collins as well as Levi were, albeit unwittingly, pushing the boundary of Historical Sociology outwards towards IR. And as also noted, unbeknown to them at the time, a number of IR scholars were seeking to expand the boundary of IR towards HS (eg. Ruggie, 1983; Cox, 1986; Halliday, 1987); a movement that has since begun to gain considerable momentum (e.g. Watson, 1992; Spruyt, 1994; Halliday, 1994; Thomson, 1994; Frank & Gills, 1996; Hobson, 1997, 1998; Linklater, 1998; Hobden, 1998; Hall, 1998; Ruggie, 1998; Reus-Smit, 1999; Amoore et al., 2000; Seabrooke, 2001). IR scholars became paradoxically interested in HS precisely because it appeared to offer a rich alternative to the parsimonious, static, structuralist and 'systemic' theorising associated with mainstream IR theory – neoliberal institutionalism and Waltzian neorealism in particular; 'paradoxically' because Skocpol, Tilly and others in fact utilised a neorealist definition of the international. HS appeared to offer an avenue out of the impasse by bringing 'state-society relations', 'agency', 'history' and 'change' back on to the IR research agenda. I have argued elsewhere that neither discipline can sensibly or effectively operate in isolation of the other. Neither discipline is 'self-constituting' precisely because the international and domestic realms are mutually entwined (Hobson, 1997, 1998). As soon as historical sociologists invoke the term 'international', as did Mann, Tilly, Skocpol, Collins and Levi, so it became imperative to engage with IR theory. Ironically, unbeknown to such historical sociological writers at the time, just when IR scholars were beginning to look to HS, such sociological writers were invoking a realist – or more accurately a neorealist – analysis of the international, as others have also noted (Scholte, 1993, pp. 23, 96, 101–102; Spruyt, 1994; Yalvaç, 1991, p. 94; Little, 1994, pp. 9–10). Arguably this got them into deep trouble because neorealism actually ignores or 'kicks the state back out' as a conceptual variable, and accords ontological primacy to the international to the exclusion of the domestic.[5] This led such writers – most notably Theda Skocpol to produce at the very least, inconsistent analyses (Hobden, 1998, Chs. 4–6), or at worst, to end up by completely contradicting their original claims to 'bring the state back in' (see Hobson, 2000, Ch. 6). Had they been more conversant with IR theory, such problems could have been avoided. This makes it a matter of urgency for such historical sociologists to engage with IR theory. This is the first reason why I believe that historical sociologists ought to engage with IR theory.

Moreover, by the late, 1990s, when *CDP* came out, the move within IR to reach out to HS had gained considerable momentum. It is therefore, from my point of view, disappointing that Levi – as one of the leading historical sociological theorists - has not ventured into this new and important area. Of course Levi could reply that however important the need to synthesise IR with Historical Sociology might be, this was not the intention of her recent book. Indeed in Chapter 3, she notes that a number of historical sociologists, including Mann and Hintze, have drawn attention to the relationship between the international and state reform. But while noting the importance of these, she goes on to state that her objective in this particular chapter is to provide an alternative approach: 'to provide a narrative of the factors influencing the form of government demands for military service and citizen responses from the late eighteenth century through the early twentieth' (Levi, 1997, p. 44). And she also correctly notes that IR theorists have themselves failed to shed light on the domestic factors that enable a state to choose a particular military format – in this case universal conscription policy (Levi, 1997, p. 4). But my main point here is that not only are her arguments on conscription limited by her omission of the international, but more importantly, such an omission brings into question her claim in Chapter one, that studying conscription policy enables her to construct a 'better' theory of the state (Levi, 1997, pp. 4–5). This is the second reason why I believe that historical sociologists should engage with IR theory – the need to advance state theory, which can not be adequately achieved within Sociology in isolation of International Relations (as well as vice versa).

I would argue – and I would be surprised if Levi would not agree – that no theory of the state is worth its salt if it ignores or fails to take into account the *impact* of the international realm. I'm sure I don't have to elaborate on the familiar point that states are not just embedded in domestic society but also international or even global society. In any case, Levi, along with Mann and others was one of the first (modern) historical sociologists to recognise this broader point – something which featured strongly in *ORR*. Conscription policy could have been a strong case for exploring these wider linkages and, therefore, to advance to a 'better' theory of the state. Unfortunately, in her recent book – unlike in *ORR* – she effectively black-boxes or brackets the international, which prevents her from building on this important insight. This in my opinion, brings into some doubt her claim that she has advanced to a 'better' theory of the state. Her recent theory of the state is undoubtedly better than many theories that are currently on offer, but it is limited by its failure to consider the international dimension. Surely the challenge for the new millennium both for Historical

Sociology and IR is less to refine earlier traditional models of the state – whether they be rational choice, Marxist, statist, liberal or realist – than to develop *new* models which consider the ways in which domestic and international relations entwine to affect the state and vice versa? Historical sociologists tend to be much better at shedding light on the domestic pressures that impact upon government policy, while IR theorists have a much more nuanced understanding of the international pressures that impact upon states. Combining the insights of both would seem to me to be the best way forward for advancing state theory. This of course is no small or easy task, and it could obviously be achieved in a variety of ways. But in my opinion it is a major, if not *the* major challenge that confronts both sets of thinkers when trying to construct a more adequate theory of the state to those that are already on offer.

Not only has her omission of the international jeopardised her claim to have built a better theory of the state, but she has also missed what I believe is *the* challenge for Historical Sociology in the new millennium: to engage with IR theory in order to better understand not jut the state but above all domestic and international social relations; something which I have addressed elsewhere (Hobson, 1997, Ch. 7; 2000, Ch. 7). If *ORR* implicitly set up a potential 'historical sociology of IR', it is clear that her latest book has retreated from this frontier. This of course insulates her from the kind of critique that Skocpol and Tilly and others are open to – namely the use of a neorealist definition of the international which, unbeknown to them, leads them to contradict the very claims about the importance of the state and state-society relations that they make. But on the other hand, it also means that Levi's analysis remains within an orthodox historical sociological or even comparative political analysis divorced from international factors. Black-boxing the international realm (as in Sociology and Comparative Politics), or black-boxing the domestic realm (as in mainstream IR), can at best lead to only partial understandings and explanations of both social relations and international relations (as well as government policy). That domestic relations and international relations are mutually embedded within each other, logically requires some kind of synthesis of these two important disciplines. This is the third reason why I believe that historical sociologists, as well as comparative political scholars should engage with IR theory.

In terms of her latest book we might ask the following questions: Have international forces or factors played a part in the development of conscription policy? If so, how have they led to changes at the domestic level to meet the adequate policy response? How have international forces and domestic forces combined to enable the development of conscription policy? But at a deeper level, we could also consider the following questions: when do international forces take precedence over domestic forces in the shaping of government policy and vice versa? Is the international a social realm or an anarchic system comprising conflicting states? Put differently, are states motivated by considerations of national interest, or can they form a cooperative and collective identity in the international realm? Does the national interest take precedence over domestic social forces? Can states shape the international realm free of international constraints, or are they required to conform to international structural imperatives? Do states construct the international realm free of domestic constraints? These are only a few questions that could be asked. But such questions could enable the advancement of historical sociological theory and simultaneously push the frontier of Historical Sociology outwards towards IR.

None of this is to say that Levi's recent work is not important in its own right. In studying conscription, she has certainly done a service in drawing attention to the important issues of governmental legitimacy, compliance, consent and obligation. My ultimate aim here is less to criticise Levi's work, but – at the risk of sounding pompous – to invite her to consider a broader research agenda which addresses the wider issues that an 'internationalised' historical sociology/comparative political theory could bring. Engaging in such an enterprise is, of course, not one without its risks given the frankly anachronistic outlook that many theorists/purists/gatekeepers still have, concerning the 'need' to resist what they perceive to be 'extra-disciplinary contamination' (such people exist within Sociology and Comparative Politics no less than in International Relations!). But from what I know of Levi's work, I would be very surprised if she was one of them. Historical Sociology as a discipline has unfortunately been slow to pick up on the moves that a growing number of IR theorists are making to incorporate, or at least draw upon, HS insight to enrich 'their' discipline. Combining IR and HS could not only improve upon the theories and approaches developed within both of these disciplines, but could also offer a potentially new research agenda that would go beyond the confines of an unreconstructed or 'one-eyed' HS or IR. I have elsewhere called this 'World Sociology' and have laid out a research agenda that would be of interest to both of its constituent disciplines (Hobson & Hobden, 2002). This is in fact the fourth reason why I believe that historical sociologists and IR scholars need to enter into a dialogue. Only when the anachronistic borders that separate the various disciplines have been transcended can we advance Social Science in general, and knowledge of the world in particular. To conclude then, I sincerely ask in a spirit of *genuine* intellectual enterprise that she consider in engaging in this larger framework, within which her work could be well-positioned to make a rich contribution.

NOTES

1. I add the prefix 'neo' so as not to confuse it with integrationist theory in International Relations, associated with functionalist and neo-functionalist writers such as David Mitrany and Ernst Haas respectively. Two excellent examples of neo-integrationist theory can be found in Risse-Kappen (1995) and Evans, Jacobson and Putnam (1993). For my own efforts at constructing such an approach, see Hobson (1997, Ch. 7; 2000, pp. 223–235).

2. As Michael Mann has candidly put it, 'Some IR practitioners have been examining the impact of social relations on geopolitics for well over a decade. Sociologists did not respond as helpfully as we might. It was over a decade ago that some sociologists became aware that our specialism was neglecting the impact of geopolitics on social relations. We first borrowed precisely the traditional form of realism from which many IR practitioners were then fleeing . . .. We passed each other in the night' (Mann, 1996, p. 223).

3. Tsarist autocracy sought to enhance its despotic power over society, and accordingly repressed all social groups, whereas Imperial Germany was embedded in the dominant classes – especially the Junkers – but sought to repress the lower social classes.

4. Or what Gourevitch (1978) calls a 'second image-reversed' approach'.

5. Many IR scholars have incorrectly assumed that neorealism is 'state-centric'. In a recent book however, I argue that neorealism – as best represented in Waltz (1979) – is not state-centric but 'structure-centric' because it makes the international political structure ontologically primitive. There is simply no room in Waltz's model for the impact of the state as a conceptual variable – such is the stuff of 'second image theory'; something which he defines his approach negatively against. The same is true of neorealists such as Krasner and Gilpin. For a full discussion see Hobson (2000, Ch. 2).

DEMOCRATIC STATES AND SOCIETIES AT WAR: THE GLOBAL CONTEXT

Tarak Barkawi

A great strength of the rational choice tradition is its commitment to explicit assumptions and rigorous conduct of inquiry. Indeed, with work of the highest quality, to grant all the assumptions is to risk being led to the same conclusions as a matter of deductive logic and evidence. Unfortunately, this commitment to explicit analytic assumptions is not matched by equal awareness of the political perspective underlying inquiry in this tradition. As Max Weber reminded us, all inquiry in the social sciences necessarily proceeds from an evaluative standpoint of some kind (1949). For all its apparent hard-nosed realism, the core assumption that humans are instrumentally rational individuals who calculate material costs and benefits is, in its modern form, a product of liberal political theory. Thomas Hobbes' mythical state of nature was a brutal one because he assumed egoistic calculations of survival and wealth, a world of bourgeois subjects without the coercive powers of state to protect life and property. For alternative traditions of social and political inquiry, humans cannot be understood apart from the social relations in which they are embedded, relations which involve community, solidarity, and sacrifice as well as authority, domination and exploitation.

Margaret Levi's *Consent, Dissent, and Patriotism* is firmly grounded in the imagined world of liberalism (1997). She frames her analysis of conscription in democratic states in the terms of liberal democratic theory, using concepts such as consent, fairness and obligation. Her book deals with a version of the basic

The Comparative Study of Conscription in the Armed Forces, Volume 20, pages 361–376.

ISBN: 0-7623-0836-2

conundrum of rational choice theory: how is it that apparently egoistic individuals come to cooperate beyond the point explicable either by analysis of costs and benefits or by coercion. Mass consent to conscription, involving as it does submitting to military discipline at potential risk of life, is certainly a 'puzzle' from the standpoint of egoistic calculation. Her solution is that liberal democratic citizens consent when they perceive their governments to be fair and trustworthy according to the normative standards of the day and when other citizens are reciprocating by complying. When these conditions are not met, citizens are likely to express dissent and resist conscription. Citizen consent to conscription is therefore contingent on the perception of trust in government, fairness in policy, and the 'ethical reciprocity,' or compliance, of other citizens. The demand for fairness and "equality of sacrifice" in democracies creates a tendency towards universal conscription policies and the elimination of 'substitution,' 'buying out' and other inequities (p. 132).

A critical flaw in Levi's research design is the failure to consider conscription in non-democratic states. By framing analysis of the mobilisation of democratic populations for war in the terms of liberal democratic theory, Levi obscures the common processes by which all modern states militarise their populations. She simply assumes with little comment that conscription in states such as Imperial Germany or the Soviet Union is a different matter, not subject to the same terms of analysis. As a consequence, she fails to consider adequately the roles of nationalism and ideology, the articulation of masculinity with military service, the ways in which the passions of war exert their grip over populations, or, most significantly, the operation of modern disciplinary structures in producing subjects who obey authority (e.g. Gillis, 1989). All of these factors are common to the analysis of war and society in modern states. To invoke them is not to deny that there are differences between democratic and other forms of the legitimation of power. Rather it is to suggest that the similarities may be more significant, that the decisions of Americans and Germans, British and Japanese, French and Soviets to answer affirmatively the call to arms were governed by common processes.

In order to conceive military service in democratic states differently, inquiry must proceed from an alternative set of assumptions than Levi's. An obvious route of critique is to question the various ontological and epistemological bases of the rational choice tradition. Such criticism frequently focuses on methodological individualism. Assuming that the basic 'atoms' of the social are individual rational choices makes it very difficult to account for obvious features of 'actually existing' societies, such as cooperation and social solidarity. This review essay takes a different approach, however. Levi makes a set of often implicit assumptions regarding states, military power and populations as well as the relations between and among them. Taken together, these amount to a position of methodological nation-statism. That is, Levi conceives of states as individual 'cases' in which state-society relations are located within sovereign, territorial boundaries (cf. Tilly, 1997). She then uses liberal democratic categories to analyse relations between democratic states and their populations. Within Levi's own terms, her analysis is tightly constructed, logically argued, and backed up by evidence regarding levels of compliance with conscription policies. However, by placing the military service of democratic populations in global social and historical context, an alternative account can be outlined. Doing so requires challenging Levi's key assumptions regarding states, military power, and populations, each of which are dealt with in turn below. In the concluding section, this alternative account provides the basis for critical engagement with Levi's liberalism.

This essay deploys a different set of political and social scientific categories than does Levi. As a consequence, it is not really about her book in the sense of direct engagement by a critic who lives in the same intellectual world. Rather, it situates Levi's object of analysis, conscription in democratic societies, within another perspective. From such a standpoint, social phenomena and political issues obscured by Levi's approach are illuminated.

States

Levi makes two important but implicit assumptions about states. First, modern states are fundamentally distinguished by regime type. Second, they are self-contained, sovereign entities which can be conceived as individual cases to be studied using the standard comparative methods of similarity and difference. By combining these assumptions, Levi arrives at a theory of conscription applicable only to democratic states through comparison of France, Great Britain, the U.S., New Zealand, Australia, and Canada. Her notion of 'contingent consent' is developed through analysis of conscription policy and degrees of consent and dissent among the citizenry in these cases.

A basic difficulty with Levi's approach to regime types is the specification of 'democracy.' All of the cases she deals with were not, by contemporary liberal standards, 'democracies' over the entire period of Levi's book. Most of these states denied the franchise to women before the First World War. Moreover prior to 1914, Imperial Germany, with its constitutional monarchy and well-developed social welfare system, was often considered by contemporaries in the West to be among the most advanced states of Europe (Oren, 1996). The a-historicity of Levi's regime typology allows her to use liberal political categories of dubious historical and social validity. For example, throughout her book people are 'citizens' rather than 'subjects.' The use of such categories for analysis produces the problem of the degree to which they are identical with, or at least adequately capture, social relations and processes. Liberal political principles are conditioned and transformed by their embeddedness in practices and institutions that are not wholly or only liberal. In particular, it is puzzling that capitalism does not merit a single index entry nor any extended discussion in Levi's book, since the history of 'actually existing' liberalism in the West is inseparable from its capitalist context (e.g Jessop, 1978; Marx, 1843[1975]). Other categories of analysis, such as imperialism, nationalism, bureaucracy and gender, similarly draw attention not only to the common social and political context of Western states but to phenomena which modify liberalism in practice.

The notion that states are fundamentally distinguished by regime type allows Levi to study conscription in democratic states with little reference to conscription in states not considered to be democratic. When events in Prussia appear to contradict her argument that the historical development of conscription policy was towards universal conscription without provision for substitution and 'buying out,' they are dismissed because Prussia was not a democratic state (p. 106). The problem here is that it is precisely the impact of democracy upon conscription that Levi is attempting to establish. Without consideration of non-democratic cases, it is impossible to know whether Levi is correct that the more democratic a regime and the more 'universalistic' its laws, the more likely citizens are to comply with a policy of universal conscription (pp. 109, 123–133). How are we to assess high levels of compliance with conscription policy in a state like Nazi Germany? Is that a completely different phenomenon than conscription elsewhere? What of factors such as nationalism which were significant in compliance with conscription in *all* states during the World Wars? By ignoring non-democratic states, Levi is able to concentrate on the 'democratic' features of her cases, hence she can analyse recruitment policy with a democratic language of consent, fairness and obligation. This enables her to exclude phenomenon common to all Western states and societies which, regardless of regime type, played a role in military mobilisation.

Processes such as the rise of mass society, the bureaucratisation of politics, and the development of industrial forms of production were found in all modernizing states. All of these processes shaped the ways in which states prepared for and waged war. Other military organizational imperatives, such as the necessity for large, rapidly mobilisable reserves, were a consequence of inter-state competition. In all the major states, modern industry enabled General Staffs to uniform and equip burgeoning populations; modern science developed ever more effective weaponry; the disciplinary processes of the regular military transformed recruits into credible soldiers; and the efficiency of modern bureaucratic organisation could mobilise, transport and feed armies of increasing size. Taken together, these processes were part of the totalisation of modern conventional warfare. States like Imperial Russia and Austro-Hungary which failed to adapt successfully suffered the consequences. The teleology of this process, more or less reached in both World Wars, was total organisation of the state into "a single national firm for waging war" (McNeil, 1982, p. 317). In all the combatant states, this process involved the mobilisation of ever-increasing percentages of their populations. To be sure, there were differences in military recruitment policy in each country due in part to politics and military tradition. But the overall historical context of conscription policy was that of the progressive totalisation of war, a context which cannot be understood through a focus on relations between regimes and their citizens alone (Shaw, 1988, 1991).

Another feature of the organisational imperatives of total war calls attention to Levi's second major assumption regarding states, that they are self-contained sovereign entities which can be studied as individual cases. Organisation for total war was transnational in nature (McNeil, 1982). The British waged war as an empire, not as a nation-state. It is unclear how Levi can conceive of Australia, New Zealand, Canada and the U.K. as separate entities over much of the period of her study. Canada was a Dominion of the British Commonwealth until 1931, Australia until 1942 and New Zealand until 1947 (Fieldhouse, 1966, p. 268). Official and informal ties continue to this day. Together, Commonwealth states amount to half of her six cases. As she herself notes, identification with Britain in these countries was a powerful incentive to serve, whether voluntarily or through conscription (pp. 116, 140). More generally, the question of how it is that the Commonwealth states even came to be involved in European wars cannot be answered without reference to the British Empire. Levi's focus on conscription 'policy bargains' between citizens and their local states misses the forest for the trees, as the relevant political community was an imperial one.

Levi is by no means alone in assuming a nation-state ontology of the international system consisting of territorially-defined sovereign units (cf. Agnew & Corbridge, 1995; Barkawi & Laffey, 1999). But in fact empire has been the dominant form of polity in the modern international system (Shaw, 1997, p. 499). Indeed, some of the most successful empires were also liberal states, e.g Holland, France, Great Britain and the U.S. Imperial rule involves the governance of internally differentiated and territorially dispersed populations. Generally, only metropolitan populations were governed according to democratic principles. A significant portion of the military power of these imperial states was constituted from 'foreign' rather than national, or metropolitan, populations (e.g. Barkawi, 2001; Clayton, 1988; Perry, 1988). This is a point of direct significance for consideration of the conditions under which democratic states conscripted metropolitan populations, an issue taken up below.

The military service of democratic societies must be placed in the larger international context. The states which governed these societies were international in nature, ruling abroad as well as at home. Consideration of local relations between states and citizens can only ever be part of the picture. Such relations are in constant interaction with their international context, which shapes and conditions the constitution and use of military power, leading to transformation in state forms. For example, total war was of necessity alliance warfare. Over the course of the twentieth century, the military complexes of Western states were increasingly integrated, a process which culminated in NATO. In the contemporary era, most of these states lack political-military autonomy; they cannot wage war independently, but only as part of NATO or another U.S.-led coalition. Hence, along the core dimension of state power-force – these states are no longer independent, sovereign entities. Equally, there has been increasing transnational organisation of the capitalist world economy, in which local relations are reworked according to the will of international agencies such as the WTO. Theorising in International Relations has turned towards concepts of transnational, international and internationalised states to account for an emergent Western state with global reach, which rules through a variety of domestic and international agencies (e.g Agnew & Corbridge, 1995; Panitch, 1996; Picciotto, 1991; Shaw, 1997). Analysis of state-society relations according to the principle of methodological nation-statism, which fails to take into account these larger international realities, is simply not credible. To see how such realities impact on the military power of democratic states, and condition the military service of democratic populations, it is necessary to turn to the critique of Levi's assumptions regarding military power.

Military Power

The military power available to states is historically consequential but it is not only 'national' manpower that matters. In the autumn of 1914, the small regular British Army was exhausted. It had fought continuously since August and one corps in particular required relief after the First Battle of Ypres. There were no trained British or Commonwealth divisions available, nor had the new volunteers of 'Kitchner's Army' reached the front. Luckily for the British, and for the defeat of the first German attempt at European hegemony in the twentieth century, a corps of professionals from the British Indian Army arrived in the nick of time. The four Indian divisions held one-third of the British sector until Christmas. Without them, it is unlikely the line could have been held (Mason, 1974, pp. 412–414; Trench, 1988, pp. 31–32). Elsewhere, France's North and West

African divisions were in the line and well over 200,000 French colonial troops were deployed on the Western Front by 1918 (Clayton, 1988, p. 98). The victory of the 'democratic' powers in the spring of that year was possible only because of the availability of military forces recruited, in many cases by conscription, from colonised populations. The contribution of such forces to Allied victory in the Second World War was equally significant.[1]

The military manpower policies of democratic states were not restricted to their 'home' or metropolitan populations. The French had hoped in both World Wars to offset Germany's demographic advantage with an African 'reservoir of men' (Davis, 1934; Echenberg, 1991). The British Empire, and the wealth and power that went with it, could not have been secured without its Indian Army (Robinson, 1972). Levi's conscription 'policy bargains' struck between states and metropolitan populations were fundamentally conditioned by the availability of imperial manpower. In focusing on national military personnel policy alone, Levi's work reflects a widespread, but flawed, assumption regarding relations between states, militaries and populations: that the military power of states is recruited from within the 'bordered power container' of national homelands and then projected outwards (Giddens, 1985; cf Agnew & Corbridge, 1995). The prevalence of this assumption is apparent in Janice Thomson's widely cited *Mercenaries, Pirates, and Sovereigns*, to which Levi refers (Levi, 1997, p. 52; Thomson, 1994).

Thomson conflates the monopolisation of armed force by sovereign states with the elimination of the use of foreign military manpower. Her argument is that over the course of the nineteenth century states gained a monopoly on the authoritative use of external violence from non-state actors. For example, colonial trading companies were deprived of their private militaries and states stopped hiring foreign mercenary companies. A fundamental problem with Thomson's approach is that she identifies the state with the formal, 'official' or juridical apparatus of rule. That is, a broader conception of the state which encompassed political and economic power would not make a fundamental distinction between the British state and the British East India Company simply because the latter was legally a private corporation (e.g Carnoy, 1984; Hay, 1999).[2] But more important for present purposes is Thomson's argument that as part of the process of monopolising violence, states' coercive apparatuses came to be based within their sovereign, territorial homelands (1994, p. 3). She makes this argument by confusing mercenarism in early modern Europe with the use of foreign military forces more generally. She assumes that because mercenarism ended, so did the widespread use of foreign military forces. Thomson shows how, over the course of the nineteenth century, European states passed laws preventing the enlistment of foreigners in their national militaries. This brought to an end the previously widespread practice of using foreign mercenary companies in the armies of Europe's sovereigns. Thomson carefully documents this process and considers the few surviving twentieth century 'anomalies,' such as the French Foreign Legion or the Gurkha Regiments of the British and Indian Armies (pp. 89–97). She states categorically, however, that "[t]he last instance in which a state raised an army of foreigners was in 1854" when Britain hired some mercenary companies for use in the Crimean War (p. 88). What Thomson fails to consider is that it was precisely over the course of the nineteenth century that European powers raised large standing armies recruited from colonised populations. The British Indian Army numbered approximately 160,000 in 1900 and was to reach a strength of nearly two million during the Second World War (Perry, 1988, p. 116). These colonial armies do not fit into the categories of Thomson's argument: they were both foreign *and* under the sovereign control of European states. In conflating the military service of foreigners with mercenary companies, Thomson has effectively written colonial armies out of history, subsuming them under the nationality of their imperial occupiers.

Of what significance is the existence of such armies for Levi? Her focus on conscription policy for the 'home' population represents only one aspect of the military personnel policy of imperial states. The need for metropolitan manpower was reduced by the availability of imperial manpower. Britain could manage with a small, volunteer regular army for so long only because it could rely largely on the Indian Army and the various African formations to maintain order in the empire and serve as a 'fire brigade' in the event of major war. Similarly, the volunteer traditions of the 'white' Commonwealth states, with their rag-tag citizens' militias, were sufficient for defence only because the Royal Navy made invasion nearly unthinkable. Only by ignoring the transnational constitution of military power, can Levi focus on 'bargains' over conscription struck between democratic states and their citizens without reference to the military service of non-democratically governed, colonised populations. Colonial armies reduced the need for metropolitan manpower and often left citizens, or at least those who could afford to, free to enjoy the benefits of wealth and privilege while others waged their wars. This has implications for just how democratic Levi's states and citizens are – an issue taken up in conclusion.

The use of foreign military forces did not end with the passing of the formal European empires. Among the 'anomalies' of twentieth century mercenarism that Thomson cites are the U.S. funded South Korean, Thai and Philippine troops used in Indochina, as well as General Westmoreland's rather obscure interest in hiring demobilised Gurkhas (p. 94). She is apparently unaware of other foreign elements of the U.S. coercive apparatus such as the multinational staff of the CIA's covert action arm or the 30,000 strong Hmong forces in Laos

(Prados, 1996, p. 272). More significantly there is no mention of the million-man Army of the Republic of Vietnam (ARVN) (Kolko, 1985, p. 234). In 'official,' juridical terms the ARVN was the army of a sovereign state, South Vietnam. But in historical and social terms, the origins of the ARVN are to be found in the French colonial army and throughout its existence it was utterly dependent upon U.S. 'advise and support.' The U.S. clothed, supplied, armed and trained the ARVN, as well as advising it in combat down to the company level. It played a central role in U.S. power projection in Indochina, providing the bulk of the forces for maintaining the U.S. client state in South Vietnam as well as for the invasions of Cambodia and Laos. Elsewhere, too, in the Third World domains of the 'free world' the U.S. maintained order by relying on the armies of client states. As President Eisenhower noted, since the U.S. could not deploy conventional forces everywhere, it sought "to develop within the various areas and regions of the free world indigenous forces for the maintenance of order, the safeguarding of frontiers and the provision of the bulk of the ground capability" (Quoted in Gaddis, 1982, p. 153).[3] While colonial armies were composed of foreigners but under the sovereign control of European states, client armies were juridically independent in sovereign terms but were in fact part of the U.S. 'external state' (Latham, 1997). Thomson is correct that states, properly understood, control large scale, organised violence; she is mistaken that this process can be understood solely in national and sovereign terms.

As a consequence of her assumption that military power is national, Levi is able to concentrate on the various inequities of selective service in the U.S., the dilemmas of conscience which agonised U.S. citizens during the Vietnam War, and the resulting policy bargains with no consideration of the role of foreign soldiers in maintaining U.S. power. With the exception of the latter stages of its involvement in Indochina, the U.S. could wage the Cold War in the Third World without making politically intolerable demands on its citizens because of its extensive apparatus for the military mobilisation of client populations. Such forces bore the brunt of the fighting, and suffered the bulk of the casualties, in wars fought to maintain Western-oriented, narrowly-based client regimes in the face of popular insurgency (Kolko, 1988).

The widespread and effective military service of colonial armies and other 'foreign forces' raises questions about another basic presupposition of Levi's: that military service should be thought of in terms of 'political obligation.' For her, military service is reflective of legitimate political authority, of the identification of soldiers with their democratic nation states. "Young men fight in war because they are patriots . . ." (Levi, 1997, p. 213). The scale of military mobilisation is seen as evidence of states' popularity and level of consent they achieve. In fact, war and the military exert a powerful attraction *of their own,* especially for young men, whether they be colonised subjects or metropolitan citizens. Levi is not unaware of this, but working within a liberal tradition, she primarily conceptualises war in terms of costs and risks, something egoistic individuals would avoid if they could. But for many, and by no means only those who have yet to experience their rigors, war and military service are sought after. War, also, is popular. The extraordinarily close relationship between masculinity and war is only one indication, albeit a very important one, of war's hold over the human imagination. Achieving male adulthood is often bound up with warrior ideals, whether or not one actually fights (Gibson, 1994; Jeffords, 1989). Warrior constructions of masculinity are both cause and consequence of war.

The nature of the relations between factors such as masculinity and conscription are subjects for additional research.[4] For present purposes, the ways in which the reproduction of gender structures are implicated in war suggests a different way of conceptualising the populations which fight it. Levi conceives of populations as composed of individuals who act on the basis of cost/benefit calculations. Conscription is seen as being about the self-interested and ethical consent of citizens.[5] Alternatively, populations can be conceived as the effect of the historical and social structures which shape and condition their nature. Analysis focuses on the structures themselves, and the discourses which constitute them, rather than on the calculations of individuals. The question becomes how are the kind of citizens who participate in militarisation historically produced?

Populations

In her concluding chapter 'The Democratization of Compliance,' Levi places the 'behavioral consent' of the conscripted in the context of obedience with the demands of authority. Her argument is that democratic institutions facilitate the compliance of rational and ethical actors, i.e democratic citizens. Invoking Weber on legitimate authority, consent to law is conceived as a function of the voluntary compliance of citizens who demand fair and impartial treatment from each other and their government (pp. 202–204).[6] In a brief section on 'other studies of compliance,' she fails to consider adequately alternative conceptualisations of obedience to authority (pp. 214–217). The notion of 'compliance' already directs attention to the decisions of individuals, rather than to the *social production of obedient subjects.*

In fact, Weber belongs in quite another tradition of inquiry regarding the nature of obedience than Levi places him in. Weber was interested in the historical and social *origins* of the type of human Levi and Hobbes assume is natural, that capable of instrumentally rational action. A central question of Weber's was the relation between social and political orders and the 'types of humans' they produced, what can be termed his 'characterology' (Hennis, 1988). In particular, he was concerned with the fate of humans in modern bureaucratic organisation, in which individuals became cogs in administrative machines. Following some ideas from Friedrich Nietzsche, he developed an account of how humans became able to lead a 'rational' life and so play their part in constructing and maintaining the modern world order. In the *Genealogy of Morals,* a text Weber read closely, Nietzsche addressed the historical development and social location of modern moral values (Nietzsche, 1989[1887]). Nietzsche was concerned, in part, with the nature of asceticism, and the psychological consequences of denying what he saw as basic human urges and passions. Asceticism, the capacity for self regulation and the deferment of pleasure, was the precondition for living a 'rational' life, for humans to become 'necessary, regular, calculable' (Nietzsche, 1989, p. 59). In the *Protestant Ethic and the Spirit of Capitalism* and elsewhere, Weber placed Nietzsche's insight in sociological context. A conjunction of religious and social phenomena in early modern Europe developed a type of person capable of economically rational conduct on the basis of the idea of a profession, or calling (Weber, 1930, pp. 26–27, 180–181).

This type of human is well-suited to service in the various public and private bureaucratic structures of the modern order, such as the military. Their lives revolve around the discharge of their duties and the receipt of their salaries. Bureaucracies and the individuals who staff them are ideally efficient means to achieve given ends, such as production for profit in the case of capitalist enterprises. What bureaucracies and bureaucrats lack are means of assessing the 'value rationality' of the ends they serve, such as the making of ever more money. As Mark Warren puts it, the experiences and responsibilities of bureaucrats "train them to disregard the rationality of the organization's goals and the ultimate consequences of those goals" (1988, p. 35). For Weber, the fundamental political problems of modernity were how bureaucratic structures could be made to serve value rational ends; and how space could be made within the modern economic order, "which to-day determine[s] the lives of all individuals who are born into [it] . . . with irresistible force", for humans to live their lives according to their highest ethical and spiritual ends (1930, p. 181). Far from finding modernity 'legitimate,' Weber was perhaps its most powerful critic.

The contemporary thinker most representative of the Nietzsche-Weber view of modernity, and the ways in which it shapes and conditions humanity, is of course Michel Foucault, especially his seminal *Discipline and Punish* (1977). Levi attempts to reconcile Foucaultian-inspired, as well as other, studies of 'compliance' with her own approach: "Reading this material in light of the model of contingent consent, the evidence appears overwhelming that contingent consent (or something remarkably like it) exists and motivates large numbers of people" (p. 217). But as should now be clear, this represents a fundamental misreading of an alternative tradition of social inquiry. Foucault, like Weber, is not interested in 'motivation' narrowly-conceived, but rather in how modern disciplinary processes produce obedient subjects capable of self-regulation. The implications of this tradition of inquiry for study of obedience to authority are numerous. Only the aspect most relevant to the study of the military mobilisation of populations is mentioned here.

Both Weber and Foucault recognised in regular military discipline the model of modern forms of bureaucratic organisation (Foucault, 1977; Weber, 1946, pp. 255–261). The hierarchical ordering of offices, regular obedience to command, and the training of individual and collective bodies are essential features of bureaucratic social control. With the advent of capitalism and the modern state, military forms of discipline left the barracks and were incorporated in the social order (Dandeker, 1990). Certainly, these forms of discipline were transformed in their 'civilian' applications, and were not as invasive or all-encompassing in the same ways as life in the actual military. But the basic premises for instilling self-regulation and the habit of obedience to authority are similar. They can be found in primary school as in basic training, in capitalist enterprises as in military formations. Moderns are bred for obedience.[7] The implication of this insight is that the differences between the civilian world and the military world are not as great as liberal conceptions of the civil/military divide suggest (cf. Drake, forthcoming). Disciplinary processes are already instantiated in the compliance of civilians with conscription and other forms of military mobilisation. Another example of war's everyday presence is its significance for gender relations in 'civilian' society. Levi notes the 'white feather' campaigns in which women pilloried men who had yet to join the forces by sending them feathers as symbols of their cowardice (pp. 111, 116, 121, 151).[8] Such examples illuminate the role of warrior masculinity in structuring both gender relations and the broader social context of obedience to conscription.

While Foucault has inspired studies of 'resistance' (e.g. Scott, 1985), the overwhelming characteristic of the modern order is obedience, which is what lends modernity its machine-like nature as a form of social organisation. By and large, populations in all the major combatant states of the World Wars 'consented to,' or more accurately willingly participated in, mass mobilisation. The Weberian conception of the modern subject offers a way of addressing why the history of the institution of conscription, and more generally of mobilisation for war, is everywhere primarily one of 'compliance.'

As with states, Levi assumes that populations are differentiated by regime type. Her democratic citizens are "ethically constituted rational actors" (p. 219). By contrast, fascism and "extreme nationalism" involve a contradiction between ethics and rationality, which enable members of a polity to participate in and consent to "horrific" regimes due to a "loss of self" (pp. 202, 219). In the Weberian view there are more similarities than differences between the populations of modern states. Regardless of regime type, states effectively organised national and foreign populations for war.[9] They did so in large part through modern forms of bureaucratic organisation. Certainly these processes were shaped by the politics of different regimes, but in all states disciplinary practices organised populations for the civilian and military labours of war. It is worth noting in the context of the 'ethical' character of the citizens of different regimes, that the military forces of both sides in the Second World War proved capable of employing mass violence against civilians (e.g. Dower, 1986). Levi's work reflects a panglossian view of the ethical capacities of democratic citizens and a lack of reflexivity regarding her own location, and that of the Western democracies, in a global order characterised by horrifying divides of wealth and power.

Democratic Military Service in Global Context

In analysis of the military service of democratic populations, the basic political theoretic premise often has been that the citizenry will limit involvement of their state in wars due to the fact that they will be required to bear the burdens of the fighting. "If . . . the consent of the citizenry is required in order to determine whether or not there will be war, it is natural that they consider all its calamities before committing themselves to so risky a game" (Kant, 1983, p. 351). Much of the literature on the so-called 'democratic peace' is based on this notion (e.g Doyle, 1996; see also Levi, 1997, p. 208, n. 6). What is overlooked is that Kant had in mind a particular form of military organisation, a republican citizens' militia. In contemporary democracies, while citizens may vote for war, or more likely register their opinions with pollsters, they are unlikely to serve.[10] The existence of professional militaries severs the link between republicanism and peace that Kant's analysis relied upon (Kubik, 2001).

In placing the military service of democratic populations in global context, other ways in which the citizenry are insulated from wars waged by their states are identified. Liberal imperial states moderated their demands for military service from metropolitan populations due to the availability of foreign forces of diverse type. Moreover, the use of these forces had direct consequences for democratic control of war making powers. Without the formal approval of

Congress or the citizenry, and often without their knowledge, the U.S. became involved in continual military operations across the Third World during the Cold War. It could do so because it had developed an extensive apparatus for the constitution and use of foreign military manpower. For example, the U.S. largely fought the twenty year war in Laos with troops that were, in U.S. constitutional terms, "untraceable" (Lens, 1987, p. 105). Levi places the resistance of U.S. citizens to the draft during the Vietnam War in the context of "ethical concerns" (pp. 166, 172–177). Certainly this was the case for most conscientious objectors and many who protested against the war. Yet thousands of foreigners had been fighting in U.S.-directed wars for years and in 1968 the citizenry elected a President who promptly shifted more of the burden of the Vietnam War back on to the South Vietnamese forces.[11] Scepticism is necessary for an ethics invoked only when one is asked to fight oneself. Of Levi's argument that "equality of sacrifice" was the standard by which implementation of conscription policies was judged in democracies (p. 132), it must be asked equality for whom?[12]

As can be seen in the case of U.S. involvement in Indochina, as in Central America, the political-military value of foreign forces was considerable in part because they were often used for 'unpopular' purposes, such as securing imperial order. The wealth and privilege found in democratic societies, and enjoyed by the more fortunate of their citizens, are a direct consequence of the historical and contemporary maintenance – very often by force – of global power relations. These facts suggest that the use of liberal democratic, political theoretic categories for the analysis of the military service of democratic populations is misguided. The reason for this is quite straightforward, neither 'democratic' states nor 'democratic' populations are nearly as democratised as Levi assumes. Rather, we live in an age in which power is legitimated in liberal democratic terms.

Through a tautological sleight of hand, Levi's identification of 'democracies' implies that they are *really* democratic, enabling her use of liberal political theoretic concepts. She places contemporary liberal democracies within an historical teleology of ever-increasing standards of fairness and universalism. "Over the centuries documented in this book citizens in democracies have raised the standards for judging the fairness, impartiality, and trustworthiness of government actors in picking and waging wars" (p. 208). But 'liberal democracy' is by no means the only possible meaning of 'rule by the people.' Liberal democracy should be placed in the context of capitalist social relations which limit its democratic potential and place constraints on the prospects for democratic development beyond 'polyarchy' (Dahl, 1998, pp. 178–179). Such a context draws attention to the historical struggle *between* liberalism and democracy, and the progressive shift – very much evident in our own time – in favour of the rights of property over the rule of the people (Bowles & Gintis, 1987; Held,

1995). Certainly liberal democracy makes a difference in terms of the expression of popular interests and the protection of individual rights. But modern democracy is a form of legitimating political and economic power, rather than a genuine vehicle for popular rule, as Levi implies.

For Levi, the obedience to authority of democratic citizens is interpreted as evidence of the potential for democracies to manage a marriage of ethics and self-interest: "[t]rustworthy and responsive government and citizens concerned with promotion of their individual ends within a context of ethical reciprocity are the foundational elements of democracy – rightly understood" (Levi, 1997, p. 219). Levi's citizens are not only rational but ethical, and her democracies, to the extent they have successfully conscripted their populations for war, are fair. "Demonstrated fairness is . . . a critical element in effective and democratic governance" (Levi, 1997, abstract). To imagine a world in which 'fair and trustworthy' democracies are populated by 'rational and ethical' citizens is to be in the grip of one of the most powerful illusions of the post-Cold War era: that liberal democracy represents the best of all possible worlds. Levi places herself in a long line of liberal thinkers who have identified universal conceptions of right and rationality with the power politics of liberal states (cf Carr, 1939; Schmitt, 1996[1932]). Such imaginings obfuscate the power relations, domestic and international, by which democratic capitalist states effect their rule and maintain their global positions of wealth and privilege.

NOTES

1. The secret War Department history of the expansion of Indian armed forces in World War II states: "At the end of 1941 there were more Divisions from India serving overseas, excluding India, than from the United Kingdom or any other component part of the Empire" (p. 21, L/R/5/273, Oriental and India Office Collection, British Library, London, U.K.). At that time, British Indian forces were in Malaya, Burma, Iraq, the Mediterranean, and East and North Africa. In 1942, 6 of 14 divisions in the Middle East were Indian (Narain, 1992, p. 31).

2. Since 1785, the Company had been subject to a 'board of control' set up by Parliament that, in the words of one specialist, "converted the company into a quasi-state department" (Quoted in Keay, 1991, p. 391).

3 When Eisenhower was asked whether or not the idea was to have other nationalities bear the brunt of future fighting, he replied "that was the kernel of the whole thing" (Quoted in Gaddis, 1982, p. 153). A U.S. general, training South Koreans to put down the peasant insurgency in the South in the late 1940s commented "KMAG [U.S. Military Advisory Group Korea] is a living demonstration of how an intelligent and intensive investment of 500 combat-hardened American men and officers can train 100,000 guys to do the shooting for you" (quoted in Cumings, 1990, p. 475).

4 The connections between masculinity, military mobilisation and conscription are evident in the experience of one World War II British conscript interviewed by the

author for another project. When the war broke out, he did not volunteer: "No, no, you wouldn't get me in the Army." He changed his mind when his mates returned home on leave wearing their uniforms and asking why he was not in the forces. He then tried to volunteer twice, but was refused because he worked in a steelworks. He remained at his job until he was conscripted a few months later. In this case, with respect to his motives for compliance with military mobilisation, there was no practical difference between volunteering and conscription.

5. Interestingly, if citizens have 'ethical' capacities, it suggests that the collective action problem of obedience to conscription does not in fact exist. That is, Levi's thesis undermines the very basis of the 'puzzle' her book seeks to address.

6. *Herrschaft* which Levi, following many American interpretations, renders as 'authority' also denotes 'domination'(Roth, 1978, p. LXXXVIII; Turner, 1992, p. 28).

7. Invoking Weber again, Levi considers 'habitual' or 'customary' obedience as an alternative explanation for consent to conscription (28–29). She considers this form of obedience an 'incentive-based' behaviour compatible with rational choice approaches but one not susceptible to investigation in historical case studies. This is a misreading of Weber's concept of traditional social action and it is obscure why such action is any more or less susceptible to historical inquiry (Kalberg, 1994, p. 26). In any case, Levi's notion of habitual obedience is not the one sketched out here.

8. Likewise, conscientious objection was articulated with homosexuality (Levi, 1997, p. 172).

9. Germany and Japan also made extensive use of foreign-recruited military forces in the Second World War (e.g. Stein, 1966, Ch. 6 & 7; Lebra, 1977).

10. While 76% of Americans supported U.S. involvement in the Gulf War, less than 2/10 of one percent of them served (Kubik, 2001, p. 20).

11. Not only did Nixon 'Vietnamize' the war, but his Doctrine was specifically concerned with limiting the use of U.S. national forces in insurgencies and shifting the burden onto client armies. (Gaddis, 1982, p. 298).

12. This is not to dispute Levi's claim that the citizenry to a degree demanded equal treatment for themselves, rather it is to say that putting this in terms of 'equality of sacrifice' is highly misleading.

ACKNOWLEDGMENTS

The author thanks Shane Brighton, Susan Carruthers, Mark Laffey, Daniel Nexon, and Louiza Odysseos for comments on earlier versions. This essay is based in part on co-authored and co-edited work with Mark Laffey (1999; 2001).

AN ANALYTIC NARRATIVE OF CONSCRIPTION: CASES, CONTEXTS, AND CAUSES

Margaret Levi

It is immensely flattering to have a book subject to the kind of thoughtful critical scrutiny that *Consent, Dissent and Patriotism* has received from John M. Hobson and Tarak Barkawi. Both raise serious questions that deserve equally serious responses. Despite some significant differences between them, both Hobson and Barkawi take me to task for my case selection; raise issues about important but insufficiently explored variables, especially those deriving from the international context; and question my explanatory apparatus from a Weberian perspective. Hobson is appreciative of some of my efforts but unhappy that I failed to live up to the promise he perceived in my earlier work (1988), of pushing forward a synthesis between historical sociology and international relations. Barkawi is more hostile to my arguments and approach. He pushes for an analysis that is both more Foucaultian and more Weberian (although his version of Weber is not one all of us would recognize).

Before responding directly to their critiques, I need to spell out what was evidently not clear in the text, given that both of these extremely intelligent scholars persist in the same misreading of my intentions.[1] My reason for this repetition is to ensure that the reader can adequately evaluate my justifications of choices of cases, contextual variables, and causal model. Both reviewers (Hobson, pp. 347–359; Barkawi, pp. 361–376) assert that my central claim[2] is – and they quote – "the more democratic the regime and the more universalistic its laws, the more likely it is that citizens will comply with a policy of

The Comparative Study of Conscription in the Armed Forces, Volume 20, pages 377–387.

ISBN: 0-7623-0836-2

universal conscription" (Levi, 1997, pp. 37, 109). I do say and mean this, but as an hypothesis, one among many. Moreover, they quote me out of context, failing to rehearse the theoretical discussion of *democratic* institutions from which the hypothesis derives. Obviously, coercion can also effect relatively full compliance. What it is unlikely to do is evoke consent. So, I plead guilty to infelicitous phrasing but not to a demonstrably silly proposition.

Nor does this hypothesis represent my central claim. I have two aims in the book. The first is explaining institutional dynamics, the reasons why military service requirements change and vary. Universal conscription is only one form military service may take, and it is neither the dominant nor persistent form in the countries I study. Here my argument is that norms of fairness affect popular behavior, which in turn influences the development of institutions of military service and governmental institutions more generally. I use the word influence purposively here; there are, of course, other factors at play as well, and I attempt to specify them in the text.

My second aim is to develop and test a model to account for variation in citizen responses to government demands in democracies. As Hobson notes, the model derives from arguments made in an earlier book, *Of Rule and Revenue* (1988), in which I found that even extremely autocratic rulers sought quasi-voluntary compliance, if for no other reason than that it lowered their costs of revenue extraction. However, the focus in *Of Rule and Revenue* was on rulers' policy decisions in response to the anticipated and actual reactions of those from whom they were demanding extractions. *Consent, Dissent, and Patriotism* focuses on why and when the relevant populations respond as they do. This is quite a distinct enterprise than the one undertaken in *Of Rule and Revenue.*

The dependent variable in this part of the analysis is not conscription and certainly not universal conscription; it is consent and dissent. Far from assuming consent, as Barkawi wants the reader to believe, I treat the relationship between contingent consent and the forms of military service as problematic and never fully settled. Because of the difficulties of measuring consent and dissent directly, in some chapters compliance and non-compliance are the surrogate measures and in some chapters opinion polls, protests, and other indicators of approval or disapproval of government military service policy. Again, universal conscription turns out to evoke more consent but only if certain conditions prevail, as I elaborate fully in the book and briefly in the opening summary.

So what is my central claim in regards to conscription, the subject of this special issue? My argument is tripartite. One, conscription in democracies remains and will remain a political as much as a military decision. Two, effective conscription policies depend on a considerable degree of voluntary compliance and, if possible, contingent consent. Three, citizens will only give their contingent consent if they perceive government as trustworthy and will withdraw it if the trust is nonexistent or broken. The form conscription takes in democracies reflects such factors as war or peace, demand for troops, geo-politics, military technology, and the like. But it also, and often most fundamentally, reflects a strategic interaction between government policy-makers, desiring to keep the costs of compliance down, and citizens (and not yet citizens), who need to be either coerced or persuaded to comply. The factors that affect popular reactions include assessments of their personal costs and benefits, their ethical commitments, their norms of fairness, and their assessments of the policy and the government itself according to these norms, and different segments of the population respond in systematically different ways. The populace expresses its views of the government's policy through votes, riots and protests, conscientious objection, and draft evasion. Popular behavior, in this account, affects not only military service policy but also the very evolution of democratic institutions.

CASE SELECTION

Both Hobson and Barkawi feel that my arguments are seriously damaged by failure to include non-democratic states in the analysis. But is it in fact so self-evident that my findings would be more credible if I delved into a wider range of cases? Is this a "fatal flaw" in my research design, as Barkawi insists. Actually not. Remember that I am trying to explain variation in contingent consent, not just coerced behavior. Contingent consent is possible only in democratic countries where citizens might actually have a voice in determining the policies that affect them and where they might actually have the right to refuse their consent. That makes the appropriate comparison other democracies.

I do not simply compare these six countries during one moment. I compare them over time. Although most of these countries may claim to be democracies throughout the 200 years I consider, or at least for most of that period, they are in fact in transition throughout, and their progress is neither linear nor unproblematic. There remains considerable room for improvement still and considerable basis for fear of serious backsliding. The franchise and other forms of representation expand and sometimes contract, the definition of rights is subject to continuous contestation and revision. Democratic institutions, norms, and ideology vary not only across the countries but also within the very same countries, and this variation, I argue, should correlate with changes in military service requirements and in compliance with them. And so it does.

Even among populations within the same democracy, contingent consent is systematically uneven. There are those who are excluded or treated discriminatorily. The comparison is not only among countries but also among populations within countries. Irish immigrants to Australia, francophones in Canada, blacks in the United States, and anarchists in France – to name but a few of the groups who receive some attention in the book – have different responses to military service than do the rest of the population in the relevant state. For them government is not so trustworthy, its policy implementation far from fair, the extraction of manpower an illegitimate undertaking, the justness of the war contested, or all of the above.

That being said, it would be wonderful to see the extent to which my arguments have validity (or not) in non-democratic contexts. Hobson appropriately berates me, as had others previously, for not exploring why Prussia, a constitutional but in no way a democratic state, could introduce universal conscription before more democratic polities. This led me to undertake a fuller analysis of the Prussian case, which I did in my chapter for *Analytic Narratives* (Bates et al., 1998). There I confirmed what I argued in *Consent, Dissent, and Patriotism:*

- democratic institutions, particularly the extension of the franchise, are only part of the explanation of more universalistic conscription
- elites, whatever the regime, benefit from tax and conscription policies which are more likely to evoke quasi-voluntary compliance and consent
- norms of fairness that promote increased democratization also help explain citizen demands for a more universalistic conscription policy and resistance to a more discriminatory policy
- but in the absence of democratic institutions, universalistic policies cannot be sustained.

It would of course be necessary to compare a large range of countries, characterized by diverse forms of governments and cultures, if the purpose is to illuminate "the common processes by which all modern states militarize their populations" (Barkawi, pp. 361–376). But the militarization of populations is not the object of my research here, as I hope is abundantly clear by now. Nor, must I add, am I convinced that militarization should be presumed; Barkawi seems to suggest that militarization is a given whereas it is obviously, as he elsewhere seems to recognize, a variable across time and place. On the other hand, I am sympathetic to his argument, derived from Foucault (1977), Gillis (Ed.) (1989) and others that modern disciplinary structures, including those of military origin, may be quite significant in explaining a wide-spread compliance that is more subjection than consent, even within democracies. But this is an alternative hypothesis,[3] one deserving of further in-depth empirical exploration so that we can determine more confidently which account explains more of the variation.

INTERNATIONAL VARIABLES AND CONTEXT

In the second of their common criticisms, both Hobson and Barkawi, scholars of international relations, spotlight my lack of attention to the international context and to what Hobson nicely calls the "military pressures emanating within the interstate system" (pp. 347–359).

I plead guilty to giving relatively short shrift to the international context as an explanatory factor. I do, to my very slight defense, argue that geo-politics cannot account for the differences among the Anglo-Saxon democracies in the timing of their institution of conscription of conscription or in the variation in resistance (Levi, 1997, p. 124 and ff.). Admittedly, this is an instance of what international factors cannot explain, not what they can. On the more positive side, and in regards to an issue that Barkawi particularly raises, I do consider the use of colonial soldiers, particularly as I trace the history of military service in my several countries in Chapter 3. Barkawi is nonetheless right to reprimand me for not making enough of the extent to which reliance on the armies of the countries of its empire, particularly the Indian Army, affected British domestic conscription policy.

Where I must take total exception with Barkawi, however, is his statement that one should not "conceive of Australia, New Zealand, Canada and the U.K. as separate entities over much of the period." (p. 5). It is true that the first three countries in this list were colonies or dominions during much of the time covered by my study. It is equally true, however, that they each had their own governments, made their own conscription policies, and revealed considerable variation among themselves and with Britain in the twentieth century, which is what I focus on in discussing the behavioral evidence on compliance and consent. While I am in absolute disagreement with Barkawi over his conceptualization of these countries, I do concede that the increasing interconnectedness of countries through the military alliances of the twentieth century have undoubtedly affected the nature of warfare and conscription. However, the kinds of alliances that significantly matter for conscription policy are largely a post World War II phenomenon and had little consequence for the periods I discuss in my book.

Hobson improperly takes me to task for failing to address the legitimacy of wars in my formal model (pp. 347–359). If I understand him correctly, he seems to be saying that legitimacy is objective, tightly related to the national interest of a country. Yet the book addresses the nature of the war and how citizens perceive its appropriateness in terms of both government's stated goals and the procedures for undertaking it. These factors influence the perception of trustworthiness of government and affect the choice of the dominant ethical norms among different groups of citizens. Indeed, much of what Hobson cites about the War in Vietnam appears in *Consent, Dissent, and Patriotism* when I analyze variation in the ideological and moral components of citizen consent across different wars (see, esp. Ch. 7). What I do not do – and perhaps this is the problem from Hobson's perspective-is model (or even much discuss) national interest as an independent variable. Once again, what is offered as a critique is actually a possible alternative account.

Having dealt with the particulars, I must now turn, however, to the more general issue. The larger question they both raise is how to theorize state actions within the international system. This question is, of course, highly contested, as Hobson's recent review of the literature illustrates (Hobson, 2000). It is a question, I must admit, to which I have given relatively little thought, but it is obviously one to which I must pay attention.

At the level of how the international system influences states, my work clearly speaks to the importance of wars as transformative of governing institutions and figures in the debate on war making as state making. *Of Rule and Revenue* provided some confirmation for Schumpeter's insight (1954), taken up by Mann (1986), that war permits governments to increase the tax rate and then sustain it post-war at a higher level than before the war. *Consent, Dissent and Patriotism* focuses quite directly on how wars can compel governments to make concessions and promises to the population that can lead to institutional changes and increased democratization, and it tries to lay out some of the conditions for maintaining those institutional changes in peace time.

War making involves more than the actual period of the war, however. It also implies war preparedness, in terms of developing military technology and training officers and soldiers. Here, too, the international system has consequences. Countries emulate each other; for example, late nineteenth century French conscription policy was modeled partially after Prussian due to Prussia's victory in 1870, and throughout the early part of the twentieth century British conscription regulations were considered when Canada, New Zealand, and Australia established theirs. Moreover, as Huntington argues (1957, pp. 30–39 and *passim*), competitive nationalism and new kinds of national security needs, which emerged with industrialization, capitalism, and the development of the modern, hegemonic state, were major factors in the rise of both a professional officer corps and universal military service. My analysis takes a new direction by exploring, in depth, the interaction between these international forces and the institutions, rather than the ideologies, of particular states.

At the level of how states influence the international system, my work represents an intervention in the on-going debate (see, e.g. Thompson & Rasler, 1999) about the relative weights of changes in military technology in the development of states. My cases indicate that likely compliance of populations (and the existence of institutions that affect that compliance) might precipitate technological transformations as well as reflect them.

At the level of the role the international system plays in accounting for the variation in military service policies and in contingent consent and compliance within democratic countries, my research suggests several possibilities, and both Barkawi and Hobson have taught me about others.

First, as the nature of military technology and war itself changes, there is a tendency towards homogenization of military formats. Countries learn from each other. Thus, France, defeated by Prussia, emulated certain aspects of its conscription practices.

Second, the increasing integration of countries in military alliances such as NATO creates a further tendency towards homogenization of military formats among the member countries.

Third, the extent to which a country can rely on the populations of its "empire" to carry out its wars, it will do so. This will affect not only military format but how much consent is required from the domestic population.

These factors may well lead to similar policies, but I must emphasize two additional points. National differences in practice are likely to remain for some time given the distinct histories, politics, and cultures of the countries involved. Similarities in military formats do not mean standardization of consent and compliance, which will continue to fluctuate as a consequence of the variations in governmental behavior and processes and of the variations in the ethical norms among subsets of the population.

TOWARDS A BETTER HISTORICAL SOCIOLOGY

Both of my critics advocate a program of social research that is distinct from mine. In this final section I am less interested in what they think I should have discussed than in how they argue analysis should proceed. They are self-professed, if revisionist, Weberians. Hobson prefers theories that are complex and inductive; he treats words like parsimonious and positivistic as pejoratives, as the basis for criticizing the arguments of others (Hobson, 2000, p. 30). Barkawi's meaning of theory is generally incompatible with the generation and testing of hypotheses. The analytic narrative approach, which I practice, is parsimonious and positivistic – if by that is meant a concern with assessing theories with evidence. It is also deductive but, at the same time, inductive. It relies on rational choice and game theory, comparative statics, and other such tools of modern social science, but it equally relies on detailed investigation of cases to provide the necessary specification of key actors, their preferences and their constraints. Sufficient detail is also essential to carry out adequate tests.

Hobson and Barkawi are hardly unique in their skepticism about the combination of rational choice and case studies in the service of building generalizable models. *Analytic Narratives* (1998), co-authored by me with Robert Bates, Avner Greif, Jean-Laurent Rosenthal, and Barry Weingast, has been the subject of considerable and recent scholarly assessment. Barkawi's objections to the analytic narrative project derive, however, from an ontology distinct from that of the equally dismissive Jon Elster (2000). Indeed, Barkawi's views of how to do historical and political sociology stand in sharp contrast to Elster's (1989), mine, Hobson's (here and in his 2000 book) and others who have provided evaluations of the analytic narrative approach (see, e.g, Johnson, 1999; Thelen, 1999; Downing, 2000).[4] The fact that Barkawi is at odds with so many of us does not in itself make him wrong or misguided – although I, for one, think he is both. What it does mean and which he himself admits is that he and I are not always engaging on the same terrain.

Perhaps this is the source of his misunderstanding of the kind of modeling I am doing. For example, Barkawi critiques me for assuming that conscription is "about the self-interested and ethical consent of citizens" (pp. 361–376). At the trivial level, he is simply misguided. He conflates my interest in the role consent plays in conscription with an assertion, which I certainly do not make, that conscription is always about consent. His target is really liberal democratic theory and, more to the point in my case, reliance on methodological individualism.[5] He seems to believe, whatever the arguments made in the book, that by focusing on compliance and consent, I cannot be considering the effects of norms or of social and economic structures on what people do in a given society at a given time. He even accuses me of being ahistorical, by which he can only mean that he does not believe I sufficiently emphasize the determinative role of capitalism and property rights.

Part of the misunderstanding is linguistic, but there is more to our differences than terminology. Barkawi is, of course, correct that our enterprises are quite distinct, but he is woefully off the mark in his characterization of my work and that of other comparative political economists and economic historians who have similar methodological persuasions, and Hobson sometimes shares in this misrepresentation. The kind of rational choice we practice depends fundamentally on an elaboration of: the relevant institutions, that is, rules and norms; the economic system, that is, the organization of production, property rights and class relations; and other features of the social structure, such as the religious, ethnic, and racial composition of the population. To construct analytic narratives, which an increasing number of us are doing[6] requires the kind of in-depth and theoretically-informed knowledge of time and place that Weber exemplified. In *Consent, Dissent and Patriotism*, property rights and class power play crucial explanatory roles in accounting for the forms conscription policy takes, the kind of exemptions that are granted, and among whom resistance is likely to develop.

Hobson and Barkawi are far from alone in disparaging the rational choice model of human behavior. Barkawi prefers Nietzsche's characterization of the origin of moral values, which he then traces through Weber to Foucault. Hobson perceives neglect of "significance, or autonomy, of norms and ideas" (pp. 347–359). Elster (2000), for quite different reasons, also rejects the rational choice models he once advocated so eloquently; he cites the lack of empirical support for the assumption of rationality and the importance of non-rational motivations. It is incontrovertible that full rationality is an inaccurate description of human decision making; Elster appeals to experimental and other sources of hard evidence, as do others (cf., e.g. Ostrom, 1998; Jones, 1999). But no one has yet come up with a better behavioral assumption for the microfoundations of macro research. Perhaps even more to the point in a response to critics, the model of contingent consent "melds normative argument and rational choice" (Simmons, 1999, p. 130).

Hobson's major complaint is that *Consent, Dissent and Patriotism* represents a narrowing of my research agenda. Hopeful for a synthesis between historical sociology and international relations, instead he found a book emphasizing a subset of countries and domestic politics, institutions, and behaviors. Without such a synthesis, he argues we will not achieve a better theory of the state, one of my declared aims. But I beg to differ. As I argued in *Of Rule and Revenue,* the kind of theory of the state he wants is a chimera. As I attempt to demonstrate there and in *Consent, Dissent and Patriotism,* we can nonetheless make progress on understanding how state institutions emerge and change, what constraints they impose and reflect on state actors, and what role citizens and subjects play in the selection of state policies and institutions. These issues are increasingly engaging historical sociologists, economic historians, and comparative political economists whether they label themselves historical institutionalist or new institutional economists, whether they are more Weberian or more rationalist (cf., e.g. Thelen, 1998; Hall &Taylor, 1996). The new analyzes reflect advances in theorizing (as well as some rediscovery of older and still serviceable theories), not abdication of the underlying enterprise of making sense of the state over time. My differences with my critics about how to construct a better historical sociology devolve to: what it means to build a theory; and what the criteria are for assessment. For Barkawi and Hobson, theory building is the construction of typologies that list key variables analysts must attend to. For me, theory building involves generalizations assessed by their empirical validity (Fogel, 1997). For them the criterion of a good theory seems to be the inclusion of all potentially important factors and relations; a theory must touch all the bases. They do, of course, expect it to capture reality, and Hobson is explicitly interested in adjudication with evidence. For me, the criterion is how well it captures hypothesized relationships when tested and whether there is another validated theory that captures more. Illustrative examples and counterexamples will not do, nor will appeals to famous authors. The theory must be subject to standards of falsifiability.

The bottom line is that adjudication of theoretical claims, be they deductively or inductively derived, involves getting down to the nitty gritty of data collection and hypothesis testing. The hypotheses must, of course, be derived logically, and the assumptions must be defensible. It is more than appropriate to criticize failures on either of these dimensions, and, of course, theories can be superseded by alternatives which account for more of the variation.

The debate over the most compelling account is a debate worth pursuing, and my critics offer interesting and competing hypotheses to several of mine. But it is incumbent on them to offer more than their opinions and tastes. At least in this review, Barkawi appeals less to systematic data to arbitrate disputes than to particular examples or learned authorities that make his points, which might be all one should expect in a review. Hobson offers a substitute logic of the state. Both claim to offer an alternative, not just a debunking of my claims and findings. This puts on them the burden of providing a means to investigate their proposed alternatives. Yet, they offer few clues about what kinds of evidence, tests, or other evaluative techniques would falsify my propositions and support theirs.

One of the on-going debates in historical sociology is the appropriate basis for critiquing a theory. As Arthur Stinchcombe (1968) and, more recently, Michael Hechter and Edgar Kiser (1991, 1998), among others, have argued, a theory is as good as its capacity to explain more of the variance than other theories against which it is pitted. Rational choice may not ultimately prove the best theory nor my account of compliance and consent the most convincing, but so far there is not yet a demonstrably better alternative.

I will be exceedingly pleased if *Consent, Dissent and Patriotism* continues to stimulate imaginative thinking about the determinants of conscription policy and compliance with extractive government demands. My grandest hope is that it will generate further research, especially research that ultimately provides more satisfying and powerful explanation. I wish John M. Hobson and Tarak Barkawi the best of luck should they choose to pursue this path. In the words of one of my favorite learned authorities, Karl Marx (1974[1867], p. 299), "There is no royal road to science, and only those who do not dread the fatiguing climb of its steep paths have a chance of gaining its luminous summits."

NOTES

1. For alternative summaries and assessments of my arguments, see Burk (1999); Johnson (1999); and Simmons (1999).

2. Hobson actually uses the term "central" to describe arguments and claims for more than one of my points.

3. I do attempt some contrast with hypotheses derived from models of ideological and opportunistic compliance, but what Barkawi is suggesting is something else again.

4. There is a symposium on *Analytic Narratives*, forthcoming in *Social Science History 24*(winter 2000), 4. The participants are Theda Skocpol, Daniel Carpenter, Sunita Parikh, and the authors of *Analytic Narratives*. Also see the review forthcoming by Andrew Bennett in *Journal of Politics*.

5. He does say (p. 2) that he is not focusing on methodological individualism but on "methodological nation-statism," but he in fact focuses on both in his text.

6. Recent examples include Laitin 1998,who investigates identify formation among nationality groups in post-Soviet republics, and forthcoming books by Roger Petersen, Stathis Kalyvas, and Sunita Parikh, who each investigate issues of rebellion and revolution.

REFERENCES

Abdullah, I. B. (1997). Bush path to destruction: the origin and character of the Revolutionary United Front (RUF/SL). *Africa Development*, *22*(3,4). Special Issue: Lumpen Culture and Political Violence: the Sierra Leone Civil War.

Abenheim, D. (1990). The Citizen in Uniform: Reform and Its Critics in the Bundeswehr. In: S. F. Szabo (Ed.), *The Bundeswehr and Western Security* (pp. 31–51). London: Macmillan.

Ackerman, B. (1998). We the People: Transformations. Cambridge, MA: Belknap Press.

Adams, R. (1995). Etnicidad en el ejército de la Guatemala Liberal (1870–1915). Guatemala: FLACSO.

Adams, R. (1996). La población indígena en el estado liberal. In: J. L. Muñoz (Ed.), *Historia General de Guatemala* (Vol. 5, pp. 173–198).

Adams, R. J. Q., & Poirier, P. P. (1987). The Conscription Controversy in Great Britain, 1900–1918. London: Macmillan.

Agirre, X., Ajangiz, R., Ibarra, P., & Sainz de Rozas, R. (1998). *La insumisión, un singular ciclo histórico de desobediencia civil*. Madrid: Tecnos.

Agnew, J., & Corbridge, S. (1995). Mastering Space: Hegemony, Territory and International Political Economy. London: Routledge.

Agrell, W. (1979). *Om kriget inte kommer. En debattbok om Sveriges framtida försvars-och säkerhetspolitik*. Stockholm: Liber Förlag.

Agøy, N. I. (1990a). The Norwegian Peace Movement and the Question of Conscientious Objection to Military Service, 1885–1922. In: K. Kodama & U. Vesa (Eds), *Towards a Comparative Analysis of Peace Movements* (pp. 89–104). Brookfield: Dartmouth.

Agøy, N. I. (1990b). Regulating Conscientious Objection in Norway from the 1890s to 1922. *Peace and Change*, *15*(1), 3–25.

Ajangiz, R. (2000). Política militar y movimientos sociales: el fin de la conscripción en Europa. Unpublished doctoral dissertation, University of the Basque Country, Bilbao.

Albesano, S. (1993). *Storia dell'obiezione di coscienza in Italia*. Treviso: Santi Quaranta.

Alexander, A. J. (1945a). Service by Substitute in the Militias of Northampton and Lancaster Counties (PA) during the War of the Revolution. *Military Affairs*, *9*, 278–282.

Alexander, A. J. (1945b). Exemptions from Military Service in the Old Dominion during the War of the Revolution. *Virginia Magazine of History and Biography*, *52*, 163–171.

Alexander, A. J. (1947). How Maryland Tried to Raise Her Continental Quotas. *Maryland Historical Magazine*, *42*, 184–196.

Allison, G. T. (1971). *Essence of Decision. Explaining the Cuban Missile Crisis*. Boston: Little, Brown & Co.

Amnesty International (1992). *The extrajudicial execution of suspected rebels and collaborators*. London: International Secretariat of Amnesty International, Index AFR 51/02/92.

Amnesty International (1997). *Uganda. "Breaking God's commands": The destruction of childhood by the Lord's Resistance Army*. New York: Amnesty International/Africa.

Amoore, L., Dodgson, R., Germain, R., Gills, B. K., Langley, P., & Watson, I. (2000). Paths to a Historicized International Political Economy. *Review of International Political Economy*, *7*(1), 53–71.

Anderson, B. (1991). *Imagined Communities: reflections on the origin and spread of nationalism*. (rev. and exp. ed.). New York: Verso.

Anderson, M. S. (1987). *War and Society, 1618–1789*. London: Fontana.

Anderson, M. S. (1998). *War and Society in Europe of the Old Regime 1618–1789*. Phoenix Mill: Sutton Publishing.

Anderson, P. (1978). *Passages from Antiquity to Feudalism*. New York: Verso.

Anderson, P. (1979). *Lineages of the Absolutist State*. New York: Verso.

Andrews, A. (1971). *Greek Society*. Harmondsworth: Penguin Books.

Anónimo. (1911). El Ejército y los indios. *Revista Militar Ilustrada*, 15 de septiembre de 1911, 9–11.

Anónimo. (1904). *El amigo del soldado*. Guatemala: Tipografía Nacional.

Arbatov, A. G. (1997). Military Reform in Russia: Dilemmas, Obstacles, and Prospects. *International Security*, *22*, 83–134.

Arbatov, A. G. (1998). Military Reform in Russia: Dilemmas, Obstacles, and Prospects. *International Security*, *22*(4), 83–134.

Ardant, G. (1975). Financial Policy and Economic Infrastructure of Modern States and Nations. In: C. Tilly (Ed.), *The Formation of National States in Western Europe* (pp. 164–242). Princeton: Princeton University Press.

Arendt, H. (1973). *The Origins of Totalitarianism* (rev. ed.). New York: Harcourt Brace Jovanovich.

Arlacchi, P. (1998). Opening address to the Conference on establishing the rule of law in post-conflict situations. Vienna: June 26.

Arnold, E. A. (1966). Some Observations on the French Opposition to Napoleonic Conscription, 1804–1806. *French Historical Studies*, *4*, 452–462.

Arquilla, J., & Ronfeldt, D. F. (Eds) (1997). *In Athena's Camp. Preparing for Conflict in the Information Age*. Santa Monica, CA: RAND.

Audoin-Rouzeau, S. (1989). *1870: la France dans la Grande Guerre*. Paris: Armand Colin.

Auvray, M. (1983). *Objecteurs, insoumis, déserteurs. Histoire des réfractaires en France*. Paris: Stock.

Avant, D. (2000). From Mercenaries to Citizen Armies: Explaining Change in the Practice of War. *International Organization*, *54*, 41–72.

Ayoob, M. (1995). *The Third World Security Predicament. State Making, Regional Conflict, and the International System*. Boulder, CO: Lynne Rienner.

Ayton, A., & Price, J. L. (1995). Introduction: The Military Revolution from a Medieval Perspective. In: Idem & Idem (Eds), *The Medieval Military Revolution. State, Society and Military Change in Medieval and Early Modern Europe* (pp. 1–22). London: I. B. Tauris.

Baer, J. (1978). *The Chains of Protection: The Judicial Response to Women's Labor Legislation*. Westport, CT: Greenwood Press.

Bahr, H-E. (Ed.) (1990). *Von der Armee zur europäischen Friedenstruppe*. München: Knaur.

Baker, P. (1984). The Domestication of Politics: Women and American Political Society, 1780–1920. *American Historical Review*, *89*, 620–647.

Bald, D., & Prüfert, A. (Eds) (1997). *Von Krieg zur Militärreform. Zur Debatte um Leitbilder in Bundeswehr und Nationaler Volksarmee*. Baden-Baden: Nomos Verlagsgesellschaft.

Bald, D. (1994). *Militär und Gesellschaft 1945–1990. Die Bundeswehr der Bonner Republik*. Baden-Baden: Nomos Verlagsgesellschaft.

Bald, D. (Ed.) (1987). *Militz als Vorbild? Zum Reservistenkonzept der Bundeswehr*. Baden-Baden: Nomos Verlagsgesellschaft.

Bald, D. (Ed.) (1992). *Die Nationale Volksarmee. Beiträge zu Selbstverständnis und Geschichte des deutschen Militärs von 1945–1990*. Baden-Baden: Nomos Verlagsgesellschaft.

Ball, D. Y. (1994). Ethnic Conflict, Unit Performance, and the Soviet Armed Forces. *Armed Forces and Society*, *20*(2), 239–258.

Banfield, E. (1958). *The Moral Basis of a Backward Society*. Glencoe: Free Press.

Barbalet, J. (1988). *Citizenship*. Minneapolis: University of Minnesota Press.

Barkawi, T. (2001). War Inside the Free World: the US and the Cold War in the Third World. In: T. Bakarwi & M. Laffey (Eds). *Democracy, Liberalism and War: Rethinking the Democratic Peace Debate*. Boulder, CO: Lynne Rienner Press.

Barkawi, T., & Laffey, M. (Eds) (2001). *Democracy, Liberalism and War: Rethinking the Democratic Peace Debate*. Boulder, CO: Lynne Rienner Press.

Barkawi, T., & Laffey, M. (1999). The Imperial Peace: Democracy, Force and Globalization. *European Journal of International Relations*, *5*(4), 403–434.

Barnett, M. N. (1992). *Confronting the Costs of War. Military Power, State, and Society in Egypt and Israel*. Princeton, NJ: Princeton University Press.

Barrett, F. J. (1996). The Organizational Construction of Hegemonic Masculinity: The Case of the US Navy. *Genderwork and Organization*, *3*(3), 129–142.

Bartov, O. (1991). Soldiers, Nazis and War in the Third Reich. *Journal of Modern History*, *63*, 44–60.

Bartov, O. (1994). The 'Nation in Arms': Germany and France, 1789–1939. *History Today*, *44*, 27–33.

Bartov, O. (1996). The European Imagination in the Age of Total War. In: *Murder in Our Midst* (pp. 33–50). Oxford: Oxford University Press.

Bates, R. H., Greif, A., Levi, M., & Rosenthal, J.-L. (2000). The Analytic Narratives Project. *American Political Science Review*, *94*(3), 696–702.

Bates, R. H., Greif A., Levi M., Rosenthal J.-L., & Weingast B. R. (1998). *Analytic Narratives*. Princeton, N.J.: Princeton University Press.

Battistelli, F. (1997). Peacekeeping and the Postmodern Soldier. *Armed Forces and Society*, *23*(3), 467–484.

Battistelli, F. (1997). Servizio militare e servizio civile alla vigilia della riforma. Gli aspetti sociologici. *Sistema Informativo Archivio Disarmo*, *10*(3), 1–8.

Beaufre, A. (1972). *La guerre revolutionnaire. Les nouvelles formes de la guerre*. Paris: Fayard.

Bebler, A. (1993). The Yugoslav People's Army and the Fragmentation of a Nation. *Military Review*, *73*(8), 38–51.

Bebler, A. (Ed.) (1997). *Civil Military Relations in Post-Communist States*. Westport, CT: Praeger.

Beckman et al. (1992). *The Nuclear Predicament* (2nd ed.). Englewood Cliffs, N.J.: Prentice Hall.

Beevor, A. (1991). *Inside the British Army*. London: Corgi Books.

Bellamy, C. (1996). *Knights in White Armour. The New Art of War and Peace*. London: Hutchinson.

Ben-Eliezer, U. (1998). *The Making of Israeli Militarism*. Bloomington: Indiana University Press.

Berdal, M. R. (1996). Disarmament and Demobilisation after Civil Wars. *Adelphi Papers*, *203*.

Bergès, L. (1980). Le civil et l'armée au début du dix-neuvième siècle: la résistance à la conscription dans les départements aquitains, 1798–1814. Unpublished doctoral dissertation, Ecole des Chartes, Paris.

Bergès, L. (1987). La société civile contre le recrutement à l'époque de la conscription (1794–1894), thèse de 3e cycle, Université de Paris – I.

Berghahn, V. (1973). *Germany and the Approach of War in 1914*. New York: St. Martin's Press.

Berlin, I., Reidy, J. P., & Rowland, L. S. (1992). The Black Military Experience, 1861–1867. In: I. Berlin, B. J. Fields, S. F. Miller, J. P. Reidy & L. S. Rowland (Eds), *Slaves No More: Three Essays on Emancipation and the Civil War* (pp. 189–233). Cambridge and New York: Cambridge University Press.

Bertaud, J.-P. (1970). *Valmy: la démocratie en armes*. Paris: Julliard.

Bertaud, J.-P. (1982). Du volontariat à la conscription, 1789–1815. *Revue historique des armées, 147*, 24–33.

Bertaud, J.-P. (1985). *La vie quotidienne des soldats de la Révolution, 1789–1799*. Paris: Hachette.

Bertaud, J.-P. (1988). *The Army of the French Revolution: From Citizen-Soldiers to Instrument of Power*. Princeton: Princeton University Press.

Bertaud, J.-P. (1991). The Volunteers of 1792. In: A. Forrest & P. Jones (Eds), *Reshaping France: Town, Country and Region during the French Revolution*. New York: Manchester University Press.

Best, G. (1982). *War and Society in Revolutionary Europe, 1770–1870*. London: Fontana.

Best, G. (1998). *War and Society in Revolutionary Europe 1770–1870*. Phoenix Mill: Sutton Publishing.

Betts, R. K. (1995). *Military Readiness. Concepts, Choices, Consequences*. Washington, D.C.: The Brookings Institution.

Biddle, S. (1998). The Past as Prologue: Assessing Theories of Future Warfare. *Security Studies, 8*(1), 1–74.

Birand, M. A. (1991). *Shirts of Steel. An Anatomy of the Turkish Armed Forces*. London: I.B. Tauris.

Bird, L. (1984). *Costa Rica: The Unarmed Democracy*. London: Sheppard Press.

Birnbaum, P. (1988). The State and Mobilisation for War. *States and Collective Action* (pp. 55–66). New York: Cambridge University Press.

Black, J. (1991). *A Military Revolution? Military Change and European Society, 1550–1800*. New York: St. Martin's.

Black, J. (1994). *European Warfare 1660–1815*. New Haven: Yale University Press.

Black, J. (1995). A Military Revolution? A 1660–1792 Perspective. In: C. J. Rogers (Ed.), *The Military Revolution Debate: Readings on the Military Transformation of Early Modern Europe* (pp. 95–114). Boulder: Westview Press.

Blair, D. (1991). Criteria for Planning the Transition to Lower Defense Spending. In: R. L. Pfaltzgraff, Jr. (Ed.), *New Directions in U.S. Defense Policy, The Annals of the American Academy of Political and Social Science* (Vol. 517, pp. 146–156).

Boëne, B., & Martin, M. L. (Eds) (1991). *Conscription et Armée de Métier*. Paris: Fondation pour les études de défense nationale.

Bond, B. (1984). *War and Society in Europe, 1870–1970*. London: Fontana.

Bond, B. (1994). *The British Experience of National Service, 1947–1963*. R. G. Foerster (Ed.), pp. 207–215.

Bond, B. (1998). *War and Society in Europe 1870–1970*. Phoenix Mill: Sutton Publishing.

Booth, K. (1983). Strategy and Conscription. In: J. Baylis (Ed.), *Alternative Approaches to British Defence Policy* (pp. 154–190). London: Macmillan.

Boothby, N., & Knudsen, C. (2000). Children of the gun. *Scientific American, 282*(6), 6–66.

Bordo, M. D., Eichengreen, B., & Kim, J. (1998). Was There Really and Earlier Period of International Financial Integration Comparable to Today? NBER Working Paper 6738.

Borkenhagen, F. H. U. (Ed.) (1986). *Bundeswehrdemokratie in Oliv. Streiträfte im Wandel*. Berlin: Dietz Verlag.

Boserup, A., & Mack, A. (1974). *War Without Weapons. Non-Violence in National Defence*. London: Frances Pinter.

Boudard, R. (1985). La conscription militaire et ses problèmes dans le département de la Creuse (1791–1815). *Revue de l'Institut Napoléon, 144–146*, 23–57.

Boudon, R. (1998). Social mechanisms without black boxes. In: P. Hedstrøm & R. Swedberg (Eds), *Social Mechanisms* (pp. 172–204). Cambridge: Cambridge University Press.

Bouleoiseau, M. (1968). *Le Comité de Salut Public*. Paris: Presses Universitaires de France.

Bouleoiseau, M. (1972). *La république jacobine, 10 aout 1792–1799 Thermidor an II*. Nouvelle Histoire de la France Contemporaine, Vol. 2. Paris: Éditions du Seuil.

Bourdeau, G. (1898). L'affaire de Nancy – 31 août 1790. *Annales de l'Est*, *12*, 280–292.

Bourke, J. (1999). *An Intimate History of Killing. Face to Face Killing in 20th Century Warfare*. London/New York: Granta/Basic Books.

Bowles, S., & Gintis, H. (1987). *Democracy and Capitalism: Property, Community and the Contradictions of Modern Social Thought*. New York: Basic Books.

Bowra, C. M. (1969). *The Greek Experience*. New York: Praeger.

Braun, R. (1975). Taxation, Socio-Political Structure and State-Building: Britain and Brandenburg Prussia. In: C. Tilly (Ed.), *The Formation of National States in Western Europe* (pp. 243–327). Princeton: Princeton University Press.

Brett, R., & McCallin, M. (1996). *Children: The invisible soldiers*. Vaxjo, Sweden: Radda Barnen.

Brewer, J. (1989). *The Sinews of Power*. London: Unwin Hyman.

Bridge, F. R., & Bullen, R. (1980). *The Great Powers and the European States System 1815–1914*. London: Longmans.

Brinkerhoff, J. R. (1993). Civilian Substitution. In: Dupuy (Ed.), Vol. 2, 525–528.

Brinkley, A. (1995). *The End of Reform: New Deal Liberalism in Recession and War*. NY: Alfred A. Knopf.

Brokaw, T. (1998). *The Greatest Generation*. NY: Random House.

Bronfenbrenner, U. (1979). *The ecology of human development: Experiments by nature and design*. Cambridge: Harvard University Press.

Brown, F. J., & Merrill, Jr., A. R. (1994). Challenges of U.S. Army Reserve Force Readiness. In: S. C. Sarkesian & J. M. Flanagin (Eds). *U.S. Domestic and National Security Agendas* (pp. 258–281). Westport, CT: Greenwood Press.

Brubaker, R. (1992). *Citizenship and Nationhood in France and Germany*. Cambridge, MA: Harvard University Press.

Brubaker, R. (1996). *Nationalism Reframed: Nationhood and the National Question in the New Europe*. Cambridge University Press.

Buffotot, P. (1997). Eviter la marginalisation. In: P. Buffotot (Ed.), *La défense en Europe. Les adaptations de l'après-guerre froide* (pp. 183–187). Paris: La Documentation Française.

Builder, C. H. (1997). Service Identities and Behavior. In: P. L. Hays, B. J. Vallance & J. R. V. Tassel (Eds), *American Defense Policy* (7th ed., pp. 108–122). Baltimore, ML: John Hopkins University Press.

Bullard, M. (1997). *The Soldier and the Citizen. The Role of the Military in Taiwan's Development*. Armonk, NY: M.E. Sharpe.

Burk, J. (1989). Debating the Draft in America. *Armed Forces and Society*, *15*(3), 431–448.

Burk, J. (1992). The Decline of Mass Armed Forces and Compulsory Military Service. *Defense Analysis*, *8*, 45–49.

Burk, J. (1994). Thinking Through the End of Cold War. In: J. Burk (Ed.), *The Military in New Times. Adapting Armed Forces to a Turbulent World* (pp. 1–24). Oxford: Westview Press.

Burk, J. (1999). Consent, Dissent and Patriotism: A Review. *Armed Forces and Society*, *25*, 529.

Burk, J. (Ed.) (1994). *The Military in New Times. Adapting Armed Forces to a Turbulent World*. Boulder, CO: Westview.

Burstein, P. (1991). Policy Domains: Organization, Culture, and Policy Outcomes. *Annual Review of Sociology*, *17*, 327–350.

Bushnell, J. (1980). Peasants in Uniform: The Tsarist Army as a Peasant Society. *Journal of Social History*, *13*, 565–576.

Bushnell, J. (1985). *Mutiny Amid Repression: Russian Soldiers in the Revolution of 1905–1906*. Bloomington: Indiana University Press.

Bushnell, J. (1987). Peasant Economy and Peasant Revolution at the Turn of the Century: Neither Immiseration nor Autonomy. *The Russian Review*, *46*, 75–88.

Buzan, B. (1991). *People, States and Fear. An Agenda for International Security Studies in the Post-Cold War Era* (2nd ed.). London: Harvester Wheatsheaf.

Calleo, D. (1978). *The German Problem Reconsidered*. Cambridge: Cambridge University Press.

Calleo, D. C. (1987). *Beyond American Hegemony*. Cambridge, MA.: Harvard University Press.

Cambon, P. (1976). Francs-tireurs et corps francs en 1870–1871: mythe et réalité. Unpublished mémoire de maîtrise, Université de Paris – I.

Camp, R. A. (1992). *Generals in the Palacio: The Military in Modern Mexico*. New York: Oxford University Press.

Campbell, B. (1994). *The Roman Army, 31 BC-AD 337. A Sourcebook*. London: Routledge.

Campbell, D. (1990). The Regimented Women of World War II. In: J. B. Elshstain & S. Tobias, (Eds), Women, *Militarism and War: Essays in History, Politics and Social Theory*. Savage, MD: Rowman & Littlefield.

Carmack, R. (1979). *Historia Social de los Quiches*. Guatemala: Editorial "José de Pineda Ibarra," Ministerio de Educación.

Carmack, R. (1990). State and Community in Nineteenth-Century Guatemala. In: C. Smith (Ed.), *Guatemalan Indians and the State* (pp. 116–136).

Carmack, R. (1995). Los Indígenas. In: J. L. Muño (Ed.), *Historia General de Guatemala* (Vol. 4, pp. 339–352).

Carnoy, M. (1984). *The State and Political Theory*. Princeton: Princeton University Press.

Carr, E. H. (1939). *The Twenty Years Crisis: 1919–1939*. New York: MacMillan.

Carr, F., & Ifantis, K. (1996). *NATO in the New European Order*. London: MacMillan Press Ltd.

Cassirer, E. (1945). *Rousseau, Kant, Goethe: Two Essays* (pp. 1–60). Princeton: Princeton University Press.

Cassirer, E. (1954). *The Question of Jean-Jacques Rousseau*. P. Gay (trans. and Ed.) New York: Columbia University Press.

Castel, J.-A. (1970). L'application de la Loi Jourdan dans l'Hérault. Unpublished mémoire de maîtrise, Université de Montpellier.

Cattelain, J. P. (1973). *La objeción de conciencia*. Barcelona: Oikos Tau.

Chabal, P. (1998). A Few Considerations on Democracy in Africa. *International Affairs*, *74*, 289–303.

Chafetz, G., Spirtas, M., & Frankel, B. (Eds) (1999). *Origins of National Interests*. London: Frank Cass.

Chagniot, J. (1985). *Paris et l'armée au XVIIIe siècle, étude politique et sociale*. Paris: Économica.

Chaliand, G. (Ed.) (1982). *Guerilla Strategies. An Historical Anthology from the Long March to Afghanistan*. Berkeley: University of California Press.

Challener, R. (1955). *The French Theory of the Nation in Arms, 1866–1939*. New York: Columbia University Press.

Charnay, J.-P. (1964). *Société militaire et suffrage politique en France depuis 1789*. Paris: S.E.V.P.E.N.

Chatelain, A. (1972). Résistance à la conscription et migrations temporaires sous le Premier Empire. *Annales Historiques de la Révolution Française*, *44*, 606–625.

Chatfield, C. (1995). Ironies of Protest. Interpreting the American Anti-Vietnam War Movement. In: G. Grunewald & P. Van den Dungen (Eds), *Twentieth-Century Peace Movements: Successes and Failures* (pp. 199–208). Lewiston: Edwin Mellen Press.

Chicken, P. (1996). Conscription Revisited. In: T. Chafer & B. Jenkins (Eds), *France: Form the Cold War to the New World Order* (pp. 93–103). New York: St. Martin's Press.

Choisel, F. (1981). Du tirage au sort au service universel. *Revue historique des armées, 143*, 43–60.

Chorley, K. (1943). *Armies and the Art of Revolution*. Boston: Beacon Press.

Christian Aid (1999). Sierra Leone: what price peace? An analysis of the Disarmament, Demobilization and Reintegration Plan. Unpublished report, December 1999.

Christian Children's Fund (1998). *Final report: Project of reintegration of child soldiers in Angola*. Luanda: Christian Children's Fund.

Cilliers, J., & Mason, P. (Eds) (1999). *Peace, Profit or Plunder? The Privatisation of Security in War-Torn African Societies*. Halfway House, South Africa: Institute for Security Studies.

Clayton, A. (1988). *France, Soldiers and Africa*. London: Brassey's Defence Publishers.

Clifford, D. L. (1990). The National Guard and the Parisian Community, 1789–1790. *French Historical Studies, 16*, 849–878.

Cobb, R. (1988). France and the coming of war. In: R. J. W. Evans & H. Pogge von Strandmann (Eds), *The Coming of the First World War* (pp. 124–144). Oxford: Oxford University Press.

Cohen, E. A. (1985). *Citizen and Soldiers. The Dilemmas of Military Service*. Ithaca and London: Cornell University Press.

Cohen, E. A. (1994). The Strategy of Innocence? The United States, 1920–1945. In: W. Murray, M. Knox & A. Bernstein (Eds), *The Making of Strategy: Rulers, States and War* (pp. 428–465). Cambridge: Cambridge University Press.

Cohen, W. B. (1980). *The French Encounter with Africans: White Responses to Blacks, 1530–1880*. Bloomington: Indiana Press.

Cohn, I., & Goodwin-Gill, G. (1994). *Child soldiers*. Oxford: Clarendon Press.

Coleman, J., & Brice, Jr., B. (1962). The Role of the Military in Sub-Saharan Africa. In: J. Johnson, (Ed.), *The Role of the Military in Underdeveloped Countries* (pp. 359–405). Princeton: Princeton University Press.

Colley, L. (1996). *Britons: Forging the Nation 1707–1837*. London: Vintage.

Collier, P. (2000). *Economic causes of civil conflict and their implications for policy*. Washington: The World Bank.

Collins, A. (1997). *The Security Dilemma and the End of the Cold War*. Edinburg: Keele University Press.

Collins, R. (1986). *Weberian Sociological Theory*. Cambridge: Cambridge University Press.

Congressional Record (1943). Washington, D.C.: Government Printing Office.

Connell, R. W. (1995) *Masculinities*. Cambridge: Polity Press.

Cortright, D., & Watts, M. (1991). *Left Face. Soldier Unions and Resistance Movements in Modern Armies*. Wesport CT: Greenwood Press.

Corvisier, A. (1979). *Armies and Societies in Europe, 1494–1789*. A. T. Siddall (trans.), Bloomington and London: Indiana University Press.

Corvisier, A. (1985a). Les circonscriptions militaires de la France, facteurs humains et facteurs techniques. In: *Les hommes, la guerre, et la mort* (pp. 39–48). Paris: Economica.

Corvisier, A. (1985b). Quelques aspects sociaux des milices bouregoises au XVIIIe siècle. In: *Les hommes, la guerre, et la mort* (pp. 221–257). Paris: Economica.

Corvisier, A., Vidalenc J., Devos, J. C., & Waksman, P. (1975). Les réactions des divers milieux sociaux et des troupes devant les différentes obligations militaires depuis le XVIIe siècle jusqu'à la Guerre de 1914. *Bulletin d'Histoire Moderne et Contemporaine, 9*, 5–16.

Cosidó, I. (1994). *El gasto militar. El presupuesto de Defensa en España (1982–1992)*. Madrid: Eudema.

Cosidó, I. (1996). Factores económicos que condicionan la profesionalización. In: M. Aleñar (Ed.), *La profesionalización en los ejércitos. Un cambio radical de mentalidad para un Estado moderno* (pp. 137–162). Madrid: Fundación Cánovas del Castillo.

Cowley, R., & Parker, G. (Eds) (1996). *The Reader's Companion to Military History*. Boston: Houghton Mifflin.

Cox, R. W. (1986). Social Forces, States and World Orders: Beyond International Relations Theory. In: R. O. Keohane (Ed.), *Neorealism and its Critics* (pp. 204–254). New York: Columbia University Press.

Craig, G. (1966). Europe Since 1815 (2nd ed.). New York: Holt, Rinehart and Winston.

Craig, G. A. (1955). *The Politics of the Prussian Army, 1640–1945*. London: Oxford University Press.

Cramer, B. (1984). Dissuassion infra-nucleaire. L'armée de milice suisse: mythes et réalites stratégiques. *Cahiers d'études stratégiques, 4*. Paris: CIRPES.

Crépin, A. (1994). Le mythe de Valmy. In: M. Vovelle (Ed.), *Révolution et République: l'exception française* (pp. 467–478). Paris: Editions Kimé.

Crépin, A. (1998). *La conscription en débat, ou le triple apprentissage de la Nation, de la Citoyenneté, de la République, 1798–1889*. Arras: Artois Presses Université.

Cress, L. D. (1982). *Citizens in Arms: The Army and Militia in American Society to the War of 1812*. Chapel Hill: University of North Carolina Press.

Creveld, M. V. (1991). *The Transformation of War*. New York: The Free Press.

Creveld, M. V. (1994). *Conscription Warfare: the Israeli Experience*. Foerster (Ed.), pp. 227–240.

Creveld, M. V. (1998). *The Sword and the Olive. A Critical Story of the Israeli Defense Force*. New York: Public Affairs.

Crowder, M. (1967). *Senegal: A Study in French Assimilation Policy*. London: Methuen.

Crowder, M. (1978). Blaise Diagne and the Recruitment of African Troops for the 1914–1918 War. In: M. Crowder (Ed.), *Colonial West Africa: Collected Essays* (pp. 104–121). London: Frank Cass.

Cumings, B. (1990). *The Origins of the Korean War: The Roaring of the Cataract 1947–1950*. Vol. II. Princeton: Princeton University Press.

Cumings, B. (1992). *War and Television*. London: Verso.

Dahl, R. (1998). *On Democracy*. New Haven: Yale University Press.

Danapoulos, C. P. & Zirker, D. (Eds) (1996). *Civil-Military Relations in the Soviet and Yugoslav Successor States*. Boulder, CO: Westview Press.

Dandeker, C. (1990). *Surveillance, Power & Modernity*. Cambridge: Polity.

Dandeker, C. (1994a). A Farewell to Arms? The Military and the Nation-State in a Changing World. In: J. Burk (Ed.), *The Military in New Times. Adapting Armed Forces to a Turbulent World* (pp. 117–139). Oxford: Westview Press.

Dandeker, C. (1994b). New times for the military: some sociological remarks on the changing role and structure of the armed forces of the advanced societies. *British Journal of Sociology, 45*(4), 637–654.

Dandeker, C., & Segal, M. W. (1996). Gender Integration in the Armed Forces: Recent Policy Developments in the United Kingdom. *Armed Forces and Society, 23*(1), 29–47.

Davenport, B. A. (1995). Civil-Military Relations in the Post-Soviet State: "Loose Coupling" Uncoupled? *Armed Forces and Society, 21*(2), 175–194.

Davis, P. (1994). *Planning Under Uncertainty Then and Now: Paradigms Lost and Paradigms Emerging*. In: Idem (Ed.), pp. 15–58.

Davis, P. (Ed.) (1994). *New Challenges for Defense Planning. Rethinking How Much is Enough*. Santa Monica, CA: RAND.

Davis, S. C. (1934). *Reservoirs of Men: A History of the Black Troops of French West Africa.* Chambery: Imprimeries reunies.

Davis, S. C. (1934). *Reservoirs of Men: A History of the Black Troops of French West Africa.* Published Ph.D. Thesis, The University of Geneva.

Dawes, A., & Donald, D. (2000). Improving children's chances: Developmental theory and effective interventions in community contexts. In: D. Donald, A. Dawes & J. Louw (Eds), *Addressing Childhood Adversity* (pp. 1–25). Cape Town: David Philip.

de Cardenal, L. (1911). *Recrutement de l'armée en Périgord pendant la période révolutionnaire, 1789–1800.* Paris: Perigeux.

de Cardenal, L. (1912). *Du service par enrôlements volontaires au service obligatoire et personnel: Etude sur le recrutement de l'armée de 1789 à l'an VI.* Paris: Henri Charles-Lavauzelle.

de Tocqueville, A. (1955). *The Old Regime and the French Revolution.* S. Gilbert (trans.). Garden City, NY: Doubleday Anchor Books.

de Tocqueville, A. (1966, 1969). *Democracy in America.* J. P. Mayer (Ed.), G. Lawrence (trans.). New York: Anchor Books.

Deibel, T. L. (1993). *Strategy, National Security.* In: Dupuy (Ed.), Vol. 5, pp. 2577–2581.

Delbrück, H. (1990[1920]). *The History of the Art of War. Vol. 4: The Dawn of Modern Warfare,* W. J. Renfroe, Jr. (trans.). Lincoln: Bison Books of the University of Nebraska Press.

Della Porta, D., & Rucht, D. (1995). Left-Libertarian Movements in Context: A Comparison of Italy and West Germany, 1965–1990. In: J. C. Jenkins & B. Klandermans (Eds), *The Politics of Social Protest. Comparative Perspectives on States and Social Movements* (pp. 229–272). London: UCL Press.

Dertouzos, J. N., & Nation, J. E. (1993). *Manpower Policies in the U.S. and NATO.* In: Dupuy (Ed.), Vol. 4, pp. 1630–1640.

Desch, M. E. (1999). *Civilian Control of the Military. The Changing Security Environment.* Baltimore, ML: John Hopkins University Press.

Desert, G. (1965). Le remplacement dans le Calvados sous l'Empire et les monarchies censitaires. *Revue d'Histoire Économique et Sociale 43*, 66–85.

Diamond, L., & Plattner, M. F. (Eds) (1996). *Civil-Military Relations and Democracy.* Baltimore, ML: John Hopkins University Press.

Dietz, P. J., & Stone, J. F. (1975). The British All-Volunteer Army. *Armed Forces and Society, 1*(2), 159–190.

Doel, T. v. d. (1994). A Review of Dutch Defense Policy: Challenges and Risks. In: J. G. Siccama & T. van den Doel (Eds), *Reestructuring Armed Forces in East and West* (pp. 57–67). Oxford: Westview Press.

Doorn, J. v. (1975). The Decline of the Mass Army in the West. General Reflections. *Armed Forces and Society, 1*(2), 147–157.

Doorn, J. v. (1976). The Military and the Crisis of Legitimacy. In: G. Harries-Jenkins & J. Van Doorn (Eds), *The Military and the Problem of Legitimacy* (pp. 17–40). London: Sage.

Dorman, A. M., & Treacher, A. (1995). *European Security. An Introduction to Security Issues in Post-Cold War Europe.* Cambridge: Dartmouth Publishing Company.

Douglas, M. (1987). *How institutions think.* Routledge: London.

Douglas, M. (1993). *In the wilderness: the doctrine of defilement in the Book of Numbers.* JSOT Press: Sheffield.

Douglas, M., & Ney, S. (1998). *Missing persons.* Berkeley: University of California Press.

Dower, J. W. (1986). *War Without Mercy: Race and Power in the Pacific War.* London: Faber and Faber.

Downes, C. (1988). Great Britain. In: C. Moskos (Eds), *Just Another Job?* London: Brassey's.

Downes, C. (1988). Great Britain. In: C. C. Moskos & F. R. Wood (Eds), *The Military, More than Just a Job?* (pp. 201–228). Washington: Pergamon-Brassey's.

Downing, B. M. (1992). *The Military Revolution and Political Change: Origins of Democracy and Autocracy in Early Modern Europe*. Princeton: Princeton University Press.

Downing, B. M. (2000). Economic Analysis in Historical Perspective. *History and Theory*, *39*, 88–97.

Doyle, M. (1996). Kant, Liberal Legacies, and Foreign Affairs. In: M. Brown et al. (Eds), *Debating the Democratic Peace* (pp. 3–57). Cambridge: MIT Press.

Doyle, M. (1997). Liberalism and World Politics. In: F. Zakaria, (Ed.), *Foreign Affairs Agenda: The New Shape of World Politics* (pp. 39–66). New York: Foreign Affairs.

Drake, M. S. (Forthcoming). *Problematics of Military Power: Government, Discipline and the Subject of Violence*. Ilford: Frank Cass.

Dumoulin, A. (1997). La vocation internationale croissante des forces de défense. In: P. Buffotot (Ed.), *La défense en Europe. Les adaptations de l'après-guerre froide* (pp. 45–57). Paris: La Documentation Française.

Dunivin, K. O. (1994). Military Culture – Change and Continuity. *Armed Forces and Society*, *20*(4), 531–547.

Dupuy, R. (1972). *La Garde Nationale et les débuts de la Révolution en Ille-et-Vilaine, 1789–1793*. Paris: Klincksieck.

Dupuy, T. N. (Ed.) (1993). *International Military and Defense Encyclopedia*. Washington, D.C.: Brasseys, U.S.

Duyvendak, J. W. (1995). *The Power of Politics. New Social Movements in France*. Boulder CO: Westview Press.

Däniker, G. (1987). *Dissuasion. Schweizerische Abhaltestrategie Heute und Morgen*. Frauenfeld: Huber.

Däniker, G. (1995). The Guardian Soldier: On the Nature and Use of Future Armed Forces. Research Paper 36 (Geneva: UNIDIR).

Echenberg, M. (1991). *Colonial Conscripts: The "Tirailleurs Sénégalais" in French West Africa, 1857–1960*. Portsmouth, NH: Heinemann/London: James Curry.

Economist (1999). Children Under Arms: Kalashnikov Kids. Vol. 352, no. 8127, 19–21.

Edmonds, M. (1988). *Armed Forces and Society*. Leicester: Leicester University Press.

Ehrenreich, B. (1997). *Blood Rites. Origins and History of the Passions of War*. London: Virago Press.

El Imparcial (1940). January 2 and July 10, 1940.

El Liberal Progresista (1941). February 14, 1941.

Elias, N. (1994). *The Civilizing Process*, Vol. 2. Oxford: Basil Blackwell.

Elron, E., Shamir, B., & Ben-Ari, E. (1999). Why Don't They Fight Each Other? Cultural Diversity and Operational Unity in Multinational Forces. *Armed Forces and Society*, *26*(1), 73–98.

Elster, J. (1989). *Nuts and Bolts for the Social Sciences*. New York: Cambridge University Press.

Elster, J. (1989). *The Cement of Society*. Cambridge: Cambridge University Press.

Elster, J. (1998). A plea for mechanisms. In: P. Hedstrøm & R. Swedberg. (Eds), *Social Mechanisms* (pp. 32–44). Cambridge: Cambridge University Press.

Elster, J. (2000). Rational Choice History: A Case of Excessive Ambition. *American Political Science Review*, *94*, 685–695.

Elting, J. R. (1988). *Swords Around the Throne: Napoleon's Grande Armée*. New York: The Free Press.

Engels, F. (1972). Die preußische Militärfrage und die deutsche Arbeiterpartei. In: K. Marx & idem, *Werke* (Vol. 13, pp. 39–78). Berlin: Dietz Verlag.

Enloe, C. (1980). *Ethnic Soldiers: State Security and Divided Societies*. Athens, GA: The University of Georgia Press.

Enloe, C. (1980). *Police, Military and Ethnicity: Foundations of State Power*. New Brunswick: Transaction Books.

Enloe, C. (2000). *Maneuvers: The International Politics of Militarizing Women's Lives*. Berkeley: University of California Press.

Estrella, R. (1993). *Military Trends Within the Atlantic Alliance Sub-Committee on the Future of the Armed Forces*. NATO Report AK76 DSC/AF(93)1.

Evans, P. (1995). *Embedded Autonomy: States and Industrial Transformation*. Princeton: Princeton University Press.

Evans, P. B., Jacobson, H. K., & Putnam, R. D. (1993). *Double-Edged Diplomacy*. London: University of California Press.

Fabyanic, T. A. (1976). Manpower Trends in the British All-Volunteer Force. *Armed Forces and Society*, *2*(4), 553–572.

Faragher, J. M. et al. (2001). *Out of many: a history of the American people* (combined ed., brief, 3rd ed.). Upper Saddle River, N.J.: Prentice Hall.

Ferguson, E. (1938). *Guatemala*. New York: Alfred A. Knopf.

Ferguson, N. (1992). Germany and the Origins of the First World War: New Perspectives. *The Historical Journal*, *35*, 725–752.

Ferguson, N. (1994). Public Finance and National Security: The Domestic Origins of the First World War revisited. *Past and Present*, *14*, 141–168.

Ferguson, N. (1999). *The Pity of War: Explaining World War I*. New York: Basic Books.

Ferrill, A. (1985). *The Origins of War. From the Stone Age to Alexander the Great*. London: Thames and Hudson.

Ferro, M. (1999). Cultural life in France, 1914–1918. In: A. Roshwald & R. Stites (Eds), *European Culture in the Great War: The Arts, Entertainment and Propaganda, 1914–1918* (pp. 295–307). Cambridge: Cambridge University Press.

Fieldhouse, D. K. (1966). *The Colonial Empires: A Comparative Survey from the Eighteenth Centurey*. London: Weidenfeld and Nicolson.

Finer, S. E. (1975). State and Nation-Building in Europe: The Role of the Military. In: C. Tilly (Ed.), *The Formation of National States in Western Europe* (pp. 81–163). Princeton: Princeton University Press.

Finer, S. E. (1976). *The Man on Horseback. The Role of the Military in Politics* (2nd ed.). Harmondsworth: Penguin Books.

Fischer, F. (1969/1975). *War of Illusions: German Policies From 1911–1914*, M. Jackson (trans.). New York: Norton.

Fitch, J. S. (1978). *The Coup d'Etat as a Political Process: Ecuador, 1946–1966*. Baltimore: Johns Hopkins Press.

Fitzpatrick, S. (1994). *The Russian Revolution* (2nd ed.). New York: Opus/Oxford University Press.

Fleming, J. (1997). Baby steps toward final peace in Angola. *Christian Science Monitor*, (February 2).

Flora, P. (1983). *State, Economy, and Society in Western Europe 1815–1975. A Data Handbook*. Vol. I. Frankfurt a. M.: Campus.

Flora, P. (1987). *State, Economy, and Society in Western Europe 1815–1975. A Data Handbook*. Vol. II. Frankfurt a. M.: Campus.

Foerster, R. G. (Ed.) (1994). *Die Wehrpflicht. Entstehung, Erscheinungsformen und politisch-militärische Wirkung*. München: R. Oldenbourg Verlag.

Fogel, R. W. (1997). *Douglass C. North and Economic Theory. The Frontiers of the New Institutional Economics*. San Diego, CA.: Academic Press.

Foner, E. (1988). *Reconstruction: America's Unfinished Revolution, 1863–1877*. New York: Harper and Row.

Forrest, A. (1981). *The French Revolution and the Poor*. Oxford: Blackwell.

Forrest, A. (1989). *Conscripts and Deserters. The Army and French Society during the Revolution and Empire*. New York: Oxford University Press.

Forrest, A. (1990). *The Soldiers of the French Revolution*. Durham, N.C.: Duke University Press.

Forster, S., & J. Nagler, (Eds) (1997). *On the Road to Total War: The American Civil War and the German Wars of Unification, 1861–1871*. Cambridge: Cambridge University Press.

Forsvarskommandoen (1998). Notat vedrørende værnepligtens betydning for forsvaret samt beslægtede problemstillinger. In: *Fremtidens Forsvar. Beretning fra Forsvarskommissionen af 1997*, Appendix Volume I, appendix 24. Copenhagen: Statens Information.

Foucault, M. (1975). *Surveiller et punir*. Paris: Gallimard.

Foucault, M. (1977). *Discipline and Punish*. London: Penguin Books.

Frank, A. G., & Gills, B. K. (1996). *The World System*. London: Routledge.

Fraser, N., & Gordon, L. (1994). Civil Citizenship against Social Citizenship? In: B. van Steenbergen (Ed.), *The Condition of Citizenship*. London: Sage Publications.

Fraser, N., & Gordon, L. (1995). A Geneology of Dependency: Tracing a Keyword of the U.S. Welfare State. In: B. Laslett, J. Brenner & Y. Arat (Eds), *Rethinking the Political: Gender, Resistance and the State* (pp. 33–60). Chicago: University of Chicago Press.

French, D. (1982). *British Economic and Strategic Planning 1905–1915*. London: G. Allen and Unwin.

Friedberg, A. L. (1992). Why Didn't the United States Become a Garrison State?. *International Security*, *16*(4), 109–142.

Friedberg, A. L. (2000). *In the shadow of the garrison state: America's anti-statism and its Cold War grand strategy*. Princeton: Princeton University Press.

Fuhrer, H. R. (1987). Austria and Switzerland: the Defense Systems of Two Minor Powers. In: L. H. Gann (Ed.), *The Defence of Western Europe* (pp. 95–125). London: Croom Helm.

Fuhrer, H. R. (1994). Das Schweizer System. Friedenssicherung und Selbstverteidigung im 19. und 20. Jahrhundert. In: Foerster (Ed.), pp. 193–206.

Fuller, W. C. (1985). *Civil Military Conflict in Imperial Russia, 1881–1914*. Princeton: Princeton University Press.

Förster, S. (1994). Militär und Staatsbürgerlich Partizipation. Die Allgemeine Wehrpflicht im Deutschen Kaiserreich, 1871–1914. In: R. Foerster (Ed.), *Die Wehrpflicht: Entstehung, Erscheinungsformen und politisch-militärsiche Wirkung* (pp. 55–70). Munich: R. Oldenbourg Verlag.

Förster, S. (1985). *Der Doppelte Militarismus: Die Deutsche Heeresrüstungspolitik zwischen Status-quo-Sicherung and Aggression, 1890–1913*. Stuttgart.

Gaddis, J. L. (1982). *Strategies of Containment: A Critical Appraisal of Postwar American National Security Policy*. Oxford: Oxford University Press.

Gaddis, J. L. (2001). The Cold War as (Really) History. The Norwegian Nobel Institute Spring Lecture for 2001, Oslo, May 30.

Gaitán, L., Herrera, J. R., Martínez Durán, C., & Martínez Sobral, H. (1940). Contribución al estudio del tifus exantemático en Guatemala. *Boletín Sanitario de Guatemala, órgano de la Dirección General de Sanidad Pública de Guatemala*, *11*(48).

Garbarino, J., & Kostelny, K. (1996). The effects of political violence on Palestinian children's behavioral problems: A risk accumulation model. *Child Development*, *67*, 33–45.

Garbarino, J., Kostelny, K., & Barry, F. (1998). Neighborhood-based programs. In: P. Trickett & C. Schelenbach (Eds), *Violence against Children in the Family and the Community* (pp. 287–314). Washington, D.C.: American Psychological Association.

Garcia, P. (1989). L'état républicain face au Centenaire: raisons d'état et universalisme dans la commémoration de la Révolution française. In: J. Bariety (Ed.), *1889: Centenaire de la Révolution française: Réactions et représentations politiques en Europe* (pp. 145–167). Berne: Peter Lang.

Gates, D. (1986). *The Spanish Ulcer. A History of the Peninsular War*. New York: W.W. Norton.

Gates, D. (1997). *The Napoleonic Wars, 1803–1815*. London: Arnold.

Geary, J. W. (1991). *We Need Men: The Union Draft in the Civil War*. DeKalb, IL: Northern Illinois University Press.

Geertz, C. (1973). Thick Description: Toward an Interpretative Theory of Culture. In: C. Geertz, *The Interpretation of Cultures* (pp. 3–30). New York: Basic Books.

Generalstab [der deutschen Armee] (1914a). *Die Franzosiche Armee nach Durchführung der Dreijährigen Dienstzeit*. Berlin. Bavarian War Ministry Archives, MKr 992.

Generalstab [der deutschen Armee]. (1914b). *Zusammenstellung der Wichtigsten Änderungen*.

Geyer, M. (1984). *Deutsche Rüstungspolitik 1860–1980*. Frankfurt a.M.: Suhrkamp.

Giap, V. N. (1970). *The Military Art of People's War. Selected Writings of General Vo Nguyen Giap*. New York: Monthly Review Press.

Gibson, J. W. (1986). *The Perfect War. The War We Couldn't Lose and How We Did*. New York: Vintage Books.

Gibson, J. W. (1994). *Warrior Dreams: Violence and Manhood in Post-Vietnam America*. New York: Hill and Wang.

Giddens, A. (1985). *The Nation-State and Violence*. Cambridge: Polity.

Giddens, A. (1991). *Modernity and Self Identity*. Cambridge: Polity Press.

Giddens, A. (1995). *The Nation-State and Violence*. Oxford: Polity Press.

Gießmann, H-J. (1992). *Das unliebsame Erbe. Die Auflösung der Militärstruktur der DDR*. Baden-Baden: Nomos Verlagsgesellschaft.

Gilbert, F. (1984). *The End of the European Era, 1890 to the Present* (3rd ed.). New York: Norton.

Giles, N. (June 1944). What about the Women? *Ladies Home Journal*, *23*, 157–159, 161.

Gillis, J. R. (Ed.) (1989). *The Militarization of the Western World*. New Brunswick: Rutgers University Press.

Gilroy, C. L., Phillips, R. L., & Blair, J. D. (1990). The All-Volunteer Army: Fifteen Years Later. *Armed Forces and Society*, *16*(3), 329–350.

Glaser, B. G., & Strauss, A. L. (1967). *The Discovery of Grounded Theory*. New York: Aldine de Gruyter.

Gleditsch, N. P. (1990). The Rise and Decline of the New Peace Movement. In: K. Kodama & U. Vesa (Eds), *Towards a Comparative Analysis of Peace Movements* (pp. 73–88). Brookfield: Dartmouth.

Gleditsch, N. P., Bjerkholt, O., Cappelen, Å., Smith, R. P., & Dunne, J. P. (Eds) (1996). *The Peace Dividend*. Amsterdam: Elsevier.

Gleditsch, N. P., Cappelen, Å., & Bjerkholt, O. (1994). *The Wages of Peace. Disarmament in a Small Industrialized Economy*. London: Sage.

Glenn, R. W. (2000). *Reading Athena's Dance Card. Men against Fire in Vietnam*. Annapolis, ML: Naval Institute Press.

Godechot, J. (Ed.) (1970). *Les constitutions de la France depuis 1789*. Paris: Garnier-Flammarion.

Godechot, J. (1985). *Les institutions de la France sous la Révolution et l'Empire* (3rd ed.). Paris: Presses Universitaire de la France.

Goldstein, Y. N. (1998). *From Fighters to Soldiers. How the Israeli Defense Forces Began*. Brighton: Sussex Academic Press.

Goldthorpe, J. (1991). The uses of history in sociology: reflections on some recent tendencies. *British Journal of Sociology*, *42*, 211–230.

Good Housekeeping (August 1943). I Looked Into My Brother's Face. 145.

Good Housekeeping (August 1944). She's the BUSIEST woman on the block. 226.

Goot, M., & Tiffen, R. (1983). Public Opinion and the Politics of the Polls. In: G. P. King (Ed.), *Australia's Vietnam*. Sydney: Allen & Unwin.

Gourevitch, P. A. (1978). The Second-Image Reversed: the International Sources of Domestic Politics. *International Organization, 32*(4), 281–313.

Gow, J. (1992). *Legitimacy and the Military. The Yugoslav Crisis*. London: Pinter Publishers.

Grab, A. (1995). Army, State and Society: Conscription and Desertion in Napoleonic Italy (1802–1814). *The Journal of Modern History, 67*, 25–54.

Gray, C. H. (1997). *Postmodern War. The New Politics of Conflict*. London: Routledge, 1997.

Gregory, P. (1983). The Russia Agrarian Crisis Revisited. In: R. C. Stuart (Ed.), *The Soviet Rural Economy*. Totowa: Rowman and Allanheld.

Griffith, Jr., R. K. (1985). About Face? The U.S. Army and the Draft. *Armed Forces and Society, 12*(1), 108–133.

Griffiths, R. J. (1995). South African Civil-Military Relations in Transition: Issues and Influences, *Armed Forces and Society, 3*(21), 395–410.

Groh, D. (1973). *Negative Integration und revolutionärer Attentismus. Die deutsche Sozialdemokratie am Vorabend des Ersten Weltkrieges*. Frankfurt a.M.: Ullstein.

Gross, A., Crain, F., & Kaufmann, B. (Eds) (1989). *Frieden mit Europa. Eine Schweitz ohne Armee als Beitrag zur Zivilisiereung der Weltinnenpolitik*. Zürich: Realutopia.

Groß, J., & Lutz, D. S. (Eds) (1998). *Wehrpflicht ausgedient*. Baden-Baden: Nomos Verlagsgesellschaft, 1998.

Gross, R. A. (1976). *The Minutemen and Their World*. New York: Hill and Wang.

Guevara, E. C. (1976). *Oeuvres 1: Textes Militaires*. Paris: Francois Maspero.

Gurr, T. (1993). *Minorities at risk: A global view of ethnopolitical conflicts*. Washington, D.C.: U.S. Institute of Peace Press.

Habermas, J. (1961). *Strukturwandel der Öffentlichkeit*. Neuwied: Luchterhand.

Habermas, J. (1973). *Legitimationsprobleme im Spätkapitalismus*. Frankfurt a.M.: Suhrkamp.

Hahlweg, W. (1986). Clausewitz and Guerilla Warfare. *Journal of Strategic Studies, 9*(2–3), 127–133.

Haldane, R. (1907). *Army Reform and Other Addresses*. London: T. Fisher Unwin.

Hale, J. R. (1985). *War and Society in Renaissance Europe 1450–1620*. London: Fontana.

Hale, J. R. (1998). *War and Society in Renaissance Europe 1450–1620*. Phoenix Mill: Sutton Publishing.

Hale, W. (1994). *Turkish Policies and the Military*. London: Routledge.

Hall, E. (1995). *We can't even march straight*. London: Vintage.

Hall, M. (1998). International Political Economy Meets Historical Sociology: Problems and Promises. *Cooperation and Conflict, 33*(3), 257–276.

Hall, P. A., & Taylor, R. (1996). Political Science and the Three New Institutionalisms. *Political Studies, 44*, 936–957.

Halliday, F. (1987). State and Society in International Relations: A Second Agenda. *Millennium, 16*(2), 215–229.

Halliday, F. (1994). *Rethinking International Relations*. London: Macmillan.

Halperin, M. H. (1974). *Bureaucratic Politics and Foreign Policy*. Washington, D.C.: The Brookings Institution.

Haltiner, K. W., & Kühner, A. (Eds) (1999). *Wehrpflicht und Miliz – Ende einer Epoche. Der europäische Streitkräftewandel und die Schweizer Miliz*. Baden-Baden: Nomos Verlagsgesellschaft.

Haltiner, K. W. (1998). The Definite End of the Mass Army in Western Europe. *Armed Forces and Society*, *25*(1), 7–36.

Haltiner, K. W. (1999). Westeuropas Massenheere am Ende? In: idem & Kühner (Eds) 21–27.

Hamilton, A. (1787). The Consequences of Hostilities Between the State. *The Federalist*, *8*.

Handy, J. (1984). *Gift of the Devil: A History of Guatemala*. Boston: South End Press.

Hansen, P. M. (2001). Militærvægring 1849–1917 – En geografisk og historisk undersøgelse af artkuleret militærnægtelse og ulovlig sessionsudeblivelse i Danmark 1849–1917. MA-diss. Roskilde University Centre, Denmark.

Harries-Jenkins, G. (Ed.) (1982). *Armed Forces and the Welfare Societies: Challenges in the 1980s*. London: MacMillan Press.

Harries-Jenkins, G., & Moskos, C. C. (1981). Armed Forces and Society. *Current Sociology*, *29*, 1–169.

Hart, B. L. (1974). *Strategy. The Indirect Approach* (2nd, rev. ed.). New York: Signet Books.

Hay, C. (1999). Marxism and the State. In: A. Gamble et al. (Eds), *Marxism and Social Science*. London: MacMillan

Hayes, D. (1949). *Conscription Conflict: The Conflict of Ideas in the Struggle for and against Military Conscription in Britain between 1901 and 1939*. London: Sheppard Press.

Hayes, D. (1973/1949). *Conscription Conflict: The Conflict of Ideas In the Struggle For and Against Military Conscription in Britain Between 1901 and 1939*. Reprint of the 1949 edition published by Shepard Press, London. New York: Garland Publishing, Inc.

Heater, D. (1992). *The Idea of European Unity*. Leicester: Leicester University Press.

Hechter, M., & Kiser, E. (1998). The debate on historical sociology: Rational choice theory and its critics. *American Journal of Sociology*, *104*, 785–816.

Held, D. (1995). *Democracy and the Global Order: From the Modern State to Cosmopolitan Governance*. Stanford: Stanford University Press.

Heller, A., & Fehér, F. (1988). *The Postmodern Political Condition*. Oxford: Polity Press.

Hennett, L. (1884). *Les milices et les troupes provinciales*. Paris: L. Baudoin et Cie.

Hennis, W. (1988). *Max Weber, Essays in Reconstruction*. London: Allen and Unwin.

Heper, M., & Güney, A. (2000). The Military and the Consolidation of Democracy: The Recent Turkish Experience. *Armed Forces and Society*, *26*(2), 635–657.

Hernández de León, F. (1940).*Viajes presidenciales; breves relatos de algunas expediciones administrativos del General D. Jorge Ubico, presidente de la República*. Guatemala: Tipografía Nacional.

Herrmann, D. G. (1996). *The Arming of Europe and the Making of the First World War*. Princeton: Princeton University Press.

Herspring, D. R. (1998). Russia's Crumbling Military. *Current History*, *97*(621), 325–328.

Higate, P. (1998). The body resists: everyday clerking and unmilitary practice. In: S. Nettleton & J. Watson (Eds), *The Body in Everyday Life*. London: Routledge.

Higate, P. (2000). Changing Times, Changing Values? An Exploration of Military Culture in Times of Conscription and Volunteering. University of Bristol: School for Policy Studies. Unpublished paper.

Higginbotham, D. (1971). *The War of American Independence: Military Attitudes, Policies and Practice, 1763–1789*. New York: The Macmillan Company.

Hilsman, R., Gaughram, L., & Weitsman, P. A. (1993). *The Politics of Policy Making in Defense and Foreign Affairs. Conceptual Models and Bureaucratic Politics*. Englewood Cliffs: Prentice Hall.

Hintze, O. (1975). *The Historical Essays of Otto Hintze*. Oxford: Oxford University Press.

Hintze, O. (1975a). Prussian Reform Movements before 1806. In: F. Gilbert (Ed.), *The Historical Essays of Otto Hintze*. New York: Oxford University Press.

Hintze, O. (1975b). Military Organization and the Organization of the State. In: F. Gilbert (Ed.), *The Historical Essays of Otto Hintze*. New York: Oxford University Press.

Hobbes, T. (1985[1651]). *Leviathan*. London: Penguin Classics.

Hobden, S. (1998). *International Relations and Historical Sociology*. London: Routledge.

Hobsbawm, E. J. (1996). *Nations and Nationalism Since 1780: Programme, Myth, Reality* (2nd ed.). Cambridge and New York: Canto Press of Cambridge University Press.

Hobson, J. M. (1993). The Military-Extraction Gap and the Wary Titan: The Fiscal Sociology of British Defence Policy, 1870–1914. *Journal of European Economic History*, *22*(3), 461–507.

Hobson, J. M. (1997). *The Wealth of States*. Cambridge: Cambridge University Press.

Hobson, J. M. (1998). The Historical Sociology of the State and the State of Historical Sociology in International Relations. *Review of International Political Economy*, *5*(2), 284–320.

Hobson, J. M. (2000). *The State and International Relations*. Cambridge: Cambridge University Press.

Hobson, J. M., & Hobden, S. (2002). On the road toward a historicised conception of world sociology. In: S. Hobden & J. M. Hobson (Eds), *Historical Sociology of International Relations*. Cambridge: Cambridge University Press.

Hoch, S. L. (1994). On Good Numbers and Bad: Malthus, Population Trends and Peasant Standard of Living in Late Imperial Russia. *Slavic Review*, *53*, 41–75.

Hockey, J. (1986). *Squaddies: Portrait of a subculture*. Exeter: Exeter University Press.

Hoffmann, S. (1965). Rousseau on War and Peace. In: Idem. *The State of War. Essays on the Theory and Practice of International Politics* (pp. 54–87). London: Pall Mall Press.

Hofmann, H. W. (1993). Land Forces, Effectiveness and Efficiency of. In: Dupuy (Ed.), Vol. 3, 1430–1437.

Hoganson, K. (1998). *Fighting for American Manhood*. New Haven: Yale University Press.

Holsti, K. J. (1996). *The State, War, and the State of War*. Cambridge: Cambridge University Press.

Honey, M. (Ed.) (1999). *Bitter Fruit: African American Women in World War II*. Columbia: University of Missouri Press.

Hooks, G., & Mclauchlan, G. (1992). The Institutional Foundation of Warmaking: Three Eras of U.S. Warmaking, 1939–1989. *Theory & Society*, *21*, 757–788.

Hopkin, D. (1997). Changing Popular Attitudes to the Military in Lorraine and Surrounding Regions, 1700–1870. Unpublished doctoral dissertation, University of Cambridge.

Horeman, B., & Stolwijk, M. (1998). *Refusing to bear arms: a world survey of conscription and conscientious objection to military service. Part II: America, former USSR, Asia and Australia, Middle East*. London: War Resisters' International.

Horeman, B., Stolwijk, M., & Luccioni, A. (1997). *Refusing to bear arms: a world survey of conscription and conscientious objection to military service. Part 1: Europe*. London: War Resisters' International.

Horne, D. K. (1987). The Impact of Soldier Quality on Army Performance. *Armed Forces and Society*, *13*(3), 443–455.

Horne, J. (1997). Introduction: Mobilising for 'total war', 1914–1918. In: J. Horne (Ed).

Horne, J (Ed.) (1997). *State, Society and Mobilization in Europe during the First World War*. Cambridge and New York: Cambridge University Press.

Howard, M. (1961) *The Franco-Prussian War: The German Invasion of France, 1870–1871*. London and New York: Routledge.

Howard, M. (1976). *War in European History*. Oxford: Oxford University Press.

Howard, M. (1976a). *War in European History*. New York: Cambridge University Press.

Howard, M. (1976b). Total War in the Twentieth Century: Participation and Consensus in the Second World War. In: B. Bond & I. Roy (Eds), *War and Society: A Yearbook of Military History* (Vol. 1). London: Croon Helm.

Huber, A. R. (1999). Erste Erfahrungen mit der Berufsarmee in den Niederlanden. In: Haltiner & Kühner (Eds), 43–53.

Hublot, E. (1987). *Valmy ou la défense de la nation par les armes*. Paris: Fondation pour les Etudes de Défense Nationale.

Hudemann-Simon, C. (1987). Réfractaires et déserteurs de la Grande Armée en Sarre (1802–1813). *Revue Historique*, *277*, 11–45.

Huesca González, A. M. (1994). La actitud de los españoles ante la multinacionalidad de la Defensa. In: Instituto Español de Estudios Estratégicos (Ed.), *Aportación sociológica de la sociedad española a la defensa nacional* (pp. 137–154). Madrid: Ministerio de Defensa.

Hughes, B. (1997). *Continuity and Change in World Politics: Competing Perspectives* (3rd ed.). Upper Saddle River, N.J.: Prentice Hall.

Human Rights Watch (1994). *Angola: Arms trade and violations of the laws of war since the 1992 elections*. New York: Human Rights Watch.

Human Rights Watch (1997). *The scars of death: Children abducted by the Lord's Resistance Army in Uganda*. New York: Human Rights Watch. Available online at: www.hrw.org/reports97/uganda/

Hunt, L. (1976). Committees and Communes: Local Politics and National Revolution in 1789. *Comparative Studies in Society and History*, *18*, 321–346.

Huntington, S. (1957). *The Soldier and the State: The Theory and Politics of Civil-Military Relations*. Cambridge: Harvard University Press.

Huntington, S. (1964). The Soldier and the State: the Theory and Politics of Civil-Military Relations. Cambridge, MA.: Belknap Press.

Huntington, S. (1965). Inter-Service Competition and the Political Role of the Armed Services. In: H. A. Kissinger (Ed.), *Problems of National Strategy* (pp. 451–476). New York: Praeger.

Huntington, S. (1991). *The Third Wave. Democratization in the Late Twentieth Century*. Norman: University of Oklahoma Press.

Huntington, S. (1997). No Exit: The Errors of Endism. In: F. Zakaria, (Ed.) *Foreign Affairs Agenda: The New Shape of World Politics* (pp. 26–38). New York: Foreign Affairs.

Ibarra, P. (Ed.) (1992). *Objeción e insumisión, claves ideológicas y sociales*. Madrid: Fundamentos.

Inglehart, R. (1976). Changing Values and Attitudes toward Military Service among the American Public. In: N. L. Goldman & D. R. Segal (Eds), *The Social Psychology of Military Service* (pp. 255–278). Beverly Hills: Sage.

Inglehart, R. (1977). *The Silent Revolution. Changing Values and Political Styles Among Western Publics*. Princeton & Oxford: Princeton University Press.

Inspector General of Recruiting (1903). *Report of the Inspector General of Recruiting [on Recruiting for the Regular Army]*. Annual Report. Published in Parliamentary Papers.

Jackwerth, C. (1998). Ökonomische Aspekte eines Vergleiches unterschiedlicher Wehrsysteme. *Österreichische Militärische Zeitschrift*, *36*(4), 375–382.

Jacobsen, J. O., & Skauge, T. (2000). The Role of the Military and the Officer Corps in Norwegian Modernisation. University of Bergen: Department of Public Administration. Unpublished paper.

Janowitz, M., & Moskos, Jr., C. C. (1974). Racial Composition in the All-Volunteer Force. *Armed Forces and Society*, *1*(1), 109–123.

Janowitz, M. (1960). *The Professional Soldier: A Social and Political Portrait*. New York: Free Press.

Janowitz, M. (1971). *The Professional Soldier: A Social and Political Portrait*. New York: Free Press.

Janowitz, M. (1972). The Decline of the Mass Army. *Military Review*, *52*(2), 10–16.

Janowitz, M. (1975). U.S. Forces and the Zero Draft. In: M. Janowitz (Ed.), *Military Conflict. Essays in the Institutional Analysis of War and Peace* (pp. 239–283). Beverly Hills: Sage.

Janowitz, M. (1977). *Military Institutions and Coercion in the Developing Nations*. Chicago: University of Chicago Press.

Janowitz, M. (1980). Observations on the Sociology of Citizenship: Obligations and Rights. *Social Forces*, *59*, 1–24.

Janowitz, M., & Moskos, C. C. (1979). Five Years of the All-Volunteer Force: 1973–1978. *Armed Forces and Society*, *5*(2), 171–217.

Janowitz, M. (1960, 1971).The Professional Soldier: A Social and Political Portrait. New York: The Free Press.

Janowitz, M. (1975). *Military Conflict*. Beverly Hills: Sage Publications.

Jauffret, J.-C. (1987). *Parlement, Gouvernement, Commandement: l'armée de métier sous la Troisième République*. 2 Vols. Vincennes: Service Historique de l'Armée de Terre.

Jaurès, J. (1972). *Democracy and Military Service: an abbreviated translation of L'Armèe nouvelle*. G. G. Coulton (Ed.). New York: Garland Publishing.

Jaurès, J. (1910). *L'Armée Nouvelle*. Paris: L'Humanité.

Jeffords, S. (1989) *The Remasculinization of America: Gender and the Vietnam War*. Bloomington: Indiana University Press.

Jessop, B. (1978). Capitalism and Democracy: The Best Possible Political Shell? In: Littlejohn et al. (Eds), *Power and the State*. London: Croom Helm.

Joenniemi, P. (1985). The Socio-Politics of Conscription. *Current Research on Peace and Violence*, *8*, 137–142.

Joffe, E. (1995). The PLA and the Chinese Economy: The Effect of Involvement. *Survival*, *37*(2), 24–43.

Johnson, J. (1999). Review of Consent, Dissent, and Patriotism, by Margaret Levi. *Ethics*, *109*, 909–911.

Johnson, W. (1966). The Ascendancy of Blaise Diagne and the Beginning of African Politics in Senegal. *Africa*, *36*, 235–252.

Joll, J. (1992). *The Origins of the First World War*. Longman: New York.

Jolly, R. (1992). *Military Man Family Man – Crown Property?* London: Brassey's.

Jolly, R. (1996). *Changing Step. From Military to Civilian Life: People in Transition*. London: Brassey's, U.K.

Jones, B. D. (1999). *Bounded Rationality, Political Institutions, and the Analysis of Outcomes. Competition and Cooperation* (pp. 85–111). New York: Russell Sage Foundation.

Joo, R. (1996). The Democratic Control Of Armed Forces. *Columbia International Affairs Online*. Columbia University Press. https://wwwc.cc.columbia.edu/sec/dlc/ciao/wps/jor01/jor01.html (June 2001).

Judt, T. (1979). *Socialism in Provence, 1871–1914: A Study in the Origins of the Modern French Left*. Cambridge: Cambridge University Press.

Kaiser Willhelm II. (1891). Kaiser Wilhelm II an den Kriegsminister Generalleutnant von Kaltenborn-Stachau. Potsdam, Neues Palais, June 15. German Federal Military Archive, Freiburg, W10/50266.

Kalberg, S. (1994). *Max Weber's Comparative Historical Sociology*. Chicago: The University of Chicago Press.

Kaldrack, G., & Klein, P. (Eds) (1992). *Die Zukunft der Streitkräfte angesichts weltweiter Abrüstungsbemühungen*. Baden-Baden: Nomos Verlagsgesellschaft.

Kann, M. (1991). *On the Man Question: Gender and Civic Virtue in America*. Philadelphia: Temple University Press.

Kant, I. (1963). *Zum ewigen Frieden. Ein philosophischer Entwurf.* Stuttgart: Reclam.

Kant, I. (1983). *To Perpetual Peace, A Philosophical Sketch.* Indianapolis: Hackett Publishing, Inc.

Karmel, S. M. (1997). The Chinese Military's Hunt for Profits. *Foreign Policy, 107*, 102–113.

Katznelson, I. (1996). Garrisons and Fleets: The Military in Antebellum America. Paper presented at the Social Science History Meetings, New Orleans.

Kaufmann, W. W. (1992). *Assessing the Base Force. How Much Is Too Much?* Washington, D.C.: The Brookings Institution.

Keay, J. (1991). *The Honourable Company: A History of the English East India Company.* New York: Macmillan.

Keegan, J. (1976). *The Face of Battle.* New York: Penguin Books.

Keegan, J. (1990). *The Second World War.* New York: Viking.

Kelleher, C. M. (1978). Mass Armies in the 1970s. The Debate in Western Europe. *Armed Forces and Society, 5*(1), 3–29.

Kellett, A. (1990). The Soldier in Battle: Motivational and Behavioral Aspects of the Combat Experience. In: B. Glad (Ed.). *Psychological Dimensions of War* (pp. 215–235). Newbury Park: Sage.

Kellett, A. (1993). Combat Motivation. In: Dupuy (Ed.), Vol. 2, 557–561.

Kennedy, P. (1987). *The Rise and Fall of Great Powers.* New York: Random House.

Kent, G. A., & Simons, W. E. (1994). Objective-Based Planning. In: Davis (Ed.), 59–72.

Kerber, L. (1998). *No Constitutional Right to Be Ladies: Women and the Obligations of Citizenship.* NY: Hill and Wang.

Kessler-Harris, A. (1995). Designing Women and Old Fools. In: L. Kerber et al. (Eds), *U.S. History as Women's History: New Feminist Essays.* Chapel Hill: University of North Carolina Press.

Kestnbaum, M. (1997). Partisans and Patriots: National Conscription and the Reconstruction of the Modern State. Unpublished doctoral dissertation, Harvard University, Cambridge, Mass.

Kestnbaum, M. (2000). Citizenship and Compulsory Military Service: The Revolutionary Origins of Conscription in the United States. *Armed Forces and Society, 27*, 7–36.

Kettner, J. (1978). *The Development of American Citizenship, 1608–1870.* Chapel Hill, NC: University.

Kier, E. (1997). *Imagining War: French and British Military Doctrine Between the Wars.* Princeton: Princeton University Press.

Kiernan, V. G. (1982). *European Empires from Conquest to Collapse, 1815–1960.* London: Fontana.

Kiernan, V. G. (1967). Foreign Mercenaries and Absolute Monarchy. In: T. Aston (Ed.), *Crisis in Europe, 1560–1660* (pp. 124–149). Garden City, NJ: Anchor Books.

Kiernan, V. G. (1973). Conscription and Society in Europe before the War of 1914–1918. In: M. R. D. Foot (Ed.), *War and Society: Historical Essays in Honour and Memory of J. R. Western, 1928–1971* (pp. 141–158). New York: Harper and Row.

Kiljunen, K., & Väänänen, J. (Eds) (1987). *Youth and Conscription.* Jyväskylässä: International Peace Bureau, War Resisters' International, Peace Union of Finland, Union of Conscientious Objectors in Finland.

Kimball, J. (1998). *Nixon's Vietnam War.* Lawrence: University Press of Kansas.

Kingma, K. (Ed.) (2000). *Demobilization in Sub-Saharan Africa. The Development and Security Impacts.* Basingstoke: Macmillan.

Kirby, S. N., & Naftel, S. (2000). The Impact of Deployment on the Retention of Military Reservists", *Armed Forces and Society, 26*(2), 259–284.

Kiser, E., & Hechter, M. (1991). The Role of General Theory in Comparative Historical Sociology. *American Journal of Sociology, 97*, 1–30.

Kitchen, M. (1968). *The German Officer Corps, 1890–1914.* Oxford: Clarendon Press.

Klandermans, B. (Ed.) (1991). *Peace Movements in Western Europe and the United States*. London: JAI Press.

Klare, M. (1995). *Rogue States and Nuclear Outlaws. America's Search for a New Foreign Policy*. New York: Hill and Wang.

Klein, P., & Zimmermann, R. P. (Eds) (1993). *Beispielhaft? Eine Zwischenbilanz zur Eingliederung der Nationalen Volksarmee in die Bundeswehr*. Baden-Baden: Nomos Verlagsgesellschaft.

Klein, P., & Zimmermann, R. P. (Eds) (1997). *Die zukünftige Wehrstruktur der Bundesrepublik. Notwendige Anpassung oder Weg zur Zwei-Klassen Armee?* Baden-Baden: Nomos Verlagsgesellschaft.

Klein, P. (Ed.) (1991). *Wehrpflicht und Wehrpflichtige heute*. Baden-Baden: Nomos Verlagsgesellschaft.

Klingenschmidt, R. (1997). *Motive und Entwicklung der Allgemein-Schulerischen Unteroffizierausbildung in der Königlich Bayrischen Armee von 1866 bis 1914*. Diplom Arbeit, Universität der Bundeswehr, München.

Kohn, R. H. (1975). *Eagle and Sword: The Federalists and the Creation of the Military Establishment, 1783–1802*. New York: Free Press.

Koistinen, P. A. C. (1997). *Mobilizing for Modern War. The Political Economy of American Warfare, 1865–1919*. Lawrence, KS: University Press of Kansas.

Kokoshin, A. (1997). Reflections on Russia's Past, Present, and Future. Columbia International Affairs Online. Columbia University Press. https://wwwc.cc.columbia.edu/sec/dlc/ciao/wps/koa01/koa01.html (June 24, 2001).

Kolko, G. (1985). *Anatomy of a War: Vietnam, the United States, and the Modern Historical Experience*. New York: Pantheon Books.

Kolko, G. (1988). *Confronting the Third World: United States Foreign Policy 1945–1980*. New York: Pantheon Books.

Kolko, G. (1994). Century of War. Politics, Conflict, and Society Since 1914. New York: New Press.

Kondapalli, S. (1996). Civilian Production of the PLA. *Strategic Analysis*, *19*(5), 707–724. New Delhi: Institute for Defence Studies and Analyses.

Koopmans, R. (1995). *Democracy from Below. New Social Movements and the Political System in West Germany*. Boulder CO: Westview Press.

Kovitz, M. 'The Enemy Within. Female Soldiers in the Canadian Forces' in Canadian *Women's Studies*, *19*(4), 36–41.

Kriegsministerium. (n.d. 1912?). Der Kriegsminister General der Infanterie von Heeringen and den Reichskanzler Dr. Bethmann-Hollweg. Number 63. German Federal Military Archive, Freiburg, W10/50279.

Kriegsministerium (1908). Kriegsminister von Einem an Herrn Reichskanzler. 27. April. Bavarian War Ministry Archives, MKr 5922.

Kriegsministerium (1912). Heeresverstärkung. Nr. 176/12.geh.A1. Berlin. 19 Januar. Bavarian War Ministry Archives, MKr 1134.

Kriegsministerium (n.d.) Zusammenstellung von Erlassen zur Verhinderung der Ausbreitung sozialdemokratischer und anarchistischer Gesinnung m Herre ud in den Betrieben der Heeresverwaltung. German Federal Military Archive, Freiburg, PH 2/470.

Krippendorff, E. (1984). *Staat und Krieg. Die historische Logik politischer Unvernunft*. Frankfurt: Suhrkamp Verlag.

Krumeich, G. (1994). Zur Entwicklung der 'Nation Armee' in Frankreich bis zum Ersten Weltkrieg. In: R. G. Foerster (Ed.), *Die Wehrpflicht: Entstehung, Erscheinungsformen und politisch-militärsiche Wirkung* (pp. 133–146). Munich: R. Oldenbourg Verlag.

Krumeich, G. (1984). *.Armaments and Politics in France on the Eve of the First World War: The Introduction of Three-Year Conscription, 1913–1914.* S. Conn (trans.). Worcester: Berg Publishers.

Kryder, D. (2000). *Divided Arsenal: Race and the American State During World War II.* New York: Cambridge University Press.

Kubik, T. R. W. (2001). Military Professionalism and the Democratic Peace: How German is it? In: T. Barkawi & M. Laffey (Eds). *Democracy, Liberalism and War: Rethinking the Democratic Peace Debate*. Boulder, CO: Lynne Rienner Press.

Kuhlmann, J., & Lippert, E. (1992). Wehrpflicht Ade? Argumente wider und für die Wehrpflicht in Friedenszeiten. In: Kaldrack & Klein (Eds), 41–76.

Kuhlmann, J., & Lippert, E. (1993). The Federal Republic of Germany: Conscientious Objection as Social Welfare. In: C. C. Moskos & J. W. Chambers (Eds), *The New Conscientious Objection. From Sacred to Secular Resistance* (pp. 98–105). Oxford: Oxford University Press.

Kuhsiek, A. G. (1915–1916). La importancia del indio para el ejército de Guatemala. Revista Militar Ilustrada; Órgano de la Academia Military del Ejército de la República. *Publicación mensual, 1*(2–3), 4–6.

Kutscher, G. (1983). The Impact of Population Development on Military Manpower Problem., *Armed Forces and Society, 9*(2), 265–273.

Königliche Bayrische Bevollmächtiger (1912a). An das k. Kriegsministerium. Betreff: Deckungsfrage. Berlin den 5. März. Bavarian War Ministry Archives, MKr 1134.

Königliche Bayrische Bevollmächtiger (1912b). An das k. Kriegsministerium. Betreff: Heeresvorlage. Berlin den 24. März. Bavarian War Ministry Archives, MKr 1134.

Laitin, D. D. (1998). *Identity in Formation : The Russian-speaking Populations in the Near Abroad.* Ithaca, NY: Cornell University Press.

Laqueur, W. (Ed.) (1978). *The Guerilla Reader. A Historical Anthology.* London: Wildwood House.

Latham, R. (1997). *The Liberal Moment: Modernity, Security, and the Making of the Postwar International Order.* New York: Columbia University Press.

Le Cour Grandmaison, O. (1992). *Les citoyennetés en Révolution, 1789–1794.* Paris: Presses Universitaires de France.

Lebra, J. (1977). *Japanese-Trained Armies in Southeast Asia: Independence and Volunteer Forces in World War II.* New York: Columbia University Press.

Leed, E. J. (1981). *No Man's Land: Combat and Identity in World War I.* Cambridge: Cambridge University Press.

Léfebvre, G. (1951). *La Révolution Française.* Paris: Presses Universitaires de France.

Legrand, R. (1957). *Le Recrutement des armées et les désertions* (1791–1815), Vol. 5 of *Aspects de la Révolution en Picardie*. Abbeville: Imprimerie Lafosse.

Lenin, V. I. (1970). Das Militärprogramm der proletarischen Revolution. In: idem. *Ausgewählte Werke* (Vol. 1, pp. 874–883). Berlin: Dietz Verlag.

Lens, S. (1987). *Permanent War: The Militarization of America.* New York: Shocken Books.

Léonard. E.-G. (1958). *L'armée et ses problèmes au dix-huitième siècle.* Paris: Plon.

Léroy, M. (1946). *Histoire des idées sociales en France de Montesquieu à Robespierre.* Paris: Librairie Gallimard.

Levi, M. (1977). *Bureaucratic Insurgency: The Case of Police Unions.* Lexington, MA: Lexington Books.

Levi, M. (1988). *Of Rule and Revenue.* Berkeley: The University of California Press.

Levi, M. (1997). *Consent, Dissent, and Patriotism.* Cambridge: Cambridge University Press.

Levitan, S., & K. Cleary, (1973). *Old Wars Remain Unfinished: The Veterans Benefits System.* Baltimore: Johns Hopkins University Press.

Levy, J. S. (1983). *War in the Modern Great Power System 1495–1975*. Lexington: Kentucky University Press.

Lieven, D. C. B. (1983). *Russia and the Origins of the First World War*. New York: St. Martin's Press.

Lindblom, C. E. (1980). *The Policy-Making Process*. Englewood Cliffs NJ: Prentice-Hall.

Linklater, A. (1998). *The Transformation of Political Community*. Cambridge: Polity.

Little, R. (1994). International Relations and Large-Scale Historical Change. In: A. J. R. Groom & M. Light (Eds), *Contemporary International Relations*. London: Pinter.

Lockman, R. F., & Quester, A. O. (1985). The AVF: Outlook for the Eighties and Nineties. *Armed Forces and Society*, *11*(2), 169–182.

Lovell, J. P., & Albright, D. E. (Eds) (1997). *To Sheathe the Sword. Civil-Military Relations in the Quest for Democracy*. Westport, CT: Greenwood Press.

Lucassen, J., & Zürcher, E. J. (1998). Conscription as Military Labour: The Historical Context. *International Review of Social History*, *43*, 405–419.

Lunn, J. (1999). *Memoirs of the Maelstrom: A Senegalese Oral History of the First World War*. Portsmouth, NH: Heinemann/Oxford: James Curry/Cape Town: David Phillip.

Luttwak, E. N. (1996). A Post-Heroic Military Policy. *Foreign Affairs*, *75*(4), 33–44.

Luttwak, E. N. (1999). From Vietnam to Desert Fox: Civil-Military Relations in Modern Democracies. *Survival*, *41*(1), 99–112.

Lynn, J. A. (1984). *The Bayonets of the Republic. Motivation and Tactics in the Army of Revolutionary France, 1791–1974*. Urbana: University of Illinois Press.

Lynn, J. A. (1989). Toward an Army of Honor: the moral evolution of the French army, 1789–1815. *French Historical Studies*, *16*, 152–173.

Lynn, J. A. (1996). *The Bayonets of the Republic: Motivation and Tactics in the Army of Revolutionary France, 1791–1794* (2nd ed.). Boulder, CO: Westview Press.

Lynn-Jones, S. M. (1995). Offense-Defense Theory and Its Critics. *Security Studies*, *4*(4), 660–691.

Lyons, M. (1999). The Grassroots Movement in Germany, 1972–1985. In: S. Zunes, L. R. Kurtz & S. B. Asher (Eds), *Non-violent Social Movements. A Geographical Perspective* (pp. 81–95). Oxford: Blackwell.

Mac An Ghaill, M. (1994). *The Making of Men*. Buckingham: Open University Press.

Machiavelli, N. (1965). *The Art of War*. New York: Da Capo Press.

Machiavelli, N. (1999). *The Prince*. Harmondsworth: Penguin Classics.

Mandelbaum, M. (1993). *The Fate of Nations: the Search for National Security in the Nineteenth and Twentieth Centuries*. New York: Cambridge University Press.

Manfrass-Sirjacques, F. (1997). Entre restructuration interne et normalisation internationale. In: P. Buffotot (Ed.), *La défense en Europe. Les adaptations de l'après-guerre froide* (pp. 15–33). Paris: La Documentation Française.

Manigart, P., & Marlier, E. (1994). La opinión pública europea sobre el futuro de su seguridad. *Cuenta y Razón del Pensamiento Actual*, *85*, 61–68.

Manigart, P. (1999). Erste Erfahrungen mit der neuen belgischen Freiwilligenarmee. In: Haltiner & Kühner (Eds), 54–63.

Mann, F.-K. (1943). The Sociology of Taxation. *Review of Politics*, *5*(2), 225–235.

Mann, M. (1986). *The Sources of Social Power: A History of Power from the Beginning to A.D. 1760*. London and New York: Cambridge University Press.

Mann, M. (1988). *States, War and Capitalism*. Oxford: Blackwell Publishing.

Mann, M. (1993). *The Sources of Social Power*, Vol. 2. Cambridge: Cambridge University Press.

Mann, M. (1995). As the Twentieth Century Ages. *New Left Review*, *214*, 104–124.

Mann, M. (1996). Authoritarian and liberal militarism: a contribution from comparative and historical sociology. In: S. Smith, K. Booth & M. Zalewski (Eds), *International Theory* (pp. 221–239). Cambridge: Cambridge University Press.

Manning, F. J. (1993). Morale. In: Dupuy (Ed.) Vol. 4, 1856–1858.

Manry, A. G. (1958). Réfractaires et déserteurs dans le Puy-de-dome sous le Directoire, le Consulat, et l'Empire. *Revue d'Auvergne*, *72*, 113–133.

Mao Tse-Tung (1975). *Selected Works of Mao Tse-Tung*, Vol. 1. Peking: Foreign Languages Press.

Markoff, J. (1996). *The Abolition of Feudalism: Peasants, Lords and Legislators in the French Revolution*. University Park, PA: The Pennsylvania State University Press.

Marshall, T. H. (1964). *Citizenship and Social Class, Class, Citizenship and Social Development* (pp. 71–134). Garden City, NY: Double Day.

Marshall, T. H. (1963). *Citizenship and Social Class. In: Class, Citizenship and Social Development* (pp. 71–134). Chicago: University of Chicago Press.

Martin, M. L. (1977). Conscription and the Decline of the Mass Army in France, 1960–1975. *Armed Forces and Society*, *3*(3), 355–406.

Martin, P., & O'Meara, P. (Eds) (1984). *Africa* (2nd ed.). Bloomington, IN.: Indiana University Press.

Marx, K. (1974[1867]). *Capital*. New York: International Publishers.

Marx, K. (1975 [1843]). On the Jewish Question. In: L. Coletti (Ed.), *Karl Marx: Early Writings*. London: Pelican.

Mason, P. (1974). *A Matter of Honour: An Account of the Indian Army its Officers and Men*. London: Jonathan Cape Ltd.

Maude, F. N. (1910–1911). Conscription. In: *Encyclopedia Britannica* (11th ed., Vol. 6, pp. 971–974). Cambridge: Cambridge University Press.

Maureau, A. (1957). Le remplacement militaire de l'an VIII à 1814 d'après les registres de notables d'Avignon – aspects juridiques et social. *Revue de l'Institut Napoléon, 131*.

Mawdsley, E. (1978). *The Russian Revolution and the Baltic Fleet: War and Politics, February 1917–April 1918*. New York: Barnes and Noble.

Mayer, A. J. (1981). *The Persistence of the Old Regime: Europe to the Great War*. New York: Pantheon.

McCallion, H. (1995). *Killing Zone*. London: Bloomsbury.

McCormick, D. (1998). *The Downsized Warrior. America's Army in Transition*. New York: New York University Press.

McCreery, D. (1994). *Rural Guatemala 1760–1940*. Stanford: Stanford University Press.

McFaul, M. (2000). Putin in Power. *Current History*, *99*(639), 307–314.

McKay, S., & Mazurana, D. (2000). Girls in militaries, paramilitaries, and armed opposition groups. Background paper for The International Conference on War-affected Children, Winnipeg, Canada.

McKenna, J. J. (1997). Towards the Army of the Future: Domestic Politics and the End of Conscription in France. *West European Politics*, *20*(4), 125–145.

McNab, A. (1995). *Immediate Action*. London: Bantam.

McNeil, W. H. (1982). *The Pursuit of Power: Technology, Armed Force, and Society since A.D. 1000*. Chicago: University of Chicago Press.

McNeill, W. H. (1995). *Keeping Together in Time*. Cambridge, Mass.: Harvard University Press.

Meinecke, F. (1977). The Age of German Liberation, 1795–1815. P. Paret (Ed. and intro.) and H. Fischer (trans.). Berkeley and Los Angeles: University of California Press.

Mellon, C., Muller, J. M., & Semelin, J. (1985). *La Dissuasion Civile*. Paris: Fondation pour les Études de Défense Nationale.

Mellors, C., & McKean, J. (1982). Confronting the State: Conscientious Objection in Western Europe. *Bulletin of Peace Proposals*, *13*(3), 227–239.

Melman, S. (1985). The permanent war economy: American capitalism in decline. New York: Simon & Schuster.

Merryman, M. (1998). *Clipped Wings: The Rise and Fall of the Women's Airforce Service Pilots (WASPs) of World War II*. New York: New York University Press.

Merton, R. (1968). On sociological theories of the middle range. In: R. Merton, *Social Theory and Social Structure* (pp. 39–72). New York: Free Press.

Mettler, S. (1998). *Divided Citizens: Gender and Federalism in New Deal Policy*. Ithaca: Cornell University Press.

Meulen, J. V. D., & Manigart, P. (1997). Zero Draft in the Low Countries: The Final Shift to the All-Volunteer Force. *Armed Forces and Society*, *24*(2), 315–332.

Micewski, E. R. (1995). Streitkräfte und gesellschaftlicher Wertewandel. Zu gesell-schaftspolitischen und militärsoziologischen Aspekten der Sicherheitspolitik. *Österreichische Militärische Zeitschrift*, *33*(3), 251–264.

Michelet, J. (1847). *Histoire de la Révolution Française*, Vol.7. Paris: Chamerot.

Michta, A. E. (Ed.) (1999). *America's New Allies: Poland, Hungary, and the Czech Republic in NATO*. Seattle: University of Washington Press.

Michta, A .A. (1997). *The Soldier-Citizen. The Politics of the Polish Army after Communism*. New York: St. Martin's Press.

Miller, S. E. (Ed.) (1985). *Military Strategy and the Origins of the First World War*. Princeton: Princeton University Press.

Millet, A. (1991). Whatever Became of the Militia in the History of the American Revolution? In: *Three George Rogers Clark Lectures* (pp. 41–63). Washington, D.C.: University Press of America.

Millett, R. L., & Gold-Bliss, M. (Eds) (1995). *Beyond Praetorianism: The Latin American Military in Transition*. Boulder, CO: Lynne Rienner.

Millis, W. (1956). *Arms and Men: America's Military History and Military Policy from the Revolution to the Present*. New York: Capricorn Books, 1956.

Mills, G. & Stremlau, J. (Eds) (1999). *The Privatisation of Security in Africa* (Braamfontein: South African Institute of International Affairs).

Minter, W. (1994). *Apartheid's contras: An inquiry into the roots of war in Angola and Mozambique*. London: Zed Books.

Misser, F., & Versi, A. (1997). Soldier of Fortune: the Mercenary as Corporate Executive. In: H. Purkitt (Ed.), *Annual Editions: World Politics 98/99* (pp. 215–218).

Mjøset, L. (2000). Stein Rokkan's Thick Comparisons. *Acta Sociologica*, *43*, 381–398.

Mjøset, L. (2001). Understandings of Theory in the Social Sciences. In: N. J. Smelser & P. B. Baltes (Eds), *International Encyclopedia of the Social and Behavioral Sciences*. Amsterdam: Pergamon/Elsevier.

Moelker, R. (2000). *Report into the Background of Repatriated Personnel of Missions to Former Yugoslavia*. Royal Netherlands Military Academy: Breda.

Moore, R. I. (Ed.) (1983). *Rand McNally Atlas of World History*. New York: Rand McNally & Company.

Morgan, D. (1987). "It will make a man of you". Notes on National Service, masculinity and autobiography.' *Studies in Sexual Politics*, No. 17, Department of Sociology: University of Manchester.

Morgan, D. (1994). 'Theater of War: Combat, the Military, and Masculinities'. In: H. Brod & M. Kaufman (Eds) *Theorizing Masculinities*. London: Sage.

Morton, L. (1958). The Origins of American Military Policy. *Military Affairs*, *12*, 75–82.

Mosch, T. (1975). *The GI Bill: A Breakthrough in Educational and Social Policy in the United States*. Hicksville, NY: Exposition Press.

Moskos, C., & Butler, J. S. (1996). *All that We Can Be: Black Leadership and Racial Integration the Army Way*. New York: Basic Books.

Moskos, C. C., & Chambers, J. W. (Eds) (1993). *The New Conscientious Objection. From Sacred to Secular Resistance*. Oxford: Oxford University Press.

Moskos, Jr., C. C. et al. (1980). Symposium: Race in the United States Military. *Armed Forces and Society*, *6*(4), 586–613.

Moskos, Jr., C. C., & Burk, J. (1994). The Postmodern Military. In: J. Burk (Ed.) *The Military in New Times* (pp. 141–162). Boulder, CO: Westview.

Moskos, C. C., & Wood, F. R. (Eds) (1988). *The Military: More Than Just a Job?* Washington, D.C.: Pergamon-Brassey's.

Mosse, G. L. (1990). *Fallen Soldiers: Reshaping the Memories of World Wars*. New York and Oxford: Oxford University Press.

Muana, P. K. (1997). The Kamajoi militia: civil war, internal displacement and the politics of counter-insurgency. *Africa Development* 22(3/4), 77–100.

Mueller, J. (1989). *Retreat from Doomsday: The Obsolescence of Major War*. New York: Basic Books.

Muhumuza, R. (1996). *Shattered innocence: Testimonies of children abducted in northern Uganda*. Kampala: World Vision & UNICEF.

Murdock, E. C. (1967). *Patriotism Limited, 1862–1865: The Civil War Draft and the Bounty System*. Kent, Ohio: The Kent State University Press.

Murdock, E. C. (1971). *One Million Men: The Civil War Draft in the North*. Madison: The State Historical Society of Wisconsin.

Murray, O. (1980). *Early Greece*. London: Fontana.

Musah, A.-F., & Fayemi, J.'K. (Eds) (2000). *Mercenaries. An African Security Dilemma*. London: Pluto Press.

Musée Calvet (1989). *La Mort de Bara: de l'évènement au mythe*. Exhibition catalogue. Avignon: Musée Calvet.

Müller, K-J. (Ed.) (1995). *The Military in Politics and Society in France and Germany in the 20th Century*. Oxford: Berg Publishers.

Møller, B. (1991). *Resolving the Security Dilemma in Europe. The German Debate on Non-Offensive Defence*. London: Brassey's.

Møller, B. (1992). *Common Security and Nonoffensive Defense. A Neorealist Perspective*. Boulder, CO: Lynne Rienner.

Møller, B. (1995). *Dictionary of Alternative Defense*. Boulder, CO: Lynne Rienner.

Narain, N. (1992). Co-option and Control: The Role of the Colonial Army in India 1918–1947. Unpublished doctoral dissertation, St. Edmunds College, Cambridge University.

Nathan, L. (1996). Civil-Military Relations in the New South Africa. In: W. Gutteridge (Ed.), *South Africa's Defence and Security into the 21st Century* (pp. 87–109). Aldershot: Dartmouth.

National Women's Party. (1946). *"Equal Rights Amendment" Questions and Answers on the Equal Rights Amendment*. Washington, D.C.: Government Printing Office.

Nelson, B. (1990). The Origins of the Two Channel Welfare State: Workmen's Compensation and Mothers' Aid. In: L. Gordon (Ed.), *Women, the State and Welfare*. Madison: University of Wisconsin Press.

Newton, D. J. (1985). *British Labour, European Socialism and the Struggle for Peace 1889–1914*. Oxford: Clarendon Press.

Nichols, T. M. (1993). *The Sacred Cause. Civil-Military Conflict Over Soviet National Security, 1917–1992*. Ithaca: Cornell University Press.

Nietzsche, F. (1989[1887]). *The Genealogy of Morals*. New York: Vintage Books.

Niezing, J. (1987). *Sociale Verdediging als Logisch Alternatief*. Van Utopie Naar Optie. Antwerpen: EPO.

Nübler, I. (2000). Human Resources Development and Utilization in Demobilization and Reintegration Programmes. In: Kingma (Ed.), 45–77.

Nye, J. (1993). *Understanding International Conflicts: An Introduction to Theory and History*. New York: Harper and Collins.

O'Brien, R. C. (1972). *White Society in Black Africa: The French in Senegal*. Evanston, IL: Northwestern University Press.

O'Neill, W. (1993). *A Democracy at War*. New York: Free Press.

O'Rourke, K. H. (1997). The European Grain Invasion, 1870–1913. *The Journal of Economic History*, *57*, 775–801.

O'Rourke, K. H., & Williamson, J. G. (1994). Late Nineteenth-Century Anglo-American Factor-Price Convergence: Were Heckscher and Ohlin Right? *The Journal of Economic History*, *54*, 892–916.

O'Rourke, K. H., Taylor, A. M., & Williamson, J. G. (1996). Factor Price Convergence in the Late Nineteenth Century. *International Economic Review*, *37*, 499–530.

O'Hanlon, M. (1995). *Defense Planning for the Late 1990s. Beyond the Desert Storm Framework*. Washington, D.C.: The Brookings Institution.

Olson, K. (1974). *The GI Bill, the Veterans and the Colleges*. Lexington: University of Kentucky Press.

Opitz, E., & Rödiger, F. S. (Eds) (1994). *Allgemeine Wehrpflicht. Geschichte, Probleme, Perspektiven*. Bremen: Edition Trennen.

Oren, I. (1996). The Subjectivity of the Democratic Peace: Changing US Perceptions of Imperial Germany. In: M. Brown et al (Eds), *Debating the Democratic Peace* (pp. 263–300). Cambridge: MIT Press.

Orren, K. (1991). *Belated Feudalism: Labor, the Law and Liberal Development in the United States*. NY: Cambridge University Press.

Ostrom, E. (1998). A Behavioral Approach to the Rational Choice Theory of Collective Action. *American Political Science Review*, *92*, 1–22.

Ottaway, M. (1999). Africa. *Foreign Policy*, *114*, 13–25.

Ottaway, M. (1999). Post-Imperial Africa at War. *Current History*, *98*(628), 202–207.

Page, M. (1987a). Introduction: Black Men in a White Man's War. In: M. Page (Ed.), *Africa and the First World War* (pp. 1–27).

Page, M. (1987b). Preface. In: M. Page (Ed.), *Africa and the First World War* (pp. xi–xii).

Page, M. (2000). *The Chiwaya War: Malawians and the First World War*. Boulder, Westview Press.

Pagnucco, R., & Smith, J. (1993). The Peace Movement and the Formulation of U.S. Foreign Policy. *Peace & Change*, *18*(2), 157–181.

Panitch, L. (1996). Rethinking the Role of the State. In: J. H. Mittelman (Ed.), *Globalization: Critical Reflections*. Boulder: Lynne Rienner.

Paret, P., Lewis, B. I., & Paret, P. (1992). *Persuasive Images: Posters of War and Revolution*. Princeton: Princeton University Press.

Paret, P. (1986). Napoleon and the Revolution in War. In: P. Paret (Ed.), *Makers of Modern Strategy: From Machiavelli to the Modern Age* (pp. 123–142). Princeton: Princeton University Press.

Paret, P. (1992a). Military Power. In: *Understanding War: Essays on Clausewitz and the History of Miltiary Power* (pp. 9–25). Princeton: Princeton University Press.

Paret, P. (1992b). Conscription and the End of the Ancien Régime in France and Prussia. In: *Understanding War: Essays on Clausewitz and the History of Miltiary Power* (pp. 53–74). Princeton: Princeton University Press.

Paret, P. (1992c). Nationalism and the Sense of Military Obligation. In: *Understanding War: Essays on Clausewitz and the History of Miltiary Power* (pp. 39–52). Princeton: Princeton University Press.

Paret, P. (1992d). The Relationship between the American Revolutionary War and European Military Thought and Practice. In: *Understanding War: Essays on Clausewitz and the History of Miltiary Power* (pp. 26–38). Princeton: Princeton University Press.

Paret, P. (1992e). *Understanding War: Essays on Clausewitz and the History of Miltiary Power.* Princeton: Princeton University Press.

Paret, P. (1993). Justifying the Obligation of Military Service. *Journal of Military History, 57*(Special Issue 5), 115–216.

Parker, G. (1996). *The Military Revolution* (2nd ed.). Cambridge: Cambridge University Press.

Parker, G. (Ed.) (1995). *The Cambridge Illustrated History of Warfare.* New York: Cambridge University Press.

Partner, P. (1997). *God of Battles. Holy Wars of Christianity and Islam.* Princeton, NJ: Princeton University Press.

Pearlmutter, A. (1977). *The Military and Politics and Modern Times: On Professionals, Praetorians, and Revolutionary Soldiers.* New Haven: Yale University Press.

Peled, A. (1998). *A Question of Loyalty. Military Manpower Policy in Multiethnic States.* Ithaca: Cornell University Press.

Peled, A. (1994). Force, ideology and contract: The history of ethnic conscription. *Ethnic and Racial Studies, 17,* 68–75.

Perry, F. W. (1988). *The Commonwealth Armies: Manpower and Organisation in Two World Wars.* Manchester: Manchester University Press.

Peters, K., & Richards, P. (1998a). "Why we fight": voices of youth ex-combatants in Sierra Leone. *Africa, 68*(1), 183–210.

Peters, K., & Richards, P. (1998b). Jeunes combattants parlant de la guerre et de la paix en Sierra Leone. *Cahiers d'Etudes africaines*, 150–152, 581–617.

Peters, K., & Richards, P. (1998). Why we fight: Voices of youth combatants in Sierra Leone. *Africa, 68*(2), 183–189.

Petersen, R. (1989). Rationality, Ethnicity and Military Enlistment. *Social Science Information, 28,* 563–598.

Picciotto, S. (1991). The Internationalization of the State. *Review of Radical Political Economics, 22*(1), 28–44.

Pleck, J., & Sawyer, J. (1974). *Men and Masculinity.* New Jersey: Prentice Hall.

Poggi, G. (1978). *The Development of the Modern State.* London: Hutchinson.

Porch, D. (1981). *The March to the Marne: The French Army 1871–1914.* Cambridge: Cambridge University Press.

Porch, D. (1981). *The March to the Marne: the French Army, 1871–1914.* Cambridge: Cambridge University Press.

Porter, B. (1994). *War and the Rise of the State.* New York: The Free Press.

Posen, B. R. (1984). *The Sources of Military Doctrine. France, Britain, and Germany Between the World Wars.* New York: Cornell University Press.

Posen, B. (1992). Nationalism, the Mass Army, and Military Power. *International Security, 19,* 80–124.

Prados, J. (1996). *President's Secret Wars: CIA and Pentagon Covert Operations from World War II through the Persian Gulf.* Chicago: Elephant Paperbacks.

Prestwich, M. (1996). *Armies and Warfare in the Middle Ages. The English Experience.* New Haven: Yale University Press.

Prunier, G. (1994). *The Rwanda crisis: History of a genocide.* New York: Columbia University Press.

Punamaki, R. (1996). Can ideological commitment protect children's psychosocial well-being in situations of political violence? *Child Development, 67*, 55–69.

Putnam, R. (2000). *Bowling Alone: The Collapse and Revival of American Community.* New York: Simon & Shuster.

Quaker Council for European Affairs (1984). *Conscientious Objection to Military Service in Europe.* Brussels: Council of Europe.

Ramos, R. (1987). Actitudes y opiniones de los españoles ante las relaciones internacionales. *Estudios y Encuestas 7.* Madrid: Centro de Investigaciones Sociológicas.

Recopilación de las Leyes emitidas por el Gobierno Democrático de la República de Guatemala, desde el 3 de junio de 1871, hasta el 30 de junio de 1881. (1881). Guatemala: Tipografía de "El Progreso".

Record, J. (1998). *The Wrong War. Why We Lost in Vietnam.* Annapolis: Naval Institute Press.

Redlich, F. (1964–1965). *The German Military Enterpriser and His Workforce: A Study in European Economic and Social History*, 2 Vols. Weisbaden: Franz Steiner Verlag.

Reichskanzler (1891). Der Reichskanzler von Caprivi an den Kriegsminister Generalleutnant von Kaltenborn-Stachau, August 27, 1891. German Federal Military Archive, Freibrug, W10/50266.

Reichstag (1912). *Kommission für den Reichshaushaltsetat.* 13 Legislatur-Periode. I Session 1912. 28 Sitzung. 3 Mai. Berlin.

Reiter, D. (1998). Democracy and Battlefield Effectiveness. *Journal of Conflict Resolution, 42*(June), 259–278.

Remington, R. A. (1996). The Yugoslav Army: Trauma and Transition. In: Danapoulos & Zirker (Eds), 153–173.

Reno, W. (1998). *Warlord Politics and African States.* Boulder, CO: Lynne Rienner.

Rétat, P. (1993). The evolution of the citizen from the Ancien Régime to the Revolution. In: R.Waldinger, P. Dawson & I. Woloch (Eds), *The French Revolution and the Meaning of Citizenship.* Westport, Connecticut: Greenwood Press.

Reus-Smit, C. (1999). *The Moral Purpose of the State.* Princeton: Princeton University Press.

Rhodes, R. (1986). *The Making of the Atomic Bomb.* New York: Simon and Schuster.

Richards, P., & Fithen, C. (2001). Making war, crafting peace: militia solidarities and demobilization opportunities in Sierra Leone. In: B. Helander & P. Richards (Eds), *No War, No Peace: Living Beyond Violent Conflict* (forthcoming).

Richards, P. (1995). Rebellion in Liberia and Sierra Leone: a crisis of youth? In: O. Furley (Ed.), *Conflict in Africa.* London: Tauris.

Richards, P. (1996). *Fighting for the Rain Forest: war, youth and resources in Sierra Leone.* James Currey, Oxford (reprinted with additional material 1998).

Richards, P. (1998). Sur la nouvelle violence politique en Afrique: le sectarisme seculier au Sierra Leone. *Politique Africaine, 70*, 85–104.

Richards, P. (1999). The war and reconstruction in Sierra Leone. *Development Outreach, 1*(2), 9–11.

Richards, P. (2001). Green Book millenarians?: the Sierra Leone war from a perspective of an anthropology of religion In: N. Kastfelt, (Ed.), (forthcoming).

Richards, P., Abdullah, I., Amara, J., Muana, P., Stanley, E., & Vincent, J. (1997). Reintegration of war-affected youth and ex-combatants: a study of the social and economic opportunity structure in Sierra Leone. Unpublished report.

Ries, T. (1989). *Cold Will.* The Defence of Finland. London: Brassey's.

Risse-Kappen, T. (1995). *Bringing Transnational Relations Back In.* Cambridge: Cambridge University Press.

Ritter, G. (1970). *The Sword and the Scepter: The Problem of Militarism in Germany. Volume II: The European Powers and the Wilhelminian Empire, 1890–1914.* Coral Gables: University of Miami Press.

Ritter, G. (1999). Gender, Labor and Citizenship from Adkins to Parrish, Presented at the Annual Meeting of the American Political Science Association in Atlanta, GA.

Ritter, G. (2000a). Gender and Citizenship after the Nineteenth Amendment, *Polity*, *32*(3)(Spring), 301–331.

Ritter, G. (2000b). A Common Citizenship for All? Veterans Benefits, Social Security, Gender and Social Citizenship after World War II, Presented at the Annual Meeting of the American Political Science Association in Washington, DC.

Roberts, A. (1976). *Nations in Arms. The Theory and Practice of Territorial Defence.* New York: Praeger.

Roberts, A. (1977). The British Armed Forces and Politics. A Historical Perspective. *Armed Forces and Society*, *3*(4): 531–556.

Robinson, R. (1972). Non-European Foundations of European Imperialism: Sketch for a Theory of Collaboration. In: Owen & Sutcliffe (Eds), *Studies in the Theory of Imperialism.* London: Longman.

Rochon, T. R. (1988). *Mobilizing for Peace. The Antinuclear Movements in Western Europe.* London: Adamantine Press Ltd.

Rogowski, R. (1989). *Commerce and Coalitions: How Trade Affects Domestic Political Alignments.* Princeton: Princeton University Press.

Rokkan, S. (1999). *State Formation, Nation-Building and Mass Politics in Europe.* Oxford: Oxford University Press.

Ropp, T. (1962). *War in the Modern World* (2nd, rev. ed.). New York: Collier Books.

Rosanvallon, P. (1992). *Le sacre du citoyen. Histoire du suffrage universel en France.* Paris: Éditions Gallimard.

Rosenau, J. N. (1994). Armed Force and Armed Forces in a Turbulent World. In: J. Burk (Ed.), *The Military in New Times. Adapting Armed Forces to a Turbulent World* (pp. 25–61). Oxford: Westview Press.

Ross, D. (1969). *Preparing for Ulysses: Politics and Veternas During World War II.* NY: Columbia University Press.

Roth, G. (1978). Introduction. In: M. Weber, *Economy and Society.* Berkeley: University of California Press.

Rothenberg, G. E. (1978). *The Art of Warfare in the Age of Napoleon.* Blomington: Indiana University Press.

Rousseau, D., & Newsome, B. (1999). Women and Minorities: the Impact of War Time Mobilization on Political Rights. Presented at the Annual Meeting of the American Political Science Association in Atlanta, GA.

Rousseau, J. J. (1966). *Du Contrat Social.* Paris: Garnier-Flammarion.

Rowe, D. M. (1999). World Economic Expansion and National Security in Pre-World War I Europe. *International Organization*, *53*, 195–231.

Rowe, D. M., Bearce, D. H., & McDonald, P. (1999). Binding Prometheus:Trade, Security, and the Decay of the British Regular Army before World War I. Paper presented to the 1999 Meetings of the American Political Science Association, September 1–5, Atlanta.

Royle, T. (1997). *The Best Years of Their Lives. The National Service Experience, 1945–1963* (enlarged 2nd ed.). London: John Murray.

Royster, C. (1968). 'Marchands d'hommes' et sociétés assurance contre le service militaire au XIXe siècle. *Revue d'Histoire Économique et Sociale, 46*, 339–380.

Royster, C. (1979). *A Revolutionary People at War: The Continental Army and American Character, 1775–1783*. New York: W. W. Norton & Company, for the Institute of Early American History and Culture.

Royster, C. (1986). A Society and Its War. In: M. Ultee (Ed.), *Adapting to Conditions: War and Society in the Eighteenth Century* (pp. 174–187). Birmingham, AL: University of Alabama Press.

Rubin, E. (1998). Our children are killing us. *The New Yorker*, March 23, 1998.

RUF/SL (1995). *Footpaths to democracy: towards a new Sierra Leone*. No stated place of publication: the Revolutionary United Front of Sierra Leone.

Ruggie, J. G. (1983). Continuity and Transformation in the World Polity: Towards a Neo-Realist Synthesis. *World Politics, 35*(2), 261–285.

Ruggie, J. G. (1998). *Constructing the World Polity*. London: Routledge.

Rutter, M. (1979). Protective factors in children's response to stress and disadvantage. In: M. Kint & J. Rolf (Eds), *Primary Prevention of Psychopathology, Vol. 3: Social Competence in Children* (pp. 49–74). Hanover, NH: University Press of New England.

Rödiger, F. S. (1994). Wehrstruktur und Rekrutieringssysteme weltweit. In: Opitz & idem (Eds), 195–206.

Sales de Bohigas, N. (1968). Some Opinions on Exemption from Military Service in Nineteenth-Century Europe. *Comparative Studies in Society and History, 10*, 261–289.

Sales, N. (1974). *Sobre esclavos, reclutas y mercaderes de quintos*. Barcelona: Ariel.

Sandler, T., & Hartley, K. (1995). *The Economics of Defense*. Cambridge: Cambridge University Press.

Sangier, G. (1965). *La désertion dans le Pas-de-Calais de 1792 à 1802*. Blangermont: CNRS, et chez l'auteur à Blangermont.

Sarkesian, S. C., Williams, J. A., & Bryant, F. B. (1995). *Soldiers, Society, and National Security*. Boulder, CO: Lynne Rienner.

Schmitt, C. (1996[1932]). *The Concept of the Political*. Chicago: The University of Chicago Press.

Schnapper, B. (1968). *Le remplacement militaire en France: Quelques aspects politiques, économiques et sociaux du recrutement au XIXe siècle*. Paris: S.E.V.P.E.N.

Schneider, B. R., & Grinter, L. E. (Eds) (1995). *Battlefield of the Future. 21st Century Warfare Issues*. Maxwell Air Force Base, Alabama: Air University.

Scholte, J.-A. (1993). *International Relations of Social Change*. Milton Keynes: Open University Press.

Schumpeter, J. A. (1954). The Crisis of the Tax State. In: A. T. Peacock & R. Turvey (Eds), *International Economic Papers* (pp. 5–38). New York: Macmillan.

Scott, J. C. (1985). *Weapons of the Weak: Everday forms of Peasant Resistance*. New Haven: Yale University Press.

Scott, S. F. (1978). *The response of the Royal Army to the French Revolution: the Role and Development of the Line Army, 1787–1793*. Oxford: Oxford University Press.

Scott, S. F. (1984). Foreign Mercenaries, Citizen-Soldiers, and Revolutionary War in the Late Eighteenth Century. *War and Society, 2*, 41–58.

Scott, S. F. (1986). Military Nationalism in Europe in the Aftermath of the American Revolution. In: R. Hoffman & P. Albert (Eds), *Peace and the Peacemakers: The Treaty of 1783* (pp. 160–189). Charlottesville, VA: University Press of Virginia.

Seabrooke, L. (2001). *U.S. Power in International Finance*. London: Macmillan.

Sealey, R. (1976). *A History of the Greek City States ca. 700–338 B.C.* Berkeley: University of California Press.

Seegers, A. (1993). South Africa: From Laager to Anti-Apartheid. In: C. C. Moskos & J. W. Chambers (Eds), *The New Conscientious Objection. From Sacred to Secular Resistance* (pp. 127–134). Oxford: Oxford University Press.

Segal, D. R., & Tiggle, R. B. (1997). Attitudes of Citizen-Soldiers toward Military Missions in the Post-Cold War World. *Armed Forces and Society*, *23*(3), 373–390.

Segal, D. R., & Verdugo, N. (1994). Demographic Trends and Personnel Policies as Determinants of the Racial Composition of the Volunteer Army. *Armed Forces and Society*, *20*(4), 619–632.

Segal, D. R. (1989). *Recruiting for Uncle Sam*. Lawrence, KS: University Press of Kansas.

Segal, L. (1990). *Slow Motion*. London: Virago.

Servan, J. (1780). *Le Soldat citoyen*. Neufchâtel: Dans le Pays de la Liberté.

Shafquat, S. (1997). *Civil-Military Relations in Pakistan*. Boulder, CO: Westview Press.

Shambough, D. (1996). China's Military in Transition: Politics, Professionalism Procurement and Power Projection. *The China Quarterly*, *146*, 265–298.

Sharp, G. (1985). *Making Europe Unconquerable. The Potential of Civilian-Based Deterrence and Defence*. London: Taylor & Francis.

Shaw, M. (1988). *Dialectics of War: An Essay in the Social Theory of Total War and Peace*. London: Pluto.

Shaw, M. (1991). *Post-Military Society: Militarism, Demilitarization and War at the End of the Twentieth Century*. Cambridge/Philadelphia: Cambridge University Press/Temple University Press.

Shaw, M. (1997). The State of Globalization: Towards a Theory of State Transformation. *Review of International Political Economy*, *4*(3), 497–513.

Shearer, D. (1997). Exploring the limits of consent: conflict resolution in Sierra Leone. *Millennium: Journal of International Studies*, *26*(3), 845–860.

Shearer, D. (1998). Outsourcing War. *Foreign Policy*, *112*, 68–81.

Shearer, D. (1998). Private Armies and Military Intervention. *Adelphi Papers*, *316*.

Sheehan, J. J. (1989). *German History, 1770–1866*. Oxford and New York: Oxford University Press.

Sheehan, J. J. (1992). State and Nationality in the Napoleonic Period. In: J. Breuilly (Ed.), *The State of Germany: The National Idea in the Making, Unmaking and Remaking of a Modern Nation-state*. London and New York: Longman.

Shills, E. (1977). A Profile of the Military Deserter. *Armed Forces and Society*, *3*(3), 427–431.

Shklar, J. (1991). *American Citizenship: The Quest for Inclusion*. Cambridge, MA: Harvard University Press.

Showalter, D. (1971). The Prussian Landwehr and its Critics, 1813–1819. *Central European History*, *4*, 3–33.

Shy, J. (1973). The American Revolution: The Military Conflict Considered as a Revolutionary War. In: S. G. Kurtz & J. H. Hutson (Eds), *Essays on the American Revolution* (pp. 121–156). Chapel Hill and New York: North Carolina University Press and W. W. Norton and Company for the Institute of Early American History and Culture.

Shy, J. (1990). *A People Numerous and Armed: Reflections on the Military Struggle for American Independence* (2nd ed.). Ann Arbor: University of Michigan Press.

Silver, A. (1994). Democratic Citizenship and High Military Strategy: The Inheritance, Decay and Reshaping of Political Culture. *Research on Democracy and Society* (pp. 317–349). Greenwich, Ct.: JAI Press.

Simmons, B. A. (1999). Review of Consent, Dissent, and Patriotism. *Comparative Political Studies*, *32*, 130–133.

Sinaiko, H. W. (1990). The Last American Draftees, *Armed Forces and Society*, *16*(2), 241–249.

Sivan, E. (1995). The enclave culture. In: M. Marty (Ed.), *Fundamentalisms Comprehended*. Chicago: Chicago University Press.

Skelly, A. R. (1977). *The Victorian Army at Home: The Recruitment and Terms and Conditions of the British Regular, 1859–1899*. London: Croom-Helm.

Skocpol, T. (1979). *States and Social Revolutions*. New York: Cambridge University Press.

Skocpol, T. (1992). *Protecting Soldiers and Mothers: The Political Origins of Social Policy in the United States*. Cambridge, MA: Belknap Press.

Skocpol, T. (1996). Delivering for Young Families: The Resonance of the GI Bill, *The American Prospect*, (Sep.–Oct.), 66.

Skocpol, T. (1994). Social Revolutions and Mass Military Mobilization. In: *Social Revolutions in the Modern World* (pp. 279–298). Cambridge: Cambridge University Press.

Smet, L. d. (1990). The Belgian Peace Movement Polled. In: K. Kodama & U. Vesa (Eds), *Towards a Comparative Analysis of Peace Movements* (pp. 235–253). Brookfield: Dartmouth.

Smillie, I., & Gberie, L. (2000). Diamonds, children and the political economy of conflict: The experience of Sierra Leone. Background paper for The International Conference on War-Affected Children, Winnipeg, Canada.

Smith, P. (1995). *Democracy on Trial: The Japanese-American Evacuation and Relocation during World War II*. NY: Simon & Shuster.

Snider, D., & Carlton-Carew, M. A. (Eds) (1995). U.S. Civil-Military Relations. In: *Crisis or Transition?* Washington, D.C.: Center for Strategic and International Studies.

Soboul, A. (1973). *Mouvement populaire et gouvernement révolutionnaire en l'an II (1793–1794)*. Paris: Flammarion.

Soboul, A. (1975). *Précis d'histoire de la Révolution Française*. Paris: éditions sociales.

Spiers, E. M. (1980). *The Army and Society, 1815–1914*. London: Longman.

Spruyt, H. (1994). *The Sovereign State and Its Competitors*. Princeton, NJ: Princeton University Press.

Stanley, S. C., & Segal, M. W. (1993). Women in the Armed Forces. In: Dupuy (Ed.), Vol. 6, 2945–2951.

Stavrou, S., Stewart, R., & Stavrou, A. (2000). The re-integration of child soldiers and abductees: A case study of Palaro and Pabbo, Gulu District, Northern Uganda. Background paper for The International Conference on War-Affected Children, Winnipeg, Canada.

Stein, G. H. (1966). *The Waffen SS: Hitler's Elite Guard at War*. Ithaca: Cornell University Press.

Stephan, C. (1998). *Das Handwerk des Krieges*. Berlin: Rowohlt.

Stevenson, D. (1996). *Armaments and the Coming of War: Europe 1904–1914*. Oxford: Clarendon Press.

Stewart, J. H. (1951). *A Documentary History of the French Revolution*. New York: Macmillan.

Stinchcombe, A. (1968). *Constructing Social Theories*. New York: Harcourt, Brace and World, Inc.

Stone, N. (1984). *Europe Transformed: 1878–1919*. Cambridge: Harvard University Press.

Stone, N. (1975). *The Eastern Front, 1914–1917*. New York: Charles Scribner's Sons.

Storz, D. (1992). *Kriegsbild und Rüstung vor 1914: Europäische Landstreitkräfte vor dem Ersten Weltkrieg*. Berlin: E. S. Mittler und Sohn.

Straker, G. (1992). *Faces in the revolution*. Cape Town: David Philip.

Sude, G. (1993). Strategy. In: Dupuy (Ed.), Vol. 5, 2573–2577.

Sumler, D. E. (1970). Domestic Influences on the Nationalist Revival in France, 1909–1914. *French Historical Studies*, *6*, 517–537.

Suratteau, J.-R. (1974). Note sur quelques problèmes de l'histoire de la Révolution française : application des lois militaires, désertions, insoumission, «objection de conscience». In: *Recrutement, Mentalités, Sociétés, Actes du 2e Colloque International d'Histoire Militaire* (pp. 137–146). Montpelier: Centre d'Histoire Militaire et d'Études de Défense Nationale de Montpelier et Université Paul Valery.

Szarka, J. (1996). The Winning of the 1995 French Presidential Election. *West European Politics*, *19*(1), 151–167.

Sørensen, H. (1993). Denmark: The Vanguard of Conscientious Objection. In: C. C. Moskos & J. W. Chambers (Eds), T*he New Conscientious Objection. From Sacred to Secular Resistance* (pp. 106–113). Oxford: Oxford University Press.

Sørensen, H. (2000). Conscription in Scandinavia During the Last Quarter Century: Developments and Arguments. *Armed Forces and Society*, *26*(2), 313–334.

Tallett, F. (1992). *War and Society in Early-Modern Europe, 1494–1715*. London: Routledge.

Tanner, F. (1992). Versailles: German Disarmament after World War I. In: idem (Ed.), *From Versailles to Baghdad: Post-War Armament Control of Defeated States* (pp. 5–25). New York: United Nations/Geneva: UNIDIR).

Thaler, R. H. (Ed.) (1991). *Quasi-Rational Economics*. New York: Russell Sage Foundation.

Thelen, K. (1999). Historical Institutionalism in Comparative Politics. *Annual Review of Political Science*, *2*, 369–404.

Thomas, L. (1966). *The Virgin Soldiers*. London: Picador.

Thompson, D. (April 1944). The Stake of Women in Full Postwar Employment, *Ladies Home Journal*, 6 & 183.

Thompson, W. R., & Rasler, K. (1999). War, the Military Revolution(s) Controversy, and Army Expansions. *Comparative Political Studies*, *32*, 3–31.

Thomson, J. E. (1994). *Mercenaries, Pirates and Sovereigns: State-Building and Extraterritorial Violence in Early Modern Europe*. Princeton: Princeton University Press.

Thomson, J. E. (1995). *Mercenaries, Pirates, and State Sovereignty*. Princeton: Princeton University Press.

Thorne, T. (1998). *Brasso, Blanco & Bull*. London: Robinson Publishers.

Thuysbaert, G. (1994). Restructuring the Armed Forces of Belgium. In: J. G. Siccama & T. Van den Doel (Eds), *Reestructuring Armed Forces in East and West* (pp. 51–56). Oxford: Westview Press.

Tilly, C. (1964). *The Vendee*. Cambridge, MA.: Harvard University Press.

Tilly, C. (1985). War Making and State Making as Organized Crime. In: P. Evans, D. Rueschemayer & T. Skocpol (Eds), *Bringing the State Back In* (pp. 168–191). Cambridge: Cambridge University Press.

Tilly, C. (1990). *Coercion, Capital and European States, AD 990–1990*. Oxford: Basil Blackwell.

Tilly, C. (1992). Where do rights come from? In: L. Mjøset (Ed.), *Contributions to the Comparative Study of Development* (pp. 9–36), Oslo: Institute for Social Research, Report 92:2.

Tilly, C. (1995). The Emergence of Citizenship in France and Elsewhere. In: C. Tilly (Ed.), *Citizenship, Identity and Social History* (pp. 223–236). Cambridge: Cambridge University Press.

Tilly, C. (1997). Means and Ends of Comparison in Macrosociology. *Comparative Social Research*, *16*.

Trench, C. C. (1988). *The Indian Army and the King's Enemies 1900–1947*. London: Thames and Hudson.

Trice, R. H. (1983). The Policy-Making Process: Actors and their Impact. In: J. F. Reichart & S. R. Sturm (Eds), *American Defense Policy* (5th ed., pp. 504–507). Baltimore: John Hopkins University Press.

Tucker, R. C. (1977). *Stalinism: Essays in Historical Interpretation*. New York: Norton.

Turner, B. S. (1992). *Max Weber: From History to Modernity*. London: Routledge.

U. S. Department of State (1999). *Angola country report on human rights for 1998*. Washington, DC: Department of State.

U. S. Senate (September 28, 1945). Equal Rights Amendment: Hearing Before a Subcommittee of the Committee on the Judiciary. Washington, D.C.: Government Printing Office.

UNICEF/Sierra Leone (2000). Case study of children from the fighting forces in Sierra Leone. Background paper for The International Conference on War-Affected Children, Winnipeg, Canada.

United States of America Department of Defense (1994). World-Wide Conventional Arms Trade (1994–2000): A Forecast and Analysis. Center for Defense Information.

Useem, M. (1973). *Conscription, Protest, and Social Conflict. The Life and Death of a Draft Resistance Movement*. New York: John Wiley & Sons.

Vallée, G. (1936). *La conscription dans le département de la Charente, 1789–1807*. Paris: Sirey.

Vallée, G. (1937) (1926). Le remplacement militaire en Charente sous le régime de la Conscription 1798–1814. *La Révolution Française: Revue d'Histoire Moderne et Contemporaine, 80*.

Vallée, G. (1937). *La Conscription dans le département de la Charente, 1798–1807*. Paris: Sirey.

Van Holde, S. (1993). State-building and the Limits of State Power: The Politics of Conscription in Napoleonic France.Unpublished Ph.D. dissertation. Cornell University, Ithaca, NY.

Van Kley, D. (Ed.) (1994). *The French Idea of Freedom: The Old Regime and the Declaration of Rights of 1789*. Stanford: Stanford University Press.

Van Steenbergen, B. (Ed.) (1994). *The Condition of Citizenship*. New York: Sage Publications.

Vassiliopulos, C. (1995). The Nature of Athenian Hoplite Democracy. *Armed Forces and Society, 22*(1), 49–63.

Vasudevan, H. .S. (1988). Peasant Land and Peasant Society in Late Imperial Russia. *The Historical Journal, 31*, 208–209.

Verhey, B. (1999). *Lessons learned in prevention, demobilization and social reintegration of children involved in armed conflict: Angola case study*. New York: UNICEF.

Vidalenc, J. (1959). La désertion dans le département du Calvados sous le Premier Empire. *Revue d'Histoire Moderne et Contemporaine, 6*, 60–72.

Vidalenc, J. (1975). Les conséquences sociales de la conscription en France, 1798–1848. *Cahiers internationaux d'histoire économique et sociale, 5*.

Vogt, W. R. (1989). Legitimitätsverfall der Sicherheitspolitik. In: *Studiengruppe Alternative Sicherheitspolitik: Vertrauensbildende Verteidigung. Reform deutscher Sicherheitspolitik* (pp. 67–101). Gerlingen: Bleicher Verlag.

Vogt, W.R. (1992). Militär – Eine Institution auf der Suche nach Legitimation. Zur Debatte über die zukünftigen Funktionen militärischer Macht im Prozeß der Friedenssicherung und –gestaltung. In: Kaldrack & Klein (Eds), 9–40.

von Clausewitz, C. (1976). *On War*. M. Howard & P. Paret (trans. and Eds) Princeton: Princeton University Press.

von Clausewitz, C. (1992). *Historical and Political Writings*. P. Paret & D. Moran (trans. and Eds) Princeton: Princeton University Press.

von der Goltz, C. (1887). *The Nation in Arms*. P. A. Ashworth (trans.). London: W.H. Allen and Co.

Walker, W. E. (1992). Comparing Army Reserve Forces: A Tale of Multiple Ironies, Conflicting Realities, and More Certain Prospects. *Armed Forces and Society, 18*(3), 303–322.

Wallach, J. L. (1994). Wehrpflicht und Berufsarmee im Alten Testament. In: Foerster (Ed.), 15–26.

Wallensteen, P., & Sollenberg, M. (2000). Armed Conflict, 1989–1999. *Journal of Peace Research, 37*(5), 635–650.

Waltz, K. N. (1959). *Man, the State and War*. New York: Columbia University Press.

Waltz, K. N. (1979). *Theory of International Politics*. New York: McGraw Hill.

Walzer, M. (1970). *Obligations: Essays on Disobedience, War and Citizenship*. Cambridge and London: Harvard University Press.

Walzer, M. (1988). *Spheres of Justice: A Defense of Pluralism and Equality*. New York: Basic Books.

Waquet, J. (1968). La société civile devant l'insoumission et la désertion a l'époque de la conscription militaire (1798–1814) d'après la correspondence du ministre de l'intérieur. *Bibliothèque de l'École des Chartres, 126*, 187–222.

Waquet, J. (1974). Pour une sociopsychologie du transit: l'exemple du recrutement militaire français et belge pendant la Révolution et la premiere moitié du XIXe siècle. In: *Recrutement, Mentalités, Sociétés, Actes du 2e Colloque International d'Histoire Militaire* (pp. 127–136). Montpelier: Centre d'Histoire Militaire et d'Études de Défense Nationale de Montpelier et Université Paul Valery.

War Office (1896). Wolsely to the Permanent Under Secretary of State for War, February 22, 1896. PRO WO 32/6357.

War Resisters International. (1990). *Conscription and Conscientious Objection: Profile of the Situation in Different Countries*. London: War Resisters' International.

Warner, J. T., & Asch, B. J. (1995). The Economics of Military Manpower. In: K. Hartley & T. Sandler (Eds). *Handbook of Defence Economics* (pp, 347–398). Amsterdam.

Weber, M. (1930). *The Protestant Ethic and the Spirit of Capitalism*. London: Unwin Hyman.

Weber, M. (1946). *From Max Weber: Essays in Sociology*. New York: Oxford University Press.

Weber, M. (1949). "Objectivity" in Social Science and Social Policy. In: M. Weber, *The Methodology of the Social Sciences*. New York: The Free Press.

Weber, M. (1958). Politics as Vocation. In: H. H. Gerth & C.W. Mills (Eds), *From Max Weber: Essays in Sociology* (pp. 77–128). New York: Galaxy Books.

Weber, M. (1964). *Economía y sociedad*. México: Fondo de Cultura Económica.

Weber, M. (1978). *Economy and Society*. Berkeley: University of California Press.

Weber, M. (1981). *General Economic History*. F. H. Knight (trans.). New Brunswick, NJ: Transaction Books.

Weiss, L., & Hobson, J. M. (1995). *States and Economic Development*. Cambridge: Polity.

Welch, Jr., C. (1985). Civil-Military Relations: Perspectives from the Third World. *Armed Forces and Society, 11*, 183–198.

Welch, Jr., C. (1987). *No Farewell to Arms?: Military Disengagement from Politics in Africa and Latin America*. Boulder: Westview Press.

Watson, A. (1992). *The Expansion of International Society*. London: Routledge.

Weatherford, D. (1990). *American Women and World War II*. NY: Facts on File.

Weber, E. (1976). *Peasants into Frenchmen: The Modernization of Rural France, 1870–1914*. Stanford, CA.: Stanford University Press.

Wessells, M. (1997). Child soldiers. *The Bulletin of the Atomic Scientists, 53*(6), 32–39.

Wessells, M. G. (1998). Children, armed conflict, and peace. *Journal of Peace Research, 35*(5), 635–646.

Wessells, M. G., & Monteiro, C. (2001). Psychosocial interventions and post-conflict reconstruction in Angola: Interweaving Western and traditional approaches. In: D. Christie, R. V. Wagner & D. Winter (Eds), *Peace, Conflict, and Violence: Peace Psychology for the 21st Century* (pp. 262–275). Englewood Cliffs, NJ: Prentice-Hall.

Western, J. R. (1965). *The English Militia in the Eighteenth Century: The Story of a Political Issue 1660–1802*. London: Routledge and Kegan Paul.

Wette, W. (1994). Deutsche Erfahrungen mit der Wehrpflicht 1918–1945. In: R. G. Foerster (Ed.), *Die Wehrpflicht* (pp. 91–106). München: Oldenburg.

Wette, W. (1994a). Wie es im Jahre 1919 zur Abschaffung der Wehrpflicht in Deutschland kam. In: Opitz & Rödiger (Eds), 67–74.

Wette, W. (1994b). Deutsche Erfahrungen mit der Wehrpflicht 1918–1945. Abschaffung in der Republik und Wiedereinführung durch die Diktatur. In: Foerster (Ed.), 91–106.

Wildman, A. K. (1980). *The End of the Russian Imperial Army: The Old Army and the Soldier's Revolt (March–April 1917)*. Princeton: Princeton University Press, 1980.

Williams, C. (1989). *Gender at Work*. Berkeley: University of California Press.

Williamson, J. G. (1995). The Evolution of Global Labor Markets since 1830: Background Evidence and Hypotheses. *Explorations in Economic History*, *32*, 141–196.

Williamson, J. G. (1996). Globalization and Inequality Then and Now: The Late 19th and Late 20th Centuries Compared. NBER Working Paper 5491.

Williamson, J. G. (1998). Globalization, Labor Markets and Policy Backlash in the Past. *Journal of Economic Perspectives*, *12*, 51–72.

Williamson, J. G. (1999). The Impact of Globalization on Pre-Industrial, Technologically Quiescent Economies: Real Wages, Relative Factor Prices, and Commodity Price Convergence in the Third World Before 1940. NBER Working Paper 7146.

Winter, J. (1995). *Sites of Memory, Sites of Mourning: The Great War in European Cultural History*. Cambridge and New York: Cambridge University Press.

Woloch, I. (1994). *The New Regime: Transformations of the French Civic Order, 1789–1820s*. New York: Norton.

Woloch, I. (1986). Napoleonic Conscription: State Power and Civil Society. *Past and Present*, *111*, 101–129.

Wolpin, M. (1994). *Alternative Security and Military Dissent*. San Francisco: Austin & Winfield.

Wood, G. S. (1991). *The Radicalism of the American Revolution*. New York: Vintage Books.

Woodward, Jr., R. L. (1985). *Central America: A Nation Divided*. Oxford: Oxford University Press.

Yalvaç, F. (1991). The Sociology of the State and the Sociology of International Relations. In: M. Banks & M. Shaw (Eds), *State and Society in International Relations* (pp. 93–114). London: Harvester.

Young, N. (1984). War Resistance, State and Society. In: M. Shaw (Ed.), *War, State and Society* (pp. 95–116). London: MacMillan Press.

Zeidler, M. (1993). *Reichswehr und Rote Armee 1920–1933. Wege und Stationen einer ungewöhnlichen Zusammenarbeit*. München: R. Oldenbourg Verlag.

Zimmerman, J. (1991). The Jurisprudence of Equality: The Women's Minimum Wage, the First Equal Rights Amendment, and *Adkins v. Children's Hospital, 1905–1923, Journal of American History*, *78*, 188–226.

Zimmermann, R. (1993). Allgemeine Dienstpflicht – eine Idee auf dem Prüfstand. In: Klein & idem (Eds), 72–80.

6, Perri. (1999). *Morals for robots and cyborgs: ethics, society and public policy in the age of autonomous intelligent machines*. Brentford: Bull Information Systems.